Application
Administrators Handbook

Application Administrators Handbook

Installing, Updating and Troubleshooting Software

Kelly C. Bourne

AMSTERDAM • BOSTON • HEIDELBERG • LONDON
NEW YORK • OXFORD • PARIS • SAN DIEGO
SAN FRANCISCO • SINGAPORE • SYDNEY • TOKYO

Morgan Kaufmann is an imprint of Elsevier

Acquiring Editor: *Steve Elliot*
Editorial Project Manager: *Lindsay Lawrence*
Project Manager: *Priya Kumaraguruparan*
Cover Designer: *Russell Purdy*

Morgan Kaufmann is an imprint of Elsevier
225 Wyman Street, Waltham, MA, 02451, USA

Library of Congress Cataloging-in-Publication Data
Bourne, Kelly C.
  Application administrators handbook : installing, updating, and troubleshooting software / Kelly C. Bourne.
    pages cm
  Includes bibliographical references and index.
  ISBN 978-0-12-398545-3
  1. Software maintenance–Handbooks, manuals, etc. 2. Software engineering–Management–Handbooks, manuals, etc. I. Title.
  QA76.76.S64B677 2014
  005.1'6–dc23

                                                                                        2013029165

British Library Cataloguing-in-Publication Data
A catalogue record for this book is available from the British Library.

ISBN: 978-0-12-398545-3

Printed in the United States of America

14 15 16 17   10 9 8 7 6 5 4 3 2 1

Working together
to grow libraries in
developing countries

www.elsevier.com • www.bookaid.org

For information on all MK publications visit our website at *www.mkp.com*

Contents

I am dedicating this book to my parents, Jack and Bev Bourne.
My parents are truly two extraordinary people.
They have been role models and an incredible inspiration to my six siblings
and me as we grew up. I can still count on their wisdom and common sense
to guide me through life.
Thanks Mom and Dad.

Acknowledgments

This book wouldn't be in your hands if not for the vision and faith that Steve Elliot of Elsevier showed in me and my proposal. Without his vision, this book would have remained just a dream. Lindsay Lawrence, also of Elsevier, has been incredibly helpful and supportive during the production and review phases of this effort. Last but certainly not least is Brian Jaffe, Technical Editor. Brian's comments, suggestions, and always extremely constructive criticism were invaluable along the way.

What Does an Application Administrator Do?

1.1 OVERVIEW OF THE POSITION

Application Administrators aren't developers and they're not users, but they are critical to keeping the applications your organization relies on running. They install, update, tune, diagnose, and babysit both internal and third-party applications. The applications they support can include ERP (Enterprise Resource Planning), CRM (Customer Relationship Management), POS (Point of Sale), BPM (Business Process Management), budgeting and forecasting, HR (Human Resources), legal matter management, AP (Accounts Payable)/ AR (Accounts Receivable), payroll, general ledger, SOX (Sarbanes Oxley) compliance tracking, training, time tracking, supply chain, database engines, and messaging, i.e., e-mail.

While software can be readily licensed from a vendor, it still requires a significant amount of effort on the part of the acquiring organization. Someone has to prepare the servers that it will run on. Then someone has to install it, configure it, load data into it, tune it, upgrade it, and generally keep the package up and running. If errors occur, someone has to report them to the vendor and work with vendor technicians to correct the problems. These are all tasks that an Application Administrator handles.

In many cases, corporations are absolutely dependent that these applications be kept running. What would be the response of employees if the payroll application broke down? What would happen to the organization's financial situation if invoices weren't sent out to customers? What if new employees couldn't be added to the HR system? The importance of Application Administrators and their level of expertise shouldn't be overlooked. Since the trend of relying upon third-party software isn't going to decrease in the foreseeable future, the role of Application Administrator won't be going away either.

Every company employs them even if their official job title doesn't sound at all like "Application Administrator." A job title of "system application administrator" might be for a position that covers both application administration and systems administration. Since there is a significant degree of overlap between these two positions, this isn't uncommon.

Any software the organization relies upon is almost certain to have an Application Administrator supporting it. This includes software acquired from a third-party vendor or from an internal development team. Development teams typically develop the application and then hand support responsibilities off to another group within the organization. For better or for worse, they don't tend to stick around indefinitely to provide ongoing production support.

1.1.1 Application administrator backgrounds

The background of IT professionals working as Application Administrators varies widely. Some have a background in software development. Others became Application Administrators because an administrator was needed and they were in the right place at the right time. Individuals without formal education or training in IT will benefit the most from this book. It will provide hands on advice on how to administer applications, troubleshoot them, and establish best practices for keeping applications running smoothly. But even the most experienced Application Administrator has weak areas that this book can help shore up.

1.1.2 Potential skillset

The list of potential skills that an Application Administrator might be required to have can be long and diverse. The skills that are being sought range from very specific technical skills to skills that are considered "softer." Virtually every posting requires some variation of excellent communication skills, troubleshooting ability, problem solving and/or analytical skills, flexibility, and understanding business needs. Some examples of requested skills are:

- Expertise and experience in *XYZ* application is a must.
- Strong experience on failover, high availability, disaster recovery, business continuance.
- Strong experience in *XYZ* version control tool.
- Good knowledge and demonstrated troubleshooting abilities on connectivity issues due to firewall, load balancer, proxy, and others.
- Experience with SOX compliance and methodologies.
- Hands on experience in process automation, best practice approach, technology efficiency, and effectiveness.
- Knowledge of Web Services and Services Oriented Architecture is desirable.
- Requires extensive knowledge of Windows 2000/2003 Server.
- Should be experienced with SQL Query Development as it relates to *XYZ* databases.
- Must demonstrate strong experience in designing, implementing, and maintaining current Windows server products including Microsoft SQL 2005, IIS, Windows Clustering, Network Load Balance, Net Environments, and ISA.
- Strong Linux experience including shell and Perl scripting for administration tasks.
- Experience with monitoring tools is a plus.
- Knowledge of Oracle Application Server, Apache Tomcat, and Microsoft IIS a plus.
- Excels at the highest technical level of all phases of applications systems analysis and programming activities.
- Understands software and hardware requirements of varied departmental systems.
- Understands the workflow and process requirements of complex application systems.
- Demonstrated ability to be the subject matter expert in supporting, maintaining, and administering complex applications.
- Excellent problem solving/analytical skills and knowledge of analytical tools.
- Display and execute logical and complex troubleshooting methods.
- Excellent verbal, written communication, and negotiations skills.
- Demonstrated soft skills required such as presentation of ideas and clearly articulate the concepts to senior management.
- Ability to effectively interface with technical and nontechnical staff at all organizational levels.
- Strong customer services and problem solving skills.
- Ability to provide outstanding customer service, be a good listener and work well with others.
- Self-motivated, able to work independently, and takes initiative.
- Ability to multitask in a fast-paced environment.
- Outstanding attention to detail with superior time and project management skills.
- Demonstrated ability to work successfully with a diverse group of customers.
- Ability to learn new content areas and new skills quickly and well required.
- Professional attitude and work habits.
- Understands business function related to the application.
- Ability to work through ambiguous work situations.

1.1.3 **Duties and responsibilities**

The list of duties and responsibilities described in some job postings is as broad and diverse as the technical skills that are required of prospective job applicants. It wouldn't be realistic to expect a single candidate to be responsible for this entire list of duties, but don't be surprised if your initial job description gets widened to include more and more responsibilities as time goes by. Some of the duties and responsibilities that an Application Administrator might be given include:

- The candidate shall monitor the *XYZ* software application, document and analyze problems, and publish maintenance schedule
- Sets up administrator and service accounts
- Maintains system documentation
- Interacts with users and evaluates vendor products
- May program in an administrative language
- Provides advice and training to end-users
- Maintains current knowledge of relevant technologies as assigned
- The candidate shall serve as part of a team responsible to maintain an *XYZ* system availability rate of 99%
- Troubleshoot, and resolve any reported problems
- Provide application performance tuning
- The candidate shall review the governing regulations to ensure proper program support
- The candidate shall monitor, update, and maintain existing legacy environment software systems interfaces to ensure that the interfaces exchange data properly and to support the current legacy environment
- This is a hands on senior technical position with Subject Matter Expertise (SME) on *XYZ* app
- Enable best practices
- Process automation
- Maintain SLA, System Availability, Capacity management, and Performance KPI
- Collaborate with hardware, OS, DBA technical teams to ensure proper integration of the environment
- Work closely with application development teams and vendors to tune and troubleshoot applications
- Plan and coordinate testing changes, upgrades, and new services, ensuring systems will operate correctly in current and future environments
- Provides second level of technical support for all corporate systems and software components
- Provide Level 3 support for the application. Must be able to support 24×7. Also enable production support team to tackle Level 2 support and issues
- Leads and participates in efforts to develop and implement processes for application and system monitoring
- Leads and participates in efforts to implement application updates to include upgrades, patches, and new releases
- Tests, debugs, implements, and documents programs. Assists in the modification of company products and/or customer/internal systems to meet the needs of the client and/or end-user
- Develops test plans to verify logic of new or modified programs
- Develop and maintain the reporting and dashboard infrastructure for the organization
- Develop work plans and track/report status of assigned projects/tasks
- Liaise with vendor support on all issues
- Fully responsible for problem management activities such as issue resolution and root cause analysis
- Daily monitoring and maintenance activities
- Assist in the day-to-day operations of Operations department

- Reviews and addresses assigned technical support tickets and calls, enters all updates related to such calls into the Help Desk ticketing system, and keeps team aware of any sensitive or escalating issues
- Provides subject matter expertise for all applications
- Participate in security and application audits
- Occasionally supporting off-hours activities. This position may require a flexible schedule
- Promote changes through the use of *XYZ* adhering to SOX policies and procedures
- Identify, download and apply *XYZ* upgrades and patches
- Research issues with application middleware, database, etc., and recommend/apply solutions such as configuration changes to O/S, WebLogic, Tuxedo, Java, etc., additional hardware, memory, CPUs, etc.
- Identify problematic SQL and work with developers, analysts, and DBAs to resolve
- Optimize and tune the *XYZ* application components
- Work with customers and analysts to develop scripts used to perform load testing
- Use load testing tool to perform tests to determine application load capabilities

As the above list makes painfully obvious, the demands put upon an Application Administrator are diverse and plentiful. It's an interesting job. It's a challenging job. It's certainly not a boring job. Every day will bring new challenges. Every problem is a learning opportunity. Every solution is an opportunity to educate your users, other professionals in the organization, or your successors.

1.1.4 Types of applications that need an administrator

Applications that are licensed from a third-party vendor and weren't custom built for an organization are frequently referred to by the acronym COTS—Commercial Off The Shelf Software. Because there are so many installations of COTS applications, they are primarily what Application Administrators support.

In addition to COTS packages, Application Administrators also work to administer Software as a Service (SaaS) applications. SaaS applications are hosted by the vendor. The client's users access it via a web browser directed to a specific URL. If the SaaS application is critical to your organization, then someone will need to function as an administrator to help users, work with the vendor when problems occur and act as an intermediary between your organization and the vendor's technical staff.

More and more enterprise-level software used worldwide is licensed from third-party vendors instead of being developed internally. This trend isn't likely to change in the future. If anything, it's likely to accelerate. Reasons for this are numerous and include the following:

- Developing a complex application is both extremely difficult and very expensive. It takes time, skilled individuals, and significant resources to develop effective, reliable software. Most organizations lack the experience to do it properly. The failure rate of large-scale software development projects is appalling high.
- Organizations like to focus on their primary business function. For most businesses, software development isn't their core function. Developing an ERP application or any other complex application reduces their ability to focus on running the business.
- Enterprise-level software is complex and becoming more so. Many, if not most, organizations extend across state or international boundaries. This requires that the software be capable of handling the laws and regulations of every state and country that it operates in. Laws and regulations tend to be extremely dynamic. It's very time consuming to modify and test software to properly handle this flood of changes.
- Software applications have to deal with dynamic environments. New versions of operating systems become available and existing ones are retired. Modifying and testing an application to deal with a new operating system is a significant commitment. New web browsers and updated versions of existing ones are released on a regular basis. Applications that rely on a web browser need to be tested, and

possibly modified, for each new browser upgrade. Database systems undergo regular upgrades and modifications. Applications that rely upon a database system need to be tested and possibly modified to deal with changes that occur within the database package.

- Security vulnerabilities are a constant threat for all software, especially ones that are widely deployed and deal with confidential or personally identifiable information (PII). The dangers to an organization's reputation and the costs of a breach are shockingly high. Staying knowledgeable about newly discovered security threats requires the focus of skilled professionals.

Due to the above points, more and more organizations are choosing to "outsource" development of software applications to specialized vendors. Acquiring a third-party application is definitely a compromise situation. None of the existing packages is likely to provide the exact features that an organization wants or needs. On the other hand, the cost and time to install an off-the-shelf application are significantly less than what it would take to develop the application internally or have it custom built by a third party.

The primary exceptions to the trend of licensing applications are when the application is "core" to the business and provides a competitive advantage. For example, Google is never going to license software from a vendor to replace its Page Ranking algorithms. Those algorithms are the heart and soul of Google and will always be kept in-house. Contrast this with an organization's payroll application. There is nothing unique or advantageous about payroll. Certainly, it's an important process, but it doesn't rise to the level of being a trade secret. It wouldn't make sense for an organization to spend millions of dollars to develop proprietary algorithms to cut paychecks. There wouldn't be any significant payback from such an investment.

1.2 QUALITIES OF AN APPLICATION ADMINISTRATOR

To be a successful Application Administrator, it helps to have a special set of qualities. The job isn't exactly like being a software developer. Some of the qualities that are good to have are described in the following sections.

1.2.1 Service mentality

You have to have a service mentality to be an effective Application Administrator. The essence of your job is to keep applications running so other people can do their jobs. Typically, you won't be in a "9 to 5" job. You have to be willing to do what it takes to keep the systems running. If the application goes down in the middle of the night and impacts users in another time zone, you'll get a call. If a patch needs to be applied and the maintenance window is from 10 pm until midnight on Sunday, then expect to be working an occasional Sunday night. If performance is slow for users on the other side of the world, then expect to be up late at night monitoring and troubleshooting the situation. You're providing a service as well as technical expertise. If the idea of providing service to internal or external clients or customers doesn't appeal to you, then you might not be suited to be an Application Administrator.

Being in an application support position means never being able to say "That's not my problem." If the users aren't able to use the application, it's your problem even if you know that the true cause of the problem has nothing to do with the application itself. You will have to work with other groups (DBAs, vendor, network team, security team, firewall team, etc.) on behalf of the users until both the application and your users are back online. Working with members of other teams will give you opportunities to learn more about the IT industry as you all work together to keep the systems running.

I'll admit that I'm more than a little bit biased on this subject, but an Application Administrator is arguably just as important to the company as the application developer. The best application in the world is worthless if it isn't installed, customized, backed up, or available to the users.

If ever the phrase "many ways to skin a cat" applied to a job position, it would be Application Administration. There are numerous ways to accomplish just about everything you will need to do. Some ways might be a little faster or more straightforward than others, but always be aware that many solutions exist. If you keep your eyes open you'll be presented with many learning opportunities as you work with other Application Administrators, Systems Administrators, Database Administrators, vendor technical reps, and other professionals. If you can pick up one or two tips from each of them, you'll be that much more valuable to your employer, your users, and your profession.

1.2.2 Persistence pays off

An Application Administrator has to walk a fine line between being persistent without being rude.

You'll need help from other people like the network team, DBAs, vendor help desk, the security team, and users at a remote site. It's tough being persistent without crossing the line and becoming annoying, but you have to keep at it. No one likes to be a pest, but the users of your application are depending on you and you can't do everything by yourself. Just keep reminding yourself that you're just trying to do your job and you are entitled to the assistance of other professionals in the organization. Don't be rude, don't be aggressive, but do be persistent. You're fighting for your applications and the users that depend on them.

1.2.3 Continuous improvements

Your job is actually more than to just keeping the applications running. Organizations are increasingly looking for ways continuously improve their processes. As part of the IT team, you will be expected to contribute to this effort. Three common ways to improve operations are:

- Documentation
- Best practices
- Process maturity

1.2.4 Document, document, document

Document everything you do. The vendor's documentation will provide some high-level examples, but specifics like server names, account names, URLs, etc., won't be included in their standard documentation. Capture screenshots of every screen that you advance through. Label screenshots thoroughly, for example, identifying which settings need to be changed on each screen.

If the application encounters a problem or has an outage, you need to document it. Write up a document that describes what happened, when it happened, who noticed it first, and how it was resolved. Your organization might call this an incident report or a root cause analysis. Make sure that your narrative is clear, concise, and accurate.

If you're doing to do an upgrade of the system, you need to write up a project plan and a test script. The project plan describes in great detail what will be done, who will do it, how long it will take, and how you'll recover if the upgrade fails. The test script lists a series of tests that need to be done to confirm that an upgrade was successful.

There will be times that when your application gets restarted. You need to document how to validate that the application came up successfully. This might be as simple as logging into the application successfully. Or it might be as complicated as confirming that application "A" can successfully pass a file to application "B." It all depends on your environment.

Take the time to accurately name each document file you create. The most detailed documentation in the world will be worthless if you can't find it. A descriptively named file will be found more quickly than a tersely or obscurely named document.

Your organization or department needs to identify a place where all documentation will be located. It doesn't really matter whether this is a SharePoint portal, a database, or a network drive. As long as it's somewhere that everyone knows about, can access it, and uses it consistently.

1.2.5 Best practices

"Best practices" is a generic term for a method or technique that has proved to result in a superior outcome. This concept is understandably vague. What are best practices for one group or organization might be worthless for another group. Your group's management needs to identify what constitutes best practices for your situation.

Where can your organization get its "best practices"? Possibilities include building them yourselves through trial, error, and observation of what works best. Acquiring them from an accredited management standards organizations like the ISO (International Organization for Standardization). A final source would be to work with a consulting firm that specializes in the area of Best Practices and have them advise you with templates applicable to IT or your specific industry.

As an Application Administrator you'll have the opportunity to ensure that all of the applications you support adhere to the best practices of the organization. It won't be done overnight, but as you improve on the current processes your job will become easier and more efficient.

1.2.6 Process maturity

Process maturity embraces the concept that your group or organization goes about its business activities in a way that improves the likelihood of success. People perform activities using the same well defined steps. This ensures that the process is repeatable. Processes are decomposed, defined, optimized, and measured. Application Administrators help insure that processes related to their applications become more and more mature.

Given all of the skills that are expected of Application Administrators and all of the conditions under which we are expected to perform reminds me of a poem from Rudyard Kipling. It's too long to include the entire poem here, but the first and last verses go like this:

If you can keep your head when all about you
Are losing theirs and blaming it on you,
If you can trust yourself when all men doubt you,
But make allowance for their doubting too;

If you can fill the unforgiving minute
With sixty seconds' worth of distance run -
Yours is the Earth and everything that's in it,
And - which is more - you'll be a Man my son!

Rudyard Kipling

1.3 WHERE DO APPLICATION ADMINISTRATORS COME FROM?

There are no undergraduate degrees in Application Administration, so no one gets a formal education for this particular position. Everyone currently in the field drifted in from another area of business or IT. Some Application Administrators, like myself, were originally software developers. Some started off with an MIS (Management Information System) degree and were assigned to be the Application Administrator for one or more of the organization's applications. Other Application Administrators may have started out as the power user of an organization's application and when someone was needed to administer the application they either volunteered or were volunteered.

1.4 WHAT JOBS CAN AN APPLICATION ADMINISTRATOR MOVE UP TO?

There really aren't any defined career paths that Application Administrators advance into. My experience and observation are that Application Administrators' career paths are as varied as the individuals in the position. One common path is to continue as an Application Administrator but for other or additional applications. Once you develop the skillset needed to be a competent Application Administrator, there are many organizations that potentially need your services.

1.4.1 IT architect

An Application Administrator works with just about every facet of the organization's IT department. He or she needs to understand how all the pieces fit together. This type of background could make an Application Administrator a potential candidate for the IT Architect position in the organization. An IT Architect is the person in an organization that works at the highest level to determine which IT investments will have the best returns for the organization. The position requires experience on both the technical side and the business side. Certifications for IT architects are offered by both Microsoft and The Open Group. If you're currently an Application Administrator and have an interest in moving up the ladder to IT Architect position, you should investigate the certification requirements and consider working toward rounding your skillset to fill in any gaps you might have.

1.4.2 Software development

If you're currently an Application Administrator and you have a software development background, then the option of moving back into development is certainly an option. The time spent supporting an application will have provided you with invaluable insight into what users expect in applications, shortcomings of current applications, and thoughts on how to write software that is easier to implement and upgrade. Developers that haven't spent time supporting applications aren't likely to have the insights you have acquired.

One warning about this career move is that software development changes incredibly quickly. If you've been out of the field for more than a few years, you can expect a steep climb to get back up to speed. If you believe this type of move is in your long-term future, then you should plan to keep up with current trends in the software development world. Read the trade journals on a regular basis, read the most respected blogs and keep your coding skills sharp. This will consume a lot of your free time, but it will be well worth it when you start submitting job applications for developer positions.

1.4.3 Work for the vendor

If you become extremely proficient with a specific software application and like working with it, then a possible career path would be to go to work for the vendor. You might consider becoming a technical analyst or system engineer for them. If you go to work for them, they will probably provide you with advanced training to learn more about internal workings of the application. You would then assist their clients with installs, upgrades, troubleshooting, etc. This position would be similar to your current position except you'll work with a number of clients instead of just your current organization.

One word of warning—the organization you work for might have an agreement with the vendor to not hire employees away from each other. If such an agreement exists, whether in writing or even just verbally, the chances of the vendor hiring you are slim. Find out if an agreement exists before approaching the vendor. It would be very awkward for everyone if you make inquiries and the vendor can't hire you due to a legal agreement with your current employer.

1.4.4 Consulting

Moving into a consulting or contract position is a possibility for anyone in IT who has demonstrated competency with a marketable set of skills. While it's possible that Application Administrators could move into a consulting position, it seems less likely for other skillsets. Application Administration is a position that's needed on a long term or a permanent basis. Most consulting or contract positions are to fill short-term positions. While this career path doesn't seem as probably as some others, it might become more common in the future. Stranger things than this have happened in the industry.

1.5 EXAMPLES OF COMMERCIAL OFF THE SHELF (COTS) SOFTWARE

Earlier in this chapter, a reference was made about COTS software. Some examples of Commercial Off The Shelf software include the following:

- ERP—Enterprise Resource Planning packages
- CRM—Customer Relationship Management packages
- POS—Point of Sale packages
- Scheduling packages
- Education/training software
- Resume processing
- Accounting packages
- Contract management software
- Medical billing
- Invoicing
- SOX compliance tracking
- Accounts payable
- Accounts receivable
- Unclaimed Property
- Sales tax processing
- Payroll tax processing
- Project Management software
- SAP
- PeopleSoft
- Sales Force
- Oracle Financials
- Oracle HR
- Warehouse management
- Order Management
- Inventory management
- Supply chain management

While every application is different, there are many common skills, techniques, and approaches that can help an application administrator support a wide variety of applications. This book attempts to document these techniques. It won't provide you with the details to install version 9.7 of the *XYZ* application, but provides a set of fundamental skills that are applicable to many if not most applications.

As an Application Administrator you have to be something of a Jack of all trades. You need to know a little about a great number of topics like operating systems, disk management, databases, networking, performance, web site, load balancing, security, backups, disaster recovery, project management, and configuration management. This book won't make you an expert in all these areas, but it will provide basic information that will enable you to do your job quickly, efficiently, and competently. Hopefully, it will provide you with enough baseline knowledge to work efficiently with experts in each of those areas.

1.6 DEALING WITH PEOPLE, LOTS OF PEOPLE

You might think that as an Application Administrator you'll spend all of your time dealing with computers and software, but that's far from reality. You'll be dealing with a LOT of people. A typical day will have you spending as much time with other people as with the application you're administering. Some of the types of people are:

- Users
- Power Users
- The application "owner"
- Your supervisor or manager
- Project managers
- Internal development team
- DBAs (Database Administrators)
- The Network team
- The Security team
- Vendor help desk personnel
- Vendor development team
- Your organization's help desk team

1.7 QUESTIONS TO ASK IF RESPONSIBILITY FOR AN APPLICATION IS DROPPED ON YOU

If you're an Application Administrator, there's a good chance that at some point in your career you'll have another application added to your list of responsibilities. If you're about to become an Application Administrator for the first time, then this is happening to you right now.

How should you respond if this occurs? You want to be a team player, but don't neglect looking out for yourself. Gather as much information on the new application as possible. A list of potential questions is provided in Chapter 6. Obviously no canned list of questions can cover every situation, but use this list as a starting point. Flesh it out with questions specific to you, your organization, and the application you're about to take responsibility for.

I hate to be a pessimist, but if the current "owner" of the application tells you the application is very easy to support, I'd take that claim with a grain of salt. After all, if it's so easy to support why is it being handed off to you?

1.8 ADMINISTERING MULTIPLE APPLICATIONS

Most applications don't require the equivalent of a full-time person administering them. This being the case, you can expect that you'll have additional responsibilities. It's entirely likely that you'll be tasked with administering multiple applications.

In my experience, the biggest challenge of administering multiple applications is balancing requests that come in for each application. Murphy's law predicts that if one application is requiring a great deal of your time and attention, that's exactly when one of your other applications will crash or require an update. The best advice I can give you is to keep your supervisor well informed about your daily activities. Work with him or her to determine which application should be your highest priority. If users or anyone else doesn't agree with it, then very diplomatically tell them to take it up with your supervisor. Letting your supervisor handle decisions like this frees up more of your time to address the problems.

If you end up being the Application Administrator for multiple applications, then you need to be as efficient as possible. You need to exploit opportunities to reuse documentation, forms, shortcuts, tips, training, DR plans, etc. Anything that can be copied and reused from one application to another will save your time. It has the secondary advantage of making your documentation and procedures more consistent between applications.

1.9 TRAINING YOUR REPLACEMENT OR BACKUP

This particular detail of your job might not be obvious, but it's one of the most important tasks to you personally. If you ever want to take any time off or be promoted or transferred, then you need to have someone who is immediately available to replace you. Nothing is worse than being on vacation or sick and getting a call telling you that the application is down and you need to address the problem immediately.

The first step in training a backup is to identify who it will be. Obviously, this decision will be made by management and not by you personally. Once the decision is made, then you need to work with your backup on a regular basis. You need to educate him or her about the application, its background, and daily activities.

You'll need to provide your backup with access to all the relevant servers and documentation. More importantly, they'll need to initially watch you and later administer it themselves. Most people seem to learn best when they actually perform the task. Application administration is no exception to this rule, so plan to have your backup watch you perform a specific task a time or two and then do it themselves the next time. You'll need to be extremely patient while they're doing any task the first time. They won't be as confident as you. They won't be as fast as you. They'll make mistakes. But that's part of the learning experience and can't be avoided.

Get in the habit of calling them over whenever you're about to do something unusual. Even if you don't think this particular task will be done again soon. It's better to let them see it done at least once than have them trying to do it for the first time when you're unavailable.

You've spent a lot of time becoming technically proficient and you enjoy having those skills. You're proud of your reputation as being someone who gets things done. It's difficult for many of us to hand tasks over to someone else, but you need to look at the big picture. Do you like being called when you're on vacation and a problem occurs? Do you want to be able to take advantage of promotions or new assignments? If you answered "yes" to either of these questions then keep that in mind as you train your backup or potential replacement.

1.10 SUMMARY

If you weren't already familiar with the position of Application Administrator, I hope this introduction has convinced you that the job is both important and challenging. It might not be a job that's suited for everyone, but it's interesting, challenging and critical to continuing the operations of the largest companies in the world. If you're already familiar with the position or are working as an Application Administrator then I hope that this book provides you with tools that will help you be a better Application Administrator.

Design

2

There's a great deal of confusion between the terms *architecture* and *design*. Both terms exist on a continuum and reasonable professionals can easily disagree on where one ends and the other picks up. A very simplistic of each of these terms could be:

- Architecture refers to the bigger picture. It deals with which framework and programming language will be used. A software framework is a reusable platform used by vendors to develop their product. Decisions related to scope and goals, i.e., what will be included in the application, are made on the architecture end of the spectrum.
- Design focuses on the smaller, tighter picture. It deals with how software modules are organized and what communications are passed between modules. Implementation and support are more on the design end of the spectrum.

As an Application Administrator you have relatively little opportunity to control either of these aspects. You're generally arriving too late in the process to impact architecture and design decisions. Generally, the application is already in place when you become involved. If you're involved in the process to acquire the software, then you may have some influence over which particular vendor's product is selected.

2.1 SPECIFICATIONS

The first step that needs to be done when either acquiring a third-party application or developing your own is to fully understand what it needs to do. The correct term for what you need the application to do is defining its specifications.

Laying out the specifications for a complex application is a very significant undertaking. Software packages exist that can help you develop specifications. Using a tool for this makes it more formal and potentially more complete, but these tools are fairly complicated to understand and learn to use. A less formal method of defining specifications is to use a combination of spreadsheets or word processing documents.

As stated earlier, most Application Administrators aren't likely to be involved in the process of gathering application specifications. This is because it's done very early in the process of acquiring or designing an application, long before an Application Administrator is involved. A second reason is that very few Application Administrators have the training or experience to develop a proper set of specifications.

2.2 INTERACTION WITH OTHER SOFTWARE PACKAGES

John Donne said "No man is an island." If it's true for people, then it's equally true for applications. In typical corporate environment applications regularly pass data back and forth. Consider the following scenario:

- A new employee is hired and has his or her personal details are entered into the HR system.
- Around the same time his or her details get entered into Active Directory (AD).

- The newcomer is assigned several courses in the Learning Management System (LMS) or training system. The Active Directory subsystem authenticates their logon information when the new user logs in to begin their training.
- Once the new hire completes their class(es), the LMS system sends a file listing the "graduates" of the course to the other applications, e.g., the Data Mart application, which creates an account for each new user. An e-mail is sent out to new users providing them with their account details.
- To get paid the HR system works with the payroll system to figure out what their net pay should be based on their base salary. It also calculates how much should be deducted from their check for federal, state, and local taxes as well as deductions for health insurance, dental insurance, etc., based on the dependent details they provided to HR.
- At the end of the year, the HR system or an income tax software package mails out the W2 statements to each employee for tax purposes.

The above examples are just a few examples of communications that exist between corporate applications. The application that you support will very likely interact with other applications. Like any other automated process, communications between two applications will occasionally fail. You need to learn the details of all interactions, so you can restore communications as quickly as possible. Listed here are just some of the basic details that you'll want to understand and document:

- How does the interaction occur? Does an API exist? Or does one application create a file that is later read by other applications?
- How many interactions does your application participate in?
- Does your application create data and send it to other applications?
- Does your application accept incoming data from other applications?
- How often does this occur?
- Is the frequency based on a scheduled time or when data becomes available?
- What is the format for the data being passed?
- What happens if the receiving application isn't available when the data is being passed?
- What happens if unexpected or garbled data is sent or received?

Besides knowing the technical details of interactions between your application and others, you have to know who to contact if another application misbehaves. Who are the Application Administrators for the applications that your application interacts with? What are their names, e-mail addresses, and phone numbers (both office and mobile)? If you get a frantic call at 2 AM telling you that a critical process has failed, then you don't want to start familiarizing yourself with the process for the first time.

2.3 CAPACITY PLANNING

Capacity planning consists of calculations done to determine what capacity is needed for a resource or an application. The business owner of the application should be able to provide the following details to you about how the application will be used:

- How many users will be on the system on average?
- How many of them will be reading data vs. writing data?
- If your application has a peak period, how many users will be using it then? For example, if you're supporting an accounting application, the peak period might be just before the end of the month. If you're supporting an application that reimburses employees for travel expenses, you might see a peak just before paychecks are cut.
- How long will the average user be logged into the application each day?

Knowing the maximum number of users that will be on the system as well as the resource utilization rate of the average transaction will enable you to estimate how much disk space, memory, network bandwidth, and other resources will be needed. This lets you accurately estimate how powerful the hardware, i.e., the server, needs to be.

Capacity planning should be done prior to acquiring the hardware for the application. You might also want to repeat it if you know the user base is going to be expanded significantly. For example, if your organization is about to merge with another company or acquire another company, then you will need to consider adding hardware resources.

If you are acquiring a COTS application, the vendor has likely already have done the capacity planning calculations for potential clients. They frequently provide a chart or a table listing the number of users broken down by whether they are constant, frequent, or infrequent users. Another table might list the number of data records or entries that will be entered into the application. Based on your answers, the vendor will recommend the number and size of servers, number of processors, amount of RAM, and amount of disk space that your hardware environment should have.

2.4 LEGACY SYSTEMS

Does your application deal with any legacy systems? In this context, a legacy system refers to a software application or computer system that is older than most. The question is significant for several reasons. A legacy system might have a lower level of support than most applications. If it's a third-party application, then the vendor might not be supporting it any longer. If it was written internally, then the developers might no longer be with the organization or they may no longer be in the development group. In either event, if something goes wrong with the legacy system, you might have to work around the problem instead of getting someone to fix it.

Another reason why you need to be aware of legacy systems is that they are more likely to be replaced than brand new applications. If they are replaced, then there likely be an impact on the application you support. The interface between applications might change when the new system is installed. Even if the replacement system duplicates the legacy system exactly, you'll still need to test the interface to confirm that everything continues to work as expected.

2.5 TYPES OF HOSTING MODELS

There are several different ways that an application can be run or hosted. Each of them has strengths and weaknesses. The most common hosting models are:

2.5.1 Hosted internally

The organization licenses the software from the vendor and runs it on in-house computers. Most of the responsibility for the application is "owned" by the organization. A support license with the vendor usually exists, so if problems occur then vendor personnel will help research and resolve the problems.

The advantage of this model is the customer retains absolute control of everything. The hardware and data are owned and administered by the customer. For an organization that likes to be in charge of its destiny this is the model to select.

The disadvantages of internal hosting are that it requires a larger financial commitment to purchase the hardware, software licenses, and hire people to support the application.

2.5.2 Hosted by the vendor

In the vendor-hosted model, all of the hardware belongs to the vendor and is at their facility. Your users connect to the vendor's servers to run the application. Depending on your contract with the vendor, you might have dedicated servers or you might have a virtual server hosted by a shared physical server. Unless you represent a very, very large installation, then you probably won't have servers dedicated to you.

There are several different terms for applications that are hosted by the vendor. One such term is ASP—Application Service Provider. Another is SaaS—Software as a Service. Another term is "software on demand." As with much of the IT industry, the specifics of vendor-hosted applications are in a constant state of flux. Specific definitions for ASP and SaaS are provided in the following sections.

2.5.2.1 Application service provider (ASP)

Typically, an ASP host application implies that each client has a specific environment built for them. The client is the "single tenant" for that environment and doesn't share it with other clients of the vendor.

2.5.2.2 Software as a service (SaaS)

Software as a Service is the term given to a model where the application software and data are hosted in the cloud. Clients potentially share the same resources, i.e., servers, software, and database. This concept is referred to as "multitenant model."

Users of the application access the application using a web browser. Business applications that are commonly available in SaaS or ASP environments include accounting applications, invoicing applications, customer relationship management (CRM) systems, human resource management (HRM) applications, and help desk management systems.

2.5.3 Advantages and disadvantages of vendor-hosted environments

Like virtually everything else in life, choosing a vendor-hosted environment has advantages and disadvantages. Some of these are listed in the following sections.

2.5.3.1 Support and updates

A significant advantage of vendor-hosted models is that you are passing all the support and update headaches to the vendor. For example, the following responsibilities now belong to the vendor instead of your organization:

- They have to keep the servers and software running.
- They have to design, set up, and test a DR (Disaster Recovery) facility.
- They have to hire and retain qualified, competent IT personnel to keep the servers running.
- They have to schedule and handle operating system upgrades of the servers.
- They have to handle upgrading the application software on all of the servers.

2.5.3.2 Stability

One significant risk when going down the vendor-hosted path is that you're relying that the vendor is competent, adequately staffed, and economically stable. If they lack any of those attributes, then you might regret your decision.

How do you know the vendor is competent, has enough technical people to support their client base, and is going to be in business for the long run? Get references from their existing clients. If it's a publically traded company, their financial information will be publicly available. Check it. Look for reviews in the industry press and blogs. Make an effort to attend a local user group meeting and talk with other clients. Attending a national conference would be even better because that gives you more people to network with.

2.5.3.3 Security

A potential vulnerability that you need to consider if you go with a hosted model is that you're giving up control of your data. If it's on someone else's box then they have access to it. Their employees have access to it or could potentially get access to it. A disgruntled employee could expose confidential information for the vendor's entire client base. On the other hand, the vendor is probably so concerned about data security that they may be able to dedicate more resources to it than your organization can.

When thinking about this potential vulnerability, you have to be realistic about your own level of security before you start criticizing a vendor's. How secure are your internal systems? Have all of the following steps been done?

- Is someone regularly applying the latest patches to the server operating systems?
- Are your servers running with the latest version of all application software?
- Have you implemented strong password requirements?
- Have you deleted or at least disabled software components on the server that aren't needed?
- Have you deactivated default accounts for the operating system and applications?
- If default accounts exist have the default passwords been changed?
- Does your organization have a dedicated, well-trained security team?
- Is penetration testing being done on your servers and network?
- Are security logs regularly reviewed?

If you can't honestly answer "yes" to all of the above questions, then your security probably isn't any tighter than the vendor you're considering going with. Perhaps the only difference is that you've been lucky so far. Or worse, maybe systems have been penetrated but you just haven't found out about it yet.

2.5.3.4 Locked in

Another point to consider is the risk and cost of being locked into any vendor's hosted application. If your organization isn't satisfied with either the application or the vendor's responsiveness, then moving to a different application won't be easy or quick. For example, if the application's performance isn't up to your expectations, there isn't a lot you can do about it. Your only solution is to work with the vendor. If the vendor isn't responsive to your concerns and requests, then you're essentially stuck with the application as it currently exists.

Moving from any application to another isn't easy, but when dealing with a hosted environment, it seems like more of your eggs are in their basket. To move off of the vendor's host site will likely require assistance or participation from them. If the reason for moving is that the vendor isn't responsive do you think they will become more responsive once they learn you are ending your contract with them?

2.5.4 Comparing costs

It's hard to compare costs between the different hosting models because it's like comparing apples and oranges. The startup costs are certainly higher for internal hosting because all of the computer hardware has to be acquired. This model also has the highest personnel costs since you're hiring people to perform numerous administrative type jobs.

The licensing fee for a vendor-hosted application will likely be higher than if you acquire the license and run it on your own hardware. But when you factor that you don't have to purchase hardware, maintain a data center, obtain licenses for a database, or hire numerous IT people then it might not be as expensive as it first appears to be.

Vendors will argue that having them host the application is cheaper because they can pool hardware, software, and personnel and prorate those costs across all of their clients. Taking advantage of economies of scale helps them provide services at a lower cost. This is a fairly persuasive argument.

If your organization already supports many applications and has a fully operational data center and the personnel to support it, then hosting internally could be more economical. In this case, then your organization is already taking advantage of economies of scale. For instance, your DBAs (Database Administrators) and database licenses are probably supporting multiple applications. The same is true for your network team, your security team, and your system administrators.

2.6 WEB APPLICATIONS VS. CLIENT-SERVER APPLICATIONS

Software applications are typically described as being made up of three major components:

- The presentation component—it's what puts the data and graphics on the users screen
- The application logic—applies business-based decisions and processes
- The storage component—stores and retrieves the data, frequently in a relational database

2.6.1 Client-server applications

A client-server application requires that software be installed on every user's desktop. This software includes the presentation logic and frequently the business logic as well. The client-server application communicates with the storage component to access the requested data, but all other processing is done on the user desktop.

This approach has advantages and disadvantages. The disadvantages included the following:

- Performance could be a major problem if the desktop computer wasn't up to the task. Insufficient disk space, slow disk drives, inadequate memory, or limited processing power can cause the application to perform at a speed unacceptable to the user.
- Software exists on every user's desktop. If a new version needs to be installed that has to be installed as well. Obviously this takes time and effort.
- If a particular user had multiple applications loaded onto their machine the application could interact with each other and cause significant problems. Frequently, this was caused when a newly installed application installed a new version of a DLL (dynamic link library). If this new version of the DLL changed an interface that an existing application required, then the existing application could stop working. This was commonly referred to as "DLL hell." New desktop operating systems allow the installation of multiple versions of DLLs, but there are a lot of desktops out there running Windows XP that are susceptible to this problem.

The advantages of a client-server approach are:

- By only requesting data from the storage component, the amount of information requested from the data storage tier was minimized. If you think of the screen of a typical application, what percentage is data and what percentage is everything else, e.g., background images, labels, buttons, framework, etc.? Typically, the data represents a relatively small percentage of what's being presented to the user. Since only the active data gets pulled down from the database, the amount of information being passed between the client computer and the storage server is minimized.
- Client-server software is relatively static. It only changes when the Application Administrator or the user chooses to update it. I have seen client-server-based applications that automatically check with the vendor's "home office" each time they are booted. If updates are available, then they are automatically downloaded.

2.6.2 **Web-based applications**

A web-based application differs from a more traditional client-server application, primarily in the presentation and application logic pieces:

- The presentation component still runs on the user workstation, but a browser, for example, Mozilla Firefox, Microsoft Internet Explorer, or Google Chrome, instead of a specialized program provided by the vendor is used as the presentation tool.
- The application logic executes on the web server instead of on the user's workstation.
- The storage component typically doesn't change much. It continues to run on a server dedicated to providing the database functionality.

Supporting a web-based application can be much more challenging than supporting a client-server application. The primary reasons for this is that the combined environment is more complicated that a traditional environment:

- More pieces of software are involved; for example, plug-ins, HTML, and Java script run behind the scenes to allow the application to function. Unless you're extremely familiar with the application you won't be aware of all the pieces involved.
- Many of these pieces are outside your control. For example, you have little control over what browser or version of browser each user has on their desktop. You can tell users over and over that application *XYZ* is only certified for Internet Explorer 9, but I guarantee you that you'll have complaints from users that the application isn't working on their computers. After you investigate it you'll determine that they're using Internet Explorer 10 or Opera or another unsupported server.
- Network throughput is vital. If the network is disrupted or slowed down significantly, then the application will get very sluggish, very quickly. I will advise you that the chances of the problem being the network are fairly slim. It's very easy to blame unknown performance issues on the network, but most of the time, it turns out to be something else. Be sure you have some proof before blaming the network. Chapter 24—"UNIX Tools" provides information on tools that you can use to determine if a problem is or isn't being caused by network issues.
- Users employ a wide variety of computers, operating systems, and Internet browsers. All of these combinations, along with the various options for configurations of settings of the O/S and browser, make it difficult to pin down exactly what the cause of a problem is.
- Firewall and port issues can be frustrating because something that worked yesterday might be failing today. Maintaining all of the rules in a firewall isn't easy and periodically that team will make a mistake and your application might be impacted. Chapter 15 provides information on tools that can be used to identify what firewall ports are open.

Overall is it harder or easier to support a web-based application than a client-server application? It's difficult to answer that question broadly. A lot of it depends on the applications themselves. Some are difficult to support, while others are significantly easier to work with.

Some things are easier under a web-based application and some things are more difficult. Bringing up a new user is easier because you don't have to load software onto his or her PC. Typically, you just have to add their account to the application and give them the URL to go to within their web browser.

On the other hand, troubleshooting access or performance problems can be more difficult due to the larger number of components and interconnections. Here are just a few possible causes that you'll have to investigate. Some of these causes apply to both client-server and web-based applications:

- Is the user entering the correct URL into the web browser?
- Is he or she using a supported browser?

- Does the user have an account in the application?
- Is the user correctly entering their ID and password?
- Is the user's application account enabled?
- Is the user's network account in Active Directory enabled?
- Is the firewall port between the user and the web server open?
- Is the DNS name being resolved correctly?
- Is the web server having resource issues, i.e., disk space, memory, database connections?
- Are the application's services running on the web server?
- Is the load balancer on the web server running correctly?
- Is the firewall port open between the web server and the database server?
- Is the database server up?
- Has the application's account on the database server expired?
- Is the database software running on the database server?
- Has the database server run out of resources, e.g., disk space or memory?

2.7 THE TOTAL COST OF OWNERSHIP (TCO) OF YOUR APPLICATION

The licensing costs that you pay the vendor are only the tip of the iceberg when it comes to the total costs of running an application. Some of the often overlooked costs are:

- Annual maintenance fees are significant. 22% of the original cost of the application isn't an uncommon percentage for this annual expenditure.
- Cost of installing the software. Be sure to include the time of your personnel as well as any consultant fees that are involved with the install.
- Cost of consulting to customize it. Many applications are so complex that an organization's employees aren't able to customize the out-of-the-box application to make it usable for the organization. Customization when done by the vendor's personnel or contractors can become very expensive, very quickly.
- Hardware—While the Moore's law says hardware is doubling in speed every 18 months, it hasn't reached the point where hardware is free yet.
- Training costs add up. Be sure to include the all of your training costs, including Application Administrators, users, and help desk personnel. You may think you're saving money if you don't train your people, but that's a false economy. You're still paying the cost in lower productivity and mistakes that untrained or under-trained employees make.
- Cost of real estate in your data center.
- Cost of electricity and cooling in your data center.
- Cost of your internal support, i.e., the network administrators, security team, server administrators, etc. These costs can be prorated across multiple applications, but they still exist.
- Cost of middleware and other support software. Some examples are the database used by the application. Don't forget to include other support software like IBM WebLogic, reporting packages, monitoring tools, backup software like CommVault.
- Cost of disk space, including that used for making backups.

Architecture

3.1 APPLICATION ARCHITECTURE

Many software development projects are built upon an underlying framework. A software framework is a reusable platform used by vendors to develop their product. Some goals of using a framework are to make the software easier to write, more consistent, and have fewer errors in the finished code.

The purpose of the framework is to provide standardized, low-level functionality so the programmers can focus on higher-level design requirements. Some examples of the functionality that a framework might provide include the following:

- Memory management, i.e., allocating and freeing up memory
- Garbage collection of unused memory
- Exception handling
- Resizing windows
- Opening and closing windows
- Moving windows
- Security
- Compilers
- Code libraries
- An Application Programming Interface (API)
- Templates
- Session management
- Caching

Examples of frameworks are:

- Spring Framework for Java
- Apache Cocoon Framework for Java
- Microsoft's .NET Framework for C# and Visual Basic
- Ruby on Rails for the language Ruby
- Django framework for the language Python
- Blueprint is a frame for CSS (Cascading Style Sheets)

The application you are supporting might or might not be based on a framework. It's not mandatory that you know whether it's built on a framework, but knowing this and the specific framework provides useful background knowledge for you.

How can you determine whether your application was built on a framework and what it is? The answer might be in the installation manual. The overview section of the installation manual might specify what framework is being used. If this isn't explicitly mentioned, then you can probably figure it out based on what software have to be loaded onto the server prior to beginning the build process of the application. For example, if one of the preliminary steps is to install .NET, then .NET is your framework. If you're required to load the JRE (Java Runtime Environment), then the language being used is Java and a framework may or may not have been used.

In addition to frameworks, there are other software components that your application may rely upon. Some of these will be explored in greater detail later in this book, but a thumbnail description of them is provided here. You won't need to be an expert regarding them, but having at least an introductory knowledge of what they are and what they do is useful.

.NET is a programming framework created by Microsoft. As of 2013, the most recent version of this package is .NET Framework 4.5. If your application was written using a Microsoft language, then you'll very likely have to install .NET prior to loading your application. Having multiple versions of .NET running on a computer is possible.

Java is a programming language that was developed at Sun Microsystems and released in 1995. Sun Microsystems was later acquired by Oracle Corporation. The basic intention of Java was to allow programmers to write code once and it would be able to run on any platform. This has largely been achieved and currently Java applications run on millions of machines. Java is particularly widely used for web applications.

There are a number of Java packages or components that you will likely run into. The major elements are:

- JDK (Java Development Kit) refers a product aimed toward Java developers. It consists of numerous tools that a programmer would use to write a Java-based application. It's very unlikely that you will be required to load the JDK onto a production application server.
- JRE (Java Runtime Environment) consists of class libraries and support files that are needed to run Java applications on a computer. If the application you're supporting was written in Java, then you will likely be required to load the JRE onto your application server. There is no licensing fee to load the JRE onto your servers.
- JVM (Java Virtual Machine) is a program that runs on your server to create its own environment, aka a virtual machine, in which Java bytecode can be executed. One advantage of running Java within a virtual machine is that it makes it easier to provide more detailed debugging information if the software errors occur. If you have loaded the JRE onto your server, then a JVM can be running on the server.

Microsoft's Internet Information Services (IIS), formerly known as Internet Information Server, is a platform for developing and hosting web applications and services. IIS runs only on Windows operating systems, for example Windows 2008 R2 and Windows 2003. The latest version of this web server is 7.5. If your application is accessed by users via a web browser, then there's a fair chance that this piece of software might be required on the server.

Apache Tomcat is an open source web server that was developed by the Apache Software Foundation (ASF). Apache is one of the most common packages used for powering web servers.

The phrase "application server" can refer to either to a piece of hardware, i.e., a server, or a piece of support software. In the context of the second definition, Application Servers support web applications by providing fundamental services for it. Examples of services that it might provide include:

- Support the construction of dynamic web pages
- Handling database connections
- Provides security-related services
- Supports the processing of transactions
- Clustering
- Failover
- Load balancing

By relying on an Application Server, the application's developers can focus on coding the high-level features of their application. An Application Server typically works with a web server, e.g., IIS or Apache, and a SQL (Structured Query Language) database. Examples of Application servers include:

- WebLogic Application Server is a Java-based application server marketed by Oracle Corporation
- IBM's WebSphere Application Server
- JBoss Application Server is an open source Java Enterprise Edition (EE)-based application server. While JBoss is open source, Red Hat charges a licensing fee for JBoss Enterprise Middleware.

Oracle Client is a middleware product that is required to connect to an Oracle database that is running on a database server. Oracle Client isn't hard to install and doesn't take up much disk space. Once installed, it provides the software layer needed to communicate between tools like SQL*Plus or SQL Developer and the database server.

JDBC, Java Database Connectivity API, is a collection of interfaces and classes that enable Java programs to interact with relational databases via SQL (Structured Query Language) statements. If your application is Java based and it connects to a relational database, then you will probably have to install some flavor of JDBC. A short list of the databases for which JDBC drivers have been written include:

- DB2
- Informix
- Ingres
- Oracle
- Microsoft SQL Server
- MySQL
- Sybase

3.2 THROUGH THICK AND THIN

One way of categorizing the design of computer system is whether the client computers are "thick" or "thin." Other common terms as "fat," "lean," or "slim." The reference to the client computer refers to how much processing it can do on its own. A thin client does relatively little processing beyond presenting data sent to it by the server. A thick client, in contrast, is capable of doing more processing itself and is less dependent on the server.

What are the advantages of each approach? A thin client needs significantly less computing power than a thick client requires, which can translate into a less expensive device. In contrast, since thick clients do more of the work, the server that supports them can be less powerful. Thick clients are able to work offline in the event that the server goes down. They also have better multimedia performance.

3.3 TIERS

When computer systems are designed, the largest components that they are made up of are frequently referred to as tiers. Figure 3.1 shows the layout of a three-tiered architecture. The three major tiers that systems are broken down into are:

- Client or presentation logic tier
- Business logic or application processing tier
- Database tier

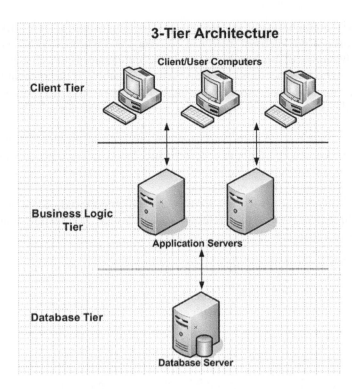

FIGURE 3.1

Three-tier architecture. (For color version of this figure, the reader is referred to the online version of this chapter.)

The presentation tier is what the users see and interact with. It displays screens with dynamic data, labels, and other objects to the users. The users interact with the application via a wide variety of controls or "widgets." Some common means of interaction are:

- Entering data into text fields
- Modifying the data in text fields
- Deleting rows in tables
- Dragging and dropping objects
- Clicking on buttons
- Clicking on menu items
- Clicking on links
- Highlighting the contents of fields and copying them

The application tier, also called the business logic tier, is the middle tier. Some examples of what this layer includes are business calculations, definitions of business objects, controlling how business objects interact, implementing security, and performing authentication. This tier requests data from the data management tier and then manipulates it according the business logic. The results are fed to the presentation layer.

The data management tier, aka database tier, is where the data resides. Typically, this layer is a relational database management system (RDBMS) like Oracle, SQL Server, MySQL, or another package. It doesn't have to be an RDBMS. It could be an object-oriented database or a collection of flat files. The only requirement is that there be a set of well-defined interfaces between the application and data management tiers.

One of the major advantages of using multiple tiers in the architecture is that changes can be made to a tier as long as the interfaces with the other tiers aren't changed. For example, if the application were using Oracle as the database package, the data management tier could be rewritten to use Microsoft SQL server. As long as the interface between the application tier and the data management tier doesn't change, this change won't cause any problems.

Another advantage is each tier can be moved from one server to another without the overall application being affected. You could increase throughput or performance by upgrading the hardware that the application or data management tiers are running on. You could even implement a load balanced package to one of the tiers without making any changes to the other tiers.

A very common architecture is a three-tier architecture utilizing the tiers listed above. Any design that includes greater than three tiers is generically referred to as an "*n*-tier" architecture. Some examples of additional tiers that can be included are:

- Web server tier—web server software that interacts with users who are using web browsers to access the application
- Workflow tier—handles workflow logic within the application
- External interface tier—handles interfaces with entities outside the application

3.3.1 Middleware

What is middleware? One analogy compares middleware with the plumbing in a home or office building. Plumbing connects various components together, for example, there are pipes connecting the water heater to the shower. Middleware that supports an application also connects components or tiers together. For example, the application probably uses libraries of functions that are called to get things done. The application developer could have written these functions from scratch, but it isn't cost effective to recreate code that already exists in readily available code libraries.

I'm reluctant to provide a list of middleware because it can become extremely technical. It can also open up arguments about exactly what is and isn't middleware. The following is a very brief list of the types of functionality that would generally be considered middleware.

- Software used to establish database connectivity
- Software used to establish network connectivity
- Software that enables RPC (remote procedure calls) interaction between servers
- Software that enables platform transparency, for example, it would translate between EBCDIC and ASCII
- Object Request Brokers
- Software that allows network transparency, for example, it might convert between TCP/IP and other protocols
- File transfer software
- Load balancing software
- Software that allows different database systems to look like a single system
- Database gateway products that allow the application to connect to more than one relational database package
- Software that allows an application to integrate with legacy applications
- Software that enables Single Sign on logins
- Transaction monitoring packages

3.4 COMPUTERS, CPUs, AND CORES

A CPU or central processing unit is the brains of a computer. A CPU can reside on a single chip within the computer. A multiprocessor computer has more than one CPU in it. Each CPU can execute instructions independently. The processors can all be on the same motherboard or on multiple motherboards. It's common for powerful computers, especially servers, to have multiple processors. If a computer has more than one processor, it will be referred to as a dual-processor, quad-processor, etc., depending on the number of processors.

A CPU can be built with more than one processor in it, i.e., there are multiple processors on the same integrated circuit. Each of these processors is referred to as a core. Each core is identical to the others on the same chip. The number of cores available within a single CPU is continuously increasing as CPU chipsets become more and more miniaturized.

The advantage of multiple processors and multiple cores is that they can run programs faster than a single core or a single processor. Virtually, every server that is bought today has multiple processors, multiple cores, or both.

The most important question of all when it comes to the number of server, processors, and cores is whether the application takes advantage of all the processors and cores that are available on the server. The answer is probably yes, but to be sure you'll have to get the answer to this question from the vendor. One source is to read through their manuals. Start with the Installation Manual or the Application Administrator Guide first. If you don't find it in the documentation, then try contacting their tech support group. It would be wasted resources to have a server with multiple processors and multiple cores being used by an application that isn't capable of utilizing them.

An easy way to determine if a Windows-based computer has multiple processors is to run "systeminfo" in a Command window. One of the sections in the output from that command tells the number of processors the computer has. Figure 3.2 shows the output for a computer with a single processor. Figure 3.3 shows the systeminfo output for a computer with multiple processors.

```
System Manufacturer:       Dell Inc.
System Model:              Inspiron 570
System Type:               x64-based PC
Processor(s):              1 Processor(s) Installed.
                           [01]: AMD64 Family 16 Model 5 Stepping 3 AuthenticAMD ~3100 Mhz
```

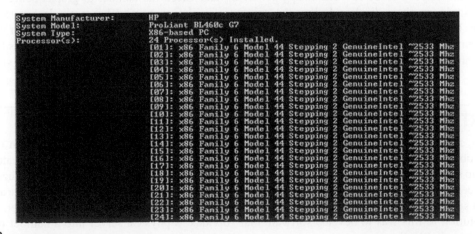

FIGURE 3.2

Output from systeminfo command.

```
System Manufacturer:       HP
System Model:              ProLiant BL460c G7
System Type:               X86-based PC
Processor(s):              24 Processor(s) Installed.
                           [01]: x86 Family 6 Model 44 Stepping 2 GenuineIntel ~2533 Mhz
                           [02]: x86 Family 6 Model 44 Stepping 2 GenuineIntel ~2533 Mhz
                           [03]: x86 Family 6 Model 44 Stepping 2 GenuineIntel ~2533 Mhz
                           [04]: x86 Family 6 Model 44 Stepping 2 GenuineIntel ~2533 Mhz
                           [05]: x86 Family 6 Model 44 Stepping 2 GenuineIntel ~2533 Mhz
                           [06]: x86 Family 6 Model 44 Stepping 2 GenuineIntel ~2533 Mhz
                           [07]: x86 Family 6 Model 44 Stepping 2 GenuineIntel ~2533 Mhz
                           [08]: x86 Family 6 Model 44 Stepping 2 GenuineIntel ~2533 Mhz
                           [09]: x86 Family 6 Model 44 Stepping 2 GenuineIntel ~2533 Mhz
                           [10]: x86 Family 6 Model 44 Stepping 2 GenuineIntel ~2533 Mhz
                           [11]: x86 Family 6 Model 44 Stepping 2 GenuineIntel ~2533 Mhz
                           [12]: x86 Family 6 Model 44 Stepping 2 GenuineIntel ~2533 Mhz
                           [13]: x86 Family 6 Model 44 Stepping 2 GenuineIntel ~2533 Mhz
                           [14]: x86 Family 6 Model 44 Stepping 2 GenuineIntel ~2533 Mhz
                           [15]: x86 Family 6 Model 44 Stepping 2 GenuineIntel ~2533 Mhz
                           [16]: x86 Family 6 Model 44 Stepping 2 GenuineIntel ~2533 Mhz
                           [17]: x86 Family 6 Model 44 Stepping 2 GenuineIntel ~2533 Mhz
                           [18]: x86 Family 6 Model 44 Stepping 2 GenuineIntel ~2533 Mhz
                           [19]: x86 Family 6 Model 44 Stepping 2 GenuineIntel ~2533 Mhz
                           [20]: x86 Family 6 Model 44 Stepping 2 GenuineIntel ~2533 Mhz
                           [21]: x86 Family 6 Model 44 Stepping 2 GenuineIntel ~2533 Mhz
                           [22]: x86 Family 6 Model 44 Stepping 2 GenuineIntel ~2533 Mhz
                           [23]: x86 Family 6 Model 44 Stepping 2 GenuineIntel ~2533 Mhz
                           [24]: x86 Family 6 Model 44 Stepping 2 GenuineIntel ~2533 Mhz
```

FIGURE 3.3

Output from systeminfo on a multiprocessor computer.

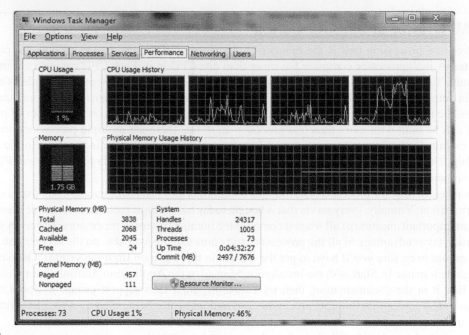

FIGURE 3.4

Task Manager showing statistics for a 4-core processor. (For color version of this figure, the reader is referred to the online version of this chapter.)

To determine how many cores a Windows computer has, open Task Manager and click on the Performance tab. The utility will show details on CPU Usage in either a single, i.e., composite, graph or multiple graphs. To switch between a composite mode and separate graphs, select menu item View | CPU History and either "One Graph per CPU" or "One Graph, All CPUs." The exact wording for the submenu might vary depending on the version of Windows that is running.

Change the display mode to "One Graph per CPU" and check the number of graphs being displayed. If only a single graph is displayed, then the computer you're examining has a single processor and a single core. If multiple graphs are being displayed, the number of graphs reflects the number of processors times the number of cores. Figure 3.4 is a screenshot taken on a single-processor computer that has four cores. The screenshot in Figure 3.5 was taken on a computer with 24 processors, each of which has a single core.

3.5 VIRTUAL SERVERS

In the past, most servers were dedicated to a single application. This made administering them easier and avoided problems that occurred when applications didn't cooperate, i.e., play well together. Dedicated servers were easy to set up and administer, but resulted in the problem of having a large number of underutilized servers in the data center. As servers become more powerful, it was seen as increasingly wasteful to dedicate a powerful server to a single application or task that wasn't fully utilizing the processing power of the server.

The solution to this was to develop software that "divides" a physical server into a number of distinct "virtual" servers. Ideally, each virtual server is completely separate from any other virtual server running on the physical device.

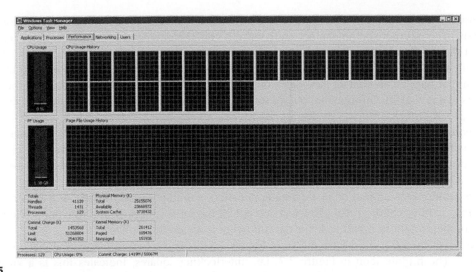

FIGURE 3.5

Task Manager showing a computer with multiple processors. (For color version of this figure, the reader is referred to the online version of this chapter.)

While virtualization software is good and constantly improving, sometimes the ideal of completely distinct virtual servers isn't always achieved. One disadvantage to virtual servers is that it can be difficult to troubleshoot performance problems. They can also be difficult to properly set up. Another downside to virtual servers is that if the physical device goes down, then every virtual server being hosted by it goes down.

The advantages of virtualization most definitely outweigh the negatives. Server consolidation is probably the primary reason that data centers are moving from physical servers to virtual ones in droves. It's much more economical to have far fewer servers hosting virtual servers than having dozens or hundreds of physical servers each running at 10-20% utilization rates. The savings will be seen in reduced power consumption, reduced cooling costs, and reduced investment in hardware. Additionally, fewer servers can be administered with fewer Systems Administrators, thus saving on personnel costs.

In addition to the obvious ability to more efficiently utilize your hardware, there are some additional advantages. Virtual servers can be created and destroyed much more quickly and more easily than physical servers. If your environment requires that new servers frequently be set up and then fairly quickly dropped, then virtualization might be your best solution. Another advantage is that it's easy to copy a template and create numerous identical servers. If you value homogeneity, then that's another reason to go with virtual servers.

As virtualization becomes more mainstream, the number of vendors in that market space has increased. Some of these products are open source and others are proprietary. Some of the most recognized of them include:

- VMWare
- Citrix Xen
- Microsoft Hyper-V
- Red Hat
- Oracle
- Proxmox
- Parallels

Not all vendors certify their software to be run on a virtual server. This is becoming less common as server virtualization becomes more commonplace and robust. If you're planning to migrate the application to virtual servers, you should get a confirmation from the vendor that this is a supported environment. The first place to check is their website. Look for a specifications page for the application you're interested in. If the information isn't on that page, then contact their sales or support groups. You could search the web for articles or white papers that reveal this information, but for something as important as this you should get it directly from the source.

If you learn from the vendor that the application is certified to run on a virtual server, then make sure you understand which ones are supported. You don't want to invest in VMware software when the only environment the application is certified for is Citrix Xen. Also make sure you know which versions of the virtualization software it will run under.

If you're taking over support of an existing application, you might want to find out whether your application servers are physical or virtual. How can you tell? If the server in question is running a Windows operating system, then log onto it and look for the following icons on the toolbar.

Hovering over the right-most icon shown in Figure 3.6 displays a tool tip indicating that the server is a physical box. The middle icon in Figure 3.7, i.e., interlocking squares, indicates this is a virtual server running VMware.

One final thing to remember about virtual servers is that virtual isn't synonymous with free. Virtualization introduces economies by reducing the number of servers in a data center. They make creating or dropping servers much more quickly than buying and building physical servers. But even with all those benefits, they still cost money. Acquiring the host server is an expense. The virtualization software can be an expensive. The time to set up a virtual server is quicker, but still exists.

One expense that can be easily overlooked is the cost of software licenses. You have to have licensed copies of software loaded on a server whether it's a physical or virtual server. For example, if you have a physical server running Windows 2008 R2 which hosts six virtual servers each running Windows 2008 R2, then you have to pay for seven copies of Windows 2008 R2. Don't forget software licensing costs when designing or pricing out your architecture.

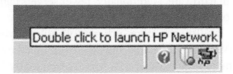

FIGURE 3.6

Icon indicating that the server is physical. (For color version of this figure, the reader is referred to the online version of this chapter.)

FIGURE 3.7

Icon indicating the server is virtual. (For color version of this figure, the reader is referred to the online version of this chapter.)

3.6 FAULT TOLERANT

A fault-tolerant system is one that continues to operate or at least degrades gracefully if one or more faults occur. An example of a fault would be if a server crashes or a disk becomes corrupted. Achieving fault tolerance isn't easy or inexpensive, so it's usually found only on systems that are critical or involve human lives. If your application is a typical business system like payroll or HR, then it probably doesn't need to be fault tolerant. On the other hand, if you're working on the avionics system of a commercial jetliner, then designing a fault-tolerant system would be appropriate.

Fault-tolerance adds complexity to a system. Additional hardware is being added, additional software is being added, or both to help ensure the system never goes down. From an Application Administrator's viewpoint, this makes the system harder to maintain. The exact ways in which it might make your job harder depend on how it was implanted, but some possible ways are:

- Installation will be more time consuming because there will be more servers to load the software onto.
- Shutting down and starting the system will be more difficult. This is because more servers are involved, but also because there are probably more stringent steps for taking the system down and bringing it back up, e.g., server "A" has to come down before server "B" can be shut down.
- Monitoring log files will be more time consuming simply because there are more of them and they are spread out across multiple servers.
- Monitoring the overall system will be more difficult because there are more servers to watch, but also because you won't want to generate false alarms. For example, if server "A" goes down in a nonfault-tolerant system that might be a fatal error and require that the monitoring system automatically restarts the server. On a fault-tolerant system if server "A" goes down then server "B" automatically assumes the primary server job. Server "A" might need to be restarted manually to ensure that it doesn't try to reclaim its job as the primary server.
- If problems occur in the hardware or software that controls the fault-tolerant nature of the system, then fixing this will very likely be very complex. More than likely you'll have to have a vendor technician involved in the process.

One additional advantage of a fault-tolerant system is that it's possible to install an upgrade without taking the system down. The method of doing this would be to

1. Take one server out of usage
2. Install the upgrade on that server
3. Bring it back into the system and make it the primary, i.e., active, server
4. Remove a second server and install the upgrades on it
5. Repeat until all servers have been upgraded

This process is more time consuming, but if your application absolutely can't be shut down, then this is a way to install upgrades with zero down time.

3.7 RUNNING MULTIPLE APPLICATIONS ON A SERVER

Should multiple applications be installed on a single, physical server? Like most other architectural considerations, there are advantages and disadvantages for each choice. Some reasons for running multiple applications on a single server are:

- Allows you to take advantage of idle CPU cycles
- Fewer physical servers means lower cost
- The data center can be smaller, cooler, and cheaper to operate

Some reasons not to run more than one application on a server

- Applications can impact each other and cause problems
- Performance impact of one application on another can be a problem, especially if one application is heavily used
- Need to coordinate down times

In an era when the cost of servers is coming down and server virtualization is widely available, the answer to this question is likely to be "no." If you have numerous applications that have lower resource requirements, you'd probably be better off installing them on their own virtual servers.

3.8 VIRTUALIZED DESKTOPS

Applications can be run on a user's desktop, on a web server, or on a virtualized desktop. One example of software that allows you to create a virtualized desktop includes Citrix XenApp. To access this last instance, the users have to log into Citrix via a browser session, connect to the application server, and within the session window run the application.

Advantages of a virtualized desktop include:

- Don't have to load the application on numerous user desktops.
- Need to purchase fewer licenses of the application since users can share the instance that is running on the virtualized desktop.

Disadvantages:

- Introduces another layer of software that has to be installed, upgraded, and otherwise maintained.
- Some software vendors don't support this way of implementing their product. If you run into problems, you're on your own.
- If the virtualized desktop layer or connectivity to it goes down, your users are out of luck.
- Possible performance issues because you're going across the network to get to the application.
- If multiple applications are running on the virtualized desktop, there may be a performance impact.

Examples of software that allows you to create a virtualized desktop include

- Citrix XenApp
- Microsoft Windows 2012 Remote Desktop Services
- VMware ThinApp

3.9 HIGH AVAILABILITY/HIGH PERFORMANCE

If the application you support has some extreme needs, then it might have been architected with high availability or high performance in mind. The following sections describe the environments.

3.9.1 Clustering

A computer cluster refers to a group of computers that are working together on similar task. The two main reasons for clustering computers are to:

1. Improve performance or throughput
2. To improve uptime by providing a backup computer in case the primary computer fails.

Before running out to purchase and install a cluster of servers for your application, you need to answer a very important question—does it need to run on a cluster? If high availability isn't critical to the organization, then is it worth paying for the extra hardware, software, and maintenance? Similarly, if the application's performance isn't a problem, then is it worth paying for a clustered environment? Investing in a single server that is more powerful might be a better solution than a cluster of computers.

If you decide to go with a clustered environment, you need to be aware that it will probably make administering the application more complicated. Some of the complications that you may encounter include the following:

- Installs will be more complicated because typically you'll have to install the application software on each cluster member individually. Once the individual cluster members have been built, then you'll go through a process of defining the members of the cluster and identify which is the primary computer and which are the backups.
- Upgrades will be similarly complicated. You'll have to apply the upgrade to each member of the cluster. If you're lucky, you might be able to apply the upgrade without taking the entire cluster down. This could be done by taking a backup server out of the cluster, updating it, returning it to the cluster, and then making it the primary server. Then you would apply the upgrade to all the nonprimary servers.
- Backups will be more complex because there are multiple servers involved. Make sure you practice restoring from backups before the clustered environment goes live. Restoring a production environment isn't something you want to practice doing when users are waiting for the application to be brought back up.
- If the application is web based, what URL do users enter to access the application? If the primary server goes down, do they continue to use the same URL or do they need to enter a different URL to access the backup server?
- You will want to create a test or QA environment that duplicates the production environment. So if production is composed of a cluster of four servers, then you'll need four servers in cluster for the QA environment. Be sure to include this additional overhead in your cost estimates.

3.9.2 Load balancing

Load balancing is a technique to use additional hardware components to increase throughput, reduce response time, and increase uptime. Examples of components that can be added in a load balanced environment are web servers, database servers, processors, network links, and disk drives.

Load balancing and clustering are similar, but not exactly the same concept. One explanation is that clustering typically includes load balancing, but load balancing doesn't necessarily include clustering. For example, an environment might be set up like the following:

1. Load balancing software captures a user's request to open a session with the application
2. The application is running on multiple, separate servers which are in different cities
3. The load balancer assigns the new request to a server based on some criteria, perhaps the server that is least busy or the server that is physically closest to the user.

The above environment describes a load balanced environment that doesn't include clustering.

Some applications are designed to work in load balanced environments, but you shouldn't make any assumptions. Read the installation documentation or contact the vendor's support team to determine if the application you're supporting can work in a load balanced environment.

3.9.3 Heartbeats and failover

A heartbeat in a computer system is a method by which computers monitor each other to make sure all of them are functioning. Suppose your environment includes a primary and backup computer. The backup computer needs to way to confirm that the primary computer is up and running. The heartbeat is a signaling method between computers that lets them keep an eye on each other. If the backup computer fails to see the heartbeat of the primary computer, then it will assume that the primary computer has failed. It will then step up and become the primary computer.

There are a great many ways that heartbeats can be designed. If your application employs a heartbeat technique, then you won't have to design or code it yourself. As an Application Administrator you will need to understand the following:

- How the heartbeat was implemented
- How it can go wrong
- How to reset it if necessary.

3.9.4 Added complexity

Adding clustering or load balancing to a system makes it more complex. This leads to increase the cost and makes it more difficult to administer. If the number of users that will be using the application is well within what a single server can handle, then you might want to reconsider setting up a clustered or load balanced environment. Why add more overhead if you don't need it?

Once again, if your production environment includes clustering or load balancing, then you'll have to create an identical environment for test or QA. This cost needs to be included when calculating the total cost of the application environment.

Your application production environment needs to be duplicated in a QA (quality assurance), test, or staging environment. If production includes complexities like clustering, failover, or load balancing, then QA, test, or staging needs to have clustering, failover, or load balancing too. The reason for this is that you never ever want to make a change in production that hasn't already been tested in an identical QA, test, or staging environment.

It will cost more to do this, but the more complex your production environment is the more valuable this advice becomes. If you only remember a couple of pieces of advice from this entire chapter, then these are two that you need to remember:

1. The production environment needs to be mirrored.
2. Never make a change on production without first having tested it in an identical environment.

3.10 OPERATING SYSTEMS

An operating system or O/S is a software that manages the computer's memory, hardware, and software. It enables the computer to communicate with hardware components like disk drives, keyboard, monitor, mouse, printers, scanners, and the network. An operating system enables multiple applications to run on the computer at the same time, switching control back and forth between them. Without a functional operating system, a computer is essentially useless.

One decision that might need to be made is whether to run a 32- or a 64-bit operating system. The application may require one or may run under either. The biggest differences between 32- and 64-bit systems are in how much memory can be accessed and how memory is managed. Applications that have been written to take advantage of a 64-bit operating system will perform better on a 64-bit system.

Operating systems come in a wide variety of sizes and level of complexity. The largest supercomputer in the world has an operating system and so does your microwave oven. The servers that your application runs on will almost certainly have an off-the-shelf, commercial operating system. The most common choices are versions of:

- Windows
- Unix
- Linux
- Apple's Mac OS X

3.11 WINDOWS VS. UNIX VS. LINUX

Arguments about which of these operating systems are the best or the worst can quickly escalate into a religious like furor. I'm not going to get into that argument. I'm also not to push one over the others. An Application Administrator doesn't get to choose the operating system of the server. Very likely one of the following situations will control that decision:

1. The O/S that the application is compatible with
2. The O/S already on the servers that will be used
3. The O/S that Systems Administrators in the data center have the most experience supporting

3.11.1 Windows

Microsoft has marketed Windows operating systems since 1985. The first version was essentially a graphical user interface for their existing operating system MS-DOS. Since then releases of Windows have been steady if not regular. The software expanded from 16-bit versions to 32 bits and then to 64 bits. Each new version generally represented an increase in the amount of memory that could be accessed, features offered, improvements in security, and more intuitive user interface.

3.11.2 UNIX

The UNIX operating system was developed at AT&T's Bell Labs in 1969. The original version was written in assembly language, but by 1973 most of it had been rewritten in C. In the years since then, it has undergone numerous revisions, spinoffs, and disagreements about what is the "official" version. UNIX is the operating system for thousands of servers around the world.

3.11.3 Linux

Linux began as a personal project to write a new operating system by Linus Torvalds. Torvalds solicited help from the programming community to expand and improve Linux. It is available free as open source software. Some companies sell versions of Linux that include installation CDs, printed documentation, installation tools, technical support, etc.

3.12 STORAGE

Every application requires storage space, i.e., files stored on a disk drive. An application server will have one or more drives. The individual drives typically contain hundreds of gigabytes (GB) of data. While that amount of storage might seem more than could ever be used, but it always seems to be consumed more quickly than you expect.

If there are more than one drives attached to a server, what goes on each drive? On a Windows server, the normal arrangement is that drive letters begin with C and go upward from there. What typically goes on each drive is shown below:

- C: Operating system (O/S) files
- D: Application files, including executables
- E: (if it exists) Data, temp, or log files

Two reasons why only O/S files should loaded onto the C: drive are:

1. It minimizes the chances that an installation of the application will corrupt O/S files
2. Data files, log files, and other output files created by applications tend to grow. If they grow on the C: drive, they can consume all the free space. If this happens, the system can crash. If they consume all the space on another drive, the application will crash, but not the server.

3.12.1 Storage area network (SAN)

A SAN is a network resource that provides disk storage to other servers, for example, application servers. Instead of having a local drive that is physically attached to it, your server would be allocated drive space on a SAN. The most obvious risk when using a SAN is that all disk I/O flows across the network between the application server and the SAN device. If your network doesn't have adequate bandwidth, then using a SAN isn't a realistic alternative.

Why would you choose to use a SAN instead of local drives? Some of the reasons for using SAN drives are:

- The organization can purchase larger, faster, more economical drives and share them across multiple application servers. This saves money and administrative effort for the organization.
- If virtual servers are being used, then SAN drives must be used because a physical hard drive can't be attached to a virtual server. Think of it this way—a virtual server doesn't have a connector that the physical drive can be plugged into.
- SAN drives are more flexible than local drives that are physically connected to the server. For example, say your application was loaded onto a 100 GB D: drive attached to the server. If all 100GB of it gets used up, what can you do? You could buy a larger drive and copy everything from the old drive to the new drive. Of course, this will require that the application be down. You could purchase an additional drive and install it as the E: drive. Then you would have to configure the application to recognize and use the new drive. You might also need to copy at least some files from the D: drive to the E: drive to free up disk space on the D: drive. If a SAN drive were being used, you would just have to contact the SAN team and request that your D: drive be enlarged. That's it. No muss, no fuss, and no down time.
- The SAN team can configure the physical drives behind the SAN using RAID (Redundant Array of Independent Disks) technology. RAID can provide faster access and redundancy so if one of the drives goes down, no data will be lost and the application can keep on working.
- As the Application Administrator, you're "outsourcing" responsibility of storage resources to a dedicated team. You don't have to become an expert in storage technology. One team is dedicated to this specialty and they make decisions for the entire organization.
- Backups can be administered for entire organization instead of on an application-by-application basis. This can make the backup process faster, more consistent, and more reliable. Again, it lets you as the Application Administrator outsource this facet to a dedicated team.

One question that you need to confirm with the vendor is whether the application supports SAN drives. Some applications aren't certified to be used with SAN drives. The reasoning behind this is that the vendor thinks that the performance of a SAN drive doesn't meet the application's needs. Essentially, if the SAN is slow, then the application will be slow. The vendor doesn't want to be blamed if the network or SAN is slow.

A word of advice here—if your application exhibits performance problems and the server uses SAN storage, it's very likely that the vendor support team will blame the problem on SAN. On the other side, your internal SAN or network team will insist that the problem isn't due to either SAN or the network. This leaves you in a very awkward position. The best you can do is to gather statistics on network performance to help identify the root cause of the problem. Better yet, have baseline network statistics from when the application's performance was "normal." This will give you something to compare the current, i.e., bad, statistics with.

Some of the most widely used SAN packages include:

- 3PAR
- Dell
- EMC
- HDS
- HP
- IBM
- Intransa
- MPC
- Sun Microsystems
- Xiotech

How can you find out if your organization is using SAN instead of local drives? The most definitive way is to ask the technical staff in your data center. There are commands that can provide this information, but there are a lot of exceptions to what they return. Asking the group that built the server will ensure you get the correct answer for all circumstances.

3.12.2 Solid-state drive (SSD)

A solid-state drive is data device that uses memory instead of disk drives to store data. The biggest advantage of an SSD is that since it is all electronic, it has no moving parts. This makes it much faster than a disk drive. In addition to being faster than hard drives, SSDs are also more reliable. The downside is that they are more expensive and don't have the capacity that a hard drive can have. As time goes by, the capacities of SSDs are going up and prices are coming down, so if they aren't practical for you today, they might be in a year or two.

Before making a significant investment in an SSD, you need to determine whether they would have a significant impact on your application. The best sources for this information include:

- Contact your application vendor's technical support group and ask whether SSD can be included in the environment advantageously. Try to get specifics like what performance improvements you can realistically expect to see.
- Network with other clients using this application that have either tested or implement this modification to their environment. If you are able to attend the vendor's user group conferences, this would be an excellent place to ask other Application Administrators about their experiences.
- If possible, get an SSD device on loan and test it in-house. You'll do this on your application's QA or test environment of course. You'll have to run stress tests before and after the SSD is installed and being used.

3.13 WHAT DOES YOUR SERVER LOOK LIKE?

By this, I'm not asking if it's an off-white box with a bunch of blinking lights on the front. I'm referring to the hardware, software, and network connections that make up the server. Some of the basic details that you should know or be able to find out about all of your servers are:

- Is it physical or virtual?
- If it's a virtual server what virtualization package is it running on?
- How many processors does it have?
- How many cores does it have?
- How fast is each CPU?
- How much RAM does it have?
- How much cache memory?
- How many NICs (Network Interface Cards) are there?
- What Operating System is running on it?
- What version and service packs?
- How many disks are there?
- How large is each disk and how much space is free?
- Are the disks connected locally to the server, SAN, or a combination?

How can you get answers to the above questions? Each operating system has tools or commands that can provide this information.

For a Windows-based server, one of the best tools is the "systeminfo" command. This command will provide most of the details you will need. Figure 3.8 shows the output from the systeminfo command.

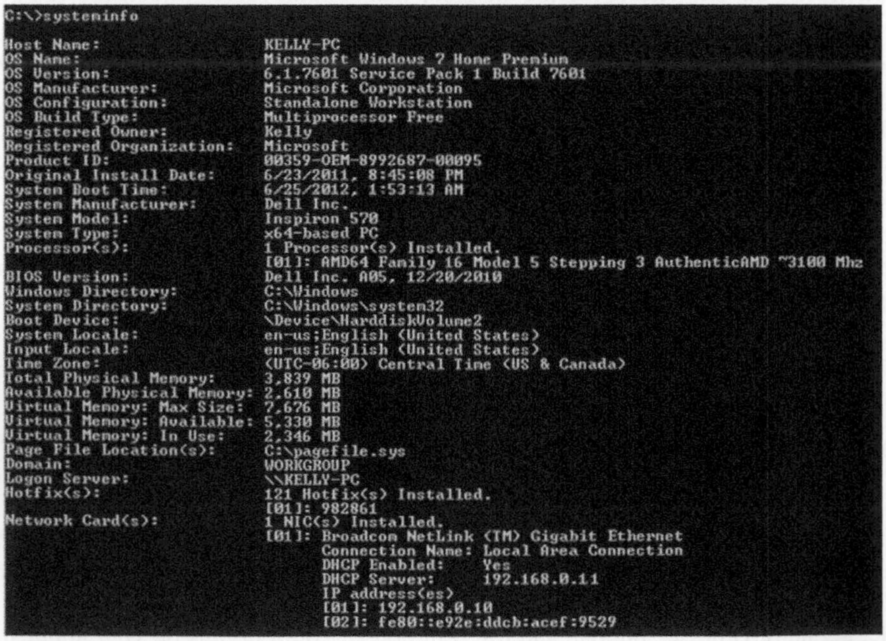

```
C:\>systeminfo

Host Name:                 KELLY-PC
OS Name:                   Microsoft Windows 7 Home Premium
OS Version:                6.1.7601 Service Pack 1 Build 7601
OS Manufacturer:           Microsoft Corporation
OS Configuration:          Standalone Workstation
OS Build Type:             Multiprocessor Free
Registered Owner:          Kelly
Registered Organization:   Microsoft
Product ID:                00359-OEM-8992687-00095
Original Install Date:     6/23/2011, 8:45:08 PM
System Boot Time:          6/25/2012, 1:53:13 AM
System Manufacturer:       Dell Inc.
System Model:              Inspiron 570
System Type:               x64-based PC
Processor(s):              1 Processor(s) Installed.
                           [01]: AMD64 Family 16 Model 5 Stepping 3 AuthenticAMD ~3100 Mhz
BIOS Version:              Dell Inc. A05, 12/20/2010
Windows Directory:         C:\Windows
System Directory:          C:\Windows\system32
Boot Device:               \Device\HarddiskVolume2
System Locale:             en-us;English (United States)
Input Locale:              en-us;English (United States)
Time Zone:                 (UTC-06:00) Central Time (US & Canada)
Total Physical Memory:     3,839 MB
Available Physical Memory: 2,610 MB
Virtual Memory: Max Size:  7,676 MB
Virtual Memory: Available: 5,330 MB
Virtual Memory: In Use:    2,346 MB
Page File Location(s):     C:\pagefile.sys
Domain:                    WORKGROUP
Logon Server:              \\KELLY-PC
Hotfix(s):                 121 Hotfix(s) Installed.
                           [01]: 982861
Network Card(s):           1 NIC(s) Installed.
                           [01]: Broadcom NetLink (TM) Gigabit Ethernet
                                 Connection Name: Local Area Connection
                                 DHCP Enabled:    Yes
                                 DHCP Server:     192.168.0.11
                                 IP address(es)
                                 [01]: 192.168.0.10
                                 [02]: fe80::e92e:ddcb:acef:9529
```

FIGURE 3.8

Output from the systeminfo command.

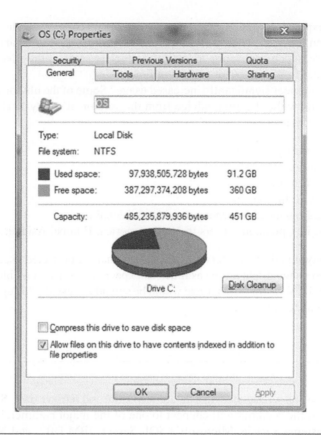

FIGURE 3.9

Properties screen under Windows Explorer. (For color version of this figure, the reader is referred to the online version of this chapter.)

To get the number of cores, you can bring up Task Manager. Figure 3.4 shows a single-processor computer with four cores.

There are a couple of ways to get the amount of total disk space and free disk space in a Windows computer. One is to open Windows Explorer. Then right-click on the disk and select Properties. A screen similar to the one shown in Figure 3.9 will be displayed. Repeat this process for any remaining disk drives on the computer.

Another way to get information on a Windows server's disk drives is from the Computer Management utility. Open Computer Management by clicking Start | Administration Tools | Computer Management. Once it's open, click on Disk Management in the left-hand panel. Figure 3.8 shows the details for the C: and D: drives on a server. The capacity and free space are shown for each drive.

3.14 SCALING UP

Applications usage always seems to either be in a state of expansion or contraction. If the application proves to be valuable to the users, then they expand their use of it. This might be done by adding more data or by using features that weren't previously being used. Adding additional users is another way that use of the application can expand. Use of the application might expand to include users in additional departments, offices, cities, or countries.

One other cause for expansion would be if your organization or company undergoes a merger or acquisition. If that happens, then the M&A team will compare your application with what the other firm is using to do the same job and decide which application to keep and which to scrap. If they decide to retain your application, then you can expect to see its usage grow significantly.

How can you scale up to meet significantly increased usage? Some of the obvious choices are listed here. Don't make these decisions without getting advice from the vendor. It's very likely that they have helped other clients with similar expansions.

- Acquire servers with faster processors
- Acquire servers with more processers
- Acquire processors with more cores
- Allocate more memory to the servers
- Set up a cluster or load balanced environment with additional servers
- Distribute the servers, i.e., position servers in North America, Europe, Asia, etc.

Before rushing out and buying additional servers, you should analyze projected usage by the new users. It's possible that the increased usage might not be as much as expected. It's also possible that the new users will be in different time zones. If this is true, then usage would be spread out evenly throughout the day without the peak usage increasing significantly.

3.15 DATABASES

All but the simplest application will connect to a database to store and retrieve data. Some applications utilize a proprietary database, but the majority will connect to one of the major commercially available relational database management systems. Oracle, Microsoft's SQL Server, IBM DB2, and MySQL are some of the most commonly used database products.

As the Application Administrator, you will want to know as much about the database as you can. Some of the details that you want to learn about are listed here. Additional information on databases is provided in Chapters 8 and 9.

- What server is the database software running on? It most likely won't be on the application server.
- What ports are used for communications between the application and database servers?
- Can you access the database independently of the application? What tool will you use?
- Is the design of the database well documented?
- Can you update or refresh statistics on the database tables?
- Can you add, drop, or modify indexes?
- How can you access any error logs that are generated by the database engine?
- Can you access database performance statistics?
- What configuration settings can be tweaked to improve performance? Are they documented?
- What information is available regarding traffic between the DB server and the application server?
- Are tools available to see the actual queries being submitted to the database server?
- Can database traffic be pinned down to specific application users?
- What account actually owns the application's database? This is frequently referred to as the DBO (DataBase Owner).
- How big is the database currently?
- How much larger can it grow before it runs into problems?

3.15.1 **Connection pooling**

When a user initiates an activity that requires that data be acquired from the database, the application could establish a connection with the database, request the data, and then close the database connection. This approach is simple, but inefficient because establishing connections with the database is relatively time consuming, it would be more efficient to reuse the connections rather than continually create and destroy them. The concept of reusing connections is called connection pooling.

To determine if your application uses "connection pooling" when it connects to the database, you need to refer to the documentation. Start by checking the Installation Manual or the Administrator's Guide. If you can't find anything about connection pooling in any of the manuals, then contact the vendor's support group.

If the application uses it, you may be able to control the maximum number of connections that can be established and pooled. This setting might be specified when the application is installed. Alternatively, it might be in a configuration file. If you change this setting, then you'll very likely have to stop and start the application for the change to be put into effect.

Be aware that each connection consumes a certain amount of memory. Setting this value too high can result in wasted memory, but having it set too small can impact performance. If you think this setting is impacting application performance, you'll need to work with the vendor and your DBAs to identify the number of connections that are needed at any given time.

The database being used by the application also has to have been written to allow connection pooling. The following relational database packages all support pooling:

- IBM DB2
- Microsoft SQL Server
- Oracle
- MySQL

3.16 **CODE BASE**

In the software development world, a code base means the collection of source code that is used to create the application. Basing the development on a single code base is desirable because then all of the focus can be on the one collection of source code. If the application has multiple code bases, then the vendor has more software to support and their resources will be spread out thinner. The end result might be a slower response when researching and correcting problems reported by clients.

If having multiple code bases is such a bad idea, why would a vendor allow them to exist? Some explanations are:

- The vendor has multiple, significantly different versions of the application in use. For example, they may be supporting versions 3.0, 4.0, and 5.0. Vendors vary in how strenuously they push clients to upgrade. Some are willing to let clients run on versions that have long since been replaced. Others are stricter about clients staying closer to the most current version of the application.
- Different code bases may run on different operating systems, for example, a Windows version and a UNIX version. If the application was written relatively recently, this shouldn't require different code bases.
- There may be a client-server version of the application and a web-based version of the application. If they were written in different languages or by different teams, then they might not share a single code base.

3.17 MIDDLEWARE

What is middleware? One analogy compares middleware with the plumbing in a home or office building. Plumbing connects various components together, for example, there are pipes connecting the water heater to the shower. Middleware that supports an application also connects components together. For example, the application probably uses libraries of functions that the application calls to get things done. The application developer could have written these functions from scratch, but it wouldn't have been cost effective to rewrite them.

I hate to provide a list of middleware because it can become extremely technical. It can also open up arguments about exactly what is and isn't middleware. The following is a very brief list of the types of functionality that would generally be considered middleware.

- Software used to establish database connectivity
- Software used to establish network connectivity
- Software that enables RPC (remote procedure calls) interaction between servers
- Software that enables platform transparency, for example, it would translate between EDCDIC and ASCII
- Object Request Brokers
- Software that allows network transparency, for example, it might convert between TCP/IP and other protocols
- File transfer software
- Load balancing software
- Software that allows different database systems to look like a single system
- Database gateway products that allow the application to connect to more than one relational database package
- Software that allows an application to integrate with legacy applications
- Software that enables Single Sign on logins
- Transaction monitoring packages

Features Common to Many Applications

4

All applications are unique, but they frequently have features that are common. By recognizing features that are shared by many applications, you can significantly reduce the learning curve for learning about new applications. Each section in this chapter describes features that are frequently offered by applications. Understanding that even very different applications have similarities will help you pick them out when you see them.

4.1 MULTIPLE MODULES IN AN APPLICATION

Applications typically offer multiple modules that can be purchased separately when the software is acquired, for example, an HR (Human Resources) module, an AR (Accounts Receivable) module, an AP (Accounts Payable) module, etc. Your organization might have purchased some or all of them. If you don't purchase them originally, the vendor would be more than happy to sell them to you at any future point in time.

At some point, you will be asked the question "which modules have been installed in our environment?" You need to be prepared to quickly and accurately answer this question. Times when it's particularly important to know the answer are when:

- Your boss asks you
- The users ask you
- The vendor's Support Desk asks you
- You're preparing to perform an upgrade
- You're documenting the system in a landscape or other technical document.

How can you identify what modules have been installed? One way is to write it down. The downside of this is that you need to keep track of that piece of paper or text file. There is also the risk that someone will add or remove a module without your knowing it, thus rendering your documentation out of date.

The best solution is to learn where to get this information from the application itself or from the server that the application is running on. Each application is different, but there are some common methods to identify what modules have been loaded and activated. These details are probably in the Administrator's Guide. If it isn't there then ask a vendor tech the next time you're working with one. They will almost certainly let you in on the secret. Some potential ways to get this information include:

- Log into the application and select the Help | About menu option.
- Log into the application and right-click on a "secret" spot on the initial screen. One application I worked with displayed version information if you right-clicked on their logo.
- Remotely connect to the application server and examine the appropriate .ini file, configuration file, or properties file.
- Remotely connect to the application server and examine the log file that is written to when the application starts up. Frequently the first few lines in these log files will identify the application version and modules that are being loaded.
- Remotely connect to the application server and look in the Windows Registry. Be very careful not to make any changes in the Registry!

- Connect to the relational database being used by the application and perform a SELECT query from the correct table. The vendor tech support will have to provide these details for you if this is how you are to determine the version.

4.2 CUSTOMIZATIONS AND CONFIGURATION CHANGES

What's the difference between customization and configuration changes? About $250 an hour. Seriously, both of these actions make changes to how the application runs and how it is seen by the user. The difference is that one of them, configuration, achieves these changes by modifying the existing code or functionality. The other, customization, requires that changes be made to the code behind the application. Changing code is time consuming, requires a significant amount of testing, and costs a lot of money. Vendors are reluctant to make coding changes unless there is a very good reason to do it.

Your vendor may refer to these terms another way, but the concepts almost certainly exist in their environment. You absolutely need to know how to achieve modifications to the application that your organization wants. If the changes can be reached via configuration changes, then that's great. If customization of the code becomes necessary, then you really need to sit back and decide:

- Are the changes really necessary?
- Is this application suitable for your needs? Of course, if you've already bought the license and installed the software then it's a little late to be making this epiphany.
- Is there another way, within the existing system, that you can get what you want? Potential workarounds might not be the most elegant solution, but it will almost certainly be faster and cheaper than going the customization route.

Some examples of modifications that can be implemented via configuration changes:

- Add fields to database tables
- Add or modify screens
- Add or modify fields on screens
- Add work flows
- Add or modify menus
- Add or modify reports
- Add or modify data structures

If you plan to change the look and feel of the application via configuration changes, then be sure you know how it's done. For example:

- Who can make configuration changes?
- Is this capability limited to just the Application Administrator?
- Can these changes be made when other users are in the application or do all users need to log out first?
- Does the application need to be stopped and started, aka bounced, for the changes to take effect?
- Can configuration changes be backed out?
- Do you need to make modifications to the database to implement configuration changes?
- Does your organization have procedures in place that require all changes be made and tested on a DEV or QA environment before made on a PROD environment?
- What types of files are used to hold configuration data? For example, ini files, .properties files, .config files, etc.

If you absolutely must have changes that are considered customizations, then you need to have a serious discussion with the vendor. The first thing you need to do is to be extremely specific about what you want.

If you aren't exceedingly precise, there's a good chance that the vendor will misunderstand what you're asking for and you'll end up being unhappy with the resulting changes.

Once you've explained exactly what you want, some of the questions to ask the vendor are:

- What will the cost be for the code changes?
- How firm is that figure?
- Who pays for the overruns if costs exceed the quoted amount?
- How long will it take to get the changes in place?
- Who will test the modified code?
- Who bears the cost if the change doesn't meet the specifications?
- Do your changes go into the code base that's shared with other clients? Does your organization consider this customization a competitive advantage that you'd rather not be made public? If this is the case, then you need to inform the vendor about this from the very beginning.
- How do updates to the application affect your customization? Will they be preserved across updates or will you have to reinstall them?

4.3 REPORTING FOR USERS

Organizations seem to live on reports. The more reports the better seems to be the logic of many organizations. Will report writing be among your responsibilities or can the more experienced users handle this? If this is something that you have to handle expect that it will take longer than you anticipate. The user community will constantly request new reports or changes be made to existing reports. It would be much better, for you, if this is a function that is handled by the more experienced members of the user community.

Whether you or someone on another team is responsible for developing the reports, is there any training or documentation for the reporting subsystem? While graphical drag-and-drop reports look easy to create, when you try to build flexible, complicated reports it's more difficult than it appears to be. Any investment in training upfront will almost certainly pay for itself in the long run.

To satisfy the need for reports almost every application includes some type of a reporting package. The report writer may have been written by the vendor specifically for their application, i.e., a proprietary report writer. More likely they licensed an existing reporting package like Crystal Reports. In either event, you will most likely have the ability to select and run an existing canned report or create a report from scratch.

If no embedded reporting exists in the application can another tool be used to create them? Can you acquire and install a tool like one of the tools listed below? You probably can, but be aware that connecting to the application's database might not be as easy as you think it will be. Even more complicated will be understanding the way the database has been designed. When a vendor designs their database, they usually aren't doing it to make it easy for a novice to understand:

- Cognos
- Crystal Reports
- Microsoft Reporting
- Oracle Reports
- Tableau
- VBA
- Scripts
- Conventional programming languages

It's very likely that the reporting package will allow you to create reports using a graphical display. It will display a list of tables or data objects. You have the ability to drag and drop the columns you want onto a template or work area. Once you've selected and arranged the data you want, then you'll be able to format and sort it. Adding summary fields is a pretty common feature. After finishing the report you save it so it can be used in the future. Reports can typically be run on demand or scheduled to run on specified days and times.

Some details you'll want to make sure you understand are:

- Who can build reports? All users, named users, or users belonging to a specific group?
- If User A builds a report can User B use it?
- If User A builds a report can User B modify it?
- If a report encounters an error what happens? Does the application write entries to a log file? Does it notify someone, for example the creator, about the error?
- Can reports handle different languages, currencies, alphabets, etc.?
- What happens if the report creates an extremely large output file? Will it keep running forever or will the system detect that it's out of control and terminate it? Is this event logged?
- Can a poorly written report impact performance experienced by other users?
- If there are updates or corrections to the report subsystem, will the vendor provide them to you or do you have to deal with the company that wrote the reporting tool?

4.3.1 Reporting without a report writer

If your application doesn't include a reporting package, it's still possible to create reports. If the application is based on a relational database, then it's possible to create decent reports using SQL commands. Of course you have to be able to write SQL or learn it very quickly.

You can create a workable reporting system that can run on either your desktop or the server. One downside to running it on your desktop computer is that if your computer isn't running when the report is scheduled to execute, then it won't be launched. Some commonly available components that can be used to create reports are:

- SQL Plus commands   to pull data from the DB
- Task scheduler   to automate running the report
- Messaging software   used to manually e-mail reports to recipients
- Excel   recipient can open CSV files with Excel

Step 1 is to write a text file with the SQL statements in it. This example creates a report from several Oracle tables. The output of the SELECT statement may look odd, but for the data to come out in a comma-separated format each column being created needs to be separated by a comma. This statement shown below does this. The query could be adapted to any number of possible reports.

4.3.1.1 Contents of file roster.sql

```
spool Roster.csv
SELECT 'Class,Student,Status,Grade,Completion Date' FROM dual;
SELECT
c.LongName||','||a.StudentName||','||a.Status||','||a.score||','||TO_CHAR(a.
DateTime,'yyyy-mm-dd')
FROM Record a, Student b, Class c
WHERE b.Student_ID = a.Student_ID
AND b.Class_ID = c.Class_ID;
spool off
exit
```

Step 2 is to write a command file to execute the query. Here is an example of a fairly straightforward command file that creates a Roster report and writes it to a CSV (comma-separated value) file. This example invokes Oracle's SQL Plus to execute the SQL statements. Another database package like SQL Server could also be used.

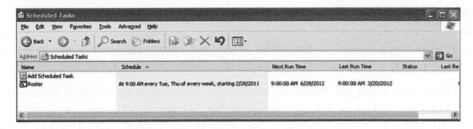

FIGURE 4.1

Windows Scheduled Tasks utility. (For color version of this figure, the reader is referred to the online version of this chapter.)

The nice thing about writing data to a CSV file is that when the recipient double-clicks the file it will open in an Excel spreadsheet. This way you get Excel to do the formatting work for you.

4.3.1.2 Contents of file roster.cmd

```
echo ****** Running Roster Query *******>> Roster.log
echo set echo off feed off pages 0          >> %0.tmp
echo whenever sqlerror exit sql.sqlcode >> %0.tmp
sqlplus -s /nolog @%0.tmp >> Roster.log;
Set CURRDATE=%TEMP%\CURRDATE.TMP
Set CURRTIME=%TEMP%\CURRTIME.TMP
DATE /T > %CURRDATE%
TIME /T > %CURRTIME%
Set PARSEARG="eol=; tokens=1,2,3,4* delims=/, "
For /F %PARSEARG% %%i in (%CURRDATE%) Do SET YYYYMMDD=%%l%%j%%k
Set PARSEARG="eol=; tokens=1,2,3* delims=:, "
For /F %PARSEARG% %%i in (%CURRTIME%) Do Set HHMM=%%i%%j%%k
RENAME Roster.csv Roster_%YYYYMMDD%_%HHMM%.csv
SendEmail.vbs Roster_%YYYYMMDD%_%HHMM%.csv
```

Step 3 is to schedule the command file to run. The screenshot in Figure 4.1 shows that a single task, Roster, has been defined. In this example, Windows Task Scheduler was used to launch the script. This could just as easily be done using cron on a UNIX or a Linux server.

4.3.2 Report output formats

A detail that you'll want to get answers to is what output formats can the application's report writer create? This is important because the "reports" that you create can be used for extremely different purposes. Some of the more common output file types are listed in Table 4.1.

Table 4.1 File Formats and Their Typical Use

Output File Format	Typically Used for
xls	Spreadsheet file, e.g., Microsoft Excel
csv	Can be opened with Excel. Also frequently used for batch input files
txt	Easily opened and read by users
HTML	Easily opened and read by users
PDF	Easily opened and read by users
XML	Batch input files

4.3.3 **Report distribution**

Reports have to be distributed to the people who need them to be of any value. So another capability of the reporting package that you'll need to understand is how can the reports be distributed? Some available options are:

- The report itself is e-mailed out. While this method is convenient to the recipient, it can put a significant strain on the system. For example, what if a 20-page report is sent out to 1000 recipients once every day? How wasteful of bandwidth is this situation? This would be especially troubling if the majority of the recipients never even look at the report.
- An e-mail is sent out telling the recipient that the report is available. If the recipient wants to see the report, they click on a URL embedded in the e-mail that acts as a link. The web page that comes up displays their report. Sending out a simple e-mail rather than a sizeable attachment is obviously much more efficient.
- Report output can be ftp'ed to another server. Users who want the report know to pick it up at that location.
- If the user interface with the reporting system is a web page, then the report can be downloaded directly from the web page. For example, the user might right-click on the report and select "Save As" to have it copied to his local hard drive.
- Reports can be posted on SharePoint or another portal system. Users go to the portal to pick up the reports they want to see.

4.3.4 **Bursting reports**

Bursting is a process of running a report a single time and selectively distributing the output to multiple recipients. For example, a sales report can be run for the entire organization. Each regional manager will receive a single e-mail with the sales figures for just their region. The concept of bursting reports is used to distribute reports to a list of intended recipients.

When defining the report to be burst you will have to provide additional details, for example, a burst key that defines how to split the report. In the example above the burst key would be region. The second key, commonly called the "recipients" key, determines how each section of the report will be distributed. If your application supports bursting reports, then the documentation will provide details on how to define these keys.

4.3.5 **Authorizing users to create reports**

Not every user of the application should be allowed to create, modify, or schedule reports. If everyone was allowed to create reports, the system could well be overrun with inaccurate, obsolete, or nearly identical reports. It's much more effective to grant the ability to create reports to a relatively small, experienced group of users. The members of this group should be determined by the business owner, not the Application Administrator.

Other report-related permissions that should be tightly controlled are:

- The ability to delete reports
- The ability to modify existing reports
- The ability to schedule reports
- The ability to modify the recipient list of reports

4.4 REPORTING FOR APPLICATION ADMINISTRATORS

Users of the application aren't the only ones who need reports. There are a number of data items that Application Administrators need to see in reports. Some examples of reports that an application administrator might want to see include:

- Number of users broken down by registered, active, disabled, etc.
- Number of users currently logged in.
- Up time and down time in the last day, week, month, quarter, and year. You might need this report to prove that you're meeting an SLA (Service Level Agreement).
- Number of transactions processed by hour, day, and week.
- CPU utilization rate for the last minute, hour, and day.
- Disk space usage broken down by space being used and space available.
- Login report showing when each user logged in and logged out. Tracking when users log out of the application can be difficult for a web-based application. This is because if the user clicks the "X" in the upper right-hand corner of the window instead of clicking on the "Log Out" button the event coded to handle log outs might not be activated. Just a friendly warning.

Is there a report on reports, i.e., a report that lists all the reports produced by the application? Details like the following would be very useful if to satisfy user requests for information:

- Report name
- Date and time it runs
- Recipients
- Last time it ran
- Status of the last run
- Who scheduled it?
- Date when it was first run
- Name of the output file

4.5 E-MAIL

It's not uncommon at all for applications to generate e-mail. Some examples of e-mails that might be created and e-mailed out include:

- Problem notification
- Distribution of reports
- Warnings to the administrator of potential problems like low disk space
- Notification that backups were successful or unsuccessful
- Login details for new accounts
- Workflow information

Some questions you need to answer to set up and maintain the e-mail of your application's capability include:

- What message server will the application be using? The name of your organization's e-mail server and possibly its type will need to be entered into a configuration file or a similar location in the application.
- If the organization's e-mail server ever changes how do you change that information in the application?

- What sender name and address will be associated with e-mails the application sends out? The application doesn't care what you enter for this, but you have to provide something. Again, this information will likely be in a configuration file.
- What port needs to be opened between the application server and the e-mail server?

A word of advice here about what to enter as the return address for e-mails the application sends out. If a recipient of one of those e-mails replies to it you want that e-mail to get to the right person or group. Don't use an individual's name or e-mail address. You should create an account for the application and use it. For example, instead of a return address like Kelly.Bourne@SomeCompany.com use ApplicationName@SomeCompany.com. This way if Kelly ever leaves the company e-mail replies will be delivered to the correct person or group. It also enables someone else to support the application while Kelly is on vacation.

You need to be aware that some types of attachments may be blocked by your e-mail server or the destination server. This is done because some file types are more likely to carry dangerous "payloads," i.e., viruses, malware, etc. Typically attached files with .exe, .jar, and .bat extensions will be blocked. The resulting error messages aren't always clear on what caused the problem. So be warned in advance that not all file attachments will reach their destinations.

4.6 USER PREFERENCES

Many applications allow individual users to define their preferences of how the application should look and feel for them. Each user can adjust the application appearance to suit himself or herself to a limited degree. It must be noted that user preferences are not the same as customizations or configuration changes. User preferences are typically relatively simple changes that are associated with individual user accounts.

Some examples of changes that can commonly be configured include:

- Language that the labels, menu items, button labels, links, etc. are be expressed in, e.g., English, French, German, Russian, etc.
- Denominations that costs or values are expressed in, e.g., Dollars, British Pounds, Euros, etc.
- Character that separates dollars from cents. Usually either a decimal point or a comma
- Time zone that the user resides in
- Days in the business week, e.g., Monday-Friday vs. Saturday-Wednesday
- Format in which dates are expressed, e.g., MM/DD/YY or DD/MM/YY
- Measurements, for example, Metric vs. English
- Holidays
- First screen that is displayed when the user logs in
- Default sorting preference, e.g., from smallest to largest vs. largest to smallest

The Application Administrator can typically set up default user preferences that are applied to new accounts. Some applications allow different sets of user preferences for groups of users. For example, all users defined to be in the region North America might have one set of default preferences. Users in EMEA (Europe, Middle East, and Africa) might have a different set of default preferences. Once a user becomes comfortable with the system, he or she can change their preferences.

You will certainly be asked questions about user preferences, so you'll want to know the answers in advance. Besides knowing what objects can be modified, you'll need to know how to set all of these preferences. You'll also need to know how to unset them in case the user gets a little too adventurous when setting their own preferences.

A valuable piece of advice would be to have a one page cheat sheet that covers the most commonly asked questions about user preferences. If you have this on hand to distribute to new users, you'll save yourself a lot of questions. You might consider sending it out to new users when they are given the logon information. Either copy it from the vendor provided documentation or write it yourself. Either way, doing this in advance will pay off in the long run.

4.7 DATA

Every application deals with data. It might be readily visible from the outside, but on the inside an application is mostly data. Without data, there is no way to record information, no way to store information, and nothing to manipulate.

4.7.1 Data types

What data types does the application support? Most applications support the "normal" data types like integer, character, float, etc. Other data types that an application might support include:

- Date
- Time
- Images
- BLOB (Binary Large Objects), commonly images
- Currency

4.7.2 Databases

Virtually every significant application, home-grown and third party, stores data in a database of some type. A very, very simple application might get by with a collection of files, but that level of application probably wouldn't need an Application Administrator. Relational databases are the most common database design. Some applications utilize object oriented databases, but those are relatively rare. If a relational database is being used, it almost certainly will not have been provided by the vendor. It will most likely be one of a handful of RDBMS (relational database management system) packages like Oracle, Microsoft SQL Server, Sybase, or MySQL.

Organizations that have more than a couple of databases will probably have one or more Database Administrators (DBAs) on staff. These IT specialists support the database software the way you support an application. Some of the duties of a DBA include the following:

- Install the database software
- Apply updates and patches provided by the vendor
- Interacting with the vendor if errors are encountered
- Create new databases
- Confirm that backups of database are being done successfully
- Restore databases that have become corrupted or need to be restored to an earlier state
- Expand the amount of disk space available to a database if it runs out of space
- Unlock accounts that have been locked or disabled
- Kill runaway queries, i.e., queries that don't appear will ever complete
- Examine SQL statements to identify ones that are inaccurate or inefficient
- Add or modify indexes to optimize database performance

In short, a DBA is a very experienced, valuable member of your organization's IT department. As with all IT professionals on the staff, try not to waste their time. You should spend a few minutes trying to figure things out for yourself before asking questions that have obvious answers.

Be sure that you learn everything you can about the database being used by your application. Some of the details you'll want to know are:

- What vendor's database is being used, e.g., Oracle, Microsoft SQL Server, MySQL, etc.?
- Is the database running on a separate server, and if so which server? Some applications, especially smaller ones, might have the database running on the same server that the application is running on. This is unusual, but it happens.
- What port is being used for communications between the application and database servers?
- Who in your organization is responsible for the database server(s)?
- How many databases does the application really have? This might seem like a strange question, but several applications that I support have multiple databases on the DB server. One has four, one has three, and one has two.
- Another odd question is whether all of the application's databases are the same? One application I support has three databases that are Microsoft SQL Server databases running on a separate server, but a fourth database runs on the application server. That one is a Microsoft Jet database. Their reasoning behind this unusual architecture is that the Jet database contains only the forms that are presented to users. There are relatively few forms and they don't change frequently. Given this, they felt the forms could be supported by a database that wasn't large and didn't have all the bells and whistles.
- How big is the database and how fast is it growing?
- How often is it being backed up?
- How long would it take to restore from a backup if the database crashed?
- How reliable are the servers that the databases are running on?
- If the database servers go down, what is the procedure for getting them back up?
- How does your application handle the situation when the database goes down? I've worked with applications that don't handle this well. If either the database went down or the application lost its connection to the database then the application would write a very specific message to its log file and then lock up. We had to put some monitoring in place to look for that log file entry and alert us if it occurred. Then we would shut down the application and restart it. Awkward, but it was better than the alternative of waiting for users to alert us that the application was down.

Relational databases that support enterprise-wide applications are themselves extremely complex. They hold both a large quantity and a wide variety of data. Modern database practice dictates that the database be designed in what's called a "normalized" design. This book isn't intended to teach database design theory so I'll summarize the impact of database normalization in five words—"lots and lots of tables." There are so many tables that only someone very experienced with the application is able to understand it. If you do go poking around in that database please be sure to do it on the DEV (development), or test environment. You don't want to be blundering about in the production database.

At some point in your career as an Application Administrator, you will probably be asked to grant a business analyst or some other number cruncher direct access to the database. He or she will blithely describe how they will use the ability of Excel, Access, or another software package to extract just the data they want and nothing else. Resist such requests at all costs! The most important reasons for this are:

- If the business analyst doesn't understand the database structure, i.e., the relationships between tables, then it's very likely that they will create a report with the wrong information on it. A mistake of this nature could have very serious business implications!

- Poorly written queries can have a significant impact on system performance.
- They will likely make numerous requests for your assistance which will be very time consuming.

If such a data request is made and can't be avoided, then try to steer it in one of the following directions:

1. Does the application include a function for exporting data? If so try to use it.
2. Create a report that extracts the desired data and writes it to an XML or CSV formatted file.
3. Pay the vendor to write a SQL SELECT statement that extracts the desired data and execute it as needed.

4.8 FEED ME! GETTING LARGE QUANTITIES OF DATA INTO OR OUT OF YOUR APPLICATION

Applications frequently provide the functionality to import or export large quantities of data into or out of the system. This capability might be to allow an easier or more accurate way to enter data. It might be to provide a way to export data that is used to feed into another application.

Some of the types of activities that you might want to perform via a bulk import include:

- Bulk registration of new users
- A merger requiring new data be added
- Consolidation of multiple, diverse, applications
- Data feeds to/from business partners, supplies, organization's subsidiaries or parent company

The specific types of data that you might need to import or export could include the following:

- Users and their details
- Groups that users are associated with
- Security
- Contracts
- Accounts
- Invoices
- Inventory details

The goal of either importing or exporting data could possibly be achieved via one or more SQL statements that select or insert data directly from the application's database. However, vendor databases are usually very complicated, i.e., highly normalized, so it's not something you should do on your own unless you're very familiar with the database design. This is especially true when importing data due to referential integrity and dependency considerations.

It's possible that the application includes a utility to import or export data. This function might be on a screen that is accessible only to someone in the administrator group. Or it might be a separate executable that is accessible via a CLI (command line interface). Check the Administrator's Guide document to see if such a capability exists.

The import functionality of the application will dictate the format of the input files. Your application may be able to handle multiple formats. The more common formats that may be available to you are:

- XML files
- CSV (comma-separated values) files
- Tab separated values files
- Fixed length fields

If you're trying to do a bulk import process, then you'll be dealing with a file that has been provided to you. Whether this file was created manually or was the export from another application you should be prepared for the data to be dirty. By this I mean that one or more of the following problems will occur:

- Data fields will be missing from some of the records. Before importing records with missing fields you need to know how that application will handle this. The import utility might accept missing fields and replace them with blanks and zeroes or it might terminate.
- The data fields won't be in the expected order.
- Name data won't be in the expected format. The input process might require that name data be broken down into separate fields, e.g., first name, middle initial, last name. The data sent to you might include the data in a single field. Another potential problem with names is that some people have either hyphenated or multiple last names.
- Invalid characters will exist in some fields. For example, if a field that should have "True" or "False" will contain the values "Yes" and "No" in some rows.
- Dates will be provided to you in an unexpected format. The import process may require that the date be in MM/DD/YYYY format. Even if you communicate this to the group that is providing the input file the file might have dates in a different format, e.g., DD/MM/YYYY or MM/DD/YY.
- If you specified that every line should end with CR/LF (character control/line feed) characters, the file may have just the LF character at the end of every line.
- Regardless of whether you specified that the file should or shouldn't have headers, there is a chance that the file you're about to import has it wrong.
- Some import processes expect that the first or last record contains special values. It might be a record count or the value "END." If the import process has requirements like this make sure the file adheres to them.
- Single apostrophes in strings, aka "ticks," can cause significant problems in an SQL insert statement. In a SQL statement, all text fields begin and end with an apostrophe, e.g., "Smith." If apostrophe occurs in the middle of the string, e.g., "O'Malley," then the SQL statement might not be successfully executed by the database engine. To get around this you might need to include a second apostrophe, e.g., "O''Malley." If this is required, you'll need to scan the input file and if any records contain extra apostrophes add the additional tick to it.
- An assumption about the currency involved that is inaccurate. For example, you assume that it's U.S. dollars when it's Euros.
- Measurement units are different, for example, pounds vs. kilograms or meters instead of yards.

You need to understand how all of the potential data anomalies will be handled by the input process. Some of these details might be specified in the application's documentation. If you have questions about how other anomalies will be handled you need to test them. Deliberately create an input file that contains the problem and import into your TEST or DEV environment to see how the application handles it. No matter what the documentation says, the acid test is to create a test file and import it.

It will take you time to clean up new files, for example, to reformat dates, fill in empty fields, confirm that records terminate correctly, etc. This is especially true the first time you receive a file from a source. Build extra time into your schedule for these potential problems. Until you've gone through the entire import process from each specific source a couple of times, expect problems to occur.

No matter how careful you are when you run an import operation there is a very real chance that things won't go the way you expect them to. I would recommend two very important pieces of advice when running an import:

1. Be sure that you have a current backup of the database.
2. Practice any bulk import or export operations on a test server before trying it in production.

How often will data files be arriving and need to be fed into the system?

- Hourly
- Daily
- Weekly
- Monthly

If data files will be arriving regularly can the process of handling them be automated? Can you write a script that kicks off the import process and schedule it via Windows Task Scheduler, cron, or Control-M?

Here are a few additional troubleshooting problems that might occur:

- What happens if the file doesn't arrive when expected?
- What happens if the file contains records that aren't in the correct layout?
- What happens if a file is inadvertently loaded a second time? Will it abend (abnormally end) or will you end up with duplicate data? Can this duplicate data be easily removed?
- What happens if the input file is empty?

How does the input process handle unexpected situations? You will want to find out, in advance, what will happen if something unexpected occurs. Will the system take one of the following courses of action?

- Will the process halt?
- Will the bad records be logged to a file and the input process continue?
- Will anyone be automatically notified, e.g., by e-mail or a text message?

4.9 APPLICATION ADMINISTRATION TOOLS

Every application provides tools and utilities that enable the Application Administrator to do things that the average user doesn't need to do. In fact, it would be best if the average user never hears about some of these tools. The best place to learn about these tools is probably in the Administrator's Guide or its equivalent. Another way to learn about these tools is if the vendor provides training for Administrators.

Some examples of the functionality that is limited to administrators includes

- A data import/export utility
- A console to configure, monitor, and control the application
- A utility or script to start and stop that application
- Creating backups
- Restoring the database from a backup file
- Creating user accounts
- Disabling or enabling user accounts
- Resetting user passwords
- Modifying details of a user's account
- Determining how many users are in the application
- Locking out users from logging into the application
- Performance monitoring of the application

Applications frequently provide two types of administrator tools: GUI based and command line based. Even if you prefer one type, you should proficient in both tools. One reason for this is that there may be times when you can use the command line-based tool, but not the GUI-based tool.

It should go without saying, but the command line-based utility is almost certainly going to be available on just the application server. You might be able to load it onto your desktop machine, but most likely, it will run only on the server.

4.10 CONSOLE ADMINISTRATOR TOOLS FOR SUPPORT SOFTWARE

The application you support isn't the only piece of software on the server that might have a console. Support software that also runs on the server can have a console administration tool through which you can control the application or its environment. Other software products that you might encounter include:

- JMX Console
- WebLogic Admin Console
- Apache/TomCat
- JBOSS
- IBM's WebSphere

WebLogic Server is a platform that supports enterprise web applications. Your application might rely upon WebLogic Server to handle low-level functions like caching, connection pooling, and security rather than have had these functions included in the application itself. Figure 4.2 shows what the Oracle WebLogic Server Administration Console looks like. If your application uses WebLogic Server, then you would have to open this console to define details of your application when it is first installed. You might also log into this console to investigate performance issues.

FIGURE 4.2

WebLogic Server Administration Console. (For color version of this figure, the reader is referred to the online version of this chapter.)

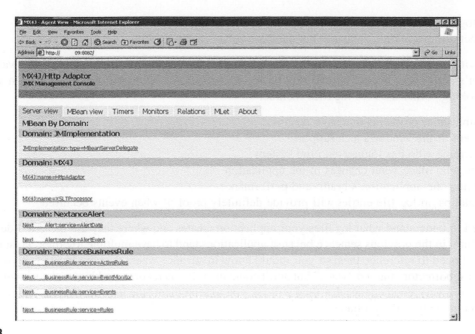

FIGURE 4.3

Screenshot of the JMX console. (For color version of this figure, the reader is referred to the online version of this chapter.)

If your application was written in Java, then you might need to bring up the JMX console to identify which services (MBeans) are registered in the application server. Parameters for these services can be modified through the JMX console. Figure 4.3 shows what the initial screen of the JMX console looks like.

4.11 LOG FILES

Log files, usually text files, are created to document activity on a computer. Most entries in a log file contain a detailed message and a time-stamp, i.e., the date and time, of when the entry was made. Log files are typically ordered chronologically, i.e., each entry in the file has a time-stamp equal to or greater than the entry before it. Some log files grow indefinitely. Others are a set size and when the end of the file is reached the next entry overwrites the first entry.

4.11.1 Application log files

Virtually every application generates one or more log files. These log files can provide the following types of insight into the application:

1. Version details, i.e., what version of the application is running
2. Startup time, i.e., when was the application last started
3. What activity has taken place in the application
4. Performance issues
5. Security issues
6. Detailed error information is written to the log file

7. User logons, i.e., who's using the application, how often, etc.

8. Connection information such as what database server the application is connecting to

Working with log files is a common activity for Application Administrators. Since you can't be watching the application's activity 24 hours you will rely on log files to learn what happened on the system while you weren't looking. Other uses for log files include:

- To troubleshoot problems that have occurred
- To be sent to the vendor's tech support
- To determine who has logged onto the system
- To track who made what changes in the application
- To monitor the application's health and performance
- Time-stamps on log file entries will provide definitely proof of when events occurred

You'll need to understand what log files your application creates and where they are located. I deliberately used the plural in the previous sentence because applications tend to have multiple log files. Trust me, eventually you'll need to reference them so you should know in advance where they are located. If you're lucky they're in a subdirectory named "\logs," but don't count on it. If you report a problem to the vendor's support team, there is a very good chance that they will ask you to send them "the log files." They will use log files entries to help analyze the problem.

4.11.2 Configuring application log files

Does your application create logs by default or does a configuration setting need to be defined to turn it on? Two very difference places where I've seen applications require a setting be changed were:

- The JMX console. One application required you to go into the JMX console to modify the logging level value. Figure 4.4 is a screenshot of how the logging level is set in the JMX console.
- A registry setting. The value of Logging, shown in Figure 4.5, is changed to determine the selectivity of what is to be logged. A value of 0 indicates no logging will be done. A value of 1 indicates only failed SQL queries will be logged. If the value is set to 2, then all SQL queries will be logged.

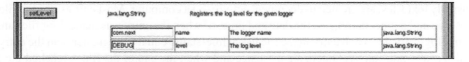

FIGURE 4.4

Setting in the JMX console for setting the logging level. (For color version of this figure, the reader is referred to the online version of this chapter.)

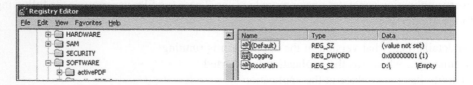

FIGURE 4.5

Registry entry that controls how much logging will be done. (For color version of this figure, the reader is referred to the online version of this chapter.)

Once you have changed the setting that indicates what level of logging should be done, does something else need to be done to activate? For example, do you need to stop and start the application for the change to take effect? Be sure you know the entire procedure required to activate logging.

Once the logging is activated where will the log entries be written? Some common locations that an application might write log entries include:

- To a log file
- To the Events area on a Windows server
- To a database table

If the application writes to a log file, you'll need to know were that log is located. Be forewarned that some applications write to more than one log file. One application I worked with writes entries related to startup operations to one log file and log entries related to ongoing application activities in a completely separate log file.

How often are log files created? Does the application continue to write a single output file indefinitely? Or is a new log file created every day with the date embedded in the file name? Does the application create a new file every time the application is stopped and then restarted?

Some applications enable you to close out old log files and create new ones on demand. If this is the only time new log files are created, are you doing this on a regular basis? There are definite advantages to creating new log files regularly. Periodically creating new log files lets you avoid having to work with extremely large log files. The larger the file, the long it take longer to open, search, e-mail to the vendor, etc. If you can automate this process then consider having it run nightly or at least weekly.

4.11.3 Log file time-stamp issues

One thing you need to keep in mind when dealing with the application's log files is the source of the time used in the time-stamp. What time zone does the time-stamp refer to? Typically the time zone used for the time-stamp is local time where the server is physically located. Keep this in mind when you're on the West Coast (Pacific Time), the server is in Omaha (Central Time) and the users are on the East Coast (Eastern Time). If the user said she did something at 3 pm, it will recorded with a time-stamp of 2 pm. This can be especially confusing because it might be 1 pm in your location.

4.11.4 Support software log files

Your application isn't the only software on the server that is writing to a log file. The list of programs that write to log files is long and varied. Some examples include:

- Operating systems like Windows, Linux, and UNIX all create log files
- If the application runs on a web server, then the web server application, e.g., IIS or Apache, also writes to a log file that track every web page request it services
- Internet browsers create log files tracking what web sites were visited
- Most third-party applications keep logs of their activities
- Security programs keep detailed log files of virtually everything that happens on a server
- Database packages like SQL Server and Oracle create transaction logs to record all of the activities they perform
- Scheduling programs like cron and Task Scheduler have log files documenting what tasks were scheduled, when and whether they were successful

4.12 NAVIGATION

Every GUI (Graphical User Interface) application provides some method for users to navigate from screen to screen. Common methods are listed here. The last three are described in more detail in the following sections:

- Using the mouse to click links
- Menus
- Function keys, aka shortcut keys
- Breadcrumbs

4.12.1 Menus

Menus will exist on virtually any application that you might support. They allow users to quickly and accurately get to the screens they want to see. When it comes to menus the question won't be whether they exist or not, it will be how configurable they are. For example, which of the following capabilities does the application give to the Application Administrator or the users?

- How many levels of menus does the application have?
- Are the menus configurable?
- Can menus be customized for each user or user group?
- If so, who can customize them? The Application Administrator or the users themselves?
- Does the application support multiple languages for the menus?
- Can menu options be activated with shortcut key combinations?
- Are the shortcut key combinations configurable? Who can configure them?

4.12.2 Function keys/shortcut keys

What shortcut keys are available in your application? Even if this is documented this is something that your users will probably ask you about. Putting together a one page document for new users is a very good investment. Including the shortcut keys available in the application on that document is a good idea as well.

If it's possible to configure shortcut keys in the application then by all means do this. Using them can make your users significantly more efficient. The only question is what shortcut keys do you want to define?

There are a few shortcut keys that are fairly common.

- F1: Brings up the help menu
- F5: Find
- Ctrl + A: Select all
- Ctrl + C: Copy
- Ctrl + F: Find
- Ctrl + S: Save
- Ctrl + V: Paste
- Ctrl + X: Cut
- Ctrl + Z: Undo the most recent change
- Ctrl + End: Go to end of file
- Ctrl + Home: Go to start of file

4.12.3 Breadcrumbs

In the original Grimm Brothers story, Hansel left a trail of bread crumbs on the ground so he and his sister Gretel could find their way home out of the forest. In a similar manner, many applications use breadcrumbs to show users how they got to the screen they are on. If an application displays breadcrumbs they are usually

FIGURE 4.6

Example of bread crumbs in an application. (For color version of this figure, the reader is referred to the online version of this chapter.)

toward the top of the browser screen, frequently just below the application's menu. Figure 4.6 shows the implementation of breadcrumbs in an application. Each screen along the path is separated by a "greater than" sign. Clicking any entry in the breadcrumb path will take you directory to that screen.

Does your application display breadcrumbs? If it does can the user click on one of them and be taken directly to that screen? One application forced users to use breadcrumbs by disabling the back arrow key in the browser. Breadcrumbs probably won't directly affect you, but you may get questions from your users about them so be prepared.

4.13 ERROR MESSAGES

Every application displays distinct error messages when something goes wrong. It would be wonderful if all software vendors coordinated their messages, but I have a very strong feeling that this isn't going to happen in our lifetimes.

See if you can get a listing of every error message that the application displays. This might be available in the Administrator's Guide. If it isn't in a manual it might be in either a text file or database table. If you're lucky you'll have access to a complete list and it will include a more detailed description of the error. Error messages displayed on the screens can be rather terse and more than a bit confusing.

Users need to be trained to always include the error number of full error message when they're reporting a problem. If possible, request that they capture a screenshot of the error message they see. Having an accurate error message will enable you, if necessary, to open a ticket with the vendor. The more accurate your information is, the more quickly the vendor's support team will be able to resolve the problem.

4.14 DASHBOARDS

A dashboard is a type of a display that communicates to the viewer important information in an easy to read format. The values that are typically displayed represent key performance indicators (KPI) for the department or organization. Frequently the chart, gauge, or other widget being used is color coded with red, yellow, and green sections indicating whether the values are bad, fair, or good.

Some dashboard-related questions that you need to have answers to are:

- Does the application you're supporting provide dashboards?
- Can user preferences be applied to them?
- How often is the data refreshed?
- What data do they contain?

- Can you create new dashboards?
- Who uses them?
- Can all users or only specific groups of users access dashboards?

4.15 LIMITATIONS

Every application has limitations regarding what other software it will work with. Some examples of limitations that it might have are:

- The application can run under Windows 2003, but not under Windows 2008 R2
- It is certified to work with Windows Internet Explorer 9, but not 10
- It may be able to export reports to Excel 6.0, but not version 7.0.

Your job is to be aware of any limitations and make sure the users are too. You can't allow your user community to upgrade to a version of Internet Explorer if the application isn't capable of working with it. I'll warn you that this will be a never ending battle. There is always a department or group that prides itself on always having the most up to date software. It will be difficult to convince them that getting ahead of the application's curve is going to cause them trouble.

4.16 WORKFLOW

Workflow is a process that allows multiple people to perform part of an overall process and then advance the object to the next person. The following might be the steps need to produce a check for an invoice:

- Invoice is received
- Accounts Payable clerk encodes the invoice with the appropriate General Ledger code
- Manager reviews invoice, makes corrections and returns it to the Accounts Payable clerk
- The Invoice is entered into the Financial System for payment
- Corporate Accounts Payable Manager signs the Invoice
- Manager of the department in question authorizes payment
- Check is cut

Many applications include a workflow component to make the business process more efficient and easier to track. The application ensures that each person in the chain completes their tasks before the object (e.g., a claim, ticket or invoice) is advanced to the next person whose attention is needed. Typically, the next person in the chain will be notified by e-mail that the object is in their queue.

If your application includes workflow functionality, there may be a lot of setup details you'll have to provide before the workflow logic will handle your objects correctly. Exactly who handles setting up the workflow depends on the application. Typically it is done by Application Administrator since it can be fairly complex to handle. In some applications, this work requires running utilities that only the Application Administrator has access to. In other applications, workflow is controlled by XML files. Users and the application owner typically aren't comfortable editing XML files.

Some of the details that might need to be defined or set up include:

- Define each task in the process to be performed
- Define the sequence in which the tasks need to be done
- Define groups

- Assign users to groups
- Assign tasks to the appropriate group
- If the assigned person doesn't complete a task within a defined amount of time a reminder will sent out
- If the assigned person doesn't complete a task within a second defined amount of time the object will be reassigned to someone else
- Who can take over a task from another worker
- Action that will take place when all steps in the workflow process have been completed

4.17 TIME ZONE TROUBLE

If your organization has offices or people located in multiple time zones, then the opportunity for time zone-related confusion exists. People typically think that the time zone they are in is the "right" one. In this regard, computer servers are no different than people. Every server has an internal clock that is usually set to the local time. The time on the server becomes important because:

- The file system uses the server's time to identify when files were created or modified
- Log file entries arc typically time-stamped with the server's time
- Transactions frequently have a time-stamp associated with them that comes from the server
- Administrative actions like backups are scheduled to occur at specific times
- Planned events like outages and reboots need to bc clearly expressed to everyone who will be affected

Other situations in which having staff or hardware in different time zones complicates your life include:

- If the Application Administrator isn't in the same time zone as the majority of users or the primary users? This becomes awkward because the amount of time when you overlap may be minimal. Is it possible to shift your work day an hour or two to come more in line with the work day of the users? The more overlap time you have with users, the more that can be accomplished in a typical workday.
- Is your vendor's support staff in the same time zone as your team? This isn't critical, but is certainly handy if vendor Support Desk is close to your time zone.
- What if your application server and database server are located in different time zones? Will they be set to a common time or will each be set to their own local time? The latter could complicate things if you ever need to correlate time-stamped entries in log files with time-stamped transactions. If you can't control a situation like this you need to be aware that it exists.

After much a herculean effort on your part you get all of your time zone-related complications worked out. You think you're in for smooth sailing, but then Daylight Savings Time rolls around! There are a number of potential problems with Daylight Saving Time that might complicate your life. Among them are the following:

- Not all U.S. states recognize DST. Most noticeably much of Arizona doesn't recognize it.
- Not all countries recognize DST.
- Countries that do recognize Daylight Savings Time don't all move onto it on the same date.
- The dates on which the United States moves onto and off of DST isn't constant.

Will your users be affected by the above situations?

From a technical point of view, will your application environment have problems similar to the ones listed below when you switch onto or off of Daylight Savings Time?

- Are your servers set to automatically change the time onto DST and back off again? Or is this a manual operation for your organization?
- What if the date on which DST occurs changes from one year to the next? Will your servers automatically recognize this?
- How will the time change affect scheduled jobs? Specifically when the time is changed backwards will jobs be scheduled a second time? If so will this cause a problem?
- How will time-stamped entries in log files be affected when the time "falls back"? Will there be multiple entries in a log file with the same date and time? Will this cause a problem for the application?
- How will time-stamped entries in database tables be affected when the time "falls back"? If the time-stamp is used as the primary key in a table could you end up with errors caused by duplicate keys?

4.18 COOKIES

A cookie, also known as a browser cookie, is a small piece of information sent by the web site the user logged into that gets stored on the user's computer. If the application was designed to use cookies, then neither the user nor the Application Administrator has any control of them. They are created automatically by the software.

One use of cookies is to personalize the web site for the user, i.e., each time he returns to the web site its appearance will be the same. Cookies might record the user details like home address so they doesn't have to added each time the user logs in. Another use of cookies is to record the contents of a shopping cart in the event that a session is interrupted.

If the application you support is web based, does it create cookies on the user's desktop? If it does create them, do you have any control over the cookies it creates? To get answers to these questions you can try examining the Administration Guide. If it doesn't answer your question, then you should contact the vendor.

Specifics About Your Application

The previous chapter describes capabilities that are common to numerous third-party applications. Now we need to ask probing questions to learn more about the application that you will be or are currently supporting. As you read this chapter, be sure to consider questions that haven't been included here. The more you let your questioning expand, the more complete your understanding of the application will be.

5.1 BROWSERS SUPPORTED BY YOUR APPLICATION

If your application is web based, what browsers is it certified to work with? This information is probably available on the vendor's website. If it isn't listed there, then check the Installation Guide. Your source of last resort, as always, is to contact the vendor's support desk. Some of the most commonly used browsers include the following

- Microsoft Internet Explorer
- Mozilla Firefox
- Google Chrome
- Apple Safari

Once you identify the list of supported browsers, you'll need to determine what specific versions of each browser that the application is certified to run on. For instance, the application may support Internet Explorer 8, but not IE9? Or Firefox 22 but not Firefox 23.

Is the application vendor responsive about supporting new versions of browsers as they are released? Or does their support lag for months after a new browser version is announced? There isn't anything you can do about this if the vendor isn't on the leading edge of browser support, but it's something you want to be aware of.

Be sure you know exactly which versions are supported because subtle problems can occur when users try to use an unsupported browser. One question that should always be asked when users report a problem is what browser, including version, was being used when their problem occurred. If the browser or version isn't supported, then your first step should be to see if the problem occurs on a supported browser. If it doesn't then, for the most part, your work on this problem is done. You should contact the vendor to see if a date for support of this browser and version has been announced. Then inform the user that they're using an unsupported browser and they need to be fall back to one that is certified.

Organizations run the gamut when it comes to controlling what software users are allowed to run on their desktops. Some tightly control this and others have a laissez-faire attitude. Where on this spectrum does your organization fall? If it's on the uncontrolled end of things, then it's up to you to inform the user community about the limitation the application imposes on their choice of browsers. They won't like it, but this is an area that's out of your control.

5.1.1 Compatibility mode

If you're using the most recent version of Microsoft's Internet Explorer (IE) browser, there is a chance that some websites won't be displaying properly. This is because some websites were designed to work with earlier versions of Internet Explorer. If the application you're supporting exhibits problems when viewed in IE, then you might have a compatibility problem.

There is a setting in Internet Explorer called the Compatibility View that displays the website as if you were using an earlier version of this browser. To work with the Compatibility View settings, you need to click on the Tools setting of the IE menu. Within the Tools menu, select the "Compatibility View Settings" option. Within the screen that will be displayed, you have the choice to viewing the current web page in Compatibility View by clicking the Add button. All websites that will be viewed in compatibility mode will be displayed in the list box shown on the screen. If you want to view all websites in Compatibility view mode, then click on the last checkbox on the screen.

5.2 IS YOUR APPLICATION BRITTLE?

Some applications seem to require constant attention. Every morning when you arrive at work, you just know that there will be e-mails from users complaining about something being wrong with the application. Or the e-mails may have come from the application itself or from your monitoring package. If applications like these were people, they would be referred to as being "high maintenance." Other applications just seem to chug along with only the minimum amount of attention being required. Which is yours? There are some very important reasons why you need to know this. The most important one being your supervisor's expectation of how much of your time needs to be dedicated to this application.

A piece of software, e.g., an application, is considered brittle if it works fine when the user does everything exactly right. But if the user deviates the way he or she is using the software, then it no longer works as expected. Often problems like these seem to occur and then disappear just as quickly. If a problem can't be readily reproduced, then it's very difficult to troubleshoot.

An application that is brittle or "high maintenance" is going to require more of your time dedicated to it, potentially a *lot* more time. As a result, an Application Administrator won't be able to support as many applications as he or she could if the application required the normal amount of maintenance. Or a single Application Administrator might not be able to support the application without assistance. You want your supervisor to know this up front so he or she doesn't think you're incompetent or goofing off.

Some examples of ways in which an application is brittle are:

- Problems occur if the users do things in a different sequence
- If the user chooses a nondefault option, then problems occur
- Problems occur if user enters an extreme, but technically valid value

No one is going to come out and say an application is brittle. There isn't a "brittle" scale on which applications are measured and compared. One way of determining whether your application is brittle or not is to listen to user complaints about problems that mysteriously "go away" or "solve themselves." These might be examples that things worked correctly until the user deviates from a specific usage pattern. They do something a little different and a problem occurs. Then the next time they do it the "normal" way and everything is OK.

Code that is brittle can't be significantly improved, i.e., be made "robust," without a significant amount of effort. Essentially, the code base that makes up the application has to be rewritten. The vendor isn't likely to do this so if the application is brittle now; it's not likely to improve in the future.

5.2.1 **Documenting brittle areas**

Perhaps, the best thing you can do to document the brittleness factor of the application is to keep detailed notes on each and every problem that occurs. You should be doing this anyway, but this is another motivation to do it. Your documentation should include the following details:

- An entry for every problem that is reported to you
- What user(s) reported the problem
- How much time it took to get details about the problem from the user(s)
- Whether you were able to resolve it yourself or was vendor assistance required
- How quickly the vendor support team responded initially
- Whether the vendor tech's first suggestion fixed the problem
- How quickly it took the user(s) to confirm that the problem has been resolved

It would be wonderful if there was a chart showing the number of man-hours needed to support every different application. Unfortunately, that's not possible because there are so many variables involved. Some of these are:

- The number of users
- The experience of the users
- Diversity of the user population
- The application's architecture, i.e., client-server vs. web based
- How flexible the application is
- Your experience in general and with this application in particular
- Whether this application is considered critical to the organization
- How quickly the vendor responds to problem tickets and how quickly they get resolved

5.2.2 **Mitigating brittleness**

It isn't possible for an Application Administrator to make an application less brittle, but there are some things you can do to mitigate the impact of a brittle application. Some possible defensive measures include:

- Document the application's idiosyncrasies as you encounter them so you're less likely to be surprised if you run into them again in the future. If run into a problem again, you'll know how to work around it.
- Report any problems to the vendor. If they aren't made aware of problems, then they can't fix them.
- Get involved with the application's user group if one exists or other Application Administrators and learn how they handle these problems. You'll be amazed at how much you can learn from your peers.
- Increase the level of logging to see if that helps identify when and why the problem occur.
- Institute a process to monitor log files looking for specific error messages related to "brittle" errors in the application. If appropriate, when the process finds an error, it will send out an alert to you so you know that it has occurred.

5.3 DOES THE APPLICATION "PLAY WELL" WITH OTHERS?

If a preexisting application, yours or another, works fine until a second application is loaded on the server or desktop and then things start degrading, then you might have a situation where one of the applications doesn't "play well" with others.

Some potential reasons why the applications don't play well together:

- They use different versions of the same DLL (Dynamic Linked Library)
- They attempt to use the same port to communicate with another computer or service
- Both applications rely heavily on a specific resource, e.g., disk I/O, network I/O, memory, CPU cycles, etc.
- One or both applications have memory leak problems which eventually causes the application or the computer to crash

The most obvious solution to this conundrum is to not force these applications to play together at all. If you're dealing with applications on a single server, then separate them. Either invest in another physical server or create a second virtual server.

If the problem exists on a user's desktop, then the solution becomes more difficult. One step would be to determine whether both applications really need to be running on the same desktop. If they must, then see if a more recent version or patch is available for one or both applications. It's possible that this is a known issue and a fix has been released that resolves the problem.

5.4 INTEGRATES WELL WITH OTHER APPLICATIONS

Many applications that your organization relies upon need to be integrated with other applications. For example, the output from your timekeeping application provides the input to your payroll application. The output from the payroll application feeds a tax application that produces tax forms for employees at the end of the year.

Some other examples of applications that can be integrated with others include:

- Supply chain management applications integrate with your inventory system
- Customer relationship management (CRM) applications integrate with your billing system
- Human Resources (HR) system integrates with your timekeeping system
- Learning Management System (LMS) integrates with your HR system
- Active Directory integrates with your HR system
- Business Intelligence (BI) integrates with numerous systems to gather data

Some applications try to provide soup-to-nuts capability, i.e., they attempt to fulfill every conceivable need that your organization might have. While this may appeal to some clients, it might not be the way you want to go. Some reasons why you might choose to integrate multiple applications instead of choosing an all-encompassing software package include:

- You're reluctant to be that dependent on a single vendor
- Your organization already has software in place which provides the functionality in question, e.g., timekeeping, and you don't need to buy a new product to handle it
- An in-house development team wrote a custom application which suits the needs of your organization perfectly
- The version associated with the new application doesn't provide all of the functionality you need
- The software you already have in place is considered the "best of breed" and you don't want to depart from it
- The cost associated with this particular package in the new application is more than you want to pay or can fund
- The package in the new application provides more functionality than your organization needs

- Government regulations restrict the software packages that can be used and the new application isn't on the approved list

Some applications seem to be better suited to integration than others. The good ones have built-in utilities or functions that make producing the output easier. They might be able to product reports in a wide variety of output formats, some of which are suitable as input for other applications.

On the other end of the chain, some applications are more flexible regarding incoming data. They can handle multiple, difference formats of incoming data. Some applications are better at handling unexpected or invalid data than other applications. You need to experiment with your application to determine how easy it is to integrate with other applications.

Applications that are extremely well suited to integrating with others have a robust, well-documented API (Application Programming Interface). An API is nothing more than a specification that documents how other software components can communicate with it. The API can take several forms. It can be language specific or language independent. It can describe how a procedural language like C would call specific functions to interact with the application. If the API is object oriented, it would describe a set of class definitions and behaviors that define how to interact with the application. As is probably obvious, the existence of an API is more flexible, but requires a higher level of technical knowledge to set up the integration.

5.5 LICENSE KEYS

Many if not most vendors use license keys to ensure that their software is only running at sites that have paid for it. This is a very reasonable requirement, but occasionally can cause problems for even clients that are properly licensed. For example, what happens if the license key expires at night, over a weekend, on a holiday or while the Application Administrator is out of the office? Murphy's Law dictates that any expiring licenses will do so at the most inconvenient time.

To be prepared for this eventually, you need to do some advanced planning. Some of the steps that you can take include the following:

- Work with your organization's procurement team to proactively deal with expiring license keys. This can ensure that the maintenance or support invoices are paid in advance and your application never experiences a licensing issue.
- Know in advance when the key expires. How to extract this information is unique to each application. You'll need to check the Administrator's Guide or contact the vendor's support desk to learn how to do this. Then you need to create a reminder, aka tickler, for yourself that will come up a week before the expiration date. This should give you ample time to contact the vendor and get the new license key.
- If you're running multiple copies of the software, e.g., a load balanced environment or separate PROD and QA environments, will their licenses all expire at the same time? It would be very nice to take care of all of your environments at one time instead of having to handle this multiple times throughout the year.
- Don't forget about your DR (Disaster Recovery) environment. If a disaster occurs, you don't want to find out that the DR site is unusable due to licensing issues that no one ever noticed.
- Does the application provide any warning that the key is about to expire? What form does this warning take?
- Will an e-mail be sent out to the Application Administrator?
- Will a warning message come up every time a user logs into the application?
- Will a warning message be buried in a log file that no one is monitoring?

Other information that you should have in advance includes knowing who to contact to get a new license key.

- Will you get the fastest response by calling the vendor's support desk?
- Are new license keys issued on their website via an automated process?
- Is there a specific person you can call or e-mail to get the new key?
- How far in advance will the vendor issue a new key?
- If a license expires outside of normal business hours, is there an emergency number you can call?
- Are the vendor's holidays the same as yours?

5.5.1 Updating license keys

One last piece of advice is that you need to know in advance how to update the license key on the server. As you might expect, every application handles this differently. Figures 5.1 and 5.2 show how to enter the new license key for one application. This process requires that you remotely connect to the server hosting the application. Once there, the first step of the process is to open that application and select the Manage | Licensing menu option. See Figure 5.1 for a screenshot of that menu option.

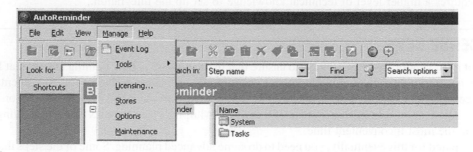

FIGURE 5.1

Accessing the Licensing Screen. (For color version of this figure, the reader is referred to the online version of this chapter.)

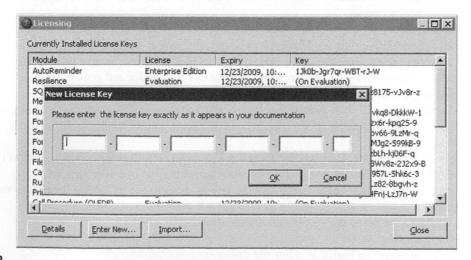

FIGURE 5.2

Entering a New License Key. (For color version of this figure, the reader is referred to the online version of this chapter.)

Once the Licensing screen is displayed, click the "Enter New" button. Enter the new licensing key that was provided to you by the vendor and then click OK. See Figure 5.2 for a screenshot of the two Licensing screens. After completing, these steps the license has been updated.

5.6 TROUBLESHOOTING ASSISTANCE

Does the application provide additional details that can assist you in the troubleshooting process? Chapter 4 described log files that applications typically create to document problems. Some examples of additional information that might be displayed which make troubleshooting significantly easier include:

- When an error occurs, a meaningful screen with details of the error is displayed.
- Each screen in the application has a unique ID so users can definitively identify the screen and pass that information on to you.
- Some applications display additional information about the current screen if a certain keystroke combination is entered or a menu item is selected.

If the application provides additional information, then you need to educate the users to capture it when they report a problem. It would be a waste not to take advantage of valuable details that the vendor took the time and effort to include in the application. Training users to provide this information from the beginning will save everyone time and trouble.

An example of an application that provides a wealth of troubleshooting information is Mozilla's Firefox. If you click menu item Help | Troubleshooting Information, the screen shown in Figure 5.3 is displayed.

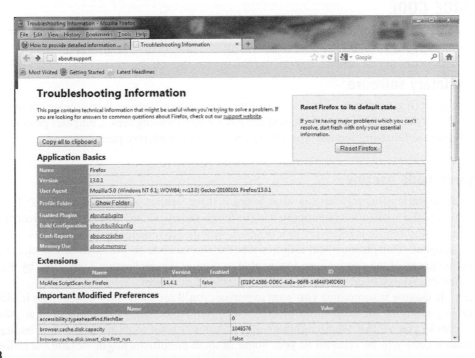

FIGURE 5.3

Troubleshooting Information available in Mozilla Firefox. (For color version of this figure, the reader is referred to the online version of this chapter.)

While not all of the information provided is applicable to a business application, it can be extremely useful when trying to troubleshoot problems with Firefox.

5.7 USING THE APPLICATION IN UNEXPECTED WAYS

Like any product, an application is designed for a specific purpose. A sports car is fast and fun, but won't carry freight the way a pickup truck will. A vacuum cleaner works great in your house, but doesn't suck up leaves and grasses clippings in your yard like a leaf blower can. My point is that the best software in the world won't work if you're using it to do the wrong job.

Some examples of how an application can be used in an environment for which it wasn't intended include the following:

- Trying to run 24×7 using an application that was designed to do batch processing
- Using a database that the application wasn't originally designed to support
- Trying to support more users, more sites, etc., than the application can handle
- Using incorrect data types, for example, an integer or float for monetary values instead of using the currency data type
- Using preexisting objects to hold data that doesn't "fit"
- Supporting data other than the designers envisioned.

5.8 SOURCE CODE

Behind every application is source code, lots and lots of source code. There are other objects like a database and business objects, but an application is composed of lots of source code.

5.8.1 Proprietary software

Vendors don't want to give access to their application's source code because then anyone could compile the application and use the resulting executable without paying the licensing fees. Computer programs or applications that require a licensing fee are typically referred to as proprietary programs.

5.8.2 Source code escrow

A concern you might legitimately have is what happens if the vendor goes out of business? If that should happen, then would the application be supported in the future and by whom? One possibility you might investigate, especially if the vendor is relatively new or small, would be to require that the source code be deposited in an escrow account. This arrangement requires that the source code be provided to a neutral third party, called an escrow agent. If the vendor is no longer able to support the application as required by the licensing agreement, then the source code would be made available to the client.

If source code escrow is something you want to pursue, you'll probably have to negotiate it with the vendor from the beginning of the acquisition process. Once they've installed the application at your site and cashed your check, you've lost your bargaining edge. You will want to define all of the conditions under which the source code will be released to you. Some of those conditions might include the following:

- The vendor declares bankruptcy
- The vendor fails to address documented errors within a certain time period, say 6-12 months

- The vendor fails to update the application to work with a new operating system version
- The vendor fails to update the application to work with a new version of the database package that it relies upon

Don't think for a minute that getting the vendor to agree to putting the source code into an escrow account is a panacea for all potential problems. If you feel that the conditions have been met that should trigger a release of the source code, you can expect that the vendor will fight it. Once source code has been released to you, their position has been significantly weakened so expect them to delay, deny, and otherwise obstruct your attempts at getting the source code.

Even after you gain access to the source code, you will still have difficulties attempting to support the application yourself. Some potential obstacles you'll have to deal with include:

- Do you have any developers on your staff that are familiar with the programming languages, the platform, and the coding style of the source code?
- Do you have enough developers on staff to fully support the application? How many technical staff members did the vendor have vs. how many do you have?
- How up-to-date is the code that was placed in escrow? The older it is, the less valuable it is.
- Were all of the libraries used by the code base included in the escrow?
- Was any documentation included in the escrow materials?

Have you defined your primary objectives for supporting the application? Unless you have an unlimited budget and personnel, you won't be able to do everything you might want to do. You'll have to prioritize the tasks you're going to undertake. Your potential objectives might include:

- Fix known errors
- Improve the performance of the application
- Increase the number of users the application will support
- Enable the application to support multiple languages
- Upgrade the application to work with a new server operating system
- Update the application to work with a new version of the database
- Add new features that will make your users more efficient or that they are specifically requesting
- Add requirements that a regulatory agency is requiring

5.8.3 Open source software

The opposite end of the spectrum on availability of source code and licensing fees is referred to as "open source software" or OSI. Often, open source software has numerous contributors during its development. Some examples of open source software projects include:

- Apache HTTP Server
- Mozilla's Firefox Internet browser
- The Linux operating system
- The Android operating system for mobile devices.

Enterprise-level open source applications are relatively uncommon, but they are beginning to emerge. As the open source movement gains strength and followers, then more and more of the types of applications that organizations depend on may become available as open source projects.

If an application you're supporting is open source, then the source code will be available to you and you're free to modify it to your heart's content. Be very aware that if you introduce errors into the software, then you're probably on your own when it comes to debugging it. You'll want to keep very close records of what changes have been made, when, and by whom so they can be undone if that becomes necessary. Chapter 7 on Change Control Management discusses methods of tracking changes to your software.

Just because the source code is readily available doesn't mean you are in a position to modify or fully support it. You have to answer many of the questions that were posed for software that's been escrowed.

- Do you have any developers on your staff that are familiar with the programming languages, the platform, and the coding style of the source code?
- Do you have enough developers on staff to fully support the application?
- Do you have the most up-to-date version of the source code?
- Are all of the libraries used by the code base available?
- Was any documentation included in the open source materials?

5.9 PHONING HOME

Like it or not, many software vendors include functionality in their applications to regularly contact the home office. The title of this section isn't intended to imply the applications would use a modem and a phone line to make these communications. The avenue of communication would in all likelihood be performed via the Internet.

There are legitimate reasons why the vendor might have included this capability in their software. For example, it might be done to report on errors that have been encountered. This has the potential to get your problem resolved faster. Other reasons why the application might be designed to phone home include:

- It might be reporting back the authorization key that is being used by the site
- It might be reporting the number of named users that are logged into the application
- It might be reporting the version of the application that is being used.

How can you find out whether your application is calling home to its mommy? Reading the documentation is one way of trying to determine this. If the Administrator's Guide doesn't mention this, you could contact the vendor's support team and ask them. If they won't give you a straight answer, then you can install software that will monitor the server for this type of activity (see Section 5.9.1).

Questions that you might want answers to on this topic include:

- Does the application you are supporting phone home?
- Is it possible to turn this "feature" off?
- What information does it send back to the vendor when it makes a connection?
- How often does the application phone home?
- Can you control how often it calls home and what it sends?
- What is the risk that this feature could be used for nefarious purposes, e.g., to send confidential information to someone outside your organization?

If you are in the process of evaluating an application, then this is a legitimate question to ask the vendor. If the application does call home and it can't be turned off then you have to decide whether this should remove it from consideration. If the sales rep or technical rep tells you that their software doesn't do this and later you find out that it does, then you have an important decision to make, do you want to work with a vendor that lies to you?

5.9.1 **Blocking phone calls home**

Antispyware packages exist that can help you prevent applications from phoning home. Once this type of monitoring package is set up, it will report any Internet access attempts. This provides you with information about what applications are trying to phone home, what ports are being used, and what the destination of the attempts are. With this information you can decide whether any communication should be allowed.

If you don't want to install antispyware package, there is another way to accomplish the same objective. Netstat is a tool that tells what ports are opened and what program opened them. Netstat is available for Windows, UNIX, and Linux. After identifying the port with netstat, you can use your firewall to stop the application from phoning home. This requires changing your firewall settings to prevent outgoing communications on the port or ports you identified with netstat.

5.10 **TRACKING DOWN CHANGES**

Who dunnit? There will come a time when you need to track down who made a change in the application, specifically a change made via the user interface. The change may have caused a problem. Everyone will deny having done it. It will be your job to play detective and figure out who "dunnit."

What facilities does the application provide for this type of investigation? Does it provide any method of researching this type of question? Does it provide any of the following capabilities and who can access them?

5.10.1 **Audit trail**

Does the application provide any kind of audit trail report? Some applications have canned reports that list exactly what you want to know. You simply bring up the report, specify a few parameters like a time range or object that was modified, and run the report. This is the optimal situation for resolving questions of this type.

5.10.2 **Log files**

If any audit report isn't available, then you're going to have to work a little bit harder to find what you're looking for. The next logical place to look would be in a log file. Depending on the application, the amount of information written to a log file varies enormously. It might go down to the level of who changed a particular field. Unfortunately, to get that level of details, some applications require that you modify the level of what is to be logged. There are two complications here. First, if the logging level isn't set at the more detailed level when the change occurs, then the information you're seeking won't have gotten logged. Second, if you ramp up the logging level so every change is logged, then it might have a noticeable impact on performance. It will certainly impact the amount of disk space being used by the log files.

5.10.3 **Database tables**

If the logs didn't record who made the change, then your next stop is the database. Many database tables include a timestamp field. If you know the specific table that the field is stored in, you can retrieve it from the database and determine exactly when the change was made. With any luck, the database table will also contain a column identifying the ID of the person who made the change. Don't get your hopes up too high because even if the table has such an ID field in it, the value in the field might be a generic ID instead of the individual user's identification. You'll have to research this, hopefully in advance, to determine what information your application retains in the database.

5.10.4 **Login reports**

If none of the above sources worked out for you, then I have one suggestion left. If you know approximately when the change was made, then you can try to determine which users were logged into the application at that time. Some applications have a report that the Administrator can access which lists when individual users logged into and out of the application. If no such report is available, then this information might get written to the log files. If these two pieces of information can narrow the potential miscreants down to a handful, then this might help you determine who made the change.

A word to the wise, if you know how to gather these details in advance, you'll be able to handle these requests more quickly. When a problem like this occurs, then people will want to know right away who did it. If you've already practiced this type investigation, then it will go much faster than if you're doing it for the first time. As always, write up your own documentation on how to gather this information. If you haven't had to do this in a while, then you might not remember the exact sequence of steps that are needed.

5.11 **USING DISK SPACE**

Every application consumes disk space, usually a considerable amount. The disk space can be broken down into two types:

1. Space that is needed initially to load the software
2. Space that will be needed as the application runs for log files, data files, images, etc.

How much disk space does your application initially require? This information will be in the Installation Guide. Very frequently during the installation sequence, the process will check to confirm that the drive you're installing the application onto has enough space to meet the recommendations. If there isn't sufficient space available, then it will give you a warning prompt and might refuse to continue the installation process.

A word of warning is called for here—take the minimum disk space recommendations seriously. The vendor probably has a very accurate handle on how much disk is needed. Don't try to squeeze by with the absolute minimum. Eventually, you'll run out of space and it will happen at an inconvenient time.

What exactly will happen if the application runs out of space? It depends on the application of course, but I can assure you that it won't be a good thing. It won't be good for the users. It won't be good for the application's availability statistics. Most importantly, it won't be good for your reputation or career.

One way to avoid having the server run out of disk space is to monitor it regularly. If you monitor the amount of available space on a regular basis, you can use those statistics to make a prediction regarding when the server will run out of disk space. The biggest questions are how often to monitor it and what will you use to do the monitoring.

A WORD OF WARNING ABOUT PREDICTIONS

Predicting when your server will run out of disk space is an admirable goal but be aware that it's not totally reliable. You may think that your server won't run out of disk space for a long time, but disk space can be used up very quickly if something unusual happens on the server. Some examples of what might cause the serve to run out of space much more quickly than you anticipated include:

- Log files can grow extremely quickly if an error situation comes up. This is especially true if all logging options are being exercised, i.e., if you're logging everything.
- Unusually heavy user activity can consume abnormal amounts of disk space.
- If the system crashes, most operating systems will create a dump file to help analyze the cause of the crash. Dump files can be extremely large. It's not uncommon for multiple dump files to have been created and overlooked on a server.

- When installing a new version of the application or updating the existing version, the process usually requires that you download a very large file with the new or modified code, libraries, etc. This file is usually zipped up and once it's unzipped, it becomes even larger. When the update is done, be sure that you delete these files.
- Backups are probably being done on your server regularly. Backup files should be moved off the server to ensure that they don't disappear if the server crashes. Make sure that old versions of the backup files haven't been left on the server.
- Testing can involve files that are extremely large. It's easy to forget that test files were loaded onto the server. If they are forgotten, they're consuming a significant amount of disk space. Once the testing is done, make sure that all test files are deleted as soon as it can be safely done.

5.11.1 Monitoring disk space

There are multiple approaches to monitor the amount of disk space available on your server. It's possible to spend as much or as little time and money on monitoring your server as you're willing to spend. Some examples of how to approach this monitoring activity are listed here.

5.11.1.1 Manually

Determining how much disk space is available isn't exactly rocket science. It only takes a couple of minutes to remote to the server and determine how much disk space is available on it. After finding out how much space is left, you can write that value to a spreadsheet. Create a chart on the spreadsheet based on the dates and sizes and bingo—instant trending. You can even delegate this activity to an intern if you have one.

5.11.1.2 Write a script to do it

One step up from manually checking the available space is to write a script to do it. The script doesn't have to be fancy. Something as simple as the UNIX df command with a grep to isolate the counts you want. Append the new value to the end of a file to capture data over time. Schedule your script to run on the server daily or weekly.

You could write a second script that e-mails you whenever the amount of disk space falls below a critical threshold, say 10%. This script should also be scheduled to run periodically. Daily or even twice a day would be very valuable.

5.11.1.3 Use an operating system feature to do it

Using an operating system feature to monitor disk space can be even easier than writing your own script. If the O/S has such a feature, then set up a monitoring task to do this. If the O/S can e-mail when the amount of available space falls below a predetermined threshold, say 10%, then this specific monitoring requirement is pretty much done.

5.11.1.4 Download a freeware tool to do it

A quick search of the Internet will list innumerable free tools that offer to monitor available disk space on one or all of your servers. Personally, I'm more than very little hesitant to load programs with an unknown provenance onto a production server, but maybe I'm a little more cautious than most. If you choose this route, you'll have many potential tools to choose from.

5.11.1.5 Incorporate it into the overall monitoring framework

Your organization might already have an enterprise monitoring tool in place. If that is the case, then you certainly want to take advantage of it instead of reinventing the wheel. Setting it up to monitoring the amount of available disk space on your server shouldn't be too hard. If you're really lucky, your organization will have an administrator for that specialty and all you'll have to do is to submit a request for him or her to add this to what's already being monitored.

5.11.2 Running out of disk space

Once you know that your server is about to run out of disk space, what should you do? Three options that come to my mind are described in the following sections.

5.11.2.1 Adding more disk space

Adding additional disk space can be very easy or very difficult depending on how your server was set up. If your server has a single drive and it's almost out of space, then that's the worst case scenario. To add space, you have to either replace the old drive with a newer, larger drive or add an additional disk drive. Both options are complicated, time consuming, and require an outage.

To replace the existing drive with a newer, larger one, you'll have to perform some variation of these steps:

- Shut down the application and the server
- Copy the contents of the old drive to the new drive
- Install the new drive as the master drive
- Restart the server and the application

If the server was built using SAN (Storage Area Network), then the steps are much simpler. Just contact the SAN Administrator and say "I need more disk space please." Of course, someone has to authorize the expansion and promise to pay for it, but it's not going to be coming out of your paycheck.

Besides being easy, expanding SAN space has another advantage. Most likely, the application won't have to come down for the SAN space to be expanded. This is especially important to you if your bonus depends on the application meeting an availability time target.

5.11.2.2 Freeing up disk space

Freeing up disk space on the existing drive appeals to the cheapskate in me. Why spend money adding disk space if a significant amount of space on the drive is being used by files that you don't need or want? The most obvious question here is what types of files can you delete if the server runs out of disk space? A brief list of candidates for deletion includes:

- Old log files
- Operating system dump files
- Install or upgrade files
- Backup files
- Test data files
- Programs or applications on the server that are no longer being used
- Modules of the application you support that are no longer being used
- Documentation files, either vendor documentation or what you've written

Of course, before deleting any files, you need to be sure that they are no longer needed. If there is any question, ask someone. Ask the users, ask the vendor support desk, ask a coworker, etc. Just be very careful deleting files that you don't know anything about.

If you're fortunate enough to have multiple drives on the application server and only one of them is becoming full, you have additional options to choose from. Listed here are several possibilities ranging from simple to a little more complicated.

5.11.2.3 Relocating files

A quick and easy solution is to just move files from the full drive to the less full drive. Of course, you can't simple move any file in sight. Any file that the application will be referencing must stay where the application expects to see it. Potential files that can be moved include:

- Old log files
- Operating system dump files
- Install or upgrade files
- Backup files
- Test data files

5.11.2.4 Modify the application to utilize another drive

Another possible solution is to modify the application to start using another disk drive for certain functions. For example, the application might have a configuration parameter that dictates where log files will be written. There's probably no reason why log files can't be written to the D: drive instead of the C: drive. If your application has \temp or a \calculation subdirectories, then perhaps those subdirectories could be moved to another drive.

It should go without saying that if you change any application setting, it needs to be tested in a nonproduction environment first. Even a change as simple as this one has the potential for unexpected side effects. Do yourself and your users a favor and test it on a QA or UAT environment before moving it into production.

5.11.2.5 Create a junction point

A junction point is essentially a directory that actually points to another directory. The idea here is to create and use a junction point so the application uses a different drive but doesn't know it. For example, say an application was loaded onto the D: drive and that drive is running out of space due to a large number of logs. Also assume you can't delete the log files or move them to another drive or subdirectory. If that server has an E: drive with plenty of space, you could create a junction point that links D:\Application\logs with E:\logs. The application would continue to write log files to D:\Application\logs, but they would actually be written to subdirectory E:\logs.

This functionality is available in many variations of Windows, UNIX, and Linux. Before assuming that you can use this technique, you need to make sure the version of the operating system on your server offers this feature. If you're working with Windows, then you may have to download either a Microsoft or third-party utility depending on what version of Windows you're using.

Be warned in advance that there are some "gotcha's" to consider when using junction points. For example, some versions require that the destination subdirectory be empty when the junction point is created. If it isn't empty, then the command will fail. You also need to confirm what your variation of this function will do if the junction point is deleted. Will the files be dropped? Or will the files continue to exist. Test this extensively before moving it into production.

As always, if you decide to use this technique, the change needs to be tested on a nonproduction environment. It would be extremely inconvenient if the application died or log files weren't being created due to this change.

Taking Responsibility for an Application

By definition, every Application Administrator gets at least one application handed to them during his or her career. When the application is being transitioned to you, there will be a relatively short "honeymoon" window. By this, I mean you'll get as much cooperation and information about the application as you're ever going to get. My advice is to make the most of this opportunity by collecting as many details about the application as possible.

The best way to gather as much information as possible is to have a very thorough list of questions ready in advance. When you are told that you're going to be responsible for the XYZ application, pull out the following list of questions and edit it to make it specific to your new responsibility. Trim out any questions or sections that don't apply to your new charge.

Feel free to modify this list of questions to suit your environment. Add, reword, and delete questions to maximize their value to you as the new Application Administrator. For example, you might want to convert this into a spreadsheet with one column for the questions and another column for the answers you expect to receive. If your organization is a heavy user of SharePoint, you could post the questions on it and request that everyone respond to them online.

One word of advice, if you distribute the list of questions to multiple people, you'll want to tailor the list to each recipient. If you send a DBA questions about the application's background, he won't be able to answer them. In fact, he might just ignore the entire list of questions altogether. Break down your questionnaire by subject and send just the applicable pieces to each coworker.

Distribute it to everyone that you're requesting assistance from. Coworkers will understand that you're new to the application and will probably be more likely to help someone who's new to the task. Some potential types that you should send a copy of your finished list to should include:

- The person(s) that previously supported the application
- The business owner of the application
- One or two of the power users of the application
- The Database Administrator
- The team that is dedicated to backups if such a team exists
- Network administrators
- Server administrators
- Security administrators

If you're new to the role of an Application Administrator, then some of the questions and concepts in this chapter may not be familiar to you. Don't be overly concerned about this. Every question and concept that is touched on in this chapter will be explained in more detail later in this book.

6.1 OVERVIEW OF THE APPLICATION

What is the name of the application?
What is the purpose of the application?
How long has this application been in use by the organization?

Who are the current administrators of the application?
If the current administrator only supported it for a short time, who supported it previously?
Will he or she be available to assist you during the transition period?

Why is this application being transferred away from the current individual or group?
Is the previous Application Administrator leaving the organization?
Is he/she available as your backup going forward?

Why is it being given specifically to you?

How is the application licensed?

There are several common licensing models for software applications

- Named user—means that only specific end users have the rights to use the application
- Seat License—company purchases the right for a certain number of users (seats) to use the application at any given time. Any employee of the company can use the application at any time as long as the number at any given times doesn't exceed the limit.
- Unlimited—any number of users can be on the application at any given time.

What documentation exists for the application?
This includes user manuals as well as documentation for administration activities.
Did the vendor provide an "Administrator's Guide" or "Installation Guide" for the application?
Does the previous App Admin have any notes, check lists, folklore, etc., on the application?

Can the existing Application Administrator provide a list of regular tasks that he or she performs and how long each task takes to perform?

Approximately how many man-hours per week or per month did the current administrator spend supporting the application?
Is that level of support expected to change in the near future?
If so, why?

Is this application SOX compliant?
Has it been audited for SOX compliancy?
If not, will it be required to be SOX compliant in the near future?

Is this application used by a single department, team, or group?

- If so which department, team, or group?
- Are there any plans to expand its use to another department, team, or group?
- If so when and who?

Are there any plans in the works for major changes to this application, for example?

- Enhancements
- Major upgrade
- Rollout to additional users or sites
- Replace this application with another new or existing application, etc.

If so, get a description of the changes, timeline, and participants.

If the organization experiences a merger or acquisition, is this application likely to be affected?

- Will it absorb additional users or departments?
- Is it likely to be replaced?

In the past, has this application required travel on the part of the administrators?

- If so, how frequently has he or she traveled?
- Why was traveling required?
- Where has he or she traveled to?
- How long does the administrator spend at the remote site?
- Would it be possible for this travel be replaced with remote access?

6.2 AVAILABILITY

What is the availability, i.e., uptime, expectation for the application? Some examples:

- During normal business hours
- 24×7
- 98% of the time
- Normal business hours plus an extra hour on either or both shoulders

What is the definition of uptime?

- How is uptime measured?
- Is it measured manually?
- Is it estimated?
- Is the application being monitoring by a process or monitoring tool?
- If so, what process is monitoring it?
- Is scheduled maintenance time counted as down time?

Has the application typically met the availability requirements?

When the application is unavailable, what are the typical reasons causing this?
Do a limited number of problems cause the majority of the unavailability events?

Has the application's availability statistics been increasing, decreasing, or remaining constant?

Does this application have a particular day of the week, week of the month, or month of the year when it is more heavily utilized?
Why is it used more heavily during this time period?
Is this usage distribution likely to change in the near future?

Is there a defined window when the application can be taken down for maintenance, e.g., to install updates, tune the database, reboot the server for performance purposes?

- What day or days is this maintenance window?
- What time does it start and stop?
- Is the maintenance window firm or only as needed?
- Do you need to contact anyone to shut, then application down during the maintenance window?

What if the application needs to come down at another time?

- Who needs to be contacted for approval?
- If the primary contact can't be reached, is there another person who can approve it?
- What types of reasons are acceptable for taking the application down?

6.3 PERFORMANCE

How is performance measured?

- Response time for the login screen
- Time to complete the most significant process
- User complaints about performance
- Reports are displayed in an acceptable time period

Are there any statistics documenting the current performance of the application?

Is the current level of performance of this application acceptable to the majority of users?
If not, what are the problems with the current level of performance?

Has the level of performance significantly changed in the recent past?
What were the causes of those performance changes?

During periods when the application doesn't meet the performance expectations, is there a documented reason for it?
Has a root cause been found for performance issues?
Has anyone worked with the vendor to resolve this issue?

6.4 USER BASE

How many users does the application have?
How many are frequent vs. infrequent users of the application?
At any given time, about how many users are actively using the application?
How is this measured?
Is there a specific number of licenses available?
What is that number and how close to it are you currently?
Can this limit be temporarily increased?
Has the size of the user base changed in the recent past? Up or down? Why?

Is the size of the user base projected to increase or decrease in the near future?
Are all users in the same city, state, country, or continent?
How many different sites have users of the application?
Are there users in all time zones or just the U.S. time zones?

What types of users exist in your environment?
Is the user community broken down by types like:

- Power users
- Read Only users
- Writer users

- Reviewer
- Approver

How many users of each type exist?

Does each site have a "super-user," i.e., an experienced user who is able to answer most of the questions that less experienced users have?

How frequently are users added, deleted, or updated?
Who is responsible for adding, deleting, and updating users?

What steps are needed to set up a new user's access to the application?
What documentation/process exists for this application relating to user set-up?

How often does the typical user log into the application, e.g., once a day, once a week.
Do users typically log into the application once a day and stay in it all day or repeatedly log into and out of the application throughout the day?

6.5 BACKUPS

Is the data for this application currently being backed up?

- If so, by who?
- How often?
- Full or incremental?
- What days and time of the day are backups being made?

Does your organization have a separate backup group or team?
If so, are they running and monitoring the backups of this application?
If no backup group exists, will you be in charge of the backups?

How exactly are backups being done?
Is a third-party tool like CommVault or Norton Ghost being used?
Is an operating system command or utility being run?

Is any group or individual verifying that all backups were successfully made?
Who?

Does the backup process create reports indicating that the process succeeded and what was backed up?
If so, who are the reports distributed to?
Who do you need to contact to get your name added to the distribution list?

Are the backup media stored onsite, offsite, or both?
If they are eventually moved offsite, how long are they onsite before being moved?
How quickly can we retrieve backup media from offsite locations?

What is the process to restore a file or an entire disk?
Who do you contact?
Is there a paper form involved or can the request be submitted online?
How long does it take to fulfill a restore request?
Can a single file be restored or just an entire backup?

Can backups be made while users are still logged into the application?
If so, does this impact performance or the validity of the backups?

What exactly is being backed up?

- The database
- Source code
- Executables
- Support files, i.e., INI files, XML files, configuration files
- The operating system on the application server
- Data files stored outside of the database, e.g., images, documents, e-mails?

What type of media are backups being made to:

- Hard drives
- Tape
- CD
- DVD
- SAN drive

If a backup fails on a given day, what happens?

- Will someone be automatically notified of the failure?
- Will that day's backup process be rerun?
- If the backup process needs to be rerun, who launches it manually?

Are the backup process and resulting media regularly tested to be certain that it works, i.e., that data being backed up actually exists on the tapes or DVDs and can be successfully restored?

- Is the restoration process documented?
- How accurate is the documentation?
- Who does this testing?
- When was the last time such a test was done?
- Was the last test restoration successful?
- When is the next test of this nature scheduled to be performed?

Is restoration an all-or-nothing process or can files be selectively restored?

When was the last time a restoration was required?

- Why was a data restoration needed?
- Who performed the restoration
- What exactly was restored, e.g., executables, data, source code
- Did it go smoothly?
- How long did it take?
- Was any interim data lost?
- Did they follow established, documented steps to perform this restoration?
- How long did it take?

6.6 PRODUCTION SUPPORT

Obtain a list of everyone who supports the application in one way or another.

Who provides for Tier 1 Technical Support?
Who provides for Tier 2 Technical Support?
Who provides for Tier 3 Technical Support?

Who provides support for overnight processing, i.e., batch processes that run overnight?

Who provides support for developing additional functionality of this application?

Can this be done internally or is the application licensed from a third party?

In the event of outages or other emergencies, who communicates with users? How is this done?

- Via an e-mail distribution list
- Via an announcements page on the application
- By contacting just the Power Users. Who actually contacts the users?

If the software needs to be installed on each user's workstation, how is it done?

- Manually? If so, by whom?
- If it needs to be installed manually, can it be done remotely?
- Automated via a tool like LANDesk?

Is there a user group (independent or vendor sponsored) for this application?

- Does it have regular local group meetings?
- Have any company personnel attended the user group meetings?
- Does the user group have a website that provides valuable support information?
- Does their website include FAQs, a knowledge base, articles submitted by users or Application Administrators, etc.?

6.7 HARDWARE

What server(s) support this application?

Compile a list of all application, development, database, and SMTP servers.

Be sure to include ALL servers

- Production servers
- Test and development servers
- DR servers
- Report servers

Can you remotely access all of the servers used by the application?

What tool is used to access them?

- RDC—Remote Desktop Connection
- WinSCP
- Putty

Are the application servers physical or virtual?

If they are virtual servers, then what software is being used? For example:

- VMWare
- Citrix XenApp
- Microsoft Hyper-V

Where are the servers physically located?

Who has physical access to them if they don't respond remotely?

What operating system is loaded on each server?

- What version of the operating system?
- What patch level or service pack?

What resources does each server have?

- Processors: make, model, and speed in GHz
- Memory
- Disk drives
- NIC (Network Interface Cards)

Is any special or unique hardware needed for this application? This would include:

- RAID drives
- Multiple processors
- Load balancers
- Clusters
- Proxy servers

Has any hardware (servers, disk drives, memory, etc.) been added recently?

- If so, what and when?
- Why was it added?
- Are any hardware additions planned for the future?

Is any of the existing hardware scheduled to be replaced in the near future?
If so, what hardware and when?

When is the "End of Life" for the servers?
What is your organization's process for replacing servers as they approach their end of life?

6.8 SOFTWARE

Was this application custom built or is it commercial-off-the-shelf software (COTS)?

Who developed this application, i.e., internal personnel or an outside vendor?
If developed by an outside vendor, does your company have a support contract with them?

- How long is the support contract scheduled to last?
- What level of support does the contract provide, i.e., 24×7, onsite, regular business hours?

Does the vendor have a website?

- If so, what is its URL?
- Does your organization have logon credentials?

Is the application currently at the current software release level offered by the vendor?

If not, why not and how many release levels behind is it?
What is the vendor's policy about support prior versions? That is, do they push clients to stay within 1 or 2 versions of the most current release?

If the application was developed internally, are the development personnel still available?

Can they provide assistance if a particularly thorny problem is encountered?
Can they act as your back up until someone else is trained for the position?

Is the application web-based or client-server, i.e., software is installed on each user's workstation?

What language is the application written in?
Do you or any of your coworkers have experience with that language?

If developed by an outside vendor, does your organization have access to the source code?
Is the source code in an escrow account in that the event the vendor goes out of business?

How often are updates typically released?
When was the last software update received and installed?
Are releases cumulative, i.e., does version 3.4 include 3.3, 3.2, and 3.1?

Are updates released to all clients at the same time or is there a staged release?
What stage is your organization in?

Some IT professionals refuse to install the first version of any software. They feel very strongly that the first version contains an inordinate number of bugs.

- Did your predecessor feel this way?
- Was there any evidence that this application or vendor has unusually buggy first releases?

How are updates distributed?

- Tape
- CD or DVD
- FTP'ed out
- Downloaded from vendor's website

When updates are published, who installs them?

- Is this something the Application Administrator can do by himself?
- Is the assistance of a vendor technician required to avoid violating the support agreement?
- Can you request the assistance of a vendor tech if the upgrade looks especially complicated?

How long does it take to install the typical upgrade?

If a significant error is uncovered in the application, how long does it take the vendor to respond with a patch or workaround?

How do your report errors in the application to the vendor?

- Website
- Phone call
- E-mail

6.9 DATABASE

Provide a description of the data used by the application.

Does this application depend on a database?
What kind of database is it, e.g., relational, XML, flat file?

What vendor produced the database, e.g., Oracle, Microsoft, IBM, Sybase?
What is the version of the database version, e.g., Oracle 11g, SQL Server 2012?

What server is the database running on?

How many databases does the application have? It's not uncommon for the application to have multiple, separate databases.
What are the name(s) of the database(s)?

Who provides database support needed by the application?

Are there any tools available to the Application Administrator to examine and/or modify the database? For example:

- SQL Plus
- Toad
- SQL Station
- SQL Developer

How many tables are in the database(s)?
Does the vendor publish any documentation describing the database tables and their interrelations?

How many megabytes or gigabytes of data are in the database?
Is the amount of data in the database expanding significantly?
If so, by how many MB of GB per month or year?
What is your organization's process to allocate more space to a database?

Does this database rely on periodic updates from the vendor a third party? For example

- Zip code data
- Tax rates
- Area code updates
- Price lists
- Government regulations

If so, how often is data updated?
How are data updates distributed; e.g., are up files mailed out, downloaded from a web site, etc.?
Does the Application Administrator have to go to the vendor website and download the updates?
How long does this take each time?
Who applies the update?
What testing is required after each update is applied?
Who does the testing?
Is data updated on DEV first, then on QA, then on PROD?
Is this entire process documented?

Does this application access data from external parties via web services?

Is there a firewall between the database server and the application server(s)?

Are there any tools to monitor the transactions between the application and database servers?

6.10 SECURITY

Does your organization have a group that focuses on security?

Do they provide vulnerability audits?
How often do they run audits?
What output do they provide to each Application Administrator?
What tool do they use? For example:

- Nessus
- Tiger
- SekChek
- WireShark
- Snort
- Backtrack

In your organization, do Application Administrators have to fix or otherwise respond to security audits?

Does each user have his or her own account?
If not, what is the justification for sharing accounts?

Who is notified when a user of the application leaves the company?
Who disables the account?
How long does this typically take?
What risk exists if a user's account isn't deleted or disabled when he leaves the organization?

Is user authentication handled within the application or by Active Directory (AD) or its equivalent?
If AD is used, then is a specific group responsible for disabling users that leave the organization?

Currently, who maintains the list of users?
Is the current user list accurate, i.e., have ex-employees been removed from the list?
How often is this list verified?
Who vouches for each user? Is each user in a group that has an authenticator in it?

What happens when users forget their password?

- Do they call the Centralized Service Desk?
- Do they open a trouble ticket?
- Do they call the Application Administrator?
- Do they just use a coworker's logon until someone figures out they're doing this?

If users exit the application improperly, are their accounts "locked"? This might happen if they exit a browser by clicking the "X" instead of the "Logout" link or if the application aborts on them.

- If they are locked out, whom do they contact to get their accounts unlocked?
- Is there a documented process to unlock accounts?
- Does someone need to grant approval before a locked out account can be unlocked?

What are the requirements of passwords?

- Minimum 8 characters
- At least one character must be capitalized
- Must include a digit

- Must include a punctuation character
- Can't be a word in the dictionary
- Is this configurable?

How often must passwords be changed?

- Every 60 days?
- Every 90 days?
- Is this configurable?

How is the password expiration requirement enforced? For example, does the application force users to change their password when the existing password has expired?

Can users immediately reuse their current passwords?
If not, how many password changes must occur before a password can be reused?

What is the process for creating a new user in this application?

- Is there a defined, documented, process?
- Where is this process posted?
- Who can authorize a new user's access to the application?
- Who actually creates new users? Help Desk? Power User? Application Administrator?
- Who decides what level of access new users will get?

Besides users, who else has access to this application? For example:

- Administrators
- Supervisors
- Approvers
- Auditors
- The Help Desk
- Security team
- The vendor

Who has access to the server(s) that the application is running on? For example:

- Application Administrator
- The Security team
- The group that runs the monitoring tool

Does the application allow new users to be added in a batch mode?
Or must every new user be added manually?

Can users be disabled but not removed from the application validation list?

6.11 TRAINING

What training is available for new or existing users of the application?

- Is the training formal or informal?
- How long does each class last?
- How many different classes are available?
- How often are training classes offered?

- Are new classes being developed and offered?
- Is web-based training available for users?
- Are users tested and graded after completing the classes?
- Do they have to attain a minimum score to obtain access to the application?

Who trains the trainer?
Is there any specialized training for the trainers?
How often is their training refreshed?

Is there any training from the vendor for Application Administrators?

- How often?
- How many classes are available?
- Are the classes online or instructor led?
- Local or do you have to travel to the vendor's site?
- Are classes included in your license cost or do they involve an extra cost?
- What prerequisites or experience is required for each class?

Does the application have a big enough presence to attract third-party training.

Are there any books written about this application?
Are any of them written by a third party, i.e., not published by the vendor?

6.12 DISASTER RECOVERY

Does the application have a DR (Disaster Recovery) Site?

- Where is it?
- Is it a duplicate of the production site?

What is currently at that site?

- Hardware
- Software
- Data

Are updates and patches that are installed on PROD also installed on the DR site?

If the server were to be destroyed, how would it be rebuilt?

- How long would this take?
- Has this been tested recently? When?
- How often is it tested?
- Who is required to rebuild a server?
- Who can authorize that a server be rebuilt?

Who will actually rebuild the server?
Do you have a contact name and number of this person or group?

Organizations typically have a large number of applications, where does your application lie in the organization's overall priority scheme? That is, if all of the organization's applications were affected by a disaster, where would this application fall? Would your application be brought back up first or last? Is the application's business owner aware of this priority?

6.13 **THE VENDOR**

If the application was licensed from a third party, what is their name and contact information?

* Is there a telephone number at which they can be reached?
* Is there an e-mail address by which vendor support can be contacted?
* How big is the vendor? For example, is it two guys in a garage?
* How long has the vendor been in business?

Does the vendor have a website? If so, does it provide the following?

* FAQs (frequently asked questions)
* The ability to open a trouble ticket
* A report of your organization's open tickets with the vendor
* A knowledge base of past tickets
* Articles submitted by users describing tips and tricks they've developed

Does the vendor sponsor a user group?

* Does the user group have regular meetings? Where?
* Do personnel from your organization attend the user groups meetings?
* Has your organization ever hosted a log user group meeting?
* Is there an annual or semi-annual user conference?

If there is a user conference, you should immediately request authorization and funding to attend it. Push for permission now by stressing that as a new administrator you'll need all the assistance you can get.

6.14 **INTERACTIONS WITH OTHER APPLICATIONS**

What are the application's data sources, i.e., where does the data it uses come from? If there is a data feed, get as much detail on it as possible.

Does this application interact, i.e., exchange data with any other applications?

* If so, what are the names of the other applications.
* Are the other applications internal or external to your organization?
* How often does this interaction occur? For example, real-time, hourly, daily, weekly?
* What data is exchanged?
* Which direction does the data flow? In? Out? Both?
* Which application drives the interaction process?

Provide specific details on the data exchange. For example, what is the purpose of the exchange?

What is the format of the data files that are exchanged?

* CSVs (comma-separated values)
* Tab-separated values
* Text file
* Binary

- XML (eXtensible Markup Language)
- HTML (HyperText Markup Language)

How are the files transmitted from one server to another?

- Transfer the file across a network
- FTP (file transfer protocol)
- Via a network drive that both servers can access
- E-mail
- Web service
- A third-party service like Dropbox
- Burned to CD or DVD and mailed to the recipient

Does the administrator or someone else have to periodically delete old files?
Or are they deleted automatically?
What is the naming format of the files being transmitted?
Does the naming format include a time or date stamp?

What happens if a scheduled interaction fails?

- Is the process restarted?
- Automatically or does a restart have to be done manually?
- Is the data lost?
- Is the data retained and then exchanged at the next scheduled interaction?
- Is a log file with meaningful information created?

Who can you contact that is knowledgeable about the other application if a problem occurs? Do you have the following for an individual or team?

- Name
- E-mail address
- Phone number, office and mobile

Do your counterparts at the other end have your name, phone number, and e-mail address?

On average, how often do problems occur?

- Daily
- Weekly
- Monthly
- Quarterly

Are the data transmissions between this application and others compressed?

- What compression algorithm is being used?
- Why is this algorithm in particular being used?

Are the data transmissions between this application and others encrypted?

- If so, who has the key?
- How often is the key updated?
- What encryption algorithm is being used?
- Is the encryption algorithm proprietary or an industry standard?
- How many bits?

6.15 OUTPUTS: REPORTS

Many, if not all, applications provide the ability to create reports. For many users of the application, the reports are the system so you need to learn as much about them as possible.

Does this application execute reports and output the results? If so, how are the results distributed?

- By e-mail
- By FTP
- Downloaded from a website
- Displayed on the user's screen

How many unique reports exist?

What is the file type of each report's output?

- xls
- csv
- txt
- html
- pdf

Is there a report or screen that shows the following:

- A list of all existing reports
- Who wrote each report?
- Who modified each report last?
- When each report was most recently modified?
- The times and dates of each scheduled report
- The recipient list of each scheduled report

Are users able to create new output reports?
Can a user create a report that only he or she can access?
Are users able to modify existing reports?

If users aren't able to create new reports, who does it?

- Application Administrator
- Report writing team

How frequently do users request new reports be developed?
How frequently do users request that changes be made to existing reports?
Is there a formal request process for such change requests?

Are report output files created on the user's PC, on the server, or both?

Are the reports run on demand, are they scheduled, or both?

- If they are scheduled, how is this done?
- What machine do scheduled reports run on?
- If a scheduled report fails, who is notified?
- Who can schedule reports, all users or just specific ones?
- If the server is down when a report is scheduled to run, will it run when the server comes back up?

6.16 OUTPUTS: LOGS

Does the application produce log files?

*   How many different log files exist?
*   Where are these log files located?

Does an administrator have to regularly monitor these log files for error conditions?

*   If so, are there any internal tools that can be used to help with this monitoring process?

Can log files be configured to produce more or less output, e.g., debug vs. errors only?

*   How is this done?
*   Does the application have to be bounced, i.e., stopped and restarted, for this change to take affect?
*   Does the server have to be bounced for this change to take affect?
*   Does running with maximum logging output impact system performance?
*   Can running with maximum logging output consume all available disk space?

Does an administrator have to periodically delete old log files?

Are log files being backed up?

6.17 CHANGING THE APPLICATION

How frequently are change requests initiated by users?

*   Daily
*   Weekly
*   Monthly

What is the nature of a typical user change request, e.g., a cosmetic change or something more significant?

Who has to approve changes requested by the user base prior to them being incorporated into the application?

Does someone filter out change requests that are completely unrealistic?

If the application was licensed from a third-party vendor, how responsive is the vendor to change requests? Will it takes months or years for a change to be made to the application code base?

Is a documented process in place for handling and documenting change requests initiated by the users?

Who fulfills user change requests, i.e., who actually does the work?
Is it internal personnel, vendor personnel, contractors, etc.?

6.18 MONITORING

Monitoring activities on an application server can reveal potential problems before they reach a critical point. If your organization has monitoring in place, you'll want to learn as much about it as possible.

Some examples of metrics that are frequently monitored are:

- CPU busy time
- Amount of disk space free
- Disk I/O
- Disk queue length
- Page faults
- Available physical memory
- Available virtual memory
- Network I/O
- Failed login attempts
- Services that are stopped

Does your organization have a team or individual that monitors application servers to make sure they are functioning correctly?

- What tool is being used by the monitoring process? Is it home-grown or a commercial tool?
- How much overhead does the monitoring process impose on the application server?
- What metrics are being monitored?
- Can you get a list from the monitoring team?
- If you want a new metric to be monitored on your application server, can it be added?
- Can actions be taken if a specific metric goes out of bounds? For example, if a specific service stops, can the application be stopped and started?
- If the monitoring team finds problems on the servers, what do they do?
- Are the steps to resolve server problems documented?

Does the application ever fill up the server disk drives?

- If the drive fills up, what happens to the server and application?
- Is anyone automatically alerted when this is about to occur?
- Can you be warned when disks get 90% full? 95% Full?

Change Control Management

Virtually every software application in existence is affected by changes. It's possible that a very small application could still be running on a DOS or UNIX machine somewhere that hasn't been changed in decades, but that would be the most extreme of exceptions. For the typical corporate application change is regular, continuous, and unavoidable.

Some examples of changes that you can expect any applications that you support to be impacted by include:

- A patch or hot fix from the application vendor. These are usually fairly limited in nature and easily installed. They are typically distributed to fix a specific problem that was uncovered in the application.
- An upgrade of the application from the vendor. A change of this variety would be larger and more time consuming to install than a patch. It would also have the potential to disrupt the application if it isn't installed correctly.
- Changes distributed by the vendor might be to the data instead of or in addition to the application's software. The application vendor might distribute SQL (Structured Query Language) statements that the Application Administrator or DBA (Database Administrator) needs to execute after connecting to the database. The commands could modify existing data, add tables, or add columns to tables. A perfect example of a data update would be tax changes. Tax rates for sales tax, property tax, income tax, withholding tax, etc., are changed regularly. Any application that deals with them must be updated regularly.
- The server's operating system will experience a steady stream of patches that need to be applied. The purpose of many of these changes will be to tighten the security of the server. To keep your environment as secure as possible, you'll need to install them as quickly as practical.
- If your application is web based, then you may receive patches or upgrades to the web server software. Some examples of this type of software include Apache HTTP Server, Microsoft IIS (Internet Information Services), and Sun Java System Web Server.
- Upgrades to the hardware will also occur occasionally, for example, the application could be moved to a newer, more powerful server for performance reasons.
- Load-balancing software and/or hardware could be added to the environment.
- The database engine that controls the data your application uses will also have patches being distributed by that vendor. These might be to correct software bugs, to enhance performance or be security related. It's entirely possible that you'll be unaware of changes being made to the database software. Your organization's DBA will receive them from the database vendor and install them on the database server.

Since changes can't be avoided, your organization needs a process in place to handle the changes that will be heading your way. This process needs to place controls on how changes are made to the code and data on production systems. It needs to be well designed, well documented, and widely publicized. It also needs to be adhered to by all concerned parties. A process that's regularly ignored is worthless.

7.1 **WHAT IS CHANGE CONTROL MANAGEMENT?**

Change Control Management is a systematic method of controlling all changes made to an environment to maximize the availability and stability of the application. When applied to the world of application administration, it's a methodical way to control the application environment. This includes the application software, the server it runs on, support software on the server, the database engine, network connectivity, and any other systems on which the application depends.

7.1.1 **Why to have change control management?**

There are many reasons for implementing a change control process. A few examples of the value that they add include:

- Documents the software and overall environment that supports the application
- Ensures that changes are made in a methodical, approved manner
- Maximizes the chance for successfully backing out changes that had a negative affect on the application
- Good communications and transparency help to avoid situations where multiple administrators are implementing separate changes simultaneously that could interfere with each other
- Adheres to the requirements of your organization's audit compliance process
- By following a systematic, methodical method you're increasing the likelihood that your change process is repeatable. Everyone likes a process that is highly repeatable and successful. The users like it. Customers like it. Management, including your boss, likes it. Application Administrators like it because it makes their lives more predictable.
- A well-designed Change Control Management process takes less of the Application Administrator's time. If Application Administrators are more efficient, the organization can fulfill the work activity with fewer IT personnel.

7.1.2 **Change control steps**

There is no magic list of steps that make up a perfect Change Control Management process. Each industry and organization has its own unique requirements. There is some basic information that should be captured about each change. Data items in this list include the following:

- Who requested the change? Typically, this would be the business owner of the application.
- The business justification for making the change.
- Origination of the change, e.g., the application vendor distributed the change to all licensees, the operating system vendor distributed the change, an Application Administrator is activating a function or capability in the application, etc.
- Date the change was requested by the business owner of the application.
- Target date when the change needs to be installed.
- Who approved the change at every step of the process.
- What applications or modules within the application the change will effect.
- A test plan to confirm that the change does what it was intended to do. The test plan should include regression testing to confirm that when it was implemented it didn't "break" unrelated existing functionality.
- When the tests in the test plan were run and by whom.
- A plan how to back out the change if it doesn't do what it was supposed to do. This might be as simple as deleting a new file and restoring the original file. On the other hand, it might be significantly more

complicated and time consuming. If the server on which the application runs is a virtual server, then backing out a change can be much easier. You can request that the Data Center staff take a snapshot of the virtual environment just before you perform the upgrade. If you need to back out the change, they can simply overwrite the current virtual server software with the snapshot. A word of advice—if the change is successful, then let the Data Center know that so they can drop that snapshot file. They'll appreciate being able to delete a multi-gigabyte file.

7.1.3 **Approvals**

To confirm that a change is being implemented correctly, the Change Control Management process requires approvals at each step along the way. There are software packages on the market that you can purchase and install to for this purpose. Examples of packages that are available include:

- Spiceworks
- SLAM's Change Management Control Software
- Pilgrim Software Change Control Management Software
- SysAid's ITIL Change Management
- Giva eChangeManager

If your organization has in-house developers, this functionality could be developed internally. One warning if your organization goes this route is that developing it will take more time and cost more than expected. There will also be an ongoing request for changes. Unless your development staff has a lot of experience and time available to work on this, you should seriously consider acquiring a third-party Change Control Management application that has already been developed, documented, and tested.

7.1.4 **Change control software**

As an Application Administrator you most likely won't have any input into what Change Control Management package is selected and installed. Most likely it will have already been selected and installed. If you are involved in the selection process when choosing a Change Control Management package, be as active as possible. Volunteer to assess the packages being considered. Provide your feedback to anyone who will listen. You'll be living with the package that is installed so take the time and effort now to help ensure the package selected is one that fits your needs, is well documented, is reliable, and is intuitive for the users. If the vendor offers any online training for their product then try to complete it. The more you know about each of the tools being considered, the more likely the best one will be chosen.

Potential steps in the process where approvals might be required are:

1. Approval by user representative authorizing installation of the change
2. Approval by IT management
3. Approval of the test plan by a user representative
4. Approval to install the change onto the UAT environment by a user representative
5. Verification that the test plan passed on UAT by a user representative
6. Approval to move the change to the production environment
7. Verification that the test plan passed on PROD by a user representative
8. Acknowledgment that the change process has been completed. This would include an e-mail sent out to all stakeholders that the change was either successful or problems occurred and the change was backed out.

7.1.5 **Workflow**

A well-designed Change Control Management package typically notifies the next approver, so the ticket doesn't languish at one step indefinitely, typically via e-mail. For example, when the user representative approves the change (step #1), the IT management team will be notified that the change is now waiting for IT approval. This notification process helps ensure the ticket continues to move along in the approval process.

Is your organization's Change Control Management process formal, informal, or absent? If a process isn't in place, then one should definitely be considered. It can be as simple or complex as you want it to be, but some process needs to exist. Without a change control process you're inviting chaos. Your environment might struggle by without it for a while, but eventually it will be needed. It's better to bite the bullet and implement the process now and begin reaping the benefits of control management sooner rather than later.

7.2 **SOFTWARE CONFIGURATION MANAGEMENT (SCM) OR CHANGE CONTROL MANAGEMENT?**

What's the difference between Software Configuration Management (SCM) and Change Control Management? To me, Software Configuration Management is the process that controls software development. Change Control Management is used to control changes to a production environment, i.e., software as well as hardware. This may not be a rigorous, academic answer, but in my experience, it seems like a very good fit.

An Application Administrator rarely if ever actually changes the application software. He can modify configuration parameters. She can determine what servers or drives the application is loaded onto. He can choose when to apply patches or upgrades that the vendor distributes. She can install new libraries or jar files. But the Application Administrator doesn't actually make changes to the application's source code. The vendor provides the new modules, e.g., executable files or library files, to you. The vendor modified the source code and compiled it into a library or executable. These new components are then distributed it to client sites like yours. If anyone is using a Software Configuration Management process to control the software it's the vendor, certainly not licensees of the software.

7.3 **CHANGE CONTROL BOARD**

Who decides what changes are going to be made to an application? The initial answer would seem to be the business owner of the application or the Application Administrator. But what if those changes have the potential to impact other applications? For example, what if a change in the payroll application requires that a change be made in the timekeeping application. Should the owner of the payroll application be able to make this decision without consulting the team that owns or maintains the timekeeping application? What if a change to the invoicing application is going to require a significant commitment from the DBA (Database Administrator) group? Can the owner of invoicing commandeer the DBA's time without input from the DBA team or other application owners that also need time from the DBAs? These examples demonstrate that the decision makers need a "big picture" view of the organization's IT operations.

At least two potential solutions exist to solve this predicament. The first is to have someone highly placed in the IT group, e.g., the CIO, make the decision. A person in that position would be both impartial and have a sufficiently "big picture" view of IT operations.

A possible second solution is to have the decision made by a group or a board. A Change Control Board could be set up to approve changes that impact multiple applications. If a change to a given application won't impact other applications, then the Change Control Board wouldn't override the application owner's decision. It would only get involved when:

- The change has the potential to impact other applications
- The change requires a significant amount of common resources like the time of DBAs, Systems Administrators, Network Administrators, etc.
- The change could impact the organization's security
- The timeframe of the change overlaps changes being scheduled by other application owners

7.3.1 Change control board membership

The membership of the Change Control Board doesn't have to be large, but it must include senior technical personnel. The organization's senior System Architect should be on the board and possibly be the chairman. Other board members could be representatives of groups in the IT department or IT managers representing the most significant applications. Application Administrators that have submitted a proposed change would be expected to attend the meeting when their change is being considered.

7.3.2 Meetings

How often they meet is up to the organization. Meeting weekly seems to be reasonable. More frequently and there wouldn't be enough changes in the queue to make the meeting worthwhile. If they meet less frequently, then changes might need to be implemented in the gap between meetings and would need to be handled in an emergency mode. Emergency changes, i.e., exceptions, are discussed in Section 7.9.

7.3.3 Proposing changes

Proposed changes could be gathered in several ways. They could be submitted to a representative of the Change Control Board via e-mail. If the organization has a formal Change Control application, then tickets that have been entered into it can be extracted via a weekly report. An e-mail listing all proposed changes gets sent out to all board members a day or two prior to each scheduled meeting.

During each meeting, they would review all application or system changes that have been submitted. The "owner" of the change briefly describes the change, the potential impact, fallback plans, and when they intend to roll it out. After his or her description, the floor is open to questions. The board votes to either approve or deny the proposed change at this time. If it is denied, the owner works with the board to resolve any objections.

7.4 ENVIRONMENTS

To minimize the chance of your application being adversely impacted by changes, it's best to have at least two environments on which the application has been installed. Changes are made first on the QA (Quality Assurance) or TEST environment. After changes are implemented and tested on the QA environment, they are moved, aka migrated, or elevated, to the Production (PROD) environment. By installing the change on TEST or QA first if there are going to be problems, then they will likely be discovered on a nonproduction environment.

An organization might need environments in addition to QA, TEST, and PROD. Other potential environments and what they are used for include:

- Development (DEV)—Typically a development environment is associated with organizations that develop or extensively modify software. Some third-party applications that are licensed from a vendor allow the client to perform a significant amount of programming even though the base code of the application isn't changed. PeopleSoft is an example of this type of application. Programmers at the client organization can write a significant amount of SQR code to provide customizations to the base product. These changes would be coded and tested on a DEV environment. Later they would be installed and tested on the QA environment. The final step would be to install them on the PROD environment.
- A staging environment can exist between the QA and PROD environments. The purpose of a staging environment is to have an environment that is physically identical to the PROD environment. An organization might want a staging environment if the architecture of the production environment includes clustered servers, load balancing, multiprocessor-based servers, RAID storage devices, or other features that don't exist on the DEV or QA environments.
- A training environment could be required if the application is particularly complicated or requires formal training for new users. If it exists, the software on the training environment should be identical to PROD. It doesn't make much sense to train new users on an environment that doesn't closely resemble what they will see when they start using the application on PROD.
- Multiple test (TEST) environments might be necessary if your usage of an application has unique testing requirements. For example, a multinational organization might divide their operations into several regions like EMEA (Europe, Middle East, and Africa), LATAM (Latin America), APAC (Asia-Pacific), etc. A testing environment might be needed for each of the regions. This would necessitate that multiple test environments be created and maintained.
- The term "sandbox" is sometimes used to refer to test or development environments. It is an environment used by one of more developers or testers. Utilizing separate environments provides protection in two directions. It protects the user that is assigned to the sandbox from changes that coworkers are making on other environments. It also protects coworkers from changes that the sandbox user is making. Only when changes have been rigorously tested will they be migrated to the code base. Once testing in sandbox is done, that environment can either be dropped or overwritten with a fresh copy of the application and allocated to another developer or tester.

Just a comment on having multiple environments, don't be afraid to use them to figure out how the application works. This is the place where you can take risks. If you want to try something new in the application or do something that isn't well documented, then a test environment is the place to do it. If your activity causes problems with the application, then just wipe the entire server clear and reload it. Better to learn about a problem here than in production.

7.4.1 The look of each environment

The closer each DEV, QA, Staging, and TEST is to your production environment, the better for the Change Control Management process. If your PROD server is running Windows Server 2008 but QA is running Windows 2003, then testing done on QA isn't as meaningful as it could be. The following objects are examples of what needs to be kept as similar as possible between the two environments:

- Version of the application software
- Version of operating system, including the service packs installed on them
- Support software like IIS, Web Logic Server, Apache, Oracle client, ODBC, etc.
- Data should be similar between the environments. It doesn't have to be identical, but the amount and diversity on each environment should be similar for testing purposes. If PROD has millions of rows of data, but QA has only a few thousand rows, then problems that occur on PROD may never appear on QA.

One warning about putting production data on a nonproduction server is that it is a security risk. Non-PROD environments never seem to be as secure that their production counterparts. If your data contain confidential information, e.g., Personally Identifiable Information (PII), it should be replaced with dummy data. This still provides valuable testing opportunities, but reduces the risk of exposing confidential data.

7.4.2 When differences are OK

There will be times when the application software differs between the QA and PROD environments. For example, if a new version has been released by the vendor, it will be installed on QA for testing purposes. It might take quite a while for the team to complete their work. During this interval, the version of the application will be different on the two servers.

7.4.3 Who can access each server?

Who should be able to access the servers or application administration features of each of the different environments? Common sense dictates that people are given the access they need to do their jobs, but beyond that access is restricted as much as possible. Your SOX compliance policy will have a great deal to say on this topic and should be the final word on the matter. As a general policy, the following groups should have the access described here:

- Developers should have unlimited access to DEV and possibly QA, but never Staging or PROD.
- Application Administrators should have unlimited access to all servers. After all, they will be the ones that load the application on each of the sites. They do need to be sensitive to the needs of whoever is currently using a server.
- Users only need to be able to run the application in production. They shouldn't be given direct access to the server on which the application runs or any administration functions that the application offers.
- The Application Business Owner might insist that they need access to all of the servers that run the application, but try to fight this as much as possible. As the person who is ultimately responsible for keeping the production application running, do you really want a lot of people to be able to log onto the server and potentially modify PROD? I certainly don't. The fewer who can access the PROD server the better.
- Testers need access to the QA or TEST environments.
- New users should only have access to the training environment until they are qualified to work on the production environment.

7.4.4 Accessing environments from outside the organization's network

If this is a web-based application, which environments can be accessed externally, i.e, from outside of the organization's network? Is there really a legitimate business requirement to allow DEV, QA, Staging, or TEST environments to be accessed from outside the firewall? If the development or test teams need to work on them remotely they should use virtual private network (VPN) access to log onto the network. If legitimate users connect to the network using a VPN, then there is no need to have the web site accessible outside the network.

What are the risks of having your nonproduction sites accessible externally? To understand the risk you have to answer the question "Do they have all the security protection that the PROD environment has?" If you answered "yes" to that question are you really sure about it? Sometimes when environments are set up corners are cut when developing nonproduction environments because people assume non-production sites don't need to be as secure as a production environment.

Any environment that contains live data, even if it's outdated, needs to be tightly secured. This is why data on a non-PROD environment shouldn't be live.

7.5 WHEN TO MOVE CHANGES INTO PRODUCTION

This might seem like an odd topic, but different people in the industry have very strong positions on when changes should be moved into production. I've worked with people that suggested different timeframes and had carefully articulated reasons regarding why their timeframes for moving changes into production was best. Some of the windows that I've heard suggested and their justifications are listed here.

- One group thought there should be no limitations on when changes can be installed. If you can get the users to agree on moving a change into production on a Monday morning at 8 am and that time works for the Application Administrator, then make the change on that date and time. Their rationale is to just let the concerned parties decide for themselves.
- Another faction thinks Wednesday and Thursday are the only days to implement changes. Their justification is that the changes need to be in place long enough before the weekend that any potential problems will have shown up. This group wants the problems to occur during the weekend when everyone who might be needed to assist with solving the problem is available. The individuals or roles they think need to be available include the Application Administrator, the application owner, the vendor's support desk, Network Administrators, Database Administrators, and System Administrators.
- The final group thinks the only time to make change is on Friday nights, specifically after the majority of the users are gone for the day. The logic behind this window is that the majority of users will be using the application during normal business hours. If the change is made Friday night and a problem occurs, then you have all weekend to fix it. If the application is down over the weekend, then the impact on the user community will be minimal.

One question that needs to be answered is when is your vendor support available. Does your support contract with the vendor require them to respond to your requests 7 days a week and 24 hours a day? If that's the case, then no matter when you make changes you can get assistance right away. On the other hand, if your support contract only provides support from 8 am to 5 pm on Monday through Friday, then you should think long and hard before rolling out a change on Friday night. If your change causes a problem that you can't resolve without vendor support, then you'll be stuck until Monday morning waiting for them to return your call.

7.6 MOVING A CHANGE INTO PRODUCTION

Typically the Application Administrator is the person why makes changes on production environments. Some exceptions can occur depending on what the organization's policies require. Many organizations have policies that restrict who can move a change into production. The restriction is that the person or team that created a change isn't allowed to migrate it to production. Allowing the same individual or team to both develop and install the same change potentially opens the door to fraud. Imposing a separation of duties might not prevent all fraud, but it makes it less likely. If your organization is limited to strictly applying changes provided by the vendor, then this restriction doesn't apply.

7.7 SARBANES-OXLEY OR SOX

Virtually everyone in IT has heard of the Sarbanes-Oxley Act of 2002 or SOX as it is commonly referred to, but relatively few know exactly how it works. Since SOX has an impact on so many applications it's being briefly covered here. For a complete understanding of the provisions of the Sarbanes-Oxley act there are numerous books on the topic. Chapter 22 will provide additional information on SOX and other ways that the government impacts your application.

The stated purpose of the SOX act is "To protect investors by improving the accuracy and reliability of corporate disclosures made pursuant to the securities laws, and for other purposes." Among the many provisions included are:

- Higher level of auditor independence
- SOX compliance is limited to publicly traded companies
- Requires executives of public corporations to sign the auditor report attesting to its accuracy
- Increases penalties, both civil and criminal, for securities violations
- Works to ensure that financial reporting is done with full disclosure

How does SOX impact IT personnel, specifically Application Administrators? If your application contains financial information for the organization, then you will be affected. Some ways in which an Application Administrator can be impacted include:

- Authentication of users
- Separations of duties, e.g., the same person can't change the code and also install the change
- Audit trails of who changed what, when a change was made, etc., need to be maintained
- Access to the application must be controlled and documented
- Activity by IT personnel outside of standardized business practices needs to be monitored

SOX provides a broad overview of what must be achieved, i.e., transparency in account practices, but leaves the details to individual organizations. This is especially true when it comes to how IT technologies are affected. SOX doesn't dictate that you have to do anything specifically. What it does say is that once you establish an SOX process then you have to adhere to it.

As an Application Administrator you won't have designed the SOX policies for your organization. The policies will already be in place and it's your responsibility to follow them. The best advice that I can give you is to get used to them from the beginning. You may not like these policies, they may seem time consuming and pointless to you, but they are the law. Resistance is futile.

7.8 SUBVERTING THE CHANGE CONTROL PROCESS

No matter what change control process your organization has in place, eventually someone will want you to push a change into place without complying with the process. They may claim that it's just a tiny little change that couldn't possible cause any problems. They may tell you that the change is needed immediately and can't wait for the normal change control process. They may swear on a stack of Bibles that they'll fill out the paperwork tomorrow to cover the change.

My advice to you is don't do it! If you do, then you're running the very real risk that either your boss or the auditor will be talking to you about your transgression. Take my word for it, you don't want to be on the receiving end of that conversation.

Another reason why you shouldn't make an exception "just this one time" is that it won't be a single time. Once you've made an exception, whoever pressured you into doing it will push you to do it a second time and a third time and a fourth time, etc. You and the users might not like the process that is in place, but you have to abide by it.

7.9 EXCEPTIONS

Rules were made to be broken and the Change Control Management process is no exception. In spite of what the previous section says, there will be times when exceptions have to be allowed. There are limitations to when exceptions should be allowed. The trick is being able to recognize the difference between a legitimate exception and someone who's too lazy to follow the established procedures.

One example of a legitimate exception is when your production site is down and absolutely has to be brought back up as soon as humanly possible. You might know from experience what needs to be done to bring it up. There isn't time to contact people for approvals so you just bring the system back up.

Another possible example of an exception would be when a critical process, say payroll processing, has aborted. If this process needs to be restarted immediately so that it can complete on time, then you probably need to do it right now. You can alert others to the problem once the system is humming again.

Making a change in production on an exception basis doesn't exempt you from the need to log a ticket on this change. You will still have to start the Change Control Management process. You may not get all the permissions at the time, but by starting the process you've documented that a change is being made. Plus an incomplete change ticket will be a constant reminder to complete the paperwork for this change.

7.10 TESTING

Any change that makes its way into production needs to be thoroughly tested. The severity of testing that needs to be done is closely related to what has been changed. A relatively small change that is isolated to a subset of the application doesn't require as much testing as a major new release of the application software that has made sweeping changes. Unfortunately, it isn't always easy to determine exactly how much testing is needed. One word of advice that I can provide is that it's better to do too much testing than too little.

Testing can be broken down into two different types: acceptance and regression. While they both test the application, they are significantly different forms of testing and require different approaches to develop and perform.

7.10.1 Acceptance testing

The intention of acceptance testing is to confirm that the modifications being tested do what they are intended to do. In a way acceptance testing is easier because you can focus directly on the areas in the application that were changed. When the vendor releases a patch or upgrade, it is accompanied with document, usually called the "Release Notes," describing what has changed. Acceptance testing for this upgrade needs to be based on what the vendor says has been changed. If the Release Notes say the input screen for zip codes, the inventory report, and the procedure that calculates withholding taxes were all modified, then your acceptance testing script needs to focus on those particular areas of the application.

The test script needs to list the steps that the tester has to make to verify that the error has been corrected. It needs to provide enough details that the tester can accurately perform the test. The script also needs to list the results that users can expect to see. If the expected results aren't displayed during the testing, then that specific test step as well as the entire test process has failed.

The spreadsheet shown in Figure 7.1 is an extremely simple example of what a test script can look like. An actual test script would probably have many more steps.

	A	B	C	D	E
1			UAT Test Script		
2			Test Case 1:		
3		Is this an Initial Test (Yes/No):	Yes	Testing Personnel:	Luis Panera
4					
5		Change Description:	Acme Inventory 9.7 upgrade	Environment:	PROD
6					
7		Test Date:	7/5/2013		
8	Task #	Action to be taken	Result Expected	Actual Result	Pass or Fail?
9	1	Confirmed that the application comes up.	Application opens up successfully		
10	2	Confirm that application is now at version 9.3d. Click on the Help | About menu item	The "About Acme Inventory" screen will be displayed and Product Version listed is v9.7		
11	3	Confirm that new currency "China - Yuan Renminbi" exists in the Currency drop down list box. To get to this screen select a currency, click on the Display tab, click on the New button, scroll down in the Currency field.	The currency "China - Yuan Renminbi" should exist in the list.		
12	4	Exit the application by clicking the "File | Exit" menu option	The application closes		
13					
14		Next action (Pass or Retest):			
15					
16	Definitions of columns				
17		Initial Test	Is this the first time test was performed?		
18		Testing Personnel	Person or persons who ran the test		
19		Change Description	Description of the change being tested		
20		Environment	Environment where test was performed		
21		Test Date	Date test was performed		
22		Task #	Task number within test script		
23		Action to be taken	Action that tester needs to take		
24		Result Expected	What should happen if test is successful		
25		Actual Result	Result that occurred		
26		Pass or Fail?	Did the Result Expected match what was expected?		

FIGURE 7.1

Simple example of a test script. (For color version of this figure, the reader is referred to the online version of this chapter.)

7.10.2 Regression testing

The purpose of regression testing is to confirm that the changes haven't broken any of the existing functionality of the application. Regression testing is more difficult than acceptance testing because it potentially requires that more testing be done. Everything in the application except what was impacted by changes in this release could be included in your regression testing.

It isn't possible to completely test even a moderately sized application. The reason for this is that as applications become more complex, the number of combinations of how it can be used increases geometrically. To thoroughly test an application, the following steps would be required:

- Every screen would have to be tested
- Every link on every screen would have to be tested
- Every button on every screen would have to be tested
- Every menu item and submenu item on every screen would have to be tested
- Every text field on every screen would have to be tested with every possible combination of input, including both valid and invalid data
- Every drop down list box and every selection within them would have to be tested
- A test database would have to contain every possible combination of data in every table
- Every possible navigation sequence would have to be tested. For example, you would have to test going from screen A to B, A to C, A to D, …, B to C, B to D, B to E, Z to A, Z to B, etc.

Now repeat each of the above test scenarios for the following:

- Every desktop operating system that the application is certified to run under

- Every server operating system that the application is certified to run under
- Every database that the application is certified to run under
- Every Internet browser that the application is certified to run under

If all of the above were done by a single tester, that still wouldn't uncover situations where multiple users using the system at the same time might interact or interfere with each other. To test this possibility you have to repeat all of the above steps for:

- Two users in the application simultaneously
- 3, 4, 5, ... users up to the maximum number of used in the system simultaneously

As you can see, complete coverage of regression testing for an application is impossible. The best you can hope for is that you cover the most commonly used features of the application. If your regression test thoroughly covers the screens and actions that are used most in the application, then you've done a better job than most sites have done.

In another way, regression testing can be easier than acceptance testing. This is because once you have developed a thorough regression test script, it can be reused again and again. Say you've developed a comprehensive regression test script for version 5.1 of an application. When version 5.2 of the application is released, then your regression test script can be reused. As new functionality is added to the application, the regression testing need to augmented to reflect them, but the majority of the test script isn't affected.

7.10.3 Who should write the test script(s)?

Barry Manilow may have written the songs that make the whole world sing, but the user community needs to write the test scripts. Scripts is plural here because the testing may be broken down into two scripts: UAT and Regression. The reasons for this are pretty simple:

- They know the application much better than anyone else.
- If they write inadequate test scripts, then they have no one but themselves to blame.

The only exception to the above rule would be that the Application Administrator needs to write the tests for a tool or utility that only he or she accesses. It doesn't make sense to require users to develop tests for a section of the application that they never see.

7.10.4 Where is testing performed?

Testing needs to be done on every environment that the updates are applied to. This includes DEV, QA, TEST, or Staging servers prior to moving it into Production. The natural progression for your testing sequence would be DEV first, TEST or QA second, and Staging next if it exists. PROD would be tested last. The reason behind this sequence is to test the changes as thoroughly as possible before they are installed on the production environment.

The results for each test step should be identical on each environment. There might be extenuating circumstance to explain why results differ on unique environments. Examples of some circumstances that might explain differences include:

- The databases on each environment are different. Different databases result in different result sets when a search is done, when lists are displayed, or when reports are created. This is very likely situation because the nonproduction environments like DEV frequently have much smaller databases than QA or PROD have.

- Performance could be significantly different because most DEV environments have fewer resources available to them. For example, DEV would have a less powerful server, a smaller amount of memory, etc.
- It's possible that a DEV environment might not have all the pieces that your PROD environment has. For example, DEV might not have reports activated. It might not have workflow on it. If this is the case, then test steps specific to those areas of the application can't be tested in that environment.

7.10.5 Who should do the testing?

Who should be performing the user acceptance and regression testing? In this case, the name says it all, i.e., user testing should be done by users. There are many reasons for this:

- They are the most familiar with using the application
- The user community is larger than the number of Application Administrators, so they can spread the load out between many more people
- Since the user community wrote the test scripts, they are the most familiar with them
- If the testing isn't done correctly, then the users have only themselves to blame

The logical exception is that the Application Administrator needs to run the tests for tools and utilities that only they can access. Frequently these pieces of the application run on the application server which users typically aren't allowed to access.

7.10.6 Testing documentation

Documentation needs to be kept on testing that was done on each different environment. A complete set documentation needs to be kept for each different upgrade. Examples of what needs to be filled out and retained include:

- The date the test was done
- Who performed the test
- Which environment this test was performed on, i.e., DEV, QA, PROD
- An indication whether this was the initial test on this environment or a repeat of the test
- The spreadsheet or document that contains all the test steps
- The results of each individual test step
- Approval by a user representative that the test was completed satisfactorily

This might or might not be obvious, but if any individual test step fails then the entire test script(s) has to be repeated. Rerunning the upgrade or changing the environment nullifies any testing that was done previously. To be confident that the change hasn't introduced new problems then the entire test script(s) need to be rerun.

7.11 APPLICATION VERSION NUMBERS

It's very important to keep track of what version of the application is running on each of your servers. You'll need it every time you open a ticket with the vendor's support desk. It seems like the two questions every vendor contact asks are what version of the application you're running and what operating system is running on the server. If your memory isn't good enough to keep track of this, then you'll need to write it down somewhere. Of course this means that now you have to remember where you wrote it down.

It would be wonderful if the way to find the version was the same for every vendor's application. Unfortunately that isn't the case. Some of the most common ways to determine the version are listed here. I'm sure there are many methods that I haven't run into yet.

- One of the most common places to determine what version of the application is running is to click the "Help" menu item and then click the "About" submenu item. Figure 7.2 shows this menu item selection. The About screen that is displayed is depicted in Figure 7.3.

FIGURE 7.2

Typical Help | About menu item to bring up the About screen. (For color version of this figure, the reader is referred to the online version of this chapter.)

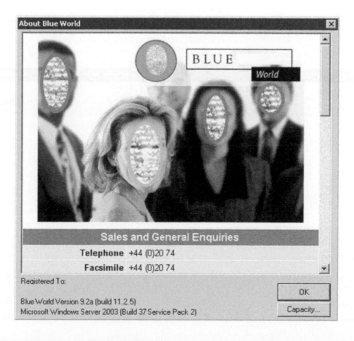

FIGURE 7.3

About screen that is displayed. (For color version of this figure, the reader is referred to the online version of this chapter.)

- For some applications if you click on their icon the equivalent of an "About" screen will be displayed. Figure 7.4 depicts the icon that would be clicked and Figure 7.5 shows the About screen that will be displayed.
- Some applications position the version information in a configuration file. File registry.xml shown in Figure 7.6 is a configuration file from an application that can be referenced to determine the current version of the application.
- Other applications write the build information to a log file each time the application is started. The log file shown in Figure 7.7 shows that version of 3.5 Update 5 (Build 2252.10) is running on the server that it came from.

FIGURE 7.4

Icon to click that brings up the About screen. (For color version of this figure, the reader is referred to the online version of this chapter.)

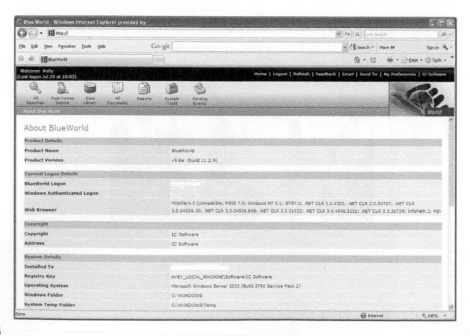

FIGURE 7.5

About screen that is displayed. (For color version of this figure, the reader is referred to the online version of this chapter.)

FIGURE 7.6

Configuration files that contain version details. (For color version of this figure, the reader is referred to the online version of this chapter.)

FIGURE 7.7

Version details that are available from a log file. (For color version of this figure, the reader is referred to the online version of this chapter.)

Installing Software

8

Every application has an installation process. If you're lucky the process of installing the software will be straightforward, logical, and well documented. If you're not so lucky, the process will be complicated, poorly documented, and will frequently fail. The worst-case scenario will require that you step back a step or two, maybe all the way back to step one, and try again. Like in so many other endeavors practice makes perfect. Practice installations on your DEV or TEST environments, so the process runs flawlessly on Production. As always, document everything you do so it can be repeated.

Each application's installation process is going to be a little different. Many software vendors use a commercial installation product. If you've installed other application that uses the same installer package, then the steps will probably be familiar to you. Some examples of like products like this are:

- InstallAnywhere
- InstallBuilder
- JExpress
- InstallShield
- Windows Installer
- Wise InstallBuilder

Installations can be designed in such a way that if the process can be run multiple times. Each fresh install overwrites the changes that were done the previous time. This isn't something that you can control, but it's nice to know if that is the way your particular application install process is set up to run. It takes a lot of pressure off you if you know that if the installation doesn't work correctly you can just start over from the beginning. If the installation documentation doesn't specify this detail, then add it to your list of questions to ask your contact at the vendor or their support desk.

One warning that I feel compelled to provide is that you need to be extremely careful when dealing with the word "server." In some situations, the word refers to a piece of computer hardware, e.g., a quad-processor server that is installed in your data center. In other situations, the word refers to a piece of software running on a computer, for example, a web server that runs on a computer to enable users to view pages. If the context in which the word is being used isn't crystal clear to you, then you need to ask for a clarification. Don't be shy about doing this because if you're confused, then it's almost a certainty that others are too.

8.1 BE THE MAN, OR WOMAN, WITH A (PROJECT) PLAN

It might seem like overkill, but creating a project plan for an application install makes a great deal of sense. Just going through the process of writing it down ensures that you'll do a better job of planning. A few other good reasons to develop a project plan are:

- Helps ensure that you don't overlook any of the preliminary steps
- Helps to sequence steps in the most efficient order

- Can help to identify the resources you'll need from other teams in the organization, e.g., DBAs, Systems Administrators, the network security team, etc.
- Provides an opportunity to identify the hardware, software, security, etc., that needs to be in place prior to when the installation can begin.
- Helps document the amount of time it took to perform the install. This will enable you to make better estimates for similar tasks in the future.

Your project plan doesn't have to be incredibly detailed, complex, or hard to understand. Theoretically, it could be written as a text file, a spreadsheet, or a Word document. If you have access to project planning software, like Microsoft Project, then it can make the process of developing the plan easier, faster, and more valuable. The more complicated your plan is, the more you'll appreciate using a specialized software tool to develop and maintain it.

An example of a project plan is shown in Figure 8.1. This particular plan isn't complicated, but includes some of the basic pieces of data for each task being scheduled. These include:

- A name or description of the task
- An estimated duration
- A projected start date
- A projected completion date
- Tasks that need to be complete before this task can be started
- Status or the percentage of the task is currently complete
- Who the task is assigned to

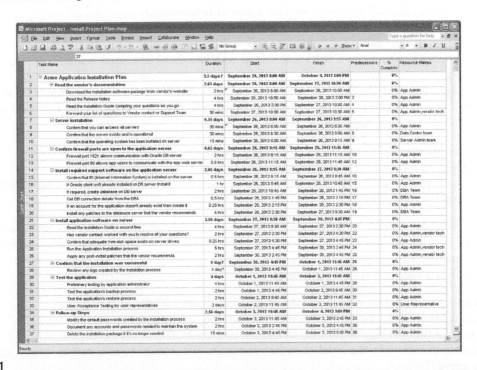

FIGURE 8.1

Example of an installation project plan. (For color version of this figure, the reader is referred to the online version of this chapter.)

8.2 HOW MANY INSTALLS HAVE TO BE DONE?

This might seem like a silly question, but how many installs have to be done for this particular application? The obvious answer of "one" isn't necessarily correct. Setting up an application's environment might require numerous, separate, installations. The following sections describe at least three situations under which there can be multiple installations. There are certainly additional situations, but those would be less common.

8.2.1 Installations on user workstations

Applications can be roughly split into two kinds: thin clients and thick clients. The difference between thin and thick refers to how much software needs to be loaded onto the user or client workstations. A thin client requires little or no software on the client machine. A thick-client design requires a significant amount of software on client machines.

The thin-client design frequently uses an Internet browser for the front end. Applications with this design model don't require an installation of any software on the users' workstation. Once you've set up the application servers, then any number of users can simply point their Internet browsers at the server and begin using the application, assuming that they have the requisite ID and password. For this reason, this model is an increasingly popular way to deliver applications to users.

If the application has a thick client, then some software, frequently a significant amount, needs to be installed onto every user's workstation. The process of installing software on user workstation may be your responsibility or it might fall into someone else's area of responsibility.

If you're not fortunate enough to have a team that handles desktop installations, then you won't have to do the work, but still need to include this task in the project plan. Be sure to add in a conservative time estimate to set up a workstation and multiple it by the total number of users that use the application.

In some cases, these installations are something the users can do for themselves. It might be as simple as them clicking on an executable for the required software to be installed. If this is the way your user workstations will be set up, then make sure to do the following:

- Test to confirm that the install works as documented in the Installation Guide
- Write up a short, nontechnical, document that will be distributed to the users
- Have a non-IT person use the document to install the software on their workstation to verify that it is both accurate and comprehensible to the average user

If the installation was successful for your non-IT test subject, then distribution the document and the executable, or its location, to everyone who needs this software on their desktop. Some potential situations that need to be considered are listed below. There is a very high probability that these situations will come up so you need to have a response ready in advance:

- What message will the user receive if the installation is successful?
- If the installation isn't successful what message will the user receive?
- If the installation isn't successful who should the user contact?
- What should the user do if the installation isn't successful, i.e., should he uninstall the app or just wait for help to arrive?
- Is the installation process different for users who are at remote sites?
- Is the installation process different for users who aren't on the organization's LAN or WAN?

8.2.2 **Application architectures can include multiple types of servers**

Some application designs include multiple types of servers in their environment. Each server provides a distinct function for either the users or the other servers. For example, an application environment might include the following kinds of servers:

- A server that supports the user interface, e.g., a web server.
- A server that supports reports
- A server that supports the database
- A server that supports business logic

Figure 8.2 shows a diagram of an environment that includes three distinct types of servers. These servers are a web server, a report server, and a database server. Environments like this are quite common.

One application I have supported had two types of servers. The first supported the user interface (UI). The second supported reports that the application generated. The vendor recommended that these distinct

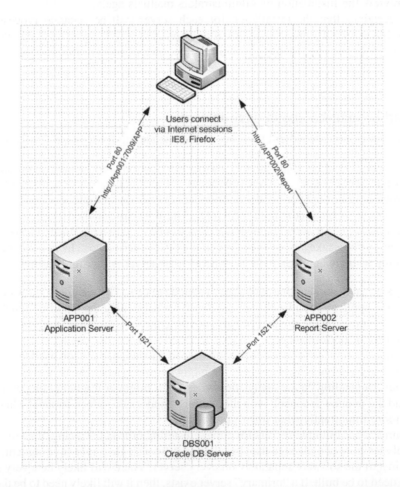

FIGURE 8.2

Diagram of an application with multiple types of servers. (For color version of this figure, the reader is referred to the online version of this chapter.)

software components be installed on separate hardware devices, although for an environment with relatively few users both components could be installed on a single hardware server.

Another application that I support also had two types of servers. The first was a web server that enabled the "normal" users to access the application via web browsers running on their desktop computers. The second type of server was accessible only to a limited number of "power" users. These users would remotely connect to the second server. Once they were connected to the server, they would run the administrative version of the application on the desktop of that server.

Both of the applications described above actually had a third type of server, the database server. It needed to be up and functional before the application software can be installed. In our organization, the responsibility for setting up database servers belongs to the DBA team so that isn't something I had to handle. My responsibility was limited to working with the DBAs to ensure that the databases were correctly created and accessible by the application and report servers.

Does the application that you're supporting have more than one server type? How many types exist? How do they interact? Which ones are dependent on the others? If you don't know the answers to these questions, then it's time to review the Installation or Administrators manuals again.

It's almost a certainty that the installation for each server will be separate process. They may be somewhat similar, but essentially are separate installation processes. When you write up the project plan and estimate the amount of time the installation will take be sure to include time for all of the installation processes.

8.2.3 Clustered or load-balanced environments

Application architectures include either clustering or load balancing for two specific purposes:

- To maximize availability of the application by having multiple servers available. If one server hangs up or dies, then the other server(s) can continue processing and the application remains available to the users.
- To increase processing throughput by distributing the load across multiple servers. The way the load is distributed between servers can be simple or complex. The most basic method is called round-robin. In it the first user request is assigned to server number one. The second request is assigned to server number two, etc. More complex algorithms take into account the complexity of each request. In this arrangement, one server might be handling a single complex request while another server is handling multiple simple requests.

Figure 8.3 displays an environment that includes clustered servers. This example shows a cluster of three servers supporting the application and a cluster of two servers supporting the reporting function. The number of hardware servers comprising the cluster can vary, but the concept is the same: multiple servers being used to enhance availability or performance.

If your application is employing either clustering or load balancing, then you need to understand exactly what benefits you're getting out of it. The objective might be to enhance system availability. It might be to enhance throughput. Depending on the application's design, it might or might not be possible to be getting both benefits. Read the manual or consult with the vendor to make sure you understand what the architecture is providing and more importantly what it isn't providing.

If your environment has multiple servers for either clustering or load balancing, then the installation process will very likely be more complicated than installation is for a single server environment. You will almost certainly have to install the software separately on every server. There will likely be a very specific order in which the servers need to be built. If a "primary" server exists, then it will likely need to be the first one that is built. The "secondary" server(s) probably will have the software installed on them once the primary server is completely operational. Be certain that you know what the process is and include all the necessary steps and sequences in your project plan.

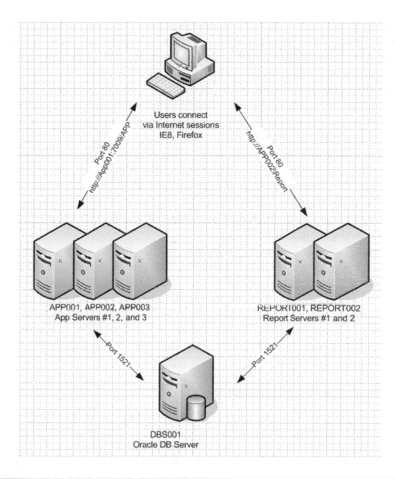

FIGURE 8.3

Diagram of an environment with clustered servers. (For color version of this figure, the reader is referred to the online version of this chapter.)

8.3 PREPARING FOR THE INSTALLATION

In my opinion, the most important steps for a successful installation aren't difficult to perform. They are the kinds of things you should be doing anyway. They are listed here. If you do these things you're chances of success are about as high as you can make them:

1. Read the Installation Guide. Reading it a second time would be even better
2. Write down any questions you have and follow up with the vendor tech to get answers
3. Fill out any worksheets included in the guide and have them available when doing the install
4. Whenever possible, practice on a Test or Development server

8.3.1 Read the installation guide

I can't emphasize how critical it is to read the Installation Guide and Release Notes that accompany the installation package you'll receive from the vendor. Read these documents as early as possible! Also, be sure not to rush through this document. Read it thoroughly. It will take time to read and assimilate the information so don't put this off until the day before the installation is scheduled.

When reading these documents make note of your questions, concerns, and anything that isn't clear to you. Don't be afraid if you're compiling a long list of questions. Take this not as a sign of weakness, but a sign that you're diligent about doing the job. If you don't understand something while reading the document, then you certainly won't understand it during the actual installation.

Once you finish reading the Installation Guide, then read it again. In my experience, reading it a second time is even more valuable than reading it the first time. During your second reading, you should frequently refer to your list of questions. You may add some questions, but it's more likely that you'll discover that you now know the answers for many of your original questions and they can be taken off the list.

Forward your list to the vendor support team to get your questions answered. Before sending it to them review your questions to ensure that they are written as clearly as possible. You don't want to waste time going back and forth multiple times explaining your questions to them. I'd advise you to pass this list to your vendor contact as early as possible. Presenting them with a long list of questions the day before your installation is scheduled doesn't leave them much time to respond. It also doesn't allow you time to react to their answers or any questions they might have for you.

You may be planning on having a vendor technician work with you to perform the installation. That's entirely appropriate in many cases, but don't think that gets you out of reading the Installation Guide. You still need to read the Installation Guide even if a vendor technician will be working with you to do the install. Believe me when I tell you that the tech wants to complete the install as quickly as possible. He or she almost certainly has another install scheduled with a different client right after he finishes working with you. They will answer your questions, but you won't have time to learn everything in detail during the process. The more you know going into this process the more you'll learn about installations.

8.3.2 Worksheets in the installation guide

Installation Guides frequently include a worksheet of information that is needed during the install process. If such a worksheet isn't in the Installation Guide, then ask a vendor technician for one. The idea is to give you a chance to gather needed information in advance and write it down in a single place.

I can't overstate how important it is to complete this worksheet thoroughly and accurately. If you don't gather this information in advance, then you'll be scrambling for it during the installation process. Installations are complicated enough without making them more difficult by not having answers to questions the vendor tech or installer program needs to know.

Examples of the types of data that you may be asked to gather include the following:

- The name of the application server(s), i.e., the hardware devices
- The version of operating system that is running on the servers
- The amount of memory on the server(s)
- Whether or not any virus scanner software on the server can be disabled during the installation process
- Whether or not you'll be using SSL (Secure Sockets Layer) and if you have the security certificate that will be needed
- The form of authentication that will be used for the application. Common choices are authentication native to the application, LDAP/AD (Lightweight Directory Access Protocol/Active Directory) or SSO (Single Sign-On)
- The name of the server, i.e., the software not the hardware
- The location where the software should be loaded, e.g., C:\AcmeApplication
- The amount of free space available on the drive where the application will be loaded
- The port(s) which users will use to communicate with the application
- Account names and passwords for the administrator account
- The location of the database client software, e.g., C:\oracle\product\11.2

- The name of the database server
- The port used to communicate with the database server
- The name of the database
- The name and password of the account which owns the database
- The name of your organization's e-mail server if the application will be sending out e-mail
- The port number used to communicate with the e-mail server

Many of the choices or settings that you will be prompted for will have defaults provided for them. Unless your organization has standards about this, I would suggest taking as many of the defaults as possible. Doing this will make it easier for vendor technicians to work with you and your system. It will also make it easier to recover this information if you forget to document it once the installation is complete.

The only obvious exceptions to the above recommendation would be for account passwords, especially the administrator account. In those cases you might want to take the default passwords initially, but change then as soon as the application is operational. Don't forget to change them! If you don't change your admin account passwords, then literally everyone in the world who has worked with or installed this application knows what your passwords are. That isn't the kind of security your bosses or application users are expecting.

8.3.3 Write a project plan for the installation

Writing a project plan for your installation will definitely be an iterative process. It's extremely unlikely that your first effort will be 100% accurate. Some of the more common mistakes that will be made include:

- Tasks will be overlooked
- Time estimates will be significantly off
- Tasks will be out of sequence
- Dependencies between tasks won't reflect reality
- The wrong people will be assigned to a task

As soon as the first version of the plan is complete, then examine it carefully for mistakes. Having an experienced project manager look it over is a good idea. If there is another Application Administrator in your group, then ask him or her to look at it.

Once you think it's ready then send it out to everyone one involved asking them to review it with a critical eye. It wouldn't hurt to schedule a short meeting with the participants. Sometimes a 30-minute meeting can clear up misunderstandings that would take days if done by sending emails back and forth.

8.3.4 Confirm the servers exist and are set up correctly

If the servers being used by this application are new, then you definitely need to confirm that they exist and had been properly set up. If your organization requires that a form be filled out when requesting that a new server be built then fill it out as early and accurately as possible. The Data Center team can't build your server the way you want it if you haven't told them what you want. Some values that you'll need to specify on a server request form could include the following:

- Requestor Name
- Who to contact if technical questions need to be answered
- Business Unit
- Date this request was made
- Date the server needs to be available
- Name that should be given to the server
- Name of application being loaded onto server

- O/S version to be loaded
- Service Pack of the O/S
- Number of processors and/or cores required
- The number of NICs (Network Interface Cards) that will be required and their specifications
- Amount of RAM required
- Number of hard disk drives and the size of each
- Whether this server will have SAN (Storage Area Network) drive space and if so, how much
- What support software needs to be loaded onto the server, e.g., IIS (Internet Information Services), Apache Tomcat, monitoring software, antivirus software, etc.
- Whether this server will be in the DMZ (Demilitarized Zone) or internal network
- Where this application requires load balancing or clustered servers
- If any service accounts need to be created on the server and if so what the ID and password should be
- Who should be included as local administrators for the servers
- If there is an existing server than can be used as a template for the new server, it is extremely helpful to mention it

When the appropriate group has completed the build of the server, they should respond back to you with some additional information about the server. For example:

- Whether or not the server set up is complete as requested
- The IP (Internet Protocol) address of the server
- The FQDN (Fully Qualified Domain Name) of the server

8.3.5 Verify that you can remotely access all the servers

Once you are told that the server(s) have been set up, then you will want to verify it. This can be done by successfully remoting to the server(s) in question. A Windows tool that is frequently used to remotely connect to another computer is RDC, Remote Desktop Connection. Figure 8.4 shows the entry screen of RDC. Use RDC to remote to the new server to verify that it exists and that you're able to access it.

8.3.6 Confirm that the operating system has been loaded

If you were able to remotely connect to the server in question, then an operating system has been correctly loaded onto the server. The only task for you now is to confirm that the correct operating system has been loaded onto it. You can identify the version of the Windows operating system that is running on a computer in the following manner. Open a command window and enter the command

FIGURE 8.4

Screenshot of an RDC connection. (For color version of this figure, the reader is referred to the online version of this chapter.)

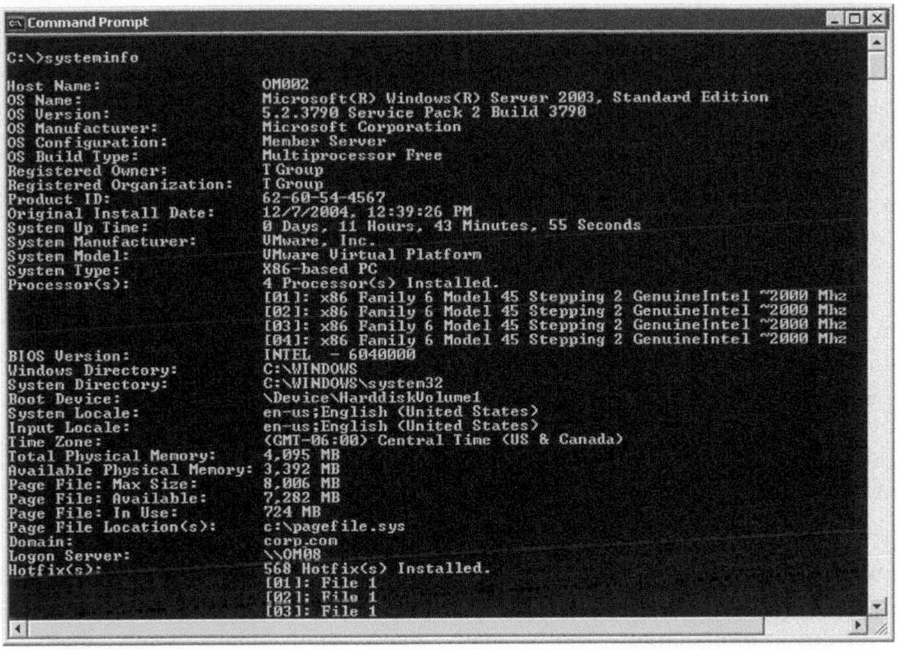

FIGURE 8.5

Screenshot of the systeminfo. (For color version of this figure, the reader is referred to the online version of this chapter.)

```
systeminfo
```

The output contains a wealth of information about this computer, including the version of the operating system that is loaded onto it. Figure 8.5 shows a screenshot of some of these details. If you run this on your workstation or computer you can scroll down to see other information including a list of all HotFixes and NIC details.

8.3.6.1 Service packs
Periodically operating system vendors issue a collection of updates, fixes, and enhancements bundled up into what is frequently called a Service Pack. For example, a given operating system might have SP1 or SP2 available for installation. The application Installation Guide might specify that a certain Service Pack be installed on the application server. Be certain that the O/S on your server has the correct Service Pack on it. The systeminfo command lists the service pack currently installed on the computer.

8.3.7 Ensure that any required supporting software has been loaded
Almost every software application requires some supporting software be loaded onto the server. Depending on the organization the Application Administrator may have to load this or there may be another group that would handle it. The list of requisite software may be short, but be assured that your application won't run without it. Some examples of the type of software that your application might require are listed here:

- IIS—Internet Information Services
- Apache Tomcat
- JRE—Java Runtime Environment

- JDK—Java Development Kit
- Oracle WebLogic Server
- IBM WebSphere
- Database user client software
- Word processing software
- Compression utilities like WinZip
- FTP software
- Software to handle PDF (Portable Document Format) documents
- BizTalk
- Tuxedo
- SharePoint
- .NET Framework
- Windows SDK—Software Development Kit
- DLLs
- Security certificates
- Virus protection software like Symantec or Norton

Unfortunately, the application installation guide might not provide you with the information you need to install these pieces of support software. If those details aren't included in the vendors list of documentation, then your best source would be to search for it on the Internet. You can also contact the vendor's Support Desk and ask them for this information.

8.3.8 Database

The application you're installing very likely requires the use of a database, frequently a relational database engine like Oracle or Microsoft SQL Server. If this is the case, then you must ensure that this component is set up before starting the application's installation process. The specific things that you need to be concerned with include the following:

- The database server must exist and be running
- The database engine software has been installed on the database server
- The database engine software is at the correct patch level
- The application server is able to communicate with the database server
- Vendor specified account(s) have been created on the database server
- Vendor specified database(s) have been created on the database server

If your organization has a DBA team, then they will be handling the bulk of these tasks. Your job will be to communicate to them the requirements specified in the Installation Guide. Be sure to contact the DBA team as early as possible. You don't want to be asking them to create a database the morning that you're planning to begin the installation.

During the installation process you may need further participation from the DBA team. The installation process may need to create database objects, e.g. tables or table spaces, under the SYSTEM account. Two common ways of doing this are listed below. I've done it both ways and they've been equally convenient. Talk to your DBA team to see which works best for them:

1. Have a DBA available so he or she can run any scripts that the vendor needs to have run at the appropriate point in the installation process.
2. Have the DBA create a temporary password for the SYSTEM account that they provide to you. Once the installation is complete they will change it.

8.3.9 **Ports**

What firewall ports does the application need open to communicate properly? The Installation Guide will provide these details. Some likely examples of ports that your application might be using are listed here:

- A port between the application server and the database server
- If the application includes multiple servers, then ports between them may need to be open
- If users interface with the application via an Internet browser, then port 80 needs to be open
- If the application generates e-mail, then a port between the application server and the mail server needs to be open
- If the environment includes either a load balancer or a cluster, then they might require that specific ports be open

If your organization has a team that handles the firewalls, then you'll need to work with them to get the necessary ports opened. Ports can be opened as incoming, outgoing, or both. Before making your request(s) make sure you know which it should be. As always, don't wait until the last minute to make this request.

8.3.9.1 *Tools to identify ports that are being used*

In a Windows environment, there are several tools that can identify what ports are open. One tool that can be used to verify that a port is open is telnet. Open a command window on the application server and enter the telnet command in it. The format of the command is:

```
telnet ComputerName port#
```

If the telnet connection is successful, i.e., the port is open to the specified computer, then the entire command window will go blank. Figure 8.6 shows a Command Window with a successful telnet command. If the port to the specified computer isn't open, then the telnet command will fail. Figure 8.7 shows a failed telnet command.

Another Windows command the displays open ports is netstat. Figure 8.8 shows the command and its output. A netstat command that is run on the application server will return a lot of output so it's convenient to filter the output to just the port you're interested in. The pipe operation and the "findstr" command can be used to perform this filtering. An example of the netstat command with this filtering is

```
netstat -aon | findstr 1521
```

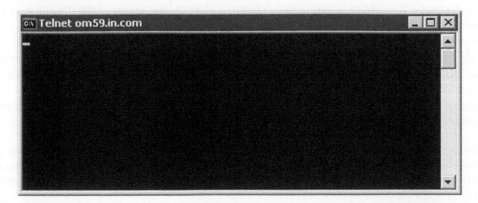

FIGURE 8.6

Screenshot of a telnet command showing an open port. (For color version of this figure, the reader is referred to the online version of this chapter.)

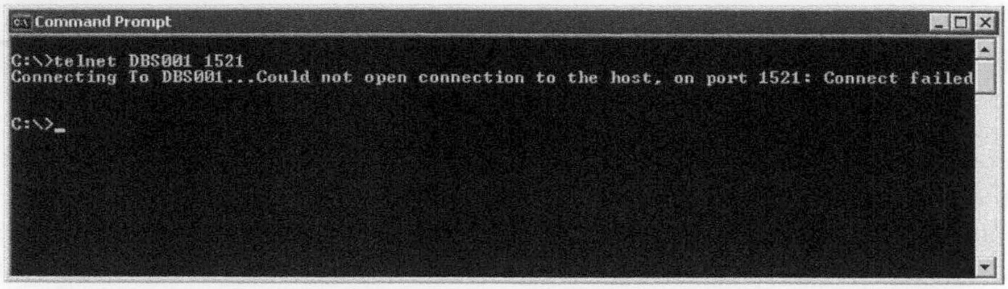

FIGURE 8.7

Screenshot of a telnet command showing a port that isn't open. (For color version of this figure, the reader is referred to the online version of this chapter.)

FIGURE 8.8

Screenshot of a netstat command showing open ports. (For color version of this figure, the reader is referred to the online version of this chapter.)

The output of the netstat command is piped to the find string command to search for string "1521." Any output lines with that string in them will be displayed. In this example port 1521 is open between IP addresses 14.11.39.48 and 14.11.39.52.

8.3.9.2 Document all the ports being used

You need an accurate list of all ports used by the application. This information should be in the Installation Guide. Unfortunately, it might be buried in that document. If an online version of the manual is available you might search if for "port."

The Installation Guide or the installer program will probably list a default number of each port that is required. My advice is to use the default whenever possible. If your organization has its own standards, then you need to follow them, but otherwise stick with the defaults. Doing this will make the installation easier and long-term maintenance easier as well.

Why does it matter? There are two extremely important reasons why you need to keep track of the ports the application will be using:

- Only one application can use a port at one time. If two applications attempt to use the same port, then neither of them will be successful. You can use the following command to identify the PID (Process ID) of the application that is already using a port where port# is the port number you're investigating

  ```
  netstat -aon | findstr port#
  ```
- Firewall ports have to be open to use them. The network security team needs to make sure that the ports in the firewall are open. If the ports aren't open, then the application won't work. When requesting that a port be open be sure to specify whether the traffic will be inbound, outbound, or both.

8.3.10 Environment variables

Environment variables are objects that the operating system uses to record details about the system's environment. Depending on the operating system, the set of environment variables can be broken into two subgroups. System variables are available to any user or process on the computer. User variables are only available to the user that created them.

The strings that hold environment variables can be used by either the operating system or applications. If software needs to be loaded onto user workstations, then it's likely that environment variables will need to be set on those machines as well.

It's common for an application's installation process to direct you to create one or more environment variables. Some of the more common types of values that an application needs defined include:

- Location of the application's source code and other files
- Location of the database's client software
- Value identifying which database character set will be used
- Location of the JRE (Java Runtime Environment)
- Location of the application's temporary subdirectory
- Location of the application's logs subdirectory
- Location of the application's output subdirectory
- Location of libraries

8.3.10.1 Two kinds of environment variables

There are two kinds of environment variables:

- User or local variables that affect only the user who created them
- System variables that affect all users and processes on the system

Depending on how long you want a variable to last and how broad you want its impact to be, then you need to create the appropriate environment variables.

8.3.10.2 Every operating system is different

Every operating system has a method of defining environment variables. Unfortunately, the method of doing this is slightly different in different operating systems, e.g., Windows 2003, Windows Server 2008 R2, etc. The basic steps to view, create, delete, and modify environment variables in Windows are listed below.

1. Left-click on the Windows icon in the bottom left-hand corner of the screen
2. Within the popup screen that is displayed right-click on "Computer" and select "Properties"
3. Click on "Advanced System Settings"
4. On the "System Properties" screen click on the "Advanced" tab
5. Click on the "Environment Variables" button
6. The screen shown in Figure 8.9 will be displayed.

8.3.10.3 Creating a new environment variable

To create a new variable click the "New" button under either the User variable or System variables sections. The screen shown in Figure 8.10 will be displayed. Enter the name and value of your new environment variable (User or System) and click the "OK" button.

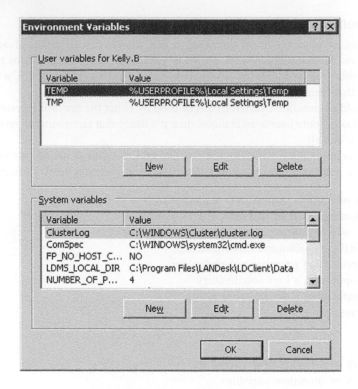

FIGURE 8.9

Screenshot of setting Path. (For color version of this figure, the reader is referred to the online version of this chapter.)

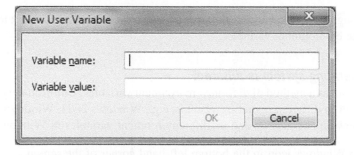

FIGURE 8.10

Screen to create a new environment variable. (For color version of this figure, the reader is referred to the online version of this chapter.)

8.3.10.4 Edit an existing environment variable

To edit an existing environment variable click the "Edit" button. Figure 8.11 is a screenshot of what the edit screen will looks like. Make the editing changes in this screen and click the "OK" button to save the new variable name or value.

One disadvantage of this screen is that it can't be resized. If the variable you're editing is longer than about 40 characters, then you won't be able to see its entire value. One trick is to copy it from this screen and paste it into a Notepad session for editing. Figure 8.12 shows the full value of the path variable displayed in Notepad.

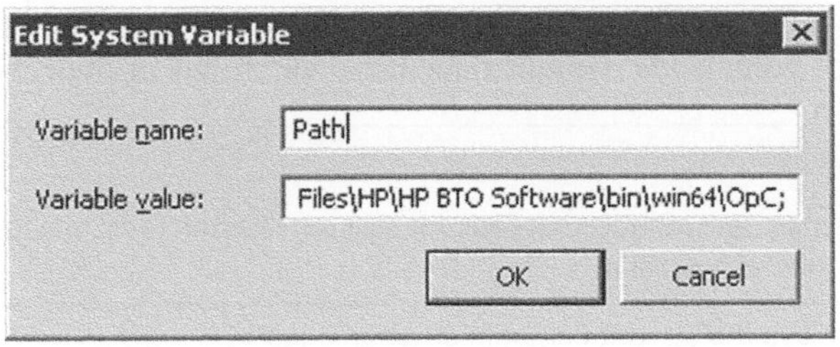

Edit System Variable   [×]

Variable name: Path

Variable value: Files\HP\HP BTO Software\bin\win64\OpC;

OK   Cancel

FIGURE 8.11

Screen to edit an existing environment variable. (For color version of this figure, the reader is referred to the online version of this chapter.)

FIGURE 8.12

Using Notepad to edit an environment variable. (For color version of this figure, the reader is referred to the online version of this chapter.)

8.3.10.5 Environment variables and command lines

If you prefer to work with the command line instead of a GUI, then you're in luck because Windows allows this. To see a list of all environment variables open a Command Window and enter the command "set." Figure 8.13 is a screenshot of the output of the set command.

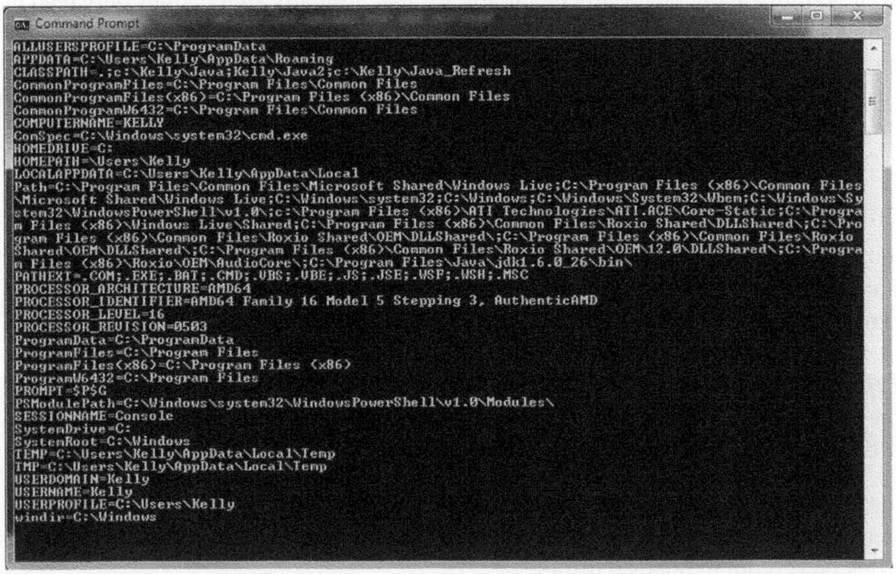

FIGURE 8.13

Output of set command used to display environment variables. (For color version of this figure, the reader is referred to the online version of this chapter.)

It's also possible to create new environment variables, delete them, and modify them from the command line. The following table of commands demonstrates these variations of the set command:

Command	Result
set testv="tester"	Creates new variable testv and loads it with "tester." This variable will only be available in the current user session
set testv	Displays the current contents of variable testv
set testv="New val"	Updates the value in testv to "New val"
set testv=	Deletes variable testv
setx NewVar New2	Creates a User environment variable named NewVar and loads it with "New2." This variable will not be available in the current user session, but will be available in all future command prompt sessions opened by the same user
setx /M NewestVar New3	Creates a System environment variable named NewestVar and loads it with "New3." This variable will not be available in the current user session, but will be available in all future command prompt sessions opened by all users To modify or delete variables created by the "setx" command the UI window shown in Figure 8.9 must be used. They can't be modified or deleted by commands entered in a command prompt

8.3.10.6 Warnings about timing and duration of environment variables

Environment variables have different "lifetimes" depending on where and how they are created. Variables created in a Windows command prompt can be of the User or System type depending on the command that is used. See the table in Section 8.3.10.4 for specific commands and durations of variables being created.

One word of warning about environment variables is that normally applications only read them when the application starts up. If a variable changes after the application is already running, then the new value won't be recognized by the application. This being the case, you should make all variable changes before the application starts up. If the application is already running, then you'll need to stop the application, create or change the environment variable, and restart the application.

8.3.11 Run the installation program

Hopefully you've done everything you can to prepare for the installation. Now it's time to start the installation by running the installer executable. Take a deep breath, turn off your phone and open up a word processing document that you'll capture screenshots in.

8.3.11.1 Typical installation questions

It's hard to predict every question that every application installer will ask, but the following is a list of fairly typical questions that you might be asked:

- Is this a new install or an update to an existing installation?
- Do you want to remove any existing files or write over them? Unless there's a valid reason, remove existing files before doing another install.
- Is this a Typical or Custom install? Make sure you understand the different between custom and typical installs. If you can live with a typical install that is usually easier and safer.
- Where do you want the software to be installed? If you can, avoid installing application software on the C: drive. It's typically reserved for the operating system.

- Do you want a shortcut installed on the desktop? If you're installing the application software on a server, there is no reason to create a shortcut. Most likely, it will be launched via services instead of you clicking on a shortcut, but create one if you want to.
- How will users be authenticated? There are several methods of authenticating users. Each of them is described in more detail in Chapter 15 on security.
  - Windows authentication—user needs to be authenticated by the Windows operating system or network first. The application software will then let them in.
  - Application authentication—user logs into the application which keeps a database of authenticated users and their passwords.
  - LDAP/AD—Lightweight Directory Access Protocol/Active Directory
  - SSO—Single Sign-On

8.3.11.2 Practice makes perfect
You should practice the installation process on a nonproduction environment first. If your organization has multiple environments, e.g., DEV, TEST, QA, and PROD, then the software should be installed on either DEV or TEST first. Make your mistakes on an environment where errors aren't critical.

8.3.11.3 Get assistance from the vendor
Don't be a hero and try to do an unfamiliar installation all by yourself. Request assistance from the vendor if this is the first time you've had to do this particular install. This is especially true if assistance during an installation is included as part of your support contract.

If you absolutely insist on doing this by yourself, then it's even more critical that you're doing it on a TEST or DEV environment first. If the first installation doesn't go well, then you would be well advised to wipe the disks clean and do the second attempt on a completely clean system.

8.3.11.4 It always takes longer than you expect
Allow yourself plenty of time to perform the installation. If the Installation Guide says it will take an hour, then assume it will take 2 or 3 hours. If it says the Installation Guide says it will take 2 hours, then assume that it will take 4-6 hours. You're always better off being conservative in your estimate regarding how long an unfamiliar installation will take. Make sure you're leaving yourself plenty of time, and not thinking it's something you can squeeze in before heading home for the weekend.

8.3.11.5 Document, document, document
Take meticulous notes of the steps you perform during the installation process. Write everything into a word processing document and save it frequently. Capture a screenshot of every screen displayed by the installation process and insert them into this document. Be sure to capture every screen on which you entered data or made some kind of selection, e.g., clicked a check box or selected a radio button.

You want to be as thorough as possible because the vendor's documentation may not be perfect. Even if it is completely accurate, your environment might require steps that aren't in the normal process. The more accurate your documentation is, the easier it will be to perform your next installation of the application. And, at some later time (e.g., months from now) when you're discussing an issue with the vendor, they may ask you a question about how the application was installed—when they do (and they will) you'll be glad you have this documentation.

8.3.11.6 After the install check for updates
It may seem like a scene from the movie "Groundhog Day," but the first thing you need to do after installing the application is to see if any patches need to be applied. This may sound downright wrong, but there's a very good reason. Sometimes the vendor finds that the installation software includes coding errors in the

application. If that happens they'll release an update, sometime called a "hotfix," to correct this type of problem. If such an update exists, then you definitely want to install it before releasing the application to the users.

8.4 USER ACCEPTANCE TESTING—UAT

A formal set of tests needs to exist that users sign off on indicating they acknowledge that the system has been installed correctly and that it fulfills their needs. Without such a test and approval agreement, you might end up in a situation where the users never formally "accept" the system. This set of tests needs to be drawn up and agreed to independent of the vendor you're acquiring the system from. If the system can do "x", "y," and "z," then it will be moved into production.

The UAT should be written by the users rather than the developer or Application Administrator. There are two primary reasons for this. First, the users are more knowledgeable about the functionality of the application. They have, or should have, a better sense of what the application should and shouldn't do.

The second reason for users to write the UAT is so the responsibility rests on them. By this I mean if the application passes the UAT but doesn't work, then the users have no one to blame but themselves. As either a developer or an Application Administrator you don't want to become the scapegoat if the application fails. If the users wrote an in adequate UAT, they should take responsibility for the application failing.

A representative of the user community should perform the User Acceptance Testing. They wrote it and they have the primary subject matter expertise so they should perform the testing. Some assistance might be required from the Application Administrator, but the vast majority of the testing should be done by users or their representatives.

The concept of a UAT applies equally to new installs and upgrades. After an upgrade you need user agreement that the upgrade was applied, it did what was expected and the system was not adversely affected otherwise. The original UAT can be the core of the testing that will be done after upgrades. Additional testing might be included, but the bulk of the tests can be the original UAT tests.

8.5 TEST DATA

Realistic testing can be only done with realistic test data. In this case, realistic refers to both volume and complexity. Suppose the production database contains millions of rows of distinct data in hundreds of separate tables. As a very simplistic example suppose the production database was projected to include 100,000 unique users and their addresses. Associated with these users might be 10,000,000 rows in the orders table. If the test database contains 100 users and 200 rows in the orders table, would your testing be realistic? Would testing with that trivial amount of database allow you to predict the performance of the application when run against the production database? I'm hoping that your answer is "no."

Creating test data isn't a trivial matter. If needs to be realistic, but not actually real. It's dangerous to use real data because people tend not to keep test data as secure as production data. Labeling this data as "test" implies that it isn't valuable or needing security.

If your organization's policy is to use production data during testing, then you need to ensure that it's treated the same way that production data get treated. Make sure that the database accounts and passwords for the test databases are as secure as they are for the production databases. Make sure that access to the test applications is as secure as it is to the production versions of the applications.

Support Software

The quote "No man is an island" from John Donne applies to software almost as well as it applies to mankind. No program, application, or piece of software stands by itself. The application(s) that you support depend on many other pieces of software which in turn rely on other pieces of code. Even the operating system requires that device drivers and other low-level software be in place to support it.

Given this almost organic interdependency of software, you shouldn't be surprised at the amount of software besides your application that needs to be loaded onto your server and possibly your users' workstations. Some of it will be loaded onto the server when the operating system is loaded. Some of it needs to be loaded prior to running your application installation. Some of it might be loaded as a part of the application installation. What's extremely important is that you know what needs to be loaded and when. Installing these pieces of support software should be included as part of the project plan you learned about in Chapter 8.

9.1 SUPPORT SOFTWARE ON APPLICATION SERVERS

While every application server has a unique environment, there are certain types of software that are commonly required on application servers. The following sections describe some of the more common types of software packages and a brief description of the functionality that they provide for applications.

It would be wonderful if this book could provide detailed information on every conceivable piece of support software that your application relies upon. Unfortunately, it would impossible for this or any book to include that level of information. It would also be outdated the moment it was committed to paper. The best course that can be taken here is to provide a high-level description of support software you're likely to encounter. More detailed information on it can be obtained either from your application's Installation Guide or directly from the vendor's support group.

The types of software described in Sections 9.1.1–9.1.12 are roughly from the bottom up. Other than the server's operating system, a framework is the most fundamental component. On top of that would be clustering and load balancing software and so on. All of them are important, but some are simply at a lower level than others.

9.1.1 Frameworks

In the world of software development and applications, a software framework is a platform that can be reused to develop applications more quickly, more efficiently, and with fewer errors. Frameworks typically include compilers, libraries, tools, and an API (application programming interface).

The application that you are supporting probably, but not certainly, was developed using a software framework. If the application was based on a framework, then you might have to make sure that required software components have been installed on the server before the application installation process can be started. If this needs to be done, then the Installation Guide will specify this and will provide installation instructions for you to follow.

The more common frameworks that your application might be built upon are Microsoft's .Net Framework and one of a variety of Java-based frameworks.

9.1.1.1 .NET framework

The .NET framework runs primarily on Windows operating systems. If your application is built upon .NET, then you will be required to install some version of .NET onto your server. Doing this isn't difficult and there is no license costs associated with loading .NET.

If multiple applications are running on a given server and each requires a different version of the .NET Framework that doesn't present a problem, different versions of .NET can be loaded onto the same machine and they'll coexist with each other.

9.1.1.2 Java frameworks

Does the application you're supporting require that Java components be installed on the server? There are many Java frameworks and each of them has their own requirements. Frameworks can be open source or proprietary, but that doesn't matter to you as an Application Administrator. The vendor who wrote the application will have decided which framework was most appropriate for their efforts and licensed it if that was necessary.

Some of the more popular Java frameworks are:

- Apache Struts
- Cocoon
- Oracle ADF (Application Development Framework)
- RAP (Rich Ajax Platform)
- WebWork

If the Java framework requires that any software components be installed on the server, then those details will be specified in the Installation Guide. As long as you follow the instructions in the Installation Guide, you shouldn't have any problems. Chapter 8 provided general application installation guidance. If problems do occur, then contact the vendor's support desk for assistance.

9.1.2 Clustering and load balancing

Clustering and load balancing are architectural techniques used to improve the availability or throughput of applications. Not all applications need higher levels of availability or performance, so most application environments don't include clustering or load balancing.

If you have chosen to employ either of these techniques, be prepared to undergo a significantly more complex installation process. This can include everything from handling additional servers, additional software, additional IP addresses, and more complicated startup/shutdown procedures.

If your organization doesn't have experience with installations of these types, you should seriously consider having either vendor technicians or experienced consultants assist you with the installation process. Be sure to factor the additional time and resources required for clusters and load balancing into your project plan.

9.1.2.1 Clustering

A cluster is defined as a group of computer servers that acts like a single system. If one of the servers fails, then ideally there should be no noticeable effect on the application's availability. There might be an impact on application performance depending on factors like the complexity of the application, the number of users accessing the application, and the number of remaining servers, but the intent is that the application will continue to be available to the users.

Clustering can be achieved by either hardware or software. If the hardware method is chosen, then specialized hardware is typically required. If the software technique is chosen, then commodity servers can be used. Since commodity servers are more economical, software clustering is the more common method chosen for creating and controlling clusters.

Some examples of clustering software are:

- Microsoft Cluster Server
- Red Hat Cluster Suite
- Solaris Cluster
- Veritas Cluster Server

9.1.2.2 Load balancing software

The objective of load balancing is to distribute the work across multiple servers, disk drives, network links, or other components in order to maximize throughput. If you have determined that your application needs load balancing, then be prepared for a more complicated installation.

There are several methods by which load balancing can be achieved. One is to have a load balancing program that receives user requests and distributes them to one of a number of "backend" servers. When a server completes the request, the results are sent to the load balancer which returns it to the requestor. As long as a backend server is available to handle the next incoming request, the user requests can be fulfilled immediately. This method hides the existence of multiple servers from users. As far as the users are aware, the load balancing program is the application.

Another approach is to have multiple "backend" servers that are exposed to the users. A user specifies a specific server when requesting a request. This approach is simpler but has the disadvantage that it puts a certain level of decision-making burden on the users, i.e., what server should they connect to. Another disadvantage with this approach is that if the server a user is accustomed to using is unavailable, the user might not be aware that other servers are available.

Some brands of load balancers that your application might be based on are:

- F5 BIG-IP Load Traffic Manager (LTM)
- Cisco IOS-based routers
- Radware AppDirector OnDemand switches
- CoyotePoint Equalizer Appliances
- Barracuda
- Riverbed's Stingray Traffic Manager
- Kemp Technologies LoadMaster load balancers

9.1.3 Web server

The term "web server" can refer to either hardware or software. If you're referring to hardware, then it's the physical devices fulfill requests for web pages made by users. When referring to software, then it's a program (see examples below) that runs on the hardware to fulfill web page requests.

If your application is browser based, then you're probably going to be working with both hardware and software versions of web servers:

- The hardware is the server that your application is installed on.
- The software is a piece of specialized code that accepts web pages requests from application users, fulfills them, and returns the results.

There are a number of widely available software servers that your application might rely upon as the web server. Some of these include:

- Apache HTTP Server, aka Apache, is one of the most popular web server programs. It's available under the Apache license, so it's open source and free to anyone who wants to use it. Apache will work on numerous operating systems, including Linux, Max OS X, Solaris, UNIX, and Windows.
- Microsoft IIS (Internet Information Services) is available for most Windows operating systems and is available as an optional component of Windows.
- Sun Java System Web Server is available from Oracle. This web server runs on AIX, HP-UX, Linux, Solaris, and Windows operating systems.

9.1.4 Software that supports applications

Application servers are designed to provide applications with the fundamentals that they need to make them functional and efficient. Some of the services that are provided for applications are security, improved availability, supports complex database access, transaction support, and mail services.

If your application depends upon an application server, the Installation Guide will provide details about it. The steps to install it will be provided. In the long run, you should learn as much about the application server as you can. (See Chapter 8 for general guides about installations.) There will be times that you have to log into its console to stop, start, or modify objects. The more familiar you are with this tool, the more competent you'll be with it.

Some of the more common application servers are:

- Oracle WebLogic Server is a Java EE platform that provides applications with access to network protocols, Java Database Connectivity (JDBC), Java Transaction API (JTA), Java Message Service (JMS), JavaMail, and other services.
- IBM WebSphere is a software suit that provides functions like a web server, website templates, development tools, configuration wizard, and the ability to access a relational database.
- Glassfish is an open source application server. It was originally developed and supported by Sun Microsystems. Currently, it is sponsored by the Oracle Corporation. The version of Glassfish that is supported by Oracle is known as Oracle GlassFish Server. Glassfish supports EJB (Enterprise JavaBeans), Java Persistence API (aka JPA), Java Message Service (JMS), and JavaServer Page.

9.1.5 Databases

Virtually, every application will connect to a database to store, update, and retrieve data needed by the application. Many, if not most, of these databases will be relational database engines like Oracle, Microsoft SQL Server, or MySQL. Some applications might have a proprietary database but those are definitely the minority.

There are a number of tasks required before an application can begin using a third-party database engine. The most common of them are listed here:

1. Install the database engine on a database server.
2. Open the firewall ports between the database server and application servers that need to communicate with it.
3. Install software on the application server that enables it to work with the database engine. This software is called the "client." For example, if the database being used is Oracle, then this version of the client software would be the Oracle Client package.
4. Create the database(s) that are needed by the application.
5. Create any administrative accounts needed by the application in the application's database.
6. Create tables that are needed by the application in the new database.
7. Populate those tables with initial data needed by the application.
8. Create user-level accounts in the application's database.

Most organizations will have one or more DBAs (Database Administrators) who are experts with the database package(s) that the organization has chosen to use. As the Application Administrator, you won't be expected to know how to perform the tasks that DBAs are trained and experienced in doing.

Of the tasks listed above, the following table shows how they are typically distributed between Application Administrators, DBAs, and other IT specialists:

Responsible Party	Task Description
DBA	Install the database engine software on any and all database servers in the organization
Security team	Modify the firewall to open ports between the application servers and database servers
Application Administrator or DBA	Install the database client software on the application servers
DBA or application installation program	Create the databases needed by the application
DBA, installation program, or App Admin	Create administrative accounts needed by the application. If the Application Administrator does this, the password to the database SYSTEM account is needed
DBA, installation program, or App Admin	Create the tables needed by the application. If the Application Administrator does this, the password to the database SYSTEM account is needed
DBA or installation program	Populate application database tables
Application Administrator or select application "power users"	Create user-level accounts. If the application has a bulk registration process, then that should be used

9.1.5.1 *Database client software*

Read the Installation Guide for details on what type of database engine is being used and whether or not it requires that client software be loaded. Not all database engines require that client software be loaded onto the application server. The following sections describe client software for several database engines.

9.1.5.1.1 Oracle client software

Oracle client software is available in 32-bit and 64-bit versions. The decision as to whether the 32-bit or 64-bit version should be loaded isn't cut and dried. If the application server's Operating/System is 32 bits, then either version of the Oracle client software could be used. Confirm which one is needed in the Installation Guide or with the vendor's support group before loading anything onto the application server. If the vendor didn't provide a copy of the client software, then it can be obtained from the Oracle website. Be absolutely certain that you install the exact version that the Installation Guide specifies. If the version of the client software installed isn't certified by the application vendor, then problems might occur now or in the future.

Loading this software should be done after the DBA has created the database and the firewall port has been opened between the application and database servers. Only after both of those prerequisites have been completed can you test the connection to verify that everything has been set up correctly.

9.1.5.1.2 IBM DB2 client software

IBM's DB2 database engine also has client software that needs to be installed on the application server. There are several versions of the DB2 client software. The largest version includes support for Java, C/C++, .NET, PHP, and Ruby. If your application requires just a single type of database connectivity support, then you can install smaller versions of the client software that support Java, .NET, or C/C++. If the vendor didn't provide the needed version, then read the Installation Guide carefully so that you can download and install the specific version that is needed.

9.1.5.2 Database access tools

As the Application Administrator, there will be times that you will need to run SQL (Structured Query Language) commands against the database. During the installation, you might need to execute an SQL script to create tables, populate tables, or create user accounts. After the application has been installed, you might need to run SQL statements or scripts when applying an upgrade. If a problem occurs with the application, it's very likely that a technician from the vendors support desk might ask you to run a script of SQL statements to gather details about the problem.

A number of tools are available to open a connection with a database and execute SQL commands. There are a number of possibilities depending on which database engine is being used. The following sections describe potential tools and how they work. Some of these tools are free and others involve a licensing fee. Some will work only with a single vendor's database, while others will work with many different databases.

9.1.5.2.1 SQL*Plus

In an Oracle environment, the most basic tool to interact with the database is SQL*Plus. Like any tool, it has pros and cons. The biggest pro for SQL*Plus is that it is available as part of the free Oracle client software. This means it's available on every workstation or server that is connected to an Oracle database. For many users, the biggest con of SQL*Plus is that it's command line centric, i.e., it doesn't have a GUI interface. Another restriction of SQL*Plus is that it can only be used to connect to Oracle databases. Figure 9.1 shows a screenshot of what SQL*Plus looks like when connected to a database.

At the prompt, you enter your SQL command and press the Enter key. The results will be displayed in the command window. If more than a few lines are being displayed, it's very useful to redirect them, i.e., spool them, to an output file. The output file can then be opened with a text editor like Notepad.

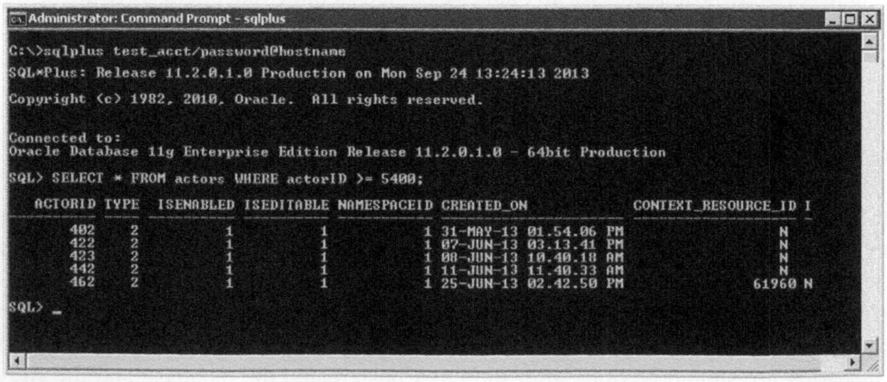

FIGURE 9.1

Example of Oracle's SQL Plus. (For color version of this figure, the reader is referred to the online version of this chapter.)

9.1.5.2.2 SQL Developer

Another tool that can be used to connect to Oracle databases is Oracle SQL Developer. SQL Developer is a GUI-based tool that might be more comfortable for those who are accustomed to working with a graphical-based tool. This tool can be downloaded from Oracle's website free of cost. Figure 9.2 shows the main screen of SQL Developer.

9.1.5.2.3 Microsoft Server Management Studio

A Microsoft tool that is available for connect to databases is SQL Server Management Studio Express. It allows the user to connect to database, execute SQL commands, and display the results. This tool is available for free to all SQL Server installations, but it can only be used to connect to SQL Server databases. Figure 9.3 contains a sample screen of this tool in use.

9.1.5.2.4 MySQL Query Browser

MySQL's equivalent tool is called Query Browser. It is also a GUI-based tool that allows the user to create and execute SQL commands and have the results displayed in an output pane. Figure 9.4 contains a screen-shot of MySQL Query Browser.

9.1.5.2.5 Toad and SQL station

The previous tools that were described, i.e., SQL*Plus, SQL Server Management Studio, and MySQL Query Browser, can only connect to those specific products. There are some tools that can be used to connect to more than one vendor's databases. Two examples of such tools are Toad and SQL Station. Each of these tools is GUI based. Their primary advantage is that they're able to connect to different vendors' databases, including Oracle, SQL Server, and MySQL. The downside is that they aren't free like the other tools that have been described.

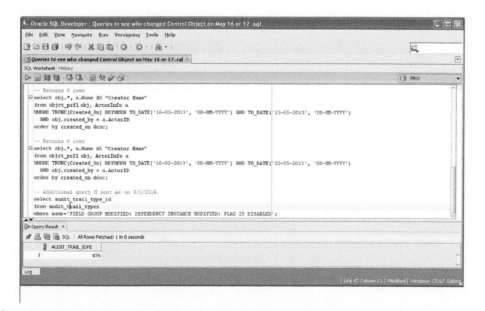

FIGURE 9.2

Example of Oracle's SQL Developer. (For color version of this figure, the reader is referred to the online version of this chapter.)

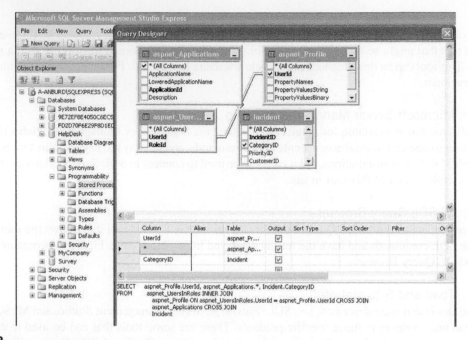

FIGURE 9.3

Example of Microsoft's SQL Server Management Studio. (For color version of this figure, the reader is referred to the online version of this chapter.)

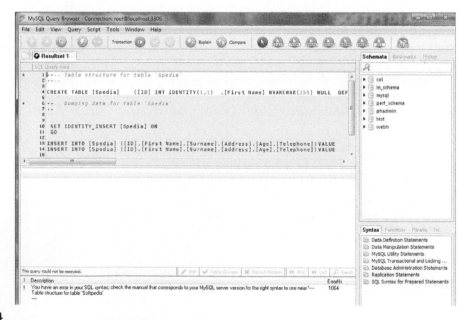

FIGURE 9.4

Example of MySQL Query Browser. (For color version of this figure, the reader is referred to the online version of this chapter.)

9.1.6 Security

Security is a major concern for every Application Administrator. The application(s) that you're supporting most likely contain a significant amount of corporate data. It might be financial data, budgeting data, accounting information, legal documents, or personal data. All data belonging to the organization needs to be kept confidential.

Many cyber criminals have come to realize the treasure trove of data that is contained within applications and their databases. As these bad actors turn their sights onto applications like the one you support, everyone in the organization needs to become more security conscious.

The following sections describe some of the types of tools that are frequently used to protect your application. There is no expectation that an Application Administrator be an expert in all of these areas, but you need a working knowledge of what they do and whether or not they have been deployed to protect your application's environment. Additional information on security is provided in Chapter 15.

9.1.6.1 Firewalls

The purpose of a firewall is to keep a network secure by controlling network traffic, both inbound and outbound traffic. A firewall can be either hardware based, software based, or a combination of both hardware and software. It analyzes data packets and determines which ones should be allowed through and which ones should be blocked based on a set of rules.

The firewall is essentially a bridge between your internal or local network and everything outside the organization, i.e., the Internet. Figure 9.5 illustrates how a firewall isolates the internal network from the outside world.

As an Application Administrator, your dealings with the firewall will be primarily to request that the security team open ports between your application server and other servers. Some examples of ports that might need to be opened in the firewall include:

- If your application uses an Oracle database, then you'll need a port opened between the application server and the Oracle database server. The default port used by Oracle is 1521.
- If the database is Microsoft's SQL Server, then a port needs to be opened between the application server and the database server that SQL Server is running on. The default port for SQL Server is 1433.
- If the application needs to communicate with an SMTP mail server, then a port between the application server and the e-mail server must be open. The default port for SMTP is 25. The default port for Secure SMTP (SSMTP) is 465.
- If the application users use an Internet browser to communicate with the application server, then a port needs to be opened for that. The default port for HTTP traffic is port 80.

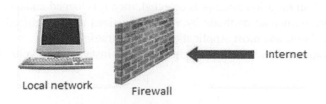

FIGURE 9.5

Illustration of how a firewall protects the organization's network. (For color version of this figure, the reader is referred to the online version of this chapter.)

9.1.6.2 Antivirus (AV) software

A computer virus is a piece of code that has the primary intent of replicating itself. It might be destructive or benign, but its primary purpose is to replicate itself to other computers. Some of the ways that viruses can be passed from one computer to another include:

- Viruses can be attached to program files like .COM or .EXE files. When infected files are executed on a new computer, it becomes infected.
- Viruses can be written as macros used by programs like Microsoft Word or Excel. When the macro is run, the computer on which it ran becomes infected.
- Viruses can infect code in specific areas of hard drives, CDs, or thumb drives, aka USB drives. If an infected CD or thumb drive is inserted into a computer, then it can become infected.

Antivirus software recognizes viruses and other malicious software like adware, Trojan horses, spyware, and worms. Once the AV software recognizes malicious software, it will block it from running. You need to understand that most AV software reacts to malicious software that has been previously identified. There is a risk that your server will be attacked by malicious code that hasn't yet been identified by the antivirus software vendors. Attacks that haven't yet been identified and for which there is not yet a solution are called "zero-day attacks."

Some examples of vendors providing antivirus software that might be running on your application server include:

- Bitdefender Antivirus Plus
- GFI-Vipre
- Kapersky Anti-Virus
- McAfee
- Microsoft
- Norton/Symantec
- Panda
- Sophos
- Symantec
- Trend Micro

As an Application Administrator, your involvement with the antivirus software is to make sure that it's running on your application server. Most AV software regularly downloads updates that it uses to recognize malicious software. The updates are referred to as signatures. If you ever notice that the AV software isn't running or new signatures aren't being regularly downloaded to your server, then you need to contact your organization's security team immediately!

9.1.6.3 Intrusion detection systems (IDS)

Intrusion detection systems are designed to prevent individuals or automated attacks from gaining access to your server or network. If an intrusion attempt is detected, then it is logged and an alert is issued to security administrators. There are numerous methods by which intrusions are recognized, but this information is beyond the scope of this book and most Application Administrators.

Some of the more common IDS tools that might have been installed onto your application server are:

- Snort
- Firestorm
- Prelude
- Dragon
- STAT

As an Application Administrator, you need to know whether or not IDS software has been installed on your server. If so, then you should know whom to contact if it generates alerts that an intrusion is occurring. The IDS should automatically notify the security team, but it wouldn't hurt for you to contact them as well if you become aware of an alert.

9.1.6.4 Log monitoring utilities

Log files are created by many different pieces of software that may be running on your application server. Some examples of components that frequently write to log files include:

- The operating system
- The application you're supporting
- Web servers
- Load balancers
- Firewalls
- ETL (Extract Transform and Load) software
- Intrusion Detection Systems (IDS)
- Backup processes

If you're like most Application Administrators, you don't have the time, inclination, or knowledge to be constantly reviewing these logs. But if no one is examining them regularly, then the valuable information they potentially contain isn't being noticed. The solution to this predicament is to have a program, called a log monitor, examine them for you.

Log monitoring utilities can be simple or complex, easy to use or complicated, and expensive or free. If your security group hasn't already selected a log monitor and installed it on your application server, then you should consider doing it yourself.

Some examples of log monitoring software are:

- GFI EventsManager
- Solarwinds
- Splunk
- Tivoli Log Monitoring Tools
- WhatsUp Log Management Suite

9.1.6.5 Security certificates

A security certificate is a key that is used to decrypt messages. If your application contains confidential information, for example, credit card numbers, then it deserves to be as secure as possible. Employing SSL (Secure Socket Layer) along with a security certificate can help provide your application with the protection that it needs.

A security certificate is obtained from a Certification Authority (CA). Each CA has its own costs, renewal details, etc. Some examples of CAs are:

- GeoTrust
- Go Daddy
- RSA
- Secure Certificate Services
- Symantec/VeriSign
- Thawte

9.1.6.6 Vulnerability scanner

A vulnerability scanner is a security tool that is used to assess the security of a server, application, or network. Fundamentally, a vulnerability scanner is a tool that thinks like a hacker. It examines the target the way a hacker would look at it, i.e., looking for vulnerabilities or weaknesses.

One approach is for the vulnerability scanner to have a database of known weaknesses. It examines the target checking to see if each of the weaknesses exists. If the weakness exists, then it will be included in the report that the vulnerability scanner prepares about the target. This explanation is for the most basic form of vulnerability scanning. Significantly more complex approaches are available, but are beyond the scope of this book.

Some examples of the types of weaknesses that a vulnerability scanner is looking for include:

- Does the application perform input validation?
- Does the server contain known configuration errors?
- Have the latest operating system patches been applied to the server?
- Have the latest patches been applied to the web server software?
- Is the application susceptible to buffer overflow attacks?
- Can attackers escalate the privileges they are granted?
- Can the application be cracked with a SQL Injection attack?
- Is the application vulnerable to an integer overflow attack?

Some examples of vulnerability scanners that are available are listed below. Some of them are open source tools, while others are commercial products. Some security experts suggest that organizations use both a commercial product and an open source tool:

- AppScan
- Arachni
- Hailstorm
- N-Stalker
- Nessus
- NeXpose
- Powerfuzzer
- Skipfish
- Wapiti
- WebInspect
- Websecurify

9.1.6.7 Update software

Updates are a way of life in an organization that depends upon technology. Software that you don't even remember you have installed on the server will eventually need to be updated. The choices are to do this manually or automate the process. If you choose the manual route for handling updates, then prepare to spend a significant percentage of your working life doing these mundane tasks.

Some examples of update software tools include the following products:

- Altiris
- AppFresh
- Desktop Central
- KACE Appliance
- LANDesk
- Synaptic/APT
- Update Notifier

As useful as these tools are, they aren't a panacea when it comes to updating software. They aren't able to update every piece of software that might exist on your server. Be sure you know what the tool you've selected is updating and what it isn't updating.

The more popular the software installed on your server is, the more likely it is that its updates can be managed with one of the update tools listed above. But, if the application you are supporting is a niche product, then it's unlikely that any of the update tools will recognize it. I would also generalize that the more complicated the software, the less likely it is that it can be automatically updated.

9.1.7 Reporting

Talk of a paperless society is, in my opinion, premature. The business world continues to run on reports and in many, many cases, those reports are being printed out on paper. To support this need virtually, every application has a reporting component. Chapter 4 contained a more complete discussion on reporting features that are common to many applications.

The reporting function is likely to be implemented in one of the following ways:

- A proprietary reporting tool that is built into the application
- A separate reporting package that was licensed from a third party
- A reporting package licensed from a third party that have been integrated into the application

As the Application Administrator, it isn't critical which of the above techniques has been chosen by the vendor to implement their reporting ability. From an administrator's viewpoint, supporting the reporting package isn't usually very difficult. The reporting tool needs to be able to connect to the database. This means you might have to tweak some configuration parameters to enable that. If reports are distributed via e-mail, then you might have to enter the name of the e-mail server into a parameter file.

If you will be personally responsible for writing reports, then of course you'll be spending a lot more time with the reporting package. If a process isn't already in place via which the users submit requests for new reports and changes to existing reports, then such a system definitely needs to be put in place. If there isn't a way to track such requests, you're in for nothing but headaches.

Some examples of third-party reporting packages that are widely used include the following:

- Business Objects
- Crystal Reports
- Cognos BI
- SQL Server Reporting Services
- Oracle Reports
- Tableau

9.1.8 Monitoring

Applications, networks, and servers have a lot of moving pieces, far too many pieces for anyone to keep track of 24 hours a day and 7 days a week. Monitoring tools are available that will keep track of all of these pieces for a busy Application Administrator. A major goal of employing a monitoring tool is to recognize a problem and hopefully get it fixed before the users become aware of it.

Some of the metrics that monitoring tools can track include the following:

- CPU load exceeds a threshold
- Network bandwidth utilization is excessive
- Network traffic monitoring to make sure thresholds aren't exceeded

- Services on the server have stopped or started
- A server has rebooted
- Available disk space falls below a predetermined threshold
- Disk I/O activity exceeds a set threshold
- A device is no longer available
- A network outage occurs
- Error files have been created.

The capability of monitoring tools varies widely. Some are just capable of logging events if a metric goes out of bounds. Others can send out an alert via e-mail if a metric goes out of whack. Some are able to take an action if a specific event occurs. For example, if an application stops, then the monitoring tool would recognize this and restart it.

Some monitoring tools use software, called an agent, which is loaded onto each server that is to be monitored. The agents actually monitor activity on each server and then sent the details back to the "master" server where the monitoring tool was loaded. Tools that don't require agents are called "agentless." These tools acquire activity details by using monitoring functionality embedded in the operating system running on application servers.

There are many monitoring tools to choose from. Some are simple and others are much more complex. Some are open source, i.e., free and others are expensive. A short list of monitoring tools is listed here:

- Cacti
- Nagios
- HP's OpenView
- Orion SolarWinds
- Zabbix
- Monit

Possible roles and responsibilities for the Application Administrator when it comes to monitoring software are listed here:

- Are you responsible for loading monitoring software onto the application server?
- Are you responsible for activating monitoring software onto the application server?
- Does the monitoring software send out alerts when something unusually or unexpected occurs on the application server?
- If so, who gets those alerts and how?
- If a server has to be stopped for any reason, e.g., during an upgrade process, can the monitoring software be temporarily disabled so alerts aren't sent out?
- Do activity reports get created by the monitoring software?
- Are activity reports created automatically or manually?
- How are activity reports distributed and who gets copies of them?

9.1.9 Backup software

The world is an uncertain place. Anything bad that could go wrong eventually will go wrong. If your application isn't backed up, then when the worst thing happens you won't be prepared. To be prepared, you need to have the server backed up on a regular, reliable, predictable cycle.

Not every file or other software component that is loaded onto your server needs to be backed up. This may seem counterintuitive to the reader, so let me explain. If your disk drive crashes and becomes unusable, it will need to be rebuilt. Some of the software that was previously on that drive can be obtained from other sources. For example, the operating system can be obtained from installation CDs or downloaded from the vendor's website. Similarly, the executable files, libraries, and other relatively static components of the application can be obtained from installation CDs or from the vendor's website. The same is true of the support software described in this chapter.

What really needs to be backed up is described in the following list. This list is essentially everything that can't be loaded from software that the vendor provides to all its customers:

- Data
- Customizations to the application
- Reports that have been written or modified locally
- Changes to screens and menus
- Workflow details created to reflect your organization's way of doing business
- The user list as well as the permission details for each user
- Details about user groups, especially if they are unique to your organization

Some examples of backup software include:

- CommVault
- IBM Tivoli Storage Manager
- NetVault Backup
- NTBackup
- Norton 360
- EMC RecoverPoint
- Yosemite Server Backup

As the Application Administrator you need to have answers to the following backup-related questions:

- Does the application software include its own backup functions?
- Does any specific backup software or package need to be loaded onto the application server?
- If this is needed then who will do it?
- Who will schedule backups?
- Are the users able to be logged into the application while backups are running?
- If not, are they aware of this or are they prevented from logging in during the backup window?
- Who will verify that backups completed successfully?
- If the backup fails, will anyone be notified?
- Where does the output of backups get sent?
- How many instances of backup files are kept?
- How are old backup files deleted?

9.1.10 **Utilities**

There are a few tools or utilities that don't neatly fall into the previously described categories. Examples of these utilities are described here:

- FTP (File Transfer Protocol) software that is used to move files between servers.
- Compression software to compress files, i.e., makes them smaller without losing any data integrity. This is needed because disk space even with today's large hard drives is limited. Some files can be compressed to a small percentage of their original size.
- Encryption software to protect your data from prying eyes.

9.1.11 Scheduling

It might not be obvious, but even a relatively simple application probably has activities that need to be launched at specific days and times. To satisfy these needs, a scheduling package might be installed on your application server. Some examples of tasks that need to be done at a scheduled date or time include:

- Perform backups
- Create and send out reports
- Export data files and transmit them to another application or server
- Bounce, i.e., stop and start, the application for performance purposes
- Capture a snapshot of server or application statistics

There is an extremely wide variety of scheduling packages. You can choose a very basic tool or one with all the bells and whistles. You can use a tool that is built into the operating system. You can download an open source package for free or choose to spend top dollar for an industry leading, state-of-the-art scheduler.

The number of tasks that need to be scheduled will likely dictate what type of tool is acquired and used. It would be pretty foolish to purchase an expensive scheduling tool if the number of tasks that needs to be scheduled is extremely limited.

Some of the scheduling tools that are available are listed here:

- Cron is built into UNIX and Linux operating systems
- Windows Task Scheduler is built into all Windows operating systems
- BMC Control-M
- Open Source Job Scheduler
- JAMS Scheduler
- Tivoli Workload Scheduler
- VisualCron
- ActiveBatch
- Advanced Job Scheduler

As the Application Administrator, you must be able to answer scheduling-related questions like the following:

- Does your application require any scheduling be done?
- If so, what scheduling tool will be used to accomplish it?
- Does any scheduling software need to be loading onto your application servers?
- What tasks are being scheduled, specifically what tasks, what days, and what time?
- Who is responsible for setting up those scheduled tasks?
- Will anyone, e.g., you, be notified if a scheduling task fails?
- If scheduling for one or more tasks fails, do you know how to reset the scheduler?
- If the schedule is running from a "master" computer, what will happen to your tasks if scheduling software is down when one of your tasks is supposed to run?

9.1.12 Extract, transform, and load

ETL is the generic name given to software that performs the following data-related tasks:

1. Extracts data from multiple and/or external sources
2. Transforms the data to fit the needs, format, or expectations of the destination
3. Loads the data into the destination database, datamart, or data warehouse

If the application that you are supporting has ETL software, then you need to consider the following questions:

*   Who will be loading the ETL software?
*   Is it loaded onto your application server?
*   If not, where does it need to be loaded?
*   Is it internal to the application or is it a separate software component?
*   Do ETL tasks needed to be added to the scheduler?
*   Who will monitor that ETL tasks completed successfully?

9.2 SUPPORT SOFTWARE ON USER WORKSTATIONS

The overwhelming bulk of an application's software is loaded onto the server, but it's possible that some components will need to be loaded onto the users' workstations. As the Application Administrator you need to examine the Installation Guide closely to understand exactly what software, if any, needs to be loaded onto the user's computers.

While the amount of software involved is relatively limited, it's complicated by the fact that there are potentially a large number of such workstations. Even worse, these devices can be spread throughout the building, city, country, or even the world. Communicating or working with the user community can be complicated by time zones, language barriers, a variety of hardware that users have, and widely varying levels of technical competence among users.

You need to understand how this software will be loaded. Some of the possibilities are:

*   Does your organization have a group responsible for loading software onto user desktops?
*   Will you be responsible for loading it?
*   Did the vendor provide a script or utility to load it?
*   Are the users capable of loading it for themselves if provided with accurate and readable instructions?

Types of software that might need to be loaded onto user workstations are described in sections 9.2.1 through 9.2.4. These descriptions are kept fairly brief because much of this software was described in the section on server software. Where necessary a more detailed description has been provided.

9.2.1 Internet browser

If users will be using Internet browsers to connect to the application, then you need to know which browsers and versions are certified by the vendor. While users might get away with using an unauthorized browser most of the time they most likely will run into problems eventually. You need to *strongly* suggest that they stick to the list of authorized browsers provided by the vendor.

Whenever a user reports a problem, one of the first questions you should ask is what browser they were using when the error occurred. If an unsupported browser or version was used, then ask them to repeat the steps they took on a supported browser and see if the problem recurs on it.

9.2.1.1 Browser plug-ins

A browser plug-in is a software component that is added to the browser to add a specific capability or feature to the functionality of the browser. Some applications that are accessed via a web browser require that specific plug-ins be loaded onto each user's workstation.

If the application you support has this requirement, then you need to document exactly how this will affect the users. Some details that should be included in this document are:

- The exact steps to install the plug-in
- The location where the user can access any files needed to do this installation
- How long this process will take?
- Does the user's workstation need to be rebooted after the process in complete?
- What message will the user see if the install is successful?
- What message will the user see if the install isn't successful?
- What the user should do if the install isn't successful, e.g., try to install it again, call someone, etc.

Some examples of functionality that a plug-in might add to the browsers for your application include:

- Add the ability to display new file formats, e.g., image file formats
- Functions to encrypt and decrypt files
- To support programming languages

9.2.2 Database

If the application requires that a piece of presentation software be loaded onto the users' workstations, then there is a possibility that the workstation will be communicating directly with the database. If this is the case, then database client software might need to be installed on each user workstation. Two ways to confirm that this need exists and to prepare for it are:

1. Read the Installation Guide
2. Set up a test workstation that mimics a typical user workstation

9.2.3 Document viewers

If the report package for the application creates reports in a format other than ASCII text, then there is the possibility that some form of viewing software will need to be installed on user workstations. Some possible examples of this type of documentation include:

- Microsoft Office, specifically Microsoft Word and Excel, if reports are created as .doc or .xls files.
- Adobe Reader to open a pdf (Portable Document Format) file. Adobe Reader can be downloaded and installed without a license fee. There are so many pdf documents on the Internet that it's very likely that all of your potential users already have this installed on their workstations.
- If the application creates HTML (HyperText Markup Language) documents that users need to access, this shouldn't present any problems. Internet browsers routinely read HTML documents and it's almost a certainly that all of your user's workstations will already have an Internet browser like Internet Explorer or Firefox installed on them.

9.2.4 VPN software

If users need to access the application when their computers aren't connected to the organization's network, then you'll want to make their connections as secure as possible. One method of securing these connections is to use VPN (Virtual Private Network) software to establish the connection.

If your users are already connecting remotely to access other applications, then there is a good chance that VPN software has already been loaded onto their computers. If this isn't the case, then you'll have to explain to them what a VPN is and why they need it to connect to the network remotely. A detailed explanation of VPN software is included in Chapter 15.

Potential types of VPN software that your organization might recommend using include:

- Cisco VPN Client
- CyberGhost Premium VPN
- Juniper VPN
- OpenVPN
- StrongVPN
- VPN4ALL Basic

Updates and Patches

10

Once you've completed installing your application, you may think that you can relax and enjoy yourself. I hate to burst your bubble, but that's not going to happen. Before you know it there will be updates to apply to your shiny new application. So stay alert and always be ready for updates to arrive unexpectedly. Over the lifetime of the application you'll certainly do more upgrades than installations so be prepared for them.

Does your license or maintenance plan with the application vendor entitle you to all of their updates? The answer to this might seem to be an obvious "yes," but unlimited updates aren't always included in licenses. For example, you might get the minor releases but not the major releases. Before making an assumption check with the vendor or review your license to absolutely sure what updates you're entitled to.

10.1 WHAT NEEDS TO BE UPDATED?

You will be surprised at how many updates need to be done on the server(s) where your application runs. An even bigger surprise is the variety of software that eventually will need to be updated on your server.

10.1.1 The application

To a beginning Application Administrator you'll probably be curious why updates are necessary. After all, it seems like just yesterday you installed the application and now the vendor is telling you that it needs to be updated? Some of the reasons that updates are released include the following:

- To fix problems that your or other users of the software have uncovered and reported. Today's applications have become increasing complex so it's understandable that errors will inevitably be encountered by users.
- To improve performance of the application by implementing improved techniques. Applications are never fast enough for users so vendors are always looking to make them faster.
- To add functionality that you or other clients have requested. No matter what the application does, there always someone would like it to do more. When requests for enhancements are submitted to the vendor, some of them are implemented and returned to you in an update.
- To keep up with changes in laws and regulations that the government imposes on commerce and industries. Some industries are more likely to be hit with these burdens than others. For example, if the application you support is related to health care, finance, insurance, or SOX compliance, then you're probably familiar with changes in regulations and their impact on software applications.

10.1.1.1 Is this update really necessary?

Not to be humorous, but is this update really necessary? If you can avoid installing an update then should you? There are several questions that need to be asked before an informed decision can be made regarding whether to install an update or not. Those questions are:

1. After reading the Release Notes that accompanied the patch or the upgrade, is it obvious that the fixes or enhancements apply to you or are something you want or need? Every update addresses a specific list of problems. Those specific problems may not apply to your organization. The issues being fixed could be in modules of the application that you didn't purchase or they may be in features that you don't use. If the fixes don't help you, then you can choose not to apply them. The business owner of the application will most likely make this decision with suggestions from you.
2. Do laws or regulations require that you apply this update? If this is the case, then you need to apply the update and be done with it.
3. If this update impacts the application's security, then it should be installed. If the vendor has distributed a security patch to repair vulnerability, then bad actors know about it as well. If you don't apply all security updates, then you have no one to blame but yourself if your application gets compromised.
4. Are updates issued by the vendor cumulative? This topic is addressed in greater detail in Section 10.2.5, but briefly a cumulative update includes all the fixes that were included in prior updates. If updates are cumulative, then you don't necessarily have to install every update because when you install the next update it will include everything the current update has in it. If they aren't cumulative then it's more likely that you'll want to install every patch that is released.

If after reviewing the Release Notes, applicable laws, and the cumulative nature of the vendor's patches, you may decide to not install this update. If the application's business owners agree with this decision, then you're free until the next patch rolls down the line.

When deciding whether or not to apply an update you need to consider the vendor's position on clients staying at the latest version of the software. Some vendors take a more hardline position on this. If you're not at the current version, or very close to it, they may not provide much support until you upgrade to the latest version. Their reasoning is that the problem you're reporting may have already been fixed by upgrades that you haven't installed yet. Not all vendors are like this, but you need to know the position that your vendor takes.

10.1.2 Support software

Updates and patches don't come just from your application vendor. Any piece of software running on your servers is a potential candidate for an upgrade. As an Application Administrator, you won't be responsible for all of these updates, but you should be aware of them. Potential software that needs to be updated includes:

- The server's Operating System
- The server's BIOS (Basic Input/Output System)
- NIC cards
- Database server
- Database drivers
- DLLs (Dynamic Link Libraries) and OCXs (OLE Control eXtension)
- Report engine
- Email subsystem
- SAN software and/or hardware
- The software that supports your VM environment
- Your Domain Name Server.

How will each of these upgrades impact your application? You need to ask some probing questions about any update being made to software that supports your application. Some examples of the questions that need to be answered include the following:

- Will patching the affected software take down a server or function used by your application?

- Does your application need to be stopped while the support software is being patched?
- Will patching the support software require that the server or the application be stopped and started, aka bounced?
- How long will the update take? You should always take a time estimate a vendor provides with a very large grain of salt. Updates almost always take longer than the vendor says they will take.
- If the update has problems how will that impact your application?
- If the update has problems how long will a recovery take?
- When can the support software be patched? For example, during normal business hour? At night? During the downtime window that was negotiated with your user community?
- Has this patch been installed in other environments or servers? If so, where, when, and how did it go there?
- How long has the update been out? Is there a degree of confidence that the update is stable and won't have any adverse impact on the application? If the patch is security related, then you might have to install it as quickly as possible.

10.1.3 Hardware

Surprisingly, there might even be hardware updates that need to be applied to your environment. Typically updates to hardware are referred to as "firmware updates." The questions that need to be asked about firmware updates are the same that should be asked about support software updates, the most essential question being "how will this affect my application?"

10.1.4 User desktops

Updates will also occur on user desktops. You probably won't be responsible for upgrading their software, but changes made to user desktops might affect their ability to access or use the application that you support.

You may not see this as your problem, but it is even if you didn't cause it or weren't aware of it. If users can't access your application or it doesn't run the way it was running before an update, their initial reaction will be to blame the application. You'll have to prove to them that the application isn't at fault. This might be a very hard case to make, especially if the application was to blame in the past.

Some examples of changes that can occur on user desktops include the following:

- A new PC or laptop is issued to a user
- A new hard drive is installed in a user's computer
- Their computer crashes and their files are restored from a backup
- A new desktop operating system is installed
- Patches to the operating system are installed
- A new or upgraded Internet browser is installed
- Upgrades to Office type software, e.g., word processor, spreadsheets, etc.
- Updates to utility software like antivirus definitions

This is just another reason to have a good relationship with the organization's desktop software team. If a user reports a problem, it would be convenient and efficient to call someone on the desktop support team and ask them if any changes were made to that user's PC recently.

10.2 TYPES OF UPGRADES AND PATCHES

Upgrades and patches aren't all the same. Some introduce substantial new software to the application, while others are intended to only fix one or more bugs in the software. You'll be able to distinguish between these types of releases fairly easily based on the number associated with the release. While every vendor has its own naming standards, in general a release that has more numbers and periods equates to a lower level release.

In general, releases can be broken down into three types. A description of the naming format and what's contained in it is explained in the following sections.

10.2.1 **Types of releases**

- Major Releases, aka Update Releases, for example, 2.0, 2.1, and 3.0
- Minor Releases, aka Fix Packs, for example, 2.0.1
- Interim Fixes (sometimes called hotfixes), for example, 2.0.1.1, are created to solve specific problems experienced by customers. Interim Fixes are only distributed to other customers that experience the same specific problem. If you don't report the problem in question to the vendor, then you won't get that Interim Fix.
- Data only updates just include new data, e.g., updated tax rates.

10.2.2 **What's included in each type of release**

- Major Releases normally include significant new functionality for the application. In some releases, the fundamental structure of the application may have been rewritten. Major Releases also include all fixes from prior patches. For example, 2.1 would include all the changes that went into Minor Fix 2.0.1
- Minor Releases contain fewer changes than a Major release. One might include new functionality as well as fixes, but wouldn't contain a restructuring of the application like a Major Release might contain. A Minor Release would normally include all Interim Fixes that have been released since the last Major or Minor Release. For example, 2.0.1 would include 2.0.0.1
- Interim Fixes are created to address specific problems. They normally include all prior Interim Fixes. For example, 2.0.0.2 would include 2.0.0.1.1 and 2.0.0.1.2
- Exceptions to the above rules do occur. If a Major Release is about to be sent out and an Interim Fix needs to be created, then it might not be included in the Major release. For example, if 2.1 is about to be released and Interim Fix 2.0.1.5 is created it might not be included in 2.1.

Another term that is used is a service pack, aka an SP, a collection of changes that are delivered in a single release. Not all vendors have service packs. Referring to the above types, a service pack would roughly equate to a Minor Release.

10.2.3 **How will you know what's in a release**

Each release is typically accompanied by Release Notes document and/or an Installation Guide. The Release Notes have a description of the changes included in this patch or fix. The changes might be broken down by the vendor's ticket numbers that are assigned to customer requests when they are opened. If you keep track of the problem tickets that you've opened with the vendor, this might be a quick way to determine whether some of your reported problems have been resolved in this release.

The Installation Guide provides details on the steps needed to install the upgrade or patch on your system. The amount of work can vary significantly between a Major Release and an Interim Fix. A Major Release might require that a large number of files be downloaded, uncompressed, and moved into a specified sub-directory. An Interim Fix might be as single as moving a single file, e.g., a jar file, into place.

One of your first tasks should be to read both of these documents. The business owner also needs to read the Release Notes. They need to know what's in the release so they can make an informed decision of whether it needs to be installed or not. If the application as it's currently running doesn't exhibit any of the problems that the release addresses, then the business owner may choose not to take the time, trouble, and risk of installing it.

10.2.4 Schedule of releases

How often does your vendor issues releases of each type? This is very specific to a vendor. Some try to issue releases on a regular basis, for example, one Major Release a year and three Minor Releases throughout the year. Since Interim Releases are driven by specific problems, they're much less schedule driven.

Your vendor might not schedule their releases as described above. They might only issues patches and fixes as they are developed. You should talk to the vendor's support group to get an idea of the release schedule. While future releases might deviate from their anticipated schedule, just knowing what the schedule is expected to be like can help you better plan the time and resources that will need to be devoted to this application's patches and fixes.

10.2.5 Are updates cumulative?

It's critical to know if the vendor's patches are cumulative or not. In the world of updates cumulative is good! Why is it so critical to know this? Because if the vendor issues patches that aren't cumulative, then you're essentially forced to install every patch as it is issued. If you don't apply a patch now, then you'll have to apply it before you are able to install then next patch. If releases are cumulative, then you'll have more flexibility to pick and choose which upgrades you want to apply and when.

How can you find this out? Ask the vendor's support desk. They may not be able to answer this for every future release, but at least they can tell whether past and upcoming releases are cumulative or not.

10.2.6 Data-only updates?

Some applications have data that needs to be updated on a regular basis. For example, if the application is used to calculate sales taxes, then it needs to know sales tax rates for every state, every county, every city, every town, and every other taxing entity in the country. The tax rates in those individual entities change on a regular basis. The new tax rates need to be available before they go into effect.

How can this data be updated on a regular basis? One solution is for the company to download a "data-only" update every month. This release usually updates just tables in the database. It wouldn't modify any of the application's software.

Be forewarned that even if the update being done is a data-only update, you still need to follow the normal protocols. This means the following steps, or something like them, need to be followed:

1. Coordinate with users for a time to update the nonproduction environment, e.g., TEST or QA
2. Back up the target environment's database before the data is modified.
3. Apply the data-only update to the database.
4. Run a UAT (User Acceptance Test) in the TEST or QA environment
5. If the UAT is successful then repeat steps 1-3 for the Production environment.

10.2.7 The curse of the first release

Many administrators are extremely reluctant or even refuse to upgrade to the first release of a major upgrade. They insist on waiting until the ".1" version of it becomes available. The reason for this is that some IT professionals feel that vendors release buggy code and expect that their customers will identify the errors in it and report them. Version ".1" is put together to fix the problems that existed in the ".0" release.

One solution would be to ask yourself if you can wait until the first ".1" update gets released. Another possible solution would be to test the ".0" release extensively on your nonproduction environment.

10.3 WHO WILL BE DOING THE UPDATES?

It's pretty obvious that updates don't install themselves. Someone has to perform the updates. Who is it going to be? To a large extent, this depends on the software being updated and the organization's structure.

10.3.1 Me, Myself, and I

In most cases, you as the Application Administrator will be performing the updates. You need to become as accomplished as possible at doing them because this activity will be a fairly common one for you. If you're relatively new to the application then it's understandable that you might want a little hand-holding from the vendor's technical people the first update or two. Fairly soon though you need to be applying updates by yourself.

If the instructions for an update don't work as documented, then don't hesitate to get the vendor involved. After checking to make sure you didn't make any mistakes then open a ticket with the vendor to explain what you were doing and what went wrong. You're not helping yourself or your organization if you continue to plod ahead after something obviously has gone wrong.

10.3.2 Getting the vendor involved

There's nothing wrong with having a vendor tech work with you to handle the first update or two. After that you need to be applying updates by yourself. Some of the reasons for doing them by yourself are:

- Most people learn more from doing than from watching.
- Vendor techs might not always be available to assist you when you want to perform the updates.
- Depending on your support contract with the vendor, your organization may be charged for these sessions. If you can avoid those charges it will help the budget and your reputation.

10.3.3 Other IT professionals in your organization

Fortunately you won't be responsible for all of the changes described above by yourself. If your organization has an IT department, the workload will be distributed across many different specialists. For example:

- Operating system updates will be applied by System Administrators
- Database updates will be applied by Database Administrators
- Network software will be handled by Network Administrators
- Internet browsers and Office type software will be handled by Desktop Software Administrators
- If your organization has a Security Team, they will handle updates being made to the antivirus software and firewalls

10.4 HOW UPDATES CAN BE DISTRIBUTED

Once an update becomes available, how will the vendor distribute it to all of its clients? This varies from vendor to vendor. Some of the more common distributions methods are described below.

10.4.1 Publicizing updates and patches

The first step in distributing updates and patches is to let clients know that is available. The principal method for doing this is via e-mail. Most vendors require that all clients provide contact information for Application Administrators and/or the Business Owners. By providing them with your e-mail address they are able to send you an email as soon as they announce that an update or patch is available.

The announcement e-mail frequently has a brief description of the fixes that were included in the release. If the business owner of the application doesn't receive the same contact, then you need to inform them as soon as possible. They'll make the decision regarding whether or not they want you to load this update. The sooner you let them know about it, the sooner you'll know whether you need to start planning for it or not.

10.4.2 Distribution

There are a number of ways that a vendor can distribute the software files for updates and patches. Some of the more common ones are listed here:

- They send out a CD or DVD via surface mail. This method has significant disadvantages compared to other methods. Primarily, it costs more and is much slower than transmitting files electronically. It's my impression that this option isn't offered by many vendors any longer.
- Via their ftp site. This method is quick, convenient, and relatively secure. The vendor provides you with the URL of their ftp site, a logon ID, and a password. Using those details you connect to their ftp site and download the software to a local drive.
- Via their website. If the files to be downloaded are fairly small, then the vendor might have them available on their website. Using an Internet browser you download the files from their website to your local drive.

10.4.2.1 What exactly are you downloading

If you're downloading a large amount of software the format might be different than if you're downloading just a file or two. In some cases what you download is not a collection of separate files, but an image of a DVD. If this is the case then the file extension might be ".ISO."

If your server isn't capable of handling ISO files, then you'll have to download a utility or driver that is capable of dealing with the ISO. Some utilities that can be downloaded to handle ISO files are:

- Undisker
- Virtual CD-ROM Control Panel for Windows XP by Microsoft
- IsoBuster
- Daemon Tools Lite
- Mount ISO Files Virtually
- Virtual CloneDrive

If you've never dealt with an ISO file before there are some fundamentals that you need to be aware of. The ISO file is an image of a DVD so you can't access it the way you access a normal drive. The first step is to mount it using the utility. Figures 10.1 through 10.3 show how this is done with a utility named Virtual CloneDrive. The first step, shown in Figure 10.1, is to select the mount option of Virtual CloneDrive.

The second step is to use the browsing option to select the ISO file that will be mounted. Figure 10.2 is a screenshot showing how this is done.

Once the ISO file has been mounted with Virtual CloneDrive, then it can be accessed like any other drive. Figure 10.3 shows that the ISO file appears like a typical drive in Windows File Explorer. When you're done working with the ISO file you can dismount it by right-clicking on the drive and selecting "Virtual CloneDrive | Unmount."

10.4.3 Download precautions

One precaution that you need to take when you're downloading updates or patches is to be absolutely certain that you're getting the correct set of files. The vendor may support numerous operating systems, versions, and languages. You need to make sure that you select the correct set of release files. If you get the wrong files, then I can guarantee you that the update or patch won't be successful. There may be different selections based on:

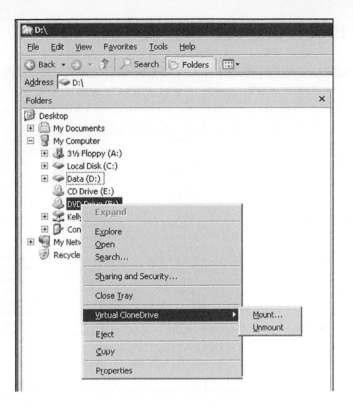

FIGURE 10.1

Mounting an ISO file using Virtual CloneDrive. (For color version of this figure, the reader is referred to the online version of this chapter.)

FIGURE 10.2

Selecting the ISO file to mount. (For color version of this figure, the reader is referred to the online version of this chapter.)

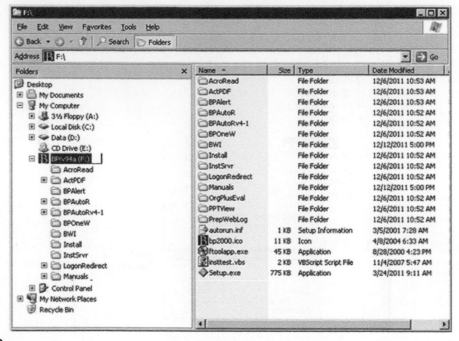

FIGURE 10.3

Accessing files within the ISO. (For color version of this figure, the reader is referred to the online version of this chapter.)

- Platform, for example PC, server, mainframe, etc.
- Operating System, for example Unix, Linux, Windows 2003, Windows 2008
- Bit size of the O/S, for example, 32 bit or 64 bit
- Language(s), for example English, French, Spanish, etc.
- File type to be downloaded, for example, zip or tar
- Download type, for example, ftp or http transfer

Another bit of advice is to download the files and move them to the destination server before you're about to start the upgrade. In many cases, the files that you'll be dealing with are quite large. Large files can take a long time to download. In addition to that, larger files seem to be more likely to have problems during the download process than smaller files. You can avoid both pitfalls by downloading the files you need and position them on the destination servers (TEST, DEV, and Production) well in advance.

This advice is especially valuable if you will be working with a vendor tech work on the updated or patch. You don't want to keep them waiting while the release files are being downloaded. There is only so much small talk you can make with them without becoming repetitive.

10.5 APPROACHING UPGRADES

You're probably going to do a lot more upgrades than installs as an Application Administrator so you need to be good at it. In general, upgrades and patches are easier to apply than installations, but you still need to have a disciplined approach if you're going to successfully apply them. The list of steps are very similar the advice for installing applications on an empty system.

10.5.1 **Read the release notes and the installation guide**

Read the Release Notes and the Installation Guide as soon as possible. They may warn you of upgrade pitfalls you want to avoid, and/or you may find you have to do a fair amount of other work (i.e., other upgrades to meet the prerequisites) before you can start installing this upgrade. Some examples of potential problems that you want to know about as early as possible include the following:

1. The new release no longer works on the operating system that your server is running.
2. The new release no longer works with the database system or version of it that you're using.
3. The new release involves significant changes to the database structure. This could impact reports, scripts, or processes you've written that access the current version of the database.
4. The new release requires more disk space, memory, or a more powerful CPU than you have.
5. The new release no longer works with the operating system that most of your users have on their desktops.
6. The new release no longer works with the web browser or version of it that most of your users have on their desktops.

Read the Release Notes and Installation Guide a second time. While reading them the second time try to answer the following questions. If you can't answer them, then you may need to contact the vendor's support team for the answers:

• Will this upgrade affect any customizations that your organization has put into place?
• Will this upgrade impact your database?
• Will this upgrade affect options like menu designs that users have set up?
• Does this upgrade change the way users access application's features? If so you should inform the users in advance rather than have them find this "problem" and report it to the Help Desk or your manager.

10.5.2 **Write up a project plan for the upgrade**

All of the reasons and justifications given for writing up a project plan for a new installation also apply to an update. Actually writing the project plan for an update is generally easier than writing one for an installation. The reason is that generally an update is less complicated, doesn't require that support software be installed, and requires the involvement of fewer people.

Project plans for updates do require some steps that weren't necessary for an installation. These additional steps are listed here and more fully explained in the following four sections:

1. Recovery steps in case the upgrade fails
2. Make a backup
3. Coordinate with the user community
4. Data Reconciliation to prove the data wasn't adversely affected

10.5.2.1 *Have a recovery plan*

If an installation process fails, the worst that you have to do is to wipe out the hard drives on the server and start the process over again from the very beginning. Since you didn't have a working system in the first place, you don't have anything to lose. The worst that can happen is that the system isn't available to the users as early as it might have been promised.

When doing an upgrade this completely flips. Now a system exists that the users are relying on. If the update fails and the system becomes unusable they won't be able to use it to perform their jobs. You will inconveniencing them, to say the least, and there most likely will be recriminations.

Having a recovery plan can help you avoid this situation. The recovery plan, if needed, is intended to get you back to a state where a working system exists. Some possible recovery plans are listed here:

- If your server is a virtual server, e.g., VMWare, then have the snapshot of it made. If the update process fails, then request that your virtual server be restored from the snapshot. Ideally, this should get you back to the exact situation where you were before the update was installed. A word of advice here—once the updated system has been tested and validated, then let the VM team know that the snapshot can be dropped. Snapshots tie up a lot of disk space and they'll want to drop it as soon as possible.
- If your environment has multiple servers, i.e., a cluster or load balancing is in place, then update them one at a time. The idea is to update one server and confirm that the application works before updating the next server. By doing this, even if an update goes badly you'll still have a workable system. You might not have all the servers operational, but at least the system will work. Having a working system should buy you some time to figure out why the update didn't succeed and correct it.
- Have the System Administrator make a clone of the server's hard drive(s). Cloning a disk involves creating an exact copy of it. If the update goes badly, then request that he or she copies the clone over the corrupted drive(s). After this is done then the system should be back to where it was when the clone was created.
- Back up everything! If you know exactly where the application software has been loaded you should be able to copy it to a safe location. If the update goes badly then you'll restore the original files and subdirectories using the copied versions. The downside to this recover plan is that it assumes you know exactly where every file that the application uses is located. If there are a few files tucked away in an unexpected or unknown subdirectory that get corrupted then this recovery plan may not work.

10.5.2.2 Make a backup
Always do a full backup before installing any upgrades, this includes the database and the source code. Most updated instructions provided by vendors recommend that this be done, but in case it's not specified do it anyway! I guarantee you that at some point in your career as an Application Administrator you'll need the backup.

Make sure that users are out of the system before you begin the backup process and that they are kept out of the system until the upgrade process is completed. Two reasons for making sure of this are:

- Some backup processes won't work if files they're trying to back up are locked by a user
- You don't want a user to make changes after the backup has been taken. Then if the update fails and you revert to a backup file the user's changes won't be there.

10.5.2.3 Coordinate with the user community
When you're doing an initial installation, the user community isn't using the application because it doesn't exist yet. But if you're doing an update then the application probably has users that are using the system. They might be relying on it to get their work done on a daily basis. If you take down the system without telling them or coordinating it with them then you're not going to be a popular fellow.

You'll want to work with the user community to find a time when the update can be done that works for both of you. You won't be asking every individual user of the application. You'll be dealing with the application Business Owner to coordinate this maintenance window. Then he or she will inform the other users about the upcoming outage.

To a significant degree, the work requirements calendar of the user community will dictate when you can install upgrades. For example, if the application deals with taxes, you won't want to do any upgrades immediately prior to the end of the tax year. If you're supporting the payroll application, then you won't want to be making changes just before paychecks are cut. If you don't know the "busy" times for your application, then you need to find this out ASAP.

Is there a formal process for requesting an outage? Is there a form to fill out or a web page to complete? If no such process exists, then you might want to put a process into place. It will save you the time and trouble of asking multiple people when you should schedule an outage.

When are the preferred days and times for making changes? Some organizations prefer the middle of the week, while others prefer Friday afternoon or evening. The rational for Friday is that if something goes wrong then you have the entire weekend to restore the application before users are back in the office. The rationale for the middle of the week is that everyone you might need to contact for help resolving the problem is more likely to be in the office. I hate to be the one to break this to you, but if your organization prefers that updates be performed outside of regular business hours, then expect to spend at least some nonbusiness hours logged into the system.

Several tips for dealing with coordinating outages:

- Upgrades can take from minutes to hours. When you tell the users how long the update will take be sure to be conservative. For example suppose that if everything goes perfectly you can apply the update in an hour, but if problems occur then you know it will take 2 hours. You'll want to tell the users it will take you either 2 hours or between 1 and 2 hours. Don't tell them the time window for the best case scenario, because that doesn't always occur.
- Do whatever you can to lock users out of the application while the update is being put into place. In some cases having a user in the application could cause problems or at least delay the process while you kick him or her out.
- What if the appointed time for the update arrives and one or more users haven't logged off as agreed? Do you have the authority to kill those sessions? Or do you have to coordinate this with a user representative? Get an agreement on this when you coordinate the update.
- Be sure you know who to contact when the update is complete and the application is ready to be tested. You'll want to have that person begin testing immediately so the application can be validated and released to the users as quickly as possible.

10.5.2.4 *Data reconciliation*

Data reconciliation is a process of proving to the users and perhaps more importantly to the auditors that the application's data hasn't been unexpectedly or adversely affected by the update process. In the simplest situation, the update won't touch the data. In more complete updates, the data might be affected in the following ways:

- Tables are created in the database
- Columns are added to existing tables
- Rows are inserted to existing tables
- Existing database values are modified

How can you prove that not a single value was unexpectedly added, deleted, or modified during an update? Short of doing a row by row, column by column comparison it isn't possible to prove that nothing was unexpectedly changed. However, there are still steps you can take to review the database to help ensure changes to the database were consistent with the release notes. This will require that you work closely with the DBAs and then end users.

What you need to keep in mind isn't that the reconciliation plan is perfect, but that it's consistent with the organization's previous practices and provides a comfort level for users and auditors. Some possible reconciliation plans are suggested here:

- If the Release Notes state that rows will be added to the currency table to reflect the change in the unit of currency in East Nowhereville, then you could run before and after queries showing the original values and new values. The number of rows affected in this example should be minimal, possible a single row, so queries to select and display them are realistic. If the number of rows affected was in the thousands, then this reconciliation plan wouldn't as acceptable.

- If the Release Notes state that no data is being affected by this update, then you could select all table names and the number of rows in each table. Run this query before and after the update is applied and dump this information into separate spreadsheets. Including formulas in the spreadsheet to count the number tables and sum up the row counts should show that no tables or rows were added or dropped.
- If the Release Notes indicate that a column will be added to a specific table, then your Reconciliation Plan could be to export the table before and after the update. If the exported values were ordered in both cases, then you could use spreadsheet functions to compare or at least spot check the two sets of data and confirm that massive amounts of table data haven't been lost or modified.

10.5.3 Practice makes perfect

Plan to apply the upgrade to your environments in an ascending priority order. Updates will always be applied to the Production server last. For example, it might be applied to environments in this order:

- Development
- Test
- Staging or QA (quality assurance)
- Production

If the update process and testing aren't successful at a given level, then you don't advance to the next level until it is successful. For example, if applying the update on the Development server doesn't go as documented then you restore the Development server to its original configuration, figure out what went wrong and apply the update a second time.

Allow yourself plenty of time to perform upgrades. It's typical for an update to take longer than you expect, especially the first time through. Once you've done it a time or two it will go much more quickly.

Keep meticulous records of what changes you've made to each server. Personally, I create a Word document for each update on each server. I take a screenshot of every screen that I encounter and paste them into my document. I also make notes of each value I had to enter and each button I click. It's time consuming, but I really only have to create this document the first time, i.e., when I update the DEV server. When I perform the update for the second server, e.g., QA, the document is pretty much complete. Normally the only changes I have to make are minor additions or to correct typos. Having such a document on hand makes applying the update to Production much faster and much less stressful.

10.5.4 Applying the patch

In my experience, most patch application processes fall into two types: manual or wizard-based patches. The following sections describe each of them in more detail.

10.5.4.1 Manual patches

If the patch process is manual, then the Installation Guide consists of a list of fairly detailed instructions that you need to follow. These instructions might be fairly similar to the following:

1. Ensure the database and application folder have been backed up
2. Stop the Acme Application services
3. Create a new folder in \Acme\software\servers and name it with the new version, e.g., 1.2.3
4. Copy the patch zip install file from the vendor's release package to the folder just created
5. Unzip the patch file in the folder just created
6. Delete the zipped patch file
7. Delete all folders and files in folder \Acme\software\servers\current

8. Copy all folders and files from \Acme\software\servers\1.2.3 to \Acme\software\servers\current
9. Start the Acme Application services
10. When the application startup is completed, open the log file and confirm that the version specified in the most recent startup entry has the correct version number, e.g., 1.2.3

Obviously, the instructions here are fairly generic and very simplistic. An actual update would have additional steps, but the above are reasonably representative of an actual application update. The steps you'll be required to perform aren't particularly difficult, but they have to be performed exactly in the prescribed order!

If a given step doesn't succeed, then you must figure out how to correct it before advancing to the next step. Hoping that a problem will go away isn't going to work. Trust me on this. I've done it and it never works. If you can't figure out what you did wrong, then immediately stop and contact the vendor's Support Desk for assistance.

10.5.4.2 Wizards or other executable processes

If the vendor has provided a wizard or other executable process to perform the upgrade, then what you end up doing is to kick it off, answer some questions, and watch the progress meter work its way across your screen.

Screens that are typically displayed to you include the following:

1. An initial welcome screen.
2. A warning screen that warns you that the application will be stopped if the upgrade is initiated.
3. A screen that requires you to accept the terms of the software license agreement.
4. A screen that confirms the name of the organization.
5. A setup type screen that allows you to choose between a typical upgrade and a custom upgrade. The complete install is easier to do, but installs all components and takes more disk space. Select a custom upgrade if you want control where the software is installed or if you don't want all components to be installed.
6. A login screen where you enter the administrative account's ID and password.
7. A screen with a progress meter that shows you the upgrade is actually being done.
8. A screen telling you the update is complete. This screen might offer to launch the application.

One thing that should be done after either a manual patch process or a wizard-based process is to check any log files created by the patch process. This is important because it's easy to miss messages that are displayed on the screen. Sometimes they are scrolled off the screen faster than you're able to read or comprehend them. Be sure that you know where the vendor writes logs to and check that once the patch is complete.

10.6 MAINTENANCE WEEKENDS, AKA PATCH WEEKENDS

Like it or not, patches are released on a regular basis by major vendors. Keeping up with this unending flood of patches will keep your organization extremely busy. Microsoft releases security patches on the second Tuesday of every month. Adobe is another software vendor that also releases their security updates, aka patches, on the second Tuesday of the month. Schedules that other vendors release patches vary widely. One releases them every 6 months. Another vendor releases patches six times a year.

Many organizations pick a specific day of the month to apply these patches on their production systems. One organization I worked for applied them the third Saturday of every month. This gave them a week and a half after receiving patches from most vendors to install them on test systems and perform a minimal level of testing to confirm that the patches didn't corrupt the operating systems, hard drives, etc.

When the third Saturday of the month arrived all of the Application Administrators knew that the Data Center staff would be taking down servers as needed to apply the patches. It was up to the Application Administrators to do the following for each of their applications:

- Inform the Business Owner that the application will be down on the Saturday
- When the patch process completed confirm that the application came back up
- Inform the business owners that the application is up and can be tested.

More detailed validity testing was the responsibility of the application business owner. For the vast majority of months, the patch process went very smoothly. In only a very small minority of cases did the monthly patches cause problems with the operating system, support software, or the application itself.

10.7 AUTOMATIC UPDATES

Does the application automatically download updates to your server? I've supported one application that checks the vendor's website for updates every time someone logs into it. This approach to distributing updates has advantages and disadvantages.

Automatic updates have the following advantages:

- Patches are applied very frequently. Since they are applied frequently they tend to be smaller and simpler. To me, a simple patch is a good patch. The more complicated they are, the more likely it is that something will go wrong.
- There is significantly less lag time between when a patch is released and when it's installed on your system. This minimizes opportunities for bad actors to take advantage of an unpatched system.
- If patches are applied automatically then you won't get behind on them.

The disadvantages of this approach are:

- Patches are unannounced. You don't get the opportunity to review and decide whether they are needed on your environment or not if they are applied automatically.
- Since patches are unannounced you can't make a backup before the update is downloaded and installed.
- You don't get a chance to test them on the DEV or QA system before they are installed on PROD. Whichever environment is logged into first will get the patch loaded onto it.
- You aren't prompted to approve loading of the patch. If you have the automatic mode turned on, then any patches available will be downloaded when someone logs into the application. The Application Administrator may not even be aware that an update has been installed. Being taken out of the loop could be inconvenient especially if the patch ends up causing problems.
- Patches can be installed at a very inconvenient time. For example, in the middle of cutting payroll checks or closing year-end books. If the patch doesn't work, this can become incredibly inconvenient to say the least.

If your application vendor offers automatic updates and you need to fully understand it before taking advantage of it. The following list of questions is just a start of what you should ask the vendor:

- Can automatic updates be turned on and off for certain times in the business calendar? For example, leading up to paychecks being cut, the accounting books being closed or taxes being filed, etc.
- Are all levels of updates, i.e., major, minor and interim, distributed via automatic updates? Or are the more significant updates distributed another way?
- Are the updates logged anywhere? If so where and what level of detail is logged?
- Is documentation on each update available?
- Can these updates be backed out?

10.8 TESTING SOFTWARE UPDATES

It's an unfortunate fact of life that people make mistakes. Despite their best efforts, vendors occasionally introduce errors into their application when they distribute updates, patches, and new versions of the application. You need to be aware of this in order to protect your organization from these potential problems.

Some of the testing-related decisions that you'll have to make include the following:

- How much testing is done after an upgrade? Usually more testing is better than less.
- Who does it? It is important to have user representatives test the majority of the application's functionality, they are the ones most familiar with the application, what it should be doing and how it works. The Application Administrator should test functions that only he or she uses.
- When is it done? As soon as possible for at least two reasons. First, if a problem has been introduced into the application, you want to know about it as soon as possible. Second, the sooner your DEV and QA environments are tested, the sooner the patch can be applied to the next higher level, ultimately to Production.
- Who approves the results? The ultimate approver has to be the business owner of the application.
- How do you document the tests and the results? Creating a spreadsheet with a description of each test, the expected results, the observed results and a pass/fail value is an efficient way of documenting the tests and results.

Vendor mistakes can take at least two forms. Your testing needs to address both types of errors that might be introduced:

- The intended fix or enhancement doesn't work as expected.
- The update breaks something else in the application that was previously working.

Your best defense against introducing these mistakes on your production system is to install all new software on a nonproduction environment and thoroughly test it before installing it on your production environment. Your testing needs to address both types of errors that can be introduced. The first type of testing is called UAT—User Acceptance Testing. The second form of testing is called regression testing.

10.8.1 UAT—user acceptance testing

First you have to test that the changes do what they are intended to do. The release notes that accompany the update will list what parts of the application are being changed. The UAT should test each area being changed.

10.8.2 Regression testing

The second type of testing that needs to be done is to confirm that the changes haven't introduced errors into the application. This type of testing, called regression testing, is by far the more difficult and time consuming of the two. Ideally, a regression test should confirm that every screen, every path, every data entry opportunity, every report, etc. gets tested. For a large, complex application this isn't practical. You'll have to balance realism with idealism to create your regression test.

One area that regression testing absolutely needs to cover is any custom changes that have been made to the application. Vendor updates have been known to overwrite or delete enhancements or customizations put into place by clients. The testing that is performed after every update must verify that your customizations are still there. This needs to be done after the first upgrade, i.e., the upgrade to your DEV, TEST, or QA environment. Don't wait until the production environment has been updated to do this testing. If testing isn't done early and thoroughly, then you might be in for a very nasty surprise when functionality that used to exist has disappeared.

Supporting Your Application

11.1 WHAT IS A SUPPORT ROLE?

The purpose of an application support role, including an Application Administrator, is to provide the day-to-day responsibility for an application once it has been put into production. If something goes wrong with the application, then the support personnel investigate it and correct it. If the application needs to be updated, then the support personnel perform the update. Ideally, the only group that would touch the application would be the application support team.

If the application is being created specifically for this organization, then the Application Administrator may participate in the review of the design specifications. This would be true whether the application is being developed internally or externally.

Installation of the application is also an area that the support team would take a leading role. Whether the application is custom developed or off the shelf, the support team will be involved. One of the more significant reasons for this is that it is an opportunity for the support team to become extremely familiar with the application by getting a great deal of hands-on experience.

A support role is significantly different than a software development position. A simple way of explaining this difference is that developers build the application and the support team makes sure it continues to work after it has been delivered and installed. If something goes wrong with the application, the support team will work with developers to gather information on the problem, but the development group will be the ones that actually write or modify the code to correct the problem. The support team will then move the changes into the QA and Production environments and test it to confirm that the fix resolves the problem.

If you came from a development background, you might have to curb your natural instincts to make changes. Initially, you may think that a support role isn't as fulfilling or rewarding as a development one, but you'll soon get over that misconception. Both jobs are needed to ensure that business users continue to have software that enables them to be productive and efficient.

11.2 SLA (SERVICE-LEVEL AGREEMENT)

An SLA is an agreement between the support group and user team that describes what the users can expect from the application. The following are examples of what might be in an SLA:

- When the application will be down for maintenance. Many applications have weekly or monthly windows during which maintenance or backups are done. Some applications can't tolerate any scheduled downtime at all. If this is the situation for your application that's fine, but everyone needs to understand it and agree to it in advance.
- The days and hours that the support team will be available, for example, Monday to Friday, 8 am to 5 pm, Central.
- If extended support hours exist during high usage calendar periods, for example, during tax season, those hours would be specified.

- Holidays during which no support is provided.
- How quickly the support team will respond when a ticket is opened. For example, if a high-priority ticket is opened, the support team will begin working on it within 30 minutes if the ticket was opened during regular business hours. For low-priority tickets, the requirement might be that the ticket is addressed within 8 business hours.
- How quickly the application will be back up after a problem occurs.
- How often backups are created and how long they will be retained.
- The maximum time it will take to restore from a database backup if that becomes necessary.
- The maximum amount of unplanned downtime that will occur, for example, the application will be up 99% of the time excepting planned maintenance times.
- Contact information for communicating with the support team during and outside of normal business hours.
- Response time of the application will not exceed a specified threshold.
- The process by which user requests for software modifications are submitted would be outlined.
- The process by which software is updated on the application servers will adhere to the change management procedures specified in the SLA.
- The process by which the support team and the user group will review software upgrades received from the vendor to determine which will be installed and when.
- Any monitoring metrics that have been agreed to. For example, the server CPU% idle time, the disk I/O time, etc.

Including response time metrics in the SLA makes it difficult to measure and to enforce. This is because there are many components that are outside the control of the application support team. The organization's local area network (LAN) is outside the control of the application support team. If the network slows down dramatically or completely shuts down, then the application will almost certainly not meet the response time metrics. While the application support team will certainly work with the network group, they have no control over the network or the team that supports it.

Each organization will have SLA provisions that are unique to their needs. For example, if the application is being used 24 × 7, then the support availability can't be limited to 9 am to 5 pm. If the user base is worldwide, then the support team may need to have personnel who are fluent in multiple languages. Exactly how many languages support will be provided in should be defined in the SLA.

It isn't very likely that the first version of the SLA will be perfect. Situations will come up that weren't covered in the SLA that need to included. The process of how the SLA can be amended must be defined. If this isn't covered, then amending the SLA will be an ongoing battle.

Where is the official version of the SLA stored? Will it be stored online? Or will the official copy be a hard copy of the document?

11.2.1 SLA metrics must be achievable

The metrics or requirements in an SLA have to be achievable. The requirement that the application be available 99.9999% of the time can't be dictated without considering the infrastructure that is needed to achieve it. For example:

- The servers would almost certainly have to be in a cluster. A single server can't realistically meet such a high uptime requirement.
- The database and/or application have to be able to create backups without taking the system down. If the system has to come down to make backups, then the availability requirement won't be met.
- All hardware beyond the servers will have to be redundant. For example, the disk drives will have to be in a RAID array, NIC cards must have backups, power supplies must have backups, communications connection must be redundant.

- Personnel, e.g., the Application Administrator, all must have full-time, dedicated backups.
- A support contract with the vendor that specifies 24 × 7 coverage.

11.2.2 Stringent SLA requirements impose a cost

An extremely high uptime requirement or extremely quick response times impose financial costs. If the business owner of the application wants very high SLA metrics, then they have to be willing to pay for them. Some examples of these costs include:

- Costs of redundant hardware
- A support contract with the vendor that specifies 24 × 7 availability
- Additional personnel costs for a full-time backup Application Administrator
- High-availability software like the operating systems and database engine
- A QA environment that mirrors the Production environment

11.3 SUPPORT STAFF

How many people support this application? The phrase Full-Time Employee (FTE) is sometimes used to describe the number of support personnel. If your application has fewer than two people assigned to it, then you might want to rethink your staffing. It isn't realistic for a single person to support an application that is operational 24 × 7. Even an application that only needs support during normal business hours, i.e., 9 to 5, is difficult for a single individual to provide the needed level of support. People take vacation time, they get sick, they have family emergencies, attend training, are traveling, and they need to sleep occasionally.

11.3.1 Priorities

Is supporting this application a full-time or a part-time responsibility for members of the support staff? Is it their highest priority or do they have other applications to support that are more critical? If they aren't full-time or this application isn't their highest priority, then you can be certain that at some point in time they won't be available when the application is down. There will come a time when both applications that they are supporting will need their immediate and complete focus. When that happens, one of the applications is going to be down longer than anticipated. It's best if everyone knows up front which of the applications has the highest priority. Is everyone in agreement on where each application is on the priority list?

11.3.2 Supervisors

Who is in charge of the support staff? To be more specific, is the supervisor in the business chain of command or in the IT (Information Technology) chain of command? This is important because the answer will probably color their view of how things are done. Someone with a strong background in IT is more likely to follow software industry practices.

11.3.3 Communicating with the support staff

How is the support staff contacted during nonbusiness hours? Do they have iPhones, Blackberries, a department smartphone, etc., that is carried at all times? These days virtually everyone has a smart phone so that's usually not a problem. The problem is making sure that all of these numbers are published so the staff can be reached when needed. Does the staff know what's expected of them when they are contact after-hours? Is there a rotating schedule of "on-call" engineers so that one person isn't overburdened with 3 am phone calls?

If there is an "on-call phone" or pager, then the staff simply needs to hand it off from the outgoing on-call person to the oncoming support person. I can remember very fondly getting rid of the department pager knowing that I was more likely to have several days or weeks of uninterrupted sleep.

If everyone has his/her own phone, then the on-call schedule needs to be posted in a place that everyone knows about and has access to. Perhaps post these numbers on a department website, portal, or with the Help Desk staff.

If things don't go as planned, then you'll end up with problems like the ones listed here. It's better to have questions like these answered in advance. No one wants to be trying to figure things out at 3:00 in the morning.

- What if the on-call support person doesn't answer their phone, respond to text messages or e-mails? How many times should they be called?
- How long should the caller wait before escalating to a more senior person?
- Who is the next person on the list that should be called?
- What are the best contact numbers for everyone on the lists?

A very important issue to the support staff is that everyone understands when they are to be called. Most support staff members understand that they'll get calls during off-hours. They realize that this is part of their job description. What they are much less understanding of is getting calls from application users who haven't bothered to follow the normal policy for contacting support staff. For example, if I'm not on call this week and the user hasn't bothered checking to see which admin is on call, then I'm not going to appreciate getting a call at 2 am no matter how important the problem is. Another example is that if password reset requests are supposed to be called into the Support Desk, which is manned 24×7, but instead a user calls an admin at 4 am. Such a call isn't going to be well received.

11.3.4 Communicating with the user community

A well-defined chain of communications with the user community needs to be defined. The Application Administrator needs to work with users on a regular basis so it's best if they know who they should be talking to. Some examples of situations that should be clarified include:

- If problems are experienced with the application who should be notified?
- During normal working hours who can approve taking the application down?
- During off-hours who can approve taking the application down?
- If those people aren't available or aren't responding who is their backup?
- Who needs to be notified when the application is back up?
- Who can authorize reverting to a backup?
- Who can authorize activating the DR (Disaster Recovery) site?

11.4 ODD HOURS

One thing that you need to know in advance is that a production support role as an Application Administrator isn't a "9 to 5" kind of job. There will be times when everything is going smoothly and you'll be able to leave whenever you want. But there will also be times when you'll be in the office much earlier or later than usual. Some examples of the reasons why you'll be working odd hours could include the following:

- To interact with users in other time zones. You'll be working with users who are in another part of the country or possibly on the other side of the world. There will be times when you have to come in early or stay late to accommodate their work schedules.

- To make changes in the system at a time when users aren't in the application. If the users of your application are limited to a single time zone or country, then there may be a time window everyday when you can take the system down and make changes without impacting users. If your application is multinational or worldwide, then you may only be able to take the system down during the maintenance window that was defined in the Service-Level Agreement (SLA).
- To monitor or change processes that run at off-hours. Many applications have processes that run at nonpeak hours to avoid impacting performance for the majority of users. Examples of these processes are lengthy reports, data dumps, data imports, database integrity checks, and backups. If processes like these need to be modified, tested, or debugged, then most likely this support activity will also be done during off-hours to avoid impacting the users.
- If the application crashed and needs to be brought up immediately, then you'll probably be getting a call, text, or e-mail. If the application isn't critical in nature and bringing it back up can wait until the beginning of the next business day, then this won't apply to you.
- To test the application after the server's operating system or support software has been updated or patched. Your data center group will dictate when patches get applied to all of the servers in the data center. For most applications that means that the application needs to come down so the server can be patched. Once the server is patched and restarted, then the application can be restarted. The application support team will need to verify that both the server and application successfully came back up. More detailed testing of the application would be the responsibility of the user team.
- Because you're making a change that requires the application be put into "single-user mode." Many applications have certain tasks that can only be performed when there is a single user logged into it. To accommodate needs like this, the application can be put into "administrative mode" or "single-user mode." If this is done during normal business hours, then all other users will be prevented from using the system. To avoid this, disruption changes that require single-user mode are typically done during off-hours.
- Because you need to run a process that will impact application performance. For example, a utility that performs batch inserts might be significantly faster than manually adding every row to the application, but the downside is that it slows the system down to a crawl. A process of this nature needs to be executed during off-hours.
- Because the task you're working on didn't get finished at 5 pm. There will be times that something you're working on needs to be finished ASAP. This means instead of knocking off for the day you keep plugging away until the job is complete.
- To interact with vendor support technicians. To a large degree you are at the mercy of these technicians' availability. When they become available to work your problem, then you make sure you're available too. These individuals could well be in another country so you may have to bend your hours to work with them. One application I supported had its primary support center in the United Kingdom. There was a problem that absolutely needed to be fixed. The tech was available on the fourth Thursday in November. To an American this particular day is known as Thanksgiving. To a citizen of the United Kingdom it's known as Thursday. I was in the office at 6 am on Thanksgiving morning to work with him to resolve the problem.

11.5 **MAINTENANCE WINDOWS**

Most applications have a time every week or month that can be used to take the system down for backups, install updates, run tests that require a dedicated server, reboot servers, etc. It may not be used for this purpose every month, but if the system is taken down then the users can't complain that they weren't aware of the possibility that it might come down.

Do you have a regular, defined maintenance window, i.e. a time when the user community knows the system will be unavailable? Is this window long enough to realistically get things done in? For example, if the system is down every night from 7 pm until 8 pm for backups but the backup process takes two hours, then your maintenance window isn't realistic.

Are users locked out of the application during this maintenance window? Or are they allowed to use it at their own risk, i.e., use it knowing that the system might come down while they are in it. If this is the case, then you had better make sure it's regularly publicized to them that the system could go down during this window. If they have been using it without being disturbed for weeks or months and suddenly they get booted off the system without warning, they aren't likely to remember that this time slot didn't belong to them in the first place.

How do you handle situations where users are logged into the application during the maintenance window? If an Application Administrator needs to take the system down, can he or she do it without notifying the user? Or does the user need to be contacted and warned? What if the user isn't really logged in? Perhaps he or she exited the application without properly logging out and now the application has a "orphan" session that isn't really active?

Does the application have to come down for a backup to be performed? If not, does the system performance from the user's perspective drop noticeably? Is this something that the users are willing to tolerate?

What happens when there is a business need for the application during the regularly scheduled maintenance window? For example, if the account department is working through the weekend to close the books, they would need the maintenance window canceled to ensure that their work isn't interrupted. Is there a process for cancelling a maintenance window so it doesn't interfere with critical work?

11.6 SUPPORTING A 24 × 7 OPERATION

Some business applications absolutely have to be operational 24 hours a day, 7 days a week. Think about the order entry system for a major website. Or a search engine. Or a metropolitan utility that customers log onto to report natural gas leakages or power outages.

How is supporting applications that can never go down different from more mundane applications like your organization's training website? I don't think it would be an exaggeration to say that supporting a 24 × 7 operation is geometrically more difficult than a "9 to 5" application. Some of the complications that arise when supporting a 24 × 7 application include the following:

- Creating backups without stopping the application. The answer to this predicament would typically come from the software vendor or the database vendor. The application has to have been designed to allow backups be made "on the fly."
- Installing updates without stopping the application. If a fix or update requires that the application be stopped and started, but that isn't acceptable from a business perspective, then life is going to be complicated. One way of resolving this is if the application is running on a cluster or multiple clusters. If this is the case, then one server can be taken out of the cluster, updated, and brought back up. If testing shows that the fix worked, then those steps would be repeated on the other servers in the cluster until all of them have been updated.
- Is the support staff adequately sized to provide 24 × 7 support for an extended period time? For the short run, a small team can handle round the clock support. But for an extended period of time, a small team will become exhausted, burned out, and error prone. The size of the support team needs to be increased if support needs to be nonstop.
- Does the support team have a formal handoff process for an ongoing problem as one shift goes off duty and another individual or group comes on? If a critical problem gets dropped in the cracks when one team leaves for the day and another takes over there will be some extremely hostile users. This problem would be more likely to occur if the shift teams aren't physically in the same location.

- Some software has errors in which memory is allocated for temporary usage, but doesn't get released to the system when it is no longer needed. This is typically called a "memory leak." If an application has this problem, a typical work-around is to stop and start the application periodically, say once a week. When the application is stopped, then all memory that was allocated to it is automatically released back to the system. If the application has to be up 24 × 7, then this method of resolving memory leaks won't be available to you.

11.7 SUPPORT TIERS

Organizations that have a Support Desk frequently categorize their support groups in escalating levels. The idea is to assign problems to the group that can most cost effectively resolve it. Many organizations define three tiers of support. If your organization doesn't have a program of support tiers in place, then this section doesn't apply to you.

11.7.1 Tier 1

Typically, when a software user calls for technical assistance, a Tier 1 technician gathers and records basic information from the caller. The tech then would attempt to resolve the problem by seeing if it falls into a list of problems that are commonly experienced by users. Problems that are more complex would be passed onto a level 2 technician.

Typical questions or problems that the Tier 1 staff can handle are:

- Register new users
- Unlock accounts that have become locked out
- Reset passwords
- Delete or disable user accounts
- Recognize error messages indicating that a web-based application is down
- Work with the user to confirm that the correct URL, logon ID, and password are being used

Turnover in the Help Desk can be high so you can't necessarily count on staff continuity. To maintain their effectiveness, Help Desk personnel either need to be well trained or need to have very effective resources available to them. An example of effective resources would be providing a document or web page that lists each problem that Tier 1 technicians are expected to encounter and handle. This information, sometimes called a "playbook" would include the following:

- Symptoms of the problem that users have experienced
- The steps that should be taken to correct the problem
- What to do if the steps listed above don't correct the user's problem
- Who should be called if the problem turns out to be more significant than expected

If the Tier 1 technician isn't able to resolve the problem, then it needs to be escalated to Tier 2 support. There needs to be straightforward instructions on how this is accomplished. It's very important that an open ticket not be dropped during this transition.

If your organization has a multitier support structure in place, who provides Tier 1 support? Do they have the information described above that can make them more effective?

11.7.2 Tier 2

Tier 2 personnel have more experience and training than Tier 1 personnel on the application. Relying on their additional expertise, they will be able to handle problems that are more complicated and less common.

When a problem is passed from Tier 1 to Tier 2 personnel, it's imperative that all of the details already gathered on the problem are provided. If this isn't done, then time may be lost repeating basic questions or investigations. If all information related to the ticket is entered into an online system, then the Tier 2 technician can access it at any time.

Some questions that might apply to your organization regarding Tier 2 support are listed here:

- Does your organization have Tier 2 assistance for this application?
- How much additional experience or training do your Tier 2 personnel have?
- Is the handoff process between Tier and 1 and Tier 2 personnel well established?
- Does a process exist by which Tier 2 staff have access to all information already gathered on a ticket as well as steps to resolve it that have already been attempted?

11.7.3 **Tier 3**

Tier 3 support personnel are responsible for handling the most difficult or advanced problems that users have with the application. These individuals have the most experience with the application. If they aren't able to resolve the issue themselves, then they will contact the vendor support team for additional assistance as needed.

As with Tier 2 technicians, when a problem is escalated to Tier 3, then the technician needs to be able to see a record of the problem. It's a waste of everyone's time if he repeats things that have already been tried by a Tier 1 or 2 staff member.

11.7.4 **Topics that affect all tiers**

Certain topics need to be described that affect all tier layers. These have been collected in the following sections.

11.7.4.1 *Knowledge base*

Supporting an application is never static. New problems will be encountered and existing ones will become less of an issue. It would make the support team more efficient if everyone became aware of new problems and the tried-and-true solutions to existing ones. How can Support Team personnel learn these new or different details? If every case coming into the team is documented, then this information can be organized into a knowledge base. Team members, especially Tier 1 and 2, can tap into this knowledge base to resolve problems that previously were only solvable by someone with more experience. The key to a valuable knowledge base is to capture every detail on every problem. If a problem in the system is described but no details on how it was solved have been recorded, then the record doesn't help anyone.

Another valuable use of a knowledge base is the possibility of extracting trend information out of it. If a certain problem has never been encountered before, but now is occurring frequently this is a trend. Using the knowledge base, it's possible to recognize trends and resolve these problems more quickly. For example, the problem might have been caused because users have upgraded their browsers. The knowledge base can provide statistics like when the first instance occurred and what browser they user had installed. Without a breadth of information, something like this might not be noticed as quickly.

11.7.4.2 *Response time*

What are the expectations of response time at each level? I'm not a big believer that response times can be predicted or commanded to an exacting degree. The difficulty is that every problem is different. What might appear to be a very simple problem can turn out to be extremely complicated. If your support staff is professional and experienced, then I believe you have to trust them to put their best efforts into solving problems as quickly as possible. If this isn't done, then time may be lost on low-priority tickets or unproductive investigations. If all information related to the ticket is entered into an online system, then the Tier 2 staff member can access it at any time.

11.7.4.3 Escalating a ticket

How do you know when a problem ticket needs to escalated from one tier to another? It's hard to put an exact time limit on this, but when a staff member hits a wall they should be able to recognize it. If they've tried everything in the knowledge base and their own personal list of tricks and aren't making any progress, then it needs to be escalated. For a Tier 1 staff member to continue trying to fix a problem by repeating solutions over and over isn't an efficient practice. Once he's tried everything that he's familiar with, it's time to push the ticket up to the next level.

Who is authorized to make the decision to escalate a ticket? I think three parties should have this authority.

1. The current support team member working on the ticket. He or she should be able to recognize when they've hit their expertise limit. If a particular member can't seem to recognize this, then his or her manager should address this as part of their personal development.
2. The Support Team supervisor definitely has the authority to escalate a ticket. The supervisor should know the team well enough to recognize when someone isn't making progress. Once that point is reached, then time and money are being wasted and the problem needs a fresh set of eyes to look at it.
3. The requester should be able to at least request that a ticket be escalated. If there hasn't been progress within a reasonable amount of time, then the request is justified in asking that the ticket be escalated. The more critical the issue, then shorter this time period would be.

11.7.4.4 Handing off a ticket

How are details captured at one tier passed along to the next tier level? A tool needs to be in place that allows the support group to gather details when a ticket is opened. Frequently, this tool is called a trouble ticket system. As each change is made to resolve this ticket, those details are captured. If a ticket is reassigned to a new support team, then an e-mail would be sent out to the new assignee alerting them of their new responsibility.

The tool to support your support staff can be developed internally or purchased from a software vendor. There are a number of readily available tools that support this need. Some examples are:

- Remedy from BMC
- iSupport Service Desk
- IncidentMonitor
- Hesk Help Desk Software
- Help Desk Software from BrightBox Solutions

11.7.5 No tiers

What if you're the only one person or one of a small number in the support team? Realistically, if the team supporting the application is limited to two or three people, then you'll be handling a significant percentage of the problems yourself. Incoming requests can be divided either by area of expertise or whoever currently has the lightest load.

If your support team is just yourself and maybe another person or two, it will be extremely important to make sure you're well organized. Since a small team can only work on a limited number of tickets at the same time, assigning a priority to each request becomes extremely important. You can't squander your limited resources working on a low-priority problem when ones of greater importance are waiting to be dealt with.

11.8 REMOTELY ACCESSING YOUR SERVERS

If you're working as an Application Administrator, you will by definition be working remotely. The servers you work on may be in another room, another building, another city, or another country, but you won't be sitting in from of them. You need to be aware of tools that will allow you to easily and efficiently connect remotely to your servers and do what needs to be done on them.

Three tools that you can use to remotely access your servers are described here. Which particular tool you choose will be driven partly by the operating systems on your servers and partly by your personal preference.

11.8.1 RDC—Remote Desktop Connection

If your desktop computer is Windows based, then you may at least consider using Remote Desktop Connection (RDC) to connect to remote servers if for no other reason than it's already loaded onto your desktop and it's free.

Figure 11.1 shows the login screen for RDC. To remotely connect to another server, you need to enter the server name that you are connecting to. As the screen states, you will be required to enter your ID and password to complete the connection.

It might be easily overlooked, but to remotely connect to another server you have to have a valid account on it. If your account doesn't already exist on the server, then you'll have to request that a System Administrator create it for you.

After successfully logging to a server, you're essentially controlling the desktop. The screen that you'll see is shown in Figure 11.2. From this desktop you can do about anything you could do if you were sitting at its console and keyboard. If you click the Start button, you have the option of opening a Command Window. If you right-click the start button, you can bring up the Windows Explorer, aka File Explorer.

After you complete your tasks on the remote server, then you'll need to log off. While this task may seem simple, it can be tricky. Select Start and then Log Off. The logoff and shutdown links are dangerously close to each other. Make sure you click on the correct one. Figure 11.3 shows a screenshot of the logoff process.

The next screen you should see is the Log Off confirmation prompt shown in Figure 11.4. If you don't see that prompt, then it's possible that you selected the Shutdown option. Continuing on this path will shut down

FIGURE 11.1

Login screen for Remote Desktop Connection. (For color version of this figure, the reader is referred to the online version of this chapter.)

FIGURE 11.2

Desktop screen for a remote server. (For color version of this figure, the reader is referred to the online version of this chapter.)

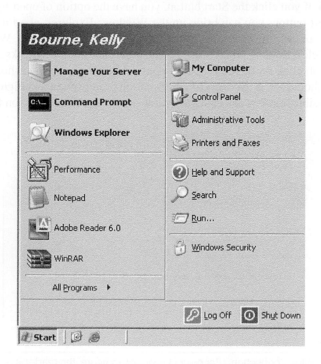

FIGURE 11.3

Log Off option. (For color version of this figure, the reader is referred to the online version of this chapter.)

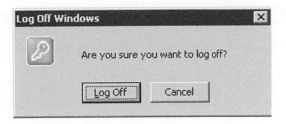

FIGURE 11.4

Log Off confirmation prompt. (For color version of this figure, the reader is referred to the online version of this chapter.)

FIGURE 11.5

Disconnecting but leaving your session open. (For color version of this figure, the reader is referred to the online version of this chapter.)

the server. Generally doing that, especially to a production server, is considered bad form. Be very careful when logging off of a server.

An extremely useful alternative to logging out of a remote server session is to close the connection but leave the session running. You might want to do this if you initiated a process that takes a long time to run. If you don't need to watch it, then you can disconnect and let it run to completion. To disconnect this way, click the red "X" in the upper right hand corner of the RDC session window. The prompt screen shown in Figure 11.5 will be displayed. Click the OK button. To restart the session, just open RDC and connect to the server like you would normally do.

One limitation that might exist in your environment is the maximum number of sessions that can be connected to a server. Each connection takes a finite amount of resources, e.g., memory, to set up and maintain. At the organization where I'm currently working, this limit has been set to two. You'll figure out what the limitations are at your location.

If those slots are already being used, then you won't be able to connect to the server. Figure 11.6 shows the message window you'll see if this is the case.

If all of the slots are being used, then you can't log onto the server until one of the current sessions is closed. However, there is a way to find out who's currently connected to the server. Once you learn that, you can contact them and politely ask them to log off so you can log on.

The way to accomplish this is to remote to a server in the same network as the server you want to connect to. For example, say you want to log onto ox002 but all of its connections are being used. You need to remote to ox001 and then open a utility called the Terminal Services Managers on ox001. Click on the Start button and then click on Administrative Tools and in the submenu select Terminal Services Manager. Figure 11.7 shows how to do this.

The default screen of the Terminal Services Manager is shows in Figure 11.8. It shows who is currently logged onto the server and his/her status. An example in Figure 11.8 shows that two users, Kelly and Cher, are logged into this server.

FIGURE 11.6

Message screen indicating all sessions are being used. (For color version of this figure, the reader is referred to the online version of this chapter.)

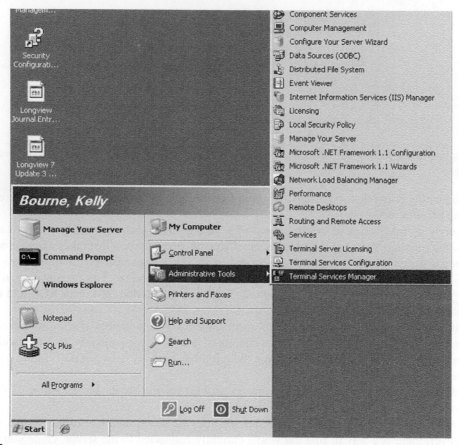

FIGURE 11.7

Opening the Terminal Services Manager. (For color version of this figure, the reader is referred to the online version of this chapter.)

To see who is currently logged into another server, select menu item Actions | Connect to Computer. Figure 11.9 shows how to select this from the menu. When prompted, enter the computer that you are really interested in seeing.

In the example shown in Figure 11.8, there are two users logged into the server. One, Kelly, has an active session. The other user, Cher, has a session that isn't active. To free up a session, you can do one of two things.

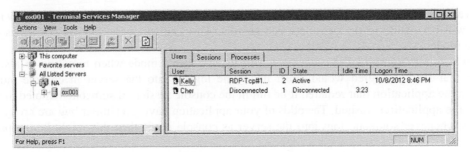

FIGURE 11.8

The main Terminal Services Manager screen. (For color version of this figure, the reader is referred to the online version of this chapter.)

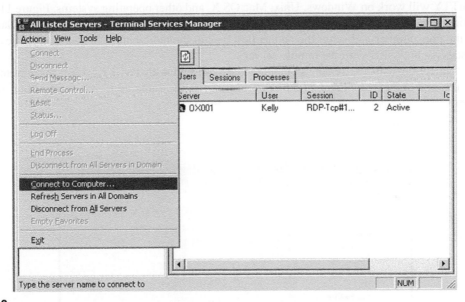

FIGURE 11.9

Connecting to another computer within Terminal Services Manager. (For color version of this figure, the reader is referred to the online version of this chapter.)

- Contact Kelly and/or Cher and politely ask them to log off of server ox011 so you can log onto it.
- Right click on one of the sessions to display a menu that allows you to disconnect the selected session. Now there will be a session available for your use. Normally, it isn't considered polite to kill someone else's session. There are exceptions to this social norm. One would be if you're dealing with an emergency situation. Another is if a session has the state of "Disconnected," which means the user is no longer using it.

11.8.1.1 Console mode

When using RDC to connect to a remote Windows server, you are effectively creating a new session and logging into it. A session, called the console session, always exists on the server. This is also referred to as "session 0." You can connect to this session by adding the parameter / console when making the connection from RDC.

The advantage of opening a session in console mode is that any applications that are currently running on the server will be visible to the console-mode session. This isn't the case when a session is opened in nonconsole mode.

There is a small degree of risk associated with using console mode when remoting to a server. One application that I administered would crash if anyone logged into the server in console mode. There was a bug in the application that required it be run in the console session. If someone remoted in as console mode, then the application crashed. The odds of your application having a similar bug are pretty small, but if it crashes whenever someone logs into the server as console mode then this might be the problem.

11.8.2 PuTTY

PuTTY is another package that allows you to remote to other servers. It's an open source terminal emulator program. PuTTY will work on Windows, Unix, Mac OS X, and other operating systems. Figure 11.10 shows the connection screen for PuTTY. The server's name or IP address is entered into the "Host Name" field. Then enter the port number and select the connection type in the radio button field. Finally, click the Open button to establish a session with the remote server.

Once a connection with the remote computer is established with PuTTY, you'll be presented with a screen like the one shown in Figure 11.11. You log in just the same as if you were sitting in front of the computer.

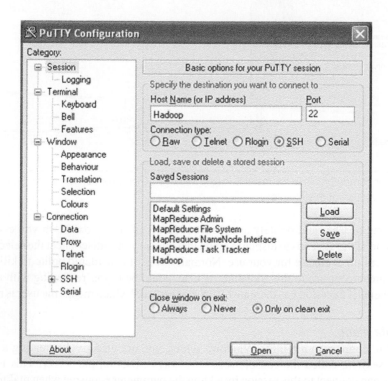

FIGURE 11.10

PuTTY connection screen. (For color version of this figure, the reader is referred to the online version of this chapter.)

FIGURE 11.11

PuTTY connection. (For color version of this figure, the reader is referred to the online version of this chapter.)

11.8.3 SmarTerm

SmarTerm is a commercial terminal emulation application that enables access to a variety of systems. It is compatible with Windows Server 2008, Windows Server 2003, Unix, and IBM mainframes. SmarTerm supports several languages besides English.

11.9 WHO IS SUPPORTING YOU?

No individual can know everything. How much support do you have for areas which you're unfamiliar with? Who can you call on for assistance when problems occur outside your application, for example, with the database or the network? Does your organization have experts in those areas that can help you investigate and correct problems that are outside of your application? Do you know now to get in contact with them? Are they generally responsive to your requests for assistance?

Hopefully, your organization has a support contract with the application vendor. No matter how much experience you have, there will eventually be a problem that you've never seen and can't handle. When this happens, it's nice to know that you can call on the expertise available on the vendor's Support Desk.

Most vendors offer various levels of support contracts to their clients. The level of assistance varies from absolutely no support all the way up to having one of their technicians sitting in the cubicle next to you. You need to know what level of support contract you have with the vendor. Make sure you know the answers to the following questions:

- What level of support do you have? For example, is it limited to regular business hours or does it extend to 24×7?
- What are "regular business hours" for the vendor? Are they in the same time zone as you?
- Do you have the current telephone number for off-hour support? Sometimes this is different than the normal number.

- Is your name on the list of authorized contacts for your organization? Some vendors allow only a limited number of people, aka contacts, from each client to call their Support Desk. Are you on that list?
- Do you know your organization's license number or client number? Some vendor's Help Desks request this question as soon as they pick up the telephone. You might want to either memorize this number or tattoo it on your wrist.

11.10 SUCCESSION PLANNING

I read once that, as soon as you get into a position, you need to start training your backup or replacement. This advice seems reasonable for all of us working as Application Administrators.

11.10.1 Why do you need a backup?

Why do you need a backup? Some reasons are listed here:

- Do you enjoy taking an occasional vacation and being able to forget about work for a week or two? Will you be able to do this if you don't have a backup? It's hard to enjoy yourself on vacation knowing that your phone could ring at any time with a crisis. Wouldn't it be more enjoyable knowing that a well-trained, experienced backup is there to handle any crisis that comes up without bothering you?
- Do you ever want to be promoted? If you're indispensable in your current position, then it's going to be hard to convince management to promote you and leave a critical application without support. If you are able to convince them to promote you, then you don't want to be doing both your new and old jobs simultaneously.
- Do you ever get ill and need to take a sick day? Have you ever tried to resolve a system outage when you're down with the flu? It makes a bad day even worse.

11.10.2 Training your backup

Everyone learns differently, but it seems to me that many people learn most effectively when a "hands-on" approach is taken. If this is true for most people, then the best method of training your replacement would be to start him or her off by watching you perform a task a time or two. Then they graduate to doing themselves under your supervision. Finally, they would do it themselves without assistance. As they master the simpler aspects of supporting the application, they need to be presented with increasingly difficult tasks.

You should start training your replacement or backup as soon as possible. This is especially true if either or both of you support other applications. If you wait until both of you have a substantial amount of "free" time, then their training will never happen. Weeks, months, and years will go by without any substantial training ever being done.

Start off with a couple of brief familiarization sessions on the application. After that, start getting them involved in hands-on sessions. To me, it's better to have a numerous short, intense sessions instead of fewer long, but tedious sessions.

11.11 CALLINGS LISTS FOR SUPPORT PERSONNEL

All support personnel need to know how to reach each other. It has to be easy to find these numbers because they'll be needed in the earliest hours of the morning. Does your organization have their list of support personnel along with their home, cell, and pager numbers available?

- Is this list on a portal?
- A web page?
- A common drive?
- Programmed into everyone's cell phones?

Does your calling list specify who should be called in what order? If the primary support person is available, then he or she should be called first. Only if they aren't available or don't respond should the next name on the list be called.

Areas of specialty within the support team should also be known. For example, your DBA team may have Oracle specialists and SQL Server specialists who don't have any expertise in the other platform. If your application is based on an Oracle database and is experiencing database issues, then it's not going to do much good to call a SQL Server expert. You need an Oracle expert and the calling list should tell you which DBA is your best prospect.

Disaster Recovery

Organizations have become increasingly dependent on their IT systems. IT has enabled businesses, government, and nonprofits to do more with fewer people. It has enabled them to communicate with their customers in ways that were unthinkable just a few years ago. The flip side is that, if these IT systems fail, then the whole house of cards could collapse.

Occasionally, unfortunate things happen that can impact a data center or an application. One might not happen to you today or tomorrow, but they happen to someone's IT environment virtually every day. Disaster Recovery (DR) is the process of planning and preparing, in advance, what you'll do if a disaster strikes your organization or application.

If a disaster strikes your data center, the consequences could be severe. The following statistic has been published by leading industry experts. If you don't have a realistic DR plan for your application, then it might be the cause of your company's downfall and/or someone (possibly you) losing their job(s).

93% of businesses that lost their datacenter for 10 days went bankrupt within one year.

National Archives & Records Administration

12.1 DISASTER RECOVERY IS NOT BUSINESS CONTINUITY

There are two terms that are commonly mentioned in the industry. The terms are "disaster recovery" (DR) and "business continuity" (BC). Despite a significant amount of overlap, they are not the same thing. In a nutshell, the difference between DR and BC is that business continuity deals with the needs of the entire organization while disaster recovery is concerned with the IT aspect of the organization.

Some examples of the major topics under BC include:

- Supply chain logistics
- Succession plans for departure of key executives
- Loss of communications, such as the organization's PBX system
- Plans for disseminating information to the public, government, and media in the event of an emergency
- Identifying and cross-training backup personal for key positions since the primary individuals may not be available during an emergency

Examples of major topics that DR addresses:

- Damage or outages at the data center (fire, flood, electrical outage, failure of key infrastructure components)
- Disruption of telecommunications

- Disruption of electricity or other utilities
- Loss of access to the data center
- Loss of use of a major IT facility such as the Help Desk
- Damage or degradation to critical business applications such as online order entry systems, customer facing websites, accounts payable, accounts receivable, inventory control, etc.

The significant amount of overlap between BC and DR requires that these plans be developed in conjunction with each other. If either of them is developed without knowing what the other is doing, it will most likely result in either duplication of effort or significant requirements being overlooked and omitted. Figure 12.1 shows a Venn diagram outlining each of them, where they overlap and where they are distinct.

As an IT professional, you may or may not have the responsible of developing the organization's business continuity plan. You might be contacted to submit your input on how the BC plan impacts the applications you support. You very likely will be involved in developing the disaster recovery plan for your application(s). If you became the administrator for the application after the DR plan was developed, then you'll still be involved when it's periodically reviewed.

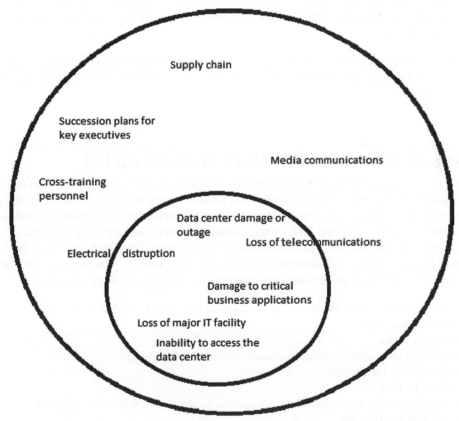

FIGURE 12.1

Venn diagram of potential problems.

12.2 WHAT CONSTITUTES A DISASTER?

One topic that your DR plan might not cover but needs to be considered is exactly what constitutes a disaster. Disasters like a complete, city-wide power outage will be obvious. But what about more limited problems? Can a disaster be declared for just a single application? For example, do the following problems constitute a disaster?

- Your application server literally catches fire and burns up. Is this a disaster? Should the application be moved to the DR site or is the best solution to acquire a replacement server and rebuild it at the production data center?
- What if an entire rack of servers burns up? Can 10, 20, 30, or 40 servers be installed and rebuilt at the production data center in an acceptable amount of time or should the applications that have been running on these crispy critters be moved to the DR site?
- What if it's the database server that crashes? Should both the database and application be ported to the DR server? To complicate the situation further, what if the hardware required for the database server isn't readily available. Does that change the decision regarding whether this constitutes a disaster or not?
- Assume you're in the potential path of a category 5 hurricane and the National Hurricane Center says there's a 90% probability that your production data center will be hit by it. Should you move tapes and people to the DR site 200 miles inland? What if the probability is 50%? Should you move to the DR site under those conditions?

The point of the previous questions is that you need to know under what conditions a disaster can be declared. Who has the power to make this decision? If the primary decision maker isn't available, then who is the backup for him or her?

12.3 TYPES OF DISASTERS THAT MUST BE PREPARED FOR

It's impossible to be prepared for every conceivable type of disaster. For example, could you effectively prepare for an extinction-sized asteroid hitting the Earth or a full-scale nuclear war? Of course, it isn't possible to plan for disasters of those magnitudes. The best you can do is to prepare for disasters that are realistic and ones that you have the resources to handle. The extreme doomsday scenarios just can't be planned for.

Some possible scenarios that must be considered are listed below. Obviously, not every type of disaster will apply to every organization. IT personnel in Nebraska don't need to plan for hurricanes and those in Florida don't need to worry about blizzards, but most of these threats are fairly universal.

- Natural disasters such as floods (natural or manmade), hurricanes, wildfires, blizzards, tornados, earthquakes, etc.
- Data center goes down
- Power outage due to weather, rolling blackouts, or technical problems
- Telecommunications interruption
- Loss of A/C or heating
- Data center is physically unreachable due to another disaster, e.g., a flood or blizzard
- Pandemic such as the bird flu
- Terrorist attack in your state or city
- Cyber-attack on your network, servers, or applications
- Train derailment that releases dangerous chemicals adjacent to your data center

It's important to note that not every disaster listed here means equipment and systems are down. Some of them are related to staffing resources where staff may be unavailable (as might be the case with widespread illness like bird flu) or simply not able to get to the workplace (as in the case of a blizzard).

12.4 ORGANIZATION-WIDE DISASTER RECOVERY PLAN

If your organization has a DR plan, then the specific plans for your application have to follow the broader guidelines. If the organization has set up a DR site at location "x," then your application's DR site will be there as well. You can't expect that another site will be established for a single application.

12.4.1 Is your organization required to have a DR plan?

While every organization should have a DR plan, some industries are required by laws or regulations to have one. Is your organization required to have a DR plan? Some examples of industries that are required to have one are:

- Banks and other financial institutions must have a DR plan as of March 2003.
- The National Association of Securities Dealers requires that its members, i.e., stockbrokers, have a business continuity plan.
- Power utilities are required by FERC (Federal Energy Regulatory Commission) to have a DR plan.
- HIPAA, the Health Insurance Portability and Accountability Act, requires that health-care providers have a disaster recovery plan.
- Radio and TV broadcasters are required by the Media and Security Reliability Council to have a DR plan.

12.4.2 Is DR taken seriously?

Is the organization's DR plan being taken seriously? The answers to the following two questions can give you great insight into whether the organization is taking DR planning seriously or not.

1. Is the DR plan being reviewed or tested periodically? If it's been years since the DR plan was reviewed or tested, then it isn't being taken seriously.
2. Has the DR plan been maintained, i.e., updated? No DR plan is perfect. Every such plan needs occasional corrections. Even if a perfect plan did exist it would become outdated as the organization's physical infrastructure, software inventory, personnel, and facility locations change. If a plan hasn't been updated in over a year, then it's almost certainly out of date. If it hasn't been updated in 5 years, then it's probably worthless.

12.4.3 Does your application exist in the overall DR plan?

What does the organization's DR plan say about your application? Is your application mentioned in it? If it isn't listed, then it might have been omitted for one of several reasons. For example:

- Your application didn't exist when the DR plan was developed. If this is the case, then it needs to be added to the overall DR plan. As the Application Administrator, you're in the best position to begin this process.
- Your application is considered low priority in the overall scheme of things and not important enough to be included in the planning process.

- It was simply overlooked. If this is the case, then you need to initiate an effort to have it included. If a disaster strikes and there is no plan for recovering your application, it won't reflect positively on either you or the application.
- Manual work-arounds will be used to replace the application during a disaster.
- No one wanted to fund the DR aspects of the application.
- The application is dependent on other resources which are not in the DR plan, so even if this application was in the DR plan, the DR wouldn't work until those resources are included.

12.4.4 What priority is your application?

Not all applications are of the same importance to an organization. This isn't an unrealistic or arbitrary observation. If every application in the organization suddenly became unavailable would the emphasis be to get a customer-facing order website up or the application that tracks internal training courses? Obviously, the first priority would be applications that generate revenue. Other priorities would be applications that dealt with personal safety. The business side of the organization, not the IT side, will make these prioritization decisions.

Frequently, applications within an organization are grouped by priority. For example, they could be grouped by how long the application can be unavailable before the organization is impacted. The groups might be defined as shown here. Of course, these are just examples and may not be applicable to your application or organization.

- High—If the application is down more than 30 minutes, then it needs to be brought up at the Disaster Recovery alternate site.
- Medium—If the application is down more than 24 hours, then it needs to be brought up at the Disaster Recovery alternate site.
- Low—If the application is down more than 3 days, then it needs to be brought up at the Disaster Recovery alternate site.

What is your application's priority? Its ranking in the corporate-wide viewpoint will have a huge impact on when it's addressed in a disaster scenario. If all of the applications are affected by a disaster, then the high-priority applications will be brought back online first. Resources like network engineers, DBAs, and System Administrators can only work on one problem at a time. Noncritical applications will be handled by the essential personnel resources once the high-priority applications have been brought back online.

12.5 DR PLAN FOR YOUR APPLICATION

Every application needs an individual DR plan. If one doesn't already exist, then it needs to be written. If one already exists, then it should be reviewed to confirm that it's up-to-date. In either case, you as the Application Administrator will have a significant part of the process.

12.5.1 Does your application already have a DR plan?

Does the application(s) that you support already have a DR plan? If so, can you answer the following questions about it?

- Who wrote it?
- When was it written?
- When was the last time it was tested?
- When was the last time it was updated?

If you don't know the answers to these questions, then you need to review the DR plan thoroughly and as soon as possible. Just because plan exists doesn't ensure that it's up-to-date or accurate.

Another question that you need to think about regarding an existing DR plan for your application is "why was it written?" This might seem like an odd question, but it's important. Was it written just so a box could be checked off? If it that is the case, then you probably want to toss it out and start over from scratch. A plan that was written just to satisfy a corporate mandate probably isn't worth the paper it's written on.

How can you recognize that your DR plan wasn't well written? One way would be to see if it looks like a template with the name of the application and a minimal number of details plugged into blank spaces. Another way is to compare it with the other DR plans for other applications in your organization. If yours looks suspiciously like the others, then it might have been created as the result of a "cut and paste" process. Either of these mass-produced-type DR plans wasn't likely to be well thought out and can probably be vastly improved upon.

12.5.2 What should be in an application's DR plan?

Every application's DR plan should include the following points. If the organization has a recommended format for DR plans, then obviously that template should be followed.

- A description of the hardware, e.g., computer servers, which are needed to support the application. This needs to include hardware used to support clustering or load balancing.
- Whether the servers are physical or virtual. If it's virtual, then a description of the virtual platform, e.g., VMware, needs to be included.
- Whether the hardware will be purchased in advance and installed at the DR site. The alternative is to order and install it after a disaster has been declared. While this approach saves money, the obvious downside is that it will take significantly longer for the application to become available to the users following a disaster.
- A description of the application software, including details like which version and what optional packages are included.
- Details on the database(s) that the application needs to function.
- A list of support software, including versions, which are needed on the application servers.
- A recovery time objective, e.g., the application will be operational no more than 24 hours after a disaster situation has been declared.
- The steps required to install the application software on the DR server. These steps should be documented and those documents should be in a location that is known to everyone involved in the DR process.
- The steps required to migrate data from the production system to the DR system.
- Roles and responsibilities of the IT and business teams that will handle the disaster incident. Primary and backups need to be identified for each role because it's very likely that not all of the primary individuals will be reachable in a disaster situation.
- Who has the authority to declare a disaster situation?
- How the IT and business personnel will communicate once a disaster situation is declared. Contact information including phone numbers (work and personal), e-mail addresses, etc., should be in the DR documentation available to everyone involved.
- How end users of the application will be notified that a disaster has occurred. They need to be told clearly when the application will be available again and how they can access the DR version.
- Description of when and how the DR plan will be tested.

The DR plan needs to be approved by both the business owners of the application and the IT group that supports it. It might also need to be reviewed by higher-level IT personnel to ensure that it conforms to the overall DR goals that the organization has put into place.

12.5.3 Types of DR sites

Not all DR environments are the same. There are multiple options regarding how to set up and maintain DR sites. One analogy is to call them cold, warm, and hot. An organization can have different types of DR environments for different applications. For example, it might have a hot DR environment for a revenue-generating application and a cold site configuration for other applications.

12.5.3.1 Hot

A hot DR site has computer equipment intended to duplicate the Production site. The hardware might not be exactly what's in production, but it's close. For example, both sites might have clustered server, but the Production site might have more servers in the cluster. The database on a hot DR site is synchronized so it is close to identical to what is on the Production site. This may include specialized software or additional network links between the Production site and the DR site.

The advantage of a hot DR site is that it can be up and running very quickly, in some cases within seconds of the Production site going down. The downside is that duplicating the hardware, software, and data is complicated and expensive. You have to purchase additional computers for the DR site that aren't being used 99.99% of the time. You might also have to purchase additional software licenses for the DR site. You should continually monitor the data synchronization process to ensure that it's always functioning and is able to take over from the Production site at short notice. It shouldn't be a surprise that a hot DR site is the most expensive of the options.

Setting up a hot DR site would only be advisable if the application being supported needs to have this level of availability. Examples of situations that might justify a hot DR site include eCommerce websites, systems for financial institutions, online stock trading systems, and government agencies that can't afford to have their applications down.

12.5.3.2 Cold

A cold DR site doesn't have computers that are up and running. In fact, initially it might not have any computers at all. Think of it more as an empty facility that gets built up only after a disaster has been declared.

The advantage of a cold site is that it's the least expensive approach. No expenditures or investments are made until or unless a disaster is declared. The disadvantage of a cold site is that it will take a significant amount of time to bring the applications up to speed. The hardware has to be acquired, delivered, installed, and then the software must be installed on it. Obviously, this type of DR site can't be used if the application in question needs to be operational in hours or even a day or two.

12.5.3.3 Warm

A warm DR site, as you might already have guessed, lies somewhere between a hot site and a cold site. It might have servers already set up, but application software might not have been installed on them yet. The data on a warm DR site is almost guaranteed to be outdated. Before the site can go into production, the latest data has to be loaded at the warm DR site.

The advantage of a warm site is that it provides a quicker response than a cold site, but at a fraction of what a hot site costs.

12.5.4 **Software licensing and your DR site**

Before acquiring and setting up DR servers make sure you understand the licensing ramifications regarding a DR site. If your DR site includes servers with software already loaded onto them, you don't want to do anything illegal. You need to consider the following questions to ensure you aren't violating your contract with the software vendor.

- Will the application software vendor allow you to load their software on a DR server without additional licensing fees?
- Does the database engine vendor allow you to load create DR database servers without additional licensing fees?
- Is all of the support software on the DR servers properly licensed?
- Is there a limit to the number of days that DR servers can be used without being considered a test or production server? Will your testing schedule violate these restrictions?

12.5.5 **Personnel staffing plans**

DR plans need to address staffing questions to be complete. Even the most well-designed DR site needs to have people involved for it to come up and stay up. A number of the personnel-related questions are outlined in the following sections.

12.5.5.1 *Who has a part in the DR plan?*

Everyone that has a responsibility in the DR effort needs to be listed by name in the DR plan. It isn't good enough to refer to them by their role. You need to include names.

The DR plan also needs to specify the name of the backup for every position in the plan. The reason for this is that a critical person might be unavailable during a disaster. He or she might have been out of town when the disaster occurred and isn't able to return due to limited travel options. A more unfortunate situation might be that critical personnel might have been killed or injured during the disaster.

Personnel turnover is one of the primary reasons that your DR plan needs to be reviewed periodically. If a critical person leaves the organization or transfers to another position, then they won't be able to fulfill their role in the DR plan. Every review of the DR plan needs to confirm that each named individual is still with the organization and still in the same position listed in the plan. If they aren't, then the plan needs to be updated with their replacement.

One final personnel question that must be considered is that their job might not be the highest priority for employees if a disaster strikes. If an employee's family is in imminent danger, it's very likely that they won't leave them to head into the office. A DR plan must take into account that not every employee will be able or willing to participate in the DR actions.

12.5.5.2 *Where will they do it from?*

Not everyone has to be physically present at the DR site. In fact, if people can perform their tasks remotely it can result in lower costs, less congestion and higher productivity. For each person who has a role to play, the DR plan needs to define whether:

- They need to be physically present
- They can work remotely

If a person needs to be physically present at the DR site, when do they need to arrive? Not everyone needs to show up on the first hour of the first day. A hardware technician that is assembling racks of servers obviously needs to be onsite at the beginning of the process. The System Administrator who loads the operating system onto servers needs to perform his or her job next. Application Administrators can't do anything until those prior steps have been completed.

How will people get to the DR site? Will they fly to it or drive there? This question is tightly tied to the location of the site. If it's relatively close to the Production site, then they can drive, but if it's 1000 miles away then driving isn't practical. Everyone needs to know where the DR site is so they can plan on how they would get there if required.

Have their accommodations been considered? If they are going to be in and out in a single day, this isn't an important question. If they're going to be onsite for days or weeks, then they need somewhere to stay. Could the organization book rooms in a nearby hotel in the event of a disaster? This would allow employees to focus on their responsibilities instead of worrying about where they'll sleep when they get the chance to do that.

12.5.5.3 Does everyone know what their responsibility is?
Everyone needs to know their responsibilities within the DR plan. They need to know what they are responsible for doing, when they need to do it, and where it needs to be done.

The DR plan needs to make sure they have the tools they need to fulfill their responsibilities. For example, if they need to access the corporate network how will they do it? The following questions outline concerns that should be addressed in the DR plan.

- Do all support personnel who will be working remotely have access to broadband Internet at home?
- Do they all have a laptop loaded with the software they need?
- Do they have a home computer that will support accessing the network?
- Do they know how to access the network from a remote location? Have they done it before? Recently?
- Is there a limit to the number of people who can VPN (Virtual Private Network) into the network at any given time? If the answer was "there is no limit," has this been tested?
- If there is a limit who has priority to get in first? How is this enforced? Have the high-priority individuals been identified?

What applications will be addressed first? This question refers back to Section 12.4.4 that prioritizes applications. Everyone needs to know what applications have the highest priority. Any time wasted arguing about this or spent bringing up a low-priority application represents a delay in getting critical applications back on line.

12.5.6 Testing your DR plan
A DR plan that hasn't been tested can't be trusted. It's all too easy to leave critical tasks off of the plan. Testing the plan from beginning to end can help to expose any such critical omissions. Testing the plan from beginning to end can also help ensure that task sequences are correct and the estimated time to complete for each task is accurate.

When preparing to test your DR plan, you need to keep the following questions in mind:

- When was it last tested?
- How did that test go?
- Were any flaws in the plan uncovered?
- Has information learned in the last test been used to improve the plan?
- Does everyone know where a copy of the DR plan is?
- Is the plan accessible if the system/network/server/data center is down?
- How much of the DR plan can be accomplished remotely?

Another question that needs to be answered is how long will it take to bring up the DR site to an operational state? This needs to be known so the users can be provided with an estimate of when each application will become available after a disaster has been declared. Questions related to the timing include?

- Has the DR plan been tested specifically for the time aspect?
- Has the ETA for each application been specified?
- Has anything changed that might cause the rebuild process to take longer now? For example, if the amount of data used by the application has tripled since the last test, it's reasonable to assume that loading it will take longer. Another example is if the application now has clustered servers, then it will take longer to load the application software on them.

12.5.7 Users and disasters

The DR plan needs to consider how users will be impacted by potential disasters. For example, if users of the application are located in the same facility or city as the primary data center, how will they be affected?

- Will they be able to continue to work in the primary facility?
- Is the plan for them to remote into the application?
- Do they have a laptop or a computer at home that will enable them to do this?
- Do they have broadband Internet access at home?
- Are they accustomed to accessing the application remotely? If not, how difficult will it be for them to learn this in a disaster situation at home?
- Are security measures in place that allows them to use the application but prevent nonqualified individuals from accessing it?

If the primary data center becomes unavailable, how will it affect users who are situated at other locations?

- Will the transition to the DR site be seamless to them?
- If not, will they know that they are supposed to connect to the DR facility?
- How will they be informed that the primary data center is no longer available?
- How will they be informed that the DR site is now available?
- Do they know how to connect to application that is running in the DR facility? If this just a matter of using a different URL in the case of a web-based application? If so, do they have the DR URL bookmarked? Will it be e-mailed to them?

12.6 THE DR SITE

Where is the DR site physically located? Is it close to the Production site? Being close has advantages and disadvantages. One advantage is that if it's close to the primary facility the staff can easily migrate between the two sites.

The disadvantage of the sites being too close is outlined in the following questions:

- Could the DR site be affected by the same disaster that impacted your primary facility?
- Are both sites on the same coast? If so, could a hurricane or tsunami affect both of them?
- Are both sites in the same earthquake zone?
- Do both sites rely on the same electrical utility?
- Do both sites rely on the same telecommunications provider?

12.6.1 Dedicated or shared DR facility?

Is the DR facility dedicated to your organization or is it shared by multiple organizations? If the facility is shared, then the following questions need to be considered.

- Who else has access to the facility?
- Can the facility host more than one client simultaneously?
- If multiple organizations need to use a shared DR facility at the same time, who has priority?
- If the answer to the previous question is "first come first serve," does this mean you should declare a disaster situation earlier than you might otherwise to ensure you have access to the DR facility?

12.6.2 Access to the DR site

Is access to the DR site restricted? If so, then you don't want the process of getting access to delay the process of getting your applications operational. Having answers to the following questions could prevent significant delays in the event of a disaster:

- If a disaster occurs, how will your IT staff get access to the site?
- Is there someone at the site 24 × 7 that is authorized and able to distribute ID cards or access cards?
- Do your key people already have keys or badges needed to get into the facility?
- If not, how long will it take to get access for them?
- Does the remainder of your team have access?
- If not how long will it take to get access?

12.7 KEEPING DR UP WITH THE PRODUCTION SITE

If the DR site has been set up in advance and is capable of being fully operational, then that's a great accomplishment. However, your Production site isn't standing still. Both the hardware and the software are continually being updated. Unless an effort is being made to keep the DR site synchronized with the Production site, then it will quickly become outdated.

Three main components that need to be synchronized between the production facility and the DR site are listed here. The following sections describe how this can be done for each component.

1. Hardware
2. Software
3. Data

12.7.1 Hardware

Synchronizing hardware between the two sites can be expensive. A cost analysis needs to be done to determine whether every hardware change on the Production site needs to be duplicated on the DR site. For example, if a newer, more powerful blade is installed in a server on the production data center does the same model need to be installed on DR? Can the existing blade on the DR site be kept until it reaches the end of its life expectancy? Changes to hardware need to be handled on a case-by-case basis.

12.7.2 Software

Earlier chapters have described how frequently software updates are made to the application itself and to its support software. These changes accumulate quickly and need to be migrated to the DR servers on a timely basis.

How can code changes be migrated from the Production environment to the DR environment? Two possible methods of implementing such a migration are to:

1. Any update that is made to the PROD server is also made to the DR server in a reasonable timeframe. Each organization has to determine what this "reasonable" timeframe is for itself.
2. Periodically, the software on the production server is copied to the DR server. This method is particularly viable if the servers in question are virtual servers.

Either method of migrating code from the production site to the DR site can be effective. Deciding which approach is to be implemented has to be made by each organization. The most critical detail though is to make sure that software migrations are being done.

12.7.3 **Data**

For most applications, data changes much faster than software. Every day new orders, invoices, purchase orders, trades, etc., are being generated. Because of this, it's imperative that an effective, consistent plan be put in place to keep the data on the DR site synchronized with the Production site.

There are many methods of synchronizing data between production and DR. Three potential methods of accomplishing are listed here.

- Real-time or near real-time synchronization of data can be accomplished if the database engine being used provides it. This functionality is sometimes called "log shipping." The advantage of this is that data is synchronized in real-time or near real-time. The potential for the loss of data is reduced from hours to minutes or seconds.

  One disadvantage of this approach is that it requires that the database engine in the DR environment must be running at all times. This might require that licenses be acquired for the database servers in the DR environment. If you haven't budgeted for those additional licensing costs, then this approach might not be economically practical.

  One caution is that not all applications are compatible with real-time data synchronization. For example, if the application stores some of its data in flat files outside of the database, then real-time synchronization of the databases won't necessarily include data in those flat files. This might eliminate this method as your solution.
- Regular backups, often nightly, are created and are written to tape. If a disaster occurs, then the most recent set of database backup tapes are sent to the DR site and loaded. All data as of the time of the last backup is now available on the DR site. A primary advantage of this approach is that it's relatively inexpensive to do.
- This approach has several disadvantages. The most significant one is that it takes time. It takes time to ship tapes to the DR site and more time to load them. Another disadvantage that is easily overlooked is that tapes aren't 100% reliable. If the most recent backup tape can't be read, then you will lose additional time it takes to ship and load the next most recent tape.

  Lastly with this method is that you will lose data entered into the system between database backups. If backups are created daily, then you could lose up to 24 hours' worth of data by reverting to the most recent backup tape.
- Nightly, backup files are created by the normal process and electronically shipped to the DR site. If a disaster occurs, then the most recent backup files at the DR site will be loaded. The primary advantage of this approach is that the backup files are available immediately at the DR site.

Another advantage of this method is that it doesn't incur additional costs of real-time synchronization. Open source code utilities are available that can automate the process of moving backup files to DR immediately after they are created. Alternatively, scripts could be written to handle this task.

A disadvantage of this method is that you will lose data entered into the system between database backups. If backups are created daily, then you could lose up to 24 hours' worth of data by reverting to the most recent backup files.

12.8 TESTING THE DR ENVIRONMENT

Your Production environment is constantly changing. To ensure that your DR plan works, it needs to be tested periodically. If your DR plan isn't tested, then you'll only discover its errors and shortcomings when a disaster occurs. Trust me, that's not the time you want to learn about its problems.

12.8.1 How often does it need to be tested?

How often is "periodically"? That's up to your organization, but annually seems to be a reasonable start. Any more often than that and people won't have time to do their jobs. Any less frequently and the risk of problems due to changes in the Production environment are rising.

If your industry has laws or regulations that require a DR plan exist, then they also probably specify how often it needs to be tested. Talk to your organization's legal department and get their opinion on this. After all, that's what they're being paid for, right?

12.8.2 What does a DR test look like?

Testing a DR plan isn't complicated but can be time consuming. Basically, you simulate that the production site is unavailable due to a disaster. Then you follow the DR plan to move IT activity to the DR site. Whatever the DR plan says needs to be done you do. Test steps might include the ones listed here. Depending on whether your DR site is cold, warm, or hot, all of the following steps might not be applicable.

- Load the operating system on the application server.
- Load the supporting software on the application server.
- Load the application on the application server.
- Confirm that the correct version of the application has been loaded.
- Load the most recent database backup onto the DR database server. This might require that you request the most recent backup tape from an offsite storage facility. The time it takes to receive the tape should match what the DR plan said it would be. Confirm that the tape can be read.
- Confirm that the application can access the database.
- Confirm that the data which was just loaded is visible in the application.
- Verify that all users have access to the application's URL.
- Verify that all users' credentials exist in the application.
- Verify that if users are supposed to be able to use a DNS value to access the application that it works.
- Confirm that users can log into the application.
- Verify that users can read, write, modify, and delete data via the application's user interface.
- If the application environment on the DR site is supposed to be clustered or load balanced, then confirm that those aspects are working.
- Confirm that everyone who should be able to remote to the application server is able to do so.

Of course, there might be some exceptions in what the DR specifies should be done. For example, if the DR plan requires that you purchase new servers, then you might want to skip doing that. Can you use existing servers and load the appropriate software onto it or them?

If your application needs to be available 24×7, then certain steps might not be practical. For example, users may specify a domain name in the URL, e.g., http://accounting.acmecorp.com, to bring up a web-based accounting application. That URL is passed to a DNS (Domain Name System) server to get translated into the production server's actual IP address. A domain name can only point to a single server at a time. It points to either the production server or the DR server but not both at the same time. If users need to access the production application while you're running the DR test, then you can't repoint it to the DR server. Perhaps you can use a second URL, e.g., http://accounting-DR.acmecorp.com, to bring up the DR version of the application.

12.8.3 Who participates in DR testing?

Everyone named in the DR plan needs to participate in the testing exercise. There two reasons for this. First, it confirms that their responsibilities are accurate. If they don't have the appropriate access rights or experience to do a task assigned in the DR plan, then it's better to learn about it sooner rather than later during a test rather than an actual disaster.

Second, by participating in the DR testing effort, personnel are practicing for a real disaster. This "trial run" will improve their effectiveness if an actual disaster occurs. If they've never performed these actions on the DR site before, then you can't expect that they'll get it right. But after participating in several DR tests, then they should be quite proficient if a real disaster occurs.

12.8.4 What is the output from DR testing

It's very unlikely that your DR tests will go perfectly. Each periodic test represents an opportunity to update your DR plan. By documenting the test results and having a postmortem to discuss the results, you can learn from each test and get closer to having the next test have better results.

Some of the things that you should be specifically looking for during the DR test include the following. Any changes that are encountered need to be updated in the DR plan.

- Additional or changed hardware
- Changes in server names
- New or changed domain names
- New or updated application software
- New or updated support software
- Database changes such as additional databases, changes in accounts needed to access the database, or updated versions of the database client software
- Changes in personnel or their responsibilities
- Additional departments, facilities, or countries that are now using the application
- Changes in locations of backup files, databases, source code, or utilities
- New or updated laws or regulations that must be followed

12.9 COMPARING PRODUCTION AND DR ENVIRONMENTS

While your DR environment doesn't have to be identical to the Production environment, you always need to be aware of where it is different. Some differences are expected and planned for, but you need to be alert for differences that haven't been accounted for. The following sections point out potential areas where the Production and DR environments can differ.

12.9.1 Backups

If the Production facility goes down and the DR site becomes Production, do you know the answers to the following questions?

- Are backups being created on your DR server?
- Are backups on the DR environment being done at the same frequency as on the Production site? Are the same things being backed up on both environments?
- Have backups created on the DR server been tested to confirm they are accurate and complete?
- Is a plan in place to move backup files offsite, i.e., away from the DR site?

12.9.2 Security

While security might not be your primary concern during the frenzy of getting the DR site setup, it's imperative that it should not be overlooked. The organization's information needs to be protected on both the primary Production site and the DR site. Some points that should be included in the test process include:

- Is the user authentication list or process the same on DR as it is on Production? Have you tested adding and deleting users on the DR site?
- Has access to user accounts been tested on the DR site? By whom? It needs to be tested by more than just the Application Administrator.
- Are user passwords the same on DR? If not, then how will the users get their new passwords?
- If your application is web based, will the users need to enter a new URL to get to the DR version of the application? If so, do they know the new URL? If not, how will it be distributed?
- Are users able to connect to the DR server through the firewall?
- Do Application Administrators have all the access they need on the DR environment?

12.9.3 Domain names

If the application is web based, then users are probably using a domain name like http://accounting.acmecorp.com to access the application. The alternative would be for users to specify the IP address, for example, http://123.345.456.678. If a domain name is being used, then the following points are applicable:

- When the DR site becomes Production, will the DNS (Domain Name Server) be updated to make the domain name switch transparent to the users?
- If so, who updates the value for the domain name in the DNS?
- How long will it take to make this change and have it be pushed out through the network?
- Will that person be automatically notified that this change needs to be made or do you have to do it manually?
- Do you have their name, e-mail address, office phone number, and cell number in the event that you need to contact them?
- Do you have the name of that person's backup and supervisor in case the main contact is unavailable?

12.9.4 Firewalls

Along with the network infrastructure, firewalls actually need to be in place before applications can be built in the DR environment. Setting up and maintaining a firewall isn't an easy task. If you have to move the production application to the DR site, then it's possible that the firewall will need to be changed to make everything work as expected. Here are some questions to make sure you have answers to.

- Have the firewall port openings in the DR environment been set up to mimic the Production environment?
- Were there any firewall issues when the DR plan was last tested?
- If changes need to be made who can handle this?
- Do you have their name, e-mail address, office phone #, and cell number?
- Do you have the name of that person's backup and supervisor in case the main contact is unavailable?
- If changes need to be made, how long does it take to make them and for them to become effective?

12.9.5 **E-mail**

If the application creates e-mails, then you need to be concerned that the DR environment can handle them. The following questions are a start toward confirming this.

- Is there an e-mail server in the DR environment?
- Has the appropriate firewall port between the application server and the e-mail server been opened?
- If e-mails are sent out, will they have the correct return address information?
- Can the DR e-mail environment handle the same volume of e-mail that PROD produces? Has this been tested?

12.9.6 **FTP transmissions**

Ftp, File Transfer Protocol, is a protocol used to transfer files across a network to or from another computer. Does your application use ftp to send or receive files to or from another server? For example, files might be sent or received with a service vendor, a partner, a government agency, or a client. If ftp is being used, then these questions need to be considered.

- Has the ftp software been loaded onto the DR server?
- Can the DR environment perform the same ftp-related tasks? Has this been tested?
- Is the DR environment authorized to communicate with another organization's ftp server? The recipient might only accept transmission from your Production environment's IP address. Someone on the other end might need to change their system to access files from the DR site's IP address.
- If files are being sent to you, do your vendors, partners, etc., know the IP address of the DR ftp server? Are they authorized to access it?
- Do you have names and contact information for people at your vendors, partners, etc., who can change ftp addresses on their end, i.e., the ability to change from the production ftp server address to the DR server address?
- Has this been tested?

12.9.7 **Batch processes**

Some applications have batch processes that run periodically to accomplish specific tasks. If your Production environment has any batch processes, then they probably need to be duplicated in the DR environment. Some points to consider are:

- Have the batch processes been set up on the DR environment?
- Is the scheduling tool used in Production also on DR?
- Frequently batch processes need to run under a service account to have access to the resources they need. Have the appropriate accounts been set up in the DR environment?
- Have the batch processes been tested in the DR environment?

12.9.8 Load balancing

Load balancing can be tricky to set up and maintain, so it needs to be explicitly tested. If your Production environment includes load balancing, then the following questions are applicable.

- Will load balancing be duplicated on the DR environment?
- If Production site has load balancing but DR site doesn't, will DR be able to support normal production activity?

12.9.9 Throughput capacity

Does the DR environment have the same throughput capacity as the Production environment? Does it need the same capacity? If not, does everyone understand that the performance users experience might be slower when the DR site is being used? They need to be warned of this in advance so they can't complain about it during a disaster.

12.9.10 Monitoring

Many data centers include monitoring tools, so alerts are sent out if critical metrics reach unacceptable levels. If your Production environment includes monitoring, will the same type of monitoring be done on the DR site? Here are some monitoring points to consider.

- Is your DR server monitored the same way your PROD server was being monitored?
- Does the monitoring process create the same alerts for the DR environment that were being created on the Production environment?
- Do the alerts go out to the same people or group distribution list?
- Has monitoring on the DR environment been tested?

12.10 COMMUNICATIONS

Communications during a disaster situation will be critical. Everyone needs to know in advance how the DR team will communication with each other. What will be your standard means of communication during emergencies?

- Phone calls between individuals
- Conference calls
- IM (Instant Messaging)
- LiveMeeting, WebEx, etc.

It's worth considering having alternate means of communications until the organization's infrastructure is operational. For example, if the organization's e-mail servers aren't functional, then everyone could have a Hotmail or Gmail account. They could also have an IM account outside of the organization's structure. If this is done, then everyone's alternate contact information needs to be documented and available to everyone.

If you're going to use conference call bridges, then certain information needs to be available to everyone prior now. This information includes the following:

- Is the access number your organization's standard number? If not, what is the number?
- Does everyone know it?
- Who can host the call?
- Does it have international capability?

12.10.1 **Contacts**

Every organization needs a contact list of people that need to be contacted if problems occur. Who should be on the contact list?

- Business owner of the application
- Application Administrators
- DBAs
- Data Center staff
- Help Desk
- Vendor Support Desk

Do you have the following information for everyone who is on the contact list?

- Name
- Position
- Backup for each person
- Home phone number
- Cell phone number
- Location, i.e., proximity to DR site

What if the person being called doesn't answer or return the call? How long should the caller wait before escalating to the next name on the list? 10 minutes? 20 minutes? 30 minutes? This should be defined in the DR plan so time isn't wasted waiting for a call that might never be returned.

12.11 **MAKING THE DECISION TO ACTIVATE THE DR SITE**

The decision to activate the DR site shouldn't be made lightly. What initially might look like a disaster could in fact be a minor issue that is resolved fairly quickly. Given the cost and effort of activating the DR site, it makes sense to do this only when it's truly necessary.

There are a number of questions that should be asked in advance about this momentous decision. For example:

- Who is authorized to make the decision to activate the DR site?
- If this person isn't available, who is the alternate decision maker?
- Does anyone at the site need to be notified and when?
- If the DR site is shared, does the owner or management of the facility need to be notified in advance?
- How will the organization's staff be notified that the DR site is being activated? Some possible methods include:
    - A calling tree
    - Automated e-mails
    - Automated phone calls
    - Automated text messages
- Do any vendors need to be contacted when the DR site is activated? For example:
    - Vendor that provides fuel for the backup generators
    - Telecommunications provider
    - The organization that provides physical security for the site
    - The vendor that provides coffee, snacks, bottled water, soda, etc.

12.12 **RETURNING TO YOUR PRODUCTION SITE**

Hopefully, your production data center hasn't been destroyed, and at some point in time, it will become usable again. Do you have plans outlining how production will move back to the original production data center? The steps for returning to the primary site will likely be very similar to the steps needed to transfer production to the DR site.

The decision to return to the primary site shouldn't be made lightly. If things are fully operational on the DR site, it would be a big mistake to move back to the primary site prematurely only to find out that it isn't as stable or functional as originally thought. It might be prudent to stay at the DR site until you are absolutely sure that the primary site is capable of supporting all production activities.

Handling Problems with an Application

I hope I'm not doing the equivalent of telling you that there is no Easter Bunny, but there is no perfect application. No matter what application you support, there will come a time when it doesn't work as advertised or as expected. This chapter describes steps that can be taken when this inevitable day comes.

13.1 HANDLING AN OUTAGE

It's Monday morning, your computer hasn't even finished booting up yet and you get a call telling you that the application is down. What do you do? What sequence of steps should you be taking to handle an outage of a production application? The following steps are what I try to do. They won't be perfect for every organization, but pick and choose what works for you.

13.1.1 Inform your boss

Keeping your boss up-to-date on any potential problems is always a good idea. You don't want him or her to find out about the outage from someone else. It only takes a minute to send out an e-mail or an IM telling him or her that the XYZ application is down and you're investigating on it. It will also let him or her to know why you're not working on another task or attending a meeting.

13.1.2 Confirm that the problem exists

I never really believe that a problem with the application exists until I see it with my own eyes. Users have been known to make mistakes. There are many reasons why the application isn't coming up for them.

- They might have entered the wrong URL into their browser.
- They might have mistyped their password. Their computer may not be connected to the network.
- The problem might be isolated to their computer or browser.
- They might be connecting remotely and forgot to go through the VPN (Virtual Private Network) before trying to log into the application.

An independent confirmation that the problem exists can be accomplished by logging into the application yourself. If I can access the application, I typically ask the user to reboot his or her computer and try logging into the application again. I also ask them to clear the cache on their web browsers. Nine times out of 10, one of these steps will solve their problem.

Determining whether the problem is isolated to a single user is a critical detail to identify. If one user can't log into the application that's a very different situation than if no one can log into it. If you can successfully log into the application, then the problem almost certainly isn't with the application. It might be a mistake the user is making or it might be something about that specific user's PC, a network problem, or a firewall issue.

13.1.3 Confirm that the server is up

Ping the application server to confirm that it's up. In Windows, UNIX, and Linux systems, the "ping" command will verify that the server can be reached across the network. If you get a response from it, then that's a definite indication that the server is up. Figure 13.1 is a screenshot of what a ping command looks like on a Windows system and what the response will typically look like. If the response you get indicates the server is unavailable, then contact the data center or System Administrator and request that it be rebooted.

13.1.4 Can you log onto the server

The next step is to attempt to remotely log onto the server to confirm that it will accept a login. If you can't log onto the server, there isn't much you can do. If neither you nor data center personnel can log onto the server, then the only option is to request that it be rebooted. Once it comes back up, check the logs for clues as to what happened.

13.1.5 Is the server extremely busy?

If the server's CPU is extremely busy, then it's likely that the application won't be performing well and may not be running at all. To determine how busy the CPU is, you ran run Task Manager on a Windows server or the "top" command on a UNIX server. If the CPU activity rate is extremely high and stays at that level, then something is obviously wrong.

Determining what processes are consuming the majority of the CPU time can provide significant clues regarding the cause of the application's problem. Figure 13.2 shows the output of the Windows Task Manager. Figure 13.3 shows the output of the UNIX "top" command. In both tools, the important columns to pay attention to are CPU and Memory. It's very helpful to click on the CPU column header in Task Manager so the processes are ordered by how much CPU they are using. Normally, the System Idle Process will be using most of the CPU time. If another process is using most of the CPU time, then that might explain why the application isn't working or is performing poorly.

The next step is to determine what the task that is consuming all the CPU time actually does. The vendor's Administrator Guide might list the processes that make up the application environment. If the active process is listed in the guide, then it will indicate what that process does.

If the overactive process doesn't belong to the application, then it might belong to some of the support software that has been loaded onto the server. For example, it might be part of the monitoring software, the backup software, or the antivirus package. One way to determine what it belongs to is to search for the

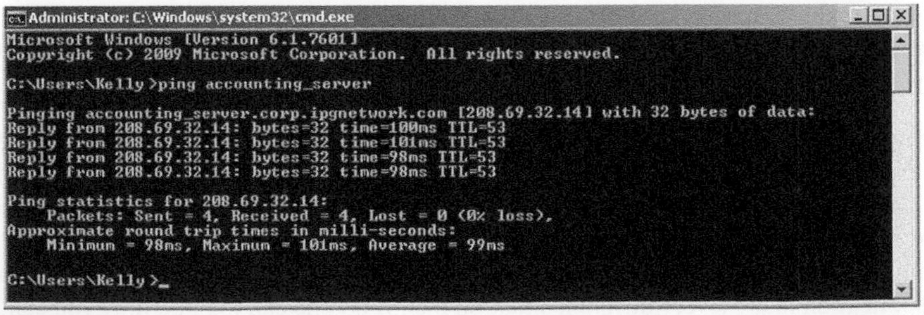

FIGURE 13.1

Ping command. (For color version of this figure, the reader is referred to the online version of this chapter.)

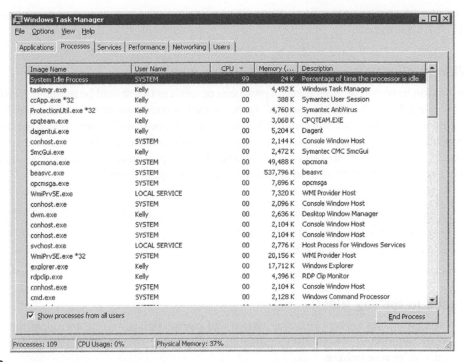

FIGURE 13.2

Windows Task Manager. (For color version of this figure, the reader is referred to the online version of this chapter.)

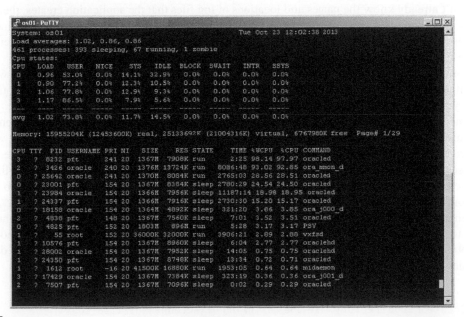

FIGURE 13.3

Output of UNIX top command. (For color version of this figure, the reader is referred to the online version of this chapter.)

process's name in an Internet search engine. There's a very good chance that you'll find the process name and an explanation of what it does.

13.1.6 What application-related processes are running?

Does the application have one or more specific processes or services that should be running? Verify that they are running by using Task Manager or the "ps" (process status) command on a Linux or UNIX server.

On a Windows server, you can bring up the Services Panel to see if application-related services are running. If the application has Windows services running, you should consider writing a batch file or script to get the status of every application-related service. Using a batch file to pull up this information is quicker and less mistake prone than doing it manually. An example of such a script is listed here.

```
REM ACCOUNTING services status
sc query AcctAdminServer | find "STATE"
sc query AcctServer1 | find "STATE"
sc query IstageBPMAdminServer | find "STATE"
sc query IstageBPMCS1 | find "STATE"
pause
```

13.1.7 What's in the log files?

Log files are created by the server operating system and many applications to document their activities, including problem situations. You should examine all available log files to see if they include details on the problem that you're researching.

Some applications maintain multiple log files. One might contain entries during the startup process. Another might contain only entries related to an administrative function. If the application maintains log files, then these are the first and best sources for details regarding any problems that it encountered.

If you don't already know the names and locations of log files that the application creates, then you need to learn this immediately. Check the Administrator's Guide for this information. If you can't find it in that document, then submit a request to the vendor's support desk asking for this information. It's crucial that you know where these logs reside so you can access them quickly when problems occur.

If you open a ticket with the vendor about a problem, there is a very good chance that they will want a copy of any and all log files that could contain details about the problem. Some vendors request that you attach log files to every ticket that you open with them.

The sooner you can capture these log files, the better. The reason for this is that log files tend to accumulate entries as time goes by. The longer you wait to copy the log files, the more entries there will be that aren't related to your problem because they were created after the problem occurred. Even worse, some logging processes create a new file at midnight each day. The longer you wait, the more difficult it will be to find the log entries you need. Do yourself and the vendor a favor by capturing log files as quickly as possible once you have confirmed that a problem exists.

If the vendor requests that you always capture and forward the same set of log files to them, then it might be efficient to write a script or batch file to automate this process. The following code example shows a batch file that captures logs files from a number of different subdirectories and copies them to a single directory to make it easier and faster to send them to the vendor.

```
REM Use this batch file to capture version 6.0 log files to send to the vendor
REM 1) Create a subdirectory like the following D:\Account\20121118_Logs\
REM 2) Copy SaveLogs60.bat to that subdirectory
REM 3) Execute SaveLogs60.bat
```

```
REM 4) Confirm that the expected subdirectories and files have been created
REM 5) Delete SaveLogs60.bat from the new subdirectory
REM 6) Zip up the subdirectories and files and send them to the vendor
mkdir DB
copy C:\Account\DB\logs\OMA001-DB.log DB\*
mkdir logs
copy C:\ Account\logs\*.* logs\*
mkdir AcctAdminServer
copy C:\Account\Domain\servers\AdminServer\logs\access.log AcctAdminServer\*
copy C:\Account\Domain\servers\AdminServer\logs\AdminServer.log AcctAdminServer\*
copy C:\Account\Domain\servers\AdminServer\logs\AcctDomain.log AcctAdminServer\*
mkdir Server
copy C:\Account\Domain\servers\OM001-Server1\logs\access.log Server\*
copy C:\Account\Domain\servers\OM001-Server1\logs\OM001-Server1.log Server\*
```

13.1.7.1 *What's in the O/S logs?*

If the server is Windows based, then the way to see O/S-related log entries is in Administrative Tools | Event Viewer. There are four primary categories of logs: Application, Security, Setup, and System. You'll need to examine each category to make sure that you don't miss anything pertinent to your problem. Figure 13.4 is a screenshot of Event Viewer. In this screenshot, the highlighted entry shows that a specific service has stopped. This could represent the application's problem.

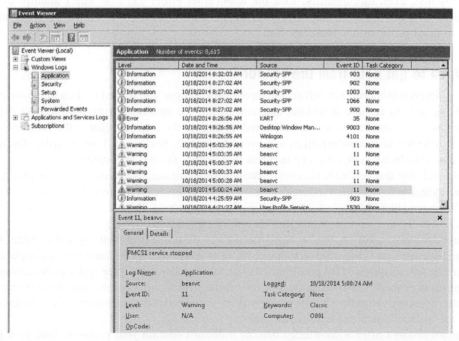

FIGURE 13.4

Windows Event Viewer. (For color version of this figure, the reader is referred to the online version of this chapter.)

13.1.8 Could the problem be related to the database?

As most applications rely upon a database, it's possible that the database is actually the cause of the problem instead of the application software. One quick way to confirm this would be to see if the database server and the database itself are up. Some steps to do this include:

- Ping the database server. If that server doesn't respond to the ping, then it could mean that the database server is down. It could also mean that there are either network or firewall problems. At this point, you should focus on the database server as the likely cause. Contact the DBA team and request that they log onto that database server to see if it's operational. If they respond saying the server and database are fine, then there could be network or firewall issues between the application server and the database server. Contact the network team for assistance.

  Once the database, network, or firewall issues have been resolved, then try to repeat the scenario within the application that caused the initial problem. If the problem can't be recreated, then you've most likely resolved the cause of your problem.

- If you were able to successfully ping the database server, then the next step is to confirm that the database itself is available. Open a connection to the database via an interactive tool like Oracle's SQL*Plus, Oracle SQL Developer, Toad, Query Browser, etc. If the connection can be established, then you can probably eliminate the database as the source of your problem.

  If the connection failed, then it's very likely that database connectivity is the cause of the problem. Contact the DBA team and ask that they confirm the database is up. Once they bring the database backup, log into the application and try to recreate the problem in it. If the problem can't be recreated, then you've most likely resolved it.

  Some applications don't handle interruptions with the database connection well. If database connectivity is lost, even momentarily, then the application either can't or won't attempt to reestablish its database connection. If it describes your application, then always restart the application after a database-related problem has been resolved.

13.1.9 When to get help from the vendor

If you've encountered this problem before and have notes on how you solved it, then you have a very good chance of being able to resolve it without assistance from the vendor. If your Application Administrator team documents every incident that is encountered, including the steps to resolve the problem, then you'll very likely be able to use that information to correct it yourself. Section 13.1.10 describes the type of documentation that should be kept on every incident that occurs for the application.

If the problem is one that you've never seen before and the above suggestions didn't help resolve it, then you'll probably need to seek help from the vendor. Vendor frequently offers several levels of assistance. The initial level of help that they would like clients to use is a searchable knowledge base. This database contains details, including potential solutions, for every problem that its clients have encountered.

If you have a support contract, you've likely been given the address of their support website. Typically, a searchable knowledge base is included on that site. It allows you to specify the version of the application you're using. Then enter a description of the problem and click the search button. If the application displayed an error number or message or wrote one to a log, then search on that error number or description. If the search returns a hit, then read it thoroughly to make sure the problem being described is the same one you've encountered. If it is, then follow the instructions listed to solve the problem.

If the vendor doesn't offer a knowledge base or it doesn't contain your problem, then your next step is typically to open a ticket with the vendor's support desk. When you create the ticket, you must be as detailed and accurate as possible when filling out information for it. The more accurate and complete your initial information is, the quicker they'll be able to respond with useful assistance.

The vendor's ticket system probably will ask for a standard set of information about the problem you've encountered. Always provide the necessary information, but don't be afraid to enter additional details as long as they are relevant. The following details should definitely be provided to their support desk:

- Your company name.
- Your name and contact information.
- The method of contact that you prefer, e.g., telephone call, e-mail, IM, via their support website.
- The name of the application being used, in case the vendor has more than one product.
- The version of the application.
- The operating system on your server.
- Whether the environment is load balanced or not.
- Whether the environment is clustered or not.
- Whether it is your production environment that is being affected.
- A detailed, accurate description of the problem. Be sure to include any error messages that are displayed as well as any log entries you were able to find. Screenshots are very helpful.
- What steps have already been taken to resolve the problem and their impact? For example, if you stopped and restarted the application, rebooted the application server, or rebooted the user workstation, then be sure to mention this. They might have been going to suggest that you perform those steps. By telling them what you've already done you'll save time.
- Whether this problem is affecting all users or just one user.
- Whether this problem is affecting a single location or multiple user locations, e.g., multiple offices, cities.
- When the problem was discovered.
- Whether this problem has ever been encountered before.
- Whether anything has been changed on the system recently. For example, patches to the O/S or support software, a recent upgrade to the application software, a new package or feature of the application is now being used, a new branch is now using the application, a change in the database server.
- Describe the scenario under which the problem was encountered. If possible, list the steps or screens leading up to when the problem occurred. This can be helpful to the vendor support team if there are multiple ways to reach that particular screen in the application.
- If vendor support typically asks that you gather and send them certain log files, then be sure to do that now. By providing this information in the initial request, you'll avoid them asking for it later and wasting the time it takes to respond.

When you open a ticket with a vendor, their first person to look at it is probably a Tier 1 support person. This tech will examine the information you provide to see if there is an obvious answer to your problem, for example, you've entered the wrong URL or a parameter that is clearly invalid. If the fix isn't obvious, then he or she will probably consult a knowledge base for tickets with similar problems. If no problem like yours exists in the database, then the ticket will be reassigned to a Tier 2 support technician.

13.1.10 Document the problem

Document everything you've done while resolving the problem in an internal document called an Incident Report. The more details you can provide, the more valuable it will be to you or someone else in the future. An example of an Incident Report is provided in a sidebar.

The exact layout of the Incident Report isn't especially important. What is vital is that this document contains specific information on that problem. One way to break it down would be to include the following sections:

- Application name
- Date/time

- Individuals involved
- Issue
- Actions/results
- Root cause
- Overview

The "Actions/Results" section needs to be especially detailed. If e-mails or IM were used to communicate while the problem was being investigated and resolved, then those messages should be summarized and inserted into the Incident Report. A complete "Actions/Results" section should include:

- A summary of the communications, including the dates and times, between people working on the problem
- Changes that were made to the system while the problem was being investigated
- The date and time when the system came back up
- Whether the application or the server was taken down and started back up
- Ticket numbers, both internal and with the vendor, that were opened for this problem
- Sources, e.g., log files, event files where information was obtained
- Whether this problem resembles similar problems that have been encountered in the past. If this is true, then include the dates of previous incidents
- Details provided to the vendor support team
- Advice received from the vendor support team
- Any recommended work-arounds that were suggested by the vendor support team
- What was done to resolve the problem? For example, a configuration setting was changed, a library file was replaced, a driver was updated, additional memory was added to the server, the system was rebooted, parameter updates in the database, table values were modified in the database, changes made on the user's workstation or Internet browser

Incident Reports need to be posted where everyone can access them. That might be a network drive or on a portal. Exactly where they are located isn't as important as being in a place that everyone can access and that everyone knows where they are.

It's best to start writing the Incident Report as quickly as possible. The earlier you start, the more accurate your memory of the event will be. The Incident Report doesn't need to be complete when it is initially created. For example, you may still be waiting for recommendations from the vendor support team. The root cause of the problem might not be available for sometime so that section can be left blank until that information has been determined. Just make sure you don't forget to go back and complete it.

INCIDENT REPORT EXAMPLE

PROD AccountingApp Server oma001
November 18, 2013
All times in this document are Central
IGG: Kelly Bourne, John Maxwell, and Shawn Torson
Vendor: Peter Hill

Issue
At approximately 4:08 am, AccountingApp services Server1 and IstageBPMCS1 stopped. This caused the AccountingApp application to go down.

Actions/Results
At 7:49 am, I received an e-mail from John Maxwell informing me that AccountingApp was down and asking me to bring it back up.

I logged onto server oma001 and determined that two of the four AccountingApp services (Server1 and IstageBPMCS1) were stopped. Since these services have to be started in a specific order, I stopped all services and restarted them using vendor-provided scripts. The app came back up.

At 8:01 am, I e-mailed John informing him that the AccountingApp was now back up.

At 8:04 am, I e-mailed our Help Desk to have a trouble ticket (# 64034) opened to cover this issue.

At approximately 8:05 am, I gathered the log files the vendor requested be provided whenever a ticket is opened. Logged into vendor's support website to open a ticket requesting assistance with this problem. The Service request number created by the vendor's ticket system was 61486.

I examined all the log files and found entries indicating the two services went down at 4:08 am.

At 10:12 am, I e-mailed Shawn asking if the critical services on the AccountingApp servers were being monitored. If they aren't being monitored, I requested that monitoring of them be started.

At 12:27 pm, the vendor support responded to the ticket asking that I look in the Event Viewer for entries that includes references to service "beasvc" stopping.

At 1:21 pm, I responded to that e-mail providing examples of entries with "beasvc service." These entries corroborated that the problem occurred at 4:08 am on November 18, 2013.

At 1:46 pm, Peter requested that I send him two specific dump files. Advice at the time was:

IstageBPMCS1 service stopped since it could no longer connect to Server1 to transfer messages.

IstageBPMCS1 and Server1 are configured as a JMS Bridge. We need to find out why Server1 was not available during that time.

At 1:54 pm, I provided the requested files to Peter.

On November 19, 2013 at 9:03 am, Peter said the log files I sent yesterday contained an indication of why service Server1 stopped. He stated "Unfortunately, none of the logs contained an indication for why Server1 service stopped on November 18th 4:08:16 am as reported by Windows Event Viewer."

At 10:23 am, he asked me to provide log files C:\ AccountingApp\Domain\hs_err_pid*.log.

At 10:28 am, I sent him the three files matching that name format.

At 11:15 am, Peter said he had identified the cause of the crash.

The crash is occurring in the JVM (Java Virtual Machine) when running the hotspot compiled code for this function: "com.accountingapp.apps.common.ButtonLoaderAction.doLoad."

Work-around for now is to run the steps below to exclude that function from being compiled.

The real fix will be in a new 7.X patch containing new version of JVM containing the hotspot compiler fix. (Release date is not known at this point.)

At 8:17 pm on November 19, Peter replied that the problem was random so if another user clicked the same button on the same page, there is no guarantee that the crash would occur again. He suggested that we implement the work-around if the crashes become more frequent.

At 10:29 pm on November 19, Shawn Torson e-mailed to say all 7 AccountingApp services (4 on application server, 3 on report server) are now being monitored. If any of them stops, an alert will be issued.

Root Cause
A coding error within AccountingApp caused the application to crash when a user performed a normal function, e.g., clicked a button or tried to bring up a form.

Overview
I was alerted that AccountingApp was down at 7:49 am on June 6, 2013. The application was back up at 8:01 am. Vendor support tracked problem to a coding error in application. Error will be corrected in a future release of app. There is no ETA for this release. Work-around is available.

I worked with Shawn Torson to have all services (4 on application server, 3 on report server) be added to what is being monitored on the servers. If any of them stops, we will be alerted.

13.2 CONTACTING THE VENDOR

Different vendors frequently provide different ways of contacting them to report problems with their applications. The three most common methods I've seen are:

1. By phone
2. By e-mail
3. Via their website

My preferences for methods of reporting problems are in the following order for the specific reasons listed here. Your experience with other vendors may be that other contact methods are preferable.

- Website—By entering a problem report into a web-based ticket system, I have a high degree of confidence that exactly what I enter is going to be recorded as the details of the problem. There isn't going to be any of the copy and paste problems that could occur with e-mails and there won't be any of the misunderstandings that can occur on a phone call.

  Another advantage of a web-based system is that certain fields have likely been designated as required. If I fail to enter values into them, then the website won't allow me to advance to the next screen until something is entered into those fields. The advantage of this is that by providing complete information in the initial request I've avoided a case where the vendor has to contact me to get the missing details.
- E-mail—While this approach has the advantage of allowing me to describe the problem in my own words, it's likely that someone on the receiving end will be copying and pasting text from my e-mail into a data entry form. If that has to be done, then there is an opportunity for errors to occur.

  Another disadvantage of opening a ticket via e-mail is that if I provide a free-form problem description, it's very possible that I'll omit some required information. The first contact made by the vendor will be to request the missing information. They won't be able to start investigating the problem until they have all of the needed information.
- By phone—I feel this is the least efficient and least accurate method of reporting a problem. The biggest problem is that I have to recite a description of my problem while someone on the other end of the line transcribes it. This is neither accurate nor efficient. It takes longer and isn't as accurate as either of the other two methods. If I have a choice, I avoid submitting problem reports by phone.

  An advantage for the phone is that is allows immediate interaction with the tech, once you get them on the line. On the other hand, challenges with language can't be minimized if the support facility is in another country.

When the vendor responds to your request, they will likely give you a ticket number. Don't lose it! Each time you want to contact the vendor about that problem you'll need to refer to that number. If you correspond with them by e-mail, then the ticket number should be included in the subject line. If you want to look up the ticket on their website, then you'll almost certainly look it up by the ticket number they gave you.

13.2.1 Who is allowed to contact the vendor?

Some vendors limit the number of individuals in your organization who are able to contact their support team. The limit might be three or four individuals. One reason for doing this is so your contacts are somewhat channeled through a small group of people. If this channeling weren't done, then duplicate requests for assistance might unknowingly be opened by different individuals in your organization.

Who will be chosen to be among this select few? In general, I would suggest that the more technical people be listed as your contacts. Many of the questions to the vendor and responses from them will be extremely technical in nature. If the contact isn't technically literate, then the possibility of confusion certainly exists.

Be sure to update the contact list promptly if one of your contacts leaves the company or changes to a new job. As soon as you're aware that someone will no longer be working with the application, then request that the vendor remove the old name and replace it with the new person's name. Be sure you know how to do this in advance so valuable time isn't lost when you need a new contact setup.

13.3 PREVENTING OR MITIGATING AN OUTAGE

Responding promptly and effectively to resolve an outage is a goal to be sought after. But is it possible to do even better? Is it possible to prevent an outage completely or respond to it so quickly that most users aren't even aware that it occurred? The answer to this is that yes, it's possible to prevent or minimize problems.

13.3.1 Monitoring

It's possible that a well-designed monitoring process can catch impending problems before they reach the level of actually causing an outage. For example, if the amount of free disk space dwindles to near zero, then the operating system or application will likely go down. If a monitoring process can alert you when the amount of free space gets below a set threshold, say 5% or 10%, then you can intervene to free up disk space and prevent a potential outage from occurring.

Monitoring other key metrics can alert you to situations that could potentially cause outages or performance issues. Some common metrics to monitor include the following.

- CPU bottleneck has occurred
- Disk free space has fallen below a warning threshold
- Disk free space has fallen below a critical threshold
- Disk bottleneck has occurred
- Memory bottleneck has occurred
- Network activity has surpassed a warning threshold
- Network activity has surpassed a critical threshold
- Network errors have occurred
- Server has rebooted
- Failed logon attempt(s) have occurred
- Cluster member was removed from cluster membership
- Service with type automatic is not running
- DNS server couldn't resolve a computer name

A well-designed monitoring implementation can be used to spot trends that predict the system is approaching its limits. Such predictions provide warning to upgrade the infrastructure before failures actually occur. This is certainly a way of preventing outages and performance issues.

To be effective, your monitoring system has to be looking at the correct metrics and if something goes wrong has to send out appropriate alerts.

- Alerts have to be sent to the correct people.
- Alerts have to be sent via the correct channel. E-mails are great, but if the recipient has gone home for the night or weekend, then a critical e-mail may not be read until Monday morning. Two ways around this limitation are:
  If you have a Help Desk or other group that is manned 24×7, then they should be copied on the e-mail. If a critical alert is received after working hours, then they would call the individual listed in the application's Playbook as the primary contact to inform him or her about the problem.
  If the monitoring system can send out text messages in addition to e-mails, then use this capability to alert people about this problem no matter when it occurs. If this option is taken, then be sure that only critical alerts are sent out as text messages. Support personnel will get very upset very quickly if they get woken up at 2 am for a routine alert.

13.3.2 Automatically handling an outage

If it's possible to automate a process that will resolve a problem that causes an outage, then consider doing so. Doing this can correct the situation no matter what time or day it occurs on. For example, an application I supported occasionally would simply stop working. The vendor said it was a known issue and would be corrected in the next major upgrade. Unfortunately, they couldn't tell us when that upgrade would be released. The interim fix was to manually stop the application when the problem occurred and then restart it.

Our organization used a monitoring package to monitor the application's service that was failing (examples of such monitoring packages are: OpenView, Nagios, and SolarWinds). If the service stopped, then a script would stop the application and restart it. By automating this, we knew that the application would be down for a maximum of 10 minutes if the problem occurred. The service was being monitoring 24 hours a day, 7 days a week, so even if the application stopped in the middle of the night it would be restored almost immediately.

The alternative was to have users report the outage as soon as they noticed it. Once the problem was reported, the Help Desk would contact an Application Administrator who would remote into the system and stop/restart the application. The end-to-end time of this could be up to an hour. Monitoring the services and automating the stop/restart process has been extremely successful.

13.3.3 Getting notified when problems occur

Getting notified when a problem occurs doesn't solve the problem, but it's the first step toward fixing it. Being notified of the problem as quickly as possible is extremely important. An automated notification process is generally better than relying on users to notice and report the problem. Does the application have some critical services that can be monitored? If so, this is probably your best method of early warning.

What if the primary Application Administrator can't be reached? If the primary contact doesn't respond within an agreed upon period of time, say 10 or 15 minutes, then the secondary contact should be called? Does the Help Desk or monitoring system know who the secondary contact is for every application? The complete contact list for every application should be in the appropriate Playbook, portal, or some other known location.

13.3.4 Monitoring tools

Monitoring techniques range from simple to complex and from free to costly. Given the available choices, there is a way to monitor your application and server for every budget and environment.

13.3.4.1 Monitoring tools

Perhaps the simplest way to monitor a service on a Windows server is an option in the Services panel. Right-click on a service and select Properties and then select the Recovery tab. The screen shown in Figure 13.5 will be displayed. This screen gives you options for handling the first, second, and subsequent situations where the service fails.

The Recovery tab allows you to set up how the server will respond if the service fails. The choices in the drop-down list box next to each failure count are:

- Take No Action—This is the default so unless you modify it no action will be taken if the service fails.
- Restart the Service—If restarting the service will bring the application back up, then choose this option.
- Run a Program—If bringing the application back up is more complicated than just restarting the service, then choose the "Run a Program" option. The program that is run can do just about whatever you want it to do. For example, it could send out an e-mail or a text message. It could run a script to capture log files. It could stop the application and then restart it. Or it could be all of the above.

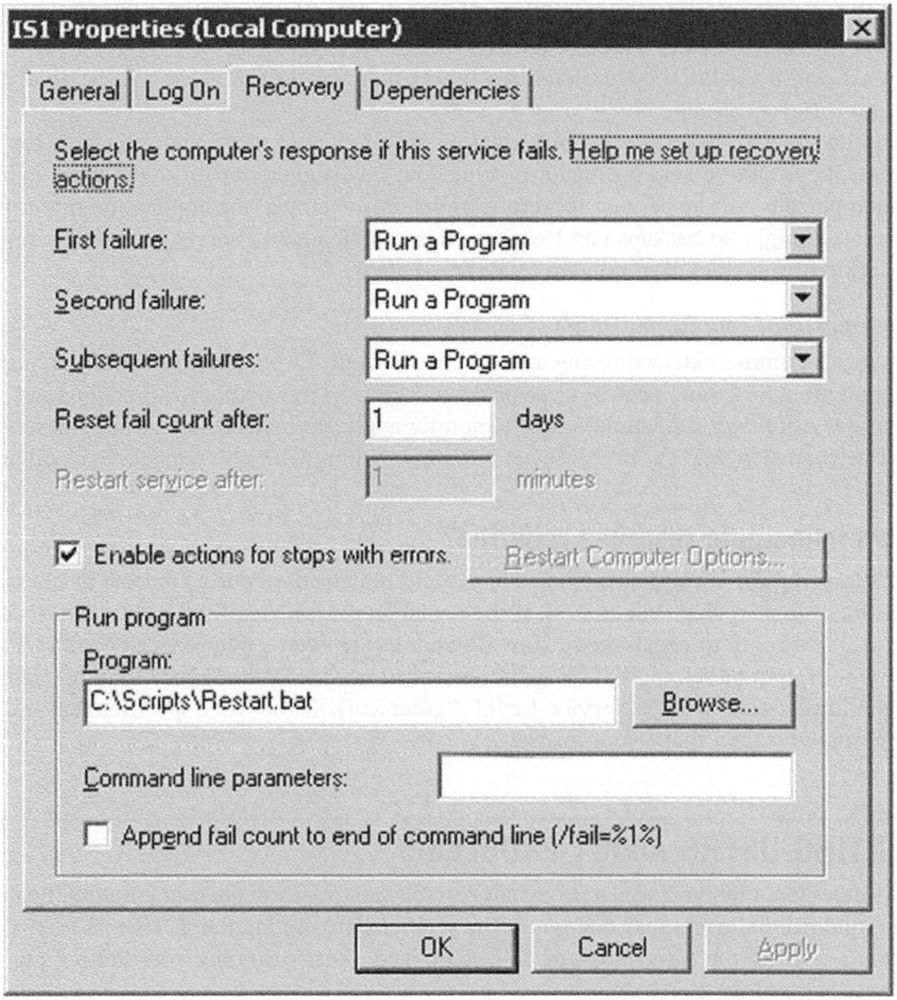

FIGURE 13.5

Recovery screen in the Windows Services panel. (For color version of this figure, the reader is referred to the online version of this chapter.)

- Restart the Computer—The final option, "Restart the Computer" would be a viable option if taking down and restarting the server was the only way to get the application back up. If multiple applications are running on the server, then this option probably isn't appropriate since it would cause an outage for them too.

13.3.4.2 Open source monitoring tools

There are many Open Source monitoring tools available if you want to go this route. Zabbix, Zenoss, OpenNMS, Nagios, and Ground Works are examples of these tools. Some of the features that Nagios offers include:

- Monitoring of system metrics, applications, and services on multiple servers.

- Sends out alerts when components fail. These alerts can be e-mails or SMS (Short Message Service) text messages sent to a mobile phone.
- If the IT staff doesn't acknowledge alerts in a timely manner, then the alert will be escalated and sent to a different group.
- Reports can be created that provide a historical record of events, alerts, and responses for review at a later time. These can be very useful for postincident investigation or for trend analysis of problems.
- Maintenance periods can be defined for applications. For example, the application might be shut down every night so backups can be taken. If an application or server goes down during these predefined time slots, then no alerts will be created.

13.3.4.3 Commercial monitoring tools

There are numerous commercial monitoring tools to choose from. Two choices are HP OpenView and Solar-Winds IT Management Software. Each of these packages offers a large number of functions and options. Like Nagios, they allow Application Administrators to monitor applications, system metrics, and services on multiple servers. Each can also send out alerts if what is being monitored deviates from defined values or statuses.

13.3.5 Is an immediate response required?

Not all applications require immediate action. They might only be used during normal business hours. They might provide functionality that isn't critical. If they crash in the middle of the night, then it's acceptable to wait until the next morning to restart them. How do you decide what's importance enough to be monitored and have alerts/notifications set up for it? Whether incidents need to be responded to immediately should be written into the application's SLA (Service-Level Agreement). If the SLA specifies that outages will be addressed immediately, then that's your answer.

13.4 ALERTING USERS ABOUT PROBLEMS

If a problem is detected, then you need to do whatever you can to inform the user community about it. If this isn't done, then additional users may encounter the problem, frustrating them. There's a good chance that multiple tickets reporting the same problem will be opened, thus frustrating you. Putting out the word on known problems is good for everyone.

There are other very good reasons for communicating with users about problems. It lets them know that the problem is actively being addressed. Knowing that you are working on the problem has a definite calming effect on users. Periodically, send them a progress report indicating the problem is still being worked. Copying your boss on these communications is a good idea too. That way he or she won't be surprised about an outage or other hit on a production application.

How can you alert the users about a known problem? The answer to this is highly dependent on your organization. The following suggestions are ways to consider informing your users. With a little imagination, you'll certainly come up with even better methods

- Sign on page—Can the sign on or log on page display a message? If so this is an extremely good solution to this problem. Make sure you don't overload this area. If you do, then users won't read it and this opportunity for informing them will be lost.
- Announcements page—Some applications have a page that precedes the sign on page that is called the Announcements page. Frequently, it just tells the users whether the application is available or down for maintenance. If you have an Announcements page, then this is another excellent place to post information about known problems.

- E-mail—If a distribution list with all application users exists, then information about known problems could be e-mailed to all users. Make sure you use this technique sparingly so you avoid overloading the users with information. For many people, the reaction to information overload is to ignore all of it.
- Inform the power users and they'll pass it along to the rest of the users. The biggest advantage of this approach is that power users will very likely understand exactly what you're talking about and can effectively pass the information along to others in their teams or sites.
- Newsletter—If your organization has a weekly or monthly newsletter and a high percentage of its recipients are users of the application, then consider including a short article about the problem. There's no guarantee that everyone will see it, but some users certainly will. With any luck, they'll educate their coworkers before or when the problem is encountered.
- Posters on bulletin boards—If all users of the application are located in the same area, then it's feasible to post information about known problems on bulletin boards in that area.

13.5 IS THERE A WORK-AROUND TO AVOID THE PROBLEM

Is there a way to work-around the problem instead of plowing right into it? Possibly, a different path to the screen in question? Maybe if a certain key combination is avoided, then the problem won't occur.

If a work-around is available, then you need to inform the user community about it. Use the same communication method you're using to for known problems to inform users about work-arounds. Helping them avoid the problem until a permanent fix can be discovered, tested, and applied makes both your life and their lives less frustrating.

13.6 SHOULD YOU GATHER DETAILS OR IMMEDIATELY GET THE SYSTEM BACK UP

There's a very delicate balance between getting the system back up ASAP and taking enough time to gather information needed to determine the root cause of the problem. Sometimes, the very act of bringing the application back up destroys or hides the evidence of what caused the outage. Getting it up fast may be good as a short-term solution, but it doesn't help you understand or prevent the problem from occurring again in the future.

One way of balancing these competing demands is to write scripts that can gather the needed information much more quickly and more accurately than a person can do it manually. Typically, vendor help desks will request that you capture a certain set of log files whenever you report an error. Take the time, in advance, to write a script or a batch file that will copy those log files to a temporary subdirectory. Then when an error occurs, you can run the script and copy them almost instantly.

Another area where a script can be useful is to display the status of processes or services. For example, an application may require that one or more services be running for the application to successfully process user requests. To check on the services, you could bring up the Windows Services panel and look at each service individually. A faster approach would be to write a script that executes the "sc query" command for each of those services. Figure 13.6 shows the output of a script that checks the status of seven services that are running on two different servers. In addition to being faster and more accurate, the output of a script like this presents the status of all the services in a single command window. Capturing a screenshot of this window would be an easy way to add documentation to an Incident Report.

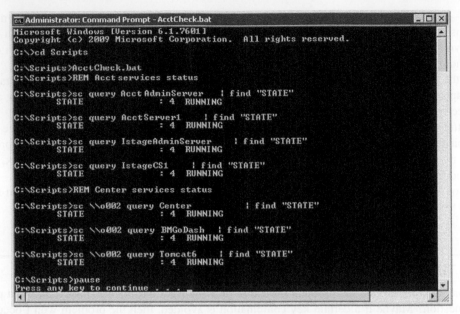

FIGURE 13.6

Script to display status of Windows services. (For color version of this figure, the reader is referred to the online version of this chapter.)

Operational Activities

While supporting an application, you will almost certainly have tasks that need to be done regularly either on demand or on a set schedule. Periodic tasks might need to be repeated every day, week, month, quarter, or year. By identifying and documenting these tasks in advance, you're less likely to overlook them. Documenting them has the additional advantage of allowing your backup to handle them if you happen to be unavailable when they need to be performed.

How frequently to perform operational activities depends on many factors. Some of them are:

- Best practices as recommended by the vendor
- Best practices as defined by your organization
- Best practices as suggested by other Application Administrators in the product's user group
- If the above sources don't cover it, then use your common sense

14.1 DAILY TASKS

Relatively straightforward tasks like those in this section will need to be done almost every day. These tasks don't take long to handle, but they aren't something you want to put off indefinitely.

14.1.1 Creating backups

The importance of successfully creating backups can't be overemphasized. It's easy to overlook the backup process once it is set up and running smoothly, but that's a huge mistake. You need to regularly confirm that the backup process is error-free, that the output is actually useable. You also need to periodically confirm that you're backing up everything that you think you are.

Most applications have a backup created every day. There are however different types of backups that can be taken of an application. Some different types are:

- Full backup—every file is backed up. Usually, this is done weekly.
- Differential—backs up the files that have been changed since the last full backup.
- Incremental—only backs up the files that have been changed since the last incremental or full backup.

14.1.1.1 What is being backed up?

Creating backups on a regular basis is a fundamental necessity, but do you know exactly what is being backed up? There are files that need to be backed up and others that don't need to be preserved. Are the correct files being backed up? Some examples of what should be backed up so that the server could be restored if the drives failed or became corrupt include the following file types:

- Data
- Executables
- Customizations your organization put into place

- Support files like the registry, ini files, resources files, properties files, xml files, etc.
- User profiles
- Log files

14.1.1.2 Backup file storage

Once backups are created, then they need to be protected. Where are backup tapes or disks being stored? Is the stage site physically secure, i.e., does it have locked rooms, sign-in/sign-out procedures, etc.? Is it protected from the elements like heat, cold, and water?

It is absolutely necessary that your backup plan includes off-site storage of backup media. This is needed because if the backup media is stored in your production site and a disaster occurs, then you could lose everything! The off-site storage could be with a commercial operation like Iron Mountain or at another location that your organization operates. You need to ensure that the storage site is distant enough that it won't be impacted by a disaster striking the production facility.

If backup media is stored off-site, then a number of additional questions need to be asked:

- What is the process for retrieving backup media from the other site?
- How quickly can it be delivered to the production or DR site?
- Where, i.e., on what drives, will it be loaded?
- Will the normal purging process of backup files delete the restored files? This could occur if your purging process is date driven, i.e., any files older than "x" days are automatically deleted.
- Has the process of requesting backup media and restoring it been tested? Has this been tested recently?

14.1.1.3 Retention

How long are your backups retained? Are critical backups, e.g., end of quarter or end of year, retained for longer periods of time? Is this retention period driven by a legal requirement for your industry?

What happens to a disk or tape once it is released?

- Are the files on it destroyed?
- If a physical media, e.g., tape, is involved, is it destroyed or reused?
- Is file destruction done in such a way it's impossible for files to be recovered?
- Does your industry have standards for how backup files are to be destroyed? Does your organization follow these standards?

14.1.1.4 Restoring from backups

Restoring from backups is a high-pressure activity. Not only is it done relatively infrequently, but most likely if it's being done then it's possible that something very bad has happened to the production environment. To maximize the chances of success, the restore process needs to be meticulously documented and regularly tested. The documentation on this process needs to be readily available to the team that will need it.

Restoring the system from backups depends on the type of backups that were made. Restoring from a full backup is strictly a matter of loading the files from backup media. If the restore is being done from a combination of full and differential or incremental files, then you need to load the most recent full backup media and then the differential or incremental media in chronological order. For example, if full backups are made every Friday and differential backups are made on other days, then the steps to restore the system on Wednesday would be:

1. Load the Friday full backup files
2. Load the Saturday differential files
3. Load the Sunday differential files
4. Load the Monday differential files
5. Load the Tuesday differential files

Doing a full backup every night would be more straightforward, but they take longer and consume significantly more storage. Combining full backups with incremental or differential backups is more efficient and requires less space, but complicates the recovery process.

Some questions that need to be thought out in advance include the following:

- Who is authorized to do decide that a restoration should take place?
- Does this person have an alternate in case the primary decision maker isn't available?
- Has the restoration process been practiced? When was the last time it was done?
- How long does it take to perform a restore?

14.1.1.5 Encryption

If your data contains PII (Personally Identifiable Information), then the backup media should be encrypted. This is especially true if it is being stored off-site. There are regular stories in the trade press about backup tapes that get misplaced. If they aren't encrypted, then any data on them is readily available to whoever found, or stole, the media.

What form of encryption is being used? Is it strong enough to keep the bad guys at bay? The field of security and encryption is changing on a daily basis. Any guidelines that I could write today will be outdated before this book hits the shelf. Your best course of action is to consult with experts regarding what encryption algorithm and key size should be chosen and deployed.

14.1.2 Backup confirmation

The common definition of the term "backup" refers to copying files from the server's disk drive to another storage media. The second storage media might be another disk drive, tape, or DVD. Typically, backups for large organizations are created using a software package like CommVault, HP's StorageWorks Enterprise Backup Solution, Sun StorageTek Enterprise Backup Software, EMC NetWorker, and IBM Tivoli Storage Manager.

Backups are created on a system to ensure that if the system fails, it can be successfully recreated from the backup media. After the backups are created, you need a confirmation that the process was successful. If the most recent backups aren't viable, then it won't be possible to recreate the system from them.

Enterprise-level backup packages like those listed above typically create reports documenting that the backup process was successful. Figure 14.1 shows the output report from the CommVault backup utility.

A warning regarding backup processes needs to be included here. You have to understand the capabilities of your backup package. It may report situations as errors that you don't need to be concerned about. One example is that some backup packages execute in two phases. During the first phase, it examines a drive's

FIGURE 14.1

A report documenting backup activity. (For color version of this figure, the reader is referred to the online version of this chapter.)

master table to identify all the files that need to be backed up. These file names are written to temporary list or table. During the second phase, the backup package attempts to copy all the files in the temporary list to the secondary storage device. If a file in the list no longer exists, then an error will be written to the report. One explanation for why a file might exist during the first phase but not the second is that it's an antivirus signature file. New AV files are loaded every day. If the backup and AV load coincide, then AV files might no longer exist on the drive during the second phase of the backup. The first error line in Figure 14.1 is an example of a file that couldn't be found during the second phase of the backup process.

Another type of error in some backup reports refers to files that can't be copied. Some backup packages aren't able to copy a file that is currently opened, i.e. in use, by another process. If they encounter an open file, an error will be included in the output report. The last two errors in Figure 14.1 refer to files that were open and therefore couldn't be backed up. Log files are the most common type of files that aren't backed up due to this situation. You will need to examine the output report because it's possible that a file critical to your application wasn't backed up for this reason.

An application that I support has a different meaning for the term "backup." This particular application depends on data that is maintained in a relational database. Additionally, pointers in the database refer to image files that are stored on the application server's file system. To this application, creating a "backup" means running a process that exports data from the database tables into flat files. Then the process creates a zip file containing both these exported database files and the image files. Everything that is needed to restore the application to a specific point in time is contained in that zip file. The vendor also supplies a restore process that takes the contents of a backup zip file and overwrites it onto the database tables and image files.

The application's concept of a backup doesn't copy the zip file to a secondary storage device. In this case, creating backups is a two-stage process. The first stage was to run the application's backup process. The second stage is to back up the zip file with a backup package like CommVault.

The application's backup process sends out an e-mail when it completes. Figure 14.2 shows what a typical successful e-mail confirmation from this application looks like. If the backup process encounters a problem and doesn't succeed, then it sends out an e-mail that clearly states the backup process failed. The text in the e-mail would be "files and databases were not backed up. Backup exited with errors. See the attached log file for more details."

These e-mails need to be distributed to more than just the Application Administrator. Ideally, they should be sent to a distribution list. If that isn't possible, then at a minimum they should go out to the Application Administrator and the alternate Application Administrator. The Business Owner of the application may also request to get copies as well.

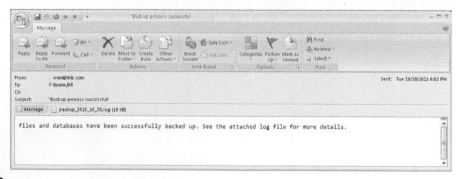

FIGURE 14.2

Examples of a backup e-mail confirmation. (For color version of this figure, the reader is referred to the online version of this chapter.)

If confirmation e-mails aren't automatically sent out, then you'll have to do a little digging to confirm the status of the backups. Log files likely contain the information you're looking for. Or you might have to examine the count and size of backup files created yesterday and compare them with the backup files that were created on previous dates.

14.1.3 Monitoring the environment

Monitoring the application on a daily basis is a very prudent thing to do. If things in the application's environment start to deteriorate and are caught quickly, you may be able to avert an outage. At the least, you may be able to prevent the situation from getting worse.

If your environment includes a monitoring package, then you can rely on it to do most of the monitoring. If you don't have a monitoring tool in place, then you should check some key metrics on a daily basis. Checking these items should be done as early in the day as possible in order to detect and correct problems before the users encounter them. Some of the items that you'll want to check are:

- Has the server rebooted since you last checked? If this has happened, then you need to investigate the cause. How can you tell if the server has rebooted? In a Windows environment, you can run the "net stats server" command in a command prompt window. Figure 14.3 shows the output line from the command that lists this in detail.
- Is the application still running? If the application isn't up, then investigating and resolving this should be your highest priority.

  There are at least two ways to check that the application is operational. The first way would be to log onto the application's server(s) and confirm that known processes or services are running. The second way to check this is to simply log into the application and confirm that it comes up. Two caveats here:
  - If the environment includes different application components, for example, a user interface and a separate reporting piece, then you'll need to log into each component to confirm that both of them are operational.
  - If the environment includes clustering or load balancing, then being able to log into the application tells you that at least one of the servers in the cluster is operational, but it doesn't tell you that all of the servers are available. To confirm that, you would have to log into each server and check it. Alternatively, you could log into the cluster administrator console, if such a tool exists, to see what servers are currently running.
- Have reports being created by the application gone out today? In the eyes of many users, the reports they receive represent the most important piece of the application. In fact, they think the reports "are" the

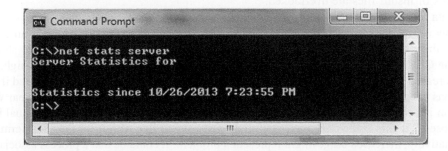

FIGURE 14.3

Windows command showing the last reboot date. (For color version of this figure, the reader is referred to the online version of this chapter.)

application. If the reports aren't being created and sent out, then many users assume that the system is down or broken. If a problem occurs with the reports, then getting them fixed should be a very high priority task.

- Did overnight processes that exist complete last night? Examples of such processes include creating export files and sending them out or receiving files from other systems and importing them into the application. These files might represent new users to be added to the application, invoices that need to be processed, transactions that need to be recorded, or changes to inventory that need to be updated. If import or export processes didn't complete, then a system somewhere doesn't have all the data it needs. Problems like this need to be addressed relatively quickly.
- Did the most recent backup processes succeed? If they didn't, then if the application or database were to crash you might lose more data than is acceptable. Resolving a problem of this type is very high priority.
- How much disk space is available on the server(s) disk drive(s)? If the current amount is dangerously low or the trend is heading in that direction, then this needs to be addressed. If the server runs out of disk space, I can all but guarantee you that the server will crash. It might not corrupt the database, but it will be very annoying for the users and a bad reflection on the support team. Murphy's law predicts that when this happens it will be at the most inconvenient possible time. Being proactive on this front will keep the users happier and make you look better.

  Running low on disk space can be caused by legitimate reasons or it can be caused if old or unneeded files aren't deleted in a timely manner. The legitimate reasons would be that the application is doing more or is being used by more users. If the storage needs are legitimate, then additional disk space needs to be added. This can be accomplished by adding more drives or replacing existing drives with larger ones. If the drives are SAN (Storage Area Network), then they can be expanded with relatively minimal effort.

  The second cause for running out of disk space is that the application, the users, or the Application Administrators aren't cleaning up after themselves properly. What kind of files can be cleaned up? A word of warning here—be sure that you don't delete files that the user community might want to retain. What looks like garbage to you might be treasure to them.
  - If the server has crashed, then there could be some very large core dump files that can be deleted.
  - There might be a large number of log files that can be compressed, archived, or simply deleted.
  - There might be test data that can be dropped.
  - There might be a large number of temp files that can be dropped. Some applications have their own / temp or /tmp subdirectory. If these exist, they should be checked for files that can be deleted.
  - If your application includes any processes that import or export data, then it's possible that old data files might exist which could be deleted.
  - Remnants of software installs or upgrades might not have been deleted. Many times the zipped versions of install files are overlooked.
  - Old data might exist on the server that can be dropped.
  - Shadow copies are snapshots of disk volumes. They are used to restore the server to an earlier state in case there is a system failure. A significant amount of disk space can be consumed by shadow copies.
- What's the CPU usage rate at? Is this rate higher than normal? If the rate is unusually high, it can reflect increased usage of the application or a problem. Increased usage might be expected if the number of users has been increased recently or if you've just entered a period of the business year when the application is being used more heavily, for example, during tax season or when the annual books are being "closed." If this is the case, then you might just have to live with it for the short term.

  Alternatively, increased usage might represent a problem. It could be that a process associated with the application or with support software is running out of control. You can use a tool like Window's Task Manager or the Unix "top" command to determine if the increase CPU utilization can be tied to a single process. If a single process is consuming the majority of the CPU time then you have probably found the culprit.

I have experienced situations where virus detection software was consuming virtually every CPU cycle that was available. That package was turned off and the problem went away. Shortly after that, we updated the virus detection software to the latest version and turned it back on. The CPU utilization problem didn't return.

- How much free memory is there? Is the amount of memory trending downward? The amount of available memory is critical to the performance of most applications. If there isn't enough memory available, then most applications won't perform as well. If the amount of available memory drops too low, then the application or the operating system can crash.

  If the amount of memory is steadily declining, it could be the result of a memory leak. An application is said to be leaking memory if it requests memory from the operating system, but doesn't free it up when it's no longer needed. Eventually it could request and leak enough memory to severely affect the server's performance.

The best solution for a leaky application is to have the code rewritten so it properly returns unused memory back to the operating system. Unfortunately, this isn't easily done. If the application is proprietary, then you won't have access to the source code. You can report the problem to the vendor, but solving such a problem may not be their highest priority.

An alternative solution is to periodically stop and restart the application. When the application is stopped, all of the memory that has been allocated to it is immediately returned to the operating system. One application I supported had memory leakage problems. The vendor support desk recommended that it be stopped and restarted weekly. We wrote scripts to stop it every Saturday morning at 1 am. A second script ran at 1:15 am to restart the application. Immediately after those scripts were put into place, performance issues with the application vanished. It wasn't the most elegant solution in the world, but it worked.

14.1.4 Investigate any alerts you receive from monitoring utilities

If you are fortunate enough to have monitoring software in place, then you'll need to pay close attention to any alerts that it issues. It might recognize and alert you to the problem, but the burden of investigating and fixing it is strictly your responsibility.

14.1.5 Follow up on user problems

When users of the application encounter problems, then one of your responsibilities will be to investigate and resolve these problems. Some of them will be caused by user errors or misunderstandings, but a fair number will be legitimate problems in the application.

The method in which you are informed of user complaints will heavily depend on how your organization is set up. Users might create a ticket in a problem tracking system. They might send an e-mail to you or to your group. Or they might just wander over to your cubicle and talk to you in person about the latest problem they've encountered.

Regardless of how you are informed about new problems with the application, it will be expected that you and/or the Application Administrator group will resolve them. Some will be as simple as educating the users of the correct way to interact with the application. Other situations will require that you dig through your notes or documentation and use previously applied solutions to fix them. The most demanding problems will necessitate that you work with the vendor to investigate and correct them.

All users will, of course, want their problems worked on immediately, but that isn't physically possible. All open tickets have to be prioritized to determine which will be addressed first and which will need to wait. Don't attempt to make this decision on your own because no matter how you prioritize the problems someone will be dissatisfied. The best way of deciding which will be worked on first is to include input from both the technical and business side of the organization.

14.2 WEEKLY TASKS

Weekly tasks could be performed on a daily basis if desired, but doing them once a week is probably acceptable.

14.2.1 Reviewing log files

Log files can contain a gold mine of information about your application, but they're meaningless if they aren't reviewed on a regular basis. Some examples of details that might exist in your log files:

- What parts of the application are being used the most
- How frequently the application is stopping and starting
- What internal errors are occurring within the application
- Security issues
- Login attempts that are failing
- If users are incorrectly using the application
- Performance issues
- Interaction with the database, especially problems that might be occurring
- Network problems
- Timeouts that users are experiencing

Your application isn't the only source of log files on the server. Any significant piece of software on the server is likely to create log files. Some examples of software that writes entries to their own log files are:

- Scheduling packages like Windows Task Scheduler or cron.
- The operating system
- Antivirus software
- Web server applications like IIS or Apache
- Application servers like WebLogic Server or IBM WebSphere
- Monitoring packages like HP OpenView or SolarWinds

The biggest difficulties about dealing with log files are:

- Where are the log files? I'm sure they don't mean to do this, but sometimes it's crossed my mind that vendors deliberately hide their log files just to be annoying. At a minimum, they don't make them easy to find. You'll find that they are spread across the subdirectory tree and tend to be tucked away deep, deep in the bowels of the application's files.
- What do log entries mean? Log file entries tend to be short to the point of being cryptic. I understand that verbose entries take longer to write and burn up more disk space, but it seems vendors tend to be on the extreme end of the spectrum when it comes to writing short, almost coded entries in their log files.

My best advice for both of the above difficulties is to stick with it and document everything you learn. Keep a document that lists every log file you deal with for the application. Similarly, keep detailed notes on every meaningful entry that you deal with.

Another piece of advice is to pester the vendor's support team members for advice and background information about log files. Ask if the vendor has a document specifically about log files. Ask them if they have any crib notes about log files. Ask if the vendor offers any classes, seminars, or webinars about their log files. The worst they can do is to tell you no.

14.3 **MONTHLY TASKS**

Monthly tasks aren't as pressing as some of the daily or weekly ones are, but that doesn't mean that they aren't important as well. If you let them slide for too long, then one of them will eventually cause significant problems.

14.3.1 **Patch weekend**

Software needs to be updated regularly. This is especially true for software that is constantly being probed by hackers for weaknesses. Vendors of large software programs, operating systems for example, regularly release patches of their products to keep up with vulnerabilities that are detected on a regular basis.

Some vendors, Microsoft, for example, release their patches on a monthly basis. To keep up with this regular feed of patches, you might want to apply them on a similar basis. Of course, you'll want to apply the patches to a test server to make sure that they don't cause unforeseen problems with your server or application.

14.3.2 **Review performance metrics**

If your organization has monitoring in place, then reviewing the statistics it creates on a regular basis is a very good idea. Every month seems to be a good interval for this. It isn't so frequent that you have to do it all the time, but it's a large enough time span that trends can be perceived. If you can chart the major statistics, then you might be able to predict when additional hardware will be needed. Some of the statistics that should be reviewed include the following:

- Amount of disk space being used or amount of free disk space available
- Number of users of the application
- Number of users logged on at a given time
- CPU utilization rate
- Number of reports created and distributed
- Disk I/O counts

The following two figures demonstrate how valuable period statistics can be for recognizing trends. Figure 14.4 shows a system on which disk space utilization isn't significantly growing and doesn't need to be addressed. Compare that with Figure 14.5 that shows a system on which disk space is rapidly disappearing. If something isn't done quickly to either recover disk space or increase the amount of available disk space on this system, then a problem is inevitable.

14.3.3 **Identify who has access to the server(s)**

The number of people who have access to the servers, especially production servers, should be limited as tightly as possible. There are very few justifications for allowing users access to a production server. Besides the Application Administrators, the list of who has access should be short. Some examples of who might need to access the server desktop include:

- Systems Administrators
- The team that administers the backup software
- Network engineers
- The team that administers the monitoring software
- The team that administers the antivirus software

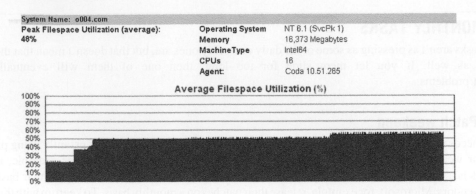

FIGURE 14.4

Statistics showing steady disk utilization. (For color version of this figure, the reader is referred to the online version of this chapter.)

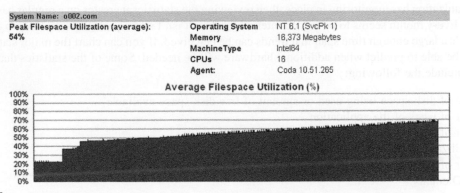

FIGURE 14.5

Statistics showing disk space is quickly running out. (For color version of this figure, the reader is referred to the online version of this chapter.)

Many organizations require that a server access report be produced periodically, say quarterly as part of their security audit process. If your organization has such a requirement, then you'll want to make sure that the process for creating this report is both accurate and well documented.

Unless you confirm who has access to your servers, it's possible that access is more widespread than you realized. To prevent this, you need to periodically confirm that no additional names or groups have been added to the access list. On a Windows server, one way to see who has access to the server is via the Computer Management tool. Click on Start | Administrative Tools | Computer Management. Under "Local Users and Groups" click on the Users and Groups to see which of each exists on the server. Figure 14.6 is a screenshot of this utility.

To see what individuals are in a group, right-click on the group's entry and select "Properties." While you need to review who belongs to each of the groups, it's critical to know who is in the Administrator group because members of it have unrestricted access to the server. Figure 14.7 is a screenshot showing the users and groups that are in the Administrators group.

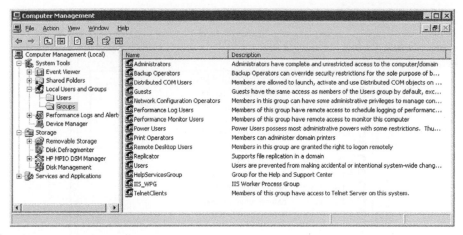

FIGURE 14.6

Computer Management tool in Windows. (For color version of this figure, the reader is referred to the online version of this chapter.)

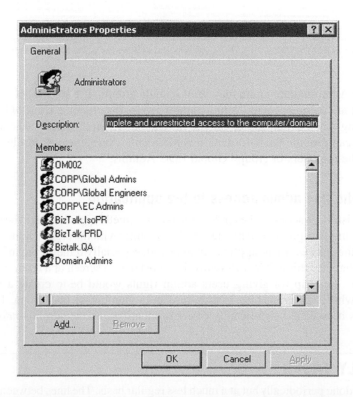

FIGURE 14.7

Members in the Administrator group. (For color version of this figure, the reader is referred to the online version of this chapter.)

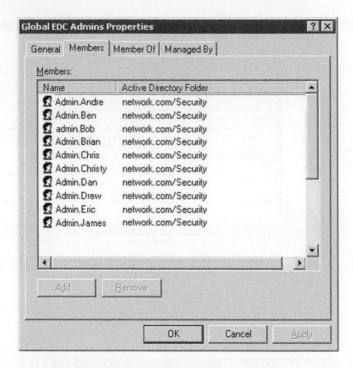

FIGURE 14.8

Members of a group in the Administrator group. (For color version of this figure, the reader is referred to the online version of this chapter.)

Unfortunately, the Administrator group may itself include groups. The screenshot in Figure 14.7 shows a number of groups that are members of the Administrator group, for example, CORP\Global Admins. It may seem like you're falling down a rabbit hole, but you need another tool to identify who are members of these groups. One tool that can provide this information is Microsoft Management Console. Figure 14.8 shows a screenshot that lists the members of group "Global EDC Admins."

14.3.4 Identify who has admin access to the application

Listing who has administrative access to the application is also something that needs to be periodically. This list should also be kept as small as possible. Anyone who is no longer with the organization or whose duties have changed should have their access to the application removed, especially if they were in an administrator role.

Every application handles this a little differently, but most have a screen or a report that lists users and the access rights each has. One tip for giving users admin rights would be to create a group or role called "Admin." Everyone who is given admin rights would be a member of that group. Doing it this way, if the application allows it, makes it significantly easier to identify who the administrators are.

14.4 QUARTERLY TASKS

Some tasks need to be done periodically but at a much less regular basis. The lines between what should be done monthly, quarterly, and annually will almost certainly vary between organizations. The suggestions here should be a guideline only. Your organization's policies, along with vendor guidance, obviously take precedence.

14.4.1 **Migrate data from production to QA, test, or DEV**

Periodically, there may be a need to migrate data from Production to another environment (QA, Test, or DEV). This might be needed to allow testing using production data to be done on a non-Production system. Users developing new reports on the QA or DEV system might need to run them against Production data.

One warning that needs to be made here is about security. If you're going to copy Production data from Production to another system, then one of the following two practices needs to be enforced:

1. The level of security on the destination system needs to be just as tight as it is on Production. Access to the servers and database needs to be the same on both environments. All security testing done on Production needs to be duplicated on the non-Production environment.
2. Personally Identifiable Information (PII) within the database needs to be obscured when it's migrated to the non-Production environment. For example, if the database contains Social Security Numbers, account numbers, birth dates, etc., then these values need to be altered so that the original values can no longer be determined.

If data is migrated from Production to another environment, then you need to have detailed documentation on this process. There are several reasons for properly documenting this process. Some of the more important ones are:

- Tasks that are done infrequently, e.g., quarterly, are more likely to have mistakes occur when they are performed. Thorough documentation will minimize this risk.
- Documentation helps ensure that the process is performed consistently, i.e., it is performed the same way every time.
- If the primary Application Administrator is no longer available, then documentation helps ensure that their replacement will be able to accomplish it successfully.
- Proper documentation can be reviewed by auditors to confirm that the process meets security requirements.
- Documentation will include a time estimate of how long the process takes to complete. This estimate can be very useful for planning purposes.

14.4.2 **Conduct a vulnerability assessment**

A vulnerability assessment is the process of identifying vulnerabilities in your application's environment. A vulnerability is defined as a weakness or flaw in the system that allows an attacker or insider to access the system in a way they're not authorized. The purpose of performing an assessment is that you can identify and correct vulnerabilities before the bad guys find and take advantage of them.

Conducting a vulnerability assessment isn't something that most Application Administrators are qualified to perform. To be done properly, it takes someone with considerable skill and experience. In addition to that, the person running the assessment needs to be able to think like a hacker. Without these skills and viewpoint, it isn't likely that the assessment will find all vulnerabilities that might exist. In many organizations a security team will run the vulnerability assessment and contact each of the Application Administrators with an assessment showing how their application did.

A very short list of vulnerabilities that need to be checked for during a vulnerability assessment include the following:

- Buffer overflows
- Input validation errors
- SQL injection weaknesses

- Privilege escalation
- Cross-site scripting (XSS)
- The existence of default accounts or passwords
- User susceptibility to social engineering attacks
- Denial-of-Service (DoS) attacks
- Weak passwords
- Versions of software that are known to be weak
- The absence of critical patches that should have been applied
- Existence of malware on the system
- The existence of software on the server that has no provenance, i.e., you can't tell that it came from a reliable source
- Integer overflow or wraparound
- Not encrypting sensitive data

There are a number of tools that might be used to help conduct a vulnerability assessment. Many of them are open source, and others are proprietary tools available for purchase from their developer. Examples of these tools include the following:

- Nessus
- OpenVAS
- SARA
- SAINT
- Core Impact
- Metasploit
- Microsoft Baseline Security Analyzer
- Retina
- Nmap Security Scanner

14.4.3 Confirm who has access to the application

Users of all applications change on a regular basis. People leave the organization. Others get a promotion or change jobs. With so much movement, it would be easy to forget to remove a former user's access from the application when they depart. Checking the list of users who have access to the application periodically is a way to confirm that someone hasn't accidentally had their unneeded access left in place.

Most applications provide a report or screen that lists all users and their level of access. A list like this can be used to confirm who should still have access. If the application documents the supervisor for each user, then break the report down by supervisors and ask them to confirm that everyone under them still needs access. If the application documents who approved each user when they were added to the system, then these approvers should be contacted to confirm that everyone on the list still needs access to the application.

In addition to making sure ex-users have their access removed, you need to confirm that users have the minimum level of access needed to do their jobs. For example, a person may have changed positions and no longer requires write access to the application. The quarterly review can be used to verify that his or her access has been changed appropriately.

In some organizations, you might not want to delete users. In these cases, you might want to disable and/or lock the user account. Anything that can be done to make the account unusable. Examples of why disabling an account might be preferable to deleting it are:

- Users might not use the application for an extended period, but will be back and will need the same accounts

- Removing users from the system might violate your audit standards
- Removing users from the application might also remove objects created or edited by them.

14.5 ANNUAL TASKS

The turning of the calendar is a natural time to review elements surrounding your application. Some of the items that should be reviewed at least once a year are listed here.

14.5.1 Review your disaster recovery plan

Chapter 12 on "Disaster Recovery" described the reasons that your DR plan needs to be reviewed and updated periodically. An annual review of this plan is a good interval. For organizations in some lines of business, it's also a requirement.

14.5.2 Test your disaster recovery plan

Chapter 12 on "Disaster Recovery" also explained why it's very important to test your DR plan. Performing this test annually is frequent enough to keep it accurate, but not so frequent that it becomes burdensome.

14.5.3 Verify what isn't being used

Usage patterns on every application change over time. Periodically, you need to review how your application is being used and whether certain pieces can be dropped. For example, if it has been a year or more since a given report has been run or requested, then it can probably be dropped.

If you find that entire components of the application aren't being used, then you might consider turning them off. If these components have an additional cost associated with them, then you might be able to experience significant savings if you update your contract with the vendor.

Even if there isn't an extra cost associated with them, it's best practice to turn off unused components. Doing this can reduce resource usage on the system as well as reducing the attack surface that an intruder might take advantage of in your environment.

14.5.4 Rebuild the system from backup tapes

One of the daily tasks was to confirm that the backup process was successful. That verification is absolutely necessary, but isn't the only testing that needs to be performed. The ultimate test is to use your backup files or tapes to recreate the system. When planning this activity, obviously you would be doing it on DR, Test, or DEV environments not your Production environment.

This activity is one that would benefit from having a project plan written for it. Writing a project plan forces you to think long and hard about the steps needed to rebuild the system. You'll want this information on paper if you ever have to rebuild the system for real. Having a plan will also give you a more accurate estimate of how long it takes to complete it.

If you already have a project plan for the system rebuild, then use this activity as an opportunity to confirm that your plan is accurate. If it isn't accurate, then update it as inaccuracies are encountered. If you ever need to rebuild the system from your backup tapes, then you'll be extremely glad that the documentation is accurate!

14.5.5 **Validate necessity of input and output feeds**

If your application requires input feeds, i.e., files, or creates output feeds being sent to other systems or applications, then you need to periodically confirm that these are still needed. Does the business need for inputs and outputs still exist? Has the functionality that these feeds support been replaced by other applications or systems? Your answer to these questions might indicate that these feeds can be dropped. If they aren't needed, then by all means delete them from the system after confirming it with the Business Owner.

Make sure that you properly document changes like this being made to the application environment. If a year from now someone comes looking to see why an input or an output feed was terminated, then you want to make sure that the justification for making this change is properly documented.

14.5.6 **Review who is backing you up**

Application Administrators as well as users change places in the organizational structure. Periodically, you need to review who supports the application as your backup, e.g. your alternate. Some of the questions that need to be answered are:

- Is the individual named as your backup last year still with the organization?
- Is he or she still in the same position?
- Has he or she received adequate training related to the application?
- When was the last time she installed an upgrade?
- When was the last time he handled a user problem?

If the answer to any of the above questions is "no" or "not in a long time," then you need to seriously reexamine your backup. The existing backup needs additional training or needs to spend more time with the application, or it might be time for a new person to have the position.

If you're the backup Application Administrator for another application, then you should review your ability to support that application. If you haven't spent any "quality time" working on it during the last year, then you need to get back into the trenches and get your hands dirty.

14.5.7 **Executing regression tests**

After each significant change to your application, it needs to be tested to validate that the change hasn't introduced problems into the application. This form of testing is called regression testing.

Periodically, the regression test needs to be reviewed to ensure that it's still meaningful. If it doesn't reflect how the application is being used, then it needs to be updated. Reviewing it at least annually with the Business Owner of the application should ensure that it still sufficiently tests the application well enough to catch problems that have been introduced.

14.5.8 **Hardware**

Software isn't the only component of the application that needs to be reviewed periodically. The hardware that makes up your application environment also needs to be reviewed periodically. The primary area to review is that references to hardware in all of your documentation are accurate. For example, in your landscape and DR documents, are the following points accurate? An annual review of your hardware is a great time to make sure that all documentation is up to date:

- IP addresses
- The amount of memory

- Size of disk drives
- Number of processors and cores
- Number of Network Interface Cards (NICs)
- The physical location of the hardware
- Load balancers
- Firewalls

Are your server(s) providing the performance that is required by the user community? If it isn't meeting user requirements, could the situation be improved by upgrading or supplementing the environment's hardware? Reviewing the application's performance on a regular basis, ideally in time to work any hardware upgrades into the annual budget, is a way to address this potential problem.

14.5.8.1 Hardware end of life

Has your hardware reached its end of life or is it rapidly approaching it? All servers reach the point where it's not economical to continue using them. Corporations typically plan to replace their server every 3-5 years. Some reasons for this are:

- They are no longer bc supported by the vendor
- Parts are increasingly difficult to obtain and when found are expensive
- New servers are more energy efficient. This is needed to make more efficient use of the finite resources in the data center
- New servers are more powerful, which is needed to keep up with growth of the application's usage

14.6 TASKS THAT ARE DONE ON DEMAND

Not all tasks need to be done on a regularly scheduled basis. Certain tasks need to be done on an as-needed basis. There will be instances when you seem to be very busy with them and at other times you won't have done it for a long while. Examples of tasks like these are listed in this section.

14.6.1 User accounts

Supporting an application means dealing with users. The higher profile or more important the application, the more users there are likely to be. Some user-related issues that need to be handled are listed in the following sections.

14.6.1.1 Adding users

One of the tasks that have to be done before an application can be used is to create user accounts.
Who will handle this task? It all depends on your organization. Some possibilities include:

- The Application Administrator
- The Help Desk
- A Super User

No matter who handles it, specific information is needed to create a new user. Develop a paper form, e-mail template, or web page that has fields for all the required information. Some of the details that need to be provided before an account can be created include the following:

- Name of user
- Employee ID number

- Network ID, for example, Jason.Smith@mycompany.com
- Phone number
- E-mail address
- Who authorized their access
- The user's supervisor
- User role being requested, e.g., reader, writer, approver, supervisor, etc.
- Organization the user belongs to
- Department the user belongs to
- Country the user resides in
- Region or state
- Default language
- Preferred date format
- Preferred number format
- Is this person an employee, contractor, consultant, intern, temporary, etc.
- When should the account be created?
- Default first screen seen by the user when the application starts

When user accounts are created make sure that a consistent naming convention is used. For example, any of the following formats could be used to create an account for user Kelly C. Bourne:

- kbourne
- KBourne
- kcbourne
- KCBourne
- kellybourne
- KellyBourne
- Kelly.Bourne
- Kelly.Bourne@mycompany.com

What's more important than the exact format that is chosen is consistently using the chosen format.

Name collisions are a problem that occurs when multiple users have names that get translated into the same user name. For example, if your naming convention is first initial and last name, then John Smith and Jerome Smith will have a name collision, i.e., they will both be jsmith.

One way of dealing with a name collision is to add a number to the new user's name. The second J. Smith added will get the user name jsmith2 which doesn't collide with jsmith. A better way of handling the problem is to use the user's e-mail address, e.g., jerome.smith@companyname.com. Since e-mail addresses must be unique, you've solved your problem by piggybacking onto an identifier that they've already been assigned.

14.6.1.2 Removing users

Just as you will need to add many users, you will have to remove or deactivate them on a regular basis. Users need to be removed for a number of reasons. They might have resigned, gotten fired, changed their duties, been transferred to a new location, etc. Any of these reasons would result in them no longer needing access to the application.

If you are the one who removes or deactivates user accounts, then how will you be informed when a user should no longer have access to the application?

- Will you get an e-mail?
- A phone call?
- A weekly or monthly terminated report?
- A post-it stuck to your monitor when you're in the break room getting a cup of coffee?

Removing users in a timely manner can be critically important to your organization's security. If users aren't removed in a reasonable timeframe, there can be an incredible amount of risk.

- Is the data in the application confidential?
- Do you want an ex-employee to continue to have access to it?
- Do you want a fired or laid-off and potentially disgruntled user to have access to it?
- Can the application be accessed from outside the corporate firewall?
- Can employees (and potentially ex-employees) VPN into the application?

Hopefully, these questions will make you aware of how important it is that application access be terminated as quickly as possible.

14.6.1.3 LDAP and SSO

If you are currently using LDAP (Lightweight Directory Access Protocol) or SSO (Single Sign-on) or plan to eventually use them, you should define your naming convention to be compatible with them. It will be extremely time consuming if you have to change all of your user's names to implement LDAP. Better to adhere to the LDAP requirements from the beginning.

The two biggest advantages of using LDAP and SSO to perform user authentication are:

1. The user doesn't have to remember yet another logon and password to log into your application. They simply use their network logon and password. If you have SSO set up, then the user will be able to access the application once he or she logs onto the network.
2. If the user leaves the company, then the LDAP team is responsible for removing his or her name from the LDAP database. From that point on, those credentials won't be able to log into your application. The same security access applies to SSO.

14.6.1.4 Problems with user accounts

Users will invariably have problems with their accounts. You need processes and policies in place to address these inevitable problem occurrences. Some of the issues that you can expect are:

- Who can reset passwords on user accounts?
- How can you verify that it is actually the user asking to have a password changed?
- Who can unlock accounts that were disabled due to inactivity, maximum number of failed login attempts, etc.?
- Who can grant users additional access within the application?

Policies need to define, in advance, what users need to do when they encounter problems and request assistance. For example:

- Who should be contacted
- How requests should be made, e.g., by e-mail, by a phone call, filling out a form, etc.
- When these problems can be handled, i.e., normal business hours or 24×7
- How quickly problems will be addressed
- How a resolution will be communicated back to the requestor

14.6.2 Software upgrades

While patches can be released on a somewhat regular basis, upgrades arrive at unpredictable intervals. The good news is that generally they don't occur too frequently. The bad news is that installing them can be time consuming. Even worse, when a new release is announced there can be a significant amount of pressure to obtain it and install it quickly.

Since you can't predict when an upgrade will be released, it's very hard to plan your time to ensure that you're available to install them. The best you can do when an upgrade is announced is to read the release notes as quickly as possible to get an estimate of how much effort it will be to install it and the urgency for installing it. With any luck, upgrades from the vendor are relatively consistent, so the amount of time the last one took is a good indicator of how long the current one will take.

14.6.3 Scheduling tasks

Many, if not most, applications have tasks that need to be scheduled. Typically, these are set up when the application is originally installed. Occasionally, it will be necessary to add a new scheduled task after the application has been up and running. The good news is that usually this only takes a few minutes to set up.

What types of tasks are typically scheduled? They can be as varied as the applications that are used by organizations. A few examples are listed here:

- Backups
- Automatically bouncing application services
- Creating reports
- Creating output files
- Picking up and/or processing input files
- Purging old files
- Log scans
- Checking disk space availability
- Handling hung processes
- Reacting to system events

14.6.3.1 Restarting the application

If your server is restarted for any reason, should the application start up automatically? Many applications already do this, for example, one or more services that make up the application are started automatically by the operating system.

If your application isn't restarted automatically then you might need to write a batch file or script to handle this. For an application running on a Windows server, you could create a task in the Task Scheduler and set it to run on system reboot. The script would then start up the application.

14.6.3.2 Bouncing the application

Does the application need to be stopped and restarted (bounced) periodically? One reason that this might need to be done is to reclaim RAM lost due to a memory leak in the application.

14.6.4 Starting up and shutting down the application

All applications have to be shut down and started up again periodically. This might be if a problem occurs, for maintenance purposes, to create a backup or to install an update. You must be very experienced regarding how to do shut the application down safely and start it up again under all conditions.

It's possible that the cause of the shutdown might be another server. If the database server has to go down for maintenance, is it possible for the application to continue to function? If not, then it will need to be stopped until the database is available again.

When you need to shut down the application, whom do you have to contact? Who needs to approve the outage? Who needs to be informed about the outage? Make sure that their contact information is readily available. What if the primary contact isn't available? Who is the backup and how can you contact him or her?

14.6.4.1 Temporarily disabling monitoring

If your environment includes monitoring tools like OpenView, SolarWinds, or Nagios, then alerts are probably sent out whenever the application stops or starts. Sending out false alarms is generally a bad idea. They either cause people to react to a problem that doesn't exist or it trains them to ignore all alarms coming out of the monitoring tool.

When you're taking down or starting up the application, you will probably want to temporarily disable any monitoring that is being done. Does the monitoring tools have a "maintenance mode" so monitoring of a server is temporarily stopped? If so, then be sure to take advantage of this whenever you're going to stop or start the application. You should also include a step to disable monitoring in the documentation you write for any activity that includes stopping or starting the application.

14.6.5 Getting the users out!

There will be times when you need to get all users out of the application. There can be any number of reasons for this. You might be:

- Executing a function within the application that requires "single user mode"
- Applying an upgrade
- Creating a backup
- Restoring from a previously captured backup

Is there a way to see whether users are currently in the application? Several of the applications I've supported have ways to determine this, each in a different way. One application had a screen available to administrators just for this purpose. Figure 14.9 is a screenshot of this capability. It shows which users are currently in the application.

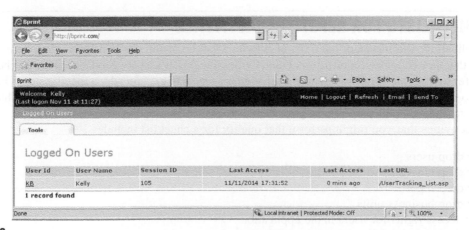

FIGURE 14.9

One example of a list of users in an application. (For color version of this figure, the reader is referred to the online version of this chapter.)

FIGURE 14.10

Second example of listing users in an application. (For color version of this figure, the reader is referred to the online version of this chapter.)

Another application I've supported has a command line interface that provides a list of users currently logged in. Figure 14.10 shows the output of this command.

A third application I've supported had a much more awkward way of determining whether users are in the application or not. You have to open a specific log file, advance to the end of it, and search backward looking for logon and logoff entries. If you find a matching login and logout entries, then it indicates a user logged in and then logged out. If you find a login entry with no matching logout entry, it indicates that the user is still logged into the application. Needless to say, this application's capability in this area was much less convenient than the previous two examples.

The point of describing these diverse methods is to emphasize that every application is different. The application you're supporting might have a convenient way of identifying logged in users, it might have an awkward method, or it might have no method at all. You need to learn which it is and be familiar with it before you need to exercise it.

Once you know whether or not users are currently logged into the application, you need to know how to force them out. Is it possible to kick users out of the application? What is the normal process? Is there emergency process for kicking users out? Can you shut down the application even if users are logged into it? You need to know how to do these things before you need to do it in a real life situation.

14.7 CHECKLISTS FOR REPETITIVE ACTIVITIES

Every Application Administrator has a list of activities that he or she performs more than once, but not so frequently that they become second nature. For activities like this, it's a very good idea to have a checklist that you can refer to when performing it. The checklist doesn't have to explain why a specific step is being done, just what to do and the order to do it in. Activities that you perform quarterly or annually seem like obvious candidates to have checklists to refresh your memory.

Some activities that you might perform that qualify for a checklist include:

- Add or drop users
- Add or drop clients
- Add or drop reports
- Add or drop business units
- Modify access rights for users in the application
- Create a new administrator for the application
- Create a backup
- Restore from a backup

- Migrate backed up data from PROD to QA or DEV
- Copying an application to a new server
- Restoring custom changes after doing an upgrade to the application
- Things to test after doing an upgrade

Creating a checklist has another valuable use. You can give it to your backup or alternate and let him or her handle some of your responsibilities. This is another way to help them gain experience supporting the application in a controlled manner.

Security

Security is a journey not a destination. As an Application Administrator, you'll need to work with other IT professionals within your organization, the vendor, and hopefully the application's user community to ensure that the application is secure. This is an area that is critically important, but traditionally underemphasized. You'll have the opportunity to learn a lot about IT security and how your organization implements it.

If your organization has a security group, then they will take the lead on many of activities described in this chapter. Some security-related steps are application specific and will be your responsibility. Others will be handled by System Administrators or DBA (Database Administrators) in your organization.

If your organization has no security group, then all security-related responsibilities might be on your shoulders. In this case, you and any other IT professionals should stress to management how important security is and request that a security position be created and filled. If your pleas go unheeded, then you'll have to use resources (like this book, as well as others dedicated to IT security) to provide the best security you can.

One point that is absolutely critical that you absorb about security is that it's not a one-time event or activity. You have to continually review security threats, policies, settings, patch levels, log files, etc. Threats against your network, server, and application are continually evolving, and your responses have to evolve too. Security is a journey not a destination.

15.1 USERS ACCOUNTS

Most computer security professionals would probably agree that people are by far the biggest threat to the security of computer systems. Their actions, or inactions, may not be malicious but frequently expose systems and applications to threats from outsiders.

15.1.1 Education

People typically resent being told that they have to perform time-consuming, inconvenient actions. If they don't understand why their passwords have to be a certain length then they resent being forced to enter lengthy passwords time and time again. If they don't understand the importance of periodically changing their passwords, they'll avoid doing it if possible. You or the security team needs to educate them of the importance of the organization's security policies. Users need to understand the threats that exist against your organization, the network, and the application that they rely upon. They may not like complying with security policies, but at least if they've been educated they'll have an understanding of why it's needed.

Like security, education is an ongoing process rather than a single event. The point in time when someone is hired or starts using your application represents an optimal time for security training to be presented. Many organizations require that a training course be completed and mastered before application credentials are issued to a new hire. You need to ensure that the training course covers the security topics needed to keep the application secure.

Like a tetanus booster shot, periodic refresher training should be provided to all users. This version of the training should contain both a summary of the original training and information on new threats that surfaced.

Refresher training shouldn't be so frequent that it prevents users from getting their work done, but on the other hand, it needs to be frequent enough to keep users aware of the organization's security needs.

15.1.2 Authentication

When users log into applications, they are typically authenticated before gaining access to it. Authentication is the process of confirming the identity of the user requesting access. There are three main ways to authenticate a user:

1. Something they know, for example, a password or PIN
2. Something they have, for example, a badge with a magnetic stripe or a smart card
3. Something they are, for example, a fingerprint or retinal scan

Most commercial applications utilize the first technique. Users are typically required to enter a valid user ID and password to the application to gain access. In the future, commercial applications may start using the other two methods in greater numbers, but that's not certain. Those methods impose significant additional costs and some experts aren't convinced the additional level of security is worth the cost.

Software that performs the authentication can either be embedded in the application or be external to the application. If the authentication process is an integral part of the application, then the application itself contains a list of user IDs and their valid passwords. This is referred to as "native authentication." Every time a user attempts to log into the application then the authentication software in the application validates that the user ID and password being entered exist in the database. If they exist, then the user is allowed to log in. If they don't exist, then the login attempt is rejected.

15.1.3 Alternative forms of authentication

Two alternative forms of authentication, i.e., external authentication, are Lightweight Directory Access Protocol (LDAP) and Single Sign On (SSO). These methods make it easier for users to log into applications.

The key question is whether both your organization and the application are capable of supporting either LDAP or SSO. To determine whether your organization supports them, contact the networking group, the security team, or other Application Administrators. To determine if the application supports them, review the application's Installation Guide or Administrator's Guide. If they don't contain references to LDAP or SSO, then you'll have to contact the vendor's support team to get your answer.

If you are intending to take advantage of either LDAP or SSO, then the application will require that some configuration settings be adjusted. Frequently, these settings are in an XML file. For example, the application will need to know the name of the LDAP server. You'll have to read the Installation Guide to identify the settings that need to be set. You'll also have to contact the group in your organization that supports LDAP to provide these details to you.

Personally, I think that LDAP authentication gives you the best return for the effort. It's true that users have to log into each application, but they don't need to remember unique logons and passwords. I also think it's significantly easier to configure applications to use LDAP authentication than SSO.

15.1.3.1 Lightweight directory access protocol

LDAP, Lightweight Directory Access Protocol, is frequently used as a central repository of information on all users. When LDAP is used to authenticate users, the application prompts the user for a logon and password as usual. After receiving these values from the user, the application passes them to an LDAP module which validates them in a centralized database. On Microsoft servers, this centralized database is frequently Active Directory (AD). If they are valid, then the application allows the user to log in. If they aren't valid, then the application rejects the login attempt. In either case, the user is unaware that an external process was used to perform the authentication.

If LDAP (or SSO) is used to authenticate users, the Application Administrator still needs to create an account within the application and assign it the appropriate access rights, starting screen, etc. What is different is that the account is tagged as using LDAP or SSO authentication instead of native authentication. So, this account needs to exist and be active in both LDAP (or SSO) and the application. If it's disabled in either of these locations, then the user isn't able to log into the application.

15.1.3.2 Single sign on

SSO, Single Sign On, is a method that allows users to log into the organization's network and from that point onward they are automatically able to access other applications without the need to log into each one. He or she just has to bring up the application, but is never presented with a logon screen.

Some of the more common SSO implementations that are available include:

- Kerberos ticket-granting ticket (TGT)
- One-time password (OTP) token method
- Security Assertion Markup Language (SAML)

15.1.3.3 Advantages of LDAP and SSO

There are numerous advantages of implementing LDAP or SSO as the authentication method for your application. Some of them are listed here:

- If network credentials are used to access applications, then users don't need to memorize separate logons and passwords for every application they use. The more applications that users log into, the more important this advantage becomes.
- If the user leaves the organization, then his account would need to be disabled in each application he has access to if native authentication is being used. If the application uses LDAP or SSO, then disabling his account in Active Directory (AD) effectively locks him or her out of every application in a single action. The Application Administrator will eventually want to delete the disabled account, but it isn't critical to do it immediately.
- If a user forgets their network password, then he or she could contact a centralized group like the Help Desk to reset it instead requesting that the Application Administrator reset it. The Help Desk is more likely to be operating 24/7 than an Application Administrator is, so users are likely to get their password reset much quicker.
- LDAP and SSO allow tighter password controls than some applications. For example, requiring users to change their network passwords on a regular basis, typically every 30, 60, or 90 days.

15.1.3.4 Disadvantages of LDAP and SSO

No advance in technology is without its disadvantages and authentication by LDAP or SSO is no exception. Some of the disadvantages are listed here:

- If the centralized database, frequently Active Directory, used for authentication isn't available for any reason, then any application that relies on LDAP or SSO won't be able to authenticate users. All user attempts to log in will fail until then centralized database becomes available again. For this reason, some application vendors recommend that an administrator account be set up that doesn't use LDAP- or SSO-based authentication.
- Not all third-party applications are designed to work with LDAP or SSO authentication. Your organization might have some applications that rely on LDAP or SSO and others that don't. This can be

confusing to users and create additional challenges/work for the Application Administrator and security teams.

- If a user's network password is cracked or otherwise becomes known, then every application that uses LDAP or SSO authentication, including yours, is compromised.
- Converting from native authentication to LDAP or SSO authentication might require that every user's profile in your application be updated.
- Not all implementations allow users from different domains, e.g., North America, Europe, Asia, etc., be supported by LDAP or SSO. This is something you need to confirm before converting to it from native authentication.
- What if a specific user doesn't have a network account, e.g., a contractor, vendor, outside client, etc.? LDAP or SSO authentication might not work for users like this.
- Implementing either of them requires configuration changes within the application.
- If you're choosing to go with SSO, it might require that additional software be acquired and installed.

15.1.4 Terminated users

It's a fact of life that users don't stay with an organization forever. On a regular basis, users retire, resign, get fired, get laid-off, change jobs, or even die. When events like this occur, their access to the application needs to be terminated.

The responsibility of who will disable their access needs to be crystal clear to everyone. The following questions need to be explicitly documented in your organization's policies:

- Will HR (Human Resources) initiate a request or announcement regarding this when the user turns in his or her notice?
- Will their supervisor submit the request or notification to terminate access?
- Is access turned off when an employee or user turns in their notice or on their final day of service?
- How does your organization know which applications this person has access to? Is this documented somewhere?
- Do the applications he or she have access to use native authentication, LDAP or SSO?
- How is the Application Administrator informed that an account should be disabled? Is this included in an e-mail, a report, a phone call?
- How quickly is the Application Administrator informed that an employee has been terminated? Real-time, end of day, weekly, monthly?
- Who actually removes application access for a terminated employee? HR, the Help Desk, their supervisor, the Application Administrator, the Active Directory team, the Network team, a Security team, or a combination of the above?

Just because an ex-employee will no longer be walking through the door doesn't mean that they can no longer access the application. Is the application accessible outside the corporate network, i.e., via the Internet? What are the ramifications if a terminated employee's access isn't disabled? Will they have access to confidential information? Can they modify confidential information?

All of their accounts need to be disabled as quickly as possible. The word "all" in the previous sentence isn't a typo since users can have multiple accounts for a given application. For example, they might have accounts on:

- The Production server
- The DEV server
- The Test server

- The DR server
- The database server

But the work doesn't stop with just disabling their personal accounts. What accounts, other than their own, might a terminated employee have had access to?

- Did they have access to an administrator account?
- Did they know the passwords for any test accounts on any of the environments listed above?
- Did any of their coworkers reveal the password to their accounts?
- Would they have known any database accounts associated with the application?

You need to immediately change the passwords on all accounts that the departing user might have known. It's better to be overly cautious and change too many passwords than not enough.

15.1.5 Security groups and users

In a Windows-based computer, users are granted access to the machine by adding them to a security group in the Computer Management utility. To open this tool, click on Start | Administrative Tools | Computer Management. To see what users and groups have been defined on this server, expand folder "Local Users and Groups."

To add a user, right-click on the "Users" folder and select the "New User" menu option. The screen shown in Figure 15.1 will be displayed. Enter the details for the user and click the Create button.

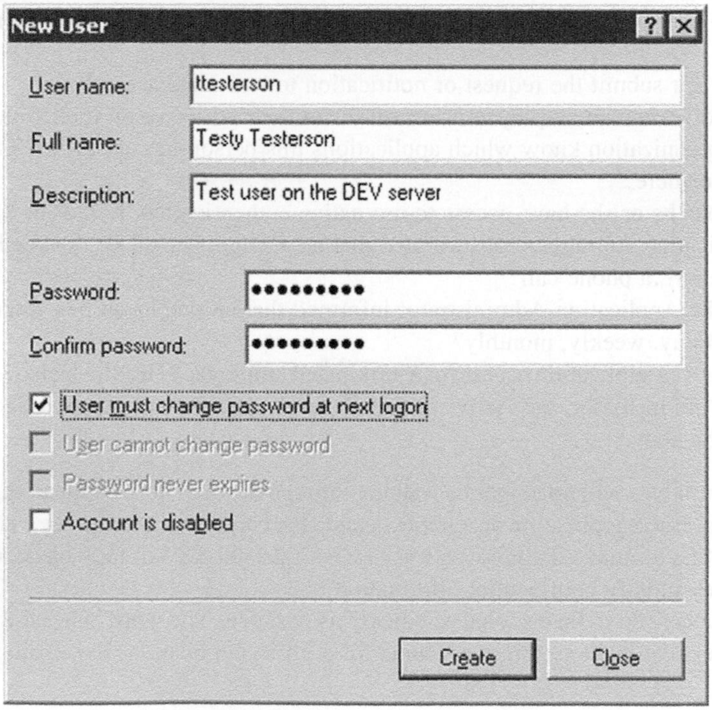

FIGURE 15.1

Adding a new user on a Windows server. (For color version of this figure, the reader is referred to the online version of this chapter.)

Once the account has been created, you need to grant it the access it needs to do things. This can be accomplished in a structured way by adding this user to an existing group instead of granting permissions to the user individually. For example, a new user might be added to the "Reader" or "Writer" group.

There are many advantages to creating groups with certain privilege sets and then assigning users to them instead of granting those same privileges to individual users. Some of these advantages are:

- It's less work to grant permissions because you only do it once, i.e., when the group is set up. After that, adding users to the group is easy.
- It allows greater visibility as to which users have which permissions.
- Maintenance is easier. If you make a change to the group's privileges, then all users in that group are automatically and immediately updated. The alternative is to modify every user's access privileges.

To add a user to one or more groups, right-click on the group in Computer Management and select the Properties menu option. Then click the "Member Of" tab. If you want to add this account to a new or additional group, click on the "Add" button, enter the name of the security group and click. Figure 15.2 is a screenshot of adding a user to the Administrator group.

15.1.6 Limiting access to a server

There are two complete different meanings to the word "access" when referring to an application. The first is access to the application, i.e., the ability to use it. All users have access to the application. They access it by bringing up the logon page and entering their credentials. The second form of access is the ability to establish a connection to the physical server on which the application software runs. This type of access should be limited to the Application Administrator and other IT professionals who need access to it to maintain it.

The number of people with access to the application server should be kept as limited as possible. There is no reason for the typical application user to be given access to the server. In some cases, the business owner or power user of the application will make a claim that they need access to accomplish their job. This may or

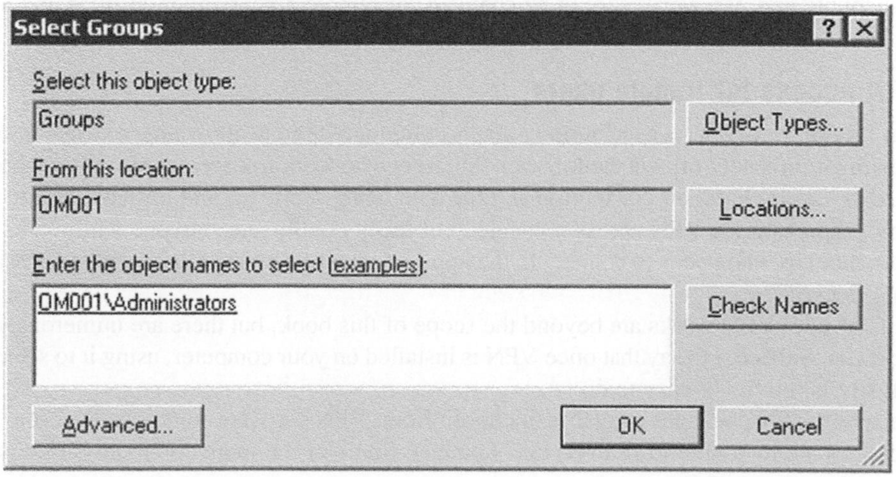

FIGURE 15.2

Adding a user to existing groups. (For color version of this figure, the reader is referred to the online version of this chapter.)

may not be accurate. To confirm this, read the application's Administrator Guide or consult with the vendor's technical support team.

It might be politically difficult, but best practices and common sense say to keep all users off the application servers, especially production. The more people that can remote to the server, the more likely it is that someone will inadvertently modify something or take the server down. If something like this were to happen, then it will also be more difficult to determine who made the change that caused the problem.

Your organization should have policies regarding the following security-related questions. If policies controlling the following don't exist, then they need to be defined and agreed to. Once the policies are established, don't ever violate them:

- Who approves creating a new user on the server?
- Who actually creates new users?
- Who approves creating new groups on the server?
- What privileges do users in each group automatically get?
- Does someone confirm that each user, group, and group member is still needed?
- Does a report exist that lists all users, groups, and group members on this server? Is it run periodically?

15.1.7 Remote access

Unless an organization has a team onsite 24×7, it will most likely allow the IT staff to remotely administer application servers. If remote administration is to be allowed, then access needs to be done as securely as possible. The following suggestions should be strongly considered:

- Include a strong authentication method like public/private key pair or two-factor authentication.
- Restrict who can remote access the server to authorized users or named IP addresses.
- Only protocols that provide encryption of both passwords and data should be used. Examples are SSH (Secure Shell) and HTTPS (Hypertext Transfer Protocol Secure).
- Accounts used to access the system remotely should have the principle of least authorization applied to them.
- Default accounts and passwords should be changed for remote authorization utilities and applications.

15.1.8 VPN access for remote users

VPN (Virtual Private Network) is a technology that is commonly used to allow remote users to securely connect to an organization's network via the Internet. All users who work from remote locations should be using VPN software to ensure that their connection and the data being sent back and forth are secure from prying eyes. In many organizations, VPN access is handed out fairly readily, e.g., anyone who works from home, from another office, or who needs to connect to the application while on the road is given VPN access to the organization's network.

The details of how VPN works are beyond the scope of this book, but there are numerous websites that provide the details. Suffice it to say that once VPN is installed on your computer, using it to securely connect to your work site is relatively easy to do.

There are many VPN packages available to choose from. VPN software comes as open source or proprietary, so packages are available to fit everyone's budget. Some of the more commonly used packages are:

- Cisco's VPN Client
- Juniper Network
- OpenVPN

- FreeS/WAN
- LogMeIn Hamachi
- Shrew Soft
- Windows Built-In VPN

15.1.9 **Least privilege for all users**

The concept of providing least privilege for users is that they are provided with the absolute minimal set of privileges they can have and still accomplish their jobs. The purpose for doing this is to minimize the changes that they'll, deliberately or inadvertently, damage the application, its data or the organization.

For example, support security roles like "reader," "writer," and "approver" have been defined in an application. If a user is only cleared to read existing documents, but not modify them or create new ones, then he or she would be assigned to the "reader" role. A reader could certainly complete their tasks if they were in the "writer" or "approver" group, but they don't need the extra access those groups grant to them.

Another reason for implementing a policy of least privilege is to minimize the damage that can be done by hackers, malware, and other bad actors. If a user has malicious software on his PC, then a hacker could be monitoring the user's actions. If the user is a reader instead of a writer or approver, then the hacker will be able to do less damage.

A word of advice to Application Administrators here, the concept of least privilege doesn't only apply to users. It also applies to you. Of course as the administrator, you should know the password for the admin account but that doesn't mean you should always use it. If you're doing something that requires the admin account, then by all means log into it. But if you're doing an activity that doesn't specifically require the admin account, then you should log in using your regular nonadministrative individual account.

15.2 BEST PRACTICES FOR USERS ACCOUNTS

Properly setting up accounts that grant access to the application has a significant impact on the security of the application. If handling accounts isn't done properly from the outset, then security will be compromised from day 1.

15.2.1 **Sharing accounts shouldn't be allowed**

As a matter of security best practices, every user should have their own account. Account sharing leads to situations where users aren't accountable for their actions. For example, if data is leaked or destroyed, the existence of a shared account might prevent you from identifying the perpetrator. You might be able to identify which account caused it, but if multiple users regularly use that account it might not be possible to determine the guilty party.

It should be repeatedly stressed to your users that they should never share their accounts with anyone else. Some organizations consider violating this security policy as a cause-for-termination offense. Being this strict might not be appropriate for all organizations, but if users are found to be sharing their account information with anyone else, then there should definitely be a resulting punishment.

One paradoxical exception to the rule of not allowing shared accounts is the administrator's account. Frequently, there are functions that can only be done by that account. If this is the case for your application, then you might have no choice but to give the account ID and password to both the primary and backup Application Administrators. Obviously, the number of people who know this account's details should be kept to an absolute minimum.

15.2.2 Remove or disable all unneeded accounts

Applications frequently come with default accounts. You may or may not need them. Make sure that one of your first steps after installing an application is to remove or disable all accounts that aren't needed. If you need to keep an account, then be sure to change the password. The names and passwords of default accounts are well known throughout the hacking community. If you leave any of them open, it won't be long before someone takes advantage of your oversight.

In addition to default application accounts, this advice also applies to software including the operating system and databases. Is there anyone who doesn't know that the default ID and password of a certain database package at one time were "scott" and "tiger"?

15.2.3 Define user groups

You should define a set of user functions that your users will be performing within the application. For example, these functional roles might be "reader," "writer," "approver," and "admin." Once the roles have been defined and reviewed, then create them within the application. As user accounts are created they are assigned to the appropriate group(s). Assigning new users to a preexisting set of roles is faster, more accurate, and more consistent than granting every new user all the access rights and privileges associated with the role.

Another advantage of defining roles is that if the role needs to have privileges added or removed, then this can be done very quickly. If this change had to be performed for each and every user in the group, it would take longer and quite likely wouldn't be done accurately.

15.2.4 Test accounts

Periodically, you will need to log into the application and see it as a user sees it. This might mean having significantly fewer rights than the admin account or even your personal account has. When accessing the application this way, you'll want one or more test accounts that have the same privileges that user groups have.

These accounts are needed to truly validate the application. If you have logged in as the admin account, you're seeing it differently than a user will see it. For the testing to be completely accurate, it needs to be done from within the same user group that users are in. So if your functional roles are "reader," "writer," "approver," and "admin," then you should create a test account for each group. Ideally, each account will have a name that makes it clear what role it belongs to. Obvious names for these test accounts would be test_reader, test_writer, test_approver, and test_admin.

The team that will be responsible for the testing effort should have access to the test accounts. This might be you and the other Application Administrators or a group of users that have been drafted because they are the best and the brightest.

Once the testing has been completed, you need to make a decision about what to do with the test accounts. At a minimum, they need to be disabled. If further testing will be done in the near future, then you might just disable them. If the testing effort is completed for the foreseeable future, then they should probably be deleted altogether.

15.2.5 Server administrative accounts

The list of people who should be admin rights on the application server should be short. The Application Administrator and his or her backup need to be an admin on the server. The others will depend on what types of technical teams your organization has. The following list of teams have legitimate needs to have admin rights on an application server:

- Server administrators
- The team that administers the monitoring software
- The team that administers the antivirus software
- The network team
- The security team
- The team that administers Active Directory
- The team that administers the backup software

15.2.6 Passwords

Many computer security types predict that the days of accounts relying on passwords to keep them secure are numbered. Passwords may or may not be around in the years to come, but for now they are critical for keeping accounts secure. To help ensure this level of security, your organization needs to develop policies that lay out what are acceptable passwords. The following points are some that should be covered:

1. What makes up acceptable passwords? This includes the length and complexity of passwords.
2. How often do passwords need to be changed?
3. When can a password be reused?
4. How many failed login attempts are allowed and what happens when the limit is reached? A limit of three is fairly common. Some applications lock the account until it's unlocked by an administrator. Other disable the account for a configurable period of time, say 1 or 2 minutes.
5. All failed login attempts need to be logged.
6. New users are forced to change their password on first sign in.
7. Uses are forced to change the password every 30, 60, or 90 days
8. Who has the authority to change passwords and/or unlock accounts?

15.2.6.1 Strong passwords

Many applications can be configured to enforce the first six points in the above list. Check the Administrator's Guide to determine how your application handles passwords. Applications that authenticate passwords frequently allow admins to enforce settings similar to these to force users to utilize strong passwords:

- Minimum length
- Requires at least one uppercase and one lowercase character be included in the password
- Requires a letter, digit, and a special character be included in the password
- A previously used password can't be reused for a certain number of days, frequently 60 or 90
- Password can't be the same as the account ID
- Password can't contain words found in the dictionary

15.2.6.2 Weak passwords

A recent trade journal article said that the most popular password found by a hacker on a popular social networking site was "123456." Other common passwords were 12345, 123456789, Password, iloveyou, princess, rockyou, 1234567, 12345678, and abc123. Can you prevent your users from picking easily guessed passwords such as these? Would the CIO at your organization be satisfied if corporate secrets were protected by these flimsy bits of security?

15.2.6.3 Who can reset passwords?

The last item in Section 15.2.6 represents a policy decision in your organization. If a Help Desk exists that's the logical group to change or reset passwords and unlock accounts. Of course, policies need to be set up so the Help Desk can verify that the requestor really is the user and not an imposter. The policy might be that the new password is sent to the user's e-mail account instead of given verbally over the phone. Of course, if the password is needed to access the user's e-mail account, then it would have to be given to them in another way.

15.2.6.4 Default passwords

It may sound obvious, but passwords are supposed to be kept secret. If possible, all users should be forced to update their password the first time they logon. There are two equally good reasons for doing this. First, it's so users don't continue to use a default password like "secret1" or "welcome2" that the administrator set up as their initial password. Second, it's so whoever reset the password won't know it once the user changes it. It isn't likely that the Help Desk guy or the Application Administrator wants to know Joe User's password, but if the user is forced to change it, then there is no question that the password is a secret.

Default accounts created by the vendor when the application is installed usually have the same default password at every installation site. If you don't change the initial passwords, then everyone who works for the vendor as well as every administrator at every site using this software in the entire world knows what your password is. If that concerns you, then change your passwords as soon as possible.

15.2.6.5 Managing your passwords

As an administrator, you'll have many passwords that you need to know. You won't need all of them on a regular basis, but will need to get your hands on them occasionally. How can you keep them straight without writing them down on a Post-It note? There are a number of utilities that will hold your passwords in an encrypted format to keep them safe. Examples of these utilities include:

- Password Safe
- Dashlane
- Hitachi ID Password Manager
- KeePass
- Kapersky Password Manager
- IronKey Personal S200

However, with all of these, the IDs/passwords are secured with a "master password" for the utility. So, there are obvious challenges if this master password is exposed, breached, or forgotten.

15.2.6.6 Unanticipated consequences of changing passwords

When a password is updated, you need to make sure that you don't stumble into any unanticipated consequences. The most likely way you'll get burned is if the account and its password are hardcoded somewhere. If it's being used in other locations, it will certainly fail its intended action. Some of these possible situations are:

- Scheduled events in the Windows scheduled
- Scripts that are run to import or export data

The solution to this is to create accounts, possibly local, that are used exclusively for that specific task. Grant it the least privilege set possible that still enables it to run the tasks it must accomplish.

15.2.7 Admin account

Every application has an Application Administrator or Super User account. Anyone logged into the application's administrator account can do just about anything in the system. Like Peter Parker's (Spiderman) uncle Ben said "With great power comes great responsibility," so make sure it's used wisely.

15.2.7.1 When to use the admin account

The rule of thumb for a super user account is only to use it only when it's absolutely necessary. Doing things like installing an upgrade, making changes directed by the vendor, restoring from a backup, etc. For activities like learning the application or testing, a problem a "normal" account should be used. The chances of causing widespread damage with the admin account make the risk of using it on a regular basis too high.

Obviously, the passwords for admin accounts should be even more tightly controlled than normal user accounts. Why should this password be so tightly controlled?

1. If multiple people know the password of any account, then you have no accountability if it was used incorrectly. Each user can deny that they were they the ones who did it. If the application's logging system records the IP address of each login operation, then you might be able to trace it back to the culprit.
2. The admin account has the ability to do a lot of damage. It can delete all objects, change them or rename them, etc.
3. If you're logged in as the admin account and a virus, malware, or Trojan horse gets installed during your session, then it has the highest level of access. The damage it could do is almost limitless.

15.2.7.2 Who should know that admin account password?

Who should know the Application Administrator account? Only the Application Administrators.

You probably want at least two people to know it: the Application Administrator and his or her backup.

Don't let any users (or your manager) talk you into giving them access to this account. If they need a higher level of access, then grant it to their individual account or role, but don't give them the super user account password!

15.2.7.3 When to change the admin account password

When do you need to change the Application Administrator account password?

- The most common situation is when it expires.
- An often overlooked time to change it is when someone who knows it leaves the company or is transferred to another job.
- One other situation when it needs to be updated is if you suspect that someone who shouldn't know it has learned it.

15.2.7.4 Is the admin account password out there somewhere?

Does the super user password exist somewhere in the files on the server? Is it embedded in any scripts, batch files, command files, etc.? You had better know the answer to this if you change it!

You don't want to find out when your nightly backup process fails.

15.3 APPLICATION SECURITY

Some steps that should be done when installing an application to help secure are:

- Confirm that the version of the software being loaded doesn't have known vulnerabilities.
- Apply patches or upgrades to address any known vulnerabilities.

- Remove or disable all unneeded default user accounts created by the application software, or change the passwords for those that have to remain.
- If any default accounts are needed to modify, the password so the default isn't being used.
- Remove all of the manufacturer's documentation from the server.
- Remove all examples or test files from the server.
- Remove any unneeded compilers, utilities, libraries, etc. from the server.
- For externally facing servers modify welcome banners to remove any specific details, e.g., O/S type and version, name and version of the application software.
- Display warning banners that advise that this is a secured system and any unauthorized persons logging in will be prosecuted to the full extent of the law.

15.3.1 Known vulnerabilities

Some of the more common vulnerabilities that exist in application software are:

- Cross-site scripting
- SQL injection
- Insecure cryptographic algorithms
- Cross-site request forgery
- Buffer and integer overflow

Finding out whether the applications your organization depends on contain vulnerabilities isn't an easy thing to do. There are a number of resources that are available and all should be checked for this critical information.

One unbiased list of potential vulnerabilities is the National Vulnerability Database (NVD). The website, http://nvd.nist.gov, allows you to search for software packages known to have vulnerabilities. Before you get your hopes up, the packages in the list tend to be operating systems, database packages, web browsers, office suites, network switches, network routers, and firewalls. It makes sense that packages like that have more patches simply because they are loaded on more servers and are the obvious targets of hackers. It will take time to search through the NVD list, but this resource should be scoured to see if your application has any known vulnerabilities.

Asking the vendor directly about the application's vulnerabilities can be done, but don't expect to be given a list of their product's shortcomings. The era of full disclosure when it comes to vulnerabilities hasn't arrived yet and may never arrive.

If there is a user group dedicated to the application, then become active in it. This is especially true if the group is independent from the vendor. Networking with your peers, i.e., other Application Administrators, is an excellent source for learning about potential vulnerabilities.

If possible, attend user conferences set up for the application. As well as an excellent time to attend presentations and network with your peers, conferences give you opportunities to meet one on one with the vendor's technical staff. They are the people that would be the most knowledgeable about potential vulnerabilities of the application.

One last method of learning about flaws in the software is to acquire and run vulnerability scanning tools on your server. The tools are designed to subject servers and applications to known vulnerabilities and determine whether the software is protected against them. On the downside, these tools can only test for vulnerabilities that have already been identified. If a brand new vulnerability, i.e., a zero-day vulnerability, is identified, these tools won't recognize then until the tool is updated.

15.3.2 **Apply patches**

The vendor's website should be referenced to get a list of patches that need to be applied to protect the application from known vulnerabilities. It's desirable to stay as close as possible to the current release level of the software. Of course, you'll want to install the patch on a test or development server first to confirm that it doesn't introduce problems for the application's use in your organization or environment.

15.3.3 **Known file locations**

Most application software is installed in widely known and predictable directories, executable names, etc. Hackers either know these details or can learn them in a matter of minutes. To avoid probes that search for known locations, consider installing the application software with nonstandard executable and directory names. This may cause some additional work during the software install and upgrades, but if it prevents you from being the victim of a hacking incursion, then it is worth it.

15.3.4 **Disable any default accounts that you don't use**

Applications frequently are installed with default accounts. If you aren't using them, then they should absolutely be either disabled or deleted. Leaving them enabled is like leaving your front door open when you're on vacation. Both are an open invitation for an intruder to walk right in.

How can you determine if your application has created any default accounts? Read the documentation looking for explicit lists of accounts or examples that use a default account. Search the vendor's knowledge base if one exists. Ask the vendor's support desk for a list of default accounts and what they are used for.

15.3.5 **Turnoff unused features**

If you're not using a feature in the application and it can be turned off, then do that. Doing this reduces the features that an intruder can potentially exploit. It also reduces the chances of a legitimate user of inadvertently using the feature and causing problems.

15.3.6 **Automatic logoffs**

Unattended application sessions represent a security threat. If a legitimate user steps away from their workstation and leaves the application running, then anyone could walk up and cause mischief. At a minimum, doing this would give them access to any confidential information that the user is allowed to bring up.

If the application has the ability to automatically logout inactive users that can minimize this security issue. If this is a configurable option, then it should probably be invoked. The biggest question now becomes what the inactive period should be set to. Your choice on this time period reflects the struggle between security types who want a short inactive period and users who want a longer inactive period.

15.4 **SERVERS**

Servers are the crown jewels of the data center. If a hacker can gain access to one of them, then the amount of damage that can be done is almost limitless. Since they are so valuable, they need to be protected to the greatest extent possible. As an Application Administrator, you probably won't be solely in charge of your server's security, but you'll want to do everything you can to help protect them.

15.4.1 Physical security

The most basic form of security is to provide physical protection for your servers. If an intruder can gain physical access to your server, then they own the box. Is the data center physically secure? Is physical access to the server room protected with locks, card readers, or guards? The same questions and concerns exist for the server, disk drives, etc.

15.4.2 Remote access to the server

Assuming physical security to the data center and servers has been put into place then the next concern is remote access to the servers. Do you know who has remote access to your application server? Can the network group in your organization provide you with a list of everyone who can access it?

It isn't consistent with "best policy" to allow users to have the ability to remotely access the application servers. If they have access to the servers, then you have no control over what they might do. For example, they might

- Delete software or files that are needed by the application
- Launch processes that consume server resources
- Inadvertently allow viruses, malware, or Trojan horses to infect the server
- Consume disk space
- Stop or interfere with application processes or jobs
- Schedule jobs that interfere with existing application-related tasks

Is there a legitimate business need for users to log directly onto the application server? They might claim that certain application functions can only be run on the server. If the users claim that this is the case, then you need to verify this with the vendor. If their claim is accurate, then you might want to investigate options like the following that enable them to do their job with a minimum of risk to the server:

- The functionality might be available remotely
- The process that they need to run could be scheduled to run at specific intervals
- An Application Administrator could run the process on the server for the users
- The user provides a batch or script file that the Application Administrator executes on the server
- The Application Administrator could use session sharing software like WebEx, NetMeeting, etc., to allow the user to kick off the process on the server via the App Admin's desktop
- An account on the server could be enabled specifically for the tasks to be run and then disabled
- Create an account on the server that can do absolutely nothing except the task in question

15.4.3 Maintenance patches

Maintenance patches can refer to changes in the application's software or support software on the server. Many patches for support software address vulnerabilities that have been identified by the vendor. Once a patch has been released, then everyone, including the bad guys, knows that the vulnerability exists. This means that you need to install these patches as quickly as reasonably possible. If your organization has a data center team, then they probably already address this type of patches.

Patches to the application's software typically come less frequently than those for support software. Application software patches generally address problems other than security. Some examples of what these patches address include:

- Fix a problem in the application
- Improve performance of the application
- Add functionality to the application

- Enable the application to work with additional databases, web server applications, etc.
- Support additional languages that users speak
- Support new forms that a government agency requires
- Handle changes to government rules or regulations, e.g., changes in the tax code

Vendor patches typically include a "read me" file that describes the changes that the patch will make. Review this file to determine if your site needs to install the patch. If the users choose not to install it, then get their decision in writing or e-mail just to be safe. If the patch needs to be installed, then install and test it on the test or development server before modifying the Production server.

15.4.4 ACLs (access control lists)

An ACL (access control list) is a method of restricting access to objects, typically files, by maintaining a list of the users and processes that are allowed to access them. ACL entries specify the type of access that is allowed, for example, read, write, create, delete. Examples of the types of files that should be protected are:

- Application executables
- Application libraries
- Configuration files
- Password hash and other authentication files
- Cryptographic keys
- Log and audit files
- Data files

15.4.5 Antivirus (AV) and malware detection tools

All computers are subject to attacks by computer viruses, Trojan horses, rootkits, and other malware. Tools exist to detect and remove malicious software. These detection tools need to be installed and maintained on application servers. Some examples of these tools include:

- Kaspersky Anti-Virus
- Norton Anti-Virus
- VIPRE Antivirus
- Webroot SecureAnywhere Antivirus
- Bitdefender Antivirus Plus
- Panda ActiveScan

If your organization doesn't have a security team that handles these tools, then the Application Administrators will need to install and maintain it. It's very important to keep these tools up to date. Antimalware software that isn't current can provide a false sense of security that can be dangerous.

15.4.6 Intrusion prevention system (IPS)

An Intrusion Prevention System (IPS) monitors the system and/or the network for activities that could be malicious. For example, attempts to access the server by unauthorized parties. If invalid activity is detected, then it will be logged. Alerts can also be sent to security or application personnel by the IPS to alert then about suspicious activity.

Some examples of IPS packages that are available are:

Check Point IPS-1
Cisco IPF Series

eTrust Intrusion Detection
IBM Security Network Intrusion Prevention System
NetScreen-IDP
Proventia
Snort
TippingPoint Intrusion Prevention System

15.4.7 Audit log files

Logging is a significant component of server security. Most applications generate log files and document problems and unusual events in it. The operating system on the application server creates a log file and writes entries to it that reflect system activity, both normal and abnormal. Intrusion Prevention System (IPSs) log suspicious activity to log files. Antivirus-scanning utilities write entries to a log file that identifies potentially dangerous software that it has found. In short, a tremendous amount of information is written to a number of log files scattered throughout the server's file system.

Mark Twain once said "a man who doesn't read good books has no advantages over the man who does not know how to read them." To me this also applies to log files. An administrator who doesn't read or review log files is no better off than one who doesn't keep log files. Log files are worthless if they aren't reviewed. Unfortunately, Application Administrators are extremely busy individuals. The last thing they need to add to the "to-do" lists is to review log files on a daily or hourly basis.

Fortunately, there are many tools, including some open source ones, exist that automate the process of reviewing log files. Acquire one, install it, and use it. Some examples of tools that scan log files looking for significant events are:

- Splunk
- PCS Log Scanning
- Nagios has plug-ins that perform log scanning
- IIS Logfile Analyser
- LogFusion
- Microsoft Log Parser

15.4.8 Encrypt disk drives

If an attacker or a malicious insider gains access to your application server, then any files on the drives are potentially accessible to them. One security technique that could thwart such a threat is to encrypt the contents of all files on the drives. Implementing encryption is not something that should be done lightly. It's also not something that should be developed locally. Acquiring a professional grade encryption product is definitely the route that should be taken. You also need to confirm with the application vendor that their package is capable of working with an encrypted environment.

Some tools that are available to encrypt disk drives are:

- FileVault 2
- BitLocker Drive Encryption
- GNU Privacy Guard
- PGP
- BitArmor DataControl
- Check Point Full Disk Encryption
- McAfee Endpoint Encryption

15.4.9 **Hardening the O/S**

Once all upgrades and patches have been applied to the operating system, the server administrator should take additional steps to harden the server. Another phrase used to describe this activity is "reducing the attack surface." Essentially means that you reduce the software on the server to the absolute minimum needed to do the job. Another possibility is to disable unnecessary services built into the operating system. The purpose of this is to minimize opportunities for attackers to exploit vulnerabilities on the server.

Specific steps that should be taken include removing unnecessary services, applications, and network protocols. If unnecessary components can't be removed, then they should be disabled. Specific examples of things that should potentially be removed include:

- File and printer sharing services, e.g., NetBIOS, NFS, FTP
- Wireless networking services
- Remote control and remote access programs, e.g., Telnet
- Directory services, e.g., LDAP, NIS
- Web servers and services
- E-mail services, e.g., SMTP
- Language compilers and libraries
- System development tools, e.g., Visual Studio, Eclipse, etc.
- System and network management tools and utilities, e.g., SNMP

15.5 **FIREWALLS**

A host-based firewall helps protect the server from unauthorized access. It does this by controlling the incoming and outgoing traffic between the network and the server. Each packet in a message is examined and if its contents are determined to be potentially dangerous then it will be blocked.

A set of rules are used to determine whether each message should be allowed through the firewall or not. Some examples of rules that can be defined are:

- Block all traffic from a specific IP address or block of IP addresses
- Allow traffic from only a set of known domain names
- Always allow traffic from domains with certain extensions, e.g., .edu or .mil
- Allow or block specific protocols, e.g., SMTP, FTP, UDP, Telnet, SNMP, or TCP
- Traffic to or from specific ports can be allowed or blocked
- Messages can be searched for specific keywords. If they are found, the message would be blocked.

Setting up the rules for any firewall can be complicated and requires ongoing attention. Unless the Application Administrator has significant experience dealing with firewalls, this responsibility should be assigned to the security team. If your organization doesn't have a security team, then petition management to add someone with this background. This type of security package definitely isn't something than can be installed and then forgotten.

15.5.1 **Ports**

In the world of computers, the term *port* refers to an interface that can exist between a computer and another device. The device can be internal or external. Examples of internal devices include hard drives, DVD drives, and USB devices like thumb drives. External devices include other servers on the far side of a network.

For a computer to use a port to communicate with an external device, the port has to be open. This means that if a firewall exists in your network architecture, then the firewall knows that communication packets are expected on the port and should be passed along. Packets may be sent from the computer to the external device and from the external device to the computer.

15.5.1.1 How applications use ports?

Most applications use at least a few ports. For example, if the application accesses an Oracle database to acquire data, then port 1521 probably needs to be open between the application server and the database server. If the application sends out e-mail, then port 25 is probably open between the application server and the mail server. If the user interacts with the application via a web browser, then port 80 is open.

15.5.1.2 What ports does your application use?

To determine what ports need to be open for your application to run you need to get the list of ports that it uses. This information can be provided in the following sources:

- The Installation Guide
- The Application Administrator's Guide
- Configuration files

If you aren't able to find the list of ports in any of the above locations, then contact the vendor's support team. They should have a complete list of ports used by the application and how they are used. If you're in the process of installing the application, then you'll need to be certain that all ports to be used by the application are open.

15.5.1.3 Commonly used ports

There are a significant number of ports that are commonly used by applications and other software. The following list provides some of them, but certainly doesn't include them all. If the software that is using a port is executing on your server, then the port will be used. Otherwise, it shouldn't be open.

Port	Usage
20	File Transfer Protocol (FTP)
21	File Transfer Protocol (FTP)
23	Telnet
25	Simple Mail Transfer Protocol (SMTP)
53	Domain Name System (DNS) service
66	Oracle SQL*NET
80	Hypertext Transfer Protocol (HTTP)
109	Post Office Protocol (POP)
111	SUN Remote Procedure Call
161	Simple Network Management Protocol (SNMP)
194	Internet Relay Chat Protocol
443	Hypertext Transfer Protocol Secure (HTTPS)
1433	Microsoft SQL Server
1434	Microsoft SQL Server
1494	Citrix Metaframe
1521	Oracle database
1524	Ingres database
1723	Microsoft VPN
3306	MySQL database
5432	Postgres

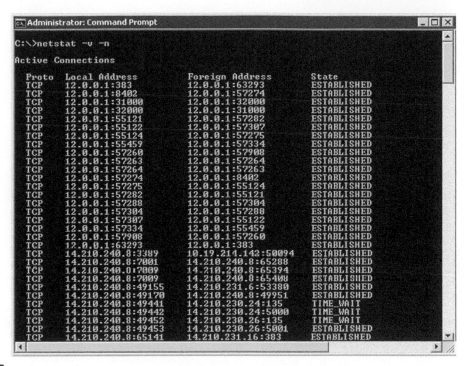

FIGURE 15.3

Output from netstat command. (For color version of this figure, the reader is referred to the online version of this chapter.)

15.5.1.4 Identifying ports being used

Ports that aren't being used should be closed to avoid allowing them to be used improperly. Once you've identified the ports being used by your application and all support software, then you can close any other ports. More realistically, the security team will be handling this, but it's good for all Application Administrators to have a fundamental understanding of how it's done.

Running a port scan can tell you what ports are open and which are blocked. One tool that scans ports on a Windows-based computer is "netstat." Entering the command "netstat –v –n" in a command window will list all ports and how they are being used. Figure 15.3 shows an example of the ports being used by a server. The first part of each address, i.e., before the colon, is the IP address of the computer. The part of the address after the colon is the port number.

15.6 WHERE IS YOUR SERVER LOCATED?

A question that the application vendor is likely to ask is "Where is your server located?" This question isn't referring to its physical location. It means where is it located in relation to the Internet, your organization's internal network, and your organization's firewall. The two possibilities are that the application server is in the DMZ, i.e., the area between the Internet and the internal network, or it's located in the organization's internal network.

Figure 15.4 shows the application server in the DMZ. This configuration would be typical if the application can be accessed from the Internet.

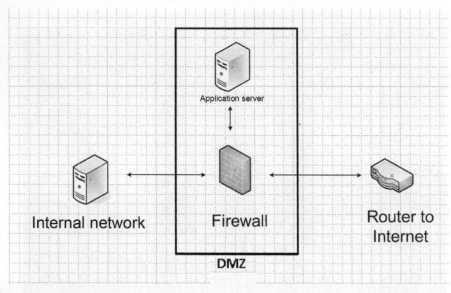

FIGURE 15.4

Application server located in the DMZ. (For color version of this figure, the reader is referred to the online version of this chapter.)

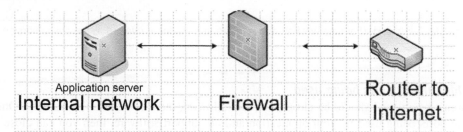

FIGURE 15.5

Application server located on the internal network. (For color version of this figure, the reader is referred to the online version of this chapter.)

Figure 15.5 shows a configuration with the application server inside the organization's internal network. This is the configuration that would be used if the application can only be accessed internally within the organization.

15.7 WEB BROWSERS

A web browser is a software application that was written to present pages from the World Wide Web to a computer user. Third-party applications that are web based require that users access their application via a web browser. The primary advantages of this are:

- By using a browser the vendor doesn't have to code the presentation component
- The typical computer user is already very familiar with using a browser

The most widely used web browsers, in random order, are:

- Mozilla Firefox
- Google's Chrome
- Microsoft Internet Explorer
- Opera
- Apple's Safari

15.7.1 **SSL—Secure Sockets Layer**

Secure Sockets Layer (SSL) is a protocol that manages security of messages transmitted on the Internet. SSL uses an encryption system that uses public and private keys to maintain the security of transmissions. Web browsers like Firefox and Internet Explorer can run SSL to secure data that is sent to and from the browser.

To implement SSL, an SSL certificate must be obtained from a certification authority. This certificate contains the public and private keys that are needed to encrypt messages that will be transmitted. Certificates are valid for between 1 and 3 years. Examples of certification authorities include:

- Symantec
- VeriSign
- GoDaddy
- Comodo

15.7.2 **HTTPS (Hypertext Transfer Protocol Secure)**

A website with an URL that begins with "HTTPS" is using SSL to secure transmissions between it and the browser. Your application might be able to utilize SSL to increase security. To determine whether it can or not refer to the Installation Guide or the Administrator's Guide. If information on HTTPS or SSL isn't in either document, then contact the vendor's support team to learn about this.

15.7.3 **Trusted sites**

A "trusted site" is a website that you have determined can be accessed and won't cause damage to your computer. If the security level on your browser is set to a high level, then you'll need to identify trusted sites in order to access them. If your application is web based, then your users might need to add the application's URL to the list of trusted sites in order for them to visit it.

15.7.4 **Time-outs**

There are many situations where you don't want a connection to stay active indefinitely. If the connection were to stay active forever, it could represent a security risk. In most cases, if the connection isn't used for a configurable period of time, it will be terminated. Examples of such places where a time-out might be desired include the following:

- If the application hasn't been used for a significant amount of time, then it will be closed
- Connections to the database are closed if no new requests are forthcoming
- If transmissions to or from the network cease, then the connection will be closed
- If the user doesn't use the mouse or keyboard for an extended period of time, then the PC will be locked

Do you have the ability to set up time-outs or determine the amount of time that must go by before an application session times out? Is it secure to accept the default time-out values? Before increasing the time-out value, make sure that you understand the implications of your actions. You don't want to make the application less secure by changing default time-out values.

15.7.5 Pop-up blockers

Many Internet browsers allow you to block online advertising that "pops up" during an Internet session. This ability is referred to as a "pop-up blocker." It's possible that your application might create additional screens to show information the user has requested. If this occurs, the browser might think that these new screens are advertisements and try to block them. If this happens, then the user will need to specify in the browsers that pop-ups from the application's website are to be allowed.

Every browser has a different method of enabling pop-ups. In Firefox, the steps to do this are:

1. Click on Tools in the main menu
2. Click on the Content tab
3. Click on the Exceptions button next to the checkbox "Block pop-up windows"
4. Enter the application's web URL and click the "Allow" button

15.7.6 Cookies

Cookies are small files created by web browsers to record information about user sessions. Web browsers can be set to disable cookies. If your application requires that cookies be created on the user's desktop machine, then users need to configure their browsers to allow them.

15.8 HACKING

Hacking is the activity of finding weaknesses in computer software, networks, or systems. Every computer that is connected to a network is a potential hacking target. If your application runs on a server that is connected to a network, then it too is a potential target. If your organization has a security team, then protecting your server will be their responsibility.

Dozens if not hundreds of books have been written about computer security and hacking. I have no delusions that this section will make the reader an expert, but providing you with a grain of knowledge might spark your interest to learn more on the topic.

15.8.1 Types of attacks

A brief list of the types of attacks that might be used against your server and application are listed here:

- SQL Injection
- Buffer overrun
- Phishing
- Spear phishing
- Botnets
- Root Kit
- Virus
- Trojan Horse

- Worm
- Denial of Service (DOS)
- Distributed Denial of Service (DDOS)

Is your app susceptible to various forms of attacks like the ones listed above? Without extensive testing, it would be hard to determine this. Some methods of learning which, if any, types of attacks it might be susceptible to are:

- Ask the vendor
- Ask the independent user group, if one exists
- Test it yourself if you have the skill, experience, and persistence
- Have a penetration test performed by a qualified, reputable security consultant or firm
- Talk to other Application Administrators who support this application
- Search the Internet for information on it
- Check the government website that tracks vulnerabilities (nvd.nist.gov)

15.8.2 **Social engineering**

A social engineering attack typically doesn't have to involve high technology. It's the art of manipulating people into giving out information that shouldn't be revealed. Some examples of social engineering techniques are:

- A hacker calls or emails a user and tells her that her account has a problem and needs to be corrected. The caller requests the user's ID and password to "fix" the problem.
- A hacker loads a thumb drive with a virus or Trojan horse and leaves it somewhere that it will be easily found. If the drive is found and connected to a PC, then the malware loads itself and enables the hacker to gain access to the system or network.
- An attacker simply follows a legitimate user through a locked entry to gain access to a secure area. This is known as "tailgating" and is especially effective if the attacker is carrying packages which prevent him or her from using their own card key to open the door.

Users need to be educated about what social engineering is and how it might be used to trick them into revealing confidential information. They should be taught that systems or Application Administrators don't need a user's password to test the system. Administrators can create test accounts or use their own accounts for testing purposes. This training needs to be repeated periodically to ensure that it isn't forgotten.

15.9 **TESTING**

You can't know if your new or existing application server is secure if it has never been tested. Testing a server to determine how secure it is brings up questions, such as:

- Who will do the testing? If the tester isn't adequately experienced and motivated, the resulting testing will be of little value.
- How often should the server be tested? Annually? Monthly? Just when it's built?
- Is it prudent to run security testing on a Production server? Will it impact your users? Could it cause a Denial of Service (DoS) situation? Could it have a major impact on performance?
- Does the server contain confidential data? If so, is it wise to subject it to security testing?

- It might be better to subject a QA server to security testing. Be aware that even if the QA system is identical to the Production system there are almost certainly some differences. Whether those differences represent additional vulnerability is difficult to say.

15.9.1 Penetration testing

According to the Committee on National Security Systems, penetration testing is "Security testing in which evaluators attempt to circumvent the security features of a system based on their understanding of the system design and implementation." Servers that hold critical information should be penetration tested. Pen (penetration) testing can't be relegated to a new hire or summer intern. It must be done by a skilled IT professional with the experience and more importantly the mindset of a hacker. The benefits of penetration testing are:

- The network and server(s) will be attacked using the same tools and methods that a hacker will use.
- If vulnerabilities exist, the intention is that pen testing will expose them so they can be corrected before the bad guys exploit them.
- Provides a sense of "realism" that many people, e.g., upper management, need to truly understand how vulnerable a server might be.
- Pen testing can determine how susceptible the organization is to "social engineering." This isn't something that can be accurately measured without an actual test.

15.9.2 Vulnerability testing

A vulnerability scan is performed by a tool that has designed to identify known vulnerabilities on servers. These tools, called Vulnerability Assessment Tools, automate the steps that a hacker would take to exploit vulnerabilities on a server. The advantages of creating a tool to automate these steps are that it can do it faster, more consistently, and on multiple servers automatically.

Some examples of vulnerabilities that these tools can find include the following:

- Open ports
- Software that isn't needed on the server
- Outdated software
- Patches that haven't been applied
- SQL injection attacks
- Buffer overflows
- Cross-site scripting (XSS)
- Capturing banners that identify the version of software on the server
- Least privilege violations

There are many tools of this nature available. Some are open source and others are proprietary. Examples include:

- Beyond Security Automate Vulnerability Detection System
- eEye Retina Network
- DragonSoft Vulnerability Management
- IBM Proventia Network Enterprise Scanner
- Lumension Scan
- McAfee Vulnerability Manager
- Microsoft Attack Surface Analyzer

- HP WebInspect
- SAINT
- Tenable Nessus

Vulnerability scans should be performed on your servers at specific points in their lives and at regular intervals. Examples of when they should be performed include:

- When the server is built, but before it going into service
- When new software is loaded onto the server
- When news of a new threat comes out
- Periodically, e.g., every 6 months

Are your application servers being scanned for vulnerabilities? If your organization has a security team, then they are probably doing this, but you need to know for sure. Contact them and request that you be made aware of when the servers are being scanned and what the results are. If your organization doesn't have a security team, then you need to bring this oversight to the attention of management and request that such scans be initiated.

The output of a vulnerability scanning isn't a checklist telling you what to do to make the server secure. Its results require a labor-intensive examination by a skilled IT professional to completely understand the vulnerabilities that might or might not exist. The results typically included numerous false positives, i.e., vulnerabilities that don't really exist.

One final recommendation when using vulnerability scanners—two are better than one. None of the available scanners are perfect. Using two scanners in combination is more likely to result in catching all vulnerabilities than just using a single one.

15.9.3 Who should be aware of testing in advance?

If you are going to subject your application servers to penetration and/or vulnerability testing, should anyone, in particular, be alerted to this in advance? Or would it be better if the testing wasn't announced? Unannounced testing are more realistic since most hackers don't call organizations up in advance and provide warnings that they are about to be attacked.

The Server

The application you support almost certainly runs on a server. The exceptions to this would be a very limited application that is loaded directly onto a user's workstation. Applications of this nature certainly aren't available enterprise-wide and wouldn't typically require the services of an Application Administrator.

The singular nature of this chapter's title is somewhat misleading. Your application may very well involve multiple servers. This is the case if any of the following is true:

- The application has separate servers for functions like the user interface, reporting, a dedicated database server, etc.
- The application environment includes load balancing or a cluster of servers
- There are separate environments for production, QA, testing, or development

There are many types of servers to be found in a large organization. Your application may include some of the following types. It's also possible that your organization has servers dedicated to the following functions that your application makes requests to. It's extremely common for one server to request services from another server. Some examples of server types are listed here:

- Database servers—Run database engines like Oracle, DB2, and SQL Server. These servers respond to requests from other servers, for example, an application server, with data that is needed to fulfill a user-requested page or function.
- Web servers—Host websites that respond to requests by users for web pages. It's fairly common for a third-party software application to run on a web server.
- File servers—Contain files that can be accessed by uses or other servers in the organization's network.
- Print servers—Prints jobs, for example, reports, checks, etc.
- Ftp server—Provide the service of transferring files into or out of the organization's network. Many applications create a daily file and then use an ftp server to transmit it to a client or a vendor organization.
- Application servers—Run applications like the one(s) you support.
- DNS (Domain Name Service) servers—Resolves the host names of servers to IP addresses. If a user enters the URL www.google.com into their browser, the DNS server is called to translate that name into the IP address that is needed before the web page can be accessed and displayed.
- Security & Directory servers—Authenticate users that request access to the network or applications.

There are numerous differences between a computer built to act as a server and the typical desktop computer. Some of these differences are:

- Powerful—A computer that is going to be used as a server typically has significantly more computing power than an individual workstation. This is achieved by having multiple processors and/or multiple cores per processor. There are exceptions to this comparison, for example, a user's workstation that has been designed for a computationally intensive task like graphics processing might have more raw CPU power than some servers.

- Resources—A generic user PC contains 4-8 GB of RAM and hundreds of gigabytes of disk space. A server might have twice as much RAM and 10-100 times more disk space.
- Reliability and Stability—Servers have to be significantly more reliable than computers used by individuals because numerous users depend on them. A server might run for months without being rebooted. It's doubtful that the average home computer could function that long continuously without crashing.
- Redundancy—Servers typically have redundancy built into them to ensure reliability and stability. For example, they might have redundant power supplies that can provide power if the primary one goes down. It might also have redundant NIC (Network Interface Card) cards for communicating with the network. If the primary card ceases to function, then communications are automatically routed through the secondary card.
- Hot swappable—In addition to having redundant components, a server may have the ability to replace components without stopping. For example, either of a server's redundant power supplies could be removed and replaced without stopping the server.
- Scalable—A server is more scalable that a typical user workstation. It has more slots that can be used for additional processors, RAM, NICs, etc.

SERVER TRIVIA

Server Trivia
Servers that don't have a monitor or other input device are said to be running in "headless" mode.

In 2010, it's estimated that servers consumed 2.5% of the energy in the United States. An additional 2.5% of all US energy consumption was needed to cool the servers.

16.1 DIFFERENCES BETWEEN SERVERS

While all servers have a great number of similarities, there are many differences. They were typically designed and built for different purposes. The two biggest differences in servers are described in the following sections.

16.1.1 Physical or virtual

A server can be either a physical device that can be seen and touched or it can be virtual. A virtual server runs on a physical server, but there is an additional layer of software that allows multiple, completely separate virtual servers to run simultaneously on a single physical server. Some of the advantages of virtual servers are:

- Running multiple virtual servers on a host server is a more efficient use of the device.
- Fewer physical servers translate into lower electrical and cooling costs.
- Virtual servers can be created and dropped much faster than physical servers can be set up.
- Each virtual server can be an identical copy of a "gold standard" that has been defined by the organization. Having each server be a clone makes the environment more consistent.
- It's relatively easy to move a virtual server from one physical server to another physical server.

The disadvantages of using virtual servers are:

- Not all application vendors certify their software to run on virtual servers. If their software isn't certified for use on a virtual server and you encounter problems on one, the vendor might not provide any assistance. More likely, they will request that you recreate the problem on a physical server before they will assist you with it.

- If the host server, i.e., the physical server, goes down, then all the virtual servers it supports will also go down.
- Virtual servers add a level of complexity that needs to be managed. This area will require someone with experience. The typical Application Administrator won't be able to support the virtual server layer.
- Problems, including performance issues, are more difficult to troubleshoot due to the additional layer of software and complexity.
- Application and operating system licenses need to be acquired for each virtual server as well as the physical server. Plus there's the cost of the virtualization software.

16.1.2 Operating system

The most common operating systems found on servers can be boiled down to three main choices:

- Linux
- Unix
- Microsoft Windows.

Each of these operating systems has variations. For example, you can be running Red Hat Enterprise Linux or SUSE Linux Enterprise. UNIX-based operating systems include Oracle Solaris and Free BSD. The two most recent "flavors" of Windows that were designed to run on servers are Windows Server 2008 R2 and Windows Server 2012.

The choice of which operating system your server runs can be determined by many things that are outside your control. For example:

- Your organization might be a UNIX or a Windows shop
- The vendor's software may only run on a specific operating system
- Your organization may be extremely sensitive to the licensing costs of operating systems
- The choice of operating systems was limited by the hardware being used.
- If data center personnel in your organization are very experienced, they may be more inclined to run the newer or build-it-yourself versions of what they are most experience with.

16.1.2.1 Operating system size

Once the type of operating system has been decided upon (Windows, UNIX, or Linux), the next decision is how many bits it should have. The choices are 32 or 64 bits. From a functional viewpoint, a 64-bit operating system handles twice as many bits as a 32-bit machine. Its registers are twice as large, 64 versus 32 bits. The addressing scheme in a 64-bit machine can access significantly more memory than a 32-bit machine. The ability to access more memory means that 64-bit machines have the potential to be faster than 32-bit machines, but this isn't always the case.

The biggest factor in the 32- or 64-bit question is what the application is certified to run under. Generally, 32-bit applications can run on a 64-bit, but applications that were written for a 64-bit computer can't be run on a 32-bit machine. The vendor's software specifics are likely to make this decision for you. Third-party applications typically can only operate on one or the other, but not both. Examine the Installation Guide for any operating size restrictions that might exist. If you can't find this specification, then you need to contact the vendor's support desk. If the wrong version of the operating system is installed on the server, then you'll lose time removing it and reinstalling the correction version.

16.2 SERVER HARDWARE

Every server requires hardware to function. The basic hardware components of servers are similar in every server, but there is room to build a server that's adapted to the needs your application will require of it. The basic hardware building blocks of a server are listed and described in the following sections.

16.2.1 Motherboard

The motherboard of a server is the circuit board that all of the other components are either mounted on or connected to. If comparisons to the human body are useful to you, then it's reasonable to compare the motherboard with either the skeleton or the backbone.

16.2.2 Processors

The processor(s) in a server are chips or chip sets that are the "brains" of the computer. General purpose processor chips are built by a limited number of companies. Two of the largest CPU (Central Processing Unit) chip manufacturers are Intel and AMD. The processors that power your server will more than likely have been provided by those vendors. Servers typically have multiple processors which each can have multiple cores.

New models of processors become available extremely quickly, so I won't list the current versions here. In general, faster processers are better than slower ones but at the same time newer processors cost more than the models that came out last quarter. The newer, faster ones might not be worth the added expense for your particular application.

16.2.3 Bus

A bus in terms of a computer is the electronic channel that data and instructions travel on from one part of the computer to another. In a comparison to the body, the bus would be the central nervous system. There are more than one kind of buses in a typical server. For example:

- System bus—communicates between the CPU and the cache memory or main memory. Also referred to as the front-side bus or local bus.
- I/O bus—used to communicate with external devices like disk drives. These are also referred to as the external bus or expansion bus.

Buses can have different speeds. A bus that is slow might be the bottleneck for the server's performance. In general, new bus types are faster than the older types of buses. The ISA (Industry Standard Architecture) bus was used in early models of the PC. More recent bus variations include the PCI (Peripheral Component Interconnect) Bus.

16.2.4 Memory

Computer memory, frequently referred to as RAM (Random Access Memory), is used to store data and computer instructions while the server is operational. If the computer shuts down, then the contents of the memory are lost.

Servers typically contain large amounts of memory, significantly more than a desktop workstation is able to address, i.e., use. Specifications provided by the software vendor will probably dictate the minimum amount of memory that your servers should have. Don't try to cut corners when it comes to memory. Your server should have at least the minimum amount specified by the vendor. Including additional memory certainly won't hurt the application's performance. In some instances, adding more RAM can change a relatively poor performing system into one that is much, much more responsive.

16.2.5 Disk drives

Disk drives are where servers permanently store data and programs. The amount of free disk space your server needs will be specified by the vendor. Don't forget that the amount listed in their documentation is what is needed over and above what is being used by the operating system and the support programs on the server.

16.2.5.1 How many drives?

How many disk drives does your application server need? While it would work to have a single, very large disk drive, there are advantages to having multiple, smaller drives. Three advantages of multiple drives are:

1. Response time can be improved because each drive can be working simultaneously. One drive can be retrieving data at the same time something is being written to a second drive.
2. If one drive crashes, then everything isn't lost.
3. More drives means that the overall storage capacity of the system is greater.

16.2.5.2 What goes on each drive?

If the server has multiple drives, there are rules of thumb regarding how files should be distributed across them. The biggest rule is that one drive, typically C: in a Windows environment, is dedicated to the operating system. The second drive typically contains the application files, e.g., libraries and executables. If a third drive exists, it could contain temp space used for calculations or log files. In most enterprise applications, data is stored on the database server so it's not impacting the local drives.

16.2.5.3 Partitions

Disk drives can be divided into separate partitions. Each partition is treated by the operating system as if it were a completely separate disk drive. Creating multiple partitions on a disk drive has the following advantages:

- The operating system can be on a separate partition from the application
- A separate partition can be defined for the paging area
- Log files can be located on a partition so they can't consume more disk space that was allocated to the partition
- Different partitions can have different Operating Systems, thus enabling the server to come up under Windows, UNIX, or Linux
- If an application and the data files it uses are on the same partition, they will be located near each other, thus minimizing the latency time, i.e., time delays for the drive to access files

16.2.5.4 Local or network drives?

Disk space can be either on a drive that is physically attached to the server or on a storage device somewhere on the network. If your server utilizes storage that resides on a SAN (Storage Area Network), then it's taking advantage of remote storage.

SAN storage had definite advantages over local drives:

- You don't have to administer SAN drives. That's the responsibility of the SAN Administrator.
- It's significantly easier to expand a SAN drive then it is to add another physical drive to your server or replace an existing local drive with a larger one.

16.2.5.5 RAID drives

RAID is an acronym for Redundant Array of Inexpensive Disks. A RAID array is a collection of drives that are treated as a single device. The purpose of implementing RAID is to make disk storage faster, fault tolerant, or both. If your disk space is on SAN storage, it's possible that it's actually residing on a RAID array.

RAID arrays can be set up in different configurations, called levels, depending on whether the intention is faster access or greater fault tolerance. Some of the basic levels are:

- RAID 0—block striping across all the drives in the array. Improves performance, but provides no fault tolerance.
- RAID 1—each drive is mirrored. Improves both performance and fault tolerance, but requires twice as many drives as RAID 0.
- RAID 3—data is byte striped across all drives. One additional drive is required for parity. Provides fault tolerance more cheaply than RAID 1 does.
- RAID 5—data is striped at the block level. Provides fault tolerance at a more efficient rate than RAID 1 and better performance than RAID 3.

16.2.5.6 Shared drives

A shared drive is literally a drive that is shared with other server(s). Shared drives provide a relatively easy method of moving files between servers. Your application might create output for a process that runs on another server. If you create a shared drive, then a specific account on that server can pull the output file off your drive.

If shared drives are created, then be sure to restrict access as tightly as possible. For example, you would want to do the following:

- Restrict which account(s) can access the share
- Specify the subdirectory that is being shared
- Restrict what can be done on the share, e.g., read, write, delete

In a Windows environment, setting up a shared drive is relatively easy. The basic steps are:

1. Open Windows Explorer
2. Browse to the subdirectory that is to be shared
3. Right-click on the subdirectory that is to be shared and select "Sharing and Security." Figure 16.1 shows this step of creating a shared drive
4. Click the "Permissions" button
5. Enter the person who is being granted access to the shared drive and the lever of access that is being granted. Figure 16.2 shows that Kelly Bourne i.e., account KB@public.com, has been granted read access to shared subdirectory tmp_tax.

16.2.6 Network information cards

A NIC (Network Information Card) supports communications between the server and the network. NICs plug into the motherboard of the server and in turn are connected to the network, typically by a cable. Servers can have multiple NICs to provide either additional throughput or fault tolerance by connecting them to different network switches.

The application installation process may prompt you for the number of NICs that the server has. This is done so it is aware of each NIC that exists. On a Windows server, you can determine how many NICs exist by entering the command "systeminfo" in a command prompt. Details on the NICs connected to the server are shown toward the bottom of the output. Figure 16.3 shows the output of the systeminfo command.

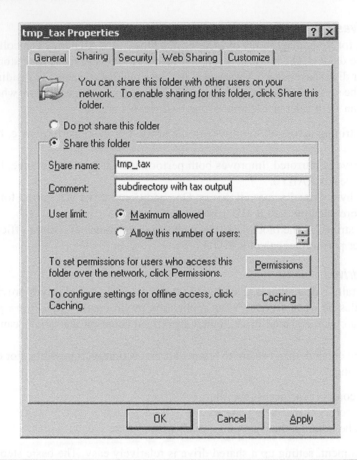

FIGURE 16.1
Defining a shared drive. (For color version of this figure, the reader is referred to the online version of this chapter.)

16.2.7 Power supply

A power supply converts AC power, i.e., wall power, to the low-voltage DC power needed by the server. Servers tend to have power supplies with greater capacity that a standard desktop computer because they tend to have more components than a desktop PC. Your server might have dual power supplies so it can stay online even if one power supply malfunctions. This is an example of redundancy, i.e., having at least one independent component to ensure system availability.

16.3 BACKGROUND PROCESSES

Operating systems have the ability to run computer programs as background processes. Background processes on a server generally don't interact with the computer console's keyboard, monitor, or mouse. They are typically initiated when the server boots up but can be launched at any time either manually or programmatically. On a Windows system, these programs are called services. On a UNIX or Linux system, they are called daemons.

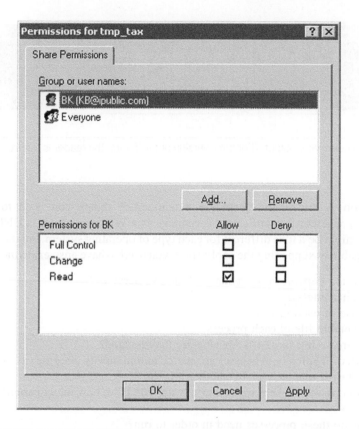

FIGURE 16.2

Granting access to a shared drive. (For color version of this figure, the reader is referred to the online version of this chapter.)

Some examples of Windows background processes and what they do are:

- 3CDMINIC.exe—driver suite for 3COM network cards
- AcroRD32.exe—Adobe Acrobat Reader program used to manage PDF files
- ALUNotify.exe—Automatic Live Update Notification for Symantec's antivirus package
- EventMgr.exe—background task for Microsoft Event Manager
- Explorer.exe—executable that runs when Windows Explorer is open
- MMC.exe—Microsoft Management Console
- Spoolsv.exe—a Windows spooling service that manages fax and print jobs
- Svchost.exe—a process that hosts processes that run from DLLs instead of EXEs
- Javaw.exe—component of Sun's Java for Windows
- Taskeng.exe—is responsible for activating legacy tasks
- Taskhost.exe—hosts UBPM-registered tasks

Most if not all third-party application requires that one or more programs be running on the server in the background to respond to user requests. They don't require intervention or handling by the Application Administrator or anyone else unless something goes wrong. The Application Administrator's Guide should provide information on whether or not your application depends on background services and what their name(s) are.

```
Command Prompt                                                    _ □ ×
Network Card(s): 1 NIC(s) Installed.
                [01]: VMware PCI Ethernet Adapter
                      Connection Name: Local Area Connection 2
                      DHCP Enabled:    No
                      IP address(es)
                      [01]: 44.61.340.6

C:\>
```

FIGURE 16.3

NIC listed in systeminfo command output. (For color version of this figure, the reader is referred to the online version of this chapter.)

As an Application Administrator, there are a number of things you need to know about them. These questions apply whether the application is running on a Windows server, a UNIX server, or a Linux server. The verbiage might be a little different for each type of operating system, but the fundamentals are the same. To be fully capable of supporting the application, you need to have answers to the following questions:

- Does your application depend on daemons or Windows Services?
- If so, what are their name(s)?
- What is the purpose of each service?
- Where is the executable file of each process?
- Do the processes create log files? If so, where are they located?
- How are they started? Typically, processes are started automatically after the operating system boots but they can also be started manually or by another process.
- Are any parameters passed to them when they are started? If so, how many parameters and what are the expected values?
- What permissions do these processes need in order to run?
- What name or account do they run under?
- If you need to stop them, how is it done?
- If multiple processes exist, what order should they be stopped and started in?
- Is this order critical or simply recommended?
- Do you need to pause after starting one process before starting the next process in the sequence? If so, how long should the delay last?
- Will the application continue to function if one or more of the processes are stopped?
- Is there a script that installs (creates) the services?
- Is there a script that drops (deletes) the services?

16.3.1 Windows services

On a Windows-based machine, these background services are called "Windows Services." If your application runs on a Windows-based server, it's a good bet that it will have one or more Windows Services doing the background processing.

16.3.1.1 Windows services panel

To see a list of the services that exist on the server you need to open the Windows Services panel. There several ways to bring up that screen:

- Start | Administrative Tools | Services
- Start | Settings | Control Panel | Administrative Tools | Services

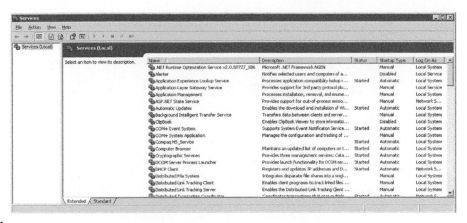

FIGURE 16.4

The Windows Services panel. (For color version of this figure, the reader is referred to the online version of this chapter.)

- Open a command window, enter "services.msc" and press the Enter key
- Start | Control Panel | Administrative Tools | Computer Management then expand "Services and Applications" at the bottom of the screen. Click on the "Services" icon.

Figure 16.4 is a screenshot of the Services panel. The most important columns are:

- Name—This is the name by which the vendor techs and documentation will refer to the service
- Status—Tells you whether or not the service is currently running. "Started" means it's running. A blank value means it isn't running.
- Startup Type—Tells you whether this service is started up automatically when the server boots. The alternatives are that it is started manually or it's currently disabled.

To get additional details on a specific service, right-click on it and select "Properties." Figure 16.5 is a screenshot of the properties of a service. The most useful detail on the General tab is the location of the executable file for the service. This screen also gives you control over the following details:

- The Startup Type drop down allows you to select whether the service should be started automatically when the server reboots, be started manually, or be disabled.
- Buttons enable you to start, stop, pause, or resume execution of the server.
- Parameters can be defined that are passed to the service when it starts execution.

The Log On tab of the Services is where you define what account the service will execute under when it is launched. The account that is specified must exist, must be active, and must have the permissions and authorization that the service needs to function. It's fairly common that the application's installation process will include a step that instructs you to create an account that all services will run under. Figure 16.6 is a screenshot of the Log On tab. In this example, the service runs under account Bprint Service.

The Dependencies tab of the Windows Services panel contains details that identify dependencies between services. In this context, dependencies means that a service requires another service be running before it can run. The screenshot shown in Figure 16.7 informs us that service Bprint AutoReminder can't be started until service TCScheduler is running. If we examined the Dependencies screen for service TCScheduler, it would list service Bprint AutoReminder in the upper panel, i.e., the area with the label "This service depends on the following system components."

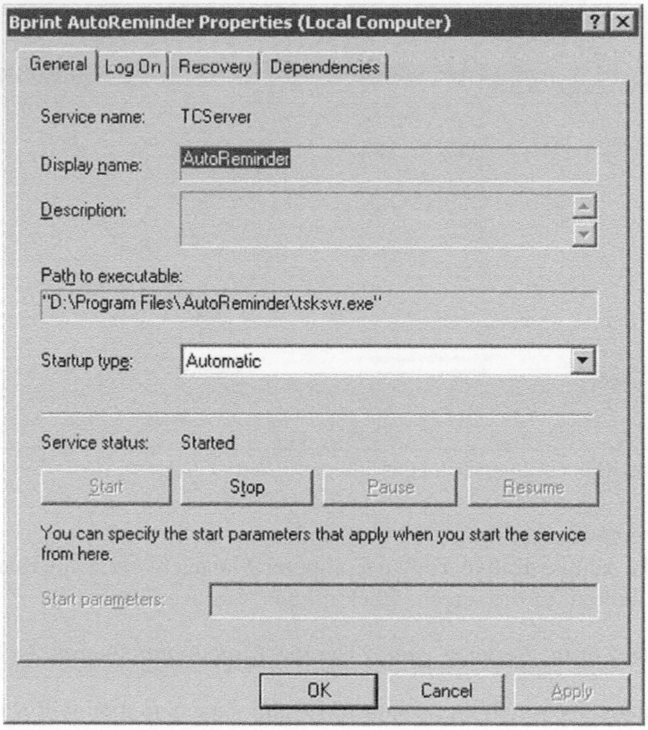

FIGURE 16.5

Properties of a specific service. (For color version of this figure, the reader is referred to the online version of this chapter.)

16.3.1.2 Command line control of windows services

Windows Services can also be administered in a command window. The basic commands for doing this are listed below:

- sc start <service-name>—starts the service
- sc query <service-name>—queries the current status of a service
- sc stop <service-name>—stops the service
- sc create <service-name>—creates a service
- sc delete <service-name>—deletes the service.

To see a list of all "sc" commands, open a command window, enter "sc ?" and press the Enter key. To see additional details for a specific command, enter "sc command ?" in a command window and press the Enter key.

16.3.1.3 Controlling windows services on another server

One feature of Windows Services commands it that it allows you to control services running on another server in your network. For example, your application might have two servers in its architecture. If you're logged onto the first server, you can use "sc" commands to control services running on the second server. This can be

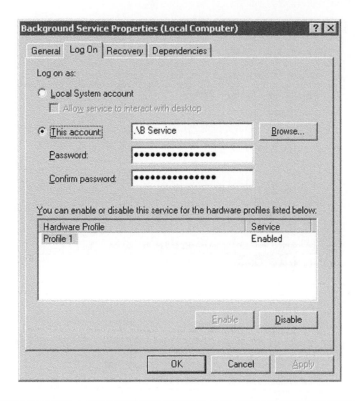

FIGURE 16.6

Log On details for a service. (For color version of this figure, the reader is referred to the online version of this chapter.)

a convenience since you don't have to log onto the other server to manipulate services on it. For example, this command:

```
sc \\opp002 stop ServiceX
```

can be issued on server opp001 to stop a service on the server named opp002.

16.3.1.4 Creating a windows services

While you might not need to know how a Windows Service is created, it's something that is useful to be aware of. It's common for the vendor to use a batch file to create the services used by the application. The batch file will likely be executed during the installation process, so you most likely won't have to execute it manually.

It's very possible that you will have to modify the Windows Services during an upgrade or while troubleshooting a problem. Knowing about the batch file, where it is located and what is in it will make it easier for you to work with a vendor tech or by yourself to debug problems.

The code shown in Figure 16.8 is an example of a batch file used by one vendor to create the Windows Service it relies upon. Batch files used by other vendors probably won't look anything like this example, but it's worth seeing one vendor's approach to creating a Windows Service.

The first statement calls another batch file, SetEnv.bat, that defines variables that are referred to in command lxasrvc. These variables contain information about the locations of files being used. The parts of the statement that actually create the service are:

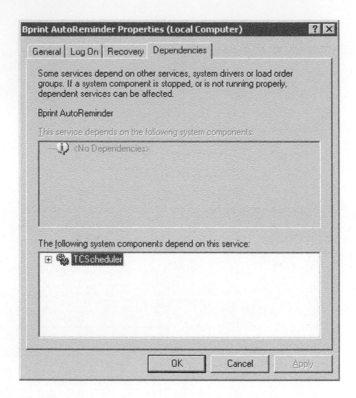

FIGURE 16.7

Dependencies details for a service. (For color version of this figure, the reader is referred to the online version of this chapter.)

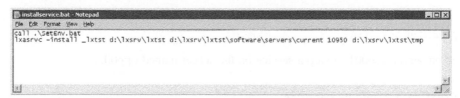

FIGURE 16.8

Contents of the batch file that creates a Windows Service. (For color version of this figure, the reader is referred to the online version of this chapter.)

1. lxasrvc is an executable provided by the vendor
2. The second parameter directs lxasrvc to do an "install" of the service
3. The name of the service will contain the suffix "_lxlwtst." The prefix for this application is always the name of the application.
4. The directory that contains the executable, i.e., . . .\software\servers\current
5. 10950 is a port that the service will use
6. The final parameter is a directory that will be used by the service to hold temporary files.

16.3.1.5 Monitoring windows services

If your application depends on a service that is critical for the application to function, then you will want to make sure it's always running. There are at least two ways to monitor it:

1. Utilize functionality that is available within the Windows Services panel.
2. If your organization already uses a monitoring tool like OpenView, Nagios, or SolarWinds, then set up that tool to monitor the application. The limitations of that monitoring tool will dictate how you can respond to the service failing. See Chapter 13 for a detailed discussion of monitoring.

If the application's service stops, then you will have to decide what you want to happen. Figure 16.9 is a screenshot of the Recovery tab in the Windows Services panel. You have four options for responding to a service's failure:

- Take No Action—Nothing will be done if the service fails. This is the default option.
- Restart the Service—The simplest response is to just restart the service. This would likely get your application up and running again, but doesn't provide you with much insight into why and how often this is happening.
- Run a Program—Allows you to run a program if the service fails. You could write a program or script that would take or all of the following actions: alert you to the problem, capture logs, and then restart the service. If you choose to run a program, then click the Browse button, navigate to the location of the program, and select it.
- Restart the Computer—An extreme choice, but could be the correct one for some applications.

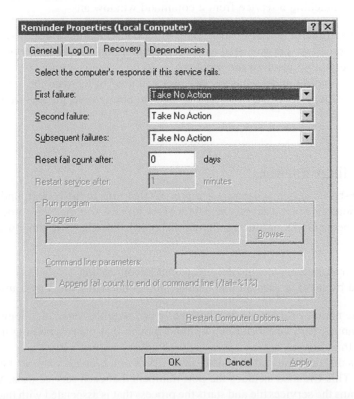

FIGURE 16.9

The Recovery tab of the Windows Services panel. (For color version of this figure, the reader is referred to the online version of this chapter.)

Note that you can have different responses depending on how many times the service has failed within a configurable number of days. The first failure might merit just restarting the service. If it fails a second time in a day, you might want to send out an alert, capture logs, and then restart it. Failures beyond the second one might motivate you to have the server restarted.

16.3.1.6 Launching a windows service from a command window

Launching services from the Windows Services panel is the way they would typically be run, but there are times you might want to launch them from a command window. To do this, open a command window, navigate to the directory that the service executable resides in, enter the name of the executable, and press the Enter key.

There are advantages of doing this when you're debugging a service. These advantages are:

- The command window will stay open, so any output created by the service is available to you. If the service is launched via the Services panel, you won't see any output from the service.
- You can pass parameters to the executable when launching it. While debugging a service, it might be helpful to pass a parameter that forces the service to perform additional logging that is be useful to the troubleshooting activity.

Two disadvantages to launching a service from a command window are:

- The service won't start automatically if the server is rebooted. During a troubleshooting effort, this isn't usually a problem, but you need to make sure that you enable the service in the Services panel once you've resolved the problem.
- The service will be running under whatever account you used to log onto the server. You need to ensure that the account being used has the appropriate permissions the service needs to execute properly.

16.3.2 UNIX and linux daemons

On a UNIX- or Linux-based server, a daemon is a process that runs in the background, typically for a long period of time. Historically, to be a daemon, the parent of the process was the "init" process. Init is always the first process started when a UNIX or Linux computer is booted. There are two other ways that a process can become a daemon:

- If the parent of a process dies, then its defacto parent becomes "init"
- Processes initiated by inetd, a daemon that manages other daemons, are also considered daemons

In a UNIX system, the names of daemons conventionally end with the letter "d." Some examples are inetd, xinetd, httpd, nfsd, named, ftpd, and ldp. Keep in mind though that there is nothing that forces third-party vendors to adhere to this rule.

The list of services that are managed by indetd on an UNIX or a Linux system can be found by examining the /etc/services file. This file also includes the port numbers that each service uses. When inetd detects a request on a port, it scans the services file and starts the process that is associated with that port. The following code snippet shows examples of entries that might exist in a services file. The meaning of each field in these lines:

service-name	port#/protocol-name	aliases	# comment
tcpmux	1/tcp		# TCP port multiplexer
tcp	6/tcp		# transmission control protocol
echo	7/tcp		
echo	7/udp		
ssh	22/tcp		#Secure shell Remote Login Protocol
ssh	22/udp		#Secure shell Remote Login Protocol
telnet	23/tcp		
smtp	25/tcp	mail	
time	37/tcp	timeserver	
time	37/udp	timeserver	
rlp	39/udp	resource	# resource location
nameserver	42/tcp	name	# IEN 116
domain	53/tcp	nameserver	# name-domain server
domain	53/udp	nameserver	
pop3	110/tcp		# POP version 3
pop3	110/udp		

16.4 WHAT'S RUNNING ON YOUR SERVER?

You may think you know what software is running on your server, but do you really know? Your organization may have standard packages of software that are loaded onto every server when it is built. You may not have asked for certain packages to be loaded, but they get installed nonetheless. Are any of the following types of software running on your server?

Types of Software	Examples
Antivirus software	Symantec, Norton AntiVirus
Firewall	WatchGuard, Symantec, Juniper
Monitoring software	HP Open View, SolarWinds
Backup software	CommVault
Delivery software	LAN Desk
Web server software	Apache, IIS, WebLogic
Database software	Oracle, SQL Server, MySQL
Email software	Outlook, SMTP
FTP server software	FileZilla, Cerebus FTP Server
Log monitoring software	Splunk, SolarWinds Log, and Event Manager
Reporting software	Crystal Reports
Load balancing software	Big IP, ACE
VM software	VMWare
Utilities	Process Explorer
Scheduling software	Control-M, Tivoli Workload Scheduler
Malware detection software	Spybot, Ad-Aware

16.4.1 How can you identify what's running on your server?

There are several methods of determining what software is running on a server, although none of them provide you with all of the details you are likely to want. One tool that can be used on a Microsoft server is the msconfig utility. The steps to use it are:

1. Click on your "Start" button and select Run
2. Type "msconfig" into the "Open" text field and press the OK button
3. The System Configuration Utility will be displayed
4. Select the "Startup" tab. All programs that are started when the server boots will be displayed. Figure 16.10 is a screenshot of this utility's Startup tab.

The Windows utility Task Manager lists all of the processes that are currently running a Windows computer, workstation, or server. Unfortunately, while it can provide some details about all of the processes, it won't tell you what each process is doing. To learn that information, your best bet is to search for it on the Internet. This tool is described in Chapter 27.

A third tool that can be used to list software on a Windows server is the Programs and Features screen in the Control Panel, specifically the "Uninstall or change a program" screen. To bring up this tool, click Start | Control Panel | Uninstall a Program. Figure 16.11 is a screenshot of this display. It lists all software that has been installed on the server. From this screen, you can modify or uninstall an application.

Both of these tools tell you what's loaded onto the server. What they can't tell you is what each of the programs does, why they were loaded, who loaded them, or whether they're really needed or not. To figure that out, you'll have to do some research. Two potential sources of this information are described here:

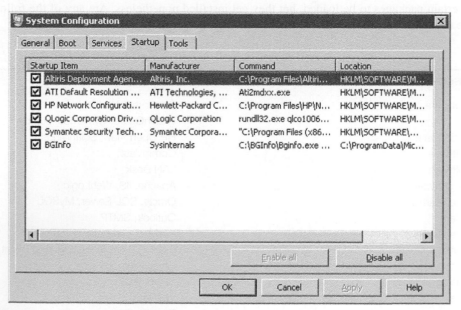

FIGURE 16.10

The Startup tab of the Windows Services panel. (For color version of this figure, the reader is referred to the online version of this chapter.)

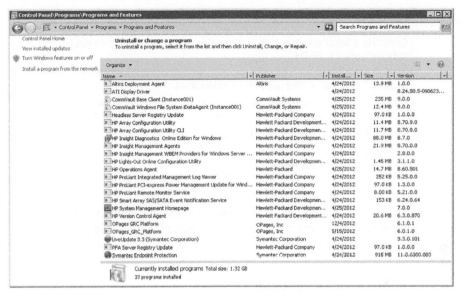

FIGURE 16.11

Microsoft uninstall a program. (For color version of this figure, the reader is referred to the online version of this chapter.)

1. Programs required by your application will likely have been listed in the vendor's Installation Guide. Checking this list should allow you to eliminate some of the programs on the server.
2. Contact the group within your organization that actually built the server. They can tell you what standard software packages were loaded onto it and what function each performs.

Anything left on the two lists of programs that haven't been accounted for yet needs to be investigated. You may have found software that can be removed from the server, but you need to proceed cautiously with this. You should contact the vendor's Support Desk to make sure you aren't about to delete software that is necessary for the application to function. You should also contact to user team to make sure it isn't something that they requested be installed on the server.

16.5 ENVIRONMENT VARIABLES

Environment variables are named values on a computer that can be dynamically changed. They can be accessed by users, applications, and processes. Environment variables exist in Windows, UNIX, and Linux-based computers, although the specific details differ for each environment.

The application you support will almost certainly refer to some environment variables. The Installation Guide will provide specifics on which environment variables need to be created before the application can be installed. You should be comfortable displaying, creating, and modifying environment variables on the operating system that your server runs on.

Some of the more common environment variables that you might encounter are listed in the following table. Of course, any given application may only refer a fraction of the environment variables that have been defined on a server.

Variable Name	What It Is Used for
PATH	Contains a list of subdirectories. When the O/S is looking for an executable, it will search all subdirectories in PATH
PATHEXT	Contains a list of file extensions, e.g., bat, cmd, and ext. When the O/S is looking for a program to launch, it will look at files with these extensions
USERNAME	The name of the user that is currently logged into the computer
JAVA_HOME	Directory where Java files will be found
ORACLE_HOME	Directory where Oracle-related files will be found
TEMP	Directory where temp files will be positioned
TMP	Directory where temp files will be positioned

To see all of the environment variables in Windows, UNIX, and Linux systems, enter the command "set" in a command window. Every currently defined environment variable on the server will be displayed in the window. Figure 16.12 is a screenshot of this command executed on a Windows server.

16.5.1 Managing variables in windows

To create or change an environment variable on a Windows server, the "set" command is used. Additional parameters determine whether the variable is being created, read, or destroyed. In the following commands, quotation marks can optionally be used to surround a text value.

To create an environment variable, the command is as follows:

```
set NEW_ENV_VARIABLE="new value"
```

To display the contents of a variable the command is:

```
set NEW_ENV_VARIABLE
```

To change the contents of a variable, the command is just like creating it:

```
set NEW_ENV_VARIABLE="new value"
```

To delete an environment variable, enter the set command, including the equal sign, but no value:

```
set NEW_ENV_VARIABLE=
```

Another method of viewing and modifying environment variables in Windows is to bring up the Advanced System Settings window in the System display. To access this screen on a Windows 2008 server, do the following:

1. Right-click on the Computer icon and select Properties
2. Click on the Advanced System Setting link
3. Click Advanced tab
4. Click the button labeled Environment Variables

The screen that is displayed will list all local and system variables. The local variables are accessible by only the account that you're logged in under. System variables are accessible by all programs and accounts. To create a new variable, edit an existing one or delete one click the appropriate buttons. Figure 16.13 shows the Environment Variables screen. If you're not comfortable using the command line, then it's a better alternative for managing variables.

FIGURE 16.12

Output of the 'set' command. (For color version of this figure, the reader is referred to the online version of this chapter.)

16.5.2 Managing variables in UNIX

On a UNIX server, the commands to create, modify, display, and delete an environment variable depend on which shell is being used. The commands for the C shell are:

To create an environment or change the value in an existing variable, the command is as follows:

```
setenv VARIABLE_NAME value
```

To display the contents of a variable, the command is:

```
printenv VARIABLE_NAME
```

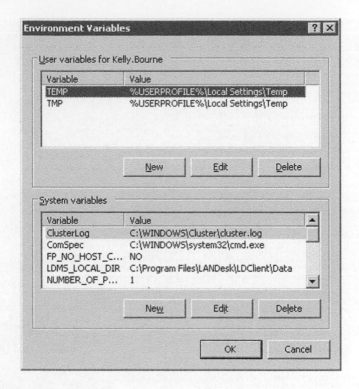

FIGURE 16.13

Environment variables on a Windows computer. (For color version of this figure, the reader is referred to the online version of this chapter.)

To delete an environment variable, enter the set command, including the equal sign, but no value:

```
unsetenv VARIABLE_NAME
```

On UNIX and Linux systems, the names of environment variables are case sensitive. For example, "HOME" and "home" are two separate variables. On Windows system, the names are not case sensitive. "WIN_HOME" and "win_home" would both refer to the same environment variable on a Windows computer.

16.6 PATH

Path is a special instance of an environment variable. It is so widely used that it needs to be discussed separately. The value held in this variable contains a list of directory names that are used to identify where executable programs or libraries are located. Every time a program needs to start the O/S will look in the directories specified in Path. If the program isn't in one of these directories, you'll get an error. If so, the choices are to:

1. Specify the exact path of the program,
2. Move the program into one of the directories specified in the Path environment variable,
3. Change the Path environment variable to include the directory that has your program.

FIGURE 16.14

Displaying the path variable on a Windows computer. (For color version of this figure, the reader is referred to the online version of this chapter.)

Programs can access the path environment variable and search each of the directories in it for files they need. On a UNIX or a Linux system, the individual directories are separated by a colon. On a Windows system, they are separated by semicolons.

During their installation process, applications may modify the value of PATH to include directories it will be referring to. This might be done by the installation program or the person installing it might have to do it manually. It's extremely important that any changes to the path variable are done without corrupting its existing contents. If that were to happen, then the new application would work, but existing software might no longer function.

To see the contents of the path variable on a Windows computer, open a command window, enter the command "path," and press the Enter key. Figure 16.14 shows the results after entering the path command. Typically, the value being held in the path environment variable is fairly lengthy. Due to this length, you might find it easier manipulating the path command using the GUI described.

16.7 ACCOUNTS ON THE SERVER

You need to keep access to a server as restricted as possible, but there are legitimate requirements for accessing it. You need to know who requires an account on the server and what rights are needed. Some examples of accounts that need to exist include the following:

- Accounts that the application requires—These are sometimes called "service accounts." They generally don't allow a user to log onto the server. Instead they're used by a program or process that runs on it. The Installation Guide will tell you whether or not a service account is needed on the server for the application.
- Vendor support accounts—You need to be very leery of giving a vendor unrestricted access to your server. If you give the vendor an account, not only are you allowing their personnel to access your server, but also you're making the assumption that security on their servers and network is good enough to keep hackers out.
- Application Administrator account(s)—The Application Administrator and his or her backup need to have accounts on the server. You will be spending a significant amount of time on this server and your account will need to have full access to it.
- Server Administrators—If your organization has a team that handles server administration, i.e., building and maintaining servers, then this group will need to be able to access your application server.

Other teams or functions in your organization that might need to access your server include:

- The team that supports the backup process
- The team that supports the monitoring software
- The team that supports the operating system
- The team that supports the antivirus software

16.8 TROUBLESHOOTING SERVER PROBLEMS

No matter how well written and well behaved the application is there will come a day when a problem occurs with it. On that day, you will have to remotely connect to the server and figure out how to fix it. Your effort is complicated by the reality that you really have two tasks to accomplish:

1.   Get the application backup as quickly as possible.
2.   Understand the root cause of the problem, so the problem can be prevented in the future.

There are times when these tasks are mutually exclusive. If you restart the application before gathering logs or other details, you can destroy or overwrite information that can identify the root cause of the problem.

The sections below describe a few of the problems that can occur on the application server. Of course, it isn't possible to include every problem that could occur on every application server, but the list gives you a brief list of problems that might occur.

16.8.1 Low disk space

Servers have a finite amount of disk space when they are built. From that day onward, the amount of free space tends to steadily decrease. If the amount of free disk space reaches a critically low amount, then it's very likely that the server will crash.

This metric is definitely something that should be monitored on a regular basis. If your organization doesn't have a monitoring package like OpenView, Nagios, or SolarWinds in place, then you should seriously consider writing a script that will do this. Writing such a script doesn't need to be complicated. Commands are available in Windows, UNIX, and Linux that return that amount of available free space. If that amount is lower than a predetermined threshold, an e-mail alert should be sent out.

When the amount of free disk space is below this level, there are a number of places that should be checked first to see if they are the ones consuming the disk space. These "usual suspects" in my experience are:

* Log files—Log files can grow extremely quickly, especially if something has gone wrong. Be sure you review any log files for errors before deleting them. You'll also want to get permission from the users before deleting log files or any other type of files. An alternative to deleting log files is to compress them. Since log files are usually text, the compression factor you'll experience could be 10:1 or higher.
* Temporary files—Some applications create temporary files during the course of their execution. If something goes wrong, then the temp files might not get deleted at the appropriate time. Over time, temp files can consume a significant amount of disk space. Unless you are extremely familiar with the nature of temp files, you shouldn't delete them without getting approval from the user community or more likely the vendor's support group.
* Calculation files—Like temporary files, some application creates calculation files to be used during processing. Calc files sometimes aren't deleted when they're no longer needed.
* Reports—If your application creates report files on the application server, there is the chance that old, no longer needed reports aren't being deleted regularly. Unless you have an agreement on this topic with the user community, don't delete report files without checking with them.
* Installation files—When the software is being installed, there are typically some extremely large files that need to be positioned on the server. Once the installation is completed and validated, these files are no longer needed. It's very easy to forget to delete them once the installation has been validated. This is a case where you don't need to check with the users before deleting files.

- Upgrade files—Like installations, upgrades typically require that sizeable files be downloaded onto the server. Once the upgrade has been applied and validated, these files can be deleted. If you forget to delete them, they can consume a significant amount of disk space.
- Shadow Copies—Windows operating systems provide a function that can automatically or manually make backup copies of files. This technology is referred to as Volume Shadow Copy Service or VSS. One common use of VSS is to create a read-only copy of files that are about to be backed up. By creating a snapshot of these files at a point in time, the backup tool can store a consistent backup set. Occasionally, the backup tool doesn't drop the Shadow Copy files when it exits. Since these files tend to be large, they can have a significant impact on the drive's free space.

You can determine if any Shadow Copies exist on the drive by right-clicking on the drive in Windows Explorer and selecting the "Shadow Copies" tab. Figure 16.15 is a screenshot showing that the E: drive on this server contains a 21GB Shadow Copy of the C: drive. You can drop this file by clicking the Disable button.

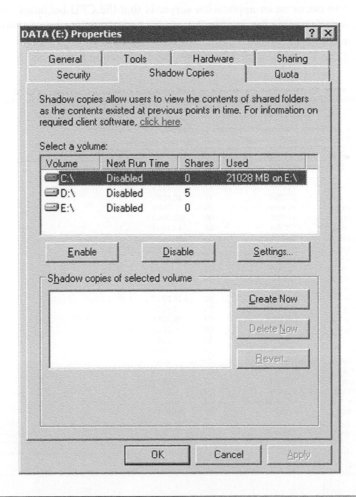

FIGURE 16.15

Identifying a Shadow Copy in Windows Explorer. (For color version of this figure, the reader is referred to the online version of this chapter.)

If the above list of locations doesn't reveal any large files that can be deleted, then you'll have to dig a little deeper. Open an instance of Windows Explorer and search the drive(s) in question, focusing on large files. I usually start with files that are at least 10 or 20 MB. Once the search completes, then sort the list by file size in descending order so you can target the largest files first. Hopefully, this process will identify files that can be deleted and will relieve your free disk space crisis. As always, be absolutely certain that deleting the files in question won't cause any harm to the application before actually deleting them.

One last word of advice on recovering disk space: if you delete files in the above locations, then it's possible that they will be moved to the Recycle Bin on the server. To reclaim the space, you might need to right-click the Recycle Bin and select the "Empty Recycle Bin" submenu item. To avoid having the file moved to the Recycle Bin when deleting a file in Windows Explorer use the Shift-Delete key combination.

16.8.2 CPU excessively busy

Another problem that can occur on an application server is that the CPU becomes extremely busy. If this occurs, then application performance for users will degrade. A very quick way to see how busy the processor is on a Windows server is to bring up the Task Manager. Right-click on the task bar, e.g., the bottom of the screen. A screenshot of the Task Manager's Processes tab is shown in Figure 16.16. Normally, the System

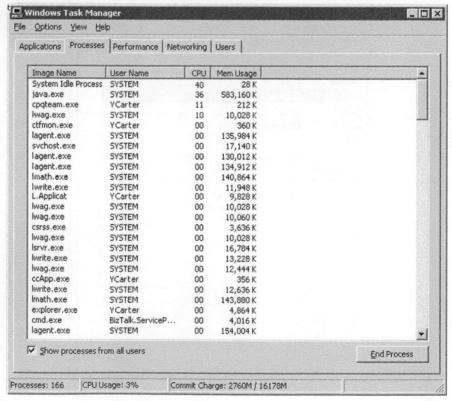

FIGURE 16.16

Performance tab in Task Manager. (For color version of this figure, the reader is referred to the online version of this chapter.)

Idle Process consumes the vast majority of CPU time on a server. If another process is consistently using up a significant percentage of CPU time, then it might be malfunctioning.

The status bar, i.e., the bottom line, of Task Manager provides a quick reference to some useful information. For example, it lists:

- The number of processes currently running
- The amount of CPU time being used
- The amount of memory being used.

To understand what is typical vs. atypical, you need to view the Processes screen when the application is functioning normally. If a process that normally uses only a percent or two of the CPU is now using the majority of CPU time and continues this pattern for an extended period of time, then it might need to be killed. To kill a process in Task Manager, right-click on it and select submenu item "End Process" or "End Process Tree."

Before killing an unfamiliar process, you should consider contacting the vendor's Support Group to help understand what the process in question is doing. If it isn't associated with the application, then you can do an Internet search for it to learn exactly what it does and why it might be malfunctioning.

16.8.3 Services that have stopped

If the application stops responding to user requests, it might be because one or more of its services have stopped executing. To confirm this, bring up the Services panel. See Figure 16.4 for a refresher on how to do this. If one of the application's services has a status other than "Started," then this might be the cause of the problem.

To get the application back online, you'll need to restart the service, but before doing this you should consider the following two points:

1. What caused the service to stop? Check the application's log files for clues behind what might have caused the problem. Since you might need to contact the vendor's Support Group for help, it is advisable to make a copy of the application's log files in case they ask for them. It's best to capture the log files before you take any additional steps like restarting the stopped service.
2. If the application has multiple services, do they need to be started in a specific order? If so, you might need to stop all of the services and restart them in the proper sequence.

16.8.4 Database connections

If your application depends on a database like Oracle or SQL Server, then any database problems have the potential to disable the application. The database doesn't necessarily have to be down to cause application problems. I've supported more than one application that weren't very sophisticated when dealing with database connectivity problems. If the connection to the database was lost, even momentarily, the application ceased to function. To get it up again, the application be stopped and then restarted.

To determine whether a database problem is causing issues with your application, there are two steps you can take:

1. Check in the application log files for an entry indicating that the database connection was dropped. Open the logs and search for terms like "database" or "connection." If terms like that don't result in a hit, then you'll have to scan the log manually. Start at the current time and move backward until you either find a database-related entry or reach a point in time when the application was functioning correctly. If you find

an entry that documents a database connection problem, you'll definitely want to make a note of the error message text for future reference.

2. Try to establish a database connection using a tool like SQL*Plus or Toad.
   • If you can't connect to the database, then the database could be down. Contact the DBA team and ask them to investigate.
   • If you can connect to the database, then it's possible that access to the database was momentarily lost. If this is the case, the resolution might be to shut down the application and restart it.

16.8.5 Web server problems

If your application is web based, then it's possible that the web server application your application relies upon is experiencing problems. If software like Microsoft IIS (Internet Information Services) or Apache Tomcat is running on your application server, then you should check those software packages to confirm that they are running.

The steps to check on IIS are described here:

1. Click on Start | Administrative Tools | Internet Information Services (IIS) Manager
2. If necessary, click the "+" sign next to the computer name to expand it
3. If necessary, click the "+" sign next to the Web Sites folder
4. If the website associated with your application has status stopped after it, then it needs to be restarted. Figure 16.17 is a screenshot of the IIS Manager that shows website "BpOWorld" has stopped
5. To restart a website, right-click on it and select submenu item "Start."

If your application's website is the only one defined on this server, then you can stop and restart IIS instead of a specific website. The steps to do this are:

1. Open a command window
2. Enter the command "iisreset" and press the Enter key
3. Messages indicating Internet services have been stopped and started will be displayed

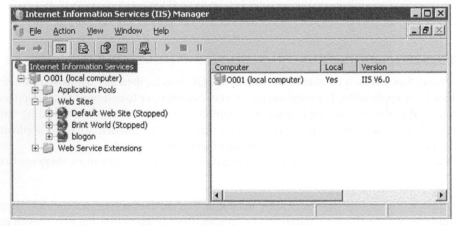

FIGURE 16.17

Determining the status of IIS. (For color version of this figure, the reader is referred to the online version of this chapter.)

16.9 REBOOTING THE SERVER

If stopping and restarting the application's services doesn't resolve the problem, then you might have to stop the operating system on the server itself. This is frequently referred to as "bouncing the server." If this doesn't solve your problem, then the problem is a significant one.

It isn't hard to stop a Windows server if you have administrator rights on it. Right-click on the Start button and select "Shutdown." You'll be presented with a window asking you what the computer should do next. The choices are "Log off the current user," "Shutdown," "Restart," "Stand by," and "Disconnect." Select the "Restart" option and click OK. The shutdown process will be initiated. The time it takes to shut down, reboot the server, and restart the application depends on your environment. This piece of information is something you should know so that you can recognize if the server doesn't restart in a timely manner.

There are a number of points to keep in mind before you bounce the server. This list depends on your organization's processes and procedures, but some points that you need to consider are:

- What are the odds that this will resolve the problem? If past experience has shown that bouncing the server won't improve the situation, then don't bother doing it.
- How long does it take to bounce the server?
- Are there any users currently logged into the application?
- How inconvenienced will logged in users be? For instance, if they're in the middle of a data entry transaction, will they lose any data that has already been entered?
- What's the risk? Is there a realistic chance that the application won't come back up?
- What approval is needed to bounce the server? For example, do you need to contact the Business Owner of the application or a user team representative for permission? Is it considered good manners to warn users in advance that the server is about to go down?
- Does your organization have any monitoring software, e.g., OpenView or Nagios, running on the application server? If so, do you need to disable it or put the server into "maintenance mode" to avoid sending out spurious alerts about the server stopping?
- Does each reboot need to be documented somewhere, for example, in a log book?
- Do you need to complete an "outage report" each time the server goes down?
- Will this action affect uptime metrics maintained on the server?

Performance Tuning

17

Performance tuning is the process of trying to improve the performance of an application or a system until it meets or exceeds performance objectives. Tuning is a complex subject that requires input from a number of sources, including the operating system, support software, the database, and the application itself. Tips that are helpful on one application might not be useful or even possible on another application. While reading this chapter, keep in mind that not all of these tips or techniques will apply to your environment. Tools that are mentioned might not be available to you. Server or application settings that are mentioned might already be at their optimal values.

The following advice applies to every environment when it comes to tuning an application. Following this advice will make it easier to learn what helps and what doesn't help. More importantly, it can help you back to the original state if changes you make actually degrade performance.

- Make changes one at a time. If you make multiple changes simultaneously, you won't know what affect each change actually had.
- Keep detailed documentation on what has been changed, the original value, the new value, the date, the time, and how the change affected performance.
- After making each change, test the application using a consistent test script. The same tests should be done in the same order after each change is made. The response time or other metric being observed should be recorded after each test.
- All other activities on the application should be minimized or eliminated if possible. If collateral activity can't be eliminated, then it needs to be consistent from one test run to the next. It isn't accurate to compare a test being made when one user is on the system vs. the same test being run when 1000 users are on the system.

17.1 WHAT TUNING GOALS ARE DESIRED?

The old saying about "if you don't know where you're going, then you won't know when you get there" applies to tuning. Before you start altering the environment, you need a clear understanding of what you're trying to achieve. For example, your goal might be to:

- Improve response time experienced by the application users
- Make batch processes complete more quickly
- Reduce the amount of network traffic
- Improve availability of the application
- Use less memory on the server
- Free up disk space
- Determine if performance improves if resources, e.g., memory, processors, are added

All of the above are legitimate tuning goals. Probably, the most common target is to improve the response time for users, but you need to know what your goal is before you start making changes.

One warning regarding tuning efforts is that many times the potential goals can be conflicting. Efforts to improve one facet of performance might actually reduce performance of another facet. For example, improving the throughput of batch jobs could reduce the response times seen by users and vice versa. Examine your goals to ensure you're not in a no-win situation.

17.1.1 Measuring response time

In order to determine whether you're meeting a performance standard, everyone needs to agree on what the standard means. For example, if your goal is to measure and improve response time, then you need to agree on the response to do what? Is it the time it takes to:

- Log into the application?
- Bring up the average screen, but which screen is the "average" screen?
- Bring up a screen that has static text, but no dynamically populated fields?
- Bring up a screen with numerous graphical icons?
- Bring up a screen that includes complex calculations?
- Bring up a screen that includes many rows of data in a table?
- Refresh any of the above screens?
- Perform a complicated search operation to find a single record?
- Create a new record?
- Modify an existing record?
- Delete an existing record?
- Run a report?

Another question that needs to be answered is when the above operations will be tested. Performance for the same operation can differ drastically depending on when it's run. For example, consider the following times of execution:

- 10:00 pm if that is when the nightly backup process is launched
- 12:10 am if that is when a daily import process is run
- 5:00 am when very few users are logged into the application
- 8:30 am when the majority of users have gotten their coffee are logging into the application
- Noon when most users are either out to lunch or aren't actively using the application
- The day before the company closes its books on the month or quarter
- Sunday evening when virtually no one is in the office or remotely accessing the application
- The week between Christmas and New Year's Day when most users are either out of the office or chatting with their coworkers
- The day of the month that payroll checks are processed

As the above lists demonstrate, the typical user in an enterprise-level application performs many different operations under vastly different levels of system utilization. Some operations can be expected to complete very quickly no matter when they run. Others take much longer to execute even if they're the only thing happening on the system. Which ones represent "average" activity and conditions?

If you're going to define what acceptable response time is, then your definition needs to be fairly specific. Don't let the definition of response time be either nebulous or immeasurable. Push to have the definition include the following:

- How long it will take to log onto the system at a specific time of day?
- How long specific screens will take to come up at specific times of day?

- How long do batch processes take to complete at their scheduled time of day?
- How long do specific reports take to complete when run at their scheduled time of day?

17.1.2 What's "normal" response time?

If you don't document a specific list of expected response times for specific screens, then you need to develop a good feel for what response time is like on a normal day. This knowledge will help you recognize if performance degrades. If you don't know what "normal" response times are, then when people complain that the system is slow you can't dispute them.

Some screens will always be slow. One application I supported had a screen that included hundreds and hundreds of objects listed on it. No matter how carefully the system is tuned that screen will always be slow. Your application most likely has similar screens. If you know which screens are always slow to come up, then if users complain about them you'll be able to truthfully respond that today they aren't any slower than normal. On the other hand, if a screen that is normally displayed in less than a second is taking 30 seconds, then you know that something is wrong.

If it's possible to know how long it takes screens to come up that would be valuable information to have. Examine the software's Administrator's Guide or contact vendor support to get answers to the following questions:

- Does the application already capture this type of information?
- Can logging be enhanced to capture it?
- If the application was written by an internal development team, could this capability be added?
- Can an automated testing tool be used to bring up screens and record the time each takes to come up? Some examples of these tools include Watir, Selenium, Visual Studio Test Professional, and Rational Functional Tester.

One caveat when dealing with capturing these statistics is that application logging consumes CPU cycles, disk I/O, and disk space. If an extensive level of logging is enabled and left active for too long a period of time, its activity can degrade the application's performance.

The best time to capture performance statistics would be on a "normal" day, i.e., not before the books are closed, when a batch file is running or when a complex search is being run. It would be even better if you captured these statistics on a regular basis, say every week or every month. This would allow you to observe trends in the performance that users are experiencing.

17.1.3 Did performance degrade instantly or over time?

Performance for a significant application is never going to be static because the environment is both complicated and dynamic. The following are just a few examples of what can be different every time a user logs into the application.

- Vendor-issued upgrades have made changes to the application
- Support software, including the operating system, is typically updated even more frequently than the application
- The number of rows in the database is always changing
- Utility software updates or operations (like an antivirus scan) can adversely impact performance
- The number of users accessing the application is likely to be different each time a user logs in
- Network and server loads change on a minute-by-minute basis if not every second
- The number of programs running on a user's workstation can vary widely from hour to hour or day to day.

If you make the effort to capture performance statistics on a regular basis, you'll be able to recognize trends in performance. Recognizing a performance trend can help you identify the cause of performance issues.

17.1.3.1 Instantly

If performance degraded instantly or relatively quickly, then it's likely that something significant in the environment has changed. Some questions that you can ask yourself that might help uncover what has changed are:

- Was any software changed on the server recently? This could include both the application and the support software. For example, did the performance go downhill right after the last upgrade of the application or the day after the most recent maintenance patches were applied to the operating system?
- Has any hardware failed? If your disk storage includes a RAID array and one or more drives crashed, the array may continue to function, but won't perform as well. If your environment includes a cluster of servers, did one or more of them drop out of the cluster? Did your NIC drop from operating at 100 Mbps to 10 Kbps?
- Is something else running on the application server, network, DB server, or user workstation that normally isn't running at this time? For example, are the nightly backups still running at 7 am? If they are, then it wouldn't be a shock if your application is running slower than molasses in January.
- Have there been any changes to your antivirus software recently? Could the level of scanning have been heightened? For example, is it scanning every file that is accessed now but it used to only scan files being copied onto the server?
- If network access seems to be slower than normal, could it be caused by changes to the firewall? Maintaining a firewall is complicated. If significant changes were made recently, it's possible they are slowing down packets going to or coming from the network.
- Did someone recently enable extensive logging within the application? Some applications have different levels of logging that can be enabled. The lowest level just logs errors, but the highest level logs virtually everything that the application does. This level of logging has its place, but can have a significant impact on performance.

The answers to these questions may not be easy to find. You'll have to partner with other groups within the organization that are the experts in specific technology niches. It takes time and most of your questioning may end up getting you nowhere, but if application performance degraded very quickly then something caused it and you need to search until you find the cause.

17.1.3.2 Over time

If performance degraded over time, then the cause is probably something different than if the change came about overnight. Some potential causes are suggested here.

- If the amount of free disk space becomes too low, the server's performance can degrade or the server could crash. Log files and temporary files tend to accumulate over time if not pruned on a regular basis.
- A shortage of free memory on the server will definitely affect performance. Potential solutions are to add more RAM or reduce the number of processes that are running on the server. One potential cause of low memory is if the application has a memory leakage problem. Processes request that memory be allocated to them and when they are done with it they return it to the operating system. If your application continuously allocates memory but never returns it, then eventually all available memory will be exhausted. This lost memory can be recovered by stopping the application. If it's possible to stop and restart the application on a regular basis, say weekly, it might mitigate the leak issue.
- Applications that have been useful or even critical to an organization tend to add users over time. If this is true for your application, then the additional usage load might be the cause of performance problem. One possible solution might be to upgrade the hardware being used by the server. For example, additional CPU power can be allocated to the server by replacing the existing CPU with a more powerful model, adding additional servers to the cluster, or if the server is virtual, increase the number of processors allocated to it. Adding memory or disk drives are two other resources that might improve performance.

- A database that has become too large or bloated can hinder a number of activities including user response time and the length of time it takes to complete backups. Some applications are designed to never actually delete data. If you delete records, what actually happens is that they are flagged to be hidden from the users. Even though they are hidden, they still need to be searched and backed up. If this is how your application handles record deletes and you know that a very significant amount of obsolete data is contained in the database, then you might want to consider exporting all active data from the database and then importing it into an empty database. This will have the effect of truly purging the database of obsolete data. Before embarking on an effort like this, you'll want to confer with the vendor's support desk to see if it's possible and/or advisable. You'll also want to ensure that the original database gets backed up.
- Applications that are initially used locally eventually might attract users from across the enterprise and possible across the country or world. If your system has this history, you might need to consider steps to improve performance for your far-flung application users. Would it be possible to improve network throughput? Does the application allow the possibility of multiple, geographically dispersed application or database servers? These steps may sound extreme, but if your application is critical to worldwide users, then steps such as these might need to be considered.

17.2 TOOLS TO MEASURE PERFORMANCE

To measure performance, you need tools that can capture specific metrics. You can't count "one Mississippi, two Mississippi" under your breath as a screen comes up and expect to get an accurate measurement. There are a number of tools available to help you, but it doesn't hurt to start out with what's already available on your operating systems.

17.2.1 Windows tools

Every operating system comes with some forms of performance management tools and Windows is no exception. The following sections describe some of the tools that come with Windows. There are many other, open source and proprietary, tools that you can load onto your server.

17.2.1.1 Task manager

On a Windows computer, the performance-related tool that is the easiest to access is Task Manager. Open it by right-clicking the Task bar at the bottom of the monitor and select Start Task Manager. Pressing the key combination Ctrl-Alt-Delete and selecting Start Task Manager will also bring it up.

The three tabs in Task Manager that will be helpful when trying to tune your server are the Processes, Performance, and Networking tabs. Figure 17.1 is a screenshot of the Processes tab. It shows the active processes, how much CPU time and memory each is using. Normally, the System Idle Process consumes the majority of CPU time, but a CPU that is being heavily utilized may show other processes using significant percentages of CPU time. If a process has a CPU usage rate that is consistently higher than all other processes, it could mean there is something is wrong with it. If nothing else, it's certainly a candidate for being looked at to see if it can run more efficiently. Sorting the display by either CPU or Memory (by clicking the column heading) makes it easy to see which processes are using the most resources.

The Performance tab presents CPU and memory usage in a chart format. Figure 17.2 shows the Performance tab. As new readings are acquired, the chart slides from right to left and the new reading is added at the right margin. The time interval between readings can be adjusted by selecting menu option View | Update Speed. Displaying the CPU and memory usage in a chart makes it very easy to identify when spikes in usage are occurring. If a spike occurs, you can shift to the Processes tab to see which specific process is consuming the resources at that moment.

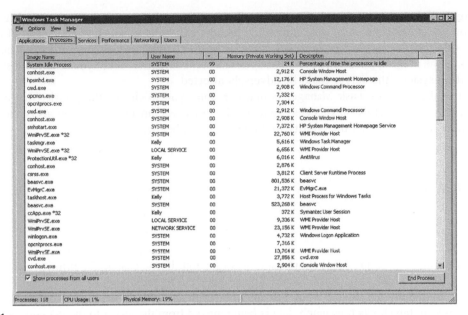

FIGURE 17.1

Task Manager Processes tab. (For color version of this figure, the reader is referred to the online version of this chapter.)

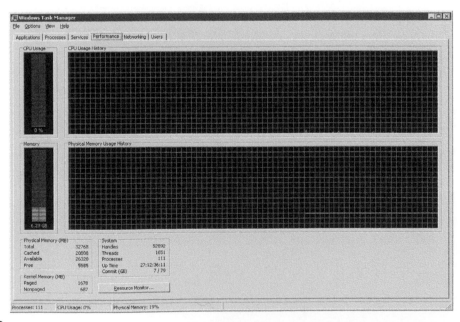

FIGURE 17.2

Task Manager Performance tab. (For color version of this figure, the reader is referred to the online version of this chapter.)

If you right-click on a process on the Processes tab, two of the options are "End Process" and "End Process Tree." If you select "End Process," that individual process will be terminated. If you select "End Process Tree," then that process and any processes it launched will be terminated. Ending processes entails some risk. If you kill one of the application's processes, you or a user could lose data. If you kill a process belonging to the operating system, the server could be adversely affected.

An additional feature of Task Manager is that it enables you to change the priority that a process is executing at. If you right-click on a process name on the Processes tab, one of the options is "Set Priority." The submenu allows you to set the priority to the levels listed below:

- Realtime
- High
- Above Normal
- Normal
- Below Normal
- Low

A word of warning is to be judicious about using this function. If you change the priority of everything to "Realtime," that won't make the system faster. You also need to be careful not to lower the priority of unfamiliar tasks to extremely low levels. They just might be critical to the smooth operation of the server.

The Networking tab shows how much data is being moved from the server to the network or vice versa. If you think that the application's performance is being limited by network I/O, then this screen will provide insight into that resource's utilization. Figure 17.3 shows the layout of this tab. As occurs on the Performance tab, new data is added on the right margin and existing data shifts to the left.

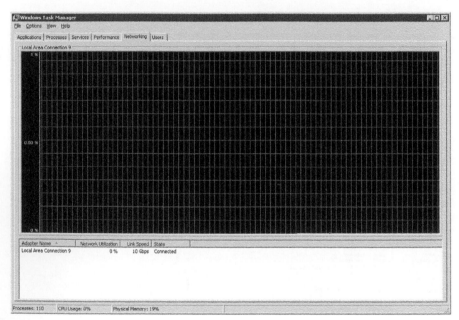

FIGURE 17.3

Task Manager Networking tab. (For color version of this figure, the reader is referred to the online version of this chapter.)

17.2.1.2 Perfmon

Perfmon, or Performance Monitor, is a more advanced performance measurement tool that comes loaded as a part of Windows operating systems. This section provides just a brief introduction of this tool. For more complete information on it, you can either perform an Internet search or click menu item Help | Help Topics. Some of the significant features of Perfmon that I've found useful are:

- You can select the statistics you want displayed from a wide range of activity categories.
- Statistics data can be exported to either a log file or a database. You can open Perfmon at a later date or time and view the statistics from those sources.
- You can control how frequently measurements are taken. Be aware that if measurements are captured too frequently, Perfmon can impact the server's performance.
- Perfmon can be set up to run continuously or it can periodically write data to a new file.
- A set of measurements being captured are contained within an object called a "Counter Log." You can have more than one Counter Log active on a server at the same time. One reason for doing this would be if each group captured different performance statistics at different frequencies.

Two ways to launch Perfmon are described here:

- In a command window, enter the command "perfmon" and press the Enter key
- Select Start | Administrative Tools | Performance

The initial screen you'll see when Perfmon is opened is shown in Figure 17.4. Some of the major points on this screen are:

- The default displays shows real-time statistics, as opposed to stats from a log file. The activities shown in the lower right panel are what is being monitored.
- The three default activities that are monitored are
  - Pages/sec which is a measurement of how much memory is being used

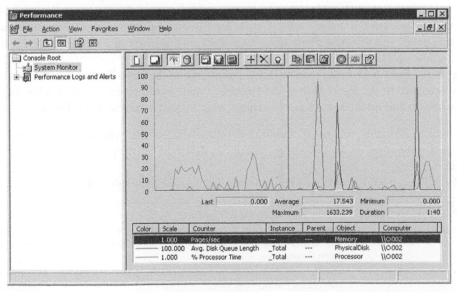

FIGURE 17.4

Perfmon's initial screen. (For color version of this figure, the reader is referred to the online version of this chapter.)

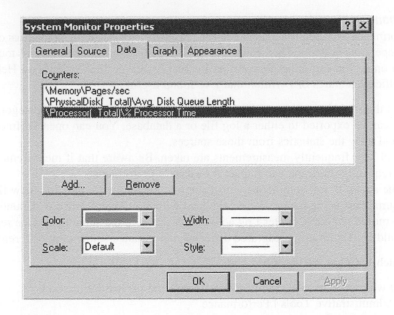

FIGURE 17.5

Adding or removing a statistic. (For color version of this figure, the reader is referred to the online version of this chapter.)

- • Average Disk Queue Length which measures the amount of disk activity
- • % Processor Time which measures how busy the CPU is
- Expand "Performance Logs and Alerts" in the left panel to list Counter Logs or create a new one.
- The solid vertical red bar moves from left to right. When it reaches the right hand edge of the screen, it reappears at the left hand margin. The most recent statistics are written to the left of the vertical bar.
- Each statistic is assigned a unique color. Colors for statistics can be reassigned by right-clicking on the chart panel and selecting Properties. Then click on a statistic and change the color by selecting a new color in the drop-down list box.
- Clicking on the light bulb menu icon will highlight in white the chart for the statistic that is currently selected. In the figure below, the Page/sec status would be displayed in white instead of blue. Use the up and down arrow keys to change which statistic currently has focus.

To change which statistics are being monitored right-click on the window and select "Properties." Figure 17.5 is a screenshot of the Properties screen. To delete an existing statistic, select it and click the Remove button.

Some of the more useful counters in Perfmon are listed in the following table.

Processor\% Processor Time	Shows how busy the CPU is
Processor\Interrupts/Sec	The number of times the CPU is interrupted per second, e.g., by a disk controller or NIC. If this value is consistently over 1000, there might be a problem with one or more device
System\Processor Queue Length	The number of threads that are queued up and waiting for CPU time. If this value divided by the number of CPUs is less than 10, the system is probably running smoothly
Memory\Pages Input/Sec	If this counter is consistently above zero, it indicates the there isn't enough RAM

Memory\Available Mbytes	Shows the amount of memory available for new or existing processes
Physical Disk\Bytes/Sec	The number of bytes being transferred to/from the disk per second
Physical Disk\% Disk Time	Indicate how busy the disk drive is. If this value consistently approaches 100%, then the disk drive could be a bottleneck
Physical Disk\Current Disk Queue Length	If this value is too high, it's telling you that the disk drive is being used excessively. This count should generally be no higher than 2 or 3
Processor\% User Time	Percentage of time spent running application code. Generally, the higher this value, the better
Network Interface\Bytes Total/Sec	Number of bytes sent to or received from the network
Network Interface\Output Queue Length	Shows the number of packets queue up to be sent across the network via an NIC. If this value is consistently above 2, then you might have a network bottleneck

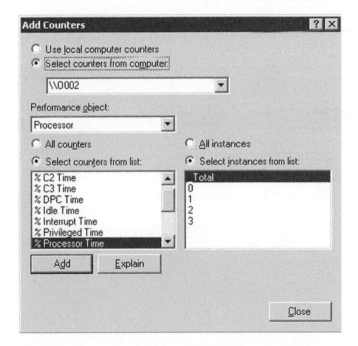

FIGURE 17.6

Adding a statistic to be monitored. (For color version of this figure, the reader is referred to the online version of this chapter.)

Adding a new statistic to the list of what is being monitored is relatively easy to do. Perfmon provides so many choices that it can be difficult to identify which one it is that you want. Figure 17.6 is a screenshot of the screen that the following steps refer to. The steps to add a statistic are:

1. Click the Add button
2. Select a value from the Performance object drop-down list box
3. Select one or more counters in the list box labeled "Select counters from list"
4. Select one or more instances from the list box labeled "Select instances from list"
5. Click the Add button
6. Repeat steps 1-5 for the next statistic that you want to be captured

7. Click the Close button
8. Click the OK button

It's extremely useful to set up Perfmon to capture statistics and write them to either a log file or a database. For example, you can have statistics captured on a server constantly and have a new log file created every night at midnight. Then on the following day, you can review the statistics captured to see if anything unusual happened. To display statistics that were captured in a log file or a database, right-click on the main Perfmon screen area, select Properties, and click the Source tab. Figure 17.7 shows the screen from which you select the source of statistics.

To display statistics from a log file, follow these steps:

1. Click on the "Log Files" radio button option
2. Click the Add button
3. Select the log file that contains the desired stats
4. Click the Open button
5. Click the Time Range button
6. Click the Apply button

FIGURE 17.7

Selecting a log file as the source of Perfmon statistics. (For color version of this figure, the reader is referred to the online version of this chapter.)

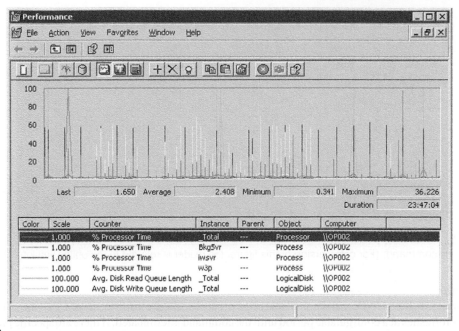

FIGURE 17.8

Displaying statistics that have been captured in a log file. (For color version of this figure, the reader is referred to the online version of this chapter.)

Figure 17.8 shows the statistics that were captured the previous day and written to a log file. The collection of statistics being displayed was defined to troubleshoot performance problems with a specific application. The statistics that are being collected fall into three categories:

- The first measurement is the total CPU processing time expressed as a percentage
- The next 3 measurements are the percentage of CPU time three specific processes consume
- The final two measurements show busy the disk is

As this screenshot demonstrates, Perfmon allows you to capture statistics that are either generic to the server or specific to your environment.

17.2.2 UNIX/Linux

UNIX and Linux also have their share of tools that can help identify performance problems. As one might expect, tools on these systems are more likely to be of the command line variety than what's available on a Windows system.

17.2.2.1 ps

The ps (process status) command in Linux and UNIX displays all processes that are running on the computer. If you suspect that a process is consuming an excessive amount of resources, the ps command can help determine if this is correct. Figure 17.9 shows the output of the ps command. If you want to terminate a process that has been identified as using too much CPU time, you can use the "kill" command to do that. Just enter the command "kill pid," where pid is the process ID number shown in the ps command output.

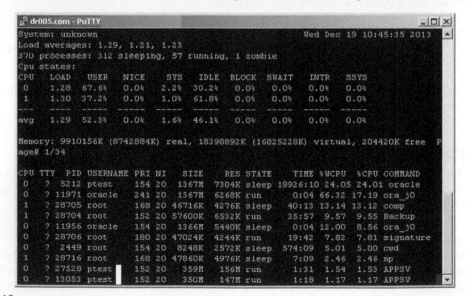

FIGURE 17.9

Output of the ps command. (For color version of this figure, the reader is referred to the online version of this chapter.)

17.2.2.2 top

The top command in both UNIX and Linux displays the processes that are using the most CPU time. The display of top processes refreshes at a configurable period until the command is terminated. If there are specific processes that you want displayed the -p parameter allows you to specify this. Figure 17.10 shows the output of a top command.

17.2.3 Database activity

Frequently, if an application is slower than expected, the subsystem that is blamed is the database. Realistically, unless your application generates an inordinate amount of database activity or the database being accessed is extremely large, it isn't likely that an enterprise-level database engine like Oracle or SQL Server

FIGURE 17.10

Output of the top command. (For color version of this figure, the reader is referred to the online version of this chapter.)

is your problem. Even with this word of advice, many Application Administrators will still cast a suspicious eye on the database so some tuning suggestions will be discussed.

There are several things that can be done to test whether the database engine is the cause of your problem or not. The first step would be to determine how busy the database server is. If its CPU is typically 99% idle and its disk queues are empty or extremely short, then it's very unlikely that the database is the source of your problem. On the other hand, if a tool like Perfmon or the UNIX top command shows that the CPU is extremely busy or the disk I/O activity is approaching capacity, then the database just might be your bottleneck.

Tuning a database can be as complex as tuning an application. Some obvious candidates for tuning the performance of a database are:

- Do the database tables have the appropriate indexes? A database query can either read every row in a database table looking for the values it's seeking or it can use an index to speed up the search. For example, suppose the application allows you to search for all orders with a value of $1000 or more. If the Orders table has an index on the column Order_Value, then a search by order value can be executed very quickly. If no such index exists, then the query will result in a table scan that is much, much slower. When the application and database were being designed, the analysts should have identified which columns needed indexes and built the database appropriately.
- Have usage statistics for the database been refreshed recently? Database engines use statistics on tables to enable them to decide which index or indexes can speed up a query. If the statistics are out of date, then queries won't be optimal. Work with the Database Administrator (DBA) to determine whether or not your database's statistics are up to date.
- Does the database engine have enough memory on the server? If not, then the queries will take longer to complete. The application or database vendor should have recommendations on how much memory to allocate to the database engine. Work with the DBA or Systems Administrator to ensure that at least the minimum recommended amount is allocated to it.
- Enterprise database engines aren't monolithic software entities. They have multiple components that together support the database. In some cases, performance can be improved by starting multiple instances of a component. For example, it's possible to make your Oracle database respond faster by starting multiple copies of the "Oracle Listener." Your DBA or the vendor technician would be in a position to know whether this will improve your application's performance.

Enterprise databases like Oracle or SQL Server allow the DBA to monitor the SQL (Structured Query Language) queries being executed. You can work with your DBA to identify which queries are being submitted to the database by the application. Two very valuable pieces of information can be gleaned from the list of queries:

1. Which queries are being executed most frequently?
2. Which queries are consuming the most time and effort to execute?

If you can identify queries that are executed most frequently and are costly in terms of CPU time and disk I/O, then your DBA might be able to optimize them. For example, if a query includes multiple tables that are all located on the same disk drive, you might be able to move one or more tables to another drive. Minimizing disk head contention this way could improve performance.

17.2.4 Network activity

For most Application Administrators, the network is a bit of a mystery. Sometimes, it works just fine and other times it has problems. A book on application administration can't teach you to be a Network Administrator, but it can provide you with a few basic tools to recognize network problems. Once you recognize a

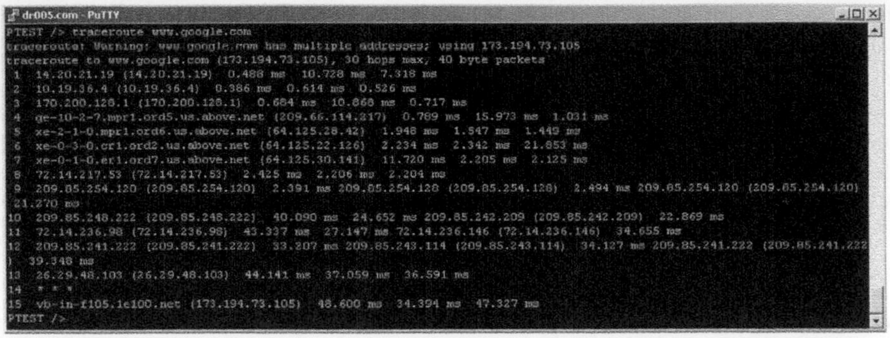

FIGURE 17.11

Output of the traceroute command. (For color version of this figure, the reader is referred to the online version of this chapter.)

specific problem with the network, then you can contact the network group at your organization to get assistance in resolving it.

My first bit of advice is to not blame your performance issues on the network unless you have credible evidence. Network Administrators, like Application Administrators, are busy and don't like unwarranted accusations that their domain is causing problems. If you have a suspicion, but no proof that the network is the problem then at least phrase your requests in a less accusatory manner to avoid alienating them from the outset.

The following are some basic network commands or tools that might help you determine if there is a problem on the network.

17.2.4.1 ping

ping is a command run that sends a message to another computer. The format of a ping command is *ping target_computer* where the target can be either a computer name or an IP address. The output displayed by the ping tells you whether the message was able to reach the destination computer and how long it took.

17.2.4.2 traceroute

The UNIX/Linux traceroute command (tracert on a Windows computer) identifies the route a packet takes between your computer and the destination computer specified in the command. As a rule, you have very little or no control on how a packet gets from point A to point B. What traceroute offers beyond the ping command is that it lists every hop along the path between the two computers. This can help you identify if communications are taking too many hops in the wrong direction or whether certain nodes are out of commission. Figure 17.11 shows the output from a traceroute command.

As with many troubleshooting and tuning operations, it is a good idea to use the traceroute command when the network is functioning properly. This will give you a good idea of what the route, the number of hops taken, and the overall times are like when conditions are normal. This will provide you with a basis for comparison so when things aren't working properly you'll recognize the difference.

17.3 POTENTIAL BOTTLENECKS

There isn't likely to be a single place in your application environment that you can point out and adjust to fix all your problems. Too often tuning an application requires that you make adjustments, usually minor, in a lot of different places until performance improves to the level you want. The difficulty is knowing where these places are and knowing exactly how to adjust them. Some potential places that might need to be investigated and potentially tuned are:

- The application server
- The application
- Support software like IIS, antivirus products, and backup software
- Scheduled activities on the server
- The database
- Services that the application calls
- The network
- User workstations
- User browser software

17.3.1 The application server

The server that your application runs on should be first on your list of what to check when trying to tune the application. Your initial checks should be to confirm that it has all of the hardware and software resources that the vendor recommends. For example, does the server have at least the minimum recommendation listed in the Installation Guider for the following?

- Processor speed—The speed of a processor is rated in Hertz or cycles per second. The typical server processor speed is likely to be in the 2-5 GHz range. You can see how fast your Windows processor is by entering "systeminfo" in a command window.
- Processors—If the vendor recommended that your server has multiple processors, then you can be certain they had a good reason for doing that. The number of processors is also listed in the systeminfo output.
- Memory—The importance of sufficient memory can't be overemphasized. Make sure the amount that is available is at least the minimum recommended by the vendor. The price of RAM is low enough that adding extra memory isn't that expensive and can't hurt. The amount of memory on your server is listed in the systeminfo command.
- Disk space—The price of disk space is also relatively inexpensive so make sure you have more than the vendor recommends. You can see how much free space you have by right-clicking the Start button and selecting "Open Windows Explorer." Then right-click on the disk(s) and select "Properties."
- Network bandwidth—If your network doesn't have sufficient bandwidth, then your application is almost certain to operate more slowly than you want it to. Finding the network speed takes a few steps. Consult your organization's Network Administrator for advice.
- Operating system—If the vendor recommends a specific version or size, i.e., 32-bit or 64-bit operating system, then make sure that's what is running on the server.
- Does the vendor support their software being run on virtual servers? While virtual servers have many advantages, if the vendor hasn't approved them then you should be running the application on one. One excellent reason for following the vendor's recommendation is that they may choose to not provide support if you have disregarded their requirements in this area.

17.3.2 The application

The second step in your quest to improve performance should be the application itself. Many applications have a number of settings, config files, or other ways to adjust how the application executes. It would be difficult if not impossible for you to figure the optimum settings on your own. You need to contact the vendor's support desk and ask for any documentation that they have on tuning or performance optimization. One vendor whose application I supported had a document titled "Configuring for Security and Performance on Windows Server."

Armed with their recommendations you need to ensure that your environment is set up correctly. Step through the documentation carefully and document any changes you make. You should also change only one setting at a time to enable you to observe the effect it has. Hopefully, their documentation will provide concrete details on what can be done to optimize application performance.

17.3.3 Support software

As stated before, the application you're supporting isn't the only software running on the server. If your examination of the server and the application haven't resolved your performance issues, then the next step is to start looking at the support software that's also running on the server. Any of those programs could be something that affects the performance of your application. For example, one of them might be consuming an excess amount of CPU time, memory, or disk I/O operations.

One of the first considerations is to make sure that all support software running on the server is the most recent version. Newer versions of the software typically run faster or more efficiently than older versions. Newer versions are also intended to be more secure and to have resolved problems. There are exceptions to these rules, but for the most part, newer is better.

Turn off or remove any software running on the server that isn't specifically needed by the application. Doing this has multiple benefits. It frees up resources like memory, CPU cycles, and disk space. Removing unused software also has the benefit of reducing the attack surface that a hacker might use to compromise your server. Some examples of software that might exist on the server that can be removed are:

- File and printer sharing services like NetBIOS, NFS, and FTP
- Wireless networking services
- Remote control and remote access programs like telnet
- E-mail services like SMTP
- Language compilers and libraries
- System development tools like Visual Studio and Eclipse

17.3.3.1 IIS

If your application is web based, there is a reasonable chance that IIS (Internet Information Services) is running on the server. If your application depends on IIS, there are some settings on it that can potentially make your application run faster. Before making any of the following suggestions, you should check with the vendor's support group to make sure doing it won't cause a problem. It would also be an excellent idea to test these changes on a development, test, or QA environment before making them on your production environment.

The following are some IIS adjustments that might help improve your application's performance:

- A setting exists that determines whether HTTP files should be compressed or not. Compressing HTML data can reduce the amount of data passed between your server and the user's browser by a factor of 5 or more.
- Cache limits related to ASP can be increased. The number of ASP files being cached and the number of scripts engines that are cached can be increased.
- Logging being done by IIS can be adjusted to be more appropriate to your environment. Cutting down on the amount of logging reduces disk I/O activity as well as the amount of disk space being consumed.

- Sessions that are inactive for a configurable amount of time are terminated by IIS. You have the ability to set this amount of time. This setting is very sensitive from both a user convenience and security aspect. If the session timeout value is too low, then users will have their application sessions terminated inconveniently early. If it's too high, then it might leave sessions open so long that other people can access it if the user walks away from his PC.
- IIS uses Application Pools, which are Windows operating system processes. User session state information is held within the Application Pool. There are a number of settings for Application Pools that can affect the application's performance. For example, how often worker processes are recycled and how long worker processes have to be idle before they are shut down.

17.3.3.2 Antivirus software

If your server has antivirus software running on it, then it's entirely possible that the AV software could affect performance on the server. To know whether this is true or not, you should know exactly what it is doing. If you can't answer the following questions, then you should research it so you more fully understand whether the AV software could be at the root of any performance issues on the server.

- Does it use signature-based detection, heuristics, or both identify viruses?
- What are the names of the processes it runs on the server?
- Are those processes running at the kernel level?
- How many false positives does it generate?
- What percentage of CPU time does each process typically consume?
- Does it examine every file that is?
- Does it examine every file that is opened?
- Does it automatically download new virus signatures?
- How often does it do this?
- What time of day do these downloads occurring?
- How much data is downloaded every time?
- Does it perform a regular scan of the server? On what schedule?

17.3.3.3 Distribution software

Does your organization have software in place that pushes updates out to servers and user workstations? These tools allow a Systems Administrator to automate the process of distributing changes to multiple servers and user PCs. Examples of such packages are:

- Altiris
- LANDesk
- SCCM
- System Center

If a package like one of the above exists on your server, it can have an effect of the server's performance. You need to know the answers to the following questions.

- Does the package have an agent or process on your server?
- What is being pushed to your server? Operating system changes? Support software changes?
- How often are changes pushed out?
- Can you prevent an update from being pushed out?
- Once installed, can an update be backed out?
- Are these changes tested on another server in your organization before being distributed?
- What time of day are changes pushed out?

- What happens if the update requires that the server be rebooted for changes to take effect?
- Does your server need to have distribution software on it? Or can it be removed?

17.3.3.4 Backup software

Every server needs to have its contents backed up on a regular basis. This is true for development servers, test servers, QA servers, and most importantly production servers. Your organization certainly has the choice regarding what software is going to be used to do the backups. Your organization might have developed its own backup process and software. Or it might have installed a package to handle this important process. Either way, a backup process moves a lot of data back and forth, so it can cause performance problems on a server.

You need to know the answers to the following backup-related questions:

- What backup-related processes are running on the server?
- What days do they run?
- What time do they run?
- What time do they usually complete?
- What happens if the backup doesn't complete, either at all or by the normal time?
- Does the application have to be stopped for the backup process to run?
- If the application doesn't have to stop, will users see performance degradation while backups are running?
- How are backups scheduled and launched?
- What drives, directories, and files are being backed up?
- What drives, directories, or files are exempted from being backed up?
- Is a full backup done every day or are full backups combined with incremental backups?
- Can the backup software copy a file if another process has it open?
- Can regularly scheduled backups be suspended or avoided during critical times of the month, quarter, or year to ensure processes that take longer than normal will complete?

17.3.4 Scheduling activities

If your application has activities that are run on a regular basis, they have the potential to impact application performance. Examples of such activities are backups, calculations, reports, data warehouse activities, and data extractions. Does the Application Administrator have the ability and authority to schedule when jobs are run? If so, you should endeavor to run them at a time when the majority of users are not using the system. If that isn't entirely possible, then can you attempt to stagger these tasks so they aren't all running at the same time?

17.3.5 The database

If the application makes calls to a database package to pull data, then this is an area that needs to be examined. To be bluntly honest, you're not likely to find much room for improvement here.

A competent vendor has already looked at these things. It's worth pursuing because if the database is poorly set up, then tuning can make a big difference, but realistically it's not likely this is the source of your problem.

Some areas that can be addressed to improve database performance include:

- Can the queries that the application passes to the database be optimized?
- Can indexes be added to tables that could make the queries faster?
- Can the statistics used by the database engine be refreshed more frequently to optimize query execution?

- Can additional memory or disk drives be added to the database server to enhance performance?
- Can additional processes like listeners or writers be created to improve performance?

17.3.6 **The network**

It's very easy to blame all performance issues on "the network." Don't fall for this trap. Unless you can prove that the network is causing the problem, it isn't productive to throw the blame on it. Some areas that can be examined are:

- Is the NIC (Network Interface Card) on the server functioning correctly?
- Is the NIC outdated?
- Does the NIC have the latest software drivers on it?
- What DNS (Domain Name System) server is being used?
- Has a backup DNS server been defined?

17.3.7 **User workstations**

You won't have much control over them, but user workstations can have an impact on performance. If a user's computer doesn't have sufficient memory or if it has too many processes running, it can slow down the application's performance.

As an Application Administrator, you certainly won't have control over users' workstations, but if a user complains about performance you might diplomatically suggest steps they can take to help themselves. Some possible actions they, or the appropriate group in your organization, can take include:

- Remove spyware, adware, and other malware from the workstation. There are a number of products that will scan a PC and remove these kinds of software. Spybot and Adaware are two examples.
- Remove as many unneeded disk files as possible. For example, there might be a considerable amount of disk space being used by photographs, games, songs, and movies.
- Uninstalling programs that aren't being used or have never been used.
- Run a defragmentation utility on the disk drive.
- Run a disk cleanup utility.
- Reduce the number of programs that are automatically launched when the computer starts up.
- Check for disk errors. On a Windows PC, you can do this by right-clicking on the drive, selecting Properties, and then the Tools tab.
- If none of the above steps help, you might consider adding additional memory to the computer. RAM is relatively cheap, although if this needs to be done for a large number of users the costs will add up.

17.3.8 **Web browsers**

If your application is web based, then the users will be using an Internet browser to interact with your application. There are a few performance-related tips that can be tried to improve performance.

- The choice of web browsers can have a huge effect application performance. I've seen applications where a specific page took 2 minutes to come up using one of the most popular web browsers, but only 2 seconds when a different browser was being used.
- If the application's website isn't listed in the approved list, then it may not work at all.
- Clearing the browser's cache can improve application performance. In Firefox, select the Tools menu item and then Options. Select the Advanced tab and then on the Network tab. Click on the "Clear Now" button in the Cached Web Content section.

- Increasing the temp file size can improve performance. The steps to do this in Internet Explorer are to click on the Tools menu item and then on the General tab. In the Browsing history section, click on the Settings button. A screen will be displayed with field named "Disk space to use (8-1024 MB)." If the current value is on the low size, then increase it and click the OK button. Exit Internet Explorer and then reenter it so the new setting takes effect.

17.3.9 Cache

The term "cache" has several meanings in the computing world. In general, the concept refers to storing data or code in an area that can be accessed very quickly. Some variations of cache that you might encounter when dealing with your application are:

- Cache memory is used by the server's CPU to hold instructions or data that have been used recently and will likely be used again in the very near future. Cache memory can make a relatively slow CPU outperform a faster CPU that has little or no cache.
- Your application might use memory to hold data it has requested from the database or file system. Subsequent use of that data will pull it from the cache instead of from the database.
- Applications can use a cache to hold security credential information. One application I supported had a reporting component that used a cache to hold account ID's and passwords for scheduled reports. If a user changed his password, the report might not run because the cache contained the old password. To make sure this problem didn't prevent reports from running, we had to periodically "clear the cache." This had a slight performance impact but guaranteed that the reports would run successfully.
- If your application is web based, then the web server, e.g., IIS, almost certainly uses a cache to retain web pages that are frequently requested. By storing them in a cache, the software avoids reading them from disk for subsequent requests.
- If your application uses a relational database engine like Oracle or SQL Server, then the database engine uses cache to minimize disk I/O and improves overall performance.
- If your application is web based, the users will be accessing it via a web browser like Internet Explorer, Chrome, or Firefox. Each of these browsers uses a cache to hold pages or data that has been retrieved from the web server. If they are requested again, they can be retrieved from the cache much faster than from the web server.

17.3.9.1 Cache questions

When used properly, cache can have a significant impact on performance at all levels of the application stack. There are several questions that you should have the answers to in order to determine if performance can be improved by caching.

- Can you determine how much cache is available at every level in the environment? For example, how much cache does the application have available to it? How much cache does IIS have available to it? The only level that you might not be able to get this information on is the database server. You can certainly ask the DBA for it, but you won't have much influence on changing cache usage on the database server.
- Can you allocate additional cache? If there a setting that determines how much cache the application uses? Do you know where it is? Do you know if additional cache can be allocated to the web server application?
- Would allocating more cache improve performance? What does the vendor's documentation say about the optimum cache size? What is your current setting compared to what the vendor recommends?

- If you are going to adjust the size of cache in an attempt to improve performance, you should do the following:
  - Change the cache size incrementally
  - Test performance after each change to a cache to document what the impact was. If there was no improvement, then you might consider changing it back to the original setting.

17.3.9.2 Flushing the cache

Another cache-related concept you need to be familiar with is "flushing the cache." This concept means to clear out the cache so fresh data can be loaded into it. For example, certain changes to an application may not become apparent until the cache has been flushed. You need to know whether or not it's possible to flush your application's cache and how to do it. This process might be as simple as deleting a temporary subdirectory, but each application can be different so get specific instructions from the vendor.

17.4 MAINTENANCE TASKS CAN HELP PERFORMANCE

There are some maintenance tasks that when done on a regular basis can help improve the performance of an application. Actually, it might be more accurate to say that when done on a regular basis they help avoid having the application's performance degrade. Some examples of these tasks are:

- If the database engine doesn't automatically refresh database table statistics, then this should be done on a periodic basis. A DBA can write and schedule a script to run at the most appropriate interval, e.g., daily or weekly.
- Disk drives that have very little free space can cause performance issues so you should periodically examine them and free up space when necessary. If your organization has monitoring software in place, then have it check on disk free space.
- An excessive number of log files have the potential to impact performance. If old log files can be deleted without impacting the application, then they should be deleted on a regular basis.
- Periodically shutting down and restarting the application can recover memory that has been lost if the application has a memory leakage problem.
- Malware running on your server takes up disk space and consumes CPU cycles. It also has the potential of being a security vulnerability. Regularly running detection software to uncover viruses, adware, and Trojan Horses is desirable from both a security and performance point of view.

17.5 CHANGING THE LANDSCAPE

If some of the earlier suggestions haven't help to tune your application's performance to the desired level, then it might be time for more drastic measures. Changing the hardware or software landscape might be the next logical progression. Before making any such drastic steps, you'll need to coordinate changes with the application's business owner. You'll also want to test changes on your development, test, or QA system before modifying the production environment.

17.5.1 Adding or replacing hardware

If you've monitored the application's environment and identified a hardware resource as the bottleneck, then adding more of that resource might solve your problems. Replacing the existing devices with faster versions might also solve the problem.

Can you predict in advance that adding hardware will improve performance? Unfortunately, it isn't always possible to know in advance that your hardware investments will have a significant impact on performance.

Some potential resources that can be considered are described in the following sections. These suggestions apply to a physical server. If your server is virtual, then adding resources is much simpler. Contact the group in your organization that administers virtual servers to have your virtual server beefed up.

17.5.1.1 Memory

Adding memory is one of the easier hardware changes that can be done. It can also yield a significant performance improvement for the price. If you go down this route, you need to keep a few things in mind. For example:

- Make sure the server can actually use the additional memory. It's a waste of time and money to add memory that can't be used by the application or operating system.
- It might not possible to mix old and new memory chips. You might have to replace all of the existing memory with new RAM chips. This will result in a higher than expected cost.
- Allocate the memory in the manner in which it will help the most. This might mean, for example, increasing the application's cache size.

17.5.1.2 Processors

If monitoring activities have identified the CPU as the performance bottleneck, then you can consider adding processors to enhance performance. Unfortunately, adding processors isn't as easy as adding memory. The server's motherboard may not have sockets for additional processor chips. Before seriously considering this action, you'll need to contact either the System Administrators in your organization or the vendor that supplied the server.

Another method of adding more processors would be to utilize either a cluster or load balancing. These changes are described in a section later in this chapter.

17.5.1.3 Disk drives

Two ways in which disk drives can affect the performance of your application are:

- A computer that is running out of free space on the disk drive can generate errors, create log entries, and generally run slower than if sufficient free space was available. Two solutions to this are to either free up space on the existing drives or add more space. The second solution is described in the following paragraphs.
- Disk activity can easily slow down an application's performance. Disk drives, being mechanical devices are much slower than all electronic devices like a CPU or memory. If your application generates an excessive amount of disk I/O, then it's very possible it can slow the application down. Potential solutions to this performance problem are described in the following sections.

17.5.1.3.1 Adding drives

Adding one or more drives to a server is relatively easy and inexpensive to do. This change has the potential to solve both of the problems described in the previous section. It's pretty obvious that adding another drive will instantly create a significant amount of free space. What's not so obvious is that doing this might also solve performance issues. If commonly accessed files are distributed across the existing and new drives, the response time for disk activity can be improved, potentially significantly. Before attempting this, make sure the application is able to recognize multiple drives.

17.5.1.3.2 Replacing existing drives with larger ones

Replacing an existing drive with a larger one is more difficult than adding an additional drive. To do this, you'll have to transfer the files from the existing drive to the new one. This might be your only choice if the server is out of slots or the power supply won't handle an additional device.

One bright side to adding a larger disk drive is that it will probably be faster than the original drive. If that's the case, then by replacing the drive you will have additional space and might improve disk performance at the same time.

17.5.1.3.3 RAID

RAID (Redundant Array of Independent Devices) arrays use software to combine numerous drives together to make them appear as a single device. There are several levels of RAID that emphasize increasing performance, enhancing redundancy, or both.

Implementing a RAID array for your application isn't without certain drawbacks. Some potential downsides of implementing a RAID array are:

- It's another layer of complexity that needs to be managed. If neither you nor your organization has experience with RAID arrays, then this is an additional area of expertise that needs to be acquired.
- It isn't free. There is a cost to the additional disk drives and the software that manages a RAID subsystem. Be certain that the benefits outweigh the costs for your installation.

17.5.1.3.4 Solid-state drives

A solid-state drive, or SSD, is essentially memory that is being used to act as hard drive storage. From the application's viewpoint, an SSD looks and acts just like a hard drive, albeit usually a relatively small one.

Solid-state drives have definite advantages and disadvantages. Having no mechanical parts, they are significantly faster than hard drives. The negatives are that they are much more expensive per GB and don't have the same capacity as a typical hard drive.

If your application relies heavily upon a relatively small amount of data or files, then utilizing SSD might be effective. To make sure you're not wasting your time and money, you should discuss this with the vendor before making a financial commitment.

17.5.1.4 NICs

If your network performance has slowed down significantly, the problem could be with your NIC (Network Interface Card). Some potential aspects of the NIC that you can examine are:

- If the NIC is old, it could be woefully out of date. Upgrading to a new card that has a higher speed could significantly improve both network and application performance.
- Does your NIC have all the latest driver updates? Installing the latest version of this critical software can improve error handling and overall performance.
- There are some functions that can be modified on an NIC. For example, disabling offloading functions, for example, "Large Send Offload," can improve performance problems under some circumstances.

Making changes to a hardware device like an NIC is probably out of the experience and comfort level of most Application Administrators. If your organization has a Data Center group, then you should contact them and discuss your concerns about network performance and the possibility that the NIC should be examined.

17.5.2 **Load balancing**

Load balancing is a method of distributing the application activity imposed by used across multiple servers. It is employed to increase performance and improve availability of the application. Load balancing is achieved via hardware, software, or a combination of both methods. It can also be handled internally by the application or via a third-party package. Some vendors and their load balancing tools are:

- Barracuda's Load Balancer
- F5 Networks Big-IP
- Cisco ACE Application Control Engine Module
- KEMP LoadMaster

17.5.3 **Clustering**

Clustering, like load balancing, is used to improve performance and ensure high availability of the application. Clustering is typically implemented via a software-only technique. Some application server software that provides clustering capability are:

- Oracle/BEA WebLogic
- IBM WebSphere
- Oracle Application Server

Both load balancing and clustering are achieved with additional costs. Some these costs include:

- Hardware—additional servers, a load balancing appliance, or both
- Software licenses
- An additional layer of hardware or software to maintain
- Expertise that your organization needs in its IT staff or contractors

17.5.4 **Upgrade the application**

If you are experiencing performance issues that haven't been resolved by any of the above suggestions, then open a ticket with the application software vendor asking them to work with you to address it. They have almost certainly dealt with performance problems of many clients. If they offer a list of things to check or changes to make, then you should strongly consider working with them.

Your vendor might suggest that upgrading the application to the most recent version will improve performance. This is a legitimate suggestion, but before being talked into this you need to be sure that it has a reasonable chance of solving the problem. One way to help you decide is to determine whether the performance issues are occurring on all platforms running the same version of the application. For example, assume your Production and QA platform have the same version of the application. If one runs more slowly than the other, then the application software may not be the cause. If the version were to blame, then both environments would have similar performance levels. If one is fast and the other is slow, then the problem is probably something other than the application software version.

If you decide to upgrade the application, you should test the new version on a development, test, or QA server before modifying your Production environment. As I've said before, never modify the Production environment without testing the change on another platform first.

The Network

18

As an Application Administrator, you'll have to have a basic understanding of networks. This knowledge will be needed when you're setting up the application, tuning it, and troubleshooting any problems that occur. While you won't need to be a network expert, you'll need to know enough about networks to work with the Network Administrators in your organization and the vendor's support team.

Every enterprise-wide application depends on a network to a significant extent. If the application's presentation tier, i.e., the software used to present data to the user, is web based, then the primary communications route will be between the user workstations and the application or web server is the network. If the database is on a separate server, then there will also be a significant number of transmissions across the network between the application server and the database server.

If the presentation tier is on the user workstations, aka a client-server application, then the communications will be across the network between workstations (the client) and the database server (the server). See Chapter 3 (section 3.3) for a refresher of the three-tier architecture common to many applications.

The only type of application without a network dependency would be one that exists entirely on a single computer. An application that fits into this design would be very limited in scope. It would probably be sitting on a user's workstation and would be used exclusively by a single user. An application thus limited most likely wouldn't require the services of an Application Administrator.

18.1 LANs, WANs, AND OTHER "AN's"

There are a number of different types of networks that can be utilized in an enterprise-wide application. The Internet is the mother of all networks, but within the corporate environment, you may hear about other types of networks being mentioned. Some of them are:

- LAN—Local Area Network connects devices across a relatively limited distance. If your organization occupies a single floor or a single building, then your "network" is probably a LAN.
- WAN—Wide Area Network is used to connect a collection of LANS across a wider distance. If your organization has multiple facilities in the same state or country, then it might have a LAN at each site and all of the LANs are connected via a WAN.
- MAN—Metropolitan Area Network is like a WAN, but smaller. If your organization has all of its facilities in a single city, then you might be using a MAN to communicate.
- SAN—Storage Area Network is a network set up to allow servers to access storage devices, i.e., disk drives or RAID arrays.

18.2 ADDRESSES

Just like a house or an apartment, every computer device has an address to enable other devices to communicate with it. Actually, each device on the network has two addresses. These addressing schemes are described in the following sections.

18.2.1 MAC addresses

A MAC (Media Access Control) address is a unique identifier assigned to every device that can connect to a network. This identifier is burned into a device's memory when it is manufactured. The devices that you'll most commonly deal with that have MAC addresses are NICs (Network Interface Cards). Every device, e.g., user workstation or server, connected to a network has a NIC. If your server has multiple NICs, then each one of them has their own MAC address.

The format of a MAC address is six groups of two hexadecimal digits separated by colons or hyphens. The first half of the address indicates the manufacturer while the second half is the serial number assigned to the specific device by the manufacturer. An example of a MAC address is 01:23:45:67:89:ab or 01-23-45-67-89-ab.

You can see the MAC address of the NIC on a Windows computer by entering the command "ipconfig / all" in a command window. Figure 18.1 shows the output of this command. In this screenshot, the MAC address, aka the Physical Address, of the NIC card is F0-4B-A2-B4-DE-D7. The Linux and UNIX equivalent of this command is "ifconfig."

18.2.2 IP addresses

The second address associated with a network device is the IP (Internet Protocol) address. The IP address designates the network and location on that network of the device. The IP address is assigned to the device when it's added to the network.

Technically, IP addresses are 32 binary digits (e.g., 74.25.227.178). To make them easier to recognize, they're typically written down as four 8-bit groups (each referred to as an octet) that are separated by a period, for example, 174.14.253.12. The current IP addressing convention is referred to as IP Version 4 or IPv4. The number of devices on the Internet has increased so much that this numbering schema is no longer large enough to provide future devices on the Internet with a unique IP address.

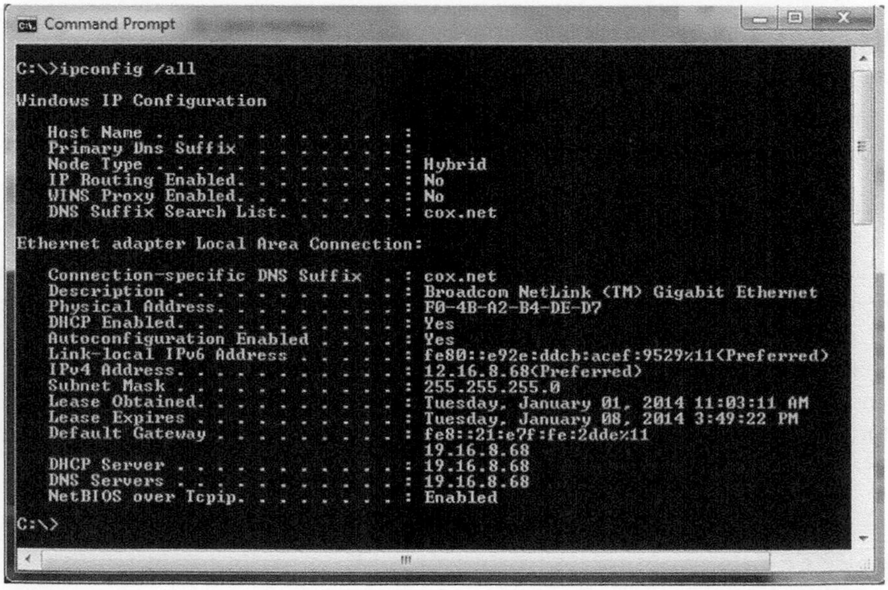

FIGURE 18.1

MAC address of a user workstation. (For color version of this figure, the reader is referred to the online version of this chapter.)

To handle all of the future devices that are anticipated to be added to the Internet, a new, expanded address has been devised. The new schema, IP Version 6, has 128 bits instead of 32 bits. An IPv6 address is written as eight 4-digit hexadecimal numbers separated by colons. For example: 2012:0CA7:BD10: ED01:0000:0000:0000:0000. If the least significant numbers are all zeros, then they can be omitted. The above IPv6 address could also be written as 2012:0CA7:BD10:ED01. Unfortunately, the two versions (IPv4 and IPv6) are incompatible, so the transition to this brave new world will likely be long and complicated.

The IP address of a device can also be obtained via the ipconfig /all command. In Figure 18.1, the IPv4 address of the NIC card is 12.16.8.68.

Each computer on the network maintains a local copy of a table called the ARP (address resolution protocol) table that maps the MAC address and IP address for each device on the network. It uses this mapping to ensure that communications are directed to the correct network device.

18.2.3 Public IP addresses vs. internal IP addresses

There are two types of IP addresses: public and private. A public IP address is one that is visible to the public, i.e., any computer in the world could potentially try to communicate with it. A private IP address can only be reached from within your organization's private network.

There are two reasons why both kinds of IP addresses exist. The first is security related. A corporation that sells its wares across the Internet, for example, Amazon, would definitely want their IP address to be public. They want everyone in the world to be able to find it, log on, and buy something. Alternatively, an organization might have a web-based employee time-entry application. There is no legitimate reason for the general public to log into Acme's time-entry system. So, access to it would be restricted to people whose computers are on the organization's private network, e.g., LAN.

If the application you're supporting is accessible from the outside world, i.e., the Internet, then its IP address is probably a public address. If it can only be used from inside the organization's private network, e.g., your LAN, then the IP address is probably private. If you need a definitive answer to whether your server's IP address is public or private, you should contact your organization's Network Administrator.

The second reason for internal or private addresses is to conserve IPv4 addresses, which are becoming a relatively scarce resource. Addresses in the Private IP address ranges can be used by any organization. Routers in these organization's local networks (LANs) know that computers with IP addresses in the private address range are for internal use only. This allows the same IP addresses to be used by many, many LANs without causing any confusion.

18.2.4 Static vs. dynamic IP addresses

The IP address assigned to a device can be either static or dynamic. The difference is that once assigned, a static IP address doesn't change. A dynamic IP address can be different each time a connection to the network is established. Dynamic IP addresses are typically assigned to devices on a LAN by a server known as the Dynamic Host Configuration Protocol (DHCP) server.

Dynamic assignments are used to conserve IP addresses, which are a finite resource. Dynamic IP addresses are typically assigned to users workstations. If your organization has a large number of users, it might not be possible to assign everyone their own static IP address. By dynamically assigning an IP address only to workstations that are connecting to the Internet, the number of unique IP addresses needed is minimized.

Your application server will almost certainly have a static IP address. This is to ensure that even if it's rebooted its IP address will stay the same. If the IP address changed each time, the application server rebooted it would be extremely difficult for users to connect to it.

You can determine whether a Windows device's IP address is static or dynamic by running the "ipconfig / all" command. If the line labeled "DHCP Enabled" has the value "Yes," then the IP Address is dynamic. If the value is "No," then the IP address is static. The screenshot in Figure 18.1 shows the "DHCP Enabled" line in the ipconfig output.

18.3 DOMAINS

In the context of computer networks, a domain is a group of computers that can be accessed and administered with the same set of rules and are administered as a group. All computers in a domain can see and be seen by all other computers in the domain. A computer can only belong to a single domain at any given time.

Your organization may have a single domain or many domains depending on how large it is and how security conscious it is. The important point for you as an Application Administrator to know is what domain the application server(s) are in. It's also useful to know what domain the users are in. Crossing domains require that firewall ports be opened, so if your servers and users are in different domains you'll probably have to submit requests for firewall ports to be opened to enable users to access the application server.

On a Windows computer, you can find out what domain it belongs to by looking at the System Properties screen. The screenshot shown in Figure 18.2 indicates that this computer is on domain network.com. You can find out what domain a Windows computer is in by following the following steps. The steps will vary slightly depending on what version of Windows you're dealing with.

1. Click on the Start menu button and click on the Control Panel option
2. Click on the "System and Security" option
3. Select the "System" option
4. Select the "Advanced system settings" option
5. Click the Computer Name tab

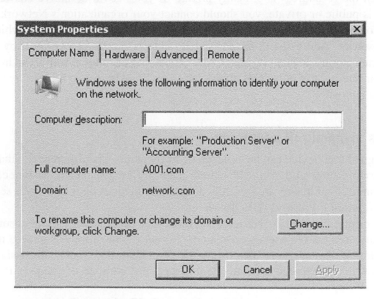

FIGURE 18.2

Determining the domain that a Windows computer is in. (For color version of this figure, the reader is referred to the online version of this chapter.)

18.3.1 Domain controllers

In a network of Windows computers, each server is either a member or a domain controller. The domain controller (DC) is a server that controls what security access each of the members is allowed to have. A domain will have a single primary domain controller and one or more backup domain controllers that take over if the primary DC fails.

Some of the security-related tasks a DC performs include:

- It holds details of all users authorized to access any server in the domain in a database
- Periodically sends copies of the security database to the backup domain controllers
- Member servers will query the domain controller to confirm that the credentials, i.e., username and password, that a user has entered are valid

This section was intended to give you a thumbnail background on Domain Controllers, which exist only on Windows computer networks. The Network Administrator will manage the domain controller. Your application server isn't going be acting as a domain controller and you won't be asked to maintain a Domain Controller.

18.4 DNS—DOMAIN NAME SYSTEM

A network of computers whether it's the Internet or the LAN used by your organization has a lot of computers. A method is needed to keep track of how a computer can contact another computer in the network. The Domain Name System (DNS) is a naming system that makes it possible to computers to "find" each other in one or more networks using names instead of IP addresses.

For example, suppose one of your users wants to access the web-based accounting application your support. He opens his web browser and enters the URL (Uniform Resource Locator) for the application, e.g., "www.accounting.acme.com." The browser takes that address and passes it to a Domain Name Server. The DNS server will translate the name entered by the user to the IP address of the web server of the application, e.g., 19.0.21.17. The browser then initiates a session with the web server software on that server. If the Domain Name System didn't exist, then users would have to enter the IP address for every server they wanted to access. This would be slow, inconvenient, and mistake prone.

As an Application Administrator, working with the Domain Name System isn't difficult. For the most part, the only times you'll need to interact with the DNS are:

- When the application servers are set up and when the application is being installed, you'll have to provide the DNS Administrator with details like the name and URL of each server.
- If the application servers have their IP addresses changed, for example, if the server is moved from one domain to another, then its IP address will be changed. The new address needs to be provided to the DNS Administrator, so he or she can update the DNS database.
- If additional application servers are added to support the application, you'll have to provide the new server names and IP addresses to the DNS Administrator, so the DNS database can be updated with them.

If your application's DNS entry is changed, then you need to be aware that these changes aren't made instantly. One delay is that the DNS Administrator might only make changes to the Domain Name Server at a certain time of day, for example, late at night.

Another potential source of delay in distributing new DNS entry data is that changes made to the DNS aren't immediately sent out to all computers on the network. Instead, each Domain Name Server caches its entries and only refreshes them when they have gotten old, i.e., when they have "timed out." The administrator of the DNS server sets the refresh time which is called the time to live (TTL). The TTL value can range from seconds to days. The rationale behind holding this data in a cache is that it is relatively stable. If every computer submitted a request to the DNS server every time it communicated with another computer, the DNS server would be overwhelmed with requests. By having this data held in a cache of individual computers, the number of such requests is significantly reduced.

18.5 FIREWALLS

The purpose of a firewall is to keep a network secure by acting as a barrier between what's outside, i.e., the Internet and a LAN or personal computer. A firewall works by analyzing incoming and outgoing network traffic to determine whether it should be allowed through the network or not. A good firewall recognizes and blocks attempts to connect to your computer or network by an uninvited visitor. It will also filter out contact attempts by websites that are known to be the source of attacks.

If your organization is particularly security conscious, the local network might have multiple firewalls. The closest to the outside world is referred to as the "front-end" firewall. The interior firewall is called the "back-end" firewall. The area in the network between the two firewalls is referred to as the DMZ, aka the demilitarized zone. If your organization does have two firewalls, then it's possible that they will be from different vendors. This provides an additional layer of protection. Section 18.6 describes the purpose of the DMZ.

A firewall can be based on either hardware or software. In either case, it is positioned between the outside world and your LAN. Firewalls need to be set up and maintained by a trained or experienced professional to ensure their effectiveness. The responsibility for maintaining your organization's firewall will be either the Network Administrator or the security group. As an Application Administrator, you won't likely be responsible for this type of maintenance activity.

18.6 DMZ—DEMILITARIZED ZONE

A DMZ is a method of providing an additional layer of security for your network. If your network has two firewalls, then the area between the firewalls is considered the DMZ. Figure 18.3 illustrates a network that has two firewalls and a DMZ between them.

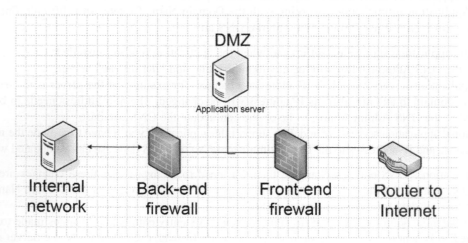

FIGURE 18.3

DMZ created by having two firewalls on a network. (For color version of this figure, the reader is referred to the online version of this chapter.)

If your organization provides services that are available to users outside of the LAN, i.e., to the outside world, then the servers that provide those services would be located in the DMZ. This allows them to be accessed from the outside world but protects the rest of your network from external exposure. Examples of services that might be available to the outside world are:

- Mail servers
- FTP servers
- Web servers

Whether or not your organization's network has a DMZ or not doesn't have a significant bearing on supporting your application, this is just a bit of knowledge that is valuable for you to know. The application vendor may ask you whether your servers are in the DMZ or the internal network. Having this information in advance and understanding what it means will make your job just a little bit easier.

18.7 WHAT'S ON YOUR NETWORK

A network can be a big, busy, and diverse kind of place. It's a good idea for an Application Administrator to have an idea of the types of devices that can reside on a network. The following sections provide a very brief description of what might be on your organization's network.

18.7.1 User's workstations

Users' workstations are probably the most numerous type of device on most networks. The users of your application need to be connected to the network to access it. The same is true for all of the other applications that support the organization's business needs.

18.7.2 Servers

A server is a computer that provides one or more services to users or other computers on the network. While it's possible for any given computer to provide multiple different services, typically each supports just a single service. Some examples of the types of servers that might exist on a network are listed here.

- Application servers—dedicated to running application software, such as the application you support. Depending on the variety of software needed by the organization, application servers might be the most common type of servers on the network.
- Web servers—run software that service web page requests submitted by users. Three common web server packages are Apache HTTP Server (Apache), Microsoft Internet Information Services (IIS), and Sun Java System Web Server.
- Database servers—software that maintains information in a database, frequently a relational database. It responds to requests from users and other servers to insert, update, delete, and select information into or from the database. Common relational database management packages are MySQL, Microsoft SQL Server, IBM DB2, and Oracle.
- Mail servers—use the Simple Mail Transfer Protocol (SMTP) to transmit e-mail across networks. Examples of the software that runs on a mail server include sendmail, Postfix, or Exim if the server is UNIX or Linux based. On Windows servers, the most common e-mail software is Microsoft Exchange Server.
- File servers—support users and other servers by containing files that are accessible by anyone on the network.

- FTP servers—exist on the network to facilitate the transfer of large files to and from the network. If applications used by your organization transfer files to or from clients, vendors, business partners, or government entities, then an FTP server might be used to fulfill this business need.

18.7.3 Printers

Almost everyone needs to print something out occasionally. Instead of each user having a small printer directly connected to his or her PC, most organizations have larger printers that are connected directly to the network. Any user that has been given access to the printer can use it to print out his or her reports, code listings, or recipes.

18.7.4 Routers

A router is an electronic device that forward data packets from one network to another, thus joining multiple networks together. If your organization supports multiple networks, e.g., one in each of several cities, then a router probably exists where they meet. Another example is if your local area network (LAN) is connected to the Internet, then there is a router on the LAN at that connection point.

18.7.5 Switches

A switch is an electronic device on a LAN that accepts messages from any device on the LAN and forward it to just the intended device. If your LAN has more than a handful of devices on it, then it probably contains one or more switches.

18.7.6 Network drives

A network drive is a storage device, like a drive, that is available to users and other servers on the organization's network. Each user needs to be granted access to the device by a System Administrator before they are able to access it. Network drives enable multiple users or servers to share subdirectories and files to facilitate collaborative work efforts.

Another example of how a network drive might be used is if an organization maintains all of its documents on a specific drive and if I need access to one of these documents, I could be granted access to the drive. Then I could map, i.e., define, the drive from my workstation. After mapping the drive, I could access the drive at any time.

18.7.7 Subnets

It's possible for an organization to divide their network into multiple pieces. If they choose to do this, then each of these subdivisions is called a subnet. One reason for doing this might be to have all of the computers in a specific building be on the same subnet. Assuming most of the computers on a subnet communicate primarily with each other, then traffic can be concentrated within the subnet. By doing this, the efficiency of the network is enhanced. If your organization has 50 computers, this won't make much of a difference, but if it has 1000 computers, it definitely will make a difference.

Your Organization

As an Application Administrator you'll spend most of your time working on technical topics, but you'll rely on the rest of your organization for a great deal of support. No one knows everything about either all of the technical topics they will encounter or everything about how their organization does its business. You'll need to work with your supervisor, peers, and other technical professionals in your organization to get your job done.

19.1 WHOM DOES THE IT DEPARTMENT REPORT TO?

If you're in the IT group it's important to understand who the group reports to. Does the IT group report to the CEO? Finance? Research and Development? None of the choices are specifically "bad," but it's an indication of IT's role in the organization. Many feel that if the CIO (Chief Information Officer) reports to the CEO, then IT has a little more prestige and status since it's obviously important to the CEO.

19.2 INNOVATION

Another way of looking at your IT department is whether it's innovative or not. Does your IT department just take orders for new hardware or does it provide leadership and vision for the organization? An IT department that sees its role as partnering with the business to drive revenue, and helping create investments in new products and new markets is likely to provide more variety and more new technology to work with than an IT department that just installs replacement servers.

19.3 TECHNOLOGY GROUPS THAT SUPPORT YOU

An Application Administrator needs the assistance of other technical teams to fully support his or her application. One of the most important things you need to know about your organization to be effective is whom to contact for assistance when your application encounters a problem with another system. Knowing the group that handles each area is a good start, but it's invaluable to know and have a good working relationship with your peers in other groups.

Learn whether your organization has groups that perform the functions listed below. Be aware that not every organization has all of the following groups. Organizations with smaller IT departments will likely have combined several functions into a single group. For example, the System Administrators might also handle network administration and security:

- Active Directory Administrator—maintains the Active Directory subsystem by managing user accounts, ensuring that user accounts have the correct security access, creates and assigns users to the correct roles, provides guidance when an application changes to LDAP or SSO authentication, etc.

- Backup and Recover Administrators—schedule and monitor backup processes that run on servers enterprise wide. Work with Application Administrators to ensure that all of the necessary drives and directories are being backed up. Set up reports for the administrators of each application to allow them to verify that backups are successful. This team also works with you if you need to load a backup file that has been stored on secondary media like tape or DVD.
- Computer Operators—work in the data center to ensure that all of the servers are operating correctly, monitoring tools, receiving alerts, escalating issues, etc. May be responsible for kicking off batch jobs and verifying that those jobs complete successfully. If a problem occurs during nonbusiness hours, they will attempt to deal with it. If the problem is severe or unusual, they will likely call the Application Administrator that supports the application to get assistance or turn the problem over to him or her.
- DBA (Database Administrators)—support the databases that your application(s) and others rely upon. They are responsible for applying updates to the database software, tuning the databases when performance is a problem, verifies that databases are being backed up, maintains database user's accounts, etc. When you are setting up a new application or applying changes to an existing one, you will call upon them if database changes are required.
- Desktop support—works with users to make sure that their desktop software and hardware is working. This team will perform installs and updates of desktop O/S software, applications, etc. Will work with users if their problems accessing your application appear to be on the desktop rather than in the application itself.
- DNS (Domain Name System) administrators—responsible for ensuring that all DNS entries needed by the organization exist and are accurate. Will be involved in the activities if the DR site is ever activated to enable users to access DR web servers.
- E-mail Administrator—responsible for any e-mail servers and software that the organization relies upon to generate and receive e-mail. If it appears that your application isn't sending out the reports or other e-mails you're expecting then you'll work with this administrator to resolve the problem.
- Help Desk—First tier of support that users have contact with. They will resolve the problems they're familiar with or can look up in a knowledge base. More difficult or unusual problems are forwarded to the second tier support personnel.
- Network Administrators—are responsible for maintaining the hardware and software that make up the organization's computer network. If it appears that the application's performance has slowed down significantly, the Network Administrators will work with you to either improve network performance or demonstrate that the network isn't the cause.
- SAN (Storage Area Network) team—Responsible for disk storage that exists on a storage area and available to anyone on the corporate network. If your application needs additional disk space, this might be the team that provides it for you.
- Scheduling Application Administrator—Installs, maintains, and supports an enterprise-wide scheduling tool like Control-M.
- Security Administrators—are responsible for IT-related security. This group probably handles requests to open firewall ports. They may also periodically run vulnerability scans with a tool like Nessus to identify and correct vulnerabilities before the bad guys access them.
- Software Development—the team that develops software applications. They are responsible for enhancing it, tuning it and fixing any problems that are identified in the software that they developed. Some organizations don't do a significant amount of internal development. Instead they rely on licensing third party applications to fulfill their IT needs.
- Systems Administrators, aka sysadmins—responsible for installing fundamental software like the operating system on servers. They also apply upgrades and patches to the operating system when needed.

- Monitoring Software Administrator—responsible for enterprise-wide monitoring software like Nagios, SolarWinds, and OpenView. If you need something on your server to be monitored, this is the group that you turn to for assistance.
- Web Server Administrator—maintain the web server packages like IIS and Apache.

19.4 DOES YOUR ORGANIZATION HAVE A DATA CENTER?

A data center is a facility that houses an organization's computers, network hardware, storage subsystems, communications connection, cabling, etc. It will likely have environmental equipment like air conditioners to keep the environment in the optimal temperature for the hardware. Many data centers have redundant power suppliers and/or a UPS (uninterruptible power supply).

If your organization has more than a handful of servers, then it's likely they are all located in a data center. It's also likely that the data center has security in place to prevent intruders from having physical access to the hardware. Security can include locked doors, guards, coded badges to restrict access, and closed circuit television cameras.

You probably won't be able access to the database center on your own due to these security precautions. If you don't have access on a regular basis, you should see if it's possible to take a tour of it. While you don't actually need to know what it looks like, to me there is some value in actually knowing where the servers you work so hard to keep running are and what they look like.

Is the data center manned 24×7? This will become important to you if the server hosting your application ever hangs up and needs to be rebooted. While there are many problems that can be resolved remotely, there are times when there is no substitute for someone pushing the switch to kill the power.

If the data center isn't manned 24×7 when is it and isn't it manned? What are your alternatives if a crisis occurs during the "off" hours? In an emergency how quickly can someone hustle down to the data center to handle a problem? The answers to these questions need to be reflected in your application's SLA (Service Level Agreement). You don't want to promise the users that the application will come back up within 10 minutes of an outage if it will take a data center staffer 60 minutes to arrive onsite over the weekend.

Do you know how to contact the data center if the need arises? It's great if the data center is constantly manned, but unless you know how to reach them it doesn't help much:

- Is there a phone at a desk that is constantly manned?
- Is there a mobile phone that is carried by an on duty data center technician?
- Is there an on-call list that identifies who to contact in the data center each week?
- Is there an e-mail address that is being monitored by data center staff?

19.5 ARE THERE SIMILAR APPLICATIONS IN THE ORGANIZATION?

If there are other applications that are administered similarly to yours in the organization, is it possible to take advantage of this situation? Applications that are similar in nature make natural opportunities for cross-support. There might be business, regulatory, or security reasons why this can't be done, but if it's possible to work together then that should be explored.

Some possible ways that you can take advantage of similar applications are:

- Can Application Administrators for the different application be quickly and easily cross-trained to back each other up?
- Can an Application Administrator support multiple applications if they are extremely similar?

- In an emergency situation can Application Administrators of similar applications support other applications without training in advance?
- Can procedures, processes, documentation, and automated tasks from similar applications be reused to avoid reinventing the wheel?

19.6 LEARN FROM OTHER APPLICATION ADMINISTRATORS

If I have learned one thing in my years in the IT field it's that everyone can learn something from everyone else. You may think that the way you administer your application can't be improved upon, but I guarantee you that if you talk to other Application Administrators you'll find a better way of doing something. If you don't learn something then you're either extremely closed-minded or you're the most competent professional our industry has ever seen.

Just a short list of what you can learn from other Application Administrators includes:

- What are its SLA (Service Level Agreement) details?
- How do they implement their change control?
- How do they take their backups?
- What clever little scripts do they have to automate mundane tasks? Every application has tasks like running backups, clearing out old files, and reviewing log files that need to be done but are time consuming and are great candidates for automation.
- What do they use to monitor their servers and everything that is running on them?
- How do they document application outages?
- What do they learn from each outage that helps them prevent or minimize future outages?
- How do they document their best practices?
- How do they synchronize their production and DR systems, both data and software?
- How do they coordinate with the user community regarding outages?
- How do they cross-train their backups and future replacements?
- How are they alerted when the application goes down?
- Do they have processes in place to restart the application if it goes down?
- What do their UATs (User Acceptance Tests) look like?
- Who writes their UATs?
- Who runs their UATs?
- How do they perform stress testing? Do they use a formal tool? Have they written scripts or batch files to impose a load on the application? If they have a group of users accessing the application simultaneously to impose load on it how do they coordinate them?
- What vulnerabilities have they identified in their applications and on their servers? How did they find these vulnerabilities and what have they done to protect against them?

Getting to know other Application Administrators in your organization and talking shop with them is a very good idea. If you can develop contacts with Application Administrators in other organizations, that can also be very productive. Of course you have to give to receive. You need to be willing to share some of your "secrets" to expect them to share theirs.

19.7 APPLICATION PRIORITIZATION

In the eyes of an organization not all applications are created equally. The ones considered most important are those that generate income or fulfill a function that is critical to the organization. Applications that don't meet those criteria aren't at the same level or importance.

Organizations typically rank the applications that are being used internally to fulfill needs. The more important an application is to the organization, the higher the rating. An application's rating determines points like the following:

- The resources devoted to it. An application that generates income for an organization is likely to have more resources allocated to it than one that doesn't generate income.
- What level of support is specified in the SLA. For example, normal business hours or 24×7. Critical applications are more likely to be expected to be available around the clock.
- How quickly it will be brought up at the DR (Disaster Recovery) site. High priority applications will be first in the queue to be brought up at the DR site if that eventuality ever occurs.
- Any support contract with the application vendor is more likely to include 24×7 support and possibly onsite consultants if it's critical to the organization's future.

A common way to prioritize applications is to assign each application a priority of high, medium, or low. Examples of priority levels and what that means are listed below. Obviously each organization will have its own definitions and criteria of what applications in each category:

High
- Applications that either generate income for the organization or are considered critical. Some examples of high priority applications include the e-commerce interface with the client/customer base, the DNS (Domain Name System) server, the application that backs up all servers and applications required to meet government regulatory requirements would candidates for high priority status.
- High-level applications are expected to be available at all times.
- If a high-level application experiences problems, it is expected to be repaired within a few hours no matter what time of day or day of the week it goes down.
- A "hot" or prebuilt server to support each high-level application already exists at the DR site. This enables the application to be brought up relatively quickly in the event that a disaster occurs.
- Data for a high-level application is backed up to the DR site on a regular basis. This might be done hourly or it might be done on a real-time basis.

Medium
- Applications that the organization can function without for a brief period of time would be assigned to a medium priority. Examples of applications that might be assigned to a medium priority could include the application that pushes updates out to user workstations or a trouble ticket tracking application.
- Medium-level applications are expected to be available during normal business hours.
- If a medium-level application experiences problems, it is expected to be brought back up within a business day.
- If a disaster occurs medium priority applications could be installed on physical or virtual servers that already exist at the DR site.
- Data for a medium-level application is backed up to the DR site on a daily basis.

Low
- Applications that the organization can function without for an extended period of time would be assigned to a low priority. Examples of them include LMS (Learning Management Systems), an application to track unclaimed property, or an application that tracks employee vacation requests.
- Low-level applications are expected to be available during normal business hours.
- If a low-level application experiences problems, it is expected to be brought back up within up to a week.

- If a disaster occurs low priority applications will be addressed after all high- and medium-level applications are operational. The hardware for low priority applications will be ordered after a disaster has been declared.
- Data for a low-level application is backed up to the DR site on a daily basis.

19.8 CHANGE CONTROL

Every organization's application software undergoes changes on a regular basis. Most of them attempt to control how and when these changes are made. Examples of these controls include the following:

- A complete and accurate description of the change being made needs to be approved by the user representative before any changes are made.
- Changes are initially made on a test and/or QA system. If they are successful at that level, they are promoted to the production system.
- Each step in the process requires approval by an authorized person. Examples of positions that can approve are user representative, IT representative, application business manager, development group representative, and the person who actually installed the changes. Dividing the approval responsibility is a way of ensuring that all affected groups have a say in the change process.
- A UAT (User Acceptance Test) is created in advance for each change that is being made.
- The UAT is executed by a user representative on each system, e.g., DEV, QA, and Production.
- A data reconciliation process must be established to verify that the change has affected only the expected set of data. This process also needs to define how data would be rolled back to its original state if unexpected data changes are observed.
- A rollback plan must be created to establish how the system will be restored to its initial state if the change doesn't work as expected.

Does your organization use a formal tool or a homegrown process for change control? Neither approach is right nor wrong, but you need to understand the process that is in place. If a locally developed process suits your organization's needs, then it's the best tool to use. Some questions to ask about the capabilities of the tool being used are:

- Does the tool include a workflow component so the process is locked for everyone except the person(s) authorized to approve the next step of the process?
- Does the tool send out e-mails to the person(s) who needs to advance it past the current stage? If the current approver isn't made aware of their pending responsibility, then a significant amount of time can be wasted waiting the change to be approved and advanced.
- Does the tool make it clear which steps have been completed so far for each change?
- Does the tool produce reports to document what changes have been made so far to a given application or during a given time period?
- Is the tool accessible to the auditors so they can confirm documented change control procedures have been followed?
- Does the tool allow for exception situations, for example, if the payroll application crashes during the middle of the monthly check-cutting phase? There may not be time to go through the full approval cycle if it needs to finish running by a specific time. Will the tool allow a change to be made immediately and be approved during the next business day by the appropriate personnel?

Does your organization have preferred or mandated times to roll changes out to the Production system? Some examples of restrictions or preferences that might be in place include:

- Changes should only be made after all users are out of the application for the day.
- Changes should only be made after the users in the primary business location, e.g., the East Coast, are out of the application for the day.
- Changes should be made, when possible, on a Friday. This allows the entire weekend to recover the application if problems occur.
- Changes can only be made on Tuesday, Wednesday, and Thursday. This makes it more likely that all necessary support personnel are available to address the problem.
- Changes can only be made during maintenance times that are published in the SLA (Support Level Agreement).
- Changes cannot be made in the days or weeks leading up to the end of the year or quarter.

19.9 DOCUMENTATION

There are several types of documentation about applications that are fairly standard within organizations. If your organization doesn't already have standards, then you may need to write these documents yourself or work with the group in your organization that is responsible for developing them. Examples of types of documents that commonly exist are:

- Technical landscape document
- Operational Support document
- Service Level Agreement (SLA)
- Verification testing
- Disaster Recovery (DR) plans

19.9.1 Technical landscape

A technical landscape document shows the hardware needed to support the application. Having a single document that includes all the essential information about a server will be quite valuable. Figure 19.1 shows an example of a technical landscape diagram. It can as simple or detailed as your organization or department wants it to be. A very simple version would simply list the servers, their IP addresses, and the communication lines between them. A more complicated version could list the following:

- Server names
- IP addresses
- Operating system and version on each server
- Whether the server is physical or virtual
- Disk drives and their sizes
- Version of the application
- Ports that need to be open between servers
- Whether the server(s) are load balanced
- End of life for physical devices like servers

If you have multiple environments each should be displayed separately. They can be on the same or different worksheets, but they need to be recognized as separate environments. Typical environments include the following:

- Development (DEV)
- Testing (TEST)
- Quality Assurance (QA), also called User Acceptance Test (UAT)
- Production (PROD)

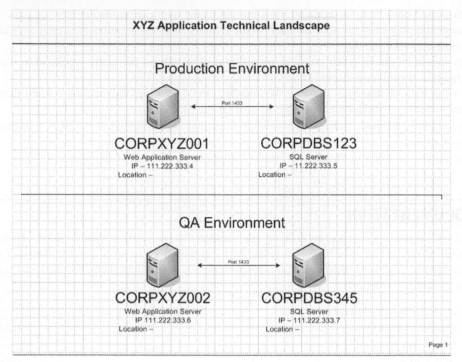

FIGURE 19.1

Example of a Technical Landscape Diagram. (For color version of this figure, the reader is referred to the online version of this chapter.)

There are many tools available that can be used to produce technical landscape diagrams. Just a few examples include:

- Microsoft Visio
- Dia
- Lucidchart
- draw.io
- Pencil Project
- Apache OpenOffice Draw

Some of these tools are open source or shareware or offer free downloads for trial periods. Other packages, which are more expensive, are tailored specifically to developing landscape diagrams. If your organization has a standard tool for producing diagrams, then that's probably the one you should use. Otherwise ask your peers to see what others are using.

19.9.2 Operational support document

An Operational Support Document provides details on how the application will be supported by the Application Administrator's group. This type of documentation is needed to prevent misunderstandings regarding the responsibilities of each group. Some examples of points that are typically covered are:

- Members of the support team, e.g., Project Manager, Documentation Manager, Systems Engineer, Test Manager, and the untitled members of the Operations Support Team
- Steps that will be done to prepare the servers prior to the application being installed

- What monitoring will be done of the application and server(s) it operates on
- Standardized procedures implemented to operate and maintain the application
- Procedures by which errors will be recognized, recorded, and diagnosed
- Security features and actions that the support group will perform
- Backup and recovery procedures that will be put into place

19.9.3 Service level agreement

A Service Level Agreement (SLA) is a contract between the support group and the customers, i.e., the users of the application, documenting what availability and performance they can expect from the application. Regardless of whether the users are internal or external, an SLA is still needed. If the application stops working or doesn't meet the performance expectations, the users don't care whether someone inside or outside the organization developed it.

Items that are typically covered in an SLA include:

- The hours and days that the application will be operational
- System availability level, for example, 98% of the time
- Response time when a problem is reported for each of priority levels: High, Medium, and Low
- Response time based on how the business is being impacted: system is completely down, system is partially available, system performance is slow, noncritical aspects of the system are down, and a work-around is available for the problem
- Procedures to escalate a problem that has been reported
- The metrics on the server that will be monitored and reported
- Hours of Help Desk coverage
- Time and days when backups will be performed
- Maintenance window during which the system can be taken down, for example, the third Saturday of every month from 8 am until 6 pm Central
- Contact information for the IT support team
- Escalation contacts if the first contact individuals aren't available or don't respond in an agreed upon interval
- Whether support is available on public holidays, including a definition of those holidays
- Method by which the requestor is notified that a reported problem has been resolved
- Periodic, e.g., weekly, reports listing all reported problems, including the status of each

An SLA can also list what isn't supported. This might include points like the following:

- Types of desktop computers that the application runs on or doesn't run on
- If the application is web-based, then a list of supported browsers and versions should be included

19.9.4 Verification testing

Verification testing is done to verify that the application is performing as expected. Some of the situations under which verification testing needs to be done are:

- After the application is initially built
- After the application has undergone an upgrade or patch
- After support software, e.g., the operating system, has been upgraded or patched, e.g., maintenance weekend for the operating system

- After changes to the database, especially after structural changes
- When a new browser or a new version of an existing browser is being used

The group that should create the actual tests for verification testing is the user community. They have a much better idea of what the application should and shouldn't do than anyone else. An Application Administrator has a basic idea of what the application does, but certainly wouldn't be as familiar with the screens and functionality as an experienced user should be. Users might resist, but at a minimum they need to be involved in developing these test scripts.

There is one very important additional reason for having the users or user representatives create the verification testing document. If they create it and approve it, then after the system passes this testing regimen they can't later say the tests weren't accurate or comprehensive enough. If the tests aren't thorough enough or aren't accurate, then they have no one to blame but themselves.

19.9.5 Disaster recovery plan

No one likes to think of the worse possible scenarios that could impact your organization and its data center. Just thinking about it can be depressing, but someone has to think about it and plan how the effects can be mitigated. Chapter 12 contains a more detailed description of the Disaster Recovery. There are many possible disaster scenarios that can be envisioned. Some very realistic possible disasters include the following:

- A tornado hits your data center or very close to it
- Your data center is flooded by leaking pipes, a river, flash flood, or tsunami
- A fire occurs in your data center
- Your data center loses power due to a natural disaster, blackouts, or brownouts
- An earthquake destroys your data center or renders it unusable
- Civil insurrection breaks out in your city, state, or country
- Wildfires shut down the data center or render it unreachable
- A terrorist attack targets your organization, data center, or city
- A disaster (tornado, earthquake, tsunami, wildfires, etc.) occurs. It doesn't physically damage the data center but prevents your employees from getting to work

The odds of the above disaster affecting you personally may seem microscopically small, but across the country and world-wide they are occurring regularly. Do you want to take the chance that no disaster will ever impact you? What will you say to defend yourself if the "impossible" does occur? If you haven't properly prepared you may be looking for a new position.

Every application the organization has needs to be evaluated individually and have an appropriate DR (Disaster Recovery) plan developed. Application users and owners may be reluctant to admit it, but not all applications are created equal. Some, for example, a website where customers make purchases, is critical to the revenue stream for an organization. Other applications, for example, ones that create quarterly or annual reports, can be down for extended periods without serious repercussions. The DR plan for the former application would be significantly different than a DR plan for the latter.

What should a DR plan look like? They can range from complicated and expensive all the way to extremely simple. The high dollar end of the spectrum might include duplicated servers at a remote DR facility with real-time transmissions to keep the production and DR databases synchronized. The low end might be the recognition that replacement servers would be acquired once the disaster occurs and loaded with software acquired from the vendor. The database would be restored from the most recent backup tapes once the DR servers have been built. As long as they are appropriate for the application in question neither of these plans is "wrong."

What is absolutely necessary is that the DR plan clearly lay out what will be done and who will do it. Some steps have to be done in advance of the disaster. Other steps would only be done once the disaster occurs. Don't forget that each application requires its own individual DR plan. The following are just a few examples of what should be included in the DR plan:

- What needs to be put in place at the DR site now? Steps that can be done in advance include acquiring servers, loading the operating system on them, loading support software, loading the application software, testing connectivity with the database, etc.
- Will the DR site have adequate power, network bandwidth, heating, and air conditioning?
- Who has the authority to declare a disaster and authorize the application being moved to the DR site? Can just one application be moved or will all applications in the organization be moved at the same time?
- Who will handle each setup task?
- When will each step be completed?
- What steps will be performed when a disaster occurs?
- Who will communicate with the users, IT support team, etc. when a disaster occurs?
- Will the move to the DR servers be completely transparent to the users or will they have to make minimal adjustments? For example, will they have to use a new URL to access a web application running at the DR site? Or will the DNS entry be repointed to the DR server so absolutely no changes need to be made?
- What is the plan to keep the DR server synchronized with the PROD server? For example, when the O/S or application software is updated on the PROD server, the same updates need to be made on the DR server.
- How will the application be migrated back to the production server when the disaster has passed? Who will make the decision and how will it be done?

A DR plan that hasn't been thoroughly tested can't be trusted. Until it's been tested you won't know if it contains omissions or errors. The DR plan needs to be tested initially. It also needs to be tested on a regular basis going forward.

Everyone needs to know what the DR plan is and where it's stored. Positioning all DR plans in a known location, e.g., on a SharePoint server or network server, allows everyone to access it. Keep in mind that the very disaster you're preparing for might well make that location inaccessible. All DR plans should be on both the normal PROD site and the DR site. Everyone involved should be aware of both locations.

Review every DR plan regularly, e.g., annually, to confirm that it is still appropriate. An application that wasn't very important 5 years ago may now be critical to the survival of the organization. Conversely, other applications may have been retired and no longer need DR coverage. If the DR plan isn't reviewed on a regular basis, changes like these won't be noticed.

Another aspect of the DR plan that needs to be reviewed regularly is the personnel assigned to each task. People leave the organization on a regular basis. If someone who's no longer with the organization is assigned a critical task in the DR plan, this could be a disaster in itself. As well as leaving, employees have a tendency to move around within the organization. Someone who was responsible for application XYZ 2 years ago may still be with the company, but in a completely different role now. All personnel assignments in all DR plans need to be reviewed regularly.

19.10 DOCUMENTATION LOCATION

Every organization requires documentation be written, developed, or maintained in support of applications. Depending on the organization, the catalogue of documentation that has been generated can be very long or relatively short. Some examples of documents that you might have to create include the following:

- Project plans detailing how an upgrade will be installed
- Request forms for new servers being built
- UATs (User Acceptance Tests) that are required for every change being made
- DR (Disaster Recovery) plans need to be developed for every application
- Succession plans are developed to lay out who will support your application when you are promoted or hit by the proverbial bus
- Backup plan details how the database for your application is backed up and validated on a regular basis
- Validity testing that will be done after each month's maintenance support software updates are installed
- Requests for new user authorization to access the application

Once you created all of the documentation described above, it has to be stored somewhere. Does your organization have any requirements or recommendations on where it should be stored? Possible locations include:

- On your PC
- On a common network drive
- On a portal
- In a physical 3-ring binder in the organization's library
- In a tool like SharePoint

Once you figure out where to store your documents, there are some other questions that might be asked. For example,

- Who should be able to access them?
- Who can grant or change authority to access them?
- What level of access, e.g., read, write, delete, modify, should each person have to them?
- Should they be backed up? How often and how?
- How long should document be maintained before they can be deleted?
- Once it's time to delete a file or document, how should is it done?

19.11 DATA DICTIONARY

A data dictionary is a centralized repository of metadata. Metadata is data about data. Some examples of what might be contained in an organization's data dictionary include:

- The names of fields contained in all of the organization's databases
- What table(s) each field exists in
- What database(s) each field exists in
- The data types, e.g., integer, real, character, and image of all fields in the organization's databases
- The sizes, e.g., LONG INT, DOUBLE, and CHAR(64), of all fields in the organization's databases
- An explanation of what each database field means
- The source of the data for each database field
- A list of applications that reference each database field
- The relationship between fields in all of the organization's databases
- Default values that exist for all fields in all of the organization's databases
- Who has access to each field

Does your organization maintain a data dictionary? If so, does it impact the application that you support? Some ways in which it might impact you include:

- Does information applicable to your application exist in the data dictionary?
- Are you required to periodically review and validate data dictionary entries related to your application?
- Are you required to update the data dictionary if your application's database details change? For example, if new fields are added or the size of existing fields is changed, do these changes need to be reflected in the data dictionary?
- If new users are added to your application, does their access need to be reflected in the data dictionary?

19.12 CHARGEBACKS

Typically IT departments don't generate income. A common way for organizations to fund services provided by IT to users is via a method called chargebacks. User departments are charged an amount commensurate with the level of IT services they "consume." The more that the IT department does for them, the more they are charged.

Knowing whether your organization has a chargeback system in place is advisable for all Application Administrators. Knowing that user groups are being charged for your services can help make you more responsive in providing them with their money's worth. It can also help you prioritize problems that come up, i.e., you should focus on services that users are being specifically charged for.

What are user departments being charged for by a chargeback system? While every organization handles this differently, some metrics commonly used to calculate what each department is charged could be based on:

- The number of servers used by the application or servers that are dedicated to a particular user department
- The number of users of the application in each department
- The level of customization done to the application, as a whole or for specific departments
- Disk space used
- Network bandwidth utilized by each user department
- CPU time used
- Labor costs for the Application Administrator prorated by user department
- The number of reports developed specifically for a user department
- Cost of setting up and maintaining a DR server
- Cost of keeping the data and software synchronized between the primary data facility and the DR site.

In turn, the IT group that administers the application might itself incur chargeback costs from other IT groups that provide services to it. For example, the application group might experience charges similar to these:

- Cost to set up a server in the Data Center. Note that the cost of a virtual server can be significantly different that the cost of a physical server
- Ongoing administration costs of a server in the Data Center
- Cost for SAN drives based on the number of drives and storage area of each logical device
- Costs for backup operations
- Cost per database or dedicated database server charged by the DBA group
- Cost of restoring a system by reloading a backup tape or file onto the server

19.13 IMPACT OF OTHER APPLICATIONS

If your organization has numerous applications running in its data center, you need to understand whether the application you administer is being impacted by other applications or possibly impacts them. Some of the questions you need to consider include:

- Does your application server(s) support other applications? Realistically, most applications aren't using the majority of a server's capacity, but frequently the software vendors recommend that their software be the only application running on a server.
- Does the database server that supports your application also support other applications' databases? If you feel that sharing a database server with another application that is database intensive causes insurmountable performances problems for your application, then you can request that your database be moved to another physical database server. I will warn you that before making a request like this you should do some research and confirm that competition for the database server is an actual problem. If you make claims that turn out to be baseless, then no one will your next request seriously.
- Does the organization's network support packet intense applications like VOIP (Voice Over Internet Protocol), file-sharing, or large images? This might slow down your application's performance. Unfortunately, there might not be any solution to an environment like this one.
- Is there a significant timing issue between your application and other applications? For example, do multiple applications launch database or network intense activities at the same time? If your application kicks off a database-intensive report at the same time that the payroll application launches the monthly payroll process, then one of these activities should be rescheduled. Another example would be if a database intense report is launched at the same time that the backup software is running on your server and other servers.

Do "recreational applications" impact performance of the network? If the cause of network performance issues is intense activity by the Imaging department, there probably isn't anything that can be done about it. But if everyone in the organization is watching March Madness basketball games, doing their holiday shopping on Cyber Monday or watching the World Cup on the Internet then maybe something can be done about it. Some examples of recreational application include:

- Internet radio/streaming audio
- Streaming video, i.e., online movies or television shows
- On-line gaming
- File sharing or P2P (Peer-to-Peer) music sharing
- Instant Messaging
- Shopping online

19.14 THE CULTURE OF THE ORGANIZATION

Every organization has a culture, even if it doesn't intentionally intend to have one. Your coworkers may be oblivious to the culture, but one still exists. Some examples of questions you can ask that could help you understand the organization's culture include:

- Is your organization on the bleeding edge of technology or does it wait until new technology becomes more stable, widely used, and economical?
- Is your organization in a highly regulated industry and are audits a regular occurrence?

- Does your organization have a higher level of turnover than is average in the industry?
- Does your organization only make changes when it is literally forced to make them?
- Do your coworkers put in extremely long hours on deadlines that are unrealistic and ultimately unobtainable?

The advice to learn as much as you can about your organization applies to everyone, but especially to newcomers. If you were recently hired to administer an application you need to spend some time figuring out how things are done in your new workplace. You're not going to make any friends or progress if you continuously ruffle the feathers of your coworkers and management because you don't understand the organization's culture.

Users

20

Never forget that without users there wouldn't be a need for applications or Application Administrators. Try to keep this in mind the next time you get a little bit frustrated with a demanding user. The purpose of an Application Administrator is to support an application and by extension that means to support the users of the application.

20.1 USER COUNT

How many users can, or do, log into your application? Depending on the nature of the application, this apparently simple question might be surprisingly difficult to answer. If your application requires an ID and password to log into it, then it shouldn't be difficult to get a list of user IDs and just count them. On the other hand, if your application is web-based and doesn't require an ID then it might not be possible to count the size of the user community. For example, an e-commerce website doesn't require any identification until a user pays for their selections.

If it's possible to do so, it's a good idea to track your user count on a regular basis. Capturing the count of users weekly or monthly and charting it aren't difficult and can be extremely valuable. Some reasons for tracking your user count are:

- If your license allows only a specific number of users, then you'll want to know how close you are to reaching the limit. If would be extremely inconvenient to find out you've exceeded the limit when you're adding the new VP as a user.
- If you're rapidly approaching the user limit, it might pressure management into agreeing to either increase the license limit or delete users that are no longer with the organization or who no longer use the application.
- If the number of users is increasing significantly, then you might need to scale up your hardware to ensure the application performance users experience doesn't degrade.
- If the number of users is increasing but shouldn't be climbing, this might be evidence of a security violation.
- Showing your management that usage of the application is increasing might help you secure funding for the application.
- On the other hand, if the amount of user activity in the application is decreasing you or the Business Owner needs to investigate why. It could be a sign that the users aren't happy with the application. Perhaps they think that the application's performance isn't acceptable. It might mean that they are getting similar data or functionality from another source. This lack of activity might be an indication that the application is no longer critical to the organization and should be considered for retirement.

20.1.1 User activity

While it's useful to know that your application has 1001 registered users, that information by itself isn't as useful as it might be. Perhaps more useful than the absolute count would be user-related statistics like the following:

- How many users are in the application right now?
- How many users have logged into it today?
- How many users logged into it yesterday?
- Over the last week, month, or year what was the maximum number of simultaneous users?
- Which user logs into the application most frequently?
- Which group or department has the most users in the application?
- What is the average time each user spends in the application?
- During what hours of the day is the application most heavily used?
- During what hours of the day is the application least heavily used?
- How much activity (e.g., number of transactions, reports, etc.) did users generate?

Does your application provide any means of answering usage-related questions like the ones listed above? Some applications provide system-level reports that provide log-in details. Reports of this nature are frequently referred to as audit trail reports.

If the application doesn't directly provide usage information, is it possible to gather these details indirectly? Does the application write a time-stamped log entry every time a user logs into or out of it? If the log files contain this level of detail, it might be possible to write a script to scan log files, capture usage-related details, and write them to a file or database. If you have the user ID, log-in time, and log-out time for every user connection then you can derive a great deal of usage-related statistics from that data.

20.1.2 Problems with log files

A word of warning regarding log-in and log-out entries in log files. In my experience, they never seem to line up perfectly. I've worked with a number of applications and these entries have never been easy to deal with. What tends to happen is the log-in entries are always there, but some of the log-out entries are missing. One reason the log-out entry might be missing is if the application crashed while the user was logged into it.

In many applications, this log-out entry will be missing if a user exits the application incorrectly. If the user clicks the "Exit" button or clicks the "log-out" menu option, then logic in the application writes a log-out entry into the log file. However, if the user clicks the "X" in the upper right-hand corner of the screen, then there might not be a log entry written to document the log-out event.

Another way these entries can get scrambled is if users are allowed to have multiple sessions open simultaneously. If this is allowed, it can be very difficult to correctly associate log-in entries with the matching log-out entries in the log file.

Even if some log-out entries are missing or users are allowed to have multiple connections, the data you can extract from log files can still be very useful. The count of users who logged in will be accurate. You just might not be able to accurately calculate how long each user was in the application.

20.1.2.1 Time-stamp issues with log files

Another potential source of confusion in log files is the time-stamps. For example:

- Does the time-stamp value increase as you move down the log file or as you move up in the log?
- Does the time represent the local time of the user who generated the activity?
- Is the time in UT, formerly known as GMT, time, or the time of the application server's location?
- How does the logging process handle situations when the time on the server is changed? For example when Daylight Savings Time causes the hour to "fall back"?

20.1.3 Are some users more equal than others?

All users are not created equal. Some of them will only occasionally log into the application and have minimal privileges. Other users seem to be in the application all the time.

It will be to your benefit if you know which users are the most important ones. Users with high privileges, like write or approval permissions, tend to be higher in the organization's hierarchy than users that have read-only access. If a highly privileged user experiences a problem, then that problem needs to be investigated and corrected as quickly as possible.

20.1.4 User locations

Life would be much easier for Application Administrators if all users of the application were in a single city or better yet in the same building. Unfortunately, there are probably very few of us in that position. Most of Application Administrators have users spread across the country or around the world. Some of the specific complications associated with multiple user locations are described in the following sections.

20.1.4.1 Time zones

One reason that geographic diversity complicates support is because it means users are in numerous time zones. Some reasons time zones complicate support are:

- Users in other time zones need or want support while you're sleeping. To support the application 24×7 requires three or more shifts of Application Administrators.
- Multiple time zones make it harder to find a maintenance window when no one is using the system so it can be taken down.
- It's impossible to contact everyone at the same time because some users will be out of the office at any given time.

20.1.4.2 Lack of face-to-face support

Support can certainly be done remotely, but I think everyone would agree that distance makes providing support more complicated. Using communication tools like e-mail, phone calls, and best of all sharing a screen can make remote support easier, but it's still more difficult than standing behind the user and seeing exactly what he or she is doing.

20.1.4.3 Cultural differences

Having users in distance countries implies that the users will be from different countries. This means that they'll speak multiple languages and come from different cultures. Cultural differences among users make remotely supporting an application that much more difficult. In general, the best advice I can provide is to have patience with all users.

20.1.5 Access to what?

What exactly do your users need to access? Some potential objects that you'll be granting access to are described in the following sections. Keep in mind though that different classes of users will need to access different objects.

20.1.5.1 The application

By definition users need to be able to access the application. Different groups or classes of users need to access different components of the application. Hopefully, you have created different roles, e.g., reader, writer, reviewer, approver, etc. that users can be assigned to. Assigning users to a role that suits their needs will make it much easier to support them.

Does the application have the ability to limit access based on the day of the week or the time of day? If there is not a legitimate business reason for a given user to access the application during nonbusiness hours, is it a good idea to impose such a limitation? Restricting access in this way might make the application more secure. On the other hand, if there is a crisis or an overwhelming amount of work that need to be done, it might prevent users from putting in overtime when it's desperately needed.

What if your application doesn't provide the ability to restrict the times that users can log into the application, but that is a desirable security feature? If you're using Active Directory (AD) or Single Sign On (SSO) do either of them provide this ability? If Active Directory (AD) is being used for authentication, can you use it to enforce limitations on when users can log into the application?

20.1.5.2 Multiple sessions

Can a user open multiple sessions of the application at the same time? Some applications allow users to do this and others don't. You should know whether your application does or not. There are pros and cons on this question. In some applications, this is a setting that you can flip one way or the other. Allowing multiple simultaneous sessions might enable the user to be more productive, especially if the response time is slow. On the flip side, having multiple sessions could corrupt the data if the user attempts to modify the same or related data items from multiple sessions.

Another reason not to allow this is for security purposes. If a bad actor logs in as a legitimate user and the real user tries to log in, then a meaningful error message will tell her that someone is using her account. Users should be educated that if they experience this they should contact their supervisor or the Application Administrator immediately!

20.1.5.3 Reports

If the application has reporting functionality, then at least some users will need access to it. Some examples of access that a user might need for the report subsystem are:

- Run existing reports
- Create new reports
- Modify existing reports
- Delete existing reports
- Schedule reports
- Modify the details of a scheduled report
- Change the distribution list of a scheduled report

20.1.5.4 The server

You may be faced with a situation in which users claim that they need access to the application server. These users may tell you that there are certain functions that can only be performed on the server. If you're presented with claims like this, your first step should be to determine whether their claims are accurate. Review the documentation to see what it says on the topic. If the details it provides aren't conclusive, then you'll need to contact the vendor support group to verify this claim.

If it turns out that there are functions that can only be performed on the server, then you need to consider ways of handling this situation. Some possibilities are:

- Can the task be automated? Would possible to add this task to a scheduler and run it on a regular basis?
- Can you remote to the server and execute the task for the users? If it needs to be performed infrequently, say once a month or less, then this might be a feasible solution. If this task needs to be done daily or even weekly, then this might not be acceptable to either you or the user in question.
- Can the user write a script or batch file that you execute for them on the server? If they can't write the batch file, then you could write it and demonstrate it to them.
- Can you share your desktop with the user after setting up a remote connection? Then you give them control of the session and allow them to launch the task in a controlled environment.
- Enable their access only when a user needs to do something on the server and revoke their access immediately after they are done with the task. At all other times, their account on the server is disabled.
- Grant access to the server to an extremely limited number of users. To me this is the least acceptable of all the possible solutions.

Here's some advice that I've learned the hard way. Think long and hard before giving out access to a production server. The more people who have access to it the more likely that something will go wrong and the more finger-pointing there will be to figure out who caused the problem.

Another reason not to give out access to the server is the auditing process that might be in place at your organization. If your application has to adhere to SOX or another set of government regulations, then restricting access to the server is very likely already mandated. In a way this can be turned to your advantage. You can tell the user they can't have access to the server and blame it on the auditors!

20.1.5.5 The database

Eventually you may receive a request for direct access to the application's database. The requestor may be a user, but it may be someone from another group in your organization. They will explain that they want read-only access to the database to extract a very specific set of data from the database. You'll be assured that their activities will have no impact on the users of the application. You need to patiently, but sternly talk them out of their misconceptions. There are some very good reasons to reject their requests:

- It would be a very unusual for anyone isn't extremely experienced with it to understand how to properly pull data from a fully normalized relational database. Vendors don't design their database to be understandable by outsiders. Databases are designed to be efficient. Efficient and being easily understood have nothing in common.
- No matter how strongly they reassure you, they can't guarantee that the select queries they run won't impact user performance. It's very possible their SQL query could end up performing full table scans. If that happens, then the database queries generated by the application on behalf of user requests could slow to a crawl.
- It's very likely that the data they extract from the database will be inaccurate. If this is the case, then any decisions based on it are going to make someone look bad. You may not have written the queries, but just be being in the neighborhood you're likely to get a share of the blame.
- Tweaks of the query they want to run will never end. There will always be "just one more little change" that needs to be made to the query of the output file. You'll be pestered for assistance for the foreseeable future.

A very good alternative would be to write a report that pulls all the data they want. If you aren't capable of writing this report, then consider having the person making the request work with the vendor write it. Have the report export the data as either a csv (comma-separated value) or an XML (eXtensible Markup Language) file. Files of these formats can very likely be imported into whatever tool or system they need to work with.

20.1.6 **Internal vs. external users**

Users can be internal or external and I mean this both physically and figuratively. Life would be easier if all of your users were employees sitting in their cubicles who are connected directly to the corporate network. Unfortunately, that isn't always the case these days. Many of your users are employees, but others can be vendors, consultants, outside attorneys, contractors, interns, clients, etc. Some employees will be located in the home office, but others will be at remote sites, working from home or on the road visiting a client. They will also need to access the application.

Some users might not even have a defined relationship with the organization yet. For example, if you support an application that accepts and processes job applications, then your "users" are job seekers. The individuals don't have a relationship with the organization yet, but they will be accessing your application.

20.1.7 **Approvers**

To become a legitimate user someone has to approve the request for access. The "someone" who OK's the request is considered an approver. Every application needs one or more people who fill this role. Their job title might not include that specific word, but they have the needed authority to approve who can access the application. Frequently the person who gives approval to new users is either the Business Owner or the Application Owner.

As the Application Administrator you need to understand how the approval process is set up. Some organizations have a very formal approval process and others have a much more relaxed way of doing things. No matter how your organization works you need to be able to answer the following questions. If you can't, then submit a list of questions to clear up your misgivings to either your supervisor or the application owner (or both):

- Who are the approvers that determine who should be able to access the application?
- Do approvers have backups? If so, who are they?
- Who will inform you that an approver's access to the system should be terminated?
- How do they communicate to you that user "x" should be granted access?
- How do they indicate what level of access a new user should be given?
- How do they inform you that an existing user is to be removed from the access list?
- How are you told when an existing user's access is to be changed?
- Is the list of users reviewed periodically?
- Is the list of approvers reviewed periodically?
- Are exceptions ever made to the normal approval process? When are they made and how are they handled?

It's important to know that even though you may take the specific steps to provide someone with access, your role as Application Administrator is not to approve users and their access levels. This comes from the people identified above. You may have some input into the process, like offering advice and guidance as to risks and potential impact associated with granting certain types of access, but the final decision rests with the approver.

20.2 **TIPS FOR DEALING WITH USERS**

The following is a list of tips that I've found useful for dealing with users. Use what works for you and ignore the rest. As you work with your own users I'm sure you'll come up with tips of your own that you find helpful. It wouldn't hurt to develop your own list to share with your peers or the person that you're training as your backup or eventual replacement:

- The best single piece of advice for dealing with users that I can give you is to have patience. The vast majority of users don't mean to be annoying, frustrating, or difficult. They just want help learning how to use the application to do their job.
- Don't talk down to people just because they aren't technical. You may be technically more literate than them, but they're almost certainly more business literate than you are.
- Don't assume they have specific technical knowledge unless they have demonstrated it. As an IT type, it's easy to assume that everyone knows how to open a command prompt or how to take a screenshot, but that isn't the case. Unless you know the user is technically competent it's better to assume they don't know a great deal of technical details.
- Don't tell provide technical details that aren't needed. For example, users don't care what language the application is written in, they don't care how many cores the CPU has. Providing too much information takes time, is confusing, and takes the focus off the task you're trying to accomplish.
- Don't use jargon, abbreviations, or acronyms when dealing with users. It leads to confusion, misunderstandings, and resentment.
- Don't be surprised to hear frustration in their voices. Stay calm and explain things in laymen's terms.
- Demonstrate, don't dictate. Show them what they need to do, but don't get upset if they do things slightly differently than you do. Their way of doing it might not be as fast or as efficient as yours, but if they're comfortable with it then it's best for them.
- Watching someone do something on a computer can be extremely frustrating. They go slower than you do. They make mistakes that you don't make. They don't know the fastest way to do things. Avoid the temptation to give too much advice. Just smile and be patient.
- Seeing how the user operates can be very insightful. You may discover certain assumptions they are making (perhaps due to a confusing UI), or that they are using a keystroke combination that works in another application, but causes your application to abort.

20.2.1 The simplest solution is probably correct

Ockham's Razor is a hypothesis that in general the simplest explanation is probably correct. This concept definitely applies to application support. If something is all of a sudden wrong with your application, try solving it by looking for the simplest fixes first:

- Is it user (cockpit) error? I hate to point fingers, but in my experience this is the leading cause of "problems" with the application. This is especially true if only a single user is experiencing the problem.
- Has anything changed? Has the user loaded any new software onto his/her computer? Does the user have a new PC? Has the user recently change physical locations, domains, networks, etc.?
- Is a new version of the application being used? If you just upgraded to a new version of the application, then it's very possible that it still have a few bugs in it.

20.2.2 Be clear

Always be ready to clarify questions you ask users. It might seem crystal clear to you, but might not be clear to them. If they don't understand your questions, their answers are likely to send you off on a wild goose chase. Better to be sure they really understand your questions before you invest a lot of time responding to their answers.

20.2.3 **Trust but verify**

I like users. Some of my best friends are users. But I never believe anything they say without verifying it. This is especially true when technical terms are coming out of their mouths or out of their keyboards.

Today I encountered a perfect example showing why Application Administrators need to verify what users say. The primary user of an application I support sent me an e-mail which said "I've had a few problems with templates this week and the vendor told me that we need to restart the database on the server. Please do this ASAP." It sounded pretty straightforward. The DBA said if we restarted the database on the database server it would impact a number of other applications. I replied to the user telling her restarting the database wasn't possible. I asked her to have the vendor technician e-mail me explaining exactly what he wanted done. A few minutes later I got an e-mail that said "On the server go to Control Panel | Administrative Tools | Services and restart the 'XXXX background service'. Then restart IIS." Those two requests are not even remotely similar. How she confused the restarting the database with restarting a Windows service and IIS is hard to understand. If I had blindly fulfilled her first request, it would have inconvenienced many other users and wouldn't have solved the problem. Never forget this phrase - "trust, but verify."

20.3 **THE USER'S VIEWPOINTS**

It shouldn't surprise you that users don't see the world the same way that IT people see it. Users typically are neither as comfortable nor as enamored with technology as IT types are. To them what's important is that the job get done as quickly, accurately, and perhaps most important as easily as possible.

Neither of the user's viewpoint nor the IT staff's viewpoint is wrong. Neither is inherently more valid than the other. They reflect the reality that organizations are complex and staffed by people with different views of things. It's very important to not discount someone else's viewpoint just because it's different than yours.

20.3.1 **Applications exist to support a business need**

Never forget that both the application and your job exist because there is a business requirement that needs to be filled. The organization has a business need to get something done, for example, to send invoices out to their customers. A user needs to enter data into the invoicing system, so invoices can be created and the organization can collect the money that is owed to it. Programmer, DBA, and Application Administrator positions exist to help fill the business requirement. Our jobs don't exist simply because the company likes cool software and applications. Technical staff might not understand this concept, but it's the truth.

20.3.2 **Cost of being down**

We technical types don't like it when the application goes down, but we typically don't assign a dollar cost to an outage. The users or the business owner of the application is more likely to make this connection than we are. It might be interesting to find out what the cost of each hour or minute of down time costs. If you have this figure, then you might be less likely to take risks that would cause an outage.

Having the answers to questions like the following can strengthen your background of the business side of your organization:

- Is there a cost associated with an outage or can the users "catch up" later?
- What does it cost the organization for every minute that an application is down?
- How many customers can be lost each time an outage occurs?
- Is there any impact on regulatory agencies if the application goes down?

- Are there any contractual requirements that the application not go down?
- Will an outage push down time over a threshold and trigger penalties or other repercussions?

20.4 USER COMPLAINTS

No application ever was or ever will be perfect. Even the best application will have problems. When problems occur with the application, then you can be sure that users will complain about it. This is to be expected because if they don't make you aware of problems then you can't fix them.

20.4.1 Performance complaints

In my experience, the most common user complaint about applications is that they are too slow. While the Application Administrator might not feel the response time has decreased, for someone who spends most of the day using the application performance degradation is quickly noticed.

If a user complains that the application is too slow, the first thing the Application Administrator needs to do is to get additional background information. Asking questions like the following can provide needed information details:

- Is the user having similar problems with other applications? This question is especially important if applications are similar, i.e., all of them are web-based or none of them are web-based.
- When did the performance problem first appear?
- Is the performance problem consistent or intermittent?
- Are other users in their immediate area experiencing performance problems with this or other applications?
- At the time that they first noticed the performance issue was the user working in the office or from a remote location?
- If they are working remotely, are they working from a regular location, e.g., home? Or is the remote location somewhere they've never been at before, e.g., a hotel, a coffee shop, or a client's site?
- Is the user directly connected to the organization's network or are they connected via a VPN (Virtual Public Network)?

20.4.2 Nonperformance complaints

Nonperformance-related complaints occur for all applications to. Some common types of these complaints include:

- The application doesn't come up when its icon or shortcut is clicked
- User can't log into the application
- The user's password has expired
- Objects like buttons, menu items, fields, etc., that should exist don't appear on the screen
- Unexpected error messages are displayed
- The results of requests either are never displayed or if they are displayed are inaccurate
- Reports aren't distributed as expected
- Lack of functionality
- Complex navigation paths
- A confusing UI (user interface)
- Inaccurate, unclear, or meaningless error messages
- Being required to enter the same information in multiple places.

I have found that asking the user to shut down the application and reboot their PC resolves the problem for a surprisingly high percentage of problems. The user may not be anxious to do this, but explain to them that this simple step may solve their problem much quicker than opening a ticket on it. If you explain to them that it's in their own best interest to try rebooting, then you'll more likely to get their cooperation.

If rebooting their PC doesn't solve the problem, then an incident report needs to be created. The following section describes what information needs to be gathered by the user and provided to either you or the Help Desk if they are the ones that complete incident report forms.

20.4.3 Incident report

Every problem or crash is an incident. Details on each incident need to be captured, stored, and be available for future reference. If your company doesn't have an official incident report you need to create one for your application. It can be as simple as a text or Word document stored on a common drive. If your organization already has a package like Remedy, Plain Ticket, Trac, or Request Tracker, then you'll almost certain be expected to utilize it to track your incidents.

Examples of the details that should be recorded on an incident report are listed here:

- Date and time that the problem occurred.
- Who first encountered the problem?
- The exact steps the user performed leading up to when the error occurred.
- Is the problem repeatable?
- Examples of what user sees or experiences. Screenshots of the problem should be included whenever possible.
- Error messages that are being displayed. Getting a screenshot of the error message is good, but you should also enter the error message into the incident document or tracking system. The contents of a screenshot aren't searchable, but if the error message gets typed in then it can be searched for.
- Source of the error message(s), e.g., was it created by the application, by the desktop operating system, by the database, etc.
- How many users have experienced the problem?
- What locations, i.e., which offices or facilities, are experiencing the problem?
- Is this a new or existing problem?
- Type of computer this occurred on? For example, does the user have an Apple, Dell, Compaq, tablet, etc.?
- Operating system of the user's computer that the problem occurred on?
- Version number of the application.
- Steps leading up to this problem occurring.
- Date and time that the problem was resolved.
- How the problem was resolved?
- Who helped resolve the problem? For example, the Application Administrator, vendor support team, System Administrators, Database Administrators, etc.

Whatever method you end up using to save your incident reports they should be searchable. This will enable you to quickly determine if a problem has occurred in the past and if so, how it was resolved then. The typical Application Administrator is much too busy to spend time investigating and fixing a problem that has already been experienced and fixed.

20.5 HANDLING USER REQUESTS FOR CHANGES

Does your organization have a formal way that users submit requests about an application? Does everyone know how they are supposed to submit and receive user requests? Some formal methods of submitting change requests are:

- During regularly scheduled application status meetings
- Via e-mail to an individual or group distribution list
- In writing on an existing request form
- Via a website or portal

20.5.1 Advantages of a formal request process

While it may seem overly rigid to have a method that's in place, there are definite advantages to a formal process. Some of these advantages are:

- Permanent record—There will be a permanent record of what the change was, who requested it, who approved it, and when it was made.
- Without a process it would be fairly easy for a legitimate request to be dropped or overlooked. A formal process makes this much less likely to happen.
- Duplication—avoid having identical of very similar requests submitted for changes.
- Prioritization—Enables a committee or individual to review all requests and determine which ones should be assigned the highest priority.
- Time and cost estimation—an estimate of time and cost is made for each request submitted. Without this information, it would be difficult to plan the work because you wouldn't know how long any of the changes will take to implement.
- Impact on users—once implemented how will a change impact users of the application? Will they need any retraining? Will it invalidate existing work or data? Will users need to go to new screens?
- Work planning—if everyone knows what the upcoming changes are then the plans for making them can be done more efficiently and accurately.

If your organization has a process in place for submitting requests, then it has to be used for all requests. If some requests are handled outside the normal channels, it will negate most, if not all, of the advantages of having a formal request process. Two additional reasons for not allowing changes outside the normal process are:

- Changes have a way of ballooning from small to significant.
- If you allow one exception, then that person will expect the next change (and the next one) to be exceptions too.

20.5.2 Approving change requests

Not every change that is requested deserves to be implemented. For example, one user might want a change made to the application that no one else wants. Or another requested change might be so expensive that it just makes no financial sense to do. To weed out changes that shouldn't be made, someone needs to review all requests and decide which ones are going to be made to the application and which aren't.

Has someone in your organization been empowered to approve requests before they are worked? Each organization does things their own way, but some possibilities for this position include:

- Business owner of the application
- Senior User Representative

- Senior Application Administration
- A committee composed of representatives of the above groups

20.5.3 Testing changes

Every change made to an application has the potential to cause problems. Some of the potential outcomes that could occur include:

- The change works as expected
- The change doesn't work as expected
- The change works as expected, but has causes other undesired problems
- The change doesn't work as expected AND causes other undesired problems

To avoid having unexpected and undesired side effects all changes should be installed on a test or QA system first. After being installed on a nonproduction environment they need to be thoroughly tested. Testing should be done by someone that is familiar with the application. A high level of familiarity will enable the tester to more easily recognize negative problems caused by the change that has been made. Chapter 7 provides more details on the reasons that testing has to be done whenever a change is being made.

20.6 USER PREFERENCES

Third-party software developers are typically very aware, even hoping, that their product is being used in multiple countries. To make their applications more acceptable to a wide variety of users, they allow certain characteristics of the application to be modified, based on the preferences of each user. Some examples of characteristics that can be set include the following:

- Language
- Date and time formats
- Currency formats, e.g., the use of commas vs. periods to designate decimal characters
- How negative values are displayed, e.g., with a negative sign or enclosed in parentheses
- Fonts and font size
- Language including variations within a language like English-British vs. English-American
- Background, aka wallpaper, displayed behind an application
- Animation enabled vs. disabled
- Display tool tips or not
- Sound effects enabled vs. disabled
- Starting screen selection

Does the application allow its default settings to be identified or chosen? If so the Application Administrator or the Business Owner should choose the ones that are beneficial to the largest user base. Users that don't like the defaults can alter their preferences to their own personal liking.

20.6.1 Language support

Supporting multiple languages isn't as simple as clicking "yes" on an option button when you are installing the application. You need to know what languages are needed and what the vendor's level of support is. If you don't know the answers to the following questions, then you need to start doing some research before you attempt to set up the application to support multiple languages:

- How many languages does the user community require?
- What are the most common 2, 3, or 5 languages among the user base?
- Does your help desk have multilingual staffers available?
- Does the application support multiple languages?
- How many languages are currently available from the vendor?
- Are any additional languages being developed by the vendor?
- Is there a charge for multiple language capability?
- Is it possible for your organization to add a language that the vendor doesn't support? How is this done? How much effort is it? What will it cost you? How long will it take?

20.6.1.1 Language variations

Do you know what variations of specific languages need to be supported? Is the application capable of supporting language variations? For example, different variations of the following languages are recognized:

- English: British vs. USA
- French: France vs. Quebec French
- Spanish: Spain vs. Mexico or other Latin American countries

20.6.1.2 What objects are language capable of?

Providing support for multiple languages has become the norm rather than the exception for enterprise-level applications. If your organization is multinational, or might grow into that situation, then supporting more than one language is probably mandatory rather than optional. What objects in the application can be displayed in multiple languages? For example, can the following objects have their text be displayed in each user's preferred language?

- Screen headers
- Background text
- Text on buttons
- Text on menu items and submenu items
- Help screens
- Text in prompts
- Text in error messages
- Text in tool tips
- Text on labels
- Text in links

20.6.1.3 Other aspects of language support

There are aspects of supporting multiple languages that aren't immediately apparent. In order to truly support multiple languages, the application has to go beyond just having the ability to display words in a different language. Does your application support the following language/cultural idiosyncrasies? If so, do you know how to set them or turn them on?

- Weights and measures
- Size of paper available in printers and copy machines
- Whether the writing direction is from left to right or right to left, top to bottom or bottom to top
- Telephone number formats
- Postal codes used in various countries
- Different alphabets, e.g., Arabic, Chinese, Cyrillic, Japanese, Latin, Greek, Hebrew, etc.

- Different numeral systems
- Different calendars, e.g., Gregorian, Hijri, Chinese, Hebrew, etc.
- The character used for quotation marks

20.6.1.4 Unicode

Multilanguage support extends beyond just what is displayed on the screen. If the users enter values in a character set other than English, the database system must be capable of storing what the users enter. One standard that has been developed to handle multiple character sets is called Unicode. If your application is going to accept input in multiple languages, then the database engine that supports the application probably needs to be set up to store text data as Unicode. You'll need to work with your DBA to ensure the database can utilize Unicode and that it is set up as the vendor has specified.

20.6.2 **Customizing roles**

As described in chapter 15, section 15.1.5, it's easier to handle administering users if you have defined a set of common roles and assign each user to one. For example, your application might have roles similar to the ones listed here:

- ReadOnly
- Writers
- Approvers
- Auditors
- Administrators

Once you have defined the roles, then you need to determine exactly what pieces of the application each role should be able to see and use. For example, a user who can only read records in the application shouldn't see buttons labeled "Edit," "Save," "Change," or "Delete." If a role isn't able to perform those functions, then there is no point in letting them see buttons that perform them. Some applications might display buttons that aren't active, but they are disabled so users can't execute them.

Examples of objects in the application that can differ for each role are listed here:

- Menu items
- Submenu items
- Panels
- Pick lists, aka drop down list boxes
- Images
- Buttons
- Links
- Text fields
- Radio buttons

20.7 **TRAINING**

You can't expect that a user will intuitively understand how to use an application. For users to correctly and efficiently use an application they need to be trained. Training may sound like overhead that wastes time and money, but effective training will result in fewer errors, fewer reworks, more efficient users, and more satisfied users. It's an investment that is worth making.

20.7.1 Types of training

What type of training will users, especially new users, of the application receive? Does a new user have to complete and pass a training course before their logon credentials are issued to them? Which of the following are available?

- Classroom training—training that's instructor led and probably in a classroom environment.
- Online training—provided via an LMS (Learning Management System), usually available on the user's workstation via a web browser.
- On-the-job training—perhaps provided by more experienced coworkers
- On-going training—the user get a periodic, e.g., annual, refresher training course

As the Application Administrator are you involved in the training process? If possible you should sit in on user training that is given to the user community. This is especially if you are new to the application. Some reasons for this recommendation are:

- You'll see the application from the user's viewpoint
- You'll learn from the questions that users ask
- You might be able to improve certain areas of the training
- You'll eventually have to handle questions on the app so it helps to have seen what the users were taught

20.7.2 Who trains the trainer

If you have classroom training, then who will be leading the classes? Perhaps the best possible scenario would be to bring in trainers provided by or certified by the application vendor. Trainers with this background are likely to be experienced both with the application and in the role as a trainer. The downside of this choice is that it will almost certainly be one of the more expensive options.

If the budget doesn't allow you to bring in outside trainers, then some alternative choices are:

- Your organization's in-house training department
- An experienced user
- An Application Administrator

If you're planning to use an in-house person to do the training, you should consider sending him or her out to attend the training classes offered by the vendor. This can be an effective choice if the trainer in question is experienced with the application and is comfortable speaking in front of a group.

20.7.3 Create a cheat sheet for users

It would be a very good idea to create a cheat sheet for the users that contains basic information that they need to use the app. If this isn't provided by the vendor, then this can be done by the trainer, the most experienced user, or the Application Administrator. The investment to develop this will be relatively small and it will definitely pay off in the long run. The more the users know about the application, the fewer mistakes they'll make and the fewer calls you'll get. Include items like the following. Be sure to keep this document up to date and periodically reissue it to the users. If this cheat sheet can be added to the application's help screens that would be well worth doing:

- URL(s) used to connect to the application.
- Scheduled maintenance periods, for example the application is unavailable Sunday nights between 10pm and midnight Central time.

- Who to contact if a problem occurs.
- Information they should be ready to provide when reporting a problem.
- Requirements to use the application, e.g., the operating system on their desktop, Internet browsers that are supported, plug-ins that need to be loaded onto the workstations, etc.
- Common problems they might encounter and what to do to correct them.
- Who to contact if their account is locked or they forget their password.
- Instructions for connecting to the organization's network from a remote location via a VPN (Virtual Private Network).
- Location of any user-related documentation for the application, e.g., on a common drive or portal.
- Location of a knowledge base that lists problems that other users have experienced and their solutions. Ideally all users would search the knowledge base after encountering a problem to see if the solution is listed. This has the potential to eliminate a large percentage of calls to you or the Help Desk.

20.7.4 **Technology to the training rescue**

Technology can be employed to provide some valuable additions to your repertoire of training tools. If no one else in your organization is in place to provide training aids like the following, then it may fall on your shoulders, but the results will probably be worth the efforts. Some examples of how technology can bolster your training are:

- Create video training sessions of common tasks that users frequently have problems with. Post these in a location, e.g., a network drive or website, that all users can access.
- A wiki is a website that anyone can add to or modify via a web browser. Create a wiki centered on your application. Seed it with the most common problems that users have experienced. Encourage users to add to it with their advice, shortcuts, and suggestions. If your user base contributes to it this could become an incredibly valuable reference.
- Capture all FAQs (Frequently Asked Questions) submitted by users to you or the Help Desk. Post them and the answers on a website or portal that all users can access.
- Using Webex, LiveMeeting or another screen-sharing sessions for training and investigating user problems. Tools of this nature are especially valuable when working with users at remote locations. If possible, record these sessions and post the most informative ones on a website or portal that all users can access.
- If possible, include links to your library of recorded training sessions, wiki or FAQ on the initial application screen. This will make it easy for users to access these tools.

20.8 **WORKFLOW PROCESSES**

Applications can include a functionality that is called workflow processing. One example of this is that the application automatically assists users by advancing the work process from one person to the next person who needs to deal with it. For example, a Change Control application will send an e-mail to the appropriate person for each approval step that needs to be done before a change can be moved into production. These steps might include the following:

- Business owner approval of change request
- IT approval of change request
- Development complete
- Business owner approval of UAT test

- Change installed on QA system
- Business owner validates change on UAT
- Move to Live
- Business owner validates change on UAT

If the application you're supporting includes any workflow processes, then you need to ask the following questions:

- How many workflow processes exist?
- Have the workflow processes been set up?
- What roles does each user group have in the workflow process?
- How easily can workflow processes be changed?
- If a workflow process is changed, e.g., a new step is added, what is the impact of tasks that are already in the pipeline?
- Do all of the users understand their part(s) in the workflow process?
- How difficult is it to create a new workflow from scratch?

20.9 REMOTELY ACCESSING THE APPLICATION

Do any of your application users work from remote locations, that is they aren't connected to the organization's network? For example, do some users work from home, from remote offices, from hotel rooms, or from client sites? If this is the case you need to investigate the following possibilities:

- Does the application expressly support remote access? Some applications are designed specifically for users that are frequently on the road. One example would be an application that is used by sales personnel who travel to potential client sites.
- Are there any idiosyncrasies in the application that prevent telecommuting?
- Are these specific functions in the application that can't be performed when accessing it remotely? For example, are there any administration tasks that aren't available unless the user is connected to the organization's network?
- How is performance affected when the user is accessing the application remotely? If there is an impact the users should be warned about this in advance. By informing them in advance you'll hopefully avoid some surprises and complaints about performance degradation when they are logging in remotely.

20.9.1 Telecommuting

Do you know how many of your application users currently access the application remotely, aka telecommute, or plan to telecommute in the near future? If this number is going to be increasing, will this require any changes to the following pieces of the application's architecture?

- The application
- The network
- The application servers
- The VPN (Virtual Private Network) setup being used

To get answers to this question, you might need to work with your organization's network administrators or the vendor's support group.

Leveraging the Vendor Relationship

21

When you're supporting a third-party application, the vendor will be a constant presence in your professional life. You'll communicate with them on a fairly regular basis. If you aren't exchanging e-mails about a problem that has been encountered, you'll be working with them on an upgrade that needs to be done. If you're lucky, your relationship with the vendor and their staff will be cordial and professional and will make your life significantly easier.

If you're supporting an application that was developed internally, then much of this chapter won't apply to you. In some ways working with an internal development group is more difficult than with outside vendor. Some of the reasons for this are:

- An internal group almost certainly won't have the same manpower that a vendor has
- They probably won't have a Help Desk
- Their support structure won't be as formal
- They might not have the same sense of customer service that a vendor has
- The availability of training will be limited if any is available at all
- High quality documentation tends to be a low priority for internal groups

21.1 LICENSING

This shouldn't come as a surprise to anyone, but you don't actually purchase computer software. Instead of buying it outright like most other products what you are doing is paying for the right to use the software with a number of limitations. If you don't believe me, just read one of the screens that come up when you're installing some software. It very clearly states that you don't own it and you're essentially "renting" the application.

If the application you're supporting has already been licensed and installed it's too late to change your contract with the vendor, but you should be aware of the basics of licensing agreements for future application acquisitions.

Some applications are designed and marketed as a collection of modules. For example, your organization might need an application that includes Accounts Receivable and Accounts Payable logic, but not Inventory Control. Does the vendor's application allow clients to pick and choose what modules they want? Their license costs might be a set price or based on the number of modules that you're utilizing.

21.1.1 Types of licensing models

There are several types of licensing models that describe how software is licensed. The most common models are described in the following paragraphs. It might be in your best interest see if the vendor will allow you to use a combination of licensing models. For example, you may need a per-processor license for the server, as well as CALs for the workstations. Don't be afraid to ask for something that's "off the menu" when it comes to licensing. The worst thing that can happen is they say "no":

- Individual or Single-User License—allows the software to be installed on a single computer and used by only a single user who is logged onto that computer. The program can't be accessed by any other users or computers across a network. This type of license isn't applicable to an enterprise-level application, so it most likely won't be one of the licensing options available to you.
- Server License—A license that permits the software to be installed on a specific server. Multiple users can then access the server in order to use the application.
- Per-Processor Licensing—A license is required for each processor that exists in the server that the software has been loaded onto. If your server has four processors, then four licenses need to be purchased, one for each of them.
- Per Core Licensing—A license is required for each core in the processor(s) that exists in the server that the software has been loaded onto. For example, if your server has 4 processors and each processor has 4 cores, then a total of 16 licenses need to be purchased.
- Concurrent User License—This type of license allows a specified number of users to access the application. For example, you could purchase a license that allows 25 users to access the application. If 25 users are logged in and a 26th user attempts to log in, then he'll get an error message stating the maximum number of users are in the application right now and to try again later.
- Per Seat—This license allows only named individuals to log into the application. If your license was for 50 named individuals, then a user not in that list can never use the application regardless of whether those 50 individuals are in the application or not.
- Client Access License (CAL)—Licenses need to be installed on the client, i.e., user, workstation before the application software can be legally accessed by a user. If you expect that 100 users will be accessing the application, then you would need to purchase 100 CALs. Not all vendors employ CALs in their licensing models, but you should be aware of the concept.

Make sure that you understand whether your license allows 25 users to be registered with the application or 25 users to access the application simultaneously. The difference here is crucial. For example, you might have 100 employees that log into the application, but be limited to only 25 logging in at any given time. This is very different from only having 25 employees registered.

If your license has a limitation on the number of registered users, there are additional details that should be determined before you sign on the dotted line. Some potential questions that you should ask include:

- Does a disabled user count as a "registered" user? You might have very good reasons for disabling a user with the expectation that he or she will be enabled later. For example, an employee that is on maternity leave or on a sabbatical might not be using the application for months.
- Can the maximum number of users be increased? Is the vendor flexible on this topic or is there a significant amount of red tape and lead time required?
- Can you temporarily increase this number? For example, if the application is an LMS (Learning Management System) and you have a large class of new employees coming on board. There might be an intense training period needed to handle them. Is it possible to increase the user limit for 2 weeks and then revert to the lower license count later?

21.1.2 License duration

A slightly different angle on software licensing is duration of the license. The most significant options are:

- Perpetual licenses—once purchased this license allows you to keep running and using the software indefinitely.

- Annual licenses—The license is good for a single year. If you wish to continue using the application during the following year, then you need to renew the license. Most software that is in the SaaS (Software as a Service) category will have an annual license.

An annual license may appear to be cheaper, but it must be renewed every year. If you intend to be using this application for a significant number of years into the future, a perpetual license might be a better choice if that option is available.

21.1.3 Limitations of the license

Software licenses come with a number of limitations or restrictions. You need to examine your contract to determine exactly what limitations your license has. Some common limitations are:

- The software can only be run on the servers specified in the license agreement.
- The number of users that can access the application is limited to what is specified in the contract.
- There might be a limit to the number of users that can access the application simultaneously.
- Upgrading your hardware, i.e., installing faster servers, additional processors, or additional cores might violate your license agreement. If you do this be prepared to be charged an increase in your licensing fees.
- Reverse engineering is not allowed, i.e., trying to figure out how the vendor's software works so you could write a similar application yourself.
- You are not allowed to publish the results of any benchmark, aka performance, tests. Some vendors are extremely sensitive regarding the publication of anything that could be considered critical of their product.

21.1.4 Choosing the model that is best for you

What licensing model(s) does your vendor offer? If the vendor has multiple licensing options, you need to decide which model alternative is best for your organization. To make this decision, you need to have a detailed understanding of your environment and user base. For example, you should know:

- The number of employees that will be registered to access the application.
- The maximum number of concurrent users.
- How frequently this maximal usage occurs, for example, at month end, year end?
- The number of processors and cores in the server(s) which the application will run on.

21.1.5 Multiple licenses

If your organization has multiple license contracts with the same vendor, you might be able to turn this to your advantage. Small- and medium-sized software vendors are being acquired by larger organizations on a regular basis. The resulting landscape is that fewer and fewer vendors hold the licenses for an increasing number of software products. It's possible that your organization is licensing a number of products from a single vendor that not long ago were coming from multiple vendors. Can this situation be negotiated into a better licensing arrangement?

It's possible with multiple licenses that you might be eligible for some type of volume discount. Even if discounts aren't publicized it can't hurt to ask for one. What kinds of concessions can a high volume client possibly ask for?

- Discounted licensing fees
- Discounted support fees
- Combine multiple licenses into a single license at a lower aggregate cost
- An upgrade to your support agreement, e.g., from standard support to premium level support

Does your organization have a department, e.g., Purchasing, that has records of every current software contract? Without a list of all contracts and vendors, you'll never know if the potential for volume discounts exists.

21.1.6 Nonproduction environments

Your organization's production environment isn't the only one on which the application software will be loaded. Other potential environments that might need to exist include:

- Development
- Test
- QA—Quality Assurance
- DR—Disaster Recovery

You need to either examine the contract or hold a conversation with the vendor to get answers to the following questions about nonproduction environments. The last thing you want is to build one and then get slapped with a fine or a hike in the licensing costs when the vendor finds out that it exists. Better to know what the nonproduction-related costs and restrictions are in advance, so this knowledge can be factored into your decision-making process:

- Does your license allow these additional environments to exist?
- Are there any add-on costs for having additional, nonproduction environments?
- Are there any limitations on how much data can exist on a nonproduction environment?
- Are there any limitations on the number of users that can connect to a nonproduction environment?
- Will the vendor provide support if a problem is encountered on a nonproduction environment?
- If the DR environment is a close replica of production, can it be operational at all times or is it limited to periodic testing to ensure that it's operational?

It has been my experience that vendors realize their clients need DEV, QA, and DR environments and don't put unreasonable restrictions on them. Hopefully, the vendor(s) you're working with is equally understanding on this topic.

21.1.7 Maintenance fees

Most vendors charge an annual maintenance fee that is typically expressed as a percentage of the cost of the software. For this fee, you are entitled to patches, updates, and documentation. Check the contract with your vendor for exactly what their maintenance fees include. It may or may not include major upgrades. Some vendors have an additional charge to get major upgrades. Better that you know this in advance than be surprised by it.

Maintenance contracts and fees are different for every vendor, but in the neighborhood of 20% is fairly common in the industry. Just so you understand what this means—if you paid $1,000,000 for the software license, then every year you are required to pay the vendor roughly $200,000 for support. If you don't pay up then you'll be cut off from their support.

Just a warning if you think you can save money by not purchasing a maintenance contract and then purchasing one if only if you desperately need it. Many vendors have already thought of this. They charge a reinstatement or reinstallment fee. This fee is an additional cost to reinstate maintenance if you ever happen to go off of it. This fee is likely to exceed any savings you experienced by not renewing your maintenance contract. Before going off of support make sure you know what it will cost to come back.

21.1.8 **Versions**

Most application software undergoes fairly frequent modifications. The vendor releases new versions for many purposes. Some of these reasons are:

- To include enhancements, i.e., new features, in the application
- To improve performance
- To correct problems that have been reported by clients
- To address changes necessitated by new government regulations or industry practices
- To support new hardware or software, e.g., new browsers or operating systems
- To address potential security problems

It's useful to have an understanding of how your vendor handles versions of their product. For example:

- How often does the vendor come out with major releases of the application? Major releases like version 5.0, 6.0, or 7.0 are typically issued fairly infrequently. It's not uncommon for a year or two to pass between major releases are issued.
- How often does the vendor come out with minor releases of the applications? Minor releases, e.g., 6.1 or 6.2, are typically released much more frequently that major releases. Coming out with two minor releases a year wouldn't be uncommon for a vendor.
- Are minor releases cumulative? Does version 6.3 include all the changes that came out in versions 6.1 and 6.2? From the Application Administrator's viewpoint, cumulative releases require less effort. If releases aren't cumulative, then you will be required to install versions 6.1 and 6.2 before installing version 6.3. Most are cumulative, but confirm this in the Release Notes or with the vendor's support group.
- How many versions of the product have been released? You can probably figure this out by looking at the current release number of the product. If it's version 6.2 then there have probably been six major releases. There have also been two minor releases since the most recent major release.
- How many past versions of the product does the vendor support? If the current version of the application is version 6.2, will the vendor allow clients to continue to run version 5.x? Will clients be allowed to run version 4.x? Some clients are quite happy to run version 4.x of the product. It does what they want and they see no reason to upgrade. On the other hand, the more versions that the vendor has to support, the more effort it is for them. Their Support Group now has to be familiar with more versions. The vendor's decision on how many past versions of the product to support has to consider what the clients want versus what's easiest for the vendor.
- Are clients forced or strongly encouraged to upgrade to the latest version? This is related to the prior point because it deals with prior versions. Some vendors are much more aggressive about nudging users to keep up with the most current version than others. For example, they may take steps like the following to encourage clients to install the most recent version:
  - Publish a specific date after which previous versions will no longer be supported
  - No longer provide new security updates to previous versions of the product
  - Charge a premium to support previous versions of the product
  - Support requests for previous versions receive the lowest priority in their schedule

21.1.9 **Fixes vs. enhancements**

Here's a lame attempt at an Application Administrator humor.

Question: What is the difference between a fix and an enhancement?
Answer: About $10,000

The joke is weak, but there is more than a grain of truth in it. If you report a problem to your vendor, they will research it to determine if it's actually a problem or something the client has done wrong. If their research determines that it's a bug, they will fix it at their own expense. If this problem isn't critical, then it might be months or even years before the fix is addressed in a new version of the product.

On the other hand, if what you're asking for is a change to the product, i.e., an enhancement, then you will be expected to pay for it. The vendor will provide an estimate of the cost for the enhancement and present you with a change request, a work order, or some similarly named contract. If you agree to pay, then they will make the change and provide it to you.

One further thing you need to understand about requesting an enhancement is that very likely this change will be included in future releases of the product. Other clients will get it for free. Don't expect them to thank you because vendors tend not to attribute specific changes to the client that requested them.

21.1.10 Tech support

If you want the privilege of being able to call the vendor's support group and get assistance, then you need a tech support agreement. Some vendors include tech support in the maintenance contracts, but not all of them. You need to know whether your vendor includes tech support in their maintenance fees or not.

If the application is considered critical to your organization's operations, then you need to think long and hard before deciding not to acquire a tech support license. One way to think about it is to consider how much it will cost your organization if the application is down for an extended period of time?

21.2 WHAT SUPPORT DOES THE VENDOR OFFER?

It's a legitimate question to ask what you're getting for your organization's hard-earned money. Each of the basic elements of support contract is described in the following sections.

21.2.1 Support desk

The vendor provides a team, frequently called the Support Desk, Support Group, or the Support Team that assists clients with problems they are having with the application. They take details about the problem from the client. A ticket is opened and assigned to a technician. The technician works with the client until the problem is resolved. If he or she can't resolve it, then a more experienced technical staff member becomes involved in the effort. Eventually a resolution to the problem is found even if it means making a change to the application source code.

You want to work with the vendor's Support Desk as effectively as possible when a problem occurs. To be effective, there are details about the vendor's support team that you should find out in advance. For example:

- Is the Support Desk available 24 × 7?
- If not, what are the hours of operation for them?
- Does a premium support contract include 24 × 7 support?
- What time zone is the vendor's Support Desk in?
- Is their off-hours team as experienced and capable as the 9 am to 5 pm team?
- Are you able to request a specific technician when you open up a ticket?
- What is the most effective way for you to contact the Support Desk? They might accept submissions via e-mail, website, or a phone call. Which works best for you?
- Many vendors require that you assign a priority to new tickets. Be sure to be honest and accurate when doing this. If you tell them that every one of your problems is "critical" you will quickly lose credibility.
- Does the vendor have defined SLAs, e.g., response time for a new ticket, or escalation/resolution times for a critical ticket?

When a ticket is initially opened what set of information do you need to provide? You will save time and frustration if you provide complete and accurate details when opening up a ticket. Even if you're in a hurry to get the ticket opened it pays off to take enough time to write it up correctly and proof read it before submitting it. Examples of the types of details a vendor might request when a ticket is opened include:

- Your organization's account name and number with the vendor
- Your name and contact information
- The date and time the problem occurred
- A description of the problem
- The wording of error messages that were displayed by the application
- The exact steps the user took to create the problem
- How long the problem has existed
- Can the problem be reproduced?
- Screenshots of the applicable screens
- Is the problem occurring for just a single user or for all users?
- Version of their application that you're running
- The type of server it's running on
- Is the server a physical box or a virtual server?
- The operating system and version running on the server
- What SPs (Service Packs) are installed for their product and the O/S
- What database and version is being used?
- Is the problem occurring on a Production system or a nonproduction system?
- Describe any changes on server, network, firewall, etc. that have been made recently
- Some vendors have a list of specific log files they request when a problem occurs

21.2.2 Support levels

Some vendors offer more than one level of support. For clients willing to pay for extra support it's available. Common terms for these support levels are Standard and Premium or Gold, Silver, and Bronze.

What do the higher levels of support buy you? The high levels of support might include the following advantages:

- Support is available 7 days a week instead of 5
- Support is available 24 hours a day instead of 8, 10, or 12
- The vendor promises to respond within 30 minutes instead of within 2 hours
- Your tickets are automatically routed to more experienced technicians
- At the highest support level you could have a technician dedicated to your organization
- Additional people from your organization are on the vendor's "contact list." Normally vendors allow a limited number of people to call their support line. Premium support contracts allow you to include additional names on the list.

Does your vendor offer different levels of support? If it does what are the costs and advantages of each support level? With this information in hand you can make an intelligent decision on what level of support your organization needs and can afford.

21.2.3 Updates and patches

Application software is changed on a regular basis. The vendor will send out an e-mail notifying the Application Administrator that a patch or update is available. It may include a URL that you can follow to access a web page where the new software can be accessed.

Once you receive notification that an update or patch is available, you should download and print the Release Notes and/or the Upgrade Guide. Review this documentation to determine the following:

- Whether the change is applicable to your environment
- What the upgrade does, specifically what problems it fixes or what enhancements it provides
- Whether the change is available
- The steps to install the upgrade
- How the upgrade can be rolled back if the install isn't successful

Armed with this information on the upgrade you can knowledgeably recommend to the user base whether the upgrade should be installed or not. The Application Owner will likely make the final decision on whether your organization will perform this upgrade or not.

Once the decision is made, you'll need to develop a project plan that includes the following tasks:

- The sequence in which your environments, i.e., Development, Test, QA, or Production, will be upgraded
- Estimated date when the first or next environment upgrade will be performed
- Steps to back up the server prior to upgrading an environment
- Steps to back up the database prior to upgrading an environment
- Develop the UAT (User Acceptance Test) used to verify that the update was successful
- Who will be performing each task of the upgrade process
- Coordination between users and administrators leading up to the upgrade so users aren't on the application when the upgrade is being performed
- Verifying that the application's data wasn't adversely affected by the upgrade. This step isn't needed if the upgrade doesn't modify the application's data.
- When the UAT will be performed and by whom
- Who will sign off that the upgrade was successful
- Repeat the above steps for the next environment that will be upgraded

21.2.4 Just the FAQs please

Has your vendor published a list of Frequently Asked Questions (FAQs) about the application? If a list of FAQ's exists, then before opening a ticket about a problem it's a good idea to review the list to see if another client has encountered the same problem. If your problem exists in the FAQ, you should try the recommended solution before opening a ticket with the vendor's Support Desk. Check the FAQ list for your problem can save both you and the vendor time.

21.2.5 Training

What training does the vendor offer for its application? Typically vendors offer a selection of classes geared toward both users and administrators. Classes are frequently available in the following formats and locations:

- On site
- Online
- At the vendor's site

Other training-related questions you should consider are:

- Is training available from an independent training organization? This will be the case for only the most widely used applications.

- Are any certifications available for the application? This is also only available for the most widely used applications.
- What are the prerequisites for the vendor's classes? You may want to "sneak in" without having the recommended prerequisites, but if you do this you may not be prepared to handle the material covered in the class.
- How many people in your organization need to be trained?
- Can someone sent to training return to the office and effectively train his or her coworkers? This approach is definitely less expensive, but not everyone is capable of teaching others.

21.2.6 Knowledge base

Does the vendor provide a searchable knowledge base that answers questions about their application. A knowledge base is like an FAQ list, but more detailed and covers a wider array of topics. If the vendor does provide a knowledge base, do clients have to have a specific support level contract or is it available to all clients?

21.2.7 Documentation

What documentation is available for the application? Examples of documents that the vendor might provide include:

- Administrator's Guide
- Installation Guide
- Upgrade Guide
- User's Guide
- Advanced User's Guide
- Performance Tuning
- Tools that are available for the users or administrators
- If the application has modular components, then a document might exist for each specific component

What format is the documentation available in? In the past, clients would either purchase or be entitled to a certain number of printed documents. More recently, the documentation is available online, typically as a PDF file, which the client can download and print off for themselves if desired.

It's useful to know how often the vendor updates their documentation. You would expect that a new version be released each time a major upgrade is done. The vendor might surprise you and release new versions with each minor upgrade of the application. One vendor I've dealt with seems to change its Administrator's Guide on what seems like a monthly basis. This becomes important if you're working with a technician and the document pages he's referring to don't seem to have anything to do with the problem you're trying to resolve.

21.2.8 Onsite vendor technical staff

If your organization is both large and extremely dependent on the application in question, then you might consider contracting to have technical staff member from the vendor stationed on-site. This is an expensive undertaking and is the exception rather than the rule. For smaller organizations contracting to hire someone from the vendor's technical staff would be very unusual due to the cost.

Instead of having someone from the vendor's staff on board on a permanent basis, it would be more likely for them to be there on a temporary basis for a specific effort. Some examples of projects that might warrant this expertise are:

- An installation from scratch, especially if it has to be done very quickly and mistakes aren't acceptable
- A major upgrade being made to the application
- A conversion to this application from a different vendor's software
- Activating a significant new component of the application
- Rolling out the application to a significantly sized department, group, or country

21.2.9 Other options for support

Are there alternatives to getting support from the vendor? There are always options, but you have to decide for yourself whether they are realistic or not. If your payroll system crashes the day before paychecks are cut it would be a crisis. Because of this you don't really have much choice but to have vendor support. On the other hand, if the application in question isn't considered critical and the process could be done manually, then it might be possible to survive without having vendor support.

21.2.9.1 Is vendor maintenance and support worth it?

Many software vendors actually generate more income from support fees than from their products licenses. This shouldn't be a surprise. If the maintenance fee is approximately 20-22% of the product price and the installed base is sizeable, then the revenue generated will be very significant.

The reality is that it doesn't matter whether the vendor makes most of their money from sales or support fees. Your organization has to decide whether the product is worth the purchase price and the ongoing support fee. If it's decided that the business need isn't worth the cost of the vendor's support, then maybe the product shouldn't have been acquired in the first place.

21.2.9.2 Going without support

It's possible to forego support for the application, but it's also very rare. The application as delivered is truly a black box, i.e., you can't see into it. Without access to the underlying design or source code, then it would be all but impossible to support an enterprise-level application. For a smaller, less critical application it could be done, but the risk level is still very high.

21.2.9.3 Alternatives to vendor support

Some alternatives to vendor support exist. A brief list of alternatives includes:

- Can you hire developers or tech reps that previously worked for the vendor? It's a possibility, but it's more realistic if the vendor has gone out of business. If the vendor is still in business and marketing the application it's likely that you signed a "no poaching" agreement when you licensed the product. If you try to hire away their staff don't be surprised if the vendor warns you or initiates legal action to prevent it.
- Do any third parties offer support for the application? There have been cases where employees left a vendor and formed a corporation to market their ability to support the application. They might promise top quality support at half the price the vendor was charging. Unfortunately, many if not most of these firms go out of business fairly soon. You have to factor this corporation's long-term viability when you are deciding to do business with them.
- Can you get a contingency contract with a consulting firm? It's possible, but how good is their support and how deep is their talent? If they only have a handful of technicians that are familiar with the application you need supported, do you want to risk it?

21.2.9.4 *Networking with other application administrators*

Networking with other Application Administrators is a great thing to do, but it's not a substitute for vendor support of the application. It might allow you to purchase a lower level of support. For example, instead of purchasing the Gold level of support, you might be able to get by with the Bronze level and hope your contacts with other experienced administrators will help fill the support gap.

Some advice if you plan on networking with other administrators:

- Dig your well before you're thirsty. You need to develop relationships with other Application Administrators before you need their help. If you encounter a crisis and desperately need help, that isn't the time to be reaching out to your peers for the first time. These relationships need to be cultivated over time.
- You have to give to get. If you expect others to help you, then you need to be willing to help them when they need it. If you get a reputation as being a "taker," then don't expect much help when you're in a crisis.

21.3 MAKING THE MOST OF VENDOR CONTACTS

In a pure capitalist system, there are a large number of buyers and sellers of every product. These large numbers on both sides of the equation are what give each side relatively equal power. If you don't like the tomatoes at your local grocery store, you can drive down the road a mile to another store and buy tomatoes there. If the sticky floors at one movie theater gross you out, then you can drive a few miles to another multiplex and see the same movie there.

Unfortunately, the situation isn't like this if you're a Fortune 100 company and you need an HR application. Your choices are much more limited when it comes to enterprise-wide software vendors. Given this, you want to maintain a good working relation with the vendor. This means trying to make the most of your contacts with the vendor's organization. For example, don't be abrasive just because the old saying is "the customer is always right." You may be right but if no one from the vendor will return your calls you're only hurting yourself.

21.3.1 Who owns the vendor relationship?

In every client organization, one group "owns" the relationship with the vendor. By this I mean the group that has the most contact with the vendor. The group or individual that the vendor contacts when something has changed, or when a something becomes available, etc. This group can be either a business group or a technical group. Neither approach is right or wrong, but you need to know how your organization is handling this crucial relationship.

21.3.2 Knowledge transfer

Whenever you or anyone in your organization is working with a technical contact from the vendor, there should always two objectives in mind:

1. Fix the problem or issue that's being working on
2. Learn as much as possible about the application, i.e., knowledge transfer

You always need to ensure that you and anyone else from your organization acquire as much knowledge about the application as possible from vendor contacts. By doing this, eventually your organization will be able to rely less on the vendor's support group and more on your personnel's accumulated skills and knowledge. The alternative is to always be forced to rely on the vendor's staff to help you with everything.

21.3.3 Put yourself in the driver's seat

One way I've found to increase the amount of knowledge that is transferred is when I'm sharing a screen session with a vendor technician is to always "drive," that is always retain control of the mouse and keyboard. The reasons I think this helps me learn more about the application are:

- I learn better by doing things. Everyone may not learn best this way, but it works best for me so I make sure that I drive whenever possible.
- When I'm clicking the mouse and entering values in the keyboard I'm controlling the speed of the activity. If I allow the vendor technician to drive, then he or she inevitably moves through the screens so fast that I can't follow what is being done.
- If I'm driving then I can pause to capture screenshots of the actions and paste them into a file to document the process. Later I'll review the document and add details and explanations. The next time I perform this process again I have my documentation up and verify its accuracy. After the second iteration, it is usually both accurate and extremely helpful.

21.3.4 Getting the most out of vendor tech rep site visits

If you're fortunate enough to have the opportunity to have a technical representative of the vendor visit your shop, then you want to do everything you can to get the most out of it. Some ways of maximizing what you get are:

- Inform everyone who works with the application about the upcoming visit. The more of your group in attendance the better.
- Make an agenda of what will be covered during the visit. Distribute the agenda in advance to everyone who will be participating.
- Be sure that you've scheduled time for a Q&A session in the agenda. Encourage everyone in your team to come with a list of questions that they would like to ask the tech rep. With any luck the questions will lead to further knowledge transfer from the vendor tech to you and the rest of the staff.
- If your budget will allow it bring in lunch instead of going out. Use the time for either Q&A or an informal bull session.

21.3.5 User conferences

Does the vendor schedule an annual user conference for their product? If they do then you should do whatever you can to attend, at least once. Your boss may recoil at the expense (these events are never cheap and neither are hotel rooms in metropolitan areas) and your coworkers may tease you about going on a boondoggle, but you need to make your case for going. Some of the many advantages of attending a user conference include:

- Keynote speeches by vendor executives frequently outline the long-term goals and directions of the vendor and the application.
- Vendors frequently offer training sessions in the day or two prior to the conference. If you've wanted to take some training, this can be an opportunity to kill two birds with one airline ticket.
- Papers presented by your peers can be extremely valuable. Sometimes they've figured out a really slick way to do exactly what you're trying to accomplish.
- Networking with vendor support staff and other Application Administrators can be invaluable. Be prepared to talk to a lot of fellow techies and exchange business cards or e-mail addresses.

One way of defraying the cost of attending a user conference is to present a paper. Many conferences waive the admission fee for anyone selected to present a paper at a session. Check the vendor's website 9-12 months in advance of the annual conference to see when submissions are accepted. Then write up a proposal describing something unusual you've done with the application, a tool or script you've written to make your work like easier and hope for the best. Of course before you submit a proposal you'll want to get your boss's approval.

21.3.6 Approved vendor contact list

Most vendors have a limit to the number of people at your organization that can contact their help desk and request assistance. If your name isn't on the official contact list, they won't answer your questions. Some of the legitimate reasons for imposing these limitations are:

- To channel your organization's requests through a small group to make sure all contacts are necessary. The vendor wants to avoid having your users calling them with problems that a more experienced user or the Application Administrator could easily resolve.
- To avoid duplicating requests that someone else has already submitted.
- To ensure that the contact is able to understand the response if it's technical
- To ensure that the contact has the knowledge and permission to implement the corrective steps being suggested by the vendor.
- As a profit motive. Some vendors will allow additional contacts for an increase in the support fee that is being charged.

Some of the details you should know the answer to related to the vendor's contact list are:

- How many vendor contacts is your organization allowed?
- Are you one of them?
- Who are the contacts on the list?
- How can you get an old contact removed and a new one added? This becomes extremely important if one of the existing contacts either leaves the organization or transfers to a position unrelated to this application.
- Since the process to update the contact list can take time for the vendor to complete, you should initiate changes as soon as you know that someone needs to be removed or added to the contact list.

You should also know who the vendor will contact within your organization for various reasons. For example, who will be contacted for the following topics?

- Billing—who will the vendor send their invoices to? If this contact isn't accurate you run the risk of your bills not being paid on time. If this happens there can be a penalty fee or your support could be suspended. Neither is good.
- Updates—who will be notified if an update or patch becomes available?
- Technical issues—if the vendor needs to know something about your organization's environment, e.g., your servers, who will they contact?

21.3.7 Getting help from the vendor's support desk

No one expects you to understand everything about the application that you support. You will encounter problems that the vendor's first- and second-level support won't be able to answer. There is no shame in contacting the vendor's Support Desk when you encounter an unfamiliar problem or question. After all, that is exactly why your organization is paying for support.

21.3.8 **How to contact them**

Each vendor's approach to customer support is a little different. It's best if you know the most efficient way to contact them before a crisis occurs. Three common ways in which vendors take details on new calls are described below. You should know, in advance, which your vendor offers and which works best for you:

- Telephone calls to toll free number
- Requests must be entered into their website
- Requests must be sent to the Support Desk's e-mail address

Other questions that you should know the answers to include the following:

- What are the days and hours they are open?
- Are they staffed on holidays?
- What do you do if you have an outage in the middle of the night?
- Do they have service desks in other time zones? If so how do you contact them? Or do you call the centralized number and that connects you to the desk that is currently being manned?

21.4 **CHALLENGES WITH VENDORS**

Like any relationship, the one you'll have with a vendor won't be all peaches and cream. There will be times when things get tense. Some situations that can complicate the relation are described in the following sections.

21.4.1 **Offshore vendors**

In an effort to either cut costs or locate the support staff closer to the development staff, some vendors have moved their support staff offshore. If your vendor has done this, then be prepared for some additional complications, but it doesn't necessarily mean that things will go badly.

Working with an offshore vendor or support staff can introduce the following issues:

- The language difference is probably the biggest complication when dealing with offshore support staff. It doesn't matter how well educated, well trained, or well intentioned the technician is, if his or her native language isn't the same as yours then verbal communications will be more difficult. The best advice I can offer is to keep your patience and your sense of humor.
- Time zone differences can make it harder to work on a problem in a lengthy, contiguous block of time. I'll have to admit that most of the offshore technicians I've worked with were working the hours needed to accommodate the client.
- Cultural differences can make working together a little more difficult too. Working together with someone from another culture always seems a little stilted to me. Neither of us wants to do anything to offend the other so we always hang back when talking.
- Overseas connections can mean slower shared screen sessions and phone connections that aren't crystal clear. Combined with the language differences, this can make working on a problem over the phone extremely challenging.

21.4.2 **Follow the sun**

Vendors that are large or have clients around the world may have multiple Support Desks strategically placed around the world. Frequently, this is referred to as "follow the sun" support. If this is true for your vendor, then you may experience better than average support. Some of the advantages to this type of support for the client include:

- Support is available at all times
- Clients call a single 800 number and are connected to a Support Desk that it currently being manned.
- If the technician working on a problem is going off-shift, the problem can be handed off to another technician who will continue to work on it. While this is great in concept, sometimes the hand-off of information from one site to another isn't quite seamless. When this happens you'll be frustrated when you find yourself proving details or background information that the previous technician already asked you.

My final pieces of advice when dealing with a vendor's Support Desk are to stay calm, be patient and don't get angry while on a call. Take my word for it this won't help! The vendor's Support Desk team wants the same thing you do, i.e., to resolve your problem as quickly and efficiently as possible.

21.5 WORST CASE SCENARIOS

Unfortunately, sometimes, the worst possible outcomes occur and you may be one who experiences it. Some examples of worst case scenarios when dealing with a vendor are described in the following sections.

21.5.1 Vendor is acquired

One undesirable scenario that you could encounter is if your vendor is acquired by another corporation. To make matters worse the acquiring vendor might not intend to support the application in the long run. This might be because they don't see that application as viable or they might have their own line of products that they would like to migrate their client base to. The only bright side to this scenario is that the acquiring vendor will probably continue to support it for at least a minimal period of time. You'll need to use this time wisely to plan your course of action.

What are your alternatives if this happens?

- Drop their support and live with the application as it currently exists. This might or might not be legally possible. You'll need to review your contract with the original vendor.
- Start planning to replace the application with another vendor's product. See the steps listed in Section 21.5.3.
- Move to the vendor's other product. If this is your choice, then the acquiring vendor will provide you with the support you need to migrate data from the old application to their new product.

21.5.2 Vendor stops supporting the application

Sometimes vendors simply decide to walk away from one of their products. This might be because the product wasn't as lucrative as expected. It might be that they don't see that it's going to be profitable in the long run. In either case, you're probably going to have to migrate away from the application.

You might be faced with a vendor that doesn't formally announce the end of an application, but they simply stop supporting it. This might mean that they stop issuing updates and patches. No new features are forthcoming. The annual user conference is "suspended." They might also severely cut back the staffing of their Support Desk. If this is your situation, then you need to begin the steps to replace the application.

21.5.3 **Vendor goes out of business**

If your vendor goes out of business and you are reliant on their application, then you're in trouble. Unfortunately, there are no two ways about it. If you are very lucky, the application might continue to be supported in one of the following ways:

- Another vendor will acquire the vendor or the application and commit to supporting it
- Employees of the defunct vendor will be available to support it
- A user group could step up and commit to supporting the application

Neither of these alternatives is great or realistically even likely. A further complication is the time factor. It might take months for the rights or access to the application's source code to become available to an entity that wants to support it.

Your only solution might be to keep the application limping along without vendor support until you can migrate to another vendor's product. Depending on the size and complexity of the application, it might take an extended period of time to accomplish such a migration. Some of the steps that are involved are:

- Write up the specifications of what the replacement application has to be capable of doing.
- Issue an RFP, Request for Proposal, to vendors with products that could potentially replace your current application.
- Wait for the vendors to respond. You might need to give them 60 or 90 days to prepare their submissions.
- Rate all of the RFP proposals and choose the best alternative.
- Negotiate with the selected vendor on points where your RFP and their bid aren't identical.
- Acquire new hardware if necessary.
- Work with the vendor to install their application.
- Work with the vendor or consultants to extract data from the existing application.
- Training users on the new application.
- Cut over to the new application.
- Decommission the old software and servers

21.5.4 **Suing the vendor**

Perhaps the worst of the worst case scenarios is that the application doesn't do half of what the sales team promised it would do. Enhancements that were specifically promised had never been released. There are show-stopping problems with the application and the support staff simply stops returning your calls.

Suing the vendor is never a good idea, but your organization might feel that it has no recourse. If it comes to this, then you can expect that the process will be a protracted one. In the meantime, what kind of support do you expect to get from a vendor that is on the sharp end of a lawsuit? Trade journals carry articles about clients that are suing their vendors and it always seems to be really messy. Your best solution might be to start the process of migrating to another vendor's product about the same time the lawsuit is initiated.

The Government Gets Involved

Like it or not, the government has an impact on your organization and very likely on the applications you support. The specific effect may be that you provide data to a government body, you receive information from a government or your business has to adhere to some type of government regulations. The amount and type of involvement can vary depending on a number of parameters like number of employees your organization has, the industry (e.g., health care, financial) you're in, or whether your organization is publicly traded or not. Regardless of the exact scenarios, there is government involvement at some level.

It isn't possible for this book or any book to list or describe all the ways that organizations interact with all forms of government. Any attempt at that would be both monumental and outdated the moment the ink on it dried. What this chapter is attempting to do is to provide some insight into how prevalent governments and their regulations are on business organizations and their IT infrastructures. The examples in this chapter are primarily drawn from organization's dealings with various levels of government in the United States, but corporations in other countries have similar laws and regulations that need to be followed.

22.1 MULTIPLE LEVELS OF GOVERNMENT

When referring to "the government" it's easy to just think about the federal government. The United States and most other countries have state or provincial governments that also have an impact on businesses and nonprofit entities. Applications that are licensed to fulfill business requirements are frequently affected by not just a single government entity, but by many of them.

Examples of common business activities that are affected by multiple levels of government entities include:

- To correctly calculate sales taxes, the logic and code in an application must be current with all state sales tax rates, all county sales tax rates, and all city sales tax rates. In addition to that, it must be aware of consumer items are tax exempt, e.g., groceries or medical services, in each government entity. This labyrinth of taxes explains why many organizations don't write their own code to calculate sales tax amounts, but instead license an application that does the leg work for them.
- Employers over a specific size are regulated by a significant number of federal, state, and local government regulations pertaining to employment. These regulations can significantly complicate how your HR (Human Resources) department goes about its work.
- Income tax withholding percentages are different for every state. In addition to state income taxes, many states allow cities, counties, or school districts to level taxes on income. An organization that has a presence in numerous states needs to be aware of which government entities require income tax withholding be calculated and applied to its employee's paychecks.
- Environmental regulations can pose a significant amount of work on any organization that deals with chemicals, water, land, or potentially hazardous material. The required reports and record keeping required by the federal and state governments can be monumental.

- Unclaimed property exists when an organization can't locate the owner of items like checks that have been issued but never cashed, dormant bank accounts, stock dividends, and life insurance benefits. Every state has different rules for handling unclaimed property. A large organization can easily end up needing to adhere with the unclaimed property rules of many different states.
- Real estate taxes are also heavily affected by various levels of government bodies that have been granted the ability to levy property taxes. Some examples of these entities are counties, cities, school districts, SIDs (Sanitary Improvement Districts), and utility districts. Each government entity has its own tax rate or mill levy. An organization that needs to pay real estate taxes on its own property or calculate payments for its clients' property needs to maintain current and accurate tax rate information on all of these government taxing bodies.
- Unemployment taxes are administered by each of the states. If your organization has a presence in multiple states, then any payroll activity will have to take into consideration the rates for every state your organization is located in.

22.2 GOVERNMENT AGENCIES

There are many different U.S. federal government agencies that your organization might have dealings with. Any list of them is guaranteed to be incomplete, but some of the more noteworthy ones are:

- IRS—Internal Revenue Service: For-profit organizations are required to complete tax returns on a quarterly basis. This requires that businesses of all forms and sizes keep accurate records of their spending, incomes, costs, investments, etc.

  Organizations that have employees are required to submit W-2 forms to the IRS to document earnings and taxes that have been withheld from each employee's paycheck.

  If your organization pays out interest or dividends, then these financial distributions need to be reported to the IRS.
- SSA—Social Security Administration: Employers are required to make FICA (Federal Insurance Contributions Act) deductions from paychecks for all of their employees. Employers may also need to interact with the SSA to verify the names and Social Security Numbers of current and former employees.
- FDA—Food and Drug Administration: The FDA is responsible for protecting the public health by ensuring that drugs, medical devices, and other consumer products are safe. It is also responsible for monitoring the testing and approving new drugs that pharmaceutical companies want to market.
- SEC—Securities and Exchange Commission: The SEC is responsible for administering laws that govern the securities industry in the United States. One of the more recent laws that the SEC administers is the Sarbanes-Oxley Act of 2002. Among the goals of these laws is to prevent accounting fraud, insider trading, and other violations of securities law. Publicly traded companies, i.e., companies whose shares can be bought and sold on a stock market, are required to provide the SEC with quarterly and annual financial reports.
- OSHA—The Occupational Safety & Health Administration makes and enforces rules to ensure workplace health and safety standards. Employers are required to adhere to OSHA regulations or face fines and other punishments.
- DHS—Department of Homeland Security: Among its many obligations, the DHS safeguards surface transportation, trucks, freight trains, pipelines, and mass transit within the United States. It is also charged with inspecting goods that are imported into the United States at all port facilities. If your organization has products that are imported or transported within the United States, then it may have to obtain information from or provide information to the DHS.

- EPA—Environmental Protection Agency: The EPA is responsible for enforcing laws and regulations related to the environment. If your organization has anything to do with manufacturing goods, mining of any kind, drilling wells, transporting petroleum products, discharging liquids or other waste material, waste management, or burning fuel, then there is a very good chance that it will have to provide records to the EPA. Providing accurate and timely records almost certainly requires an IT structure to collect, monitor, and maintain output-related data.

22.3 REGULATIONS

If all of the regulations imposed on business by governments were laid end to end, they would probably reach to the moon and beyond. I have no intentions of even attempting to list them all, but will list and describe just some of the more notable ones to provide the reader with an understanding of how difficult it can be to adhere to them.

22.3.1 Sarbanes oxley

The Sarbanes Oxley Compliance Act may have had the more impact on American business than any other single regulatory act and yet it may be among the most misunderstood pieces of regulation in existence. The intent of SOX regulations is to protect shareholders and the public from fraudulent practices and accounting errors. SOX applies to U.S. publicly held companies, but other countries have enacted similar regulations.
Some of the main ways in which SOX may impact the IT department and a specific application are:

- Independent auditing of information is mandated
- Internal controls for recording financial information need to be established and maintained
- Business records, both hardcopies and electronic, need to be maintained for a minimum of 5 years for some types of business records
- IT application controls have to include completeness checks and validity checks
- Business users of applications need to be uniquely and irrefutably identified
- Only authorized users should be able to access financial applications

Some questions that an Application Administrator needs to ask regarding SOX are:

- Is the organization required to be SOX compliant? Not every organization is subject to them. For example, privately held organizations aren't subject to SOX regulations.
- Does this application have to be SOX compliant? Even for an organization that is subject to SOX regulations, not every application that the organization relies upon needs to be SOX compliant. Only the applications that deal with the financial processes like payroll, the general ledger, accounts payable, etc, for example, an LMS, Learning Management System, probably wouldn't need to be SOX compliant.
- If the application doesn't need to be compliant now will it be required to be SOX compliant in the future? Your guess is as good as anyone's.
- Has the application been audited for SOX compliancy? Did it pass? It's important to mention that SOX doesn't specify what is or isn't compliant. Each corporation works with their auditors on that, but once their procedures have been defined the corporation has to maintain compliance.
- What is the process for making changes to the application?

22.3.1.1 SOX audits
In the context of this book and this chapter in particular, an audit is an evaluation of an organization's internal controls and processes to ensure that they both comply with government regulations and are consistently being followed. If the organizations processes are ideal, but are regularly ignored, then they are worthless.

Many organizations have two audit processes. An internal audit group performs their evaluation of the processes. If they detect problems it gives the organization's staff an opportunity to improve or perfect their processes. The second audit is done by an external, independent group of auditors. The findings of the external auditors are the ones that count. If an organization fails an SOX audit, then a remedial audit will be scheduled to test the areas that had problems.

Some of the issues that an SOX audit will be looking for include:

- What actions do employees have responsibility for and does any single individual have a set of responsibilities that can undermine controls that are in place?
- Who has access to applications and systems that deal with financial information?
- Who approves users that have access to financial information?
- How often are user lists reviewed to verify that each user still needs access to financial information?
- Has a segregation of duties been instituted to minimize the possibility of fraudulent activity?
- Are business processes consistent throughout the entire organization?
- Is access for terminated employees removed as quickly as possible after their departure?
- Is the number of test accounts minimized and are they removed as soon after testing is completed as possible?
- Do procedures that deal with data interfaces into and out of all applications include error handling, validation, and authentication?
- Applications should require "strong" passwords.
- New user accounts should require that the password be changed the first time the user logs in.
- Applications developers should not have access that allows them to modify code or executables in the production environment.

22.3.2 Health insurance portability and accountability act

The Health Insurance Portability and Accountability Act, HIPAA, of 1996 was enacted to protect the health insurance coverage of workers and their families. One section of the act establishes standards for protecting the security and privacy of patient's health-related data. This is probably the portion of the act that most affects IT departments and the applications it runs.

If the organization you work for deals with the health data of patients, then HIPAA regulation will probably impact your IT department. Examples of organizations that are affected include:

- Hospitals
- Clinics
- Health insurance companies
- Organizations that provide specialized services like MRI readings
- Dentists
- Optometrists
- Schools
- Primary care physicians
- Business associates that provide services like claims processing, billing activities, accounting services, or accounting services for any of the businesses listed above

Some questions that an Application Administrator needs to ask regarding HIPAA compliance are:

- Is the organization subject to the HIPAA act?
- Is the application being supported subject to HIPAA regulations?
- If not, will it be required to be HIPAA compliant in the future?
- Has the application been audited for HIPAA compliancy?

If the application you're supporting is subject to HIPAA compliance, there are a number of potential security threats that have been identified. Software that enables access to HIPAA-related data needs to be protected against reasonably anticipated threats or hazards. You need to ensure that your application doesn't have vulnerabilities like the following:

- Software on user workstations that allows them to remotely accessed needs to be secure. One way to achieve this security is to encrypt communications to and from the workstation.
- Remote access software needs to log all remote access activity. If logging isn't performed it would be virtually impossible to identify who gained access to the system and when.
- Passwords, especially to administrator accounts, need to be changed when an employee leaves the organization or is transferred to a job that no longer requires access to the application.
- Using the same administrator password on multiple remote systems may be convenient, but makes it difficult to change all of them quickly. A departing employee may be able to access remote systems before their passwords are changed.
- Log files need to be either centralized or accessible from a central location. This makes it easier for Application Administrators to access them on a regular basis without undue effort.

22.3.3 Payment card industry data security standard—PCI DSS

The credit card industry has developed a set of standards called PCI DSS (Payment Card Industry Data Security Standard) to increase the security for handling cardholder information of credit cards, debit cards, ATM cards, and POS cards. If your organization receives payment via any of the above types of cards, it may have to adhere to the standards and requirements of PCI DSS. Organizations that fail to apply and maintain these standards face the possibility of significant fines.

A summary of the requirements put forward by PCI DSS are:

1. Firewalls are required to protect servers that contain cardholder data
2. Default passwords for administrative accounts on systems need to be changed
3. Cardholder data that is stored in databases or files needs to be protected
4. Cardholder information that is transmitted across public networks must be encrypted
5. Systems need to be protected by regularly updated antivirus software
6. Applications and systems need to be secure
7. Access to cardholder data must be restricted to users who have a legitimate need to know
8. Users must be assigned unique IDs and use them when accessing the applications and data
9. Physical access to cardholder data must be restricted, e.g., locked doors, guards, etc.
10. Access to cardholder data and network resources must be tracked and monitored
11. System security should be regularly tested
12. An information security policy needs to be developed and maintained by the organization

22.3.4 Federal information security management act

The Federal Information Security Management Act of 2002, FISMA, requires federal agencies to ensure that their information systems are secure. Some of the attributes that should be included in an effective security program are:

- Risk assessment has to be periodically reviewed. Policies and procedures need to be modified to address changes in perceived risks
- Plans for providing security for subordinate systems like networks, facilities, and systems need to be developed and implemented

- Training to educate personnel about security needs to be developed and provided
- Information security policies need to be periodically tested and evaluated
- Procedures for handling security incidents, i.e., detecting them, reporting them, and responding to them need to be developed
- Plans for ensuring continuity of operations need to be developed.

You may think that FISMA can't possibly apply to your organization, but you might be in for a surprise. The act also extends to systems and application that are provided for federal agencies by contractors or other entities. If your organization does business with a federal agency that is required to adhere to FISMA policies, then your organization might also come under this act's umbrella of security standards.

22.3.5 Fair credit reporting act

The Fair Credit Reporting Act (FCRA) is a federal law that specifies how consumer credit information is to be handled, used, and protected. If your organization deals with consumer credit, then it's likely that you'll have to deal with this set of regulations.

In addition to credit information, if your organization compiles or maintains the following types of data about consumers, then the FCRA regulations must be adhered to:

- Medical payments
- Medical records
- Tenant history
- History of home ownership
- Check writing history
- Employment history
- Insurance claims

22.3.6 Children's online privacy protection act

The Children's Online Privacy Protection Act, COPPA, specifies what personal information can be collected about children who are under that age of 13 and how that data is to be handled. The FTC (Federal Trade Commission) has been authorized to enforce COPPA and issue additional regulations. Fines up to 1 million dollars have been levied against companies that violate COPPA regulations. If your organization collects or utilized data on children, then the COPPA regulations might apply to it.

Some of the guidelines for collecting personal information on children are:

- A clear and comprehensive privacy policy must be posted on websites which describes what an organization does with the information that is gathered
- Parental consent must be obtained before personal information can be collected on their children
- Parents have to be given the option of prohibiting the organization from disclosing information on their children to third parties
- Parents must be given the ability to review their children's data and delete information from it
- Parents must be given the option to prevent additional collection and/or use of their children's personal information
- Organizations must ensure that the information collected from children is maintained in a confidential and secure manner.

22.4 PRIVACY

As of mid-2013, the United States doesn't have a federal law guaranteeing its citizens the right to privacy. If your organization does business exclusively in the United States, you may think this means you don't have any privacy standards to meet. You may be wrong and surprised at the source of the privacy standards you have to meet. If your organization's website includes a privacy policy, then the organization is obligated to meet those claims. Some claims that are commonly made on website privacy policy statements include:

- Whether or not the consumer's information will be sold, exchanged, or transferred to any other organization
- A statement indicating whether or not cookies are used by the website
- A differentiation between information collected online vs. offline
- Whether the information being collected is mandatory or optional
- What security is used to ensure the protection of consumer's information
- How the consumer can learn about changes in the security policy
- How the consumer can opt out of future contacts from your organization.

Laws in the European Union provide significantly greater privacy protection to its citizens. EU Directive 94/46/EC includes the following seven principles governing the privacy of personal data:

1. Notice: subjects whose data is being collected should be given notice of such collection.
2. Purpose: data collected should be used only for stated purpose(s) and for no other purposes.
3. Consent: personal data should not be disclosed or shared with third parties without consent from its subject(s).
4. Security: once collected, personal data should be kept safe and secure from potential abuse, theft, or loss.
5. Disclosure: subjects whose personal data is being collected should be informed as to the party or parties collecting such data.
6. Access: subjects should granted access to their personal data and allowed to correct any inaccuracies.
7. Accountability: subjects should be able to hold personal data collectors accountable for adhering to all seven of these principles.

22.5 PROTECTING PERSONALLY IDENTIFIABLE INFORMATION

Personally Identifiable Information (PII) is information that can be used to uniquely identify an individual. If a criminal obtains the personally identifiable information of someone it makes stealing their identity a very real possibility. For this reason, there are laws regulating the types of protection that organizations must provide for it. The laws on protecting PII vary from country to country. If your organization does business in multiple countries, you should know the rules for each of them.

Examples of information that constitute PII include:

- An individual's full name, if that name isn't common
- A national identity number in countries where such numbers are issued
- In the United States a Social Security Number
- Passport number
- A driver's license number
- Credit card numbers
- Date of birth

- Birthplace
- Biometric information such as fingerprints, iris scans, and facial geometry
- Home and personal cell telephone numbers
- Mother's middle and maiden names
- Military records

Some common industry recommendations for how PII should be secured include:

- If PII is stored on workstations or mobile devices it must be encrypted using FIPS 140-2 certified encryption module
- PII stored electronically should only be accessible with access controls like User IDs and passwords
- PPI stored on network drives or databases should be available on a need to know basis
- When extracts are created from PII databases, the activity should be logged including the creator, date, and the type of information extracted
- PII transmitted over the Internet must be encrypted
- PII that is transmitted by e-mail needs to be encrypted

Questions regarding PII that an Application Administrator should be able to answer include:

- Does the application you're supporting include PII?
- Are you adhering to industry best practices to protect personally identifiable information?
- What do you have to do to prove that you're following industry best practices?
- Have the application and/or your processes been audited?
- Is your data encrypted?
    - If so where is it encrypted? On the disk, in-flight or both?
    - What type of encryption is being used, for example, DES, 3DES, AES, RSA?
    - How many bits are used in the encryption algorithm?
    - How are the encryption keys managed?
- Are your backup tapes encrypted?
- Do you audit the security of your contractors?
- Do you audit the security of firms that work is outsourced to?
- Do you audit the security of your offsite storage vendor?

22.6 DISCLOSURE AFTER DATA LOSS INCIDENTS

If a data loss or a system intrusion occurs, are you required to alert customers that their data might have been compromised? Currently 46 U.S. states have laws that require organizations disclose information when a data loss incident occurs. If your organization is located in one of those 46 states, then it needs to have policies and procedures in place to adhere to state privacy laws. It needs to be stressed that state laws apply if any of the data lost belongs to a customer, employee, client, etc. who is a resident in one of those 46 states. What constitutes a data loss incident? Some common types of incidents include:

- Unintended disclosure of sensitive information. For example, a list of employees' or customers' Social Security numbers are inadvertently posted on a publicly available website.
- An outsider, e.g., a hacker, accesses a computer server, network, or database and possibly gained access to sensitive information.
- An insider, e.g., an employee or contractor, accessed or downloaded data they were not authorized to see.

- Loss of paper documents containing sensitive information, e.g., reports, job application forms, loan application forms, health records, etc.
- Loss of a portable electronic device such as a laptop, PDA, hard drive, USB drive, and backup tape that contained sensitive information. The device might have been stolen or lost.
- Loss of a stationary device like a server that contained sensitive information.

Does your organization have policies and procedures for handling such incidents? Do the policies specify what types of data or how much data has to be lost for a disclosure to be required? At some point in the future, there may be federal legislation on this topic. When that happens every organization will need to review its policies to ensure that they adhere to the federal or state laws, whichever are more stringent.

22.7 UNCOVERING DISCOVERY

In U.S. law, each party in a lawsuit is required to provide evidence to the opposing party. This pretrial phase of the legal process is called "discovery." If your organization becomes involved in a lawsuit, it will be required to cooperate fully in the discovery process. Discovery also includes the exchange of information that was originally stored in electronic format. Your company may be required to produce some or all of the following types of information:

- E-mail
- Instant message (IM) chats
- Photos
- Video files
- The contents of relational databases like Oracle, DB2, SQL Server
- The contents of desktop databases like Access
- Spreadsheets
- Structured flat files
- XML pages
- Voice mail

As an Application Administrator you might be required to participate in the effort to gather and provide electronic information for the discovery process. If this is the case you need to understand that failure to provide all of the related information, whether an omission is intentional or accidental, can result in catastrophic legal consequences. Be certain that you understand exactly what you need to provide.

22.8 DATA RETENTION REQUIREMENTS

Businesses are legally required to retain certain types of information for various periods of time. Data that is older than this can be purged at the organization's discretion. Make sure that you know whether any of the categories of data listed in the following list are applicable to the applications that you support.

Some examples of data that has to be retained are listed here. This list is solely to provide examples and shouldn't be taken as a definitive list. Legal requirements change and are different in every state and country, so it's important to have your organization's legal department research what needs to be retained and for how long.

Personnel employment applications	1 year
Purchase orders	1 year
Bank reconciliations	3 years
Physical inventory logs	3 years
Accident reports and claims	7 years
Bank statements	7 years
Commission records	7 years
Purchase orders	7 years
Copyrights	Permanently
Patents	Permanently
Mortgages	Permanently

As an Application Administrator you should be familiar with your organization's data retention policy. If the application you support contains any of the types of data specified in the organization's data retention policy then confirm that data is being retained for the appropriate period of time. If you have any questions contact your organization's data retention team or Legal Department.

22.8.1 **Legal investigations trump normal data retention practices**

In the event that your organization becomes involved in a legal investigation or lawsuit, then it becomes critical to stop deleting any form of electronic records that might be related to the case. This would include deleting files, destroying backup media, or overwriting backup tapes. The requirements of discovery supersede the normal data retention periods or practices.

Windows Tools

23.1 WINDOWS TOOLS

Every operating system has its share of tools that can make your life easier if you are aware of them and know how to use them. Windows is no exception. The tools listed in this chapter can make the job of an Application Administrator easier.

23.2 USING COMMAND PROMPT

Command Prompts, once upon a time known as DOS windows, aren't dead. As an Application Administrator, you will need to know how to use them. There are many reasons why you might need to use a Command Prompt. Some examples are:

- Many vendor installation procedures will require that you open a command prompt and perform specific steps
- It can be faster to accomplish some tasks in a command prompt compared to a GUI
- Many commands that can be run in a command prompt offer command line options that have aren't available in a GUI window

23.2.1 Opening and closing command prompt windows

There are several ways to start a command prompt.

- Left-click on the Start button. If a "Command Prompt" icon is displayed, then click it.
- Left-click on the Start icon, click on the Run option, enter "cmd," and press the Enter key.
- Create a shortcut on the desktop by dragging C:\Windows\System32\cmd.exe to the desktop and selecting "Create shortcuts here." Then double-click on the new shortcut.

To close a command prompt, you can either:

- Click on the "X" in the upper right-hand corner of the window
- Enter the command "exit" and press the Enter key

23.2.2 Advanced ways to start command prompt windows

There are several additional ways to start Command Prompt windows. These aren't applicable in all situations, but when they can be used they are very effective.

23.2.2.1 Start a second command prompt window

If you have a command prompt open, you can open a second command prompt window by entering the command "start" in it and pressing the Enter key. A new command window will be opened. The new command prompt window will be at the same subdirectory level that the original command window was running in.

The second command prompt window will be opened in the same mode as the first window. If the first window was opened in administrator mode, the second window will also be in that mode. If the first window wasn't in administrator mode, then the second window won't be either. See Section 23.2.3 for an explanation of what "administrator mode" is.

23.2.2.2 Opening a command prompt from windows explorer

If you don't want to type at all, then there's a way to open a Command Prompt window directly from Windows Explorer. Hold down the Shift key and right-click a subdirectory in Windows Explorer. When the submenu is displayed, click on the "Open command window here" option. See Figure 23.1 for a screenshot of the submenu options that will be displayed. A Command Prompt window will be opened and it will be positioned at your selected subdirectory. If the path you want the window to be at is either very deep or has a very long name, then this method of opening a Command Prompt may be the easiest way to open a command prompt.

23.2.2.3 Using drag and drop to change a command prompt's subdirectory

It's possible to use the drag and drop concept to change the current subdirectory of a Command Prompt window. The steps to do this are

1. In a Command Prompt window, enter "cd" and a space character
2. From Windows explorer, drag a subdirectory into the Command Prompt window and drop it
3. In the Command Prompt window, press the Enter key

FIGURE 23.1

Opening a Command Prompt from Windows Explorer.

The current subdirectory of the Command Prompt window will be changed to the subdirectory that was dropped onto it. This technique is very quick and useful if you don't like to type.

23.2.3 **Opening a command prompt as administrator**

There will be times when a command that you're about to enter into a command prompt will make changes to the system. In order to make changes to the system, you have to full administrator rights. This requires that the command prompt be opened as Administrator. The title of the command prompt that has been opened in admin mode will say "Administrator:Command Prompt."

Three ways to open a command prompt with these additional rights are shown here.

1. If you have the Command Prompt option in the Startup list when you click the Start icon, then right-click it and select "Run as administrator." See Figure 23.2 for a screenshot of this option.
2. A second way to open a command prompt is via the Start icon. The steps to accomplish it are:
   a. Left-click the Start icon
   b. Click on Run
   c. Enter "cmd" in the Open text field
   d. Simultaneously press the Ctrl, Shift, and Enter keys
3. If you created a shortcut for opening a Command Prompt as described in Section 23.2.1, then the shortcut can be modified to always open the Command Prompt in admin mode. The steps to do this are:
   a. Right-click on the shortcut and select Properties
   b. If the Shortcut tab isn't already selected, then select it
   c. Click the Advanced button
   d. Click the "Run as administrator" check box

FIGURE 23.2

Opening a Command Prompt as Administrator. (For color version of this figure, the reader is referred to the online version of this chapter.)

23.2.4 **Changing the appearance of the command prompt window**

The default command prompt window may be smaller than you want it to be. To make a command window taller or shorter, just grab the upper or lower edge and drag it.

Making a command prompt wider requires a few additional steps.

- Right-click on the upper border of the command prompt window and select "Properties."
- The screen shown in Figure 23.3 will be displayed.
- Click the Layout tab if it isn't already selected.
- Change the settings for Width to the desired value.
- You may be prompted to decide whether this change should affect all command prompts or just the current one.

The Properties window enables you to make a number of other changes to the command prompt. The most significant adjustments that can be made are:

- Numerous fonts are available in which text can be displayed
- Adjust the buffer that holds commands and output in the command prompt
- A select of preset window sizes, e.g., 4×6, 6×8, or 12×18 can be chosen
- Font colors for both text and background can be selected

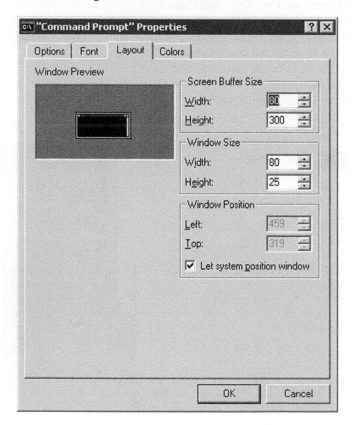

FIGURE 23.3

Properties for the Command Prompt. (For color version of this figure, the reader is referred to the online version of this chapter.)

23.2.5 Copy and paste

It's possible to perform copy and paste operations within the command prompt. This can be very helpful when you want to copy output from a command that has been executed in a command prompt. Two ways to copy text from a command prompt are:

To select everything in the command prompt, the steps are:

1. Right-click in the command prompt and select "Select All"
2. The entire screen will be displayed in reverse video
3. Press the Enter key

The contents of the screen are now in your clipboard buffer. They can be manipulated like any other buffer content.

To copy a subset of the command prompt, perform the following steps:

1. Right-click in the command prompt and select "Mark"
2. Click at the point where the copy should begin
3. Drag the mouse to the point where the copy should end
4. Press the Enter key

When using the second technique, you need to be aware that the area being copied doesn't automatically include complete lines. A rectangle is formed between the initial pixel where the mouse was clicked and the current mouse position. This rectangle won't necessarily include complete lines. If you want entire lines to be copied, then the final position of the mouse must be at the right-hand edge of the command prompt window. See Figure 23.4 for a screenshot showing an example of the mark option being used.

Pasting into a command prompt window is fairly straightforward with a single caveat. If you're accustomed to using the Control-V key combination to paste, then forget about this shortcut. To paste into a command prompt, you need to right-click in the window and select the paste option on the submenu that will be displayed.

A warning about the paste action needs to be provided here. Whatever is in the clipboard buffer will be pasted into the command prompt. This includes Control Return and Line Feed control (CRLF) characters. If you copied multiple lines from a Notepad window, then the text that precedes CRLF characters will be executed. Be very careful not to include any CRLF characters in your pasted string to avoid unwanted commands automatically executed in the command prompt.

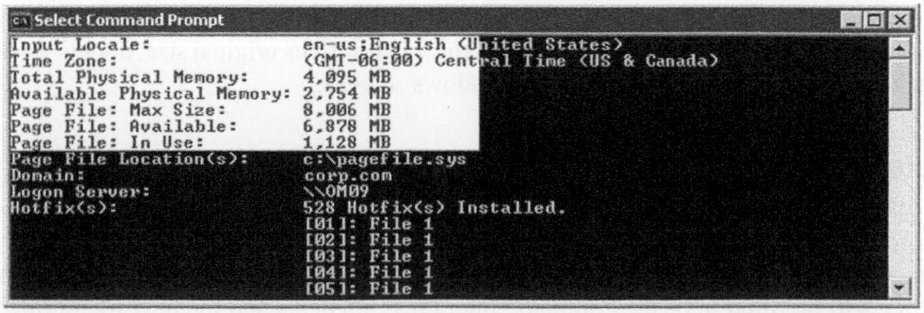

FIGURE 23.4

Copying from a command prompt with the mark option. (For color version of this figure, the reader is referred to the online version of this chapter.)

After pasting a string into the command prompt, it can then be edited. Use the left arrow key to position the cursor and then use the backspace or delete keys to remove unwanted characters. Use the keyboard to enter new text. Press the Enter or Return key to execute the command that is displayed in the command prompt window.

23.2.6 Useful command prompt features and commands

There are a large number of ways to improve your productivity while using command prompts. A few of them are described here.

23.2.6.1 Clear screen
A command that is very useful when you're copying and pasting into a command prompt is the "clear screen" command. Enter "cls" and press the Return key to have the command prompt screen blanked out. This is quite helpful when you want to copy only a single command's output.

23.2.6.2 Repeating commands
You can repeat commands in the command prompt window without re-entering them by pressing the up or down arrow keys on the keyboard. Once you've displayed the command you want, it can be edited by using the right and left arrow keys or the backspace and delete keys.

23.2.6.3 Redirecting files
The output of most commands executed in a command prompt window can be redirecting to a disk file. To do this, enter the command and then enter "> filename" in the command prompt. The output will be written to the file specified. For example, the command *systeminfo >systeminfo.txt* will run the systeminfo command and write the output to file systeminfo.txt in the current subdirectory. If the specified file already exists, it will be overwritten.

23.2.6.4 Appending files
You have the option of appending the output of a command to the existing contents of a file. The format to do that is to add ">>filename" to the end of the command. For example, the command *ipconfig >> systeminfo. txt* will append the output of the ipconfig command to the systeminfo lines that are already in file systeminfo. txt.

23.2.7 Enlarging a command prompt window

To quickly enlarge a command prompt window, just double-click on its title bar. The window will increase to the size specified in the properties window. To return the window to its original size, double-click the title bar again. This trick can be used on most if not all Windows screens.

23.2.8 Autocomplete

If you don't like typing long strings when entering subdirectory names or file names, then you'll find the autocomplete feature of the command prompt to be very useful. This features works extremely well with the change directory (cd) command. Enter "cd" and a space. Then press the Tab key. The alphabetically first file or directory will be filled in on the command line. Press tab again and the next file or directory will be displayed. This can be extremely useful for drilling down into a directory tree. It's quicker and more accurate than typing in the name manually. After using this feature for even a short period of time, you won't understand how you lived without it.

If the current subdirectory has many objects in it and the one you want is toward the end of the alphabetic list, then enter the first letter or two of the object name you want and press the Tab key. This lets you quickly reach files whose names come last alphabetically.

If you want to drill down deeply into a directory structure, the autocomplete can help. Start by entering "cd" and a space then Tab to get the directory you want. Next press the "\" key to add a backward slash ("\") in the path and then the Tab key again. Repeat this process until you have the full path you want. Finally, hit the Enter key and you'll be at the desired subdirectory. With just a little bit of practice, you'll learn to navigate subdirectories faster than you dreamed could be done.

The autocomplete can also be used to launch cmd, bat, and exe files. Press the Tab key and the command line will autocomplete with the alphabetically first object in the current subdirectory whether it's a file or a subdirectory. When the particular file you want to launch is displayed on the command line, press the Enter key and it will be launched.

23.2.9 Associate file types

When you double-click on a file in Windows Explorer, the operating system will open the file with the application that has been associated with the file's extension. For example, files that have a ".txt" extension will normally be opened with Notepad. Excel will be used to open files with an ".xls" extension. If there is no association with the file's extension type, then you'll be prompted for the application that should be used to open the file.

The "assoc" command can be used to either list or change the program associated with a specific file extension type. Typing "assoc" into a command prompt will list all file extension types and the program associated with them. Figure 23.5 shows that files ending with "csv" will be opened by Excel while those

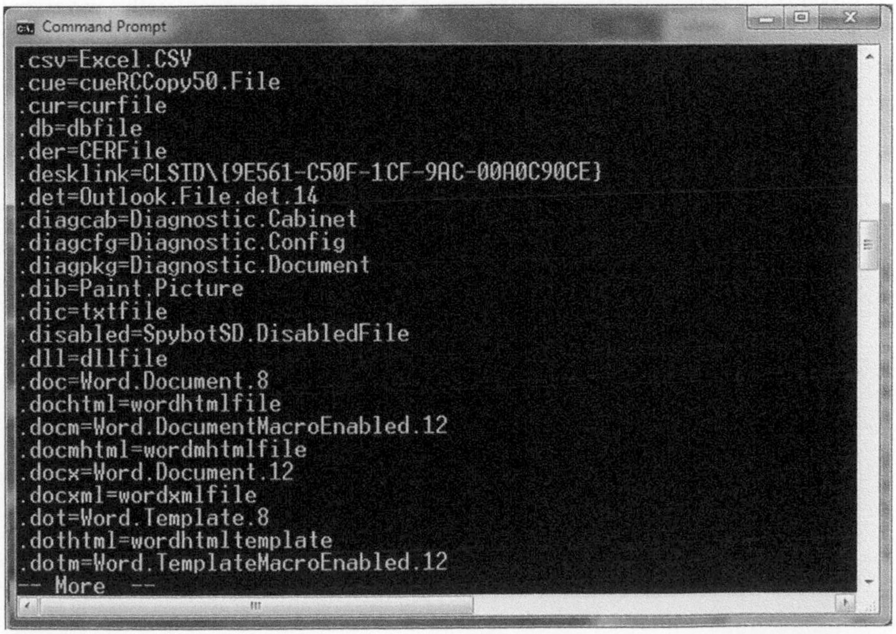

FIGURE 23.5

Listing associated file types. (For color version of this figure, the reader is referred to the online version of this chapter.)

ending with "doc" will be opened with Microsoft Word version. The next section will explain the meaning of the last line shown in Figure 23.5.

File associations can be obtained from the Windows GUI, but drilling down that deeply takes longer than using the assoc command in a command prompt. To use the GUI method of displaying file associations, do the following:

1. Click Start and select Control Panel
2. Click the "Default Programs" link
3. Click the "Associate a file type of protocol with a program" link

If you only want to see a specific association, then you can add the pipe symbol and the "find" command to list a single file type. For example, to see what program is associated with file extension "txt," enter the command *assoc | find ".txt."* The pipe symbol causes the output of the "assoc" command to be fed into the "find" command. The find command has been instruction to look for the string ".txt." Figure 23.6 shows the command and results.

If you want to remove the association between a file extension and a program, you can use the assoc command with a not value following the equals sign. For example, the command

```
assoc .txt=
```

removes the association between ".txt" files and Notepad.

The file type association can be created in the following ways:

1. Double-click on a text file in Windows Explorer and select Notepad when given the choice of what program to open the file with
2. Enter the command assoc .txt=txtfile in a command prompt
3. Bring up Control Panel | Default Programs | Associate a file type or protocol with a program then click on the "txt" entry and click the "Change Program" button. On the "Open with" screen select Notepad and click OK.

FIGURE 23.6

Listing a single associated file type. (For color version of this figure, the reader is referred to the online version of this chapter.)

23.2.10 **More**

The number of associations that will be listed using the "assoc" command can be quite lengthy. If just the "assoc" command is entered, it's likely that so many file types will be displayed that you won't be able to see them all. An alternative is to include the "more" command to what you enter. By entering the command as "assoc | more," you will have much more control over how the output is displayed. The pipe symbol ("|") causes the output of the "assoc" command to be fed into the "more" command which displays just a single screen's worth of output at a time. The screenshot shown in Figure 23.5 is the result of the command "assoc | more."

If you press the Return key, the more command will displays an additional line of output from the assoc command. Pressing the space bar displays an additional screen full of lines of output from the assoc command. The "More" command can be used in conjunction with any command that produces output in a command prompt window.

23.2.11 **Clip**

If you want the output of a command executed in a command prompt to be written to the clipboard buffer, then the "clip" command can be used. For example, to export the output of the assoc command into the clipboard buffer, enter the following command:

```
Assoc | clip
```

Like the more command, the clip command can be used with any command that produces output in a command prompt.

23.2.12 **FC—file compare**

It's not unusual for Application Administrators to have to compare different versions of a file. One example that comes to mind is to see if configuration or settings files have changed after an update has been applied. This can be done in a GUI editor like Notepad++. But it's also possible to accomplish this in a command prompt.

The command to compare two files is "fc." The syntax is to enter "fc" following by the two file names. The example in Figure 23.7 shows a comparison of the current settings.xml file with an older version of that file.

This command is great when it works, but it doesn't work on all file types. You won't be able to compare PDF documents, older versions of Word documents, or older versions of Excel spreadsheets. Actually, this

FIGURE 23.7

Using the fc command to perform a file compare. (For color version of this figure, the reader is referred to the online version of this chapter.)

limitation isn't as severe as it might sound because the ini files, config files, and parameter files typically used by applications are frequently ASCII text files.

23.2.12.1 Comp command to compare files

Another command that allows you to compare files is the "comp" command. The comp command can be launched in a command window. The format of this command is

```
comp file1 file2
```

where file1 and file2 are the files to be compared.

The comp command has the following parameters:

- /D—Displays the differences it finds in decimal format
- /A—Displays the differences it finds in ASCII characters
- /l—Displays the line numbers where differences are found
- /N-number—Compares only the first "number" lines in the files

23.2.13 Command prompt windows and function keys

Command prompt windows can be more efficient than a GUI, but if you can combine command prompts with Function Keys, then you can be really productive. The following list of function keys are available in command prompt windows:

- F1—Repeats the last command one character at a time. Each time you press the F1 key, another letter is displayed. Very useful if you're dealing with long paths or file names.
- F2—You are prompted to enter a character. When you do, the command entered on the previous line up until that character is repeated. The screenshot shown in Figure 23.8 shows the previous command and the prompt when F2 was pressed. I entered "d" in response to the prompt. Figure 23.9 shows that the previous command up to, but not including the first "d" was displayed.
- F3—Repeats the entire previous command. The result is basically the same thing as pressing the "up arrow" key a single time.
- F4—Similar to F2 but prompts you for the character to delete up to from the last command.
- F5—Allows you to display all of your previous commands. Each time you press F5, the prior command is displayed. The result is the same as pressing the "Up arrow" key multiple times.
- F6—Includes the Ctrl Z (end-of-file) to the command line.

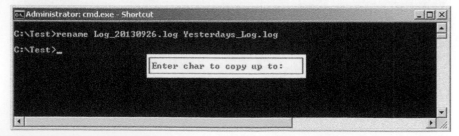

FIGURE 23.8

F2 prompt. (For color version of this figure, the reader is referred to the online version of this chapter.)

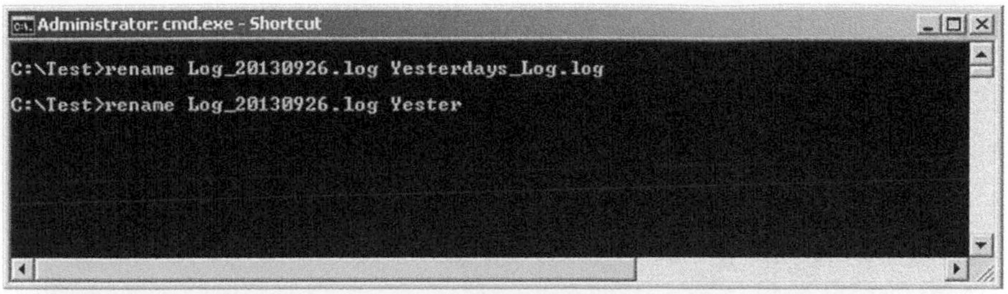

FIGURE 23.9

F2 results. (For color version of this figure, the reader is referred to the online version of this chapter.)

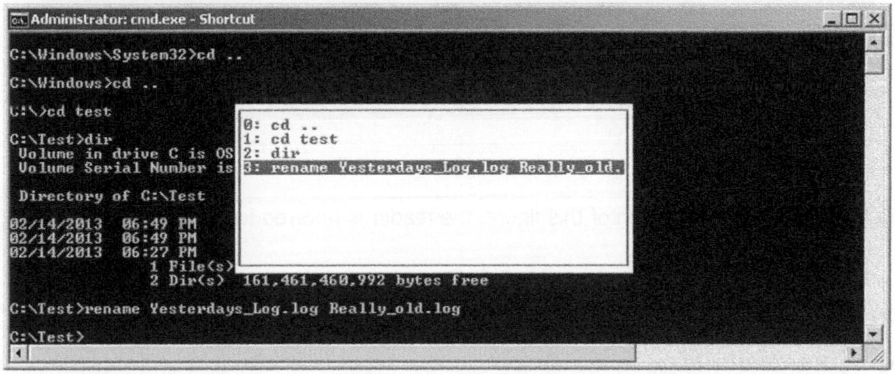

FIGURE 23.10

Window showing the command line history. (For color version of this figure, the reader is referred to the online version of this chapter.)

- F7—A prompt window lists all of the commands that have been entered in this session. You can use the up and down arrows to select a command. When you press the Enter key, the selected command will be displayed in the command line. Figure 23.10 shows the prompt window that is displayed. If you want to clear the buffer holding the command line history, press Alt + F7.
- F8—Pressing F8 cycles through the command line history that has accumulated. Entering one or more characters in the command line causes the F8 to filter what is displayed to just the commands that begin with those character(s). For example, if you enter "c" and press F8, then only commands in the history that begin with "c" will be listed.
- F9—Lets you enter a command number from the list presented by F7. You have to have a good memory or a screenshot to make the most of this function key.

23.2.14 Tree

The tree command displays the subdirectory structure of the current drive and subdirectory in a semi-graphical display. Be aware that if there are a lot of subdirectories below the current level, then much of the output from the tree command will scroll off the top of your screen. Figure 23.11 shows an example of output from the tree command.

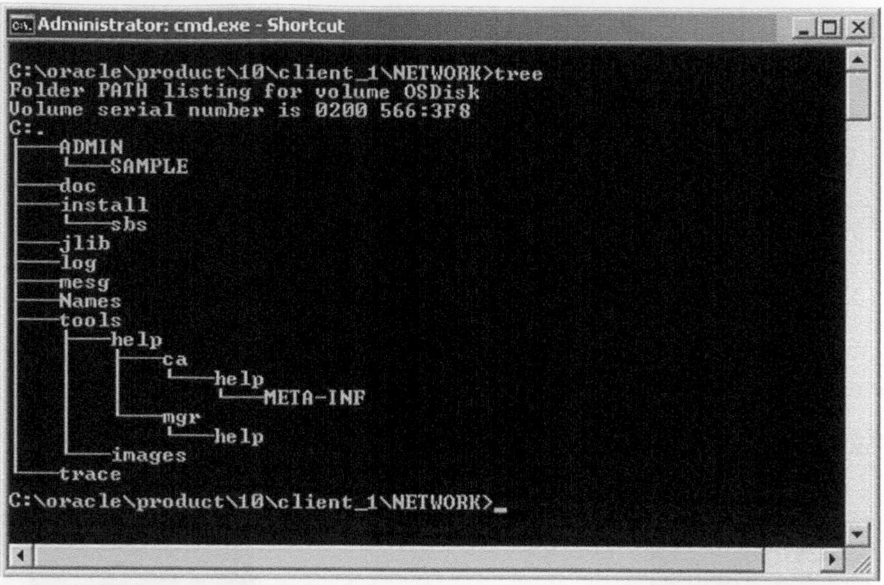

FIGURE 23.11

Tree command output. (For color version of this figure, the reader is referred to the online version of this chapter.)

23.2.15 Ctrl-C

If a command in your command prompt is returning more output or is taking longer to process than expected, then you can choose to abort it. Press the Ctrl-C keys and most commands will be terminated.

23.2.16 Prompt command

By default, the prompt in a command prompt window shows the drive and subdirectory you're currently in. This is typically not a problem, but there can be times when it isn't optimal. Two situations in which you might not want the entire path to be shown are:

1. When the path is so long that you can't enter a command on the remaining part of the command line. As you type your command will automatically scroll down to the next line, but that might not be easy to read or convenient.
2. When you're taking screenshots but don't want the actual subdirectory to be displayed. You might be creating documentation and don't want to reveal unnecessary details.

To avoid this situation, you can use the "prompt" command to change what is being displayed. The format of the command is "prompt xxxx" where xxxx is the new string to be displayed. The screenshot in Figure 23.12 shows several executions of the prompt command and the results.

- Entering "prompt C:" changes the prompt to "C:"
- Entering just "prompt" reverts to the default prompt
- Including "$g" in the command appends the ">" symbol to whatever string you've chosen. In this case, the result is "C:>"

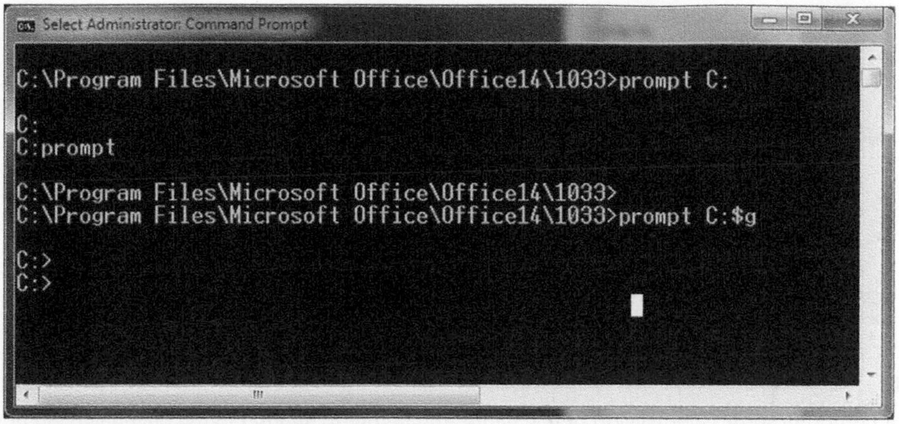

FIGURE 23.12

Changing the prompt value. (For color version of this figure, the reader is referred to the online version of this chapter.)

23.2.17 Shutdown

The shutdown command allows you to, surprise, shut down a computer. This command can be used to affect either the one you're logged into or a remote computer on the network. Obviously, since this command has a lot of power, you need to be extremely careful when using it.

Parameters that can be specified with the shutdown command are:

- /i—cause a dialog screen to be displayed
- /l—logs off the current user before the local computer is shut down
- /s—the local computer is shut down
- /m \\computername—specifies that the named remote computer be shut down
- /r—the local or remote computer is restarted
- /p—powers off the computer after the shutdown completes
- /f—forces all running programs to close without warning
- /t xxx—the shutdown will occur in xxx seconds
- /c "comment"—the comment explaining the shutdown is recorded in the Event log

23.3 LEARNING MORE ABOUT THE COMPUTER

One useful category of commands and tools will teach you more about the workstation or server that you're currently logged onto. You may know everything about your PC or laptop, but probably aren't as familiar with the server that run your applications. The commands and utilities listed in the following sections provide you with a great deal of information about a server.

23.3.1 ipconfig command

The ipconfig command displays IP address information of the computer. Figure 23.13 is a screenshot of the output after running ipconfig in a command window.

```
Command Prompt                                    _ ☐ ✕
C:\>ipconfig

Windows IP Configuration


Ethernet adapter Local Area Connection 5:

    Connection-specific DNS Suffix  . :
    IP Address. . . . . . . . . . . . : 10.10.20.5
    Subnet Mask . . . . . . . . . . . : 25.25.25.192
    Default Gateway . . . . . . . . . : 10.10.20.5

C:\>_
```

FIGURE 23.13

IP details for a computer. (For color version of this figure, the reader is referred to the online version of this chapter.)

The ipconfig command has several command line options that cause it to display additional information. The most useful of the options are:

•	ipconfig /all	Displays IP address information as well as DNS (Domain Name System). A Domain Name Server is the computer that translates a URL, e.g., www.amazon.com, into an IP address
•	ipconfig / release	Terminates active TCP/IP connections on the computer's network adaptors, i.e., NICs
•	ipconfig / displaydns	Displays all remote server names and IP addresses in the DNS cache. Useful if you want to see the IP address that a URL has translated into
•	ipconfig / flushdns	Clears the DNS cache. This command is useful if the contents of the DNS cache become corrupted
•	ipconfig / renew	Reestablished connections on the NIC

23.3.2 Hostname command

The hostname lists the name of the computer that it ran on. If you have a number of remote sessions with different servers, this simple command can help you keep track of which session is connected to which server. Figure 23.14 shows the output from a hostname command.

```
Command Prompt                         _ ☐ ✕
C:\>hostname
OP002

C:\>_
```

FIGURE 23.14

Hostname for a computer (For color version of this figure, the reader is referred to the online version of this chapter.)

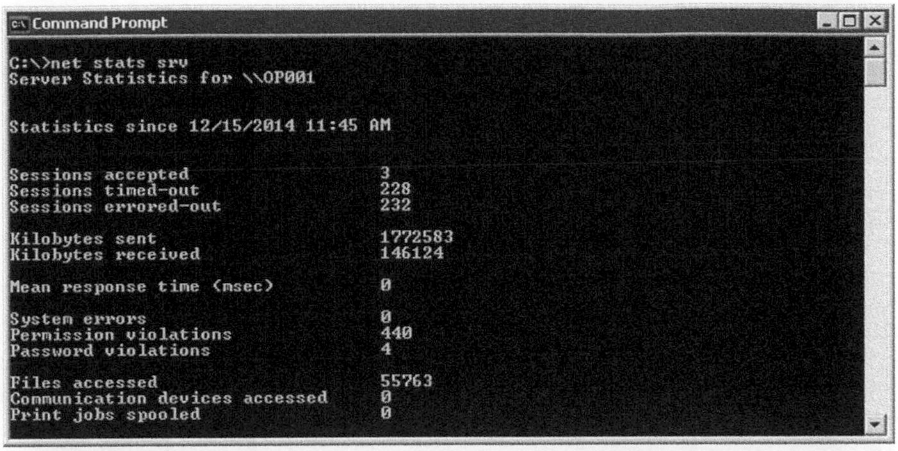

FIGURE 23.15

Uptime for a Windows computer. (For color version of this figure, the reader is referred to the online version of this chapter.)

23.3.3 net stats srv command

There will be times when you need to know how long a server have been up. On a Windows server, the command *net stats srv* provides a great deal of information about activity on the box. The first piece of information listed is the time when this computer was last rebooted. The actual label on this line is "Statistics since" and then the date and time of the reboot are listed. Figure 23.15 shows the initial lines of output from the *net stats srv* command.

23.3.4 Driverquery

The definition of a software driver is that it's piece of software written to enable a computer to communicate with a hardware device. For example, a computer needs drivers to interact with a keyboard, hard drive, monitor, mouse, printer, CD-ROM drive.

Any computer will have a number of drivers loaded on it. The specific drivers on a computer will be changed as new devices are connected to it. Updated versions of drivers might be distributed by a vendor if the newer version is more efficient or corrects errors that existed in the prior version. To see the list of drivers on a computer, you can enter "driverquery" in a command prompt window. The output of driverquery is shown in Figure 23.16.

Be prepared for a significant number of lines to be output from the driverquery command. You might want to use some of these following commands to make the output more understandable.

- More—to break output into multiple windows
- Find—to only output specific lines
- Clip—to paste the output into the clipboard buffer

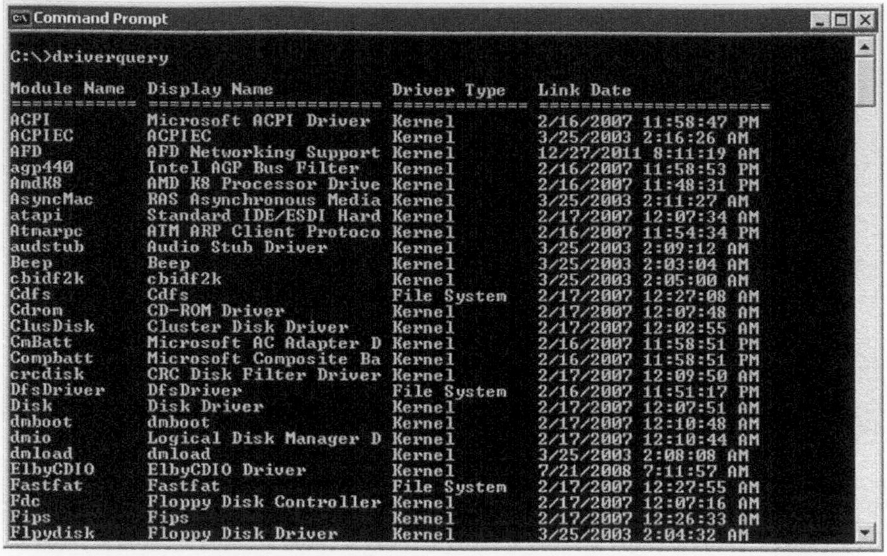

FIGURE 23.16

Output of the driverquery command. (For color version of this figure, the reader is referred to the online version of this chapter.)

FIGURE 23.17

Ways to see if Java is on a computer. (For color version of this figure, the reader is referred to the online version of this chapter.)

23.3.5 Java

Many servers, especially those that support web-based applications, have elements of Java loaded onto them. There are several straightforward commands that can be run in a command prompt to see if Java is loaded on a computer. Figure 23.17 shows the output of these commands. The commands and their meaning are:

Java -version	Determines whether the Java JRE (Java Runtime Environment) exists on a computer. Applications typically only require the JRE
Javac -version	Determines whether the full JDK (Java Development Kit) exists on a computer. The JDK is needed by developers, but not typically needed on an application server
set JAVA_HOME	If Java exists on a computer, then environment variable JAVA_HOME is normally used to define its location. The set command shows the value in variable JAVA_HOME
Echo %JAVA_HOME%	Another way to display the contents of an environment variable

23.3.6 **WMIC**

WMIC (Windows Management Instrumentation Command-line) offers an incredible amount of functionality packed into a single command. Depending on the parameters specified, it can return details about the hardware or software on a server. To really understand the full capabilities of this command, you have to play with it a lot to become proficient with it. Run it with the help option, i.e., "wmic /?" to get a list of parameters and options.

Some of the basic options of the wmic command are listed and described here.

• wmic baseboard list	Provides details about the computer's motherboard
• wmic product list	Lists software products that have been loaded on the machine
• wmic process list	Lists processes that are currently running on the server
• wmic service list	Lists services that have been defined on the server
• wmic startup list	Executables that are started when the server boots up

The output of the wmic command can be fairly long. There are several very useful options for dealing with the output. For example, you can:

- Include the "brief" option in the wmic command, e.g., "wmic product list brief"
- Specify an output file in the wmic command, e.g., "wmic output:product_list.txt product list"
- Pipe the output to a file by appending "| filename" to the end of your wmic command
- Pipe the output through the more command to have better control of the output
- Pipe the output to the clipboard buffer by appending "| clip" to the end of your command

Using the "get" option within wmic, you can specify that only certain columns be displayed. This is another way of cutting down the output of the command. Figure 23.18 shows the output of the *wmic product get name, version, vendor* command.

FIGURE 23.18

Output of the wmic command. (For color version of this figure, the reader is referred to the online version of this chapter.)

23.3.7 Terminal services

All Windows server operating systems and all Windows desktop operating systems from XP onward have a feature called Terminal Server included in them. This software allows users to remotely log onto, i.e., connect to, the computer. When a user logs in remotely using RDC (Remote Desktop Connection) for example, it creates a client session dedicated to their connection. Application Administrators frequently use RDC to monitor and control what's happening on application servers that are located hundreds or thousands of miles away.

The Terminal Services Manager provides an insight into connections on the server. For example, it lists users, sessions, and processes that are running on a server. As an Application Administrator, these details give you an overview of what's happening on the server as well as the ability to control who is currently connected to the server.

23.3.7.1 Disconnecting vs. logging off

When you are done with your remote connection to a server, you need to understand that there is a difference between logging off and disconnecting.

- When you disconnect, your remote session with the server continues to exist. Any programs that were started during your session continue to remain active. If you log in again later, you will be reconnected to the existing session and see that the programs you launched are still running.
- When you log off, your remote session is completely closed. Any programs that were started during your session are terminated.

Disconnecting instead of logging off ties up resources that will not available to other users. One specific resource that continues to be tied up is a session connection. The default for many servers is to allow only two connections to be made to it at a time. Leaving your connection in place may prevent others from connecting to the server. If you need your session to stay active that's fine, but don't leave it running if there is no need to do so.

23.3.7.2 Terminal services manager

To bring up the Terminal Services Manager, left-click on Start | Administrative Tools | Terminal Services Manager. The initial screen that you'll see is shown in Figure 23.19. It shows that a single user is connected to the server and the method of connecting was "RDP." RDP, Remote Desktop Protocol, is the protocol used by

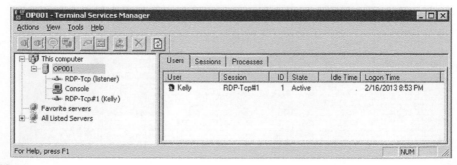

FIGURE 23.19

Terminal Services Manager. (For color version of this figure, the reader is referred to the online version of this chapter.)

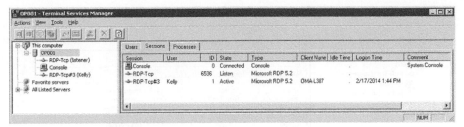

FIGURE 23.20

Session tab of the Terminal Services Manager. (For color version of this figure, the reader is referred to the online version of this chapter.)

Remote Desktop Connection (RDC) when connecting to a remote computer. The user's session is currently active.

From within the Terminal Services Manager, you can disconnect or log off any user session. To accomplish this, right-click on a user and select either "Disconnect" or "Log off" from the submenu that is displayed. Terminating someone's session might not win you any friends, but there are times it has to be done.

The second tab in Terminal Services Manager provides details on sessions that exist on this computer. The three rows in Figure 23.20 inform you that this computer only allows three sessions and currently two of them are being used. The console session will always exist and is always session 0. The value in column "Client Name" provides the name of the computer from which the remote session was initiated.

Some other features that the Terminal Services Manager provides are:

- You can send a message to users who are remotely connected to the computer by selecting the user or session and clicking the "Send Message" button, it's the third icon from the left on tool bar. You could use this to inform a user that the server is about to be taken down or if you're requesting them to log off of the server.
- Statistics regarding a session are available by clicking the "Status" button, it's the sixth icon from the left on the tool bar.
- A session or user can be disconnected by clicking the "Disconnect" button, second from the left on the tool bar.
- A session or user can be logged off by clicking the "Log Off" button, seventh from the left on the tool bar.

Figure 23.21 is a screenshot showing the third tab of the Terminal Services Manager utility. This tab shows the processes that are active on the computer. The details provided are similar to what the Task Manager provides.

23.3.8 Computer management

Computer Manager is a suite of tools and utilities that you'll use to control who has access to a server as well as how much access each person has. It's also a way to bring up other Windows tools that you will probably use. The default initial screen of Computer Manager is shown in Figure 23.22. The icons in the left-hand panel can be clicked to open other utilities or dig deeper into functionality inside Computer Manager. A brief description of these icons and what they open up are:

- Event Viewer—A utility that allows you to see events that are posted by the operating system, custom applications, generic applications, or the security software. This utility is discussed in Section 23.3.9.

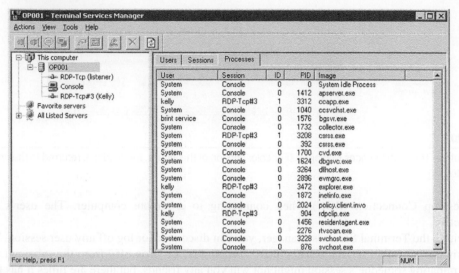

FIGURE 23.21

Processes tab of the Terminal Services Manager. (For color version of this figure, the reader is referred to the online version of this chapter.)

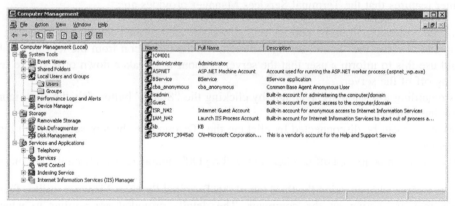

FIGURE 23.22

Computer Manager's initial screen. (For color version of this figure, the reader is referred to the online version of this chapter.)

- Shared Folders—Lists all of the shared folders that have been defined on this computer. Chapter 16 explains how drives can be shared. Sharing folders on a specific drive is just a way to limit what you have chosen to share. This feature within Computer Manager is a convenient place to review or modify any drive or folder that has set up to be shared.
- Users—Lists all users who have access to this computer. This feature of Computer Manager is described in greater detail in Section 23.3.8.1.
- Groups—Lists all groups that have been granted access to this computer. The Groups function is described in Section 23.3.8.2.

- Performance Logs and Alerts—This link takes you to the Performance Logs and Alerts utility, aka Perfmon which allows you to capture statistics on a wide range of metrics within the operating system. The Perfmon utility is described in Chapter 17.
- Device Manager—Links to screens that provide details on the devices that make up the computer or server. Some examples of these devices are disk drives, network adapters, processors, RAID controllers, keyboards, DVD drives, memory, the motherboard, and any buses that exist.
- Removable Storage—Provides insight any removable storage devices connected to the computer. For example, DVD or CD drives.
- Disk Defragmenter—A link to a utility that will defragment the server's hard drives.
- Disk Management—A function within Computer Manager that provides details on all of the hard drives connected to the server. It also provides some diagnostic capability that enables you to determine how healthy the physical drives are. This utility also allows you to determine the version of drivers running for each disk drive, update the drivers, uninstall drivers, or roll back to the previous version.
- Services—Lists the services that have been defined on this computer. The Services Panel can also be brought up by selecting Start | Administrative Tools | Services. Services are described in Chapter 13.
- WMIC Control—Clicking this icon brings up the Windows Management Instrumentation Control. Through its dialog window, you can obtain information about the computer including hardware details, operating system version, and service pack information.
- Internet Information Services (IIS) Manager—Clicking this link brings up the IIS Manager. The IIS Manager can also be started by selecting Start | Administrative Tools | Internet Information Services (IIS) Manager.

23.3.8.1 Users

Before a user is able to access a computer, they have to be defined as a user on it. The screen where users are defined can be brought up by selecting the Users icon within the "Local Users and Groups" in Computer Manager. The list of users that have been defined on server OM001 is shown in Figure 23.22. Users that have a red circle with a white "x" in it are currently disabled. Additional details about users can be obtained by right-clicking on it and selecting the "Properties" submenu option.

Looking at Figure 23.22, it should be apparent that there is more than one kind of user. Several that stand out are on this computer are:

- !OM001 is the associated with the computer itself. It is a built-in account that is used for administering the computer and domain.
- Administrator is an account that exists on servers, but is typically disabled unless it specifically needs to be used.
- Service accounts like BServer are created to support a specific application. A service most likely exists on this computer and is running under the BServer account.
- Kbourne is an example of an individual user account. In reality, this account probably shouldn't exist in this folder. Best practices are to assign individual user accounts to a group. See Section 23.3.8.2 for more information on groups.
- Guest is an account intended for people that don't have an account. Since it doesn't require a password, this account is a significant security risk. The Guest account should always be disabled as the one in Figure 23.22 is.
- Built-in accounts exist to support specific applications or services. Examples of built-in accounts on this computer are isadmin, ISR_N42, and IAM_N42.

To create a new account, right-click on the User link and select the "New User" submenu option. You'll be presented with a window where fields user name, full name, description, and password can be entered.

23.3.8.2 Groups

A group is a collection of users that all have the same access rights on a computer. It's considered best practices to define and create a limited number of groups and then assign all users to one or more groups. Reasons for this are:

- It's easier and faster to assign a new user to an existing group than to set up privileges and access for every user.
- It's more consistent because every user has the same privileges and access that every other member in the group has.
- It's easier to remove everyone with a specific privilege because you just remove every member of the group.
- It's easier to document what access users have if they are in a descriptively named group like Administrators or Remote Desktop Users.

Figure 23.23 shows a list of the groups that are defined on a specific server. To define a new group, right-click on the "Groups" icon and select the "New Group" submenu item. You'll be presented with a window where the group name, description, and members can be added.

To see a list of the members of a group, you can either double-click on the group or right-click on it and select the "Properties" submenu item. A list of the members of the group is displayed. Figure 23.24 shows the properties of the Administrators group. Membership of the group can be changed by clicking the Add or Remove buttons.

Users defined in Computer Management in either the Users or Groups areas can be local or domain wide. If an entry has a domain name separated from the name by a backslash, then the user is defined at a higher level, e.g., in Active Directory. Users "NA\Kelly.Bourne" and "NA\ovdeleguser" are both defined in the NA domain. Entries that don't have this type of prefix in front of their names have been defined locally, i.e., on the machine that you're looking at.

There are some questions related to users and groups that you should be able to answer?

- Does your audit process require you to periodically list all groups and their access rights?
- Does the audit process require that you periodically list the members of each group?

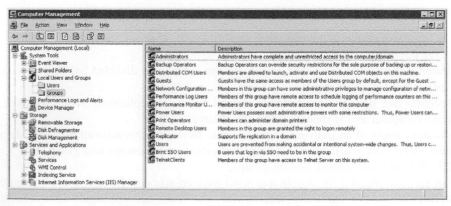

FIGURE 23.23

Group screen in Computer Manager. (For color version of this figure, the reader is referred to the online version of this chapter.)

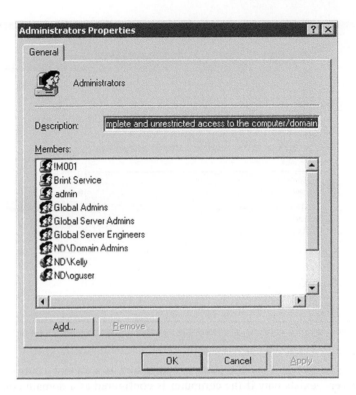

FIGURE 23.24

Users in the Administrators Group. (For color version of this figure, the reader is referred to the online version of this chapter.)

- Do you have a report or process that lists all users, groups, and group members on this computer to accommodate this audit requirement?
- Is this report or process run periodically?
- Does someone periodically confirm that each user, group, and group member is still needed?
- If a user, group, or group member needs to be dropped, is there a process for following through on this?

23.3.9 Event viewer

Windows operating systems create log entries when unexpected events or error situations occur.

These log entries can be viewed by Application Administrators by using the Event Viewer utility. This tool can be opened by selecting Start | Administrative Tools | Event Viewer. Figure 23.25 shows the default screen of the Event Viewer.

Log entries are broken down into five different categories of messages. When you click on one of these categories, the main panel in Event Viewer will list only the log entries associated with the selected category.

- Application
- Security
- Setup
- System

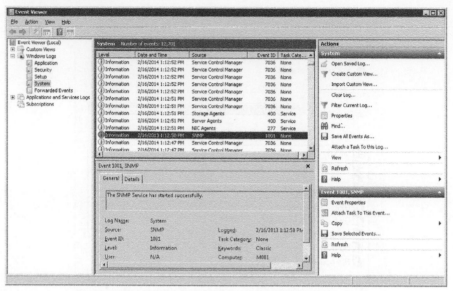

FIGURE 23.25

Event Viewer. (For color version of this figure, the reader is referred to the online version of this chapter.)

- Directory service—exists only if the computer is configured as a domain controller
- File replication server—exists only if the computer is configured as a domain controller
- DNS server—exists only if the computer is configured as a DNS server

Log entries are broken down into different levels. The levels, listed from the lowest priority to the highest, are shown here. Note that the two types of audit logging are turned off by default. If you want them enabled, the System Administrator will need to enable them.

- Failure Audit—a security access attempt that is being audited has failed
- Successful Audit—a security access attempt that is being audited has succeeded
- Information—a successful operation occurred and has been logged
- Warning—an event occurred that isn't immediately significant, but could indicate a future problem
- Error—a significant problem occurred

To view all the details of a specific entry, double-click on it. The window shown in Figure 23.26 will be displayed. You can scroll through all events in Event Viewer by clicking the up and down arrows on the right-hand column of the screen. The details for the currently selected event can be copied and pasted to the clipboard buffer by clicking on the Copy button. This can be useful if you need to document an event.

23.3.9.1 Application events

Applications are free to post entries to the Windows log files that are displayed in the Event Viewer. Some application vendors choose to post entries in the Windows log files and some choose to create their own log files. If the application's documentation doesn't specify where log entries are posted, then you should ask their Support Desk about this.

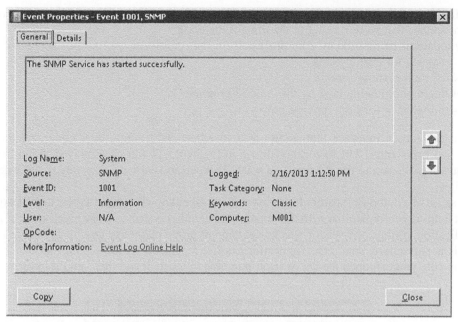

FIGURE 23.26

A specific event in the Event Viewer. (For color version of this figure, the reader is referred to the online version of this chapter.)

If the vendor has chosen to post their entries to the Windows log files, then you can access them by clicking on the Application category of log entries.

23.3.9.2 Exporting event logs

If the application you support writes entries to the Windows log files, then there is a possibility that their Support Desk may ask you to export these entries and send the export file to them. The default file extension for export files that are created with Event Viewer is "evtx." Unless you have a very good reason not to, you should stick with the default extension type.

The steps to export log entries are:

- Right-click on the Windows Logs | Application
- Select the "Save all events as" submenu option
- Enter a File name and, if desired, change the subdirectory where the file will be written
- Click the Save button.

23.3.10 Dr. Watson

When an application crashes or abends (abnormal ending), the operating system can be set up to have a tool called Dr. Watson to create a dump file. The dump file contains details about what was happening in the computer when the problem occurred. The details that are captured include:

- Name of the program that caused the crash
- Date and time of the crash
- The error that caused the crash

- Details like the computer name, the user name, session id, # of processors, operating system
- List of processes that were running at the time of the crash
- Memory locations being used by each process
- Register contents for each process
- Symbols for each running process
- Dump of the memory being used by the crashed program
- Contents of the stack for each running process

Dr. Watson has a user interface that allows you to adjust its settings. In a command prompt, enter "drwtsn32" and press enter. The screenshot shown in Figure 23.27 will be displayed. From this interface, you can adjust Dr. Watson to run the way you want. This screen is also an easy way to see where it writes the dump files.

Making sense of a dump isn't particularly easy to do. It takes knowledge and a great deal of experience. In particular, it helps if you're familiar with the hexadecimal number system to make much sense of a dump file. If your application crashes, the vendor's technical support group might ask you for the dump file that was created. This is particularly true if the application crashes repeatedly. If the vendor requests that you send them a dump file, you can open the Dr. Watson interface to locate it and then send it to them.

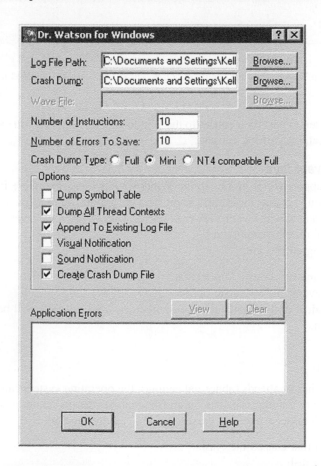

FIGURE 23.27

Dr. Watson user interface. (For color version of this figure, the reader is referred to the online version of this chapter.)

23.3.11 **Windows registry**

The Windows Registry is a database that stores details and options for any software that is designed to use it. Third-party applications may store information in the Registry or they may have been designed to retain their details in ini (initialization) or config (configuration) files. If the application writes configuration settings information into the Registry, then it almost certainly does this during the installation process.

It is possible that, under a couple of scenarios, you might have to edit the Registry. One example of a scenario would be to turn debug level logging performed by the application on or off. Making incorrect changes to the Registry can have a catastrophic impact on the application. If the vendor suggests that you make changes to it, I have some advice:

- Get the instructions in writing. This isn't an area that you want to go in and casually make changes. It's essential to have written documentation on exactly what needs to be changed.
- Strongly consider making a backup of the server or at least of the Registry before editing it. Instructions for backing up the Registry are listed in Section 23.3.11.1.
- Take notes or capture a screenshot of any Registry settings before you modify them.
- Make the changes on the DEV, Test, or QA environment before making them on your Production environment. If the changes cause problems, you don't want them to occur on Production.
- Ask the vendor's support group whether the application has to be stopped and started for the changes to take effect. Ask if the server has to be rebooted after the Registry has been changed. Also ask if users can be in the application while you're editing the Registry to make this particular change.
- Make only one Registry change at a time. Make one change and test it to confirm that it does what you expected. If it does, then go ahead and make the next change. If you make multiple changes and something goes wrong, you won't know which change caused the problem.

23.3.11.1 *Backing up the registry*

The steps to back up the Registry are listed here. This process only takes a minute or two to complete.

1. Select Start | All Programs | Accessories | System Tools | Backup
2. Click Next button
3. Select "Back up files and settings"
4. Select "Let me choose what to back up"
5. Click on the "My Computer" check box
6. When the selections under My Computer expand, click on the "System State" check box
7. Click Next button
8. Click the Browse button and select the subdirectory where the backup file will be save
9. Enter a name for the backup file or accept the default name of "Backup"
10. Click Next button
11. Click the Finish button.

You'll be presented with a "Backup Progress" screen. The backup should take less than a minute to complete.

23.3.12 **Regedit**

Regedit is a tool that is used to edit the Windows Registry. To launch it, open a command prompt window and enter the command "regedit." Figure 23.28 is a screenshot of the Regedit interface. The left-hand panel allows you to drill down to specific users, pieces of hardware, programs, or components of a software package.

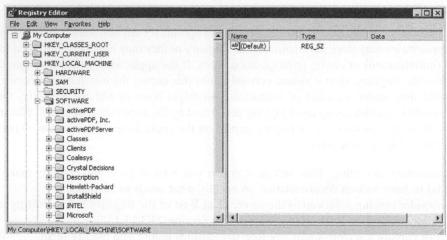

FIGURE 23.28

Regedit's interface. (For color version of this figure, the reader is referred to the online version of this chapter.)

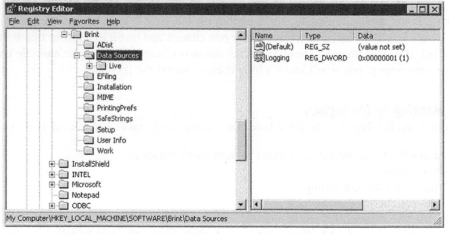

FIGURE 23.29

An application specific entry in the Registry. (For color version of this figure, the reader is referred to the online version of this chapter.)

The vendor's instructions should identify exactly what level you should drill down to and what to change. For example, one vendor's software has an entry in the Registry that enables or disables the logging feature of their application. This setting is shown in Figure 23.29. To activate logging, you must edit the "Logging" entry and change its value to 1. To deactivate logging, the value should be changed to 0.

23.3.13 Query command

Entering "query" in a command prompt will display a variety of information about system activity. This information can be obtained from other sources, e.g., Task Manager, but if you already have a command window open it's quicker and more convenient to the query command.

The options that are available are described here:

- query process—displays process owned by your account
- query process *—displays all processes
- query process username—displays processes owned by username
- query session—displays all sessions on the computer
- query session /SERVER:server_name—displays all sessions running on the remote computer
- query user—lists all users logged onto the server

23.3.14 Path

The path environment variable is used by many if not most applications. The location, i.e., the directory, of the application's executable(s) is added to the path variable by the installation program or manually by Application Administrator. This enables the operating system to find and start the application. Two commands that can be run in a prompt window to display the contents of the path variable are:

- echo %path%
- set path

23.4 WHAT'S RUNNING ON THE COMPUTER

There will be times that you need to know what processes are running on your server. Windows provides several tools that can gather this information for you. Some of them have already been described. For those tools, a very brief description will be provided and a reference to the original section where it is described in greater detail.

23.4.1 Task manager

The Windows Task Manager lists all processes that are currently running on a computer. It's installed on every Windows computer and is very easy to start and use. Task Manager is covered in Chapter 17. The default columns that are displayed for each process are:

- Process Name
- The User who launched it
- CPU times being used by the process
- Amount of memory the process is using
- A description of the process

You can easily add or remove the columns that are displayed by Task Manager. To do this, select menu option View | Select Columns in Task Manager. The screen shown in Figure 23.30 will be displayed. Check the metrics that you want displayed and uncheck the ones you don't want displayed in Task Manager.

23.4.2 Perfmon

Perfmon, Performance Monitor, is a performance measurement tool that is part of the Windows operating system. It allows you to select exactly what you want to be measured and how often measurements are taken. Perfmon is described in Chapter 17.

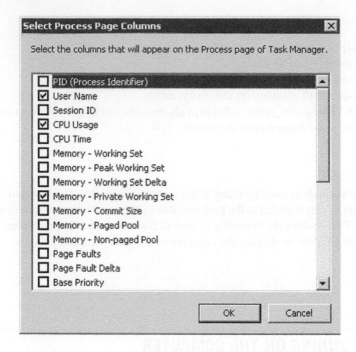

FIGURE 23.30

Adding columns to Task Manager. (For color version of this figure, the reader is referred to the online version of this chapter.)

One of the Performance objects that can be select is "Process." If this object is selected, you can select one or more counters like the following to be captured. You also have the choice of capturing this data for every process or just the processes you select.

- % Processor Time
- % User Time
- Elapsed Time
- Handle Count
- IO Read Bytes/sec
- Page Faults/sec

23.4.3 Process explorer

Process Explorer is an extremely useful tool that provides many, many features that an Application Administrator can take advantage of. It's not an exaggeration to say that, no matter how much space is devoted to this tool, it isn't enough. A partial list of what Process Explorer can do is:

- Lists all processes running on the computer along with a description and the name of the company that developed it
- Lists the CPU time used by each process
- Shows system activity, e.g., CPU usage, physical memory being used, paging activity, I/O activity, kernel memory, paging
- Via a tree-structure, it shows which processes were spawned by other processes

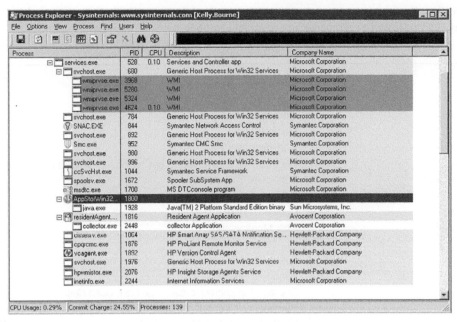

FIGURE 23.31

Process Explorer. (For color version of this figure, the reader is referred to the online version of this chapter.)

- If you hover the cursor over a process, a pop-up box shows the name and path of the executable and/or service behind the process
- Processes and their children shown in the tree-structure can be expanded or minimized. This makes it easier to focus on specific processes
- Individual processes or entire trees of processes can be killed
- Right-clicking on a process brings up a multi-tabbed window with in-depth information on the process, its executable path, performance statistics, network activity, any ports being used by the process, etc.
- Users logged onto the server are listed
- Allows you to search for the processes that are currently using a handle or DLL
- Lists all DLLs that are currently loaded into memory and what process is using them
- Makes calls to Google to find details about DLLs or processes
- Lists all handles that exist and the process that owns each
- Changes the priority of processes
- Enables you to control which processor(s) each process is allowed to run on
- Allows you to suspend or restart processes

The more you explore this tool, the more ways you'll find to use it. This is definitely a utility that you need to become familiar with. The initial screen of Process Explorer is shown in Figure 23.31.

23.5 STARTING GUI TOOLS FROM A COMMAND PROMPT

Earlier in this chapter, the power of the command prompt was described. In addition of commands that are only available in a command prompt, there are ways to open many GUI-based tools from a command prompt.

It can be significantly faster to open them from the command line, especially if you already have a command prompt open. The following commands are available to open tools or utilities

Command	Tool It Starts
Appwiz.cpl	Add or Remove Programs utility
compmgmt.msc	Computer Manager
control	Control Panel
control admintools	Administrative Tools utility
control folders	Window that allows you to set options for folders in Windows Explorer
control schedtasks	Scheduler Tasks utility
desk.cpl	Desktop Properties
devmgmt.msc	Device Manager
diskmgmt.msc	Disk Management
drwtsn32	Dr. Watson
eventvwr.msc	Event Viewer
firewall.cpl	Windows Firewall
fsmgmt.msc	Displays the shared folders that have been defined
intl.cpl	Regional and Language Options
lusrmgr.msc	Displays users and groups windows
mstsc	Remote Desktop Connection
ncpa.cpl	Network Connections utility
nlbmgr.exe	Network Load Balancing Manager
odbccp32.cpl	ODBC Administrator
perfmon.msc	Performance Monitor
regedit.exe	Launches the Registry editor
services.msc	Windows Services panel
sysdm.cpl	System Properties windows
tscc.msc	Terminal Services Manager
wuaucpl.cpl	Windows Automatic Updates utility

23.6 TOOLS TO WORK REMOTELY

As an Application Administrator, you will be working remotely every day of your career. Even when you're sitting at your desk in the office, it's very doubtful that all of the application servers will be on the desk in front of you. You'll need to remotely connect to them from your workstation or laptop to support the application. Some of the tools that are available for working remotely are described in this section.

23.6.1 VPN—Virtual private network

Virtual Private Networks, VPNs, were described in Chapter 15. In that context, VPNs were described as allowing users connect to the organization's network remotely via the Internet. As an Application Administrator, you will almost certainly be doing this as well. You may get a call in the middle of the night telling you that an application has gone down. Instead of driving into the office you can fire up your laptop, use a

VPN tool to security log into the organization's network and resolve the problem while you're still in your pajamas.

23.6.2 Remote desktop connection (RDC)

Remote Desktop Connection (RDC) is a Microsoft product that allows you to connect to remote computers. RDC is installed by default on virtually all Microsoft computers. To start RDC, click on Start | All Programs | Accessories | Remote Desktop Connection. If you use RDC frequently, you can pin it to the Start menu so it's always immediately available.

Figure 23.32 shows the screen that is displayed when you start RDC. Once you have RDC set up the way you want it, you can click the "Options" button in the lower left-hand corner. That trims the screen down to just the basics shown in Figure 23.33.

To make a successful connection to the remote computer, accurate information needs to be entered into the three fields shown in Figure 23.34. The expected values are:

- User Name—The user name that you're logging in under
- Password—The password of the above account

FIGURE 23.32

Starting Remote Desktop Connection. (For color version of this figure, the reader is referred to the online version of this chapter.)

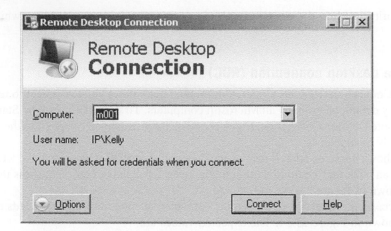

FIGURE 23.33

RDC minimal screen. (For color version of this figure, the reader is referred to the online version of this chapter.)

FIGURE 23.34

Logging onto the remote computer. (For color version of this figure, the reader is referred to the online version of this chapter.)

- Log on to—The value in this field can be either a domain or the name of the computer you're attempting to remotely connect to. If you select the local computer, then the account must be a local account on that computer. If you choose a domain, then the account must exist on the selected domain.

To be able to create a remote connection to another computer, the target computer must recognize the account. There are two ways to set up an account.

1. The account can be set up as a local account on the computer
2. The account can exist in a domain and added to the user list on the target computer.

Anyone in the administrators group can create a local account on the computer. See Section 23.3.8 on Computer Management for the steps on how to create accounts on the target computer.

In addition to having an account on the destination computer, your account must be in group "Remote Desktop Users." If you're account is a member of the administrators group, then this requirement has probably already been fulfilled.

23.6.2.1 Reusing RDC connections

If you have a set of computers that you remote to frequently, then you can save the RDC connection settings for each remote computer into a file. When you double-click on the file, then RDC will be launched and you'll go directly to the screen shown in Figure 23.34. To create these RDP files, just click on the "Save As" button on the screen shown in Figure 23.32. When prompted, name the file appropriately. Saving all of these RDP files to a single subdirectory makes it easier to see all of your connection files at one time. Figure 23.35 shows a collection of RDP connection files.

When you want to log off of a remote computer, you need to exercise some care. If you click the Start button, you will be present with up to three options depending on the operating system running on the server.

- Log Off—Most of the time this is what you want. Logging off closes the connection. This frees up the connection object so someone else can remotely connect to this server.
- Disconnect—If you choose this option, then your session remains active on the remote computer. Later on, you can use RDC to reconnect to that server and you'll be back in your original session. Taking this option is appropriate if you kicked off a process or job on the remote server that you want to keep running. You can disconnect and the job will continue running without you watching it.
- Shut Down—This does exactly what it says—it shuts down the server. Chances are this isn't what you want to do. One example of when you might want to shut down the server would be if you need to bounce the server for a change to take effect. If you do this make sure, you take the "restart" option. If you take just the "shut down" option, then the server goes come down but won't automatically start back up. To restart, it requires that someone physically push the power switch at the server.

23.6.2.2 RDC background

If you read or research RDC, you will probably come across several related terms.

- RDC was previously called Microsoft Terminal Services.
- The protocol used by RDC is Remote Desktop Protocol (RDP).

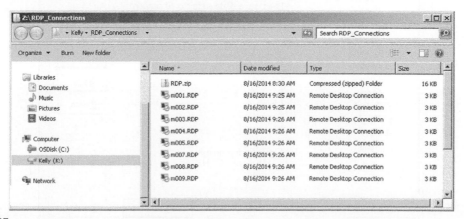

FIGURE 23.35

Setting up connection files for RDC. (For color version of this figure, the reader is referred to the online version of this chapter.)

If you hear someone talking about these terms, don't be concerned. You're probably all referring to the same product and capability.

23.6.3 Telnet

Telnet refers to a network protocol that can be used on local area networks (LANs) or the Internet to open a command line interface on a remote computer. Telnet was developed in an era when most networked computers were in academia and security wasn't thought to be particularly important. Since it by default sends its data unencrypted, the use of telnet has dropped in recent years.

To open a telnet connection with another computer, enter the following command:

telnet *computer_name port*

where *computer_name* is the target computer and *port* is the port number to be used for the connection.

23.6.4 PuTTY

PuTTY is an open source terminal emulator that can be used to create connections with remote computers. PuTTY is easy to use, powerful, and best of all it's free. Figure 23.36 shows the initial screen you'll see if you initiate PuTTY. Enter the name or IP address of the computer that you want to connect to in the "Host Name" field. If the port and connection type are set correctly, then click the "Open" button. Once the connection is established, you'll be in a standard shell session.

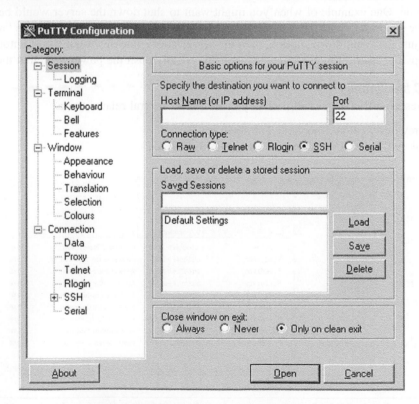

FIGURE 23.36

PuTTY's default screen. (For color version of this figure, the reader is referred to the online version of this chapter.)

23.6.5 **WinSCP**

There will be many, many times when you need to move or copy files between computers. For example, you might need to copy upgraded files from your workstation to a server or you might need to copy a backup file from the database server to the application server. WinSCP, Windows Secure CoPy, is an open source utility that allows you to securely transfer files between computers.

Figure 23.37 shows the initial WinSCP page. On this page, you create connection sessions that are later used to complete a connection to a remote computer or server. The left-hand panel allows you to define the parameters that will be used to make the connection.

Once you have selected or set up the session details, click the Login button. The screen that will be displayed is shown in Figure 23.38. The panel on the left shows the contents of the local drive while the panel on the right shows the contents of the drive on the remote computer.

Some of the actions that can be taken on this screen are:

- On the left panel, you can select from the drives defined on your local computer by selecting the drive in the drop down box
- On the left panel, you can move up or down the subdirectory structure of the local drive
- On the right panel, you can move up or down the subdirectory structure of the remote computer's drive
- After clicking on one or more files, you can press the F5 key to copy it to the other drive
- Pressing F6 moves the file from the selected drive to the other drive
- Pressing F8 deletes the selected file
- Pressing F9 shows the properties of the selected file
- Pressing Shift+F2 compares the currently selected subdirectories

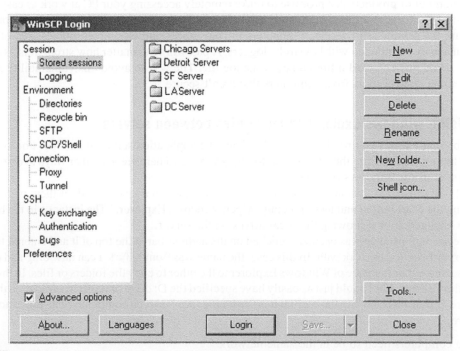

FIGURE 23.37

WinSCP connection page. (For color version of this figure, the reader is referred to the online version of this chapter.)

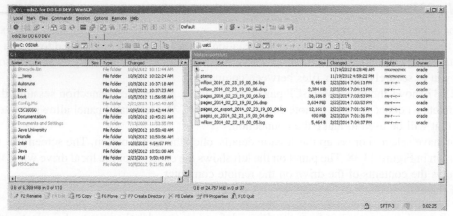

FIGURE 23.38

WinSCP transfer screen. (For color version of this figure, the reader is referred to the online version of this chapter.)

- Pressing Ctrl + F5 synchronizes the current subdirectories
- Columns can be added or dropped on both the local and remote panel
- Files can be sorted on any column on both the local and remote panel

23.6.6 Using remote control tools

There are a number of products that promise to make remotely accessing your PC at work as easy as logging into a website. While the security of these tools can be debated, what isn't in question is that the computer you use to initiate the session isn't secure. Computers in copy stores, airports, hotel lobbies, and other similar locations can easily be infected with keystroke loggers. A password, no matter how strong it is, is completely worthless if a bad guy can read it from a keystroke log file. The way to avoid this vulnerability is simple—don't use remote control tools from computers that aren't secure.

23.6.7 Using windows explorer to move files between servers

There will be many times you need to move files from one application server to another. For example, you might need to move a file from the DEV server to the QA server. There are a number ways to do this, but one of the easiest is using Windows Explorer.

Figure 23.39 shows two instances of Windows Explorer open on a server. Both of them were opened by right-clicking the Start button and then selecting "Open Windows Explorer." The instance in the background hasn't been changed so it's showing the local drives on the server.

After the second instance was opened, I clicked on the address bar at the top of it and entered the name of the other server I wanted to work with. In this case, the name was \\om003\c$. I can now drag and drop file or folder icons from either instance of Windows Explorer to the other to copy the folders or files. In this example, I specified the C: drive, but I could just as easily have specified the D: drive or a specific folder on the C: drive.

There are limitations on using this technique for moving files between computers. The limitations that I'm aware of are:

- The two computers need to be in the same network
- You must have an account on the second computer
- The drive or folder that you specify must be shared

49 items

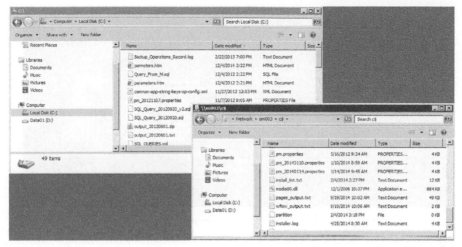

FIGURE 23.39

Moving files using Windows Explorer. (For color version of this figure, the reader is referred to the online version of this chapter.)

23.7 TOOLS TO TEST CONNECTIVITY

There will be many times where you need to confirm that two computers are able to communicate with each other. This section lists a number of tools that can be used to test connectivity.

23.7.1 Ping

Perhaps the most basic connectivity tool is ping. It tests to see if a computer is reachable on an IP (Internet Protocol) network. To run a ping test, open a command prompt and enter the command "ping" and the computer's name or IP address. Figure 23.40 shows the result of a ping command. If the destination computer is reachable, then the reply statements will indicate a successful reply was received.

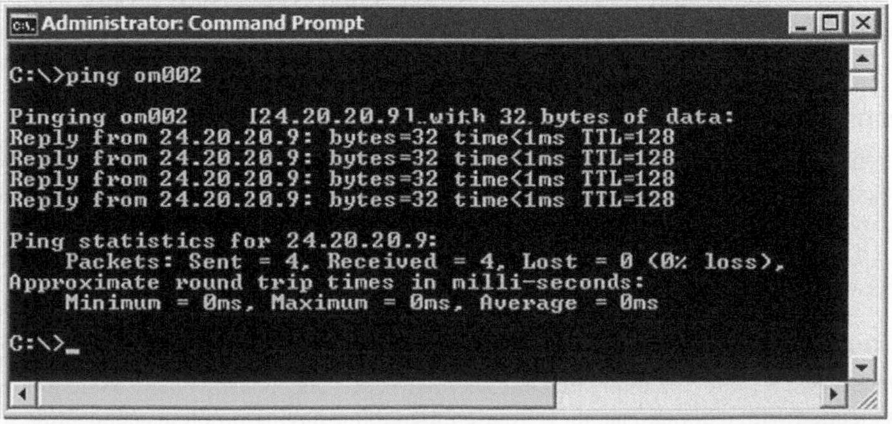

Administrator: Command Prompt
C:\>ping om002
Pinging om002 [24.20.20.9] with 32 bytes of data:
Reply from 24.20.20.9: bytes=32 time<1ms TTL=128
Reply from 24.20.20.9: bytes=32 time<1ms TTL=128
Reply from 24.20.20.9: bytes=32 time<1ms TTL=128
Reply from 24.20.20.9: bytes=32 time<1ms TTL=128
Ping statistics for 24.20.20.9:
Packets: Sent = 4, Received = 4, Lost = 0 (0% loss),
Approximate round trip times in milli-seconds:
Minimum = 0ms, Maximum = 0ms, Average = 0ms
C:\>_

FIGURE 23.40

Ping command. (For color version of this figure, the reader is referred to the online version of this chapter.)

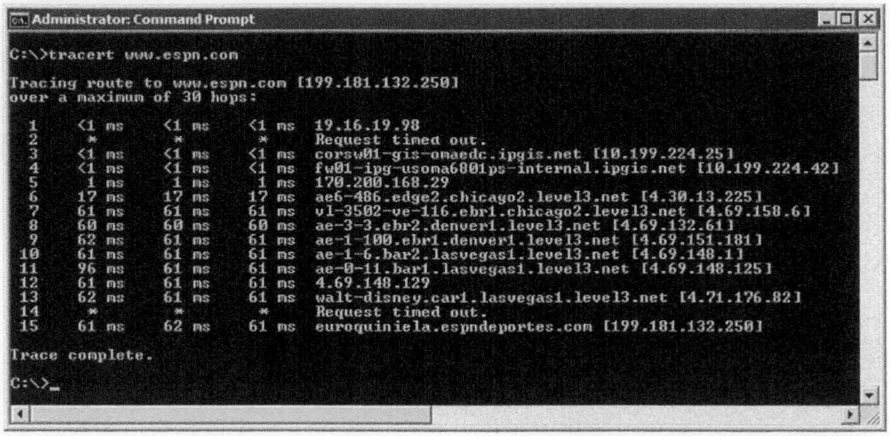

FIGURE 23.41

Tracert command. (For color version of this figure, the reader is referred to the online version of this chapter.)

23.7.2 Tracert

Tracert, or traceroute, is like ping in that it determines if a connection can be made with another computer, but it offers additional details. Tracert displays the route the packets took across the network to reach the destination. Communication packets don't move directly from the source to computer to the destination. The message passes between a number of servers along the way. Details on each hop or computer along the path is displayed on a separate line in the output.

The format and output of tracert is shown in Figure 23.41. The format is to enter the command and then the name or IP address of the destination. I deliberately chose a computer that isn't local so the output would be more interesting.

23.7.3 Pathping

Pathping is a utility that is effectively a combination of ping and tracert. It displays the intermediate servers that the message passes through while getting to its destination. Perhaps the biggest difference is that it produces performance statistics based on a longer period of time. This tends to make pathping more accurate because a single good or poorly performing transmission doesn't distort the statistics up or down.

23.7.4 Tnsping

The tnsping command allows you to determine if the listener on an Oracle database server is available. The format for the command is "tnsping service_name." The service name can be found in the tnsnames.ora file in the subdirectory where the Oracle client was installed. If the tnsping command fails, you should contact the organization's DBA (Database Administrator) team and ask them to confirm that both the database and listeners are operational (Figure 23.42).

23.7.5 nslookup

nslookup, name server lookup, is a utility that allows you to query the Domain Name System (DNS) to see the IP address associated with a domain name. If your application is having problems connecting to a particular server, running an nslookup command will determine whether a legitimate IP address is being returned by the DNS server.

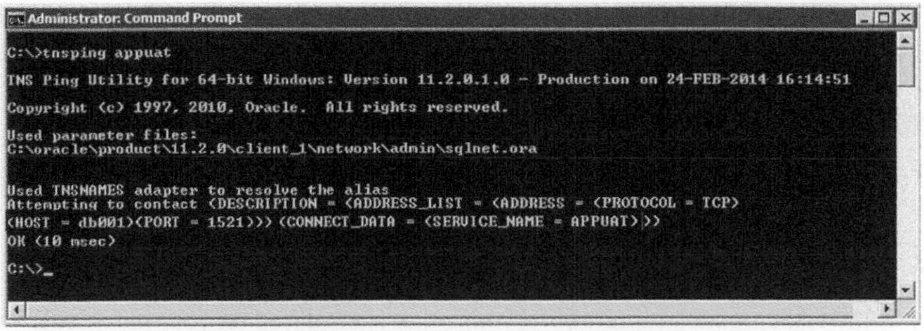

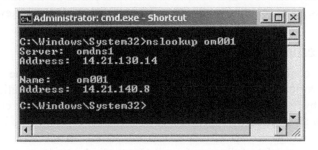

FIGURE 23.42

tnsping command. (For color version of this figure, the reader is referred to the online version of this chapter.)

FIGURE 23.43

nslookup command. (For color version of this figure, the reader is referred to the online version of this chapter.)

The format of the command is *nslookup computer_name* where *computer name* is the computer you want the IP address for. You can specify the DNS server as an optional second parameter. If this parameter isn't specified, then the default DNS server is called. If your organization has a backup DNS server, you can test it by including its name as the optional parameter.

Figure 23.43 shows a screenshot of the nslookup command and the results of a call. The first set of data returned is the name and IP address of the DNS server that was called for this lookup. The second set of data is the name and IP address of the computer specified in the command.

23.8 WINDOWS TIPS

No matter how long you've been using Windows, there are always a few tricks and shortcuts that will be new to you. I hope that this section includes at least a couple of gems that you'll learn to rely to make your job just a little bit easier.

23.8.1 Windows explorer tips

You can quickly open a command window in any subdirectory through the Windows Explorer. Hold down the Shift key and right-click on a subdirectory in Windows Explorer. Select "open command window here" in the submenu and a command window will start in that subdirectory. If the subdirectory tree is deep, this tip can save a lot of typing.

When in doubt about a file, you can right-click on it and select the Properties submenu option. This will frequently display useful information about the file, its history, etc.

23.8.2 PrtScn

If you aren't already familiar with the PrtScn button on the keyboard, then it's time to start using it. The screenshots that can be captured with the PrtScn button are perfect for documentation, reporting problems, and creating training materials.

Exactly what is captured by PrtScn is controlled by what button(s) are pressed.

- Pressing just the PrtScn button captures everything that is displayed on your monitor. If you happen to have multiple monitors, it captures everything on all of them.
- Pressing the Alt + PrtScn keys at the same time captures just the window that has focus.

The image captured by PrtScn is saved in the clipboard buffer. It can be pasted into Word documents, Excel spreadsheet cells, e-mails, Paint, or other applications by pressing the Ctrl + V key combination.

23.8.3 Paint is powerful

The Paint application that comes preloaded on Microsoft computers may not be the most sophisticated image processing utility in the world, but it is adequate for many of the needs of Application Administrators. Paste the screenshots captured by PrtScn into Paint with the Ctrl + V keys. Then you can crop and trim the image to suit your needs. You can also overwrite any sensitive information on the image before sending it to your vendor or users.

Paint can save images in any of the following formats. It can also be used to convert an image from one file type to another.

- PNG
- JPEG
- BMP (both 16- and 256-color versions)
- Monochrome BMP
- GIF
- TIFF

23.8.4 Miscellaneous windows tips

The following tips don't fit into any of the above categories so I've collected them together.

23.8.4.1 Cycling through all open processes

If you continuously press the Alt-Tab keys, then Windows will cycle through all of the sessions and tools that you have open. This can be faster that figuring out which icon on the task bar you want to bring to the foreground.

23.8.4.2 Pasting file names

There is a very quick way to open files in programs like Word, Excel, Notepad, Notepad++, etc., if the full file and path name already exist somewhere. For instance, if a document or log file has the name of a file you want to open, follow these steps:

1. Highlight the path and name
2. Press Ctrl + C to copy it to the clipboard buffer

3. In Word, Notepad, etc., click on menu item File | Open
4. Click on the "File Name" field and press Ctrl + V to paste the file name
5. Click the Open button

This can be very handy when a file name is printed to a log file and you want to open it. It saves you the time of working your way through the directory tree. This trick should work on most programs that have the File | Open function.

23.8.4.3 Recovering space from deleted files
When you delete files, they are typically moved to the recycle bin instead of actually being deleted. The space they were consuming isn't freed up until they are removed from the Recycle Bin. You can empty it by right-clicking on the Recycle Bin entry in Windows Explorer and select "Empty Recycle Bin."

UNIX Tools

This chapter is an introduction to UNIX. If you aren't familiar with UNIX, then it should be enough to provide you with a minimal understanding of some of the tasks you will encounter while supporting an application on a UNIX server. If the server's operating system is UNIX, then by all means pick up one of the many fine UNIX books that are available. In the meantime, read this chapter to get a quick taste of UNIX.

There are many instances in this chapter where a comparison between Windows and UNIX is made. The reason for this is my observation that typically Application Administrators have more experience with Windows than with UNIX. By providing a Windows comparison, I'm hoping to explain UNIX in terms and concepts that are familiar to many readers.

24.1 INTRODUCTION TO UNIX

The following sections provide just the barest background of a UNIX system. I've tried to keep this material broad and aimed at activities that an Application Administrator is required to perform during the normal course of his or her duties.

24.1.1 Shells

The interface between the user and the operating system in UNIX is called a shell. Commands entered by the user are interpreted by the shell and then executed. Scripts, collections of commands written to a file, are also executed in the shell.

24.1.1.1 Available shells

There are more than one shells available under the UNIX operating system. Each shell has its own focus and strengths. You can determine which shell you're working in by entering the command:

```
echo $SHELL
```

The most commonly used shells are:

- The Bourne shell—this was the original UNIX command line interpreter. It was written by Stephen Bourne at AT&T and released with Version 7 UNIX in 1977. Enter the command "sh" to run the Bourne shell. Full disclosure, although we share the same last name I'm pretty sure that Stephen Bourne and I aren't related.
- The C shell—was written by Bill Joy. It was based on the C language. To switch to the C shell enter the command "csh" at the command line.
- The Korn shell—was developed by David Korn while at Bell Labs. To switch to the Korn shell enter the command "ksh" at the command line.

If you want to permanently change the shell that you use it can be done. The first step is to confirm that the shell you want to change to is available on your server. Once you confirm this, then you can run the "chsh" command with the following parameters:

```
chsh -s shell_name user_name
```

where shell_name is the shell type you want: /bin/ksh, /bin/csh, /bin/sh, etc.

The final parameter, user_name, is the user account being changed.

24.1.1.2 Shell scripting

Commands that you would enter at the command line can be written to a file and executed. A file that contains such a list of commands is called a shell script. If you're familiar with DOS or Windows batch (.bat) files, then a shell script is the UNIX equivalent.

There is a significant amount of power in shell scripts, but it takes experience and practice to write them correctly. More likely as an Application Administrator you will be executing shell scripts that the vendor has provided.

If you have a programming or technical background, there is no reason you can't write your own shell scripts to streamline or automate tasks that you need to perform. My only word of advice here would be to test your new shell scripts thoroughly on a test or development platform before putting them into Production. Like any other coding change, a poorly written script file can cause a lot of damage.

24.1.2 At your command

In Windows, the default method of interacting with the system is through a graphical or GUI tool. These graphical tools are all that many or most users know about. A few quick examples are:

- Windows Explorer to display subdirectories and files
- Task Manager to show the processes that are running
- Control Panel and Administrative Tools allow you to view or modify the system
- Computer Manager enables you to add or modify users that can access the server
- The Services panel lists services that exist and their current status and properties

On a UNIX system, the command line is the primary way of interacting with the system. Everything that needs to be done can be accomplished using a command that is entered at a command prompt. Even if there is a GUI tool available to do the same thing, in most cases the command line interface (CLI) has additional functionality or options that aren't available in the GUI approach.

The screenshot shown in Figure 24.1 shows what a typical command line interface looks like. To get to this particular server I used a utility called PuTTY to connect to remote server. All of the commands shown in this chapter can be entered at the prompt shown on this screen.

24.1.3 Case sensitivity

One significant difference between Windows and DOS is case sensitivity. Names and commands in Windows are not case sensitive. On the other hand, UNIX is case sensitive. On a Windows system, the names "Test_File.txt" and "test_file.txt" refer to same file. On UNIX they represent distinct files. It's extremely common for a new UNIX user to become frustrated when a file being referenced appears not exist. Before tearing your hair out, check to make sure that the file name you've entered matches the case of the actual file name.

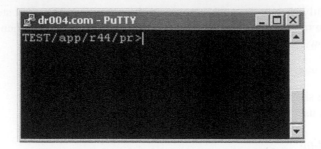

FIGURE 24.1

Typical UNIX command line interface. (For color version of this figure, the reader is referred to the online version of this chapter.)

24.1.4 Environment variables

UNIX, like Windows, has environment variables that can be set and used by applications, shell scripts, and commands entered at the command line interface. One pleasant advantage of UNIX over Windows in this area is that UNIX has virtually no limits on the number of environment variables or what they can be named. Environment variables are typically all capital letters. Although this isn't required, it makes them much easier to spot in shell scripts, files, and commands.

To see a list of all environment variables enter the command "env." Figure 24.2 shows this command and the output it creates. To see a single environment variable, enter "echo $" and then the specific variable. For example, the command "echo $SHELL" lists the current shell that is being used.

One commonly used environment variable is PATH. It is a multivalued variable that lists all of the sub-directories that will be searched when an executable is about to be run. Figure 24.2 displays the current contents of the path variable.

FIGURE 24.2

Environment variables in UNIX. (For color version of this figure, the reader is referred to the online version of this chapter.)

The following UNIX commands are available to either view or manipulate environment variables.

env	Returns all defined environment variables
setenv NEW_VARIABLE new_value	Defines a new environment variable
unset VARIABLE_NAME	Removes the definition of variable-name
unsetenv VARIABLE_NAME	Deletes the variable completely
set PATH=(/usr/local /usr/bin /bin /etc \.)	Sets PATH to be a multivalued variable. Note—if the parenthesis were left off then PATH would contain a single value
Echo $#PATH	Returns number of values in a multivalued variable
Echo $PATH[2]	Returns the second value in multivalued variable

24.1.5 Directory structure

The typical directory structure on a UNIX computer contains the following subdirectories. Of course the vendor providing the application software might require that a few additional subdirectories be added to reflect their standards:

- /root directory contains mainly subdirectories
- /bin directory contains binary or executable files
- /etc—administrative and configuration programs and files
- /lib—libraries
- /tmp—location of temporary files
- /usr—contains files used by system applications like mail spooler or print spooler

24.1.6 Information streams

There are three types of information streams in UNIX. These streams and their descriptions are shown here. These streams apply to programs and commands:

• Standard input	Input stream into a program or command. The standard input stream is what is typed into the keyboard at the system console. This input stream can be redirected, so the contents of a file are imported into a program or command. The next section describes how to redirect input and output.
• Standard output	Output from a program or command will be directed to the system console unless it is redirected. A program or command's output can be redirected to a more permanent object such as a file.
• Standard error	Error messages displayed when a program or command encounters problems are typically sent to the system console. The output can be redirected to a log file if desired.

24.1.7 Redirection of input and output streams

All streams going into or out of programs and commands can be redirected. Redirecting the input stream allows the contents of a file to feed a program or command. Similarly, the output can be sent to a file so it can be preserved. The commands used for redirection are listed here.

•	<	Read input from a file instead of standard input
•	<<	Read input from the terminal until EOF is signaled
•	>	Output written to a file
•	>>	Output appended to a file
•	|	Output written to a file
•	tee	Sends output to both the terminal and a file

Output redirection can be made to disappear with this output redirection program > /dev/null.

24.1.8 Pipes

Pipe operations are allowed in both Windows and UNIX. The pipe symbol in Windows, UNIX, and Linux is the vertical bar (|). This symbol is normally the uppercase character on the backslash key on the keyboard. Pipes allow the output from one command to be the input for another command. For example, the following command

```
ls | more
```

would execute the ls command and send its output to the more command. More makes it easier for the user to read the contents of a large set of output.

The only practical difference between using pipes in DOS and UNIX is that DOS creates interim temporary files and UNIX doesn't. From the user's viewpoint, this doesn't impact usage of pipes.

24.1.9 Running jobs

Running an application in UNIX can be as simple as typing the executable name into a command window and pressing the Enter key. Command line arguments being passed to the program, e.g., file names, follow the program name and are separated by a blank space. If command options need to be passed to the application they follow the arguments and are preceded by a hyphen (-) characters. Windows command lines use a forward slash (/) to indicate command options.

When a program or application is launched a process is started. This process represents a running copy of the program. Multiple copies of a program can be running simultaneously. For example, a user could have more than one copy of text editor vi running. Each process has a process identification number or pid associated with it. The pid is displayed by commands like "ps" that display a list of all processes that are running on the system.

24.1.10 Command search path

UNIX is quite flexible when it comes to the location of an executable file that you want to run. For example the executable can be located in:

- The current working directory, i.e., the directory that the command session is currently located at.
- Any subdirectory included in the PATH environment variable. The shell will look for the executable in every subdirectory in the PATH variable. The first instance of the executable found will be executed.
- A location that isn't in the PATH variable if that location is specified in the command launching the executable.

24.1.11 **Tar files**

The UNIX equivalent of a Windows zipped file is a tar (tape archive) file. Files or entire subdirectory structures can be compressed into a single tar file. The resulting file will typically have the extension ".tar." If the vendor provides installation software or updates for a UNIX system, then their files will almost certainly be in the tar format.

Some of the basic tar commands that you might need to execute are:

tar tvf file_name.tar	Lists the contents of tar file without extracting them
tar xvf file_name.tar	Extracts all files from the tar file
tar xvf file_name.tar /path/file1.txt	Extracts file1.txt from the tar file
tar xvf file_name.tar –wildcards "*.pdf"	Extracts all pdf files from the tar file
tar xvf file_name.tar /path/dir/	Extracts just subdirectory /path/dir/ from the tar file
tar xvf file_name.tar /path/dir1/ /path/dir2/	Extracts subdirectories /path/dir1/ and /path/dir2 from the tar file

24.2 BASIC UNIX COMMANDS

UNIX has many, many commands that can be executed at the command line or in a shell script. This section describes some of the commands that an Application Administrator is likely to encounter. Not all of these commands are available in all UNIX shells. Section 24.7 provides information on the concept of UNIX shells.

Most UNIX commands accept one or more command line arguments that influence exactly what actions the command performs. In UNIX, the command line arguments being with a hyphen (-). If multiple arguments are being entered, they are separated by a blank space. Table 24.1 lists some basic UNIX commands along with a description of each.

24.3 HELP AT THE COMMAND LINE

UNIX provides help to make using the command line easier. The following sections describe ways to make it easier to quickly and accurately enter commands at the command line.

24.3.1 **Repeating commands**

The C shell and Korn shells allow you to repeat commands that have been previously entered. They can even be displayed and edited for greater accuracy and flexibility.

The previous command can be repeated by entering !! at the command line. To repeat the last command in the Korn shell press the Escape key and then the "k" key.

Entering a single exclamation point and then one or more characters will display the most recent command that began with those character(s). For example, if you type in !ls, then the most recent ls command that you entered will be displayed. You can edit any of the command line parameters that were entered on that command.

It's also possible to repeat commands based on their position in the command history. This is done by entering a single exclamation point and then a numeral. For example, if you enter !1, then the oldest command in the history log will be displayed. The next section described how this log is sized.

Table 24.1 UNIX Commands and Their Descriptions

Command	Description of the Command
pwd	Print the current working directory
cd	Returns the current session to the user's home directory
cd ~jason	Changes the current working directory to the home directory of account jason
head filename head –n filename	Prints the first 10 lines of a file. Including command line argument "n" results in more or fewer lines being displayed
tail filename tail –n filename	Prints the last 10 lines of a file. Including command line argument "n" results in more or fewer lines being display. The tail command is especially useful to see the most recent entries in a log file
clear	Clears the session's screen
man command	Displays the manual documentation page for the command that is specified
ls	Lists files in the current subdirectory. The "ls" command has numerous command line arguments. To fully understand this command, you need to perform a search on it using a search engine or execute the command "man ls" to see the documentation on it
touch	Changes the last time the file was accessed to the current time
mkdir directory-name	Creates a directory at the current location named "directory-name"
rmdir directory-name	Removes directory "directory-name"
cp file1 new_dir	Copies file "file1" to directory "new_dir." The copy command can also have many arguments. To fully take advantage of it you need to search it or review the man page
more filename	Displays a single screen of the file. The next screen can be displayed by pressing the spacebar key. Pressing the Enter key displays one addition line from the file.
less filename	Like the more command but has more flexibility. For example, it allows the user to move up or down in the file.
grep	Searches one or more files for a specified pattern. Frequently used in conjunction with the pipe command. For example, ls	grep xyz would display all files with "xyz" in their names. grep has numerous ways in which it can be utilized so make sure you research it to take full advantage of its potential
compress filename	Compresses the file to make it smaller
uncompress filename	Restores a compressed file to its original condition
cat filename	Displays the file to the standard output device, typically the terminal
find	Finds files that meet the conditions specified in the command.
diff file1 file2	Displays the differences between two files
lp filename	Prints the specified file to the default printer. Output can be sent to a specific printer by including command parameter –dprinter_name

24.3.2 Command history

UNIX shells maintain a history of recently entered commands. The size of the history log can be displayed in a C shell by entering the command:

```
echo $history
```

The returned value is the number of commands that are remembered. If the value is zero, then this functionality is not available.

To change the number of commands that will be recorded in a C shell enter the command:

```
Set history=25
```

This will set the size of the history log to the most recent 25 commands.

24.3.3 Command line completion

Some shells allow you to enter part of a command and the remainder of the command will automatically be displayed or completed. This can be very helpful if you know that a command exists, but can't remember the complete name of it.

To activate this function you enter one or more characters of a command and then press the Tab key. If what you have entered is unique to a single command, then the auto completion will fill in the remainder of the command. If the string that you have entered applies to more than one command, then the auto completion function won't work.

24.4 RUNNING JOBS

A user can cause a job to start running by entering the program or application's name at the command line and pressing the enter key. This causes the program to be invoked. Once a program has been invoked, a process is running on the computer. When the logic in the program finishes then the process exits.

24.4.1 Foreground and background jobs

Jobs launched by a user can be either in the foreground or in the background. If a job is running in the foreground, then the command session where it was launched is tied up. Until that job completes no additional jobs or commands can be entered.

Jobs that are running in the background don't tie up the user's command session. If you know that a program is going to run for an extended period of time, it might be better to have it run in the background.

24.4.2 Starting a background job

To cause a job to run in the background add an ampersand (&) after the program name on the command line. For example, to have the calc program run in the background enter this command:

```
calc &
```

When you press the Enter key to start this job a number will be display. This is the job number of the background job that was just started.

It's important to understand that all jobs running in the background are tied to your session on the computer. If you log off of the computer, then all of your background jobs will be terminated.

There is an exception to the rule about jobs being terminated when you log off. If you kick off the command using the "nohup" command it will be immune to hangups. Output from your command will be sent to nohup.out. Input will be read from file nohup.in. The format for kicking off the calc job using nohup would be

```
nohup calc
```

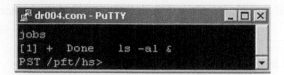

FIGURE 24.3

Output from the jobs command.

24.4.3 Keeping track of your jobs

If you enter the "jobs" command at the command line, it will list all jobs that have been started during the current session. Figure 24.3 shows a screenshot of the jobs command.

24.4.4 Changing jobs from foreground to background and vice versa

Running jobs in the background is powerful, but has a significant limitation. A background job will be suspended if it attempts to read or write from the system console. To interact with the system console a process has to be brought into the foreground.

The "fg" command will move a process to the foreground. When entered with no parameters, "fg" will move a job that is waiting for input to the foreground. Include the job identifier as a parameter to move a specific process to the foreground, for example, "fg 2" will bring job number 2 to the foreground.

Once a process has been moved to the foreground, it can write to the system console. If it is waiting for input, you can enter the expected input at the system console after the job has been moved to the foreground.

If you started a job and now want to move it to the background perform these steps:

1.   Interrupt the process with Control-Z character. The process is now suspended.
2.   Enter command bg to force the suspended process to run in the background.

Processes can be moved between foreground and background mode as many times are desired.

24.4.5 Terminating jobs

If you need to kill or terminate job that is running there are two ways to do that. If the job is running in the foreground then press the Ctrl-C key combination. This will terminate most foreground jobs. If the job you want to kill can't be terminated with the Ctrl-C keys, then try the command described in the next paragraph.

The second method of terminating a job is to enter the command "kill %n" where "n" is the job number (use the jobs command to get the job number) of the job you want to terminate. If the "kill" command doesn't do the job, then enter "kill -9 %n," where "n" is the job number of the job to be killed. The job number can be obtains via the "jobs" command.

24.4.6 Serial jobs

There may be times when it's convenient to start multiple jobs at the same time. For example, job "A" creates a file that job "B" needs as input. You could start job "A," wait until it completes and then start job "B." Or you could start both jobs and set them to run serially, i.e., one after the other. The way to start multiple jobs serially is to enter all of the job names in a command line separated by semicolons. The command shown below would start jobs "A" and "B" serially:

```
Job_A ; Job_B
```

The example above describes two jobs that happen to share a common file. There doesn't have to be any relationship between jobs to run them serially. The following command line starts three unrelated commands:

```
ls ; pwd ; mkdir joe
```

24.4.7 Parallel jobs

Just as it's possible to start multiple serial jobs with a single command, you can start multiple parallel, i.e., background, jobs with a single command. They are called parallel because they are all running in parallel or at the same time. To do, this each job name needs to be followed by an ampersand (&) symbol. The following command starts three parallel jobs:

```
Job_A & Job_B & Job_C &
```

You can use the "jobs" command listed in Section 24.4.3 to obtain the job numbers associated with each of your parallel jobs. If you want to move one of them to the foreground, you can use the technique described in Section 24.4.4.

24.5 SCHEDULING JOBS

UNIX has multiple ways of scheduling jobs to run at a future time. The methods in the following sections describe two methods of scheduling jobs. The first is simple while the second is more complicated, but has significantly more power and flexibility.

24.5.1 at

The "at" command (which is also available in Windows) can be used to schedule a job to be run a single time at some point in the future. The following command will schedule Job1 to run at 11:30 am today:

```
at 11:30 < Job1
```

Some of the parameters that can be used with "at" include are listed in Table 24.2.

Table 24.2 Parameters for the "at" Command

Parameter	Description
-f filename	File "filename" contains the command to run
-m	Sends out an e-mail out after the command has been launched
Date	Specifies the date on which the command is to be run
-l	Lists all scheduled jobs. See the "atq" command below

Two additional variations of the "at" command are:

atq	Lists all jobs that have been scheduled via the "at" command by the current user
atrm #	Removes, i.e., deletes, job number #

24.5.2 Cron

Cron is a scheduling utility that provides significantly more power and flexibility that the "at" command provides. Cron can be used to schedule repetitive tasks like:

- Creating backups every night
- Purging old files that are no longer need
- Kick off jobs to search log files
- Run reports that need to come out weekly or monthly

Some of the scheduling variations that crontab can perform include:

- Run a job when the computer starts up
- Run a job once an hour, once a day, once a week, once a month, or once a year
- Run a job on a specific day of the week
- Run a job on a specific day of the month
- Run a job with repetitions at specific intervals, e.g., every hour, every day, etc.
- Send out mail each time a job is run
- Run a job on the first through 10th of every month
- Run a job at a specific time, i.e., 9:40 pm every day
- Run a job on a specific day of the week, e.g., every Monday at 7 am

On most UNIX systems, you have to be granted permission to schedule jobs with cron from the System Administrator. If the application you're supporting is the only software running on the server, then you will probably be granted this privilege.

A file contains details for all jobs that are scheduled to be run by cron. This file can be edited by entering the command "crontab –e." The details of this file are fairly complex and are out of the scope of this book. Details on it can be found in virtually any UNIX book. They can also be obtained via the "man" page on the system or by searching the Internet. When you first start modifying crontab, you need to be extremely careful. If you inadvertently change existing entries in crontab it's possible to do a lot of damage without realizing it.

24.6 TOOLS TO LEARN ABOUT THE SERVER

There are a great many UNIX commands that provide you with information about the server that is running your application. Some of the more useful ones are listed here. Not all of these commands will work for every version of UNIX and each of the different UNIX shells. The output of commands may differ somewhat from screenshots provided here depending on the version and shell you're running under.

24.6.1 Getting to know you

Perhaps the most basic thing to know about a server is its name. This might seem obvious, but if you're remotely logged into several servers at once it's nice to have a command that will confirm which server is which. A command that will return the name of the UNIX server is "hostname."

The "uname" command returns information about the version of UNIX that is running on the server. Parameters that can be included in the uname command to elicit more information include:

•	-a	Displays basic information about the version of UNIX
•	-i	Displays the name of the hardware platform
•	-n	Displays the nodename
•	-p	Displays the host's processor type
•	-r	Displays the operating system release level
•	-s	Displays the operating system name
•	-v	Displays the version of the operating system
•	-X	Displays expanded system information, one information item per line

Running the "id" command at a command line will display information about the account that you logged in under. Specifically it lists your:

- username
- user ID (uid)
- group name
- group id (gid)

The "whoami" command also provides details about the account under which you are currently logged in.

Periodically you'll want to know how long the server has been up. Typically, this becomes important when you're troubleshooting a problem. The "uptime" command provides that information as well as some other useful tidbits. Figure 24.4 shows the output from the uptime command. The output is:

- Current time
- Number of days and hours the system has been up
- Number of users currently logged in
- The load average, i.e., amount of activity, over the last minute, the last 5 minutes and the last 15 minutes. A value of zero indicates no activity. A value of one means on average one process was running per processor. In general, the higher the number the more processes that were running.

24.6.2 **What's running on the server**

Maybe the question that you'll need answered more than any other is "what's running on the server?" This might be in response to a performance problem. It might be asked while trying to figure out why something isn't working like it should be. Or it might be asked just so you can more fully understand what is happening on the server when things are running smoothly.

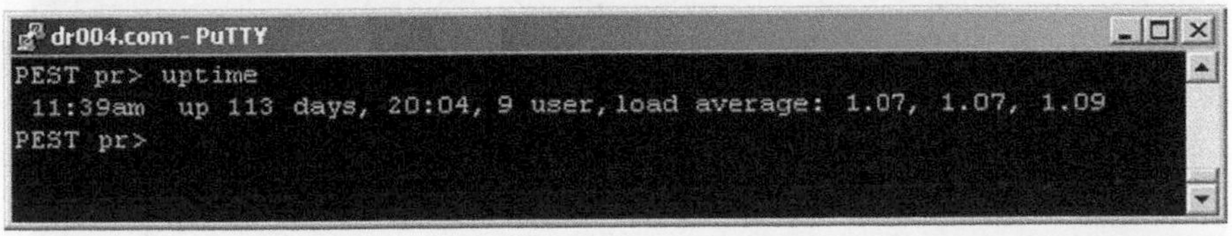

```
dr004.com - PuTTY                                                _ □ ×
PEST pr> uptime
 11:39am  up 113 days, 20:04, 9 user, load average: 1.07, 1.07, 1.09
PEST pr>
```

FIGURE 24.4

Output from the uptime command. (For color version of this figure, the reader is referred to the online version of this chapter.)

UNIX provides several commands that can help answer this question. The first command is the "ps" or process list command. The ps command has a dizzying array of options that it can be run with. Just a basic ps command with no options returns very little. Primarily just the processes you started in your command session.

Some of the parameters that can be added to ps are listed here. More than one parameter can be included in the ps command:

-a	Lists information about all process associated with a terminal
-d	Lists every process except session leaders
-e	List all processes running on the server
-f	List full details on each process
-g grplist	Lists only processes associated with group leader IDs in grplist
-j	List session ID and process group ID for each process
-l	List the long or verbose version of the output
-o format	List information on processes in the specified format
-p proclist	Lists only processes with process IDs in proclist
-u username	List all processes started by username
-P	List the processor number to which each process is bound

Figure 24.5 shows the output of the command "ps –el | more." The "e" parameter causes ps to list every process that is running. The "l" parameter specifies the long or full output list. I added "| more" to the command to have the output sent to the monitor one screen at a time.

If you want details for just a specific process you could pipe the output from ls through grep. For example "ps –el | grep test" would list all details on just the processes that have "test" in their names.

One drawback to the ps command is that it can be a little overwhelming. It displays very useful information, but on a typical server, there are a lot of processes running at any given time. It's hard to identify which processes are using the majority of CPU time when you're sifting through so many of them.

The "top" command provides the answer to the question "what processes are using most of the server's CPU time?" Top lists processes ordered by how much CPU time they're using. Figure 24.6 shows the output of the top command.

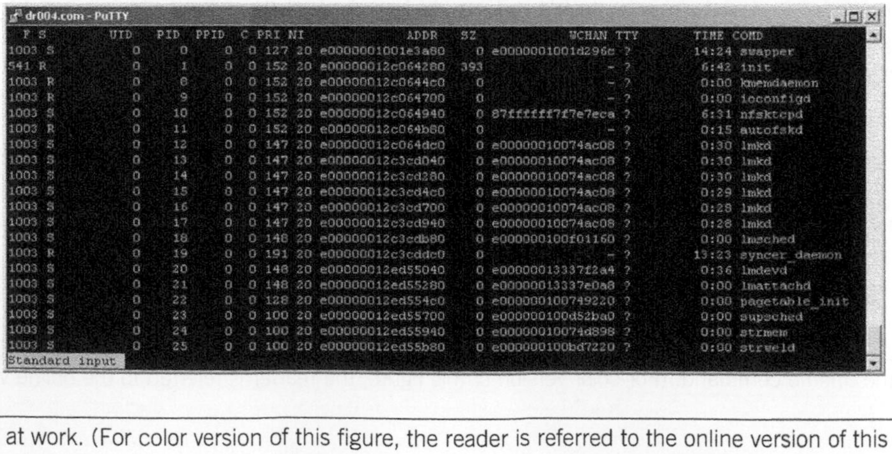

FIGURE 24.5

ps command at work. (For color version of this figure, the reader is referred to the online version of this chapter.)

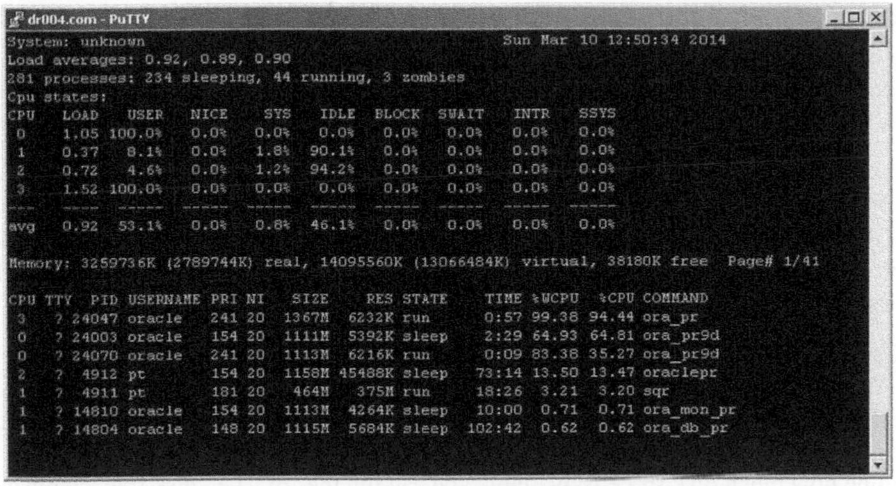

FIGURE 24.6

Output from the top command. (For color version of this figure, the reader is referred to the online version of this chapter.)

An extremely nice feature of top is that it refreshes the list of processes every few seconds indefinitely. You can terminate the top command by pressing the Ctrl-C keys. This interval can be specified by including the "-s" parameter. For example, to have it refresh every 10 seconds enter the command:

```
top -s 10
```

After running the top command you may decide that a process needs to be terminated. The "kill" command can be used to kill a process. Enter the command "kill pid" where pid is the process ID of the process that you want terminated. If the process isn't stopped then add the "-9" option to the command, e.g., "kill -9 pid." This should kill the process.

Another utility that provides information on processes is "glance." This utility is only available on HP/UX systems. Glance is much like top, but provides the information in more of a graphical format than top offers.

24.6.3 Who is logged onto the server

Typically, there should be very few people that are able to log onto an application server, especially the production server. You can use the "who" command to find out who is logged onto a server. The output from this command will tell you who is logged on and when they logged in.

Another command that can be used to find out who's on a server is the "finger" command. The output from finger provides a few additional columns that aren't available from "who," but essentially the information is the same.

One last command that might be useful is the "w" command. It's not available on all UNIX systems, but might be on yours. It's a combination of the "uptime" and "who" commands. It also lists what each user is currently doing. If you run this you'll notice that your session is currently running the "w" command.

The "listusers" command lists all users that are authorized to log onto a server whether or not they are currently logged in. This information can be very useful if you're trying to get a handle on who has access to a server. You can identify people who should never have been given access to the server or who might no longer need access because their jobs have changed or they have left the organization.

24.6.4 **Resources available on the server**

Determining what resources are available on a server is a fairly common activity for an Application Administrator. Resources that are frequently checked include free disk space, memory, and processors. Some situations when knowing the resources are:

- Most software installations processes require that you confirm the resources on the server are sufficient to meet the requirements of the application.
- Upgrades to existing applications also require confirming that certain minimal levels of resources exist.
- When performance issues are occurring one of the first checks you'll make is to confirm that there are resources for the application to run.

Some UNIX commands that can be used to see what resources are available are described in the following paragraphs. As mentioned before, not all of these commands are available on all variations of UNIX and under all shells. If a command listed here doesn't work on your UNIX server you can run an Internet search for a variation of it or of an equivalent command that works on your server.

To determine how much disk space is available you can run the "df," i.e., disk free, command. Including the –P option displays information in the following columns:

- File system name
- Total size of the file system in 512 byte units
- Total amount of the space currently being used in 512 byte units
- Total amount of free space in 512 byte units
- Percentage of space that is being used
- The root directory of the file system

The "du," disk used, command provides information about how much disk space each file or subdirectory is using. Running a du command returns two columns:

- Number of 512-byte blocks allocated for all files and subdirectories with each subdirectory
- Subdirectory name

If your server has a lot of subdirectories and files, then the output from this command will be very lengthy. You can make the output more manageable in the following ways:

- Include a starting subdirectory name as a parameter, e.g., du /tmp or du /tmp/bmp
- Pipe the du command's output to the "more" command so one screen at a time is displayed
- Redirect the output to a file, using the ">>" symbols, for later examination
- Pipe the output to grep and search for a specific subdirectory or file

The method of determining how much memory is available on a UNIX system varies greatly. The following commands provide this information depending on what version of UNIX is running on the server you're working with. Try them until you find the one that works for you:

- machinfo | grep Memory
- dmesg | grep mem
- prtconf –v | grep Memory
- dmesg | grep Physical
- show mem /page
- grep memory /var/run/dmesg.boot
- vmstat –P | grep "^Total"

Another system resource that vendor support groups frequently ask is how many processors are on your serve and how fast they are. The top section of the "top" command lists all of your CPUs.

To get the speed of the CPUs is a little more difficult. Like many other resource-related commands, there isn't always a single command that works on every UNIX system. Some common commands that can provide this information are listed here. Try them on your system and make a note of which one works for your environment:

- grep –c processor /proc/cpuinfo
- lshw –class processor –short
- dmesg | grep cpu
- dmidecode | grep –i CPU
- psrinfo –v
- /opt/ignite/bin/print_manifest | pg

24.6.5 Information about files

When supporting an application you will be working with a great variety of file types. There will be executable files, libraries, configuration files, log files, data files, and many other kinds. These files will be positioned in a great many different subdirectories. To make your professional life easier it will help if you become proficient at quickly finding the files you need. Drilling down through a lengthy path structure takes time. Some UNIX commands are described here that will help you location and work with files.

It's very likely that any application files that you have to deal with will be a subdirectory listed in the PATH environment variable. Frequently, an application's installation process adds one or more of its own subdirectories to this variable. You can use the "echo" command to display the PATH variable and see where it points. The format of the command is

```
echo $PATH
```

To find a specific file on a UNIX system you can use the "find" command. This command has many options, but the basis command to find a file by name is by calling find, the location where the search is to be made and the name of the file. File names can include wildcards like "*." For example, the command

```
find . -name "*.cfg"
```

will find all files with the .cfg extension in the current directory. You can specify that all subdirectories be searched by changing the command slightly:

```
find / -name "*.cfg"
```

You can also specify that only a specific subdirectory be searched. The following command will only search in the /usr/local subdirectory for files with the "cfg" extension:

```
find /usr/local -name "*.cfg"
```

When it comes to file names UNIX is case sensitive. If you run a find command searching for a file named "archimedes," the find command wasn't find any names with a capital letter in it. So your search won't find "Archimedes" or "ARCHIMEDES." To force the find command to be case insensitive use "-iname" instead of "-name." For example:

```
find /use/local -iname "archimedes.*"
```

If you want to learn more about a specific file the "file" command can be used. Enter "file file_name' where file_name is the name of the file. The output lists whatever the operating system knows about the file. For example:

- whether it is a text file
- whether the file contain programming code
- whether the file contains ASCII data
- whether the file is an executable
- whether the file contains scripting commands

24.7 BASIC UNIX SECURITY

Even if you're not the System Administrator for the UNIX server that your application runs on, you have a vested interest in seeing that the server is secure. Having a basic understanding of UNIX security can help you avoid exposing the server to people who might want to exploit your security missteps.

24.7.1 Superuser account

Every UNIX server has a root or superuser account. This account has the ability to do anything on the system. It can change the access permissions of any file or directory. It can modify the permissions of any user account. It can execute any command. When logged into the root account, you can accomplish a great deal or cause a great deal of damage if you're not familiar with what you're doing.

As the Application Administrator will you have access to this account? If you do then you need to be very careful. Perhaps the best advice would be to log in as root only when you absolutely need to. When you're done with the task at hand, then immediately log out of root and use your personal account the rest of the time.

To switch to the root account enter the su (switch user) command as shown here:

```
su -
```

You'll be prompted for the password to the superuser account. Enter it correctly and you'll be logged in a root. Enter "exit" to log out of root and back to your own account.

Another option for running commands that require root access is to use a program called "sudo." sudo can execute commands that are normally reserved for the root account. The format is to enter "sudo" and the command that you want to execute. For example:

```
sudo AcctgApp restart
```

If your account is in the list of users authorized to execute sudo for the entered command, then you'll be prompted for your account password. Different users can be granted different abilities by sudo. One user may be able to execute any command while another can only execute a limited set of commands.

24.7.2 Controlling file access

Access to subdirectories and files in UNIX can be tightly controlled. As an Application Administrator you'll probably have access to every file associated with the application. Periodically you may have to give access to other users or applications. An overview of the access control method used in UNIX as well as commands for granting access will be described in the following sections.

24.7.2.1 *Access to files*

Every file, which includes subdirectories in the UNIX universe, has three classes of access privileges associated with it. Different levels of permissions can be assigned to each class. The three classes are defined as:

1. The owner of the file
2. The group owner of the file
3. Users who are not in the above two classes

The possible access rights that can be given to a class are listed here. When the access rights are displayed if a user hasn't been granted a specified right, then a hyphen (-) is shown instead of one of the other letters:

- r—read, i.e., a file can be only read
- w—write, i.e., the file can be written to, deleted or a new version can be created
- x—execute, i.e., the file can be executed

The meanings of the access rights for directories have a slightly different meaning. Their meanings for directories are:

- r—the group can read the contents of the directory. Note that this doesn't imply that the user will have access to the files themselves.
- w—the group can add files to the directory, delete files from the directory, and rename files in the directory.
- x—the user can cd, i.e., change directory, into the directory in question.

The permissions granted to each class can be seen by running the "ls –l" command. Figure 24.7 shows an example of the output it produces. Every file and subdirectory has a row which describes who has access to it and what level of access.

An explanation of how to read the 10 letters signifying access privileges is provided by Table 24.3. By comparing each entry with this table we can see the following:

- InstData, the first entry, is a directory. All groups can read the contents of the directory. They can also add, delete, and rename files. Finally, all groups can cd to the directory.
- Setup.bat, the second entry, is a file. The owner has read, write, and execute access. The owner group also has read, write, and execute access. Everyone else has only read access.
- Setup.sh, the third entry, is also a file. The owner has read, write, and execute access. The owner group has read and write access. Everyone else has only execute access.

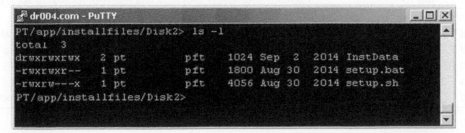

FIGURE 24.7

Access privileges shown in the ls command. (For color version of this figure, the reader is referred to the online version of this chapter.)

Table 24.3 Access Rights Shown by the ls Command

Position #	Description
1	Indicates whether the entry is a directory (d) or a file (-)
2, 3, 4	Access rights of owner in the order read, write, execute
5, 6, 7	Access rights of owner group in the order read, write, execute
8, 9, 10	Access rights of others in the order read, write, execute

24.7.2.2 Changing access rights of a file

Access to a file is not set in stone. The owner of the file or the root account, aka superuser, can change the access rights to a file. The command to do this is the "chmod" command. There are two ways to use the chmod command: numeric and symbolic.

To use the numeric method, it helps if you're good with numbers, especially octal numbers. Each combination of an access level and an access right has an octal number or mode. The modes and their meaning are as follows:

• 400	The owner has read permission
• 200	The owner has write permission
• 100	The owner has execute permission
• 040	The owner group has read permission
• 020	The owner group has write permission
• 010	The owner group has execute permission
• 004	The everyone else group has read permission
• 002	The everyone else group has write permission
• 001	The everyone else group has execute permission

To set multiple access rights in a single command you add up the ones you want. Then you specify the aggregate mode in the chmod command and the appropriate group(s) will be given the specific rights. The following examples will, hopefully, illustrate how this works. Some of these examples aren't realistic, but provide a teaching moment:

• chmod 444 test.txt	Owner, owner group, and everyone else now have read (r) access
• chmod 222 test.txt	Owner, owner group, and everyone else now have write (w) access
• chmod 111 test.txt	Owner, owner group, and everyone else now have (x) execute
• chmod 666 test.txt	Owner, owner group, and everyone else now have read and write access
• chmod 777 test.txt	Owner, owner group, and everyone else now have rwx access
• chmod 700 test.txt	Owner has read, write, and execute, aka rwx, access
• chmod 770 test.txt	Owner and owner group have read, write, and execute
• chmod 771 test.txt	Owner and owner group have rwx, everyone else has just execute

The second method of changing access rights is called the symbolic method and it doesn't involve octal numbers. Using the plus (+) and minus (−) signs you indicate what access rights should be added or removed from the current set of permissions. One clarification in this method is that:

- "u" refers to the owner of the file
- "g" refers to the owner group
- "o" refers to everyone not in the "u" or "g" groups.

The following examples should make this version of the chmod command clear:

chmod u+r test.txt	Adds read permission to what the owner already has
chmod g+w test.txt	Adds write permission to what the owner group already has
chmod o+x test.txt	Adds execute permission to what the other group already has
chmod o-x test.txt	Removes execute permission from what group other had
chmod o-w test.txt	Removes write permission from what group other had

24.7.2.3 *Changing ownership of a file*

Changing ownership of a file isn't common but sometimes needs to be done. The "chown" command exists to do this. It can only be executed by the owner of the file and the root account. The following command will change the ownership of file test.txt to the user named Jason:

```
chown jason test.txt
```

To change the ownership of every file in a directory, including all subdirectories within it, you would enter the following command:

```
chown -R jason test_dir
```

24.8 **TEXT EDITORS**

There are a number of text editors that are available on UNIX systems, but people typically associate vi with UNIX. Providing a primer for vi or any other UNIX editor is well beyond the scope of this book. I'll provide a list of text editors that are available on UNIX. If the reader needs to learn more about one of these editors, there are a number of books or tutorials about them:

- vi is found on virtually every UNIX or Linux systems. This particular editor isn't GUI oriented, but provides a great deal of power once you are experienced with it. One word of advice—until you become proficient be sure to save your changes frequently!
- Pico has a much smaller footprint and feature list than is available on vi. On the other hand, that makes it much easier to master. Pico isn't a GUI or WISYWIG tool, but has more graphical features that vi offers.
- Emacs lays somewhere between pico and vi. It offers more features than the former, but not as many as the latter. If emacs is available on your system, then it might be the one you're most comfortable and productive with.

24.9 **TUNING TOOLS**

As an Application Administrator you need to tread lightly when it comes to tuning a UNIX server. Unless you have a system administrator background, it's possible that your attempts to tune the operating system will make things worse rather than better. The paragraphs in this section can be valuable, but be careful not to venture in deeper than your ability to swim.

24.9.1 Time

If you want to get a feel for how long a command takes to run on a UNIX system the "time" command can help you. It returns information on how long a command took to run broken down into three categories:

- Real time—the amount of time, i.e., wall clock time, that elapsed while the command ran
- User time—the amount of time the CPU spent executing the command you entered
- Sys time—the amount of time the CPU spent executing system calls on behalf of the command you entered.

To use this command you enter the "time" command and the command that you want to run. For example, if you wanted to gather statistics on a job called run_accounts, then enter the following command:

```
time run_accounts
```

24.9.2 Core dumps

If a program terminates abnormally, then UNIX will typically capture a core dump of information associated with the program. If your application terminates abnormally more than a time or two, then the vendor might ask you to provide them with a core so they can analyze it. They will analyze the core to figure out what their application was doing just before it crashed.

Explaining how to read a core is way beyond the scope of this book. It requires a significant amount of experience as well as a programming background. You're probably better off providing the vendor with the core and let them analyze it.

24.9.3 Profiling

Contrary to the current usage of this word, profiling an application is a good thing. What profiling does is to examine exactly what the application is doing internally. For example, a profiling operating might capture the following statistics:

- What internal functions, c.g., subroutines are being called
- How often each function is called
- How long each call to a function takes to complete
- What percentage of overall execution time is being spent in each function

By knowing exactly what it's doing it is possible to improve how the application works. For example, if a large percentage of time is spent in a particular function, then it would be worthwhile trying to optimize it. A function that is rarely called probably isn't worth optimizing no matter how inefficient it might be.

The downside of profiling is that you have to have to source code of the application. It isn't likely that a third party vendor will provide the source code to you, but if the application was developed internally, then you might be able to improve the application using this tool.

24.9.4 Vmstat

Vmstat is a command that provides statistics on every process that is running on the system. It can help you recognize situations where specific system resources like the CPU, memory, disk I/O, or the page file are being heavily used. If you can spot situations where a resource is in short supply you can either figure out how to reduce usage of it or provide more of it. For example, if the system is always short of memory you might want to acquire additional RAM. It might also be possible and advisable to add another processor to a server to alleviate situations where the existing CPUs are running at extremely high utilization rates.

24.9.5 **nice**

The reality of most computers systems is that there are many applications, jobs, or processes competing for limited resources. If one job gets more of the limited resource, then less is left for other processes. Competition for CPU time is a common problem on many systems. There might be a small number of processes on a system that are consuming a significant percentage of CPU time. If those processes could be forced to reduce their usage, e.g., play nicely, then other processes will be able to complete more quickly.

Nice is a program found on UNIX systems that can alter the priority of a process and thus the amount of CPU time it will be allocated. If you can identify the jobs or processes on a system that are consuming an excessive amount of CPU time you can change their "nice" setting so they get less time. Alternatively, there may be a critical process that should get as much CPU time as it wants. The nice command could be used to bump the amount of CPU time allocated to a critical job.

24.10 **CONNECTIVITY**

More than likely your application server doesn't exist in a vacuum. The application might consist of multiple servers, e.g., a web server, a report server, etc. The application might be in a load-balanced environment. It might utilize a cluster to improve either performance or availability. The database very likely resides on a separate, dedicated server.

If any of the above situations exist in your environment, then you're going to be dealing with multiple servers. Multiple servers means that you'll have to understand how to communications between those servers occurs. The tools or commands listed in this section can provide insight into communications between servers or between your server and the larger world.

As an Application Administrator perhaps your most troublesome problems will be dealing with potential connectivity issues. When hunting down connectivity issues it's helpful to have a checklist of things to check and always run through them in order. After a while you'll get a feel for what's causing the issue this time. Some examples of typical connectivity-related problems include the following:

- Is the application server experiencing problems connecting to the database server?
- If the application is running on multiple servers, e.g., an application server and a reports server, are they able to connect to each other?
- Are users having problems connecting to the application server?
- Are users able to connect to the organization's network?
- Can users access the organization's network from a remote location?
- Are performance problems experienced by users being caused by the application, the database, the network, or something else?

To troubleshoot problems like the ones listed above you need to know what tools are available on your server. Every organization's environment is different, but the tools that are described in the following sections are probably available on your UNIX server. The sections are organized from the simplest check first and the most complicated checks last.

24.10.1 ping

The ping command was described in Chapter 23. It works essentially the same under Windows and UNIX. Enter "ping" and another computer's name or IP address. The format of both ping commands is shown here. Ping will determine if the destination is reachable. If ping continues to display output lines you can press Ctrl-C to kill it:

```
ping computer-name
ping IP-address
```

If you get an error message saying the ping command is not found then try entering ping as follows:

```
/usr/sbin/ping computer-name
```

There are two potential shortcomings to using the ping command. The first is that if you enter the name of the remote computer it's possible that your DNS (Domain Name System) server is translating the server name you entered to the wrong IP address. If an inaccurate IP address is being provided, this could be the source of your problem. To determine whether or not this might be the problem you should compare the IP address returned by a "ping computer-name" command with your documentation that identifies the IP address of the remote computer. If the IP address returned by the ping-by-name doesn't match your records, then a problem exists in the DNS area. Contact your network team and work with them while they resolve it.

You should also execute a ping command and specify the IP address of the remote computer. This will help you determine whether the remote computer can be accessed if an accurate IP address is being used.

The previous advice assumes that you have a "landscape" document or other documentation that shows the name and correct IP address for all of the organization's computers. If this documentation doesn't exist, then now would be a very good time to create it.

The second potential problem with a ping command is that some servers have been configured to ignore ping commands. This is done as a security measure to help protect them from DOS (denial of service) attacks. If you get the result "Request Timed Out" every time you ping a particular server, then this probably means it has been set to ignore ping commands.

24.10.2 Database connectivity

If your connectivity problem appears to be related to the database, then you should see if the database server can be accessed from the application server. There may be a tool on the application server that enables you to initiate a database session. For example, if the database being used is Oracle, then SQL*Plus has likely been loaded onto the application server. Open a SQL*Plus session with the database using a command like the following:

```
sqlplus username/password@hostname
```

If the session established, it proves that connectivity with the database server exists. If the SQL*Plus command fails, then a problem exists. The next step would be to work with the DBA team to confirm that the database engine is running. If it is, then you might need to work with the network team to verify that the application server can communicate with the database server.

24.10.3 Traceroute

If the ping-by-name and the ping-by-IP were unsuccessful, then you need to find out where along the path between your server and the destination it failed. You need to know if your computer is able to communicate with the Internet or other networks. Your organization has a device called a gateway router that acts as a gateway between your network and all other networks. Run the "traceroute" command to determine whether your communication attempts are getting out the door so to speak. If the results indicate that your traceroute attempt didn't make it past your gateway router, then you need to contact your organization's network team to resolve the problem.

traceroute, like ping, confirms whether or not connectivity to the destination computer can be established. The output from traceroute indicates how many servers or hops it takes a packet to get from your server to the destination computer. The format of the traceroute command is:

```
traceroute destination
```

where destination can be either a name or an IP address.

This command can be very informative if communications with another computer are extremely slow. It can tell you either that the packets are taking an excessive number of hops taken along the path or that a specific computer in the path is taking longer than expected to communicate. If either of these is the case these, the problem isn't with your server.

24.10.4 tnsping

tnsping is a utility provided by Oracle that determines if connectivity to the Oracle database server can be established. If your application uses an Oracle database, then you can use tnsping to determine if the application server can communicate with the Oracle database server. The format of the command is:

```
tnsping service-name
```

If you don't know the value of the service name you can find it in the tnsnames.ora file within the Oracle Client software subdirectory.

24.10.5 netstat

netstat displays the following network communications related information:

- Active ports—running netstat with the—an option displays a list of all active ports. This means a list of incoming and outgoing network connections that are currently open on the server. It also lists the process that opened each port, whether the port is open for input or output and what protocol is being used.
- Routing tables—the routing table holds the list of computers that can be directly communicated with. It might be a surprise to you, but your server isn't aware of every server on the Internet. It is aware of a few other computers which are aware of a few more computers which are aware of still more computers, etc. To view only routing table information include the –r option when calling netstat.
- Statistics by protocol can be obtained by running netstat with the –s option displays a list of statistics for each of the protocols (tcp, udp, ip, icmp, igmp) that are supported. Some of the stats that are displayed are: packets sent, packets received, connection requests, connection accepts, connections established, and timeouts.

24.10.6 ruptime

ruptime, remote uptime, shows the status of all machines on the network. It also provides information on how long each computer has been up and what its recent load level is. The formation of ruptime is as follows:

```
ruptime
```

24.10.7 **rwho**

rwho, remote who, lists who is logged onto all machines in network. Be aware that rwho isn't available on all networks due to security concerns. If you need to know who is logged into another computer and "rwho" doesn't work, then you'll have to remote to that machine and run "who" on it. The format of this command is:

```
rwho
```

24.10.8 **nslookup**

If your users or application is no longer able to connect to a server, the problem could be that the local name server has out of date or otherwise inaccurate information. The nslookup command allows you to query the Domain Name System (DNS) to gather information on domain names it contains. Using it you can learn the name and IP address of the name server that is being used. You can also obtain the IP addresses of machines that the name server is maintaining information on.

Figure 24.8 shows the results of an nslookup call to get the details on server "dr005." The nslookup command has other available parameters which can be seen on the man page for it.

24.10.9 **Firewall problems**

It's possible that your organization's firewall is causing the connectivity problems. It's not uncommon for a change in a firewall's configuration to cause problems connecting to a server that was working just fine yesterday. Depending on your level of expertise you could investigate this yourself or contact the organization's team that administers the firewall. A word of warning is definitely in order here: be very careful not to cause problems or make unapproved changes of the firewall. Doing so could cause extremely serious problems for you, your users, other applications, and their users.

If you're knowledge about the organization's firewall, you might consider checking the firewall configuration or its logs to see if there are any clues about the problem. Two commands that might provide some insight are:

iptables −n −L	Lists all rules configured in the firewall. If you're not familiar with firewall rules, then the output from this command will probably be undecipherable to you.
tail −f /var/log/ messages	Repeatedly lists the 10 most recently added entries in the log files located in directory /var/log/ messages.

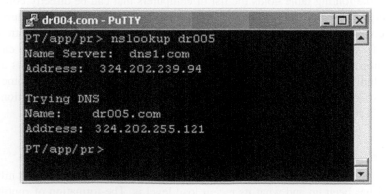

FIGURE 24.8

nslookup command. (For color version of this figure, the reader is referred to the online version of this chapter.)

24.10.10 **Network analysis tools**

There are a number of network analysis tools that can be acquired to provide detailed information on the communications between your server and other machines. Providing an in-depth description of any of them is beyond the scope of this book, but a brief description of some tools that are available is provided.

24.10.10.1 *tcpdump*

tcpdump is a packet analyzer that is launched from the command line. It can be used to analyze network traffic by intercepting and displaying packets that are being created or received by the computer it's running on. It runs on Linux and most UNIX-type operating systems.

24.10.10.2 *Wireshark*

Wireshark is an open source tool that is used for troubleshooting network problems. It runs on Linux, Windows, and many UNIX-like operating systems. You can use Wireshark to capture all packets on the network, but need to be careful that the volume of traffic being captured doesn't become overwhelming. The GUI (graphical user interface) in Wireshark makes it relatively easy to capture only the specific traffic that you're interested in.

24.10.10.3 *Cheops*

Cheops is an open source package that provides numerous network-related utilities. Using it you can locate, diagnose, and manage network resources. It can identify the operating systems of all hosts on the network. It provides a mapping of your network and if it's especially large you can break the overall map down into multiple views. A port scanner documents what tcp ports are being used.

24.10.11 *Connectivity tools*

There are a number of connectivity-related tools available in UNIX. They are described in the following sections. Application Administrators should have at least a working knowledge of connectivity tools.

24.10.11.1 *Telnet*

Telnet is a utility that enables you to remotely connect to another computer and open a terminal session on it. Use of telnet has diminished significantly because it isn't a secure communication method. If you want to log onto another computer using telnet the format is:

```
telnet remote_computer.domain.org
```

You will be prompted for an ID and password to complete the connection process. If the computer is on the same network as the computer you are logged into, then you can omit the ".domain.org" from the command.

24.10.11.2 *rsh*

Rrsh (remote shell) is another method of remotely connecting to another computer and running a terminal session on it. To use rsh to open a session on a remote computer, you must have an account on that computer. When the connection is established, you'll be prompted to enter your password. The format for using rsh is:

```
rsh remote_computer.domain.org
```

One variation of rsh is that it can be used to execute just a single command on the remote computer instead of opening a terminal session. The format for using rsh in this way is:

```
rsh -l username remote_computer.domain.org command
```

24.10.11.3 *ssh*

ssh (secure shell) is a more secure way to log onto a remote system. ssh offers similar functionality to rsh but more securely. Communicates passed between computers during an ssh session are encrypted, so they are much better protected than either telnet or rsh. The format of the ssh command to initiate a remote terminal session is:

```
ssh remote_computer.domain.org
```

You will be prompted for the password before the remote session is established.

24.10.11.4 PuTTY

PuTTY is an open source utility that allows you to connect with remote computers. Although it was originally written for Windows it has been ported to a number of UNIX platforms. PuTTY was described in detail in Section 23.5.4 of Chapter 23.

24.10.11.5 ftp

ftp, file transfer protocol, is a UNIX application that is used to transfer files between machines over a network. There are numerous GUI implementations of ftp, but most UNIX systems support the command line version of this tool. To initiate an ftp session enter the following command:

```
ftp remote_computer.domain.org
```

You will be prompted for your username and password. Once your ftp session has been established, you can use any of the following basic instructions to transfer files to or from the remote computer:

- cd—change the working directory on the remote computer
- lcd—change the working directory on your local computer
- mkdir—make a directory on the remote computer
- ls—list files in the working directory on the remote computer
- bin—sets the mode so file will be transferred in binary mode
- asc—sets the mode so files will be transferred in ASCII, i.e., characters, mode
- put—moves a file from the local computer to the remote computer
- get—retrieves a file from the remote computer to the local computer
- help—displays a list of available commands and their parameters
- quit—exit out of the ftp session

24.10.11.6 rcp

rcp, remote copy, is a UNIX command that allows you to transfer one or more files to or from a remote computer. In order to move files to or from another computer, you must already have an active account on the remote machine.

The format of a basic rcp command to copy a file to a remote computer is:

```
rcp example.txt kellyb@remote_computer.domain.org:
```

The command to copy a file from a remote computer to your local computer is:

```
rcp kellyb@remote_computer.domain.org:example.txt
```

24.10.11.7 scp

scp, secure copy, has similar syntax and functionality as rcp, but is more secure. SCP encrypts the contents of the file before transferring it. If someone is capturing and examining the packets in your file transfer they wouldn't be able to read them.

The format of a basic scp command to copy a file to a remote computer is:

```
scp example.txt kellyb@remote_computer.domain.org:
```

The command to copy a file from a remote computer to your local computer is:

```
scp kellyb@remote_computer.domain.org:example.txt
```

Linux Tools

Linux is a derivative of UNIX, so many of the commands and techniques described in Chapter 24 on UNIX apply to Linux as well. In this chapter, I tried to list only the commands and features that are unique to Linux or are significantly changed from their UNIX incantation.

25.1 INTRODUCTION TO LINUX

Linux was created to be a free alternative to UNIX. It currently runs on a diverse set of platforms from desktop machines to very large servers. Updates to Linux are provided by a dedicated collection of developers who contribute the time and expertise expecting no compensation.

25.2 SHELLS

Like UNIX systems, in Linux the shell is a program that interfaces between the user and the operating system. The primary shells associated with Linux are described in the following sections.

25.2.1 Bash

Bash or "The Bourne Again Shell," is the standard shell for Linux systems. It is a superset of the Bourne shell. Virtually, all commands and scripts that work in the Bourne shell will also work in the Bash shell.

25.2.2 tcsh

The tcsh shell is an extension of the C shell. Scripts that were written in the C shell will run in the tcsh shell.

25.3 DIRECTORY STRUCTURE

The directory structures of UNIX and Linux are almost identical. Directories that will typically be found on a Linux machine but not on a UNIX machine include the following:

- /run—used to store temporary files. They aren't placed in the /tmp directory because it can be deleted
- /selinux—used by secure Linux installations

25.4 ENVIRONMENT VARIABLES

Printenv	Like the UNIX env command, this displays all defined environment variables
Set	If no arguments are provided, this displays the values of all variables defined in the current shell
Readonly	Prevents new values from being assigned to the shell variables in the argument list of this command

25.5 BASIC LINUX COMMANDS

Some of the commands that are unique to Linux that an Application Administrator is likely to use are listed here. Many of these commands have a number of arguments that have a significant impact on the final result. To learn details about each command, you should utilize the "man" command to see the manual page on it.

Command	Description of the Command
change	Changes the expiration date of a user password
cksum	Computes the CRC (Cyclic Redundant Check) for the file(s) in the argument list. The CRC is used to verify that a file hasn't been corrupted
egrep	Produces the same result as the grep command with the -E, i.e., full regular expression pattern searching
find	Searches the directory tree for files that meet the user-entered specifications
gawk	GNU (Gnu is not UNIX) version of awk which is a pattern-matching scripting language
gzexe	Utility to compress executable files
gzip	Compresses files that are specified using the Lempel-Ziv algorithm
gunzip	Uncompresses files that were compressed with gzip
Reset	Clears the monitor. Same function as the clear command in UNIX
Sum	Calculate and print the checksum for the specified file. This checksum can be used to verify that a file was transmitted without being corrupted

25.6 HELP AT THE COMMAND LINE

Linux also provides help at the command line for the user. Some of these features are described in the following sections.

25.6.1 Repeating commands

The "fc -l" command displays a history of commands that have entered during the current terminal session. The user can specify how many commands to display and which range of commands from the complete history to display. Some examples of how this command can be used are:

fc -l 1 10	Lists the oldest 10 commands from the history log
fc -l -10	Lists the most recent 10 commands from the history log
fc -l -1 > output_file	Writes the most recent command to file output_file
fc -e vi 1 15	Opens the vi editor with the oldest 15 commands displayed in it

25.6.2 **Command history**

The Linux "history" command displays the buffer that holds the most recent commands that have been entered. You can pipe the output of history to the more command to make it easier to view this list:

```
history | more
```

Once you've displayed the contents of the history buffer, you can reexecute a specific command form it. To execute command number 5 from the history buffer, enter:

```
!5
```

To execute a command that begins with a certain set of characters, the exclamation mark is used. The format of the command to execute the most recent command that begins with "ls":

```
!ls
```

The contents of the history buffer can be purged by entering the following command:

```
history -c
```

If for some reasons you want to disable the history feature, that's possible. To disable it, enter the following command:

```
export HISTSIZE=0
```

25.6.3 **Command line autocompletion**

Linux commands aren't usually very long, but file or subdirectory names can be quite lengthy. Fortunately, Linux has the ability to autocomplete commands for you if you enter the first few characters and then press the Tab key. When you do this, the first command or name that matches what you've entered is displayed. If the command, directory, or file name you're looking for isn't the one that was displayed, then press the Tab key again and the next match will be displayed. Repeat this cycle until the command line is completed to your satisfaction.

This is an extremely useful feature but must be used with care. If you assume that the first match is what you're expecting and you automatically press the Enter key, then you just executed the wrong command. Mistakes like this have the potential to be disastrous so be careful before hitting the Enter key.

25.6.4 **which**

When a command is about to be executed, the shell searches all of the directories in the PATH environment variable for that command or program. The first command or executable that is found is the one which will be executed. This may not be the one you expected. The "which" command can be used to identify which command or program is going to be executed. The format of the "which" command is:

```
which command_name
```

The output is the full path of the command or program that will be executed.

For example, suppose the PATH variable holds the following string:

```
/app1/bin:/app2/bin
```

Also suppose that both of these bin directories contain an executable named "myapp." If you enter "myapp" at a command line, the one that will be executed is the version in /app1/bin. If you wanted to execute /app2/bin/myapp, you're out of luck. You might not even be aware that two versions of myapp exist and assume that the problem is being caused by coding errors in /app2/bin/myapp. Running the "which" command will let you identify exactly what is being executed.

25.7 RUNNING JOBS

Running a job in Linux is accomplished exactly as was described for UNIX. Just type in the name of the job into a command prompt and press the Enter key. The following sections describe tools and methods to make running jobs more flexible and productive.

25.7.1 Foreground and background jobs

Linux, like UNIX, provides the ability to create jobs in either the foreground or background. Foreground jobs tie up the command line, while background jobs don't. Jobs can be moved from one level to the other.

25.7.2 wait

The "wait" command causes execution to pause until all background jobs have completed. Two variations of the wait command are:

wait id	Waits until the process with id completes
wait $!	Waits until the most recently created background process completes

25.7.3 Terminating jobs

The following Linux commands can be used to kill one or more processes.

killall process_name	Kills the process named process_name. If multiple processes are running with that name, they will all be killed
killall5	Kills all active processes except the one that ran this command. The killall5 command can only be run by the superuser account

25.8 SCHEDULING JOBS

The same basic tools exist in Linux and UNIX to schedule jobs. The commands listed below are Linux variations on the UNIX standard capabilities.

25.8.1 atq

The "atq" command lists any pending jobs scheduled by the current user. If the current user happens to be root, i.e., the superuser, then jobs scheduled by every user are listed.

```
atq
```

25.8.2 **atrm**

The format of the "atrm" command is "atrm job#." When entered, it will delete the job associated with that job number.

```
atrm job#
```

25.8.3 **batch**

The "batch" command executes jobs that are already scheduled by the "at" command whenever the job load level drops below a certain average level. By default, this level is 0.8, but it is configurable.

25.9 **TOOLS TO LEARN ABOUT THE SERVER**

Tools that provide background information on the computer exist in every operating system. Some of the features that are available in Linux are described in the following sections.

25.9.1 **hostid**

Entering the command "hostid" causes the id of the host computer to return its numeric identifier. For a Linux machine, the host id value is the MAC (Media Access Control) address of the first Ethernet card. You should be aware that this ID number is a hexadecimal number. It might contain the letters "a" through "f" as well as digits. The format of this command is:

```
hostid
```

25.9.2 **dnsdomainname**

The command "dnsdomainname" returns the DNS domain name. This is the name of the server that translates Internet domains and host names to their corresponding IP addresses. These translations occur every time a computer attempts to connect to another machine on a network. The format of the dnsdomainname command is:

```
dnsdomainname
```

25.9.3 **What's running on the server**

The "tload" command displays a graphical representation of the system's average load. If the delay parameter (tload -d delay_count) is included in the command, then the graph will update every "delay_count" seconds. The format of this command is:

```
tload
```

To learn the process identifier (PID) of a process that is running, you can use the "pidof" command. Simply enter the name of the process in the command as follows:

```
pidof process_name
```

The process identifier (PID) value of the process will be displayed.

25.9.4 Who is using a process or file?

The "fuser" command can be used to identify the process that is using a file or directory. The format of the command is where "name" is either a file or a directory name.

```
fuser name
```

25.9.5 wall

To send a message to all users that are currently logged into this computer, the "wall" (write to all) command can be used. The format of the command is

```
wall message
```

where message is the message to be sent out. All users currently logged in will see the message on their terminal along with who sent it and the time it was sent.

25.10 BASIC LINUX SECURITY

It's probably accurate to say that Linux systems aren't attacked as often as Windows systems, but that doesn't mean that you can be oblivious to security just because the application you support runs on a Linux server. For Linux systems as well as all other operating systems, it's important to be aware of security at all levels. Hopefully, the following sections will provide you with additional knowledge on how Linux systems can be made more secure.

25.10.1 Changing access rights of a file

The "chattr" command changes the file attributes of one or more Linux files. This command is the equivalent of the UNIX "chmod" command. The format of the command is:

```
chattr [options] filename1 filename2
```

where filename1 and filename2 are the files or directories to be modified. The options can specify exactly what attributes are to be given to the file(s). Another option, the recursive attribute -R, causes access rights of directories and the files within them to be modified by the chattr command.

25.10.2 chpasswd

If you want to change the password of a single account, you would use the "passwd" command. If you have a list of accounts that need to have their passwords changed, the Linux command "chpasswd" can be extremely helpful. The format of this command is:

```
chpasswd
```

It reads the standard input expecting a user name and password on each line separate by a colon. When you have entered all of the users in your list, enter Ctrl-D to terminate input and exit the command.

If the list of user names and passwords exists in a file, you can use the redirection character to import that file into chpasswd. An example of this operation is:

```
chpasswd < user_list.txt
```

where user_list.txt is a text file containing the user names and passwords. Each pair of user names and passwords must be on a separate line and be separated by a colon. For example:

```
jkash:singer1
mdaemon:actor1
ppicasso:painter1
```

25.11 TEXT EDITORS

The choice of text editors available in Linux is very similar to what is available on UNIX systems. Some of the more popular ones are:

- vim—vim stands for "vi improved." It is distributed without a licensing fee, but if you find it a useful addition to your tool chest, you are encouraged to make a contribution to the charity that the developers support.
- Emacs—the most popular version of Emacs is GNU Emacs. It is an open source tool that can be downloaded without cost.
- nano—nano is an open source that comes with many Linux distributions. Perhaps its biggest feature is that it's easier for newcomers to use than the more comprehensive and complex text editors. nano is a WYSIWYG, i.e., "what you see is what you get," editor. If you're used to an editor with a GUI interface, then this might be the best one for you to use.

Tools for Your Toolbox

26

No matter how mature the application you're supporting is, there will always be room for tools that make you more productive. Tools can come in a variety of forms. Even a tool that seems incredibly simple can be a significant help to you. All of the following are legitimate forms of tools:

- A vendor-provided utility
- A script
- A program, simple or complicated
- A checklist

Some of the advantages of using tools or scripts are:

- It's faster than doing it by hand
- It's more accurate once the script or tool has been debugged
- It's repeatable
- You might be able to schedule it
- It can be delegated to your backup

26.1 DON'T REINVENT THE WHEEL

If a tool that you need already exists, then use it. If you're like most Application Administrators, you have plenty to keep you busy without reinventing a tool that already exists. Some potential sources for preexisting tools are listed here.

26.1.1 Does the vendor already provide the tool you need?

Before taking the time and effort to create a tool, you should read the documentation provided by the vendor to make sure they haven't already provided it. If the vendor has provided a manual similar to an "Administrator's Guide" that should be the first one you search for a list of tools. Any documents with a description "technical toolkit," "reference guide," or "tools" are also potential sources for details on tools that might be available.

Another potential source is if the vendor provides a knowledge base (KB) or list of frequently asked questions (FAQ) on their support website. These frequently contain a list of papers or tips from their own support staff as well as submissions from Application Administrators such as yourself. If a knowledge base or FAQ list is available, they are definitely worth checking to see what jewels they might contain.

One example of a tool that a vendor might provide is a batch registration utility. At one point, I was the administrator for a Learning Management System (LMS) application. Periodically, the organization I worked for underwent a merger or acquisition. When that happened, all of the new employees would have to be registered in the LMS. Sometimes this was 10 people and other times it was 100. The vendor provided a utility that could read a CSV (command separated value) file and batch register the names in it. It wasn't the most reliable or flexible tool, but 99% of the time it handled our requirements. I probably could have written a tool to duplicate or improve upon it, but that would have been a waste of my time. The existing tool wasn't perfect but did the job.

26.1.2 **Does a user group already provide similar tools?**

Does the application you support have a user group? If so, then there's a chance that it might be the source of some valuable information, including tools.

How can you find out if the user group has anything valuable? Check to see if it has a website. If one exists, then scour it looking for tools, tips, and scripts. Other ways to learn if it has anything to offer includes:

- Attend a user group conference. Many user groups offer at least one national conference a year. If you're lucky enough to be able to attend, then plan your time wisely. Choose presentations with titles or abstracts that imply they would be of value to an administrator. Many conferences either post the presentations on a website or make them available on a DVD. Get a copy even if it costs a few bucks. If you find one tool or tip, then it paid for itself.
- Attend a local meeting if there are any in your area. Local meetings won't be as large as the annual conference, but they frequently bring in someone from the vendor or an experienced user or a consultant. One advantage of a local meeting is that the most of the attendees live and work in your area. Which is a great segue into the next bullet point.
- Network, network, network. Whether you're at a national event or a local event, get to meet your peers. Exchange names, e-mail addresses, and backgrounds. The guy you have lunch with today might be able to help you with a problem a month or two down the road. But that can't happen unless you take the time and effort to reach out to people.
- Contribute to the common good. If you have a good tip or tool, then publish it on the website or present a session on it. Not only will you be helping your fellow administrators, but people will recognize you as an expert. This will help you network.

26.1.3 **Is what you're looking for available on the internet?**

The Internet presents a great source for potential tools. The number of people working with the same application is going to be a very small number, but administrators who support other applications generally have similar needs. Spend a little time doing an Internet search before you begin writing a new tool. Even if you don't find exactly what you're looking for, you might find something close enough that can be modified to make it fit your immediate need.

26.1.4 **Has a coworker created a similar tool?**

Your fellow Application Administrators may not be working on the same application as you, but their needs are probably very similar to yours. If you need a script to kick off backups and perform other tasks, there's a fair chance that someone in your organization or department has the same need. Ask around to see if the tool you're looking for already exists on someone's desktop. If no one else has written it already, then maybe you can either collaborate to build it or you can share it once you're perfected it.

If you want to be a star performer, you can put together a way for you and your coworkers to share tools that each has developed. You could do this on a portal, on a shared drive, or during a monthly lunch-and-learn session. Management should see these efforts as a great example of teamwork and recognize that you're going above and beyond the call of duty.

26.1.5 Is a commercial product available?

Developers tend to think they can quickly put together something that will meet their needs. If the objective is simple enough this very well might be true, but as the requirements of a tool become more complex then the time and development cost to develop it can easily exceed the price tag of an existing product. Use your best judgment but don't let it be clouded by unrealistic estimates of how quickly you or your team can develop a tool.

26.2 EXAMPLES OF TOOLS

Some categories of tools that will prove to be useful are described in the following sections. These are just a few suggestions of things I've encountered. Anything that you find yourself doing more than once should be a candidate for a tool. If a particular task takes more than just a few minutes to complete, then it too is a possible candidate for a tool. Keep a list of things you like to automate or script and in your spare time develop the ones that will give you the most bang for the buck.

26.2.1 Status check

If your application consists of more than one service or process running on the server, then it might be worthwhile to write a script or a batch file to query the status of the services. If you support multiple applications, it's easy to forget exactly what services support each application. Having a batch file makes it easier and faster to check the application's status, especially if something has gone wrong and you want to know about it in a hurry.

A very simple batch file, AppCheck.bat, that runs on a Windows server and returns the status of the four services behind application FIN_APP is shown here:

```
REM Returns the status of services associated with FIN_APP
sc query FinAppAdminServer | find "STATE"
sc query FinAppServer1 | find "STATE"
sc query InterstateAdminServer | find "STATE"
sc query InterstateServer1 | find "STATE"
```

The output created by that batch file would look like the screenshot in Figure 26.1. If the status of all services is "RUNNING," then the application is up. Any other status values, e.g., STOPPED, represent a problem with the application.

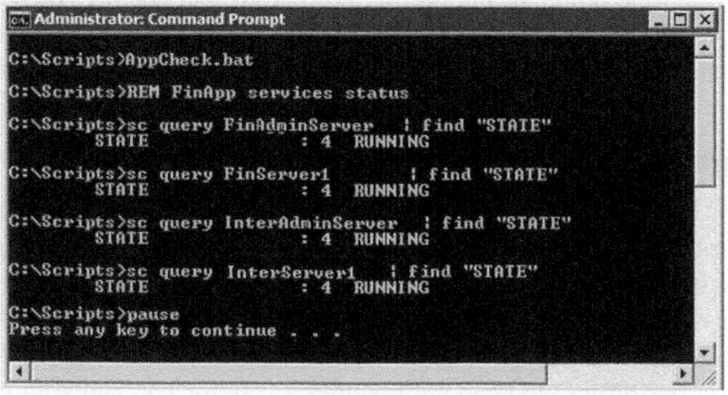

FIGURE 26.1

Application status batch file results. (For color version of this figure, the reader is referred to the online version of this chapter.)

If your application runs on multiple servers, it's possible to add query statements to check the status of services running on another server. Code to get the status from a remote server is shown here:

```
REM Returns status of services on the FIN_APP report server
sc \\finapp002 query CC | find "STATE"
sc \\finapp002 query Dashboard | find "STATE"
```

A script that would run on a UNIX server would look significantly different, but wouldn't be much more complicated. Here's an example of simple script. If one of the four processes isn't returned, then it means that particular process isn't running.

```
# Returns status of processes associated with FIN_APP
ps -el | grep FinApp
ps -el | grep FinAppServer1
ps -el | InterstateAdminServer
ps -el | InterstateServer1
```

26.2.2 Comparing servers

An earlier chapter stressed (harped?) on the need to have multiple environments for your application, e.g., DEV, QA, and PROD. There will come a time when your application runs correctly on one server, but not on another. For example, it works OK on DEV, but something is a little odd on QA. One way of determining the cause is to compare the two systems. If you have a tool to compare the following types of objects, it will make this task immensely easier and faster.

- The registry
- Directory trees
- Specific files, e.g., configuration files, properties files, initialization files
- Services
- Scheduled tasks
- Startup tasks
- DSN—data source names
- Database connection strings
- IIS entries
- Open ports
- DLL versions

Don't worry if you can't automate the entire comparison process initially. Start off small and then add more objects to the comparison process as you have time. If you can't write a script to automate the process, at least have a checklist of what needs to be compared. Working down a checklist is significantly faster and more effective than trying to remember what needs to be compared from your overworked memory.

26.2.3 Startup and shutdown scripts

In my experience, applications need to go up and down on a regular, if not exactly frequent, basis. Some examples of when you might need to bring down the application are:

- To perform backups
- To upgrade the application
- To perform maintenance on the operating system or support software

- To perform bulk inserts of data
- For hardware repairs, replacements, or upgrades
- The vendor might recommend it be bounced periodically for performance reasons
- To lock out users during critical times of the business fiscal year, for example, so the books on the previous year can be closed

If your application is straightforward, it will consist of a single service running on a single server. Stopping and starting an application like this isn't difficult. A more complex application may have numerous services running on multiple servers. In many cases, the services need to be started in a very specific sequence. If the vendor hasn't provided scripts to start up and stop the application, then you definitely want to write them yourself. Rather than trusting your memory and your typing skills, you should create a script that will start up everything in the correct order.

Other pleasant by-products of writing such scripts are:

- Running a script should be error free
- It's typically faster than doing it manually
- You can kick off a script and then work on something else until it completes
- Scripts can be scheduled to run at specific times, e.g., when a backup is being done
- They're easier for your backup to execute. You do have a backup, right?

Shutting down an application is usually simpler and faster than starting it up. Services or processes can typically be stopped in less time than it takes to start them. Usually, the order in which services are stopped is less important than the order in which they are started up. Even though it's faster and easier to stop an application, it's still handy to have a script that will do it for you. If you write a script to start up the application, you should invest the time to write a shutdown script too.

26.2.4 Data backups and restores

Application data needs to be backed up on a regular basis. The definition of "regular" depends on a lot of things. Some of these conditions are:

- Is the data mostly read or mostly written to?
- How much data is changed every day?
- Is the data critical to the operation of the organization?
- If data was lost, could it be recovered from another source or application?
- Are there legal or regulatory requirements dictating how often the data must be backed up?

26.2.4.1 Backups

Depending on your answer to the above questions, your application data may need to be backed up hourly, daily, weekly, or in real time. Is it humanly possible for you to back up the data every hour? You could conceivably do it every day, but do you want to? Typically, data is backed up during the "off-hours." Do you want to be doing a backup every night at midnight for foreseeable future? I wouldn't want to have that obligation hanging over my head.

If you can't or don't want to run the backup process manually, then you have no choice but to use a tool to perform it. If you're lucky, the vendor provided a backup script or utility. If they didn't, then you'll have to develop it yourself. If you're forced to develop the script or tool yourself, then my advice is to test, test, and then test some more. When you're done testing the backup process on your TEST or QA environment, then perform a restore and verify that every piece of data that is needed was both saved and restored.

Notice that I didn't use the phrase "database backup" or "database restore." The choice of words was deliberate. For some applications, all of the data resides in a relational database. In these cases, the backup process is straightforward and can probably be handled by features embedded in the database engine. For other applications, there might be files or other forms of data outside of the database that need to be backed up at the same time that the database gets backed up. The database backup without the external files is useless and vice versa.

26.2.4.2 Restores

Typically, data restores are done fairly rarely. Your DR (Disaster Recovery) plan might be executed and tested once or twice a year. Other than that, you might never do a recovery on a live system. The primary reasons for writing a script to restore the database are if the stuff hits the fan, then you'll want the restore to:

1. Work correctly the first time
2. Be completed as quickly as possible

If the restore process can't be automated, then at a minimum you need to write out a detailed list of steps to perform one. Don't assume that you can use a list provided by the vendor. You need a customized list that includes specifics for your environment that won't be in the vendor's list. Some potential details that are unique to your organization are:

- Names of your application servers
- Names of your database servers
- Locations of any external files being used by the application
- Location of the database backup files
- Location of the external backup files
- The amount of time your restore process takes
- Account(s) needed to perform the restore

Once you have developed a customized list, then you need to run through the restore process multiple times to ensure the list is accurate. You should be able to perform a restore on the DEV or TEST environments without impacting the users. You would be wise to practice doing a restore more often than your DR testing is scheduled. It would also be wise to have your designated backup practice performing the restore process too. You don't want to be called back from your honeymoon or family reunion because the system crashed and no one besides you knows how to restore it.

26.2.5 Who's logging onto your server?

If you took my advice about security on your application server, then the number of people who can log onto your server will be extremely limited. If you chose not to take it or have been pressured to allow people other than the administrators access to those servers, then you're in for trouble. I can all but guarantee you that someday something significant will change on the server and absolutely everyone will deny that they changed it.

If 10 people have access to the server but no one will admit that they did it, how can you determine who made the change? One way is to write a script to document who logs onto the server and when they logged on. The following command in a Windows batch file will write a record listing the date, time, username, and IP address every time someone logs onto the server using RDC (Remote Desktop Connection). This batch file needs to be located in directory C:\Documents and Settings\All Uses\Start Menu\Programs\Startup on your application server.

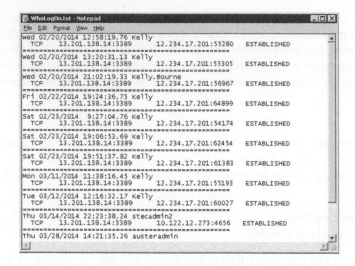

FIGURE 26.2

Who logged onto a server. (For color version of this figure, the reader is referred to the online version of this chapter.)

```
@Echo off
Echo %date% %time% %username% >> C:\Who\WhoLogOn.txt
Netstat -n -p tcp | Find ":3389" >> C:\Who\WhoLogOn.txt
Echo=================================================== >>C:\Who\WhoLogOn.txt
```

Figure 26.2 shows a screenshot of output file C:\Who\WhoLogOn.txt produced by this script. If you know a problem started occurring on a specific date, this log file can quickly narrow down who logged onto the server that day. Of course, if someone really wants to cover their tracks, they could edit this log file to remove entries showing that they logged in. This tool isn't meant to uncover high-level hackers. It's more to help you "remind" your coworkers that they logged onto the server on specific days.

26.2.6 Reporting scripts

A script that executes a SQL query to select data from a database can be a poor man's reporting tool. Such a script could do the following steps:

- Run the SQL query
- Format the data
- Name the output file appropriately, frequently with a date stamp
- E-mail the file to the interested party

The following very simplistic example of automating a report requires two files. The first file, Report1.bat, is a batch file that is scheduled to run periodically, e.g., every day or once a week. It establishes the connection to the database and then kicks off the SQL statements in the second file. A more advanced example could rename the output file with the current date and either e-mail it or ftp it out.

The contents of the batch file Report1.bat are:

```
connect username/password@DB_Host; > %0.tmp
whenever sqlerror exit sql.sqlcode >> %0.tmp
@Report1.sql; >> %0.tmp
exit; >> %0.tmp
sqlplus -s /nolog @%0.tmp;
```

The second file, Report1.sql, contains the SQL statements that extract the data from the database, format it, and write it to the output file.

The contents of SQL file Report1.sql are:

```
SET FEEDBACK OFF
SET HEADING ON
SET PAGESIZE 30000
SET LINESIZE 300
COLUMN "FIRSTNAME" FORMAT A25
COLUMN "LASTNAME" FORMAT A25
COLUMN "CLASS" FORMAT A55
COLUMN "DATE" FORMAT A11
COLUMN "GRADE" FORMAT A3
set termout off
spool Report1.txt
SELECT FirstName AS FirstName, LastName AS LastName,
LongName AS Class, TO_CHAR(DateTime, 'mm-dd-yyyy') AS Date,
TO_CHAR(WScore) AS Grade
FROM Class
WHERE a.Class_ID = 12345
/
spool off
exit
```

26.2.7 Data feed

Many applications need to generate files that feed data into other systems. For example, the application you support might need to export data to systems that belong to other departments in your organization, to clients, to suppliers, to vendors, to government regulators, etc. In many ways, this process is very similar to writing a script or batch file that creates a report.

Perhaps, the biggest difference is that a data feed probably won't have headings or fancy formatting. Most likely, the files needed have to be either a CSV (comma separated values) file or a fixed length file. A CSV file uses commas to separate fields within a record. A fixed length file has a fixed length for each field and a fixed length for the overall record length.

Figure 26.3 is an example of a CSV file, while Figure 26.4 shows what a fixed length file looks like. Both files have the same columns and data. In the fixed length example, text fields are left justified but numeric field are right justified. Be sure to coordinate this detail with the recipient of the any data feeds you create. The columns in the examples are:

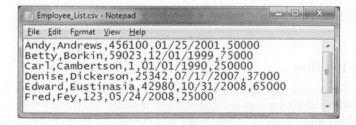

FIGURE 26.3

Example of a CSV file. (For color version of this figure, the reader is referred to the online version of this chapter.)

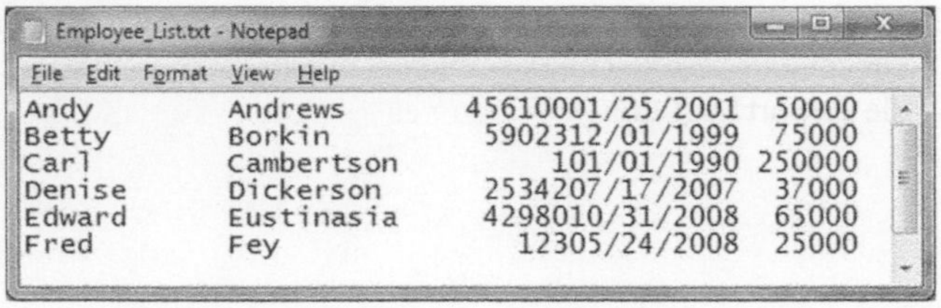

FIGURE 26.4

Example of a fixed length file. (For color version of this figure, the reader is referred to the online version of this chapter.)

- First Name
- Last Name
- Employee ID
- Hire Date (MM/DD/YYYY)
- Salary (no decimal value or commas)

If the application doesn't already provide an export utility or reporting tool to create export files, then you can accomplish this using SQL statements. Creating a CSV file with a SQL query isn't particularly difficult; it just requires that you pay attention to details. An example that would create a file formatted like Figure 26.3 is shown here. Note that you have to explicitly add the commas that will separate your fields in the output. If your data has commas in it, then that makes using a CSV file more troublesome. If that's the case, you might want to create the file in a fixed length format.

```
set pagesize 0
SELECT FirstName || ',' || LastName || ','|| EmployeeID || ',' || HireDate || ',' || Salary
FROM employee
ORDER BY FirstName, LastName;
```

Creating a fixed length file is also relatively easy. The trick, at least in Oracle, is to define the width of each field in advance. The following code would create a file like the one shown in Figure 26.4:

```
COLUMN "FIRSTNAME" FORMAT A20
COLUMN "LASTNAME" FORMAT A20
COLUMN "EMPLOYEE" FORMAT A6
COLUMN "HIREDATE" FORMAT A10
COLUMN "SALARY" FORMAT A7
SELECT FirstName, LastName, EmployeeID,
TO_CHAR(HireDate, 'mm/dd/yyyy') AS HireDate, TO_CHAR(Salary) AS Salary
FROM employee
ORDER BY FirstName, LastName;
```

26.2.8 Gathering log files

If you encounter a problem with your application and aren't able to resolve it yourself, then you will likely open up a ticket with the vendor's support team. When you open the ticket, they will want information about the problem to help them understand what happened and how it can be recreated. One additional piece of information that they will likely want is a set of log files from the server when the error occurred. These files help them piece together what happened and what went wrong.

Since you'll be gathering these log files on multiple occasions, it makes a great deal of sense to write a script to gather them. Using a script for this is faster, easier, and more accurate. An example of a batch file written to accomplish this is shown in the following code snippet. Be aware that your application will have a completely different set of log files requested by the vendor. Here is an example of a Windows batch file, SaveLogs.bat, which will copy a set of log files to a specific subdirectory.

```
REM Use this batch file to capture log files to send to vendor
REM 1) Create a directory like C:\App1\20130401 Logs\
REM 2) Copy SaveLogs.bat to that subdirectory
REM 3) Execute SaveLogs.bat
REM 4) Confirm that expected directories/files have been created
REM 5) Delete SaveLogs.bat from the new subdirectory
REM 6) Zip up subdirectories and ftp or email them to vendor
mkdir db
copy C:\App1\db\logs\db.log db\*
mkdir logs
copy C:\App1\logs\*.* logs\*
mkdir AdminServer
copy C:\App1\AdminServer\logs\access.log AdminServer\*
copy C:\App1\AdminServer\logs\App1AdminServer.log AdminServer\*
copy C:\App1\AdminServer\logs\App1Domain.log AdminServer\*
mkdir App1Server
copy C:\App1\App1Server1\logs\access.log App1Server\*
copy C:\App1\App1Server1\logs\App1Server1.log App1Server\*
```

26.2.9 Deleting old files

There are a lot of different types of files on most application servers. Many of these files are valuable for a limited period of time but after that are of diminishing value. For example, log files that are months old will almost certainly never be referred to again. Backup files are invaluable until a new one is created. Report files older than yesterday, last week, or last month are probably worth very little, especially if they can easily be recreated. If older files like these aren't deleted on a regular basis, it won't be long until the disk drive on the application server is completely full.

Writing a batch file to delete files on a regular basis isn't hard to do and can save you a lot of time. The following code deletes backup files that are no longer needed. This example has comments and writes a list of files that are being deleted to a log file. Without those lines, this batch job would have only two lines.

```
REM Batch file to delete backup files greater than 4 days old.
REM Document files that are being deleted.
echo ' >> c:\Delete.log
echo %date:~4,2%/%date:~7,2%/%date:~10,4% %time% >> c:\Delete.log
REM Output list of what gets deleted.
FORFILES /P C:\App1\backup /M *.log /D -5 /C "cmd /c echo @path being deleted" >> c:\Delete.log
FORFILES /P C:\App1\backup /M *.zip /D -5 /C "cmd /c echo @path being deleted" >> c:\Delete.log
REM Actually delete files
FORFILES /P C:\App1\backup /M *.log /D -5 /C "cmd /c del @path"
FORFILES /P C:\App1\backup /M *.zip /D -5 /C "cmd /c del @path"
```

26.2.10 **Backup of directories and files prior to an upgrade**

When doing an upgrade of an application, one of the first steps you will likely be directed to take is to back up specific files and directories. If the upgrade doesn't go well, then these backups can be used to quickly revert back to the current version of the application. It's critical to get this correct, but you also want to get it done quickly. One way of achieving both goals is to write a series of copy commands in a batch file or script. This script can be initially written when you upgrade the development environment, tested when you upgrade the QA environment, and used confidently when you're upgrading the production environment.

An example of commands that will back up directories and files on a Windows computer is shown in the following code snippet. The xcopy command is being used because it can recursively copy subdirectories within the specified directory.

```
xcopy C:\App1\reports\web\p2p\WEB-INF\lib c:\_App1_Backup\web\lib /E
xcopy C:\App1\reports\config c:\_App1_Backup\config /E
xcopy C:\App1\CC\apache-tomcat c:\_App1_Backup\CC\apache-tomcat /E
xcopy C:\App1\CC\tools\bin c:\_App1_Backup\CC\tools\bin /E
copy C:\App1\CC\registry.xml C:\_App1_Backup\registry.xml
```

26.2.11 **Monitoring tools**

If your organization hasn't invested in a commercial monitoring tool like SolarWinds or OpenView, a viable alternative would be an open source tool like Nagios. If even an open source tool isn't an acceptable option in your organization, then it's possible to write scripts capable of performing at least a minimal level of monitoring.

Relatively straightforward scripts can be written to check on the following:

- A process isn't running
- A critical file doesn't exist
- A specific error message has been written to a log file
- A port that should be open is closed
- Utilized space on a disk drive exceeds a specific threshold, say 90%, 95%, or 100% full
- The CPU utilization rate exceeds a specific threshold, say 70%, 80%, or 90%

It might take some research, some coding, and some practice but all of the above criteria can be monitored. As advised in an earlier section, ask coworkers at your organization to see if anyone has already put the type of monitoring you're looking for in place. If it doesn't exist, then dust off your reference manuals and start experimenting. Of course, you'll want to do all your development and testing on a development or test server. Only after you're confident that it works, should it be moved to the production environment.

If your application requires that a specific service or process is running, it shouldn't be hard to write a script to confirm that it's running. If the service isn't running, then send out an e-mail alerting you and others to this. Schedule this script or batch file to run every 5, 10, or 15 minutes and voilà, you have a monitoring tool.

One action that can be taken if a critical service goes down is to issue an alert about it. If the alert is going out in the form of an e-mail, it would be best to send it to a distribution list. By using a distribution list, the recipients can be changed without having to modify the monitoring program or even log onto the server.

If the application is extremely important, you might want to send out a text message to support staff. Sending a text to a cell phone is almost as simple as sending out an e-mail. Depending on your service provider, you might just need to append the service provider's domain to the cell phone number. For example, sending an e-mail to the following address would result in an IM being sent to a Sprint cell phone:

8005550100@messaging.sprintpcs.com

26.2.12 **Restart the application if a critical service goes down**

If the application downtime needs to be minimized, you could write a script to restart it if a critical process or service stops. When the monitoring tool, either something you wrote or a third-party tool, notices that a critical service has stopped, then it would restart the application. If your application involves more than a single service, it's probably a good precaution to stop all of the processes or services and then restart them all to make sure they are started up in the correct sequence. If the vendor has provided scripts to start and stop the application, that definitely reduces the amount of work you have to do.

26.2.13 **Clipboard pop**

An LMS (Learning Management System) I administered had a monthly task that required me to log into the application, bring up a list of user accounts one at a time, and disable them. There was no batch disable utility so this was a manual process. It was possible to export the list of users that needed to be disabled to a spreadsheet. I noticed that I was spending a significant amount of time copying user IDs from the spreadsheet and pasting them into a text field in the application. I wrote a quick utility program that allowed me to load the entire list of account IDs into its buffer. By clicking the "Next Value" button, the next ID would be displayed and would also be loaded into the clipboard buffer. This allowed me to very quickly paste the next ID into the application's User ID text field and click the Search button. Figure 26.5 is a screenshot of this utility's interface. By investing about an hour to write this utility, I saved myself hours of tedious keyboard work every month.

26.2.14 **How many users are logged into the application**

There will be times when you want to know how many users are currently logged into the application. One very common example is that you want to bring the application down but don't want to terminate any user sessions. If the application provides this functionality, then by all means use it. If it isn't provided, then it's probably something you should consider developing.

If this functionality isn't provided by the application, then you might have to get creative to acquire this information. One application I supported wrote all login and logout operations to a log file. A utility or script could be written to scan the log file backward from the current time and list everyone who had logged in but hadn't yet logged out.

Another possible solution is through the database. Does the application create a row every time someone logs into the application? Is the row updated to reflect that they have logged out, perhaps by writing a date and time value to a column named "logout_time" or something like that? By scanning that table for records that have no logout times, you have a list of every user who is currently logged into the application.

26.2.15 **Stop the screensaver from kicking in**

Don't tell the security team about this section, but sometimes it's really annoying to have the screensaver activate on your workstation. Having your session lock up like this has an unpredictable impact on any processes you might have running.

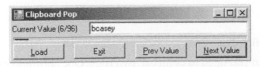

FIGURE 26.5

Clipboard Pop tool. (For color version of this figure, the reader is referred to the online version of this chapter.)

If you're working remotely and have established a VPN session, it's even more annoying if your laptop times out because then your VPN session could be lost. This requires that you log back into the network.

Wouldn't it be nice to be able to avoid having your sessions time out? It's not only possible, it's relatively easy. The code shown below in a VBS (Visual Basic Script) file, e.g., StopScreensSaver.vbs, will activate the F15 key every 120 seconds.

```
Set ws = CreateObject("WScript.Shell")
Do
Wscript.Sleep 120000
ws.SendKeys "{F15}"
Loop
```

To launch this script, you need to create a .bat file with the following command in it. The file I created was named StopScreensaver.bat.

```
cscript.exe c:\_StopScreensaver\StopScreenSaver.vbs
```

My example has these files located in a directory named C:_StopScreensaver. If you position your files in any other directory, you'll have to adjust the command in your .bat file accordingly.

26.2.16 Keystroke programs

There are times when you need to perform the same keystrokes over and over again. An excellent example would be if you're doing stress testing on an application. When doing a stress test, you want to generate as much activity in the application as possible. Repeating the same function over and over indefinitely may seem redundant to you, but it is forcing the application to respond. If you could have 10 or 100 people performing testing like this at the same time, that would be even better.

There are third-party tools capable of doing this. If you're familiar with the "macro" function in spreadsheets and word processors, the functionality is similar. Essentially, you turn on a "recorder" and then start pressing keys. When you're done, you stop the "recorder." All of the keystrokes you entered are recorded to a file. The tool can play back all of your keystrokes. Some tools allow you to edit the file. This would enable you to have it loop endlessly.

A "macro" script capability like this can be extremely handy for stress testing. You simply record all the actions you want, performed, and kick off the script. If you are able to log into the application multiple times, you could have numerous sessions running on a single workstation. Ten workstations or PCs running 25 sessions each would allow you to imitate or reproduce the activity of 250 different users.

Some examples of keyboard macros tools that are available include:

- KeyText
- Keyboard Express
- AutoIt
- Superkey

26.2.17 File comparison

There will be many times when you need to compare two files. One common example is the need to compare configuration files from before and after an upgrade. In many cases, these files will be too long or too detailed to accurately compare by eyeballing them.

In cases where the files to be compared are too complex, you'll want a tool to compare them. Some available tools are:

- The fc command in a Windows command prompt window
- The diff command in UNIX and Linux
- If you are more comfortable with a GUI tool, then Notepad++ is a very good option. It has a very convenient compare feature. To compare two files, open them both and then select menu item Plugins | Compare. Best of all, Notepad++ is an open source so it can be downloaded for free.
- WinMerge is an open source tool that identifies differences in files for Windows. It presents the differences in a visual text format that makes the differences easy to recognize and merge. WinMerge is also able to compare directory structures and display their differences.

26.2.18 Synchronizing files

There are a number of situations why you might want to or need to synchronize files between two different platforms. Some of these situations include:

- The DR (Disaster Recovery) system needs to be kept synchronized with the Production system
- Periodically, the test system needs to be synchronized with the development system
- Special purpose environments, e.g., year-end testing or global testing, need to be synchronized with the QA system
- Periodically, the contents of the production system need to be pushed out to all of the other environments

If synchronizing files between servers needs to be done, then there are at least two ways to accomplish it. The first is to write a series of copy, cp, or xcopy commands. Perhaps the biggest drawback to this approach is that it will be maintenance intensive. Each time a new file, a new directory, or a new drive is added to the system, the synchronize scripts will have to be updated.

An alternative to the manual approach is to use a tool to synchronize files between servers. One readily available tool is the "rsync" (remote sync) command. rsync was originally written for UNIX systems but has been ported to Linux and Windows platforms. The basic format of rsync is:

```
rsync options source destination
```

Source and destination values can specify server names as well as directory names. Wildcard characters can be used to allow more flexibility in what files are to be copied. A feature of rsync that sets it apart from a standard remote copy utility is that it only copies files that have changed since the last time rsync ran. Being more efficient enables rsync to generate less network traffic and complete more quickly.

Some of the options that can be specified with the rsync command are:

-c	use checksum values to determine what should be copied
-n	Perform a trial run, i.e., no files will actually be copied
-p	preserve permissions on destination server
-q	operate in quiet mode, i.e., don't display details on progress of the command
-r	recursively handle directories within directories
-R	relative path names are used
-t	preserve times on destination server
-v	verbose, i.e., display details on progress of the command
-z	compresses the files during the transfer

26.2.19 **New users**

The process of adding users seems to be different for every application. If you're lucky, the application you support has a batch registration utility. If such a utility exists, it may expect the new users to be in CSV file.

Before using this utility for the first time in production, you'll certainly want to test it in your development or QA environment. After running the batch register in QA, you should log into the application as one of the new accounts just to verify that it was created correctly. After logging in as one of the new users, run some quick checks to confirm that the account has all of the access rights it's supposed to have and nothing more.

If the application in question doesn't provide a batch registration utility, you might be tempted to find a way to add new users without having to manually enter their information into the application's data entry screens. For example, you might think that you can insert data into the appropriate database tables using SQL statements. I would strongly advice against this unless you are explicitly told by the vendor's support group that this will work correctly. Most vendor's database designs are extremely complicated and it probably won't be obvious how all of the tables are interrelated.

26.2.20 **Audits**

Many organizations require that its applications be audited on an annual basis. If the application that you support is one that undergoes an audit, you should be on the alert for ways to make the audit process more efficient, easier, and more automated. Mentally review every step in an auditing process to see if it could be automated or somehow made more efficient.

Audit requirements are specific to your organization because everyone's audit process is different. The following reports are examples of some ways of making the auditing process more efficient.

- List all users and the access privileges each user has been granted
- List all users and their supervisors
- List the last time each user accessed the application
- Approvers are people who authorize access to the application. Create a report for each approver listing every user that they have approved. These reports can be used to verify that all existing users continue to have a legitimate need to access the system.

Third-Party Tools

Some tools you can and should build for yourself, but others are significantly more complex and realistically can't be built by the average Application Administrator. They can require extensive experience coding in an area that you're not familiar with. Then there is the time factor. Most Application Administrators have a lot on their plates and don't have bandwidth to spend building significant new tools from scratch.

The following sections briefly describe tools build by others that you can use to support your application. If you're interested in one of them, you can easily do a web search to obtain more details and usually download the tools.

27.1 SYSINTERNALS UTILITIES

If your applications are running on Windows computers, then you will benefit by becoming familiar with the Windows Sysinternals Suite of tools created by Mark Russinovich. At the time of this writing, I was able to download this suite, at no cost, at URL http://technet.microsoft.com/en-us/sysinternals/bb842062. aspx. Some of these tools that I've found to be very helpful are listed here. This is not a complete list by any means.

- AccessEnum—an easy method to determine who has access to the directories, files, and registry entries on a computer.
- Autoruns—lists the programs that are started up when your system boots.
- BgInfo—automatically generates a desktop background that lists details about the server, including the computer name, IP address, NIC cards on the server, etc. Very useful to have this display on each of your servers.
- DiskView—shows disk sectors that are being used in a graphical display.
- DiskUsage—lists directories and the amount of disk being used by each. Useful if you're trying to find files to delete to free up disk space.
- Handle—shows files that are open and who has a handle for them. This can be extremely valuable to know when you're trying to delete a file but can't because a process currently has it open.
- ListDLLs—lists a process that is currently using a DLL. Useful if you want to update it and need to find out what processes will be affected by this change.
- LogonSessions—lists the current and most recent log sessions on the computer. If you include the /p parameter, then LogonSessions will list the executables that were run during each logon session.
- MoveFile—moves a file to the stipulated location immediately after the next reboot of the system. This is quite useful if the file you need to change gets opened and locked by a process shortly after the system boots. If you want to delete a file, then simply specify a pair of double quotes ("") as the destination for the MoveFile command.
- ProcDump—create a process dump for any named process. Very useful if a process is hung up but you don't have any idea why. Before capturing any process dumps, be sure that someone is available that is able to read them. It won't do you much good if you can't interpret it.

- ProcessExplorer—a utility that lists all of the processes that are running on the computers. Any process or process tree can be killed from within ProcessExplorer. It can also be used to find what process has a handle or DLL open.

One word of warning about using these tools—they are extremely powerful so be sure you know what you're doing before you do it. It would be extremely easy to add a parameter or leave off a parameter and make changes that you hadn't anticipated. The first time you use a specific command it would be a good idea to practice it on a test or development system instead of your production platform.

27.2 REMOTE SESSIONS

All Application Administrators need to be comfortable with establishing and working in remote sessions. Questions that you should ask before choosing a remote session tool include the following:

- What functionality is included? For example, remote print, file transfers, remote control.
- Does it work on the operating systems your organization has in place?
- Do any firewall ports need to be opened?
- Does a centralized server need to be contacted?
- Are any plug-ins needed?
- Does an agent need to be installed on the client side?
- What are the risks of using a tool like this?
- What encryption algorithm is used for session encoding?
- If the tool isn't free, then are you paying a one-time fee or an annual licensing fee?
- How many simultaneous sessions can you operate?
- How is the performance of the session?

There are many great tools available that can be used for remote sessions. Many of these tools are either free, come preinstalled with Windows, or have a version with limited functionality that is available for free. Some examples are listed here:

- Gbridge—this utility is free. It allows file transfers between computers. It has been ported to multiple versions of Windows. Doesn't require any firewall changes, i.e., no ports have to be opened.
- LogMeIn—this tool is also free, but a Pro version is available for an annual subscription cost. Ported to Mac and Windows PCs. Host agent needs to be installed on your PC connecting to the LogMeIn Website. Doesn't require any firewall changes. Works with a number of web browsers.
- RDC—Remote Desktop Connection—this free utility is built into all current versions of Windows. Does require that a firewall port be opened. Available on current versions of Windows and Mac.
- TeamViewer—has a free version as well as a commercial version that isn't free. Works with current versions of Windows and versions of Mac starting with OS X10.4. Requires that an agent be installed or a memory resident client be running on the remote computer.
- VNC Viewer—has a free version as well as Personal and Enterprise versions that are not free. Works with Windows, Mac, UNIX, and Linux. Doesn't require agents or a centralized server. It uses port 80, so it doesn't require any firewall changes.
- WinRemotePC—this utility is free. It runs on current versions of Windows. A firewall port must be opened for this tool to communicate with the client computer. An agent must be installed on the remote computer.

27.3 **SESSION SHARING**

As an Application Administrator, there are numerous times when you'll be sharing either your computer screen or someone else's screen. This type of communication is frequently referred to as an online meeting. Some examples of when you'd need this functionality include:

- Working with a vendor technician to install a software or resolve a problem
- Working with a user to learn about or correct a problem
- Working with a coworker on a problem or project
- Leading user training

Some of the tools described in Section 27.2 can be used for session sharing. Other tools are available that are specifically geared toward sharing sessions. Again, some are free while others will put a bite in your budget. Some examples of them are:

- Cisco WebEx—Ported to Windows, UNIX, and Linux. Browser based and requires that a browser plug-in be downloaded and installed to host a meeting. People simply joining an online meeting don't have to perform an install. Monthly licensing fee, but a free trial is available.
- GoToMeeting—browser-based tool that has been ported to Mac and PC platforms. This tool has a monthly cost, but a free trial version is available.
- Mikogo—Participants join a meeting by pointing their browser at the Mikogo website and entering a session ID. No downloads are required. Mikogo works with Windows, Apple, and Linux computers. Pricing for this tool can be paid either annually or lifetime and is available in freelancer, team, or corporate versions.
- Microsoft Lync—Microsoft's unified communications flagship product. Lync includes the ability to share screens with participants on calls. This product is not free.
- Adobe Connect—participants connect via the web browsers, so it doesn't required any software to be installed. Connect is not a free tool, there is a monthly or annual licensing fee.

One feature that can be extremely useful is the ability to record a session and play it back later. This is very helpful for training sessions. Instead of having to train every new user to the application, you can record the material once and direct new users to a link. Recorded sessions can provide the video equivalent of a FAQ list. For each problem or question user encounters, you record a session describing the problem or difficulty and how to work around it. If you think that recording sessions is something you'll want to do, then make sure that the tool you select has this capability.

27.4 **MOVING FILES**

As an Application Administrator, you'll frequently need to move files from one computer to another. This will be such a common task that you'll need to be able to complete it quickly. For example, you might need to:

- Download upgrade or patch files from the vendor's website and then move them to the application server(s).
- Upload log files from a server to the vendor's website or FTP server.
- Run SQL queries that extract data from the database and pass the resulting file to the business owner.
- Accept data files from the business owner and import them into the application via a bulk insert utility.
- Move data from the production server to the QA or development server, so the two servers can be synchronized.

- Move data or backup files from production to the DR server to test or activate your DR environment.
- Transfer the results of a scheduled report or data extract to another department, vendor, or client.

Some available tools that can be used to move files are described in the following sections. Some of them may already exist on your server. Others are open source and can be downloaded for free. Others have a licensing fee.

27.4.1 FTP

FTP, file transfer protocol, is a widely used program to transfer files across networks like the Internet. Initially, FTP client applications were command line tools. Now, there are numerous GUI or graphical user interfaces for using FTP. One example of a GUI FTP tool is FileZilla. You should use whatever interface is most comfortable for you.

A warning about the transfer type setting is an FTP session. This setting controls how the data is formatted as it is actually being transferred. The possible values are:

- ASCII—used to transfer text files between computers using the ASCII character set. PCs and servers typically use ASCII. If you're uploading a log file to the vendor's support group, then you should be using the ASCII setting.
- Binary—file contents are passed byte by byte without being converted to a character representation like ASCII or EBCDIC. For example, if you're downloading files from the vendor to apply an upgrade to your application, you should be using the binary setting.
- EBCDIC—used to transfer text files between computers that use the EBCDIC character set. Typically, mainframe computers use the EBCDIC format.

Moving a file between two systems using FTP can result in unexpected problems if you use the wrong mode. Be aware of the type of file you're transferring and adjust the transfer type setting accordingly.

The biggest shortcoming of FTP is that it isn't secure. Files are not encrypted as they are sent across the network. Anyone who has access to the network could use a packet sniffer to pluck off the packets being used to transfer your file. The packets are in plaintext, so any expectations of privacy or secrecy are unrealistic. Section 27.4.2 describes variations of FTP that include security.

There are many tools out there that implement the FTP protocol. A brief list of them includes:

- Command line tools—the biggest advantage is that many computers already have the FTP command loaded on them. The downside is that you have to learn the commands needed to set up the FTP connection and transfer files. If already experienced with DOS or UNIX commands, then learning the basics of FTP should be pretty easy.
- FileZilla—a free GUI-based FTP tool. Easy to set up and use. FileZilla is one of the most widely used GUI-based FTP tools.

27.4.2 Secure alternatives to FTP

There are a number of tools available that address the security deficiency of FTP. Some of these products are:

- WinSCP (Windows Secure CoPy)—is an open source client for SFTP, SCP, and FTP that runs on Windows client computers. In addition to file transfer functions, it can also be set up to provide file synchronization.
- FileZilla—this product was mentioned in the section on FTP tools, but it can also use the SFTP protocol to encrypt packets being transferred.

- SCP (Secure Copy)—SCP is a protocol designed to securely transfer files between two computers. A command line program, "scp," exists that uses this protocol. GUI-based tools that utilize the SCP protocol also exist.
- DropBox—a tool tool/service that allows you to easily move files from one computer to another. A free version is available but has limitations on the amount of space available. Additional space can be obtained via a license that has a cost to it.

27.5 MONITORING TOOLS

At some point in your career as an Application Administrator, you will encounter the need to figure out what's happening on a server. Your goal might be to make the application run faster. Or it might be to figure out why all of the server's memory is being used. Or it might be to figure out what process has a lock on a specific file. There are tools that can help you answer many questions including the ones I just listed. The trick is to become experienced with the tools *before* you need them. That will enable you to work on the problem instead of finding or learning about the tool.

27.5.1 Monitoring the server

The following sections describe tools you can use to decipher what activities are occurring on the server. Be aware some of these tools need to be put into place before the problem is encountered.

27.5.1.1 *Task manager*

Task Manager is one of the most basic monitoring tools on a Windows computer. It can provide you with the following insight into server processes:

- What processes are running
- The PID, Process ID, of each process
- Whether a process is 32 bit or 64 bit
- The owner of each process
- CPU time being used by each process
- Memory being used by each process
- Applications that are active
- All defined services and their current status (Stopped, Running, Disabled, Starting, Stopping)
- The command line statement that launched each service
- All users currently logged onto the system
- Scrolling charts showing the CPU usage rate and the amount of memory being used over time.

A detailed description of Task Manager and many of its features was presented in Chapter 17.

27.5.1.2 *Perfmon*

Perfmon, aka Performance Monitor, is a tool that allows you to choose what system metrics will be recorded, how frequently they should be recorded, and where the results will be written. Using Perfmon, you can monitor just about any type of activity that can occur on a server.

A few pieces of advice when using Perfmon are:

- Don't attempt to record every possible metric. The details will inundate you and might affect the performance of the server. It's better to start off capturing relatively few statistics and add to that list one by one.

- Make sure you understand the metrics you are monitoring. Don't make decisions based on what you assume a particular statistic means. Review the Help screens in Perfmon or search the Internet for a statistic if you aren't absolutely sure about it.
- Resist the temptation to capture metrics too frequently. If Perfmon runs every second, the amount data will overwhelm you and possibly impact the server's performance.
- Have Perfmon running before the problem is encountered. This will enable you to see when performance starts to degrade or exactly when a resource, like memory, becomes scarce.
- Have Perfmon create a new file at least once a day. It's easier to open and view metrics on a daily basis instead of for a week or a month at a time.

Perfmon was described in greater detail in Chapter 17.

27.5.1.3 ProcessExplorer

ProcessExplorer is a part of the Sysinternals suite of tools written by Mark Russinovich. This tool might be the most useful tool around for determining what's happening on a Windows computer. It was described extensively in Chapter 23, so I don't want to duplicate what has already been listed. This is a tool that you need to play with and explore. The more you use it, the more useful you'll find it to be.

27.5.1.4 WMIC

The WMIC, Windows Management Instrument Command, was also described in Chapter 23 but is valuable enough to be listed again. It isn't as intuitive as a GUI tool but packs an incredible range of functionality. You can use it to find out the following types of information about the server:

- Hardware details like CPU type, CPU speed, number of NICs, amount of memory, etc.
- Software that has been loaded on the server
- List user account information
- List information about active processes
- Terminate processes
- List printers and their status
- List fixes and patches that have been applied to the operating system
- Details on devices like hard drives, CD-ROM drives, and NICs

WMIC can be run in two modes: interactive and noninteractive. Interactive mode is great if you have a number of queries you want to make. Noninteractive mode is useful if you have just a single query to make. You can write multiple WMIC instructions to a file and execute the file by calling it in noninteractive mode.

27.5.2 Monitoring the Network

Every enterprise-level application ultimately depends on the network to function. User browsers need to communicate with the web server and the DNS server. The web server needs to communicate with the database server and the AD server. The database server needs to communicate with the SAN. All of these communications require the network to be functional and not overloaded.

Some of the functions that network monitoring tools can perform include:

- Provide a high-level schematic or picture of the network
- Identify links in the network that are experiencing lost packets
- Identify links that are slow
- Identify links that might be about to go down
- Network utilization rates

- Analyze routing protocols to optimize network efficiency
- Maintain historical routing information that can be compared with current statistics
- Record failures of links or hardware devices
- Monitor websites by checking HTTP pages on configurable intervals
- Provide statistics for network capacity and growth calculations
- Identify users or applications that are consuming significant amounts of network bandwidth

There are many tools that enable you to map a network and monitor it. Some of them are open source and others are commercial products that require licensing fees. Learning to monitor networks and understanding what you're seeing is a learning experience. The sooner you begin the process, the sooner you'll begin to recognize abnormal or nonoptimal situations.

27.5.2.1 SolarWinds
SolarWinds offers a suite of monitoring tools that include many focused on the network. It was first described in Chapter 13. One specific tool that is part of SolarWinds performs network traffic analysis. It monitors traffic patterns and bandwidth across the network to the lower level and presents the data in charts, tables, or dashboards. You can use this tool to identify which applications and specific users are consuming large amounts of your precious bandwidth. This product suite is not available as an open source license.

27.5.2.2 Nagios
Nagios is an open source tool that can monitor applications, servers, and networks. This tool was described in Chapter 13 but that focused on its ability to monitor applications. The design of Nagios allows plug-ins to be added so you can monitor just about anything. A wide variety of plug-ins are available for download. Alternatively, you can write them yourself if what you need doesn't already exist.

27.5.2.3 Wireshark
Wireshark isn't a generic monitoring tool like the two previous tools. It performs packet analysis of traffic moving across the network. Wireshark allows you to filter exactly what traffic will be viewed or recorded so your log files don't become unwieldy. This tool is available in both GUI and CLI (command line interface) versions. Wireshark is an open source application that can run on Windows, UNIX, and Linux platforms. This tool has a very active group of developers supporting it so its functionality is continuously expanding.

27.6 MANIPULATING FILES
As an Application Administrator, you'll be manipulating files on a regular basis. Some examples of the types of files you need to be familiar with include:

- Configuration files
- HTML files
- XML files
- Log files
- Batch files
- Scripts
- SQL queries
- Compressed files

27.6.1 **Editors**

Editing files is an everyday activity for Application Administrators. Some editors aren't able to display certain files types or if they can be displayed aren't in a particularly convenient format. For example, Notepad doesn't line up the matching elements in an XML file. If you deal with files that aren't ASCII text, then it's both convenient and productive to use an editor that recognizes different file types. Some examples of file types that you will likely encounter include:

- Configuration files, initialization files, batch files, and scripts are typically ASCII and can be edited with virtually any editor.
- Log files are also likely to be text files. One concern is that some log files will be too large to open with a simple editor like Notepad. To open a file that is tens or hundreds of megabytes in size, you need an editor that's intelligent enough not to try to load the entire file at once. If your editor tries to load the complete file, then it will take a long time to start up, be very slow, and consume most of the memory on the computer.
- XML files have matching open and close syntax that must be balanced. They can be edited with a simple text editor like Notepad, but if you are using an editor built to for XML code it's much easier. Additionally, you're less likely to make typos or other mistakes when using an XML-oriented editor.
- HTML files, like XML files, have open and close syntax that must be balanced. A simple text editor can be used, but you'll be significantly more efficient and productive if you use an editor built to handle HTML files.
- Most of the time if you have to work with a PDF file, you'll just be reading it. If you need to edit it, then you must use an editor that is compatible with this file type.
- Code files like C, C#, and Java can be edited in a simple editor. But using a specialized editor like the one in an IDE (Integrated Development Environment) will make you much more productive and cut down on your errors. Some of the features this type of editor provides include:
  - Color coding different elements like syntax words, variables, etc.
  - Autocomplete key words
  - Shows lists of parameter needed for procedure calls
  - Automatically adds closing elements like parentheses, braces, and "End" statements
- You will be creating and updating a significant amount of documents in your work day. To make these documents presentable and professional, you'll need a word processor like Microsoft Word or OpenOffice Writer.

All Windows computers come preloaded with Notepad and Wordpad. All Linux and UNIX computers come with vi. There are many, many other editors that are available. Some are open source and others incur a licensing fee. Depending on your exact needs, you should acquire one or more editors that will make you more productive with the types of files you use the most.

Some features that you might consider before deciding upon an editor include the following:

- Can the editor open a file that is locked by another process? Some can and some can't.
- Can the editor display files in the following formats: hexadecimal, octal, or binary?
- UNIX and Windows files have different line termination characters. Can the editor create files in both formats?
- Can files be opened by dragging and dropping them onto the editor?
- Is it capable of performing file comparisons?
- How does it handle extremely large files?
- Can multiple files be opened simultaneously?

If you run an Internet search for editors, you'll get hundreds of thousands of hits. It wouldn't be possible for any book to review or recommend even a fraction of such a multitude. Several editors that are available are listed below, but this list is obviously just a tiny sliver of the options available to you.

27.6.1.1 Notepad++

Notepad++ is an extremely useful open source text editor. A partial list of its more useful features includes the following:

- Allow multiple documents to be opened, each in a separate tab
- File comparison that displays a high-level view of exactly where the files differ
- Split screen editing
- Macro recording and execution
- Supports line endings for UNIX type files
- Displays source code syntax text in different color fonts
- Supports autocompletion for some programming languages
- Supports many languages including C, C++, C#, Java, JavaScript, XML, HTML
- Over 100 plug-ins are available to further extend the power of this editor

27.6.1.2 UltraEdit

UltraEdit is a commercial text editor that provides many features beyond what Notepad offers. Some of its advantages include:

- Able to handle files that are larger than 4 GB
- A powerful text comparison tool, including the ability to compare binary files
- Replace operations can preserve that case of the string that is being replaced
- Color codes syntax, variables, etc.
- Matching delimiters, e.g., opening and closing parentheses, are easy to spot
- Supports many languages including C, C++, PHP, XML, HTML, Java, JavaScript, and Perl
- Autocompletion for syntax keywords

27.6.1.3 PDF

PDF (Portable Document Format) files were developed by the corporation Adobe Systems. This format is something that the typical Application Administrator will come across regularly. In my experience, many vendors publish their manual as PDF documents. This is done because PDF files can be opened on virtually any computer. The ability to read a PDF file is available via Adobe Reader® for no cost to anyone who wants to download it from the Adobe® website.

27.6.2 Comparing

There will be many times when you need to compare two, or more, files. For example, you might want to compare version of a configuration file before and after an upgrade was done. Or you might need to compare two lists of data that is in CSV files. You should make sure that the editor you're using has the ability to compare files.

27.6.3 Compression

Application Administrators occasionally have to deal with some extremely large files. Some examples of file types that can be quite large include:

- Upgrade and install packages from the vendor
- Log files being sent to the vendor's support team
- Large export files being sent to another system or application
- Backup files
- Copying an application from one server to another

If you need to store, move, FTP, or e-mail extremely large files, it's very common to compress them first. The algorithms used by compression software can be very complex, but the concept is pretty simple. Files can be compressed by removing repetitive data. In most cases, the repetitive sections are replaced with a much smaller code value. When the file is uncompressed, the algorithm recognizes the code and restores the original value. Source code and logs files are particularly rich in duplicated text strings, so they can usually be compressed to a fraction of their original sizes.

One warning that needs to be provided here is that once a file is compressed, you typically need the same package to decompress it. There are exceptions for common compression techniques, but if you stray off the path and use an unusual compression package then you'll very likely need it to decompress that file in the future. If a nonstandard package was used to compress the file, are you certain that you'll still have the package 1, 2, or 5 years down the road when you want to uncompress it? Will that package still exist? Will it have been upgraded to work with the operating systems that are being used in the future? These are just a few thoughts to keep in mind when choosing your compression package.

There are a number of compression utilities that are available beyond what's already loaded as part of the server's operating system. One concern that you need to be aware of is that all compression tools don't create equivalent output. They can use difference algorithms so one utility might not be capable of uncompressing a file created by another utility. Some examples of compression tools that are available are described in the following sections.

Some questions you should ask yourself before choosing a compression tool are:

- Is the tool effective?
- Is it easy to use?
- Is the interface GUI or command line oriented?
- Has it been ported to all of the operating systems you work with?
- Is it capable of handling compressed file types that you typically encounter?
- Does the utility compress and decompress files quickly?
- Can multiple files or folders be combined into a single compressed output?
- Is it affordable?
- Will it be around in 1, 2, or 5 years?

27.6.3.1 WinZip

WinZip has a licensing fee associated with it, but you can download a trial version for free. It is available for Windows and Mac computers. WinZip can create files with multiple file types and uncompress files that were compressed with many of the more popular compression algorithms. One security conscious feature is that when extracting encrypted files, any temporary files created by WinZip are wiped clean so they can't be misused by others.

27.6.3.2 WinRAR

WinRAR is not a free tool, but a trial version is available so you can try it before you buy it. You can probably surmise based on its name that it runs only under Windows operating systems. It is able to compress files into the RAR and ZIP formats and can unpack compressed files that are in many files types including: CAB, ARJ, TAR, JAR, ISO, 7z, and Z. One useful feature that WinRAR has is that it can create archives that extend across multiple volumes. If you're dealing with extremely large sources, this can be very valuable.

27.6.3.3 7-Zip

7-Zip is an open source compression tool that can be downloaded for free. It is able to compress and/or decompress most of the common formats like zip, TAR, GZIP, CAB, ISO, RAR, and XAR. 7zip can be interacted with via the command line or a Windows GUI. Perhaps the greatest strength of this package is its ability to create files in its own 7z format.

27.6.3.4 FreeArc

FreeArc is also an open source compression tool. It works on both Windows and Linux systems. Their website claims that this tool is two to five times faster than other compression tools. One very nice feature FreeArc offers is that the user is able to fine-tune setting for the compression algorithms including the ability to specify the algorithm used by file type.

27.6.4 Encryption

Encryption is a very serious topic that shouldn't be taken lightly. If you have files or data that need to be protected, then you want to make sure that the encryption algorithm is secure and that the way it's being used is correct. Perhaps the most common need for encrypting files that an Application Administrator will encounter is when data is extracted from the application's database and sent to another entity, e.g., vendor, client, supplier, business partner.

Many compression utilities also include the ability to encrypt the files that are being compressed. Of the above compression utilities, all except FreeArc state on their websites that files can be encrypted while being compressed. If your files need to be both compressed and encrypted, then consider acquiring a compression utility that can do both. If you go this route, make sure that the encryption algorithm being used by the utility is sufficiently strong.

If you need only an encryption tool, there are quite a few to choose from. As was stated earlier, encryption is an important area that needs to be done right. This book isn't intended to provide advice on which algorithm to choose, what size keys to use, etc. Anyone implementing an encryption process would be wise to consult an expert in the field to ensure things are set up correctly and securely.

There are thousands of encryption packages out in the marketplace. It wouldn't be possible for even a book on encryption to review all of them. A very limited number of the encryption packages that are available are described in the following sections.

27.6.4.1 BitLocker

BitLocker uses an AES (Advanced Encryption Standard) algorithm and a 128-bit or 256-bit key to securely encrypt entire hard drives or volumes for Windows computers. This tool is provided by Microsoft with their recently released versions of Windows.

27.6.4.2 TrueCrypt

TrueCrypt was described by reviewer Seth Rosenblatt, CNET senior editor, as "the ultimate freeware encryption program." It offers numerous different encryption algorithms that can be used to store encrypted files in either file or partitions. TrueCrypt runs on Windows, Mac OS X, and Linux computers. It allows you to encrypt files in real time, i.e., as you open or close them. As with any encryption product, if you encrypt a file with a strong password and forget or lose the password, then your files are inaccessible.

27.6.4.3 PGP

PGP, Pretty Good Privacy, has been around since the early 1990s and is a leader in the encryption area. It offers the ability to encrypt entire disk drives. PGP has been ported to Windows 2008, Windows 2003, XP, Vista, and Mac OS X. It provides endpoint encryption protection for servers, laptops, desktops, and removable media like USB drives. PGP has an associated licensing cost.

27.7 THE SCREEN

It's easy to overlook, but a huge amount of information flows across your computer monitor or screen. There will be many situations when you'll want to capture something off a screen that you're looking at. What you're looking at might be on your computer, on a server's desktop, inside an application, on an Internet webpage, or maybe even on someone else's computer that they are sharing with you. You need to be so familiar with capturing data off screens that you can do it quickly and without thinking about it.

The following sections describe ways to capture what's on your screen.

27.7.1 Screen capture tools

There will be times when you want to capture exactly what you see on a screen. Perhaps the most common need for this is when you're creating documentation. You might be writing a how-to manual for the users or sending details of an error to the vendor's support group.

27.7.1.1 PrtScrn

For these or any other situations, you can very easily capture the screen of a Windows computer. Pressing the PrtScrn key will create a screenshot, i.e., capture the image of whatever is on the screen at the time.

There are some variations for the Windows embedded screen print capability. These options are described here.

- Pressing the PrtScrn key captures everything on your monitor. If you have multiple monitors, then the image captured includes everything on all of them. One disadvantage of this is that details tend to be hard to make out when multiple monitors are included in the capture area.
- Pressing the Alt + PrtScrn keys will capture just the active window. This is extremely useful when you're putting together documentation and only want to include a specific window instead of the entire monitor(s).
- Pressing the Ctr + PrtScrn keys is useful if you have multiple monitors. If you have a single monitor, it functions the same as the PrtScrn key. But if you have multiple monitors, it captures the image of the primary monitor regardless of which window has focus.

27.7.1.2 Microsoft snippingtool

This tool is preloaded on Windows 7 and Vista computers as well as the Experience Pack for Windows XP Table edition. It not only captures entire screens the way PrtScrn does but also allows you the ability to drag and capture just the part of the screen that you want. You're able to capture specific windows, rectangles, or perform a free-form capture. The image that was captured can be saved as one of several file formats including PNG, GIF, JPG, and MHT.

You can bring up SnippingTool in one of several ways.

1. Click on the Windows Orb or Start icon, click Run, and enter SnippingTool in the Open text field
2. Open a command prompt window, enter SnippingTool into it, and press the Enter key
3. Click on the Windows Orb or Start icon, click All Programs, click on Accessories, and then click on the entry for SnippingTool

The executable for this tool is located at C:\Windows\system32\SnippingTool.exe. If you're going to use this tool extensively, you can easily drag it to the desktop to create a shortcut to it.

27.7.1.3 FastStone capture

FastStone Capture is a lightweight screen capture utility that also has the ability to function as a screen video recorder. It starts during the Windows startup sequence and has an icon in the System Tray area. When activated, a small toolbar is displayed that provides the ability to screen capture and start the screen recorder. Once captured, your images can be sent to a file, a printer, an e-mail message, a word processor, or other destination types. It can save images in numerous file formats including BMP, GIF, JPEG, PCX, PNG, TIFF, and PDF. This tool is not open source.

27.7.2 Tools to capture screen activity

Being able to capture a screenshot is great, but there are times when capturing a video of screen activity is even better. Two situations when a video capture is extremely handy are:

- Training—There are times when it's significantly faster, easier, and more accurate to provide a user with a video showing how to do something instead of writing up the steps to do it.
- Error reporting—There are times when the actions that precede an error are lengthy or complicated. If a user could turn on a video capture utility and then walk through the steps that bring about the error situation, that would make it much easier for you to understand exactly how to recreate the error. You could also use this capability when providing details on an error to the vendor support team.

27.7.2.1 FastStone capture

FastStone Capture was described in Section 27.7.1. As stated earlier, it is also capable of recording screen activity. After initiating this tool, click the icon to activate the screen recorder. The computer's microphone can be used to record audio while screen activity is being captured. This enables the user to provide a running commentary of his or her actions. When your activity is complete, turn off the recorder and save the output to a file. Files containing a recorded session can be dragged and dropped onto the screen recorder's panel to play them back. A video editor allows you to add annotations to the video.

27.7.2.2 Microsoft problem steps recorder

Problem Steps Recorder (psr) isn't exactly a screen recorder. Instead, it creates a series of screenshots that are designed to show every step taken up to a specific point in time. When recording is done, the output is automatically saved in a zipped MHTML file that can be e-mailed to someone who, you hope, can help solve the problem.

The steps to start psr and record your activity are:

- Click the Windows Orb or Start icon, enter psr in the text field, and press the Enter key
- Click the Start Record button
- Perform the steps needed to reproduce the problem
- Click the Stop Record button
- You'll be prompted to enter a name for the file, type in a meaningful name and click Save
- The file that is created will have a .zip file extension
- To view the recording, open the zip file that was just created and then double-click the MHTML file
- A browser session will open and the document will be displayed in it
- To advance from one captured screen to the next, just scroll down in the browser session

The file that is displayed has the following information:

- A header area describing a functional overview of the Recorded Problem Steps tool
- Each screen that was captured has the following information:
  - An ascending step number
  - A date and time stamp of when it was captured
  - The action the user took to get there, e.g., "User left-clicked on Start (push button)"
  - A screenshot of the screen after the action was completed.
- The last section is titled "Additional Details" and shows a summary of each step including details like:
  - The Step number
  - The action the user took
  - The name of the program that was involved, including the version, maker, and executable name
  - The UI elements that were involved, e.g., the name of the button pressed, the dialog box on the screen.

I have to admit that this tool is slick! To me, it seems perfectly suited to the need it's attempting to address. The information provided is exactly what is needed to reproduce a problem. Even the most technophobic user should be capable of using this tool to provide excellent information on how to recreate a problem. On top of all of that, it's free. Who could ask for anything more?

27.7.3 Manipulation tools

Capturing a screenshot is easy enough, but sometimes you want to modify it after that.

For example, to put it in your documentation you might need to crop it down a bit to make it fit. Another example is that the screenshot might contain an account number that you don't want public. Being able to modify your images after the screenshot is captured is a very important step if you intend to use them in any form of documentation.

Tools that are capable of manipulating images are described in the following sections. As always, some are free and others have a licensing fee to acquire.

27.7.3.1 Microsoft paint

It would be easy to dismiss Microsoft Paint as a trivial app just because it's free, it's been around forever, and it comes preloaded on all Windows computers, but doing that would be a mistake. Paint is easy to use. It has a lot of features including the ability to add objects like text, circles, arrows, etc., on images to emphasize specific areas. It can save image files in the following formats: BMP, PNG, JPEG, GIF, and TIFF. Paint isn't ever going to put Photoshop® out of business, but for basic manipulation of images it provides more than enough functionality. Oh, and did I mention that it's free?

27.7.3.2 Paint.NET

Paint.NET is an open source freeware editor that allows you to modify images. Some of its functionality rivals imaging editing software packages that have a significant price tag. Just a few examples of what it can do include:

- Crop, rotate, and resize images
- Adjust colors
- Remove "red-eye" removal from photographs
- Allows the user to create layers within the image
- Capable of including special effects like sharpening, blurring, distortion, and embossing
- Save files in common image-related formats like GIF, JPEG, PNG, and TIFF

27.8 BROWSERS

Most computer users have a particular Internet browser that they use the vast majority of the time. If you don't already have a second, or third, browser available on your computer, I'd like to present some reasons why you should have an alternative readily available.

* Speed—In particular instances, some browsers are faster than others. On one application I support, a particular screen took 58 seconds to come up. We were tearing our hair out trying to figure out why it took so long. Was it a database issue? Was it a network bottleneck? As it turned out, it was the browser. Using another browser, it took only 2 seconds to bring up the same screen. Those times were consistent. Browser A always took just under a minute and Browser B always took less than 3 seconds.
* Errors—There have been many times when I've tried to bring up a web page and it wouldn't come up. Eventually, I'll try opening it with another browser and voila—it works. This seems to always happen when someone sends me an e-mail that contains a link inviting me to an online meeting.

I don't think I need to describe the following browsers to anyone familiar with a computer, so I'll just list some of the most widely used browsers. Even if you are a diehard fan of one of the browsers, it wouldn't hurt to have another one loaded on your workstation for emergency situations.

* Google Chrome
* Microsoft Internet Explorer
* Mozilla Firefox
* Opera
* Apple Safari

27.9 DATABASE ACCESS TOOLS

If you're working as an Application Administrator, you will almost certainly have to connect to the database behind the application once in a while. In many cases, that database will be a relational database. To connect to it, you need to establish a SQL session and that means you need some kind of client tool to work with.

The following sections describe some of the tools that are available. Perhaps the most important considerations are what brands of databases you need to connect to. For example, if your shop has only Microsoft SQL Server databases, then the Oracle tools won't be of much use to you.

27.9.1 Oracle SQL*Plus

SQL*Plus is typically available on your computer if the Oracle Client has been installed. You can do about anything with it, but if you're not comfortable with using a command line interface then this might not be the best tool for you. On the other hand, you might consider stretching your skills and putting in the effort to become proficient with it. Putting together a cheat sheet of tips on using this tool shouldn't take more than a few minutes.

27.9.2 Oracle SQL Developer

Oracle SQL Developer is a tool that can be downloaded for free from Oracle's website. This GUI tool is very powerful and easy to use. It offers the pretty standard worksheet interface where you type in your SQL commands and another panel displays the results of your commands. You can save your queries for use again later. SQL Developer also allows you to administer your databases. Since SQL Developer only works with Oracle databases, you might want another GUI tool on hand if your organization relies on other databases.

27.9.3 TOAD

Quest Software's TOAD is capable of connecting to a number of types of relational databases including Oracle, Microsoft SQL Server, Sybase, IBM's DB2, and MySQL. TOAD is as intuitive as any of the other GUI database access tools that are available. TOAD is not free, but a trial version can be downloaded.

27.9.4 SQL-Station

SQL-Station, from Computer Associates, is also a GUI database access tool that supports a number of relational databases. A partial list of what it can work with includes Oracle, MySQL, SQL Server, DBA, and Sybase. SQL-Station is not an open source or free tool.

27.10 PROJECT MANAGER TOOLS

As an Application Administrator, you and your application(s) will be involved in a number of projects. Potential projects that can affect you include:

- Acquiring the initial application package
- Migrating to a new or different application package
- Archiving an application
- Expanding or divesting what the application covers due to a merger or acquisition
- Upgrading to a new version of the application
- Move to new hardware, i.e., a new server
- Move to a different data center
- Adding a new environment, for example, a DR site

Some of these projects will be complicated enough to justify writing up a project plan. You will likely be requested to either write or contribute to writing the project plan. If you can get your hands on them, try to see previous project plans for your application or other applications. There's nothing wrong with basing your project plan on a similar task.

The range of tools used to develop project plans can range from a few lines in a spreadsheet to hundreds of pages in a full-blown project management tool. My advice would be to keep it as simple as possible. If your "project" includes relatively few tasks, then it could easily be managed in a text file or a spreadsheet. On the other hand, if your project will involve the efforts of dozen contributors or hundreds of separate tasks, then you definitely need a tool that was built specifically to track projects. One complication that definitely makes a project planning tool worthwhile is if some of your tasks need to be performed consecutively while others can be done at the same time.

Some of the major categories of data that you will want to capture in your project plan include:

- Task name
- Start date/time
- Duration of task in weeks, day, hours, or minutes
- Finish date/time
- Predecessor task or tasks

- Resource(s) being applied to task
- Percentage complete

Some of the available tools allow you to define high-level details such as the following. These settings are incorporated in the calculations done to determine end dates for tasks.

- Definition of the work week, e.g., Monday through Friday or Saturday through Wednesday
- Number of hours in the work days
- Company-recognized holidays
- Percentage of time each team member is to dedicate to the project

There are literally hundreds of project management tools available for you to choose from. Some are general purpose, while others are industry specific. It's very possible that your organization or group has already chosen the tool you'll be using. If the tool decision hasn't already been made for you, then prepare to do a fair amount of research before making a choice. Many of the tools are free or open source, but others are quite pricey. Of course, the costlier ones tend to include more bells and whistles.

Some examples of Project Management tools are:

- Microsoft Project
- Clarizen
- Genius Project
- Daptive PPM
- Tenrox
- PROJECT Insight
- Redmine
- Trac
- Zoho Projects

Troubleshooting Tips

28

Every application that is being used eventually encounters problems. Once a problem occurs with your application, you will be the point person and figure out what's wrong and fix it. There is no right or wrong way to troubleshoot a problem, but some ways are more efficient than others. You need to find the most efficient way for you to handle problems, document it, and then always try to consistently use that method.

28.1 OVERVIEW OF TROUBLESHOOTING

Troubleshooting problems is best accomplished if you follow a set of consistent, logical steps. Another Application Administrator or author might suggest a different version of these steps, but the following is a workable method of solving most problems that will be encountered.

1. Identify the problem
2. Gather information on the problem
3. Test possible solutions, especially solutions that have proved successful with similar problems in the past
4. If necessary, seek specialized assistance
5. Document both the problem and the solution for future reference

28.2 IDENTIFY THE PROBLEM

Until you identify the problem, you won't know how extensive it is, how significant it is, or how to address it. One way of identifying the problem is to isolate where it's occurring. For example

- Is the problem an error that a user is experiencing on his or her workstation or laptop?
- Is it occurring on the application server?
- Is it occurring within another subsystem, for example, the database, network, Active Directory, SAN?

Once you know where it is occurring from, there are specific steps and questions that need to be taken or asked. Examples of these actions are listed in the following sections.

28.3 GATHER INFORMATION ON THE PROBLEM

Don't even think about "solving" a problem until you know as much as possible about it. If you try to solve the problem before gathering adequate information, you may well find yourself solving the wrong problem.

28.3.1 **Questions to ask a user who reports a problem**

If a user reports that a problem is occurring on his or her workstation, then you need to get information from him or her about it. Not all users are equally articulate. Not all users are equally computer literate. Not all users are equally observant. To make up for the differences between users, it will be significantly more productive if you take the initiate in this situation. Instead of simply listening to their description of the situation, you should ask pointed questions about it.

You can call them and ask these questions, send them an e-mail with a checklist, or direct them to a web site where their answers can be captured. Use whichever approach works best for you and your organization. Regardless of the approach you or your organization take, you need to get answers to basic questions. The answers will help you to identify potential causes of the problem.

Your list of standard questions should be regularly reviewed with an eye toward improving it. If you find yourself frequently thinking "Gosh, I wish I had asked the user about x, y, or z," then you need to add those questions to your list. Similarly, if you're asking questions that don't contribute anything to your ability to solve the problem, then they can be dropped from your list. In general, the fewer questions you ask, the faster the process will be and the more cooperation you'll get from users.

The following questions can act as a first pass of the ones you ask your users. Don't be afraid to change this list to reflect your situation. For example, if all of your users are in the same building, then asking what city or country they're in is a waste of everyone's time. If your users can only access the production version of the application, then asking what environment the error occurred on isn't necessary.

- Name of the person reporting the problem.
- Date and time the problem occurred.
- Is this issue impacting production?
- Location (room, floor, building, city, country) of the person reporting the problem.
- Is the user on the network or working remotely? If working remotely, is he or she connected to the organization's network via VPN software?
- Description of the error, including any error numbers that are listed.
- Capture a screenshot of the error screen if possible. Note—you should have a document readily available that shows users how to capture screenshots and paste them into an e-mail or a document.
- What were the steps that lead up to problem occurring? Note—the Microsoft Problem Steps Recorder is an excellent tool for capturing the steps leading up to when problems occur. You should have a document describing how to use it ready to send to your users.
- Has this problem occurred before?
- If so, when and how frequently does it occur? For example, hourly, daily, weekly, monthly?
- Are other users experiencing this problem? Note—if the user is relatively isolated, i.e., is the only one using this application in an office or city, then you might need to contact other users to get this information. It would be wise to have a list of users in various offices, cities, countries, time zones, etc., that you can ask about this problem.
- Does the problem occur every time you take these steps?
- Can the problem be reproduced readily?
- What is the name of the user's computer? Users can get this information by Start | Run, enter sysdm.cpl and press the Enter key.
- What version of the Desktop Operating System is being used? Users can get this detail by opening Windows Explorer, right-clicking on "Computer," and selecting "Properties."
- What Internet browser and version is being used. Users can get this by selecting Help | About or something similar in most browsers.

- What network domain is your machine on? Users can get this detail by opening Windows Explorer, right-clicking on "Computer," and selecting "Properties."
- What version of the application is being used? Gathering this information will be different for every application? Is there a Help | About menu item? Is there an icon that can be clicked to display this information? As the Application Administrator, you need to provide users with guidance on how to find this information.

28.3.2 Seeing is believing

I don't mean to appear unkind or distrustful of what users report, but I strongly advise you to not believe that a problem exists until you see it for yourself. Many times the problem boils down to a misunderstanding or an error on the user's part. But you won't know this until you see for yourself what they're doing.

There are several steps you can take to get a proof of exactly what is going on. The quickest and easiest is to have them send you a screenshot of the screen showing the error. Many times this will be enough to confirm that the problem is real.

If this doesn't convince you, then ask them to run the Microsoft Problem Steps Recorder utility. This tool is extremely easy to use and will capture a series of screenshots and all user actions along the way. It can be started by clicking Start | Run and entering "psr" then pressing the Enter key. After clicking the "Start Record" button in PSR, the user performs the same steps taken when the problem was first encountered. PSR will capture screenshots and user actions of everything leading up to the problem. When the error is encountered, they click "Stop Record," name the zip file, and e-mail it to you. Using this information, you should be able to reproduce the error yourself.

The final and perhaps most conclusive approach is to use a tool that allows you to remotely view and if necessary take control of the user's desktop. If your organization has licenses for Citrix's WebEx, Microsoft's Live Meeting or Communicator, then use them. Otherwise, there are many free tools that perform that provide the same functionality. See Chapter 27 for a complete description of this type of tool. Once you're monitoring their desktop, have them walk through the same steps that earlier caused the problem to occur. If you can see what's wrong, either tell them the correct steps or take control and show them.

28.3.3 But it worked yesterday!

I can absolutely guarantee that in your position as an Application Administrator, you will hear someone claim "but it worked yesterday!" You will hear this over and over and over. In many, many cases, this claim will actually be true. I know that I've made this claim on more than one occasion.

There are some things that are worth checking if the application stops working and you know that you haven't made any changes to it recently. The items shown below are just a quick list of what might have caused an application that worked yesterday to not work today. As you encounter additional problems like the ones listed in this section, you need to update your own list of points to check.

- Did the application license expire? This happened to me while we were in the process of implementing an application. A quick call to the vendor and then to our Accounts Payable department straightened it out. If this had happened on a production platform, it would have been a much bigger problem.
- Firewall changes—contact the security team or the firewall team to see if any changes have been made in this area recently.
- O/S patches—were patches recently applied to the operating system?
- Database problems—has the database server run out of space? Is the database engine running? Are the database listeners running? Have any database accounts expired?
- DNS name isn't recognized—has the DNS server been corrupted?
- Viruses and malware—is antivirus software running on your server? Have the signature files it uses been updated recently? Has its license expired?

28.3.4 **Problems that appear on the server**

If the problem is occurring on the application server instead of on a user's workstation, then all of the details regarding the cause of the problem should be available on the server. The potential sources that should be examined are described in the following sections.

28.3.4.1 *E-mail alerts from the application*

E-mails might be sent from the application alerting the Application Administrator that a problem has occurred. All applications don't broadcast problem information this way, but it's possible that the application you support handles it using emails. Check the Administrator's Guide for details about this.

If you can receive alerts by e-mail from the application, then you'll have to provide configuration details to the application. For example, the name of your organization's e-mail server and the e-mail address(es) that alerts should be sent to. If possible, enter a group distribution list instead of individual e-mail addresses. This provides greater flexibility by allowing you or anyone else to alter the recipient list without having to access the application server.

28.3.4.2 *Error messages displayed on the application server*

It is possible that error messages will be displayed on the application server's monitor, but this isn't usually the case. The developers of enterprise application understand that administrators aren't constantly logged into the server so pop-up message boxes aren't usually displayed on the desktop of the server.

28.3.4.3 *Application log files*

Log files created by the application are the most common method of recording problems with the application. Unfortunately, applications tend to create and write to multiple log files. These files can also be spread out across the application server's disk drives. For example, if the application has multiple services, then each service may write its entries to a separate file. Some applications have log files that are dedicated to the start-up process. As the Application Administrator, you need to know the following about its log files:

- Name and location of each log file
- When it is written to, e.g., during the start-up process or during ongoing activity
- If and when the current log file gets archived and a new one is created
- The meanings of entries written to each log file
- Which log files the vendor support group will want if a ticket is opened

You should periodically review application log files looking for error or warning messages. Performing this as a part of your regular maintenance activities might enable you to spot little problems before they escalate into big ones. Reviews like this can be performed manually or you can set up a tool to automate it.

28.3.4.4 *Event viewer*

Writing entries into the Event Viewer on a Windows-based application server is a method used by many applications to record their error conditions. The Administrator's Guide or its equivalent for your application will tell you whether this is where the application writes its log entries.

To open Event Viewer, select the Start icon and then Administration Tools | Event Viewer. Once you have Event Viewer open, you have to select the specific area or folder where the entries have been written to. The primary folders are Application, Security, and System. It's possible that an additional folder will have been created by the application. One vendor whose application I supported created an additional folder named "IC Software" and wrote all of its log entries into that folder.

Once you've found the correct folder, you need to scroll through the time-sequenced entries looking for the ones related to the incident you're investigating. To cut down on the number of entries that have to be examined, Event Viewer allows you to create a filter. If you'll be doing much searching in Event Viewer, the time spent in learning to use the filter feature might be a wise investment.

28.3.4.5 Web server logs

If your application uses a web site as its method of interfacing with users, then it's possible that problems will have been documented in log files maintained by the web server software. For example, if the web server software being used is IIS (Microsoft's Internet Information Services), then error conditions may be documented in IIS log files.

The location where IIS positions the log file can be found by following these steps:

- Open IIS
- Expand the Web Sites folder
- Right-click the application's web site and select Properties
- Select the Web Site tab
- Click on the Properties button in the Enable logging section
- The location of the log file will be displayed in the "Log file directory" field

One likely location is C:\Windows\system32\LogFiles. Within this directory, there will be one log file for every date that the web site was active. The naming convention for these files is ex000000.log, where 000000 is an ascending sequence value.

The contents of these files document activity, including errors, on the web site. It has to be acknowledged that reading IIS log files isn't particularly easy. If the web site is a busy one, then there will be a lot of entries in each day's log files. Obviously, you don't want to be reading them unless you have a good reason to do so. Such reasons would be that either all other sources of information have been exhausted or the vendor's support team requested that you search the web server log files.

28.3.4.6 Levels of logging

Some applications allow you to configure how much logging will be done. For example, they might have provided logging levels similar to the ones described below. Of course, your vendor might have different names for these levels or they might have combined two or more of these levels into a single one.

- Error—only logs errors that are extremely serious. One rule of thumb is the only type of error that gets logged here would be one that is serious enough to call someone at 2 in the morning to handle.
- Warning—items that are significant enough to be tracked, but don't require immediate attention.
- Debug—logs entry and exit of nontrivial areas of code, especially events that are unusually, but not necessarily an error situation.
- Info—logs more information than the "debug" setting but not everything is being captured.
- Trace—log everything! Obviously, this level would be used in extremely rare situations, perhaps during development when the team is trying to track everything the system does.

Changing the logging setting seems to be different in every application I've supported. Examine the Administrator's Guide to understand if such configurability exists and how to modify it. Some examples of how it might be handled are:

- Editing a configuration file or a properties file
- Changes need to be made to a registry setting
- Adjustments are from within the application UI (User Interface)
- From within a "configuration" utility that is only available to Application Administrators

Be very careful when you change the logging level! If make the system log too much information, it can easily overwhelm the I/O bandwidth of your server or consume incredible amounts of disk space. A very good rule is to raise the logging level for short periods of time. Then change it back to normal while you examine the log files that were just created. As soon as it is safe to do so, you should delete any large log files that are no longer needed. Doing so can help prevent a situation where the application crashes due to a lack of available disk space.

28.3.5 Dump files

The term "dump file" refers to a file that contains a snapshot of a computer's memory at a specific point in time, i.e., when the dump file was created. Typically, a dump file is created either when an application or the operating system crashes. A dump file can provide detailed information to an analyst regarding the state of the system at the time of the crash. With experience, persistence, and a little luck, the analyst can pinpoint the cause of the crash.

28.3.5.1 Dump terminology

To the uninitiated, the terminology associated with dump files can be daunting. The definitions of some of these terms are provided here to give you an overview of what is being discussed.

- Binaries or executables—refers to files that contain the binary or executable code for a program, application, or even the operating system.
- Heap—the heap is a relatively large memory area from which blocks of memory are allocated to any process that requests memory. When a process is done using the memory block, it is returned so it can be allocated to another process in the future. If a process doesn't correctly return heap memory that has been allocated to it, this is referred to as a memory leak. Dumps can be created with or without the heap memory area being included.
- Full or complete dump—is a dump that includes all of the RAM (memory) that a computer has. In a modern server, this can be tens or hundreds of Gigabytes of memory. This version of a dump is much more complete, but is more difficult to deal with due to its size.
- Kernel dump—is a dump that is limited to the RAM (memory) that was occupied by the operating system's kernel. The kernel is core or essential portion of the operating system code. A kernel dump is significantly smaller than a full dump.
- Minidump or small memory dump—is a relatively small dump that doesn't include the binary or executable files that happened to be in memory at the time of the crash. It does include the stack for the thread or process that caused the crash to occur.
- Stack—a stack is a relatively small region of memory that is reserved for a specific process or thread. The process uses this temporary memory to hold registers and the return address when a function is called.
- Symbol information or symbol files—files that are created by the linker when executable (.exe) or library (.dll) files are created. The information in symbol files include global and local variables, function names and their address locations, and source file line numbers. This information is not needed for the executable file to run, but is extremely helpful to debug programs or when analyzing dump files.

28.3.5.2 Tools for analyzing dump files

There are a number of tools available that can help analyze dump files. Examples of the tools that can be used include:

- Debugging Tools for Windows from Microsoft is a collection of debuggers and related tools. The most recent versions are integrated into the Visual Studio development environment. This set of tools is part of the Windows SDK.

- DebugView is part of the Windows Sysinternals suite of utilities from Microsoft. It allows you to monitor debug output. This tool is available for free.
- BlueScreenView displays a report with information about crashes that result in a BSOD (Blue Screen of Death) on a Windows computer. It specifically lists the drivers or modules that potentially could have caused the crash. This utility is free, but the creator accepts donations.
- WhoCrashed is a freeware tool that examines Windows minidump files and can help isolate which new drivers or corrupted existing drivers could have caused the problems.

Some of the details that these tools extract and display from dump files include the following:

- A list of recent crashes
- The names and locations of dump files created after crashes
- A list of the processes that were running at the time of a crash
- A list of drivers that were loaded at the time of a crash
- Recreates the screen that was displayed when the system crashed
- Suggests the process or driver that it considers the most likely cause of the crash
- The call stack for the process or thread that was running when the crash occurred

28.3.5.3 Who is in the best position to analyze dumps?

The person who is in the best position to analyze dumps is probably the person that has the most experience. In your situation, that might be:

- You, the Application Administrator
- An in-house Systems Administrator
- Someone at the vendor's help desk

My advice here would be "don't try to be a hero." If you don't have experience reading dumps created by crashes, then gracefully defer to someone who has more expertise than you. If you want to develop this expertise that's great, but don't assume that just because you're enthusiastic and willing to learn that you're the best qualified. Maybe your best course of action would be to try to analyze the dump yourself and then compare your assessment of the cause with what the System Administrator or vendor support person comes up with.

28.4 TEST POSSIBLE SOLUTIONS

It seems to me that the 80/20 rule definitely applies to application problems. By this, I mean that 80% of problems are caused by 20% of the potential causes. If you check out the usual suspects, i.e., causes, then very likely you'll find the root of the problem. The following sections describe things I always check first.

28.4.1 Ask the user to perform the following steps

I can't guarantee this, but more often than not if you ask the user to perform the following steps the problem will be resolved. With luck, you can train your users to do them even *before* calling you or opening a ticket on the problem. This would save everyone a lot of time and trouble.

28.4.1.1 Exit the application

Have the user exit the application and then log back into it. There is a very good chance this will solve the problem.

28.4.1.2 Close all other applications
It never hurts to ask the user to close any other programs that are open. It may not help, but it certainly can't hurt and it's easy enough to do.

28.4.1.3 Clear their Internet browser cache
Every time a web site is brought up in a browser information is written to the browser's cache area. Eventually the cache can become cluttered with thousands and thousands of files. Ask the user to clear their browser cache and then log into the application again to see if the problem has been resolved.

Clearing the cache is slightly different for every browser, but it's never very difficult. The steps for Internet Explorer are:

- Click Tools and select Delete Browsing History...
- Deselect Preserve Favorites web site data and select Temporary Internet files, Cookies, and History
- Click Delete

If the browser being used is Mozilla Firefox, the steps are:

- Click Tools | Clear Recent History
- Select "Everything" as the time range to clear
- Click the "Clear Now" button

28.4.1.4 Connect to the network using VPN
If the user reporting the problem is working remotely then verify that they are connected to the organization's network via VPN software. If they aren't connected this way then request that they do this and try using the application again. This has resolved many, many login problems for users of the applications I've supported.

28.4.1.5 Try another internet browser
This isn't an obvious solution, but I've encountered a number of situations where a problem that occurs on one Internet browser doesn't occur when the application is brought up with a different type of browser. It doesn't seem intuitive that two browsers should act so differently, but I've seen it with my own eyes. It's definitely worth trying because it takes almost no effort and there is no risk involved.

If this resolves the problem, then you've solved one issue, but potentially created another. You now know that the original problem is a bug in the browser and not the application. You also know that a work-around is to use browser number two. If most of your users don't have that browser loaded, then they all may need to have it loaded. If your typical users don't have admin rights on their workstations, then someone else has to load the new browser for each of them.

28.4.1.6 Reboot their PC
It never hurts to ask the user to reboot their PC and see if the problem still exists. It only takes a couple of minutes to do and frequently clears up the problem.

28.4.1.7 A user session was abnormally terminated
Some applications are very, very particular about how the user is supposed to exit them. One application I supported required that the user click the "Log out" link to exit. If they happened to click the "X" in the upper right-hand corner of the window, then bad things would happen. By doing this, the user left open an entry in the application's records indicating the session was still active. The user couldn't log back into the application until that record was expunged.

If the application you support has tendencies like this, then you need to know about it and have a plan for dealing with it. Some options are

- Train, remind, and nag the users about this peculiarity of the application. Make sure they understand that they're hurting themselves if they slip and terminate the application incorrectly.
- Will the application eventually clear the "orphan" sessions automatically? If so, make sure the users know how long they have to wait before they can log back in.
- Write a script that will quickly, easily, and accurately clear the orphan record.
- Ensure that your backup knows about the application's tendency and how to handle it. If you write a script, then make sure he or she knows how to use it.
- See if the script be executed on a regular basis to clean up potential orphan sessions. You'll have to make absolutely sure that executing it won't harm legitimate session records.

28.4.1.8 Case sensitivity

There are some situations when the case, i.e., uppercase vs. lowercase, of text being entered is critical. Entering a value with the wrong case results in problems. Users need to be informed about such situations and warned of the consequences of using the wrong case. Some examples when case sensitivity might cause issues include:

- Account IDs
- Passwords
- Licensing keys
- File names, especially on a UNIX or Linux system
- Directory names, especially on a UNIX or Linux system

28.4.1.9 Special characters

There are some characters that have special meanings to computer software. If these characters are used in unexpected places or used incorrectly, they have the potential to cause problems. What makes these problems difficult to troubleshoot is that they occur very rarely and the symptoms are hard to identify. Some special characters that might cause problems are:

- Grave accents or back ticks (`) used in place of a normal apostrophe or tick (')
- Tilde (~)
- Pipe (|)
- Single quotation mark (') can cause SQL statements to fail if input strings aren't being scanned for this potential problem.

28.4.1.10 End of line characters

The way Windows and UNIX operating systems handle end of line conditions are fundamentally different. Windows represents an end of line situation with both a carriage return (CR) and a line feed (LF) characters. UNIX uses just a line feed (LF) character. If you move a file from one type of system to the other without taking this into consideration, you might be in for an unpleasant surprise.

28.4.2 Bouncing the application

There will be times when you will want to stop and restart the application to see if this solves a problem that is occurring. This is typically called "bouncing the application." Since taking the application down, even if just briefly, will affect the users, you don't want to do it without some forethought.

Each organization is different, but some steps you might want to take before bouncing the application include:

- Who is authorized to make this decision? The business owner of the application? The most senior user? The Application Administrator?
- If a maintenance window exists for the application during which it is typically stopped, can the stop/restart be done during that time frame?
- Should you alert users that the application is about to come down? How do you notify them about it?
- If you aren't able to reach all of the users, can the stop/start be done anyway?
- If the application or its processes are being monitored, then it's a good idea to disable the monitoring process during the outage. If you don't disable monitoring, then alerts will be sent out stating that the application has gone down. This might cause panic, confusion, and general mayhem.
- Should an application bounce be logged or documented? If so, where? Is there a physical notebook? A log file on a common drive? A spreadsheet on a portal?
- Will this outage affect the uptime statistics of the application? If you're required to meet certain available statistics, you might consider delaying the bounce until a maintenance window so the uptime won't be impacted.

28.4.2.1 What can bouncing the application solve

There are several situations that bouncing the application is likely to resolve. The most significant is if the application has a memory leak. Ideally, when a computer program needs memory to perform some function, it requests a block of memory from the operating system. When the program is done using the memory, it releases it, i.e., gives it back, to the operating system, thus enabling it to be used by another application at some future time. If due to a coding or logic error the program doesn't release the memory when it's done with it, then this is called a memory leak. This is bad because over time the application will request more and more memory and never give it back. Eventually, the server can run out of available memory. When this happens, the server will either crash, hang up, or start behaving oddly.

If your application has a memory leak, then stopping it releases all of the accumulated memory back to the operating system so it becomes available again. As an Application Administrator, you can't fix the application's memory leak problem. The only thing you can do is to bounce the application when the lack of available memory becomes a problem. You can also report this issue to the vendor and hope that their developers will fix it in a future release.

You can track the amount of memory being used by the application by using a tool like Performance Monitor or Task Manager on a Windows server. The TOP command on a UNIX server will show how much memory each application is using. If it becomes clear that the application continues to accumulate more and more memory and never releases it, then you can be fairly confident that it has a memory leak problem.

28.4.3 Bouncing the server

Just as stopping and starting the application can clear up some issues, starting and stopping the server can also clear up issues. It wouldn't be accurate if I didn't acknowledge that some operating systems don't need to be stopped and started on a regular basis. It seems like Linux and UNIX servers can be run for months or years without ever being restarted.

Some potential downsides to bouncing the server are:

- It will probably take longer than bouncing the application takes
- If other applications are running on the same server, they will be affected too
- Downtime statistics are more likely to be affected

Each organization is different, but some steps you might want to take before bouncing a server include:

- Who is authorized to make this decision? The business owner of the application? The most senior user? The Application Administrator?
- Should you alert users that the server and application are about to come down? How do you notify them about it?
- If a maintenance window exists for the application, can the stop/restart be done during that time frame?
- Does the application need to be shut down gracefully before the server is stopped?
- Will the application come up automatically after the server is back up or is manual intervention required?
- Does someone need to verify that the application came up cleanly after the server bounce?
- Is there a need to keep the users out of the application until everything is back up and fully functional? If this is required, then how is it accomplished?
- If the server, application, or its processes are being monitored, then it's a good idea to disable the monitoring process during the outage. If you don't disable monitoring, you might end up with a lot of people panicking and wondering what's going on.
- Should a bounced server be logged or documented? If so where? Is there a notebook? A log file on a common drive? A spreadsheet on a portal?
- Will this outage affect the uptime statistics of the application? If you're required to meet certain available statistics, you might consider delaying the bounce until a maintenance window so the uptime won't be impacted.

28.4.4 E-mail problems

If your application is capable of generating e-mail, then eventually an e-mail-related problem may occur. If a user isn't getting e-mails that he or she is expecting, the first thing I do is suggest that he or she looks in his or her "junk email" folder. This tip is especially true if the e-mails in question are new, the application has been ported to a new server, or the e-mail server has changed. This has been the source of my supposed "missing" e-mails on more than one occasion.

To troubleshoot e-mails problems, you should check the following:

- Is the e-mail server correctly defined in the application's configuration files?
- Is the e-mail server up and running?
- Is network connectivity to the e-mail server available?
- Is the port open between the application server and the e-mail server?
- Is e-mail server set up to accept e-mail from the application server and send it to external addresses?
- Do the e-mails being generated by the application have file types that are prohibited? For example, some e-mail servers won't allow "exe," "zip," or "bat" files to be attached to incoming e-mails.
- Do the e-mails being generated by the application have attached files that are too large to be processed? Some e-mail servers have an upper limit of 5 MB attachments.

If none of the above solves the problem, you might need to contact your e-mail group and ask them to examine the e-mail log files to see what exactly was sent to it. Before contacting them make sure you know the name of the server that the e-mail originated on as well as the date and times when specific e-mails should have been created. This will help the messaging team search the logs on the e-mail server(s).

28.4.5 DLL hell

In the "bad old days," it was common for users to experience a situation that was commonly referred to as "DLL hell." When 16-bit versions of Windows operating systems were prevalent, it was fairly common for multiple applications to rely on DLLs (Dynamic Link Libraries). DLLs contained routines, essentially sub-routines, which applications called for instead of duplicating the code internally. In concept, this was a great idea, but in practice problems could occur when one application upgraded a DLL that other applications were also using. Occasionally, the new version of the DLL was changed in such a way that it worked for the application that updated it, but didn't work for the other application(s). These problems were especially difficult to diagnose because it might not be obvious that a DLL had been changed. Once the root cause was identified, the choices were pretty bleak. It sometimes boiled down to Application #1 would work and #2 would be broken or #2 would work and #1 would be broken.

Fortunately, DLL hell isn't as significant a problem as it once was. There are several reasons why this former problem is no longer the menace that it once was. A primary reason is that by using 32-bit operating systems, each application runs in a separate memory space. This allows each application to use its own version of library files like DLLs.

28.4.5.1 Registering DLLs

As an Application Administrator, you might occasionally have to install and then register a DLL or OCX. Registering a DLL causes the appropriate references in the Registry to be created. From that point on, calls to that DLL can succeed. The steps to register a DLL or OCX are:

- Open a command window
- CD to C:\windows\system32
- Enter "Regsvr32.dll name," where name is the name of the DLL to be registered, e.g., librfc32.dll

28.5 SEEK SPECIALIZED ASSISTANCE

There are always some problems that are harder to resolve than others. Once you're tried the easy solutions to resolve a problem and found they don't work, then you have to dig deeper to handle the tougher problems. Every application and environment is different, but the following tips should help resolving your more difficult problems.

28.5.1 Requesting vendor support

If you weren't able to resolve the problem by applying tried-and-true fixes, then you probably need to call in the experts. To be perfectly honest, fixing the application isn't your job. Technically, your job is to make sure that your organization's instance of the application is running. These aren't the same things.

Your ability to fix what's wrong with application is severely limited due to:

- You don't have the source code for the application
- You may not be familiar with the language the application was written in
- You didn't participate in design meetings for the application
- You probably don't have documentation on the database structure
- You almost certainly don't have the time to learn all of the above

My point here is that there is nothing wrong with relying on the expertise of the vendor's support group for help. After all, they wrote the thing and you're paying them for support and maintenance. They ought to be able to fix it when it isn't working. Your responsibility is limited to:

- Open a ticket with the vendor's support desk
- Provide all of the details about the problem that are available to you

- Work with the support group as they request either additional information or want to test specific solutions
- Keep the Business Owner and your boss up-to-date on progress

28.5.2 Problems with other systems

There will be times when problems with your application will be caused by something totally outside of your control. For example, the root of the problem might be in another subsystem. If the error logs created by the application include messages indicating that the database engine isn't responding to requests, then you don't need to spend any more time looking at the application. You need to contact someone who can troubleshoot the database system.

A potential list of subsystems that might be causing problems is provided in the following sections. Depending on the size and layout of your organization's IT department, all of the teams listed here might not exist. They might have other names or multiple teams might have been combined. If you find other subsystems that are applicable in your environment, be sure to document them so you can check them again the next time a problem of this type occurs.

You need to know individuals not just the names of teams that are responsible for other systems. When you're trying to get your application operational again, you won't have time to be researching who's who in the IT department. You need to have a list of names, e-mail addresses, and telephone numbers that you can call right away if you need them.

Be sure to have a copy of those names and telephone numbers that is independent from your computer. This might mean a paper copy of them or have all of them in your cell phone. There might be a time that you need to call someone and your computer either isn't handy or isn't working. For example, when you're on vacation and didn't bring your laptop along.

28.5.2.1 Database team

As has been stated several times, most enterprise-wide applications depend on a database server to store their data. It isn't difficult to determine if your problems are being caused by the database system. Some quick checks that you can perform are:

- When you or users try to log in, do error messages include references to the database engine errors, e.g., ORA-00000?
- Do application log entries contain references to database engine errors?
- Can you successfully ping the database server?
- Can you telnet to the database server specifying the port that should be open between the servers? The default ports for some common database engines are:
  - Oracle—1521
  - Microsoft SQL Server—1433
  - MySQL—3306
- Can you connect to the database from the application server using a tool like SQL*Plus, Toad, or SQL Developer?

28.5.2.2 Virtual server team

There are many advantages to running applications on virtual servers instead of on physical servers. One major disadvantage is that it adds another level of complexity to the environment. As an Application Administrator, you almost certainly won't have the knowledge, experience, or access to install, diagnose, or correct problems with the virtual server installation. If your application is running on a virtual server and you suspect that there is something wrong with it, then you need to contact the technical specialists who support this layer on the server.

28.5.2.3 Storage subsystem

The storage subsystem, i.e., disk storage, which your application depends on, can be physical drives that are actually connected to the physical server or they are provided by a SAN (Storage Area Network) subsystem. If your server is a virtual server, then by definition SAN drives are being used. If your server is physical, then the storage subsystem could be either local drives or SAN drives.

One way to determine whether you're experiencing storage subsystem problems is to open Windows Explorer and right-click on each of the drives. If the properties look OK, then try to access a directory or file. If everything looks OK and the performance seems normal, then the storage subsystem is likely functioning correctly. Obviously, this is a very simplistic test so don't rely on it to assume that the storage system is running correctly.

If your drives are physical and are having a problem, then you need to contact the Data Center team about this. If the drives are SAN and they aren't available, then you need to contact the team that supports SAN storage.

28.5.2.4 Load balancer or cluster team

If your application environment includes a load balancer or a cluster, then you need to determine which devices are functioning and which aren't. In the case of a load balanced environment, each server has its own physical IP address. You need to ping each server to confirm that it's operational.

If the application is running on a server, then each server will have its own IP address. The cluster will also have a separate IP address. You need to ping each device and the cluster to determine which are and which aren't available.

If the entire set of devices and support structures, e.g., load-balancing device or cluster, isn't available, then you need to contact the team that supports this structure.

28.5.2.5 Network team

If you know that devices on each end of the network are functional but they aren't able to communicate with each other, then the problem is possibly within the network. For example, if you know that the application server is functioning and the DBA team has assured you that the database server is working, but the two servers can't communicate, then it doesn't seem like a stroke of genius to recognize that network issues might be causing the problem. Contact the Network team and provide them with as many details about the problem as you can.

28.5.2.6 Security team

If users are having trouble connecting to the organization's network, this might be a security-related issue. Their network accounts could have been locked or disabled.

If authentication is done via either (AD) Active Directory or SSO (Single Sign On) and if problems are occurring in those subsystems, then users most likely won't be able to log into any applications. Contact the organization's security team to find out what security-related issues might be taking place.

28.5.2.7 Firewall team

If you, your users, or your application is able to access some servers but not all of them, then it's possible that the firewall is the cause of the problem. Properly setting up and maintaining the organization's firewalls are a difficult and complex undertaking. As changes are made to them to include new users, servers, or applications, it's possible that errors are introduced. Contact the firewall or security team for help resolving these types of access issues. It will help if you can be as explicit as possible when describing the problems you're experiencing.

28.5.2.8 DNS team

If your organization has a web presence then it likely has a DNS (Domain Name System) server. The DNS server is what translates URLs like www.google.com into the underlying IP address, 74.125.142.103 in this case. If the DNS server stops responding or becomes corrupted, then users and applications running on your network may have trouble connecting to external servers or web sites on the Internet. Contact the DNS team or network team if there is no DNS team if users have trouble in accessing external web sites.

28.5.2.9 Other subsystems

Are there other subsystems or support teams that you need to be aware of and make friends with? Network with the other Application Administrators in your organization to make sure you're not overlooking groups that support subsystems that could potentially cause problems for you or the applications you support.

28.5.3 Finger pointing between vendors (or your internal teams)

One of the most difficult, time-consuming, and awkward situations you can be put into is if two different groups each says the problem is caused by the other group's software. Each would claim that their software is acting correctly and the other package is doing things incorrectly. The groups might be two different vendors, for example, the application vendor and the database vendor. It might also be an internal group and a vendor, for example, the application vendor and the network team might blame each other for slow response time being experienced by users at a remote location.

I think that even Solomon would have a difficult time dealing with this predicament. My best advice is to stay calm, stay neutral, and stay focused. Don't take sides because if you do then, you're going to lose the trust of one side. Try to maintain a professional attitude.

I've also found that it helps to get both sides together instead of acting as a go-between. If you carry messages back and forth between them, there is a very real risk that you'll misquote one side and introduce new complications into the situation. Schedule a meeting or a conference call so they can talk to each other. Also try to use desktop sharing so everyone can see the problem at the same time. If both sides see the error as it occurs, it might be harder for someone to deny that their software is the cause of the problem.

28.6 DOCUMENT THE PROBLEM AND THE SOLUTION

To be an effective Application Administrator, you need to document everything new that happens on the application. If a new problem occurs and a fix is found, you need to document both the problem and the solution. All documentation needs to be available in a location where everyone can access it. This might be on a network drive or on a portal. By doing this, you improve the organization's processes for responding to and correcting problems.

28.6.1 Document your troubleshooting tips

When things are going badly in your application's world, what do you do? What steps do you take to get the application back up and what order do you do them in? These are the kind of tips that you need to document in advance. The last thing you want to do is to be scrambling around trying to put together this information when the users and your boss are looking at you and expecting the application to be operational ASAP.

Your documentation should be as detailed as necessary to help resolve the problem. Since it might be weeks or months before you run into a given problem again it makes sense to have more rather than fewer details in your documentation. When you're trying to remember a problem and how to fix it, you'll thank yourself for having provided an abundance of details the next time it occurs.

Don't ever forget that this documentation isn't for your use alone. If your backup can use it to bring the application online in your absence, it means one less call to you while you're on sick leave or vacation. Good documentation will also enable your replacement to support the application after you've been promoted or transferred.

28.6.2 Screenshots

Taking and saving a screenshot might seem very low tech, but it can save a lot of time and confusion. I try to include as many screenshots as reasonable in my documentation. They help refresh my memory when I'm dealing with an issue that I haven't seen in months.

Capturing a screenshot is very easy to do. The following steps are all there is to it.

- Pressing the "PrtScn" key captures the entire screen and writes it to the clipboard. If you have multiple monitors, it captures both of them.
- Pressing Alt/PrtScn captures an image of just the window that has focus.
- Pressing the Ctrl/PrtScn buttons captures just the primary monitor if you're using multiple monitors.

Once the image of the screen is in your clipboard, then it's treated like any other object. You can paste it into a Word document, into an e-mail, or save it as a file. You can also paste it into an image editor like "Paint" and edit it before saving it.

Screenshots can be extremely valuable when doing the following:

- Providing details to a vendor related to a problem
- Documenting a process
- Diagnosing user problems by having them send you an e-mail with a screenshot in it.

When users have problems with an application, I always try to get a screenshot from them. Once you get the screenshot, you should first look for simple, but easily made mistakes. If it's a web-based app, look for errors like the following:

- Incorrect URL scheme, for example, https: instead of http:
- Incorrect slash marks, i.e., \\ instead of //
- wwww or ww instead of www
- Incorrect URL host name, for example, www.amozon.com instead of www.amazon.com
- The suffix is inaccurate, e.g., .con instead of .com in a URL
- Some application URLs require that a port number be specified. If your application requires this, then make sure the correct port is specified and is separated by a colon
- Is the user referring to a file or path that doesn't exist?
- Have the user left off a parameter?
- Is the user logging in correctly?

28.6.3 Develop your own troubleshooting list

You need to develop your own "Tips and Trick" documentation for the application. Every time you learn something new you should document it. It doesn't matter if you combine all of your tips into a single document or create separate documents for each tip. As long as you know where to find them or can do a search to find them that's all that matters.

What should be in your "Tips and Tricks" documents? The following are some examples, but don't be limited by this list. Basically, anything that you've ever done to improve the application or clear up a problem is a candidate for this list. Your documented tips and tricks should never stop growing.

- How to kill a user session?
- How to stop and start the application?
- How to determine if the application is responding to requests?
- How to determine if the application server is hung?
- How to unlock a user session?
- How to determine how many users are in the application?
- How to determine who changed something within the application?
- How to recompile or rebuild the application?
- How to examine log files created by the application?
- How to create a backup of the application?
- How to restore data from a backup that was previously taken?

What are the sources for your "Tips and Tricks" documents? The basic answer is everything! Everything you do, everything you see, everything you read about, every time you talk to a colleague about any application. There should be no limitation on what might serve as the source for a tip. I've woken up in the middle of the night with an insight that eventually became one of my tricks. A few practical sources are listed here, but don't be limited by this list.

- Your own experiences with this or another application
- Advice from other Application Administrators
- Innovative things you see your coworkers do
- A user might find a clever way to accomplish something in the application that's worth remembering
- Vendor documentation like the Administrator's Guide
- Vendor web sites frequently have white papers or lists of suggestions
- Presentations at user conferences
- Articles you read in trade journals
- Articles or postings you read online

Things to Do or Know How to Do in Advance

This may be hard to believe but there will be times in your professional career when things will get a little tense. Maybe the application has crashed and you need it up right now! The predicament might be that you need to shut down the application right away. Whatever the situation, there will be times when you need to do something immediately. You won't have time to look this up in a manual or Google it or contact the vendor's support. The solution is to know how to do it in advance and hopefully have written documentation about it.

The sections in this chapter describe just a few situations when you'll wish you were better prepared for if they happen to occur. As you gain experience with one or more applications, you should constantly be looking for situations where a little preparation would have helpful. Taking a few minutes to write up a description of the situation will be greatly appreciated by you or your successors.

29.1 WHO'S LOGGED INTO THE APPLICATION

There will be situations when you need to know who is logged into the system or who was logged in at a specific time. Does the application provide a way of finding out the answers to this question? Some applications provide a screen that the administrator can use to find this out. If you're really lucky, the application will also let you find out when each user logged in and what they are currently doing. You'll save both time and frustration if you know how to obtain this information in advance.

Some examples of when this knowledge might be needed include:

- You need all users to exit the application so it or the server can be rebooted. If you can quickly get this list of names, then you can contact them asking them to log off. Even better would be if you could get a list of users AND their supervisors. If they get an e-mail or IM from their boss directing them to log off, they'll probably respond more quickly.
- In my experience, there have been many times when data was changed within an application or maybe an object or a report was deleted. Something went wrong and you are asked to figure out who did it. If you're very lucky, the application will have an audit trail capability so you can run a report and see exactly who changed or deleted objects. If you're not so lucky, then the system might only provide a list of who is on the system now or was logged on at an earlier-in-time. Using that list you or the Business Owner can contact each user to try to determine who caused the problem.
- No matter how powerful the CPU, how many processors the server has, or how much memory a server has, it seems that the application never runs as fast as the users would like it to run. There will be times when they claim performance is particularly bad and insist that something be done about it. At these times, it helps to know who is logged into the application and what they are doing. Maybe someone is executing a massive search or a report that is pulling every piece of information since the beginning of time. If the application provides the ability to list the users and what screens they're on, then you're 90% of the way to having this problem solved. If you can only get a list of users in the application, then at least you have a starting point. From this point on, you have to search logs, look at which processes are running, or you could contact each active user and ask them what they're doing.

- Some applications allow a user to log into the application multiple times at a given time. Other application don't allow multiple simultaneous sessions. For some applications, this is an option that can be configured either way. If the application doesn't allow multiple simultaneous sessions for a user, then you might get a call from a user claiming that she can't log in because someone is currently logged in as her.

There are at least two explanations for such a condition. The first is that the user didn't log out of the application cleanly the last time she was in it. Perhaps her computer crashed or she used Task Manager to kill the application. The other possibility is that someone else is actually logged in as that user. In either case, if the application allows you to list all users currently in it, you can try to determine which situation it is. A step that you'll eventually need to do is to kill the current session whether it's an orphan session or a hijacked session it will need to be killed. If it turns out to be an imposter or hacker has logged in as the user, you need to kill the session and immediately change the password for that account.

29.2 TERMINATING USER SESSIONS

There are certain situations when users shouldn't be in the system at all. The presence of users could cause severe problems when certain activities are taking place. At a minimum, it will be frustrating for the user because they will very likely lose any updates they make and their session is likely to be terminated prematurely. Some examples of these situations are:

- During upgrades to either the application or the operating system
- While backups are being created
- When data is being restored from a backup file
- When the application is in the process of coming up, but isn't completely operational yet
- In the middle of a shutdown sequence
- In some applications, certain administrative functions must be done in "single user" mode
- During a maintenance window that is regularly scheduled, for example, every Sunday evening at 10 pm

If a user logs on during one of these forbidden periods, then the Application Administrator needs to know how to terminate their session.

29.3 PREVENTING USER SESSIONS

The previous section described situations when users shouldn't be logged into the application. The advice it offered was that the Application Administrator should know how to terminate those sessions. A better solution would be to prevent users from logging into the application at all. This would prevent numerous problematic situations. You need to know if there is a way to prohibit access to the application.

If such a capability exists, can it be turned on or off programmatically? If it's possible for a program or script to do this, then this functionality could be used in conjunction with backups or scheduled maintenance outages to ensure that users aren't logging in when they shouldn't be.

29.4 BRINGING DOWN THE SYSTEM

Applications typically provide a method of bringing down the executable or services. This method might not be able to bring the application down if users are currently logged into it. Is there an emergency or override version of this method?

For example, one application I support has a command line interface that allows the administrator to perform functions like

- Start the application
- Stop the application
- Display the status of the application
- List the number of users logged into the application
- Create new users
- Delete existing users
- Display details of the specified user

The "stop" command won't work if one or more users are currently logged into the application. However, there is an override for this situation. By entering the command "stop immediate," the application will be stopped regardless of whether or not users are logged in. If this command is executed, then user sessions are immediately terminated. Obviously, this should only be utilized in the most critical circumstances since forcing all processes to terminate may have an adverse impact on the user, the application, the data, or the system.

29.5 **AUTOMATE MAINTENANCE TASKS**

Most working days for Application Administrators are very busy. To-do lists always seem to be brimming with activities like applying upgrades, testing new versions of the software, and working with the vendor support group on existing tickets. There will also be unexpected events such as when users encounter problems with the application that need to be investigated and resolved.

Anything you can do to automate regular maintenance tasks will free up time that you'll need for your many other obligations. Some examples of maintenance tasks that can be automated are listed here. With a little imagination and ingenuity, you should be able to automate many tasks that would otherwise take up your valuable time. Obviously, not all of these tasks will be necessary for every application.

- Stop and start the application's services periodically to free up memory that has been leaked by the program. One application vendor recommended that their application be bounced every week to ensure memory leakage didn't become a problem. We wrote scripts to stop the services every Saturday morning at 1:00 am and start them back up at 1:15 am.
- Check the available disk space on server drives by having a script run periodically. If the amount of free space falls below a threshold, have the script send an e-mail alerting you to this potential problem.
- If your environment experiences problems with DNS names, you could write a script to periodically ping your servers by name. If they don't exist, then the script would e-mail you an alert.
- Write a script to ping your application servers to confirm that they are alive and responding. If the ping fails, then have the script send you an e-mail, text message, or page you. I've seen many application users that view the QA environment as almost a "production-light" platform. If QA goes down, they expect that this problem will be addressed immediately. A similar set of scripts could be used to check up on your nonproduction platforms, e.g., DEV.
- Write scripts that confirm that application services are active. If they aren't, then the script will send out an e-mail, text, or call alerting you to this problem. Alternatively, if the script notices that a critical service is stopped, it could bounce or restart the application.
- Periodically confirm that databases are available or the application hasn't disconnected from them. One application I supported would drop the database connection at random intervals. When that happened, the first user who noticed it would open up a ticket or call us directly. A script was written to scan the

application error logs regularly looking for a specific error code. If that code was found, the script e-mailed an administrator who would bounce the application and reestablish the database connection. If this problem had happened more frequently, we would have gone the extra step and had the script bounce the application to reduce downtime to an absolute minimum.

- Output a report by writing a script to pull that data from the database and then e-mail it to the recipient. If the application has a reporting package, this might not be needed, but there might be straightforward reports you need that can be run outside of the standard reporting package.
- Clean up log files by having a script delete them when they get to a certain age. Another option would be to have a script zip up older log files. Since they are text files and contain a high percentage of duplication, log files should compress to a very small percentage of their original size. This would allow you to keep log files for a much longer period of time without consuming valuable disk space.
- Run a script to extract data from databases that needs to sent to other applications, vendors, clients, or regulatory agencies. An Application Administrator could manually run a SQL query to extract the same data, but why tie up an administrator if a script can accomplish the same task?
- A relatively simple script could be written to search log files for specific phrases and e-mail, text, or call an Application Administrator if the phrases were found. Some examples of phrases that you might look for would include database connection errors, invalid attempts to log into the application, or attempts by users to make changes they aren't authorized to make.
- Creating scripts to FTP files to and from the server isn't difficult to do. If you've already written a script to extract data, then adding FTP statements to send it to your vendor, client, supplier, regulatory agency, etc., shouldn't be too difficult. A script could also be written to pull a file from an external source via FTP and kick off the process to import a data file into the application's database.

29.6 USER FAQs

It's been my experience that as a group users tend to ask the same questions over and over again. I'm not criticizing them for this. If a user encounters a problem once every year, it's unlikely that he or she will remember the instructions you gave them last year. Another reason why you might get the same questions asked repeatedly is because new users are regularly being added to the system.

One way of preparing for their questions is by having a list of user's FAQs ready. If you can write up answers to potential questions, then you can simply give them the appropriate document when they ask a question. You want to make sure that document you give them answers their questions so make sure it's accurate, clear, and includes screenshots where appropriate. If a user asks a question that you haven't already prepared an answer for, then write up an answer and add this question to your list of FAQs.

Ideally, you would put your FAQ list somewhere the users can access it and train them to look there before contacting you. If you are successful in doing this, then you may eliminate the majority of such questions. Examples of where these files could be listed include a portal, a common network drive, a wiki. If the application has an announcement page or a welcome page, then you should publicize the location of the FAQ files there.

Some potential FAQ topics are:

- The URL of the application if it's web based
- How to start the application if it isn't web based
- If the application isn't web based, a list of any software that needs to be loaded onto a new user's workstation
- How to change your password
- Requirements of a valid password, e.g., minimum length, mixture of characters

- Restrictions on reusing passwords
- Location of any documentation or training material for the application
- How to define a printer
- How to navigate through the application
- How to see data from last month or last year
- How to recover a data (file, folder, report, etc.) that has been deleted
- The day and times of the maintenance window, if one exists
- Time frame when the books are closed on one year and the next is opened
- What information must be included when reporting an error
- How to request that user permissions be modified
- How to request that a locked user account be unlocked
- How a user can modify their preferences
- How to change a user's name or account ID

29.7 LOG FILES

Applications can create an incredible number of log file entries, even when things are going normally. The entries can accumulate so quickly that it isn't practical to examine them manually on a daily basis. Can you set up an automated process to scan the log files for specific error entries?

29.7.1 Vendor support will request log files

Vendor technical support will frequently request that you send them one or more log files when you open a ticket on a problem you've encountered. If they normally ask for log files, then you should automatically include them when a new ticket is opened. To be able to respond more quickly, you should be familiar with the name and location of the log file(s) that the application creates. If you haven't done this already, you should write a script or batch file to automate the process of capturing the log files that the vendor typically requests.

Capturing log files is something that should be done sooner rather than later. Two advantages of copying them as soon as possible after the error has been discovered are:

1. The log file you send to the vendor will have less "post-problem" clutter in it
2. The log file won't get archived or renamed in the interim time period.

29.7.2 User logon attempts

Do the application logs show when users log on/log off? If so, this could be used to monitor legitimate and unauthorized access attempts. You won't need this knowledge very frequently, but when you're trying to identify who was on the system when a problem has occurred this information could prove to be invaluable.

29.7.3 Understanding log files

Log files don't provide any value unless they are read and interpreted. It's no exaggeration to say that reading log files is difficult. They can be extremely long. The contents of log files are pretty cryptic with their codes and abbreviations. The secret of reading log files is practice, practice, and more practice. If you need help, hopefully you can contact the vendor's technical support group for advice. Another potential source of assistance would be to check the papers presented at the user conferences to see if any provided tips on interpreting log file entries.

29.8 THINGS TO KNOW ABOUT A SERVER AND HOW TO LEARN THEM

There will be times when you need to know specific details about your servers. For example, if you report a problem to the vendor support group, they may have specific questions about the server or how the application was installed. The quicker you can respond to questions of this nature, the sooner they can help you.

Listed here are details about the server that I've had to find at one time or another. Hopefully, this list will be useful to you as well. Note—The UNIX/Linux commands listed here may not work on all variations of those operating systems.

Detail	Source
What is the name of the server	Windows In a command prompt enter the *systeminfo* command. One of the first sections is Host Name UNIX/Linux Enter the command *hostname* at the command line
What is the server's IP address?	Windows In a command prompt enter the command *sysconfig*. Look for the lines labeled IPv4 Address or IPv6 Address UNIX/Linux Enter the command *host machine-name.domain.name* at the command line Linux Enter the command *ip addr show* at the command line
What is the IP address the outside world sees for the server?	Windows In an Internet browser bring up the URL *whatismyipaddress*. The IP address that the world outside your network sees will be listed at the top of the screen
What operating system is running on the server?	Windows In a command prompt enter the *systeminfo* command. One of the first sections is OS Name UNIX/Linux Enter the command *uname -a* at the command line
What domain is the server on?	Windows In a command prompt enter the *systeminfo* command. Look for the section labeled "Domain" UNIX/Linux Enter the command *cat /etc/resolv.conf* at the command line
Is the operating system 32 bit or 64 bit?	Windows Click on the Windows icon, right-click on Computer, and select Properties. Look for the section labeled "System Type." It will specify 32 bit or 64 bit UNIX/Linux Enter the command *getconf KERNEL_BITS* at the command line Another command is *bootinfo -y*
Is the server virtual or physical?	Windows Click on the Windows icon, right-click on Computer, and select Properties. Look for the section labeled "System Manufacturer" or "System Model." If these values contain the name of a computer manufacturer like Dell, HP, IBM, etc., then the server is physical. If they contain a value like VMWare, then the service is virtual A shortcut that will tell you if a server is a VMWare server is to look for an icon in the toolbar that say "VMWare tools" UNIX/Linux Enter the command *model* at the command line Other possible commands are *machinfo* and *prtconf*

How much memory does the server have?	**Windows** In a command prompt enter the *systeminfo* command. Look for the section labeled "Total Physical Memory" **UNIX/Linux** Enter the command *top* at the command line
How much disk space does the server have?	**Windows** Bring up Windows Explorer, right-click on each drive, and select Properties. The total size and amount of available disk space are listed **UNIX/Linux** Enter the command *df* at the command line
Are the disk drives physical or SAN?	**Windows** Click on Start	Administrative Tools	Computer Management. Then click on Storage	Disk Management. Then right-click on the name of the drive, e.g., "Disk 0" and select properties. Under the General tab will be a description of the drive, for example, "VMware Virtual IDE Hard Drive" or "Hitachi." This value will indicate whether the drive is physical or SAN **UNIX/Linux** Enter the command *lsdev -Cc disk* at the command line
How many processors does the server have?	**Windows** In a command prompt enter the *systeminfo* command. Look for the section labeled "Processors." The number and type of processors will be listed **UNIX/Linux** Enter the command *top* at the command line
How many cores does the server have?	**Windows** This is a multistep process 1. In a command prompt run the *systeminfo* command and get the number of processors 2. Open Task Manager, on the Performance tab select View	CPU History	One Graph per CPU. Count the number of graphs being displayed 3. The number of graphs divided by the number of processors is the number of cores **UNIX/Linux** Enter the command *grep -ic ^processor /proc/cpuinfo* at the command line **Linux** Enter the command *grep "^core id" /proc/cpuinfo	sort -u	wc -l* to get the number of CPU cores per CPU
How many NIC (Network Interface Cards) does the server have?	**Windows** In a command prompt enter the *systeminfo* command. One of the last sections is Network Card(s). The type and number of NIC cards will be listed here **UNIX/Linux** Enter the command *netstat -i* at the command line Other commands are *ip link show*
What software is running on the server?	**Windows** In a command prompt enter the command *wmic product get name, version, vendor* The output will list all software loaded on the server **UNIX/Linux** Depending on the version of the operating system, use one of the following commands: *pkginfo* *swlist* *lslpp*

Continued

Detail	Source
What scripts, tasks, or jobs are launched at startup?	Windows There are several places to find programs that are started when a Windows server comes up 1. Click the Start icon and then the Run option. Enter *msconfig* in the text field labeled "Open." When the System Configuration screen comes up, click the Startup tab. The list of all programs that come up when the server starts is on this screen 2. Open the Services panel by selecting Start | Administrative Tools | Services. All services with Startup Type of Automatic are started when the service comes up 3. Select the Start icon then All Programs | Startup This will list additional programs that are started up when the server comes up
Who is currently logged onto the server?	Windows Bring up Task Manager and select the Users tab. The list of users currently connected to this server will be listed UNIX/Linux Enter the command *who* at the command line
Who can log onto this server?	Windows Click on Start | Administrative Tools | Computer Management and then click on Local Users and Groups | Groups. Double-click on Administrators. The list of names and groups that are able to log onto this server will be displayed UNIX/Linux Enter command *listusers* at the command line
Who has admin rights to this server?	Windows Click on Start | Administrative Tools | Computer Management and then click on Local Users and Groups | Groups. Double-click on Administrators. The list of names and groups all have admin rights to the server will be displayed UNIX/Linux The root account has admin rights to a UNIX/Linux server
When was the server last rebooted?	Windows In a command prompt window enter the command *net stats srv* The line labeled "Statistics since" indicate the date and time of the last reboot UNIX/Linux Enter command *uptime* at the command line

29.9 EMERGENCY SITUATIONS

There are some emergencies that can occur in the life of an Application Administrator that will keep your job exciting. Hopefully, these will occur few and far between, but if they occur you'll need to react immediately. You won't have time to contact vendor support, a coworker, or your predecessor. You can never completely prepare for an emergency, but if you have a cheat sheet for every potential problem that you can think of then that's about the best preparation you can perform. Of course, if you run into an unforeseen situation, you'll want to document it and add it to your list.

29.9.1 How to unlock an administrator account

Administrator accounts are special in that they allow to you perform actions that other accounts aren't able to perform. One task that they are typically capable of performing is to unlock user accounts that have somehow gotten locked. An observant reader will ask "how do you unlock an Administrator's account if it should happen to get locked?" That is an excellent question. Depending on the application, there may be several possible answers. If this isn't covered in the Administrator's Guide, then you need to contact the vendor's Support Group and get the answer.

One possibility is to create several accounts that have administrator rights. For example, you could endow your personal account with these rights. The account created for your backup should also have them. Finally, an admin account should have them. If one of these accounts gets locked, then one of the other accounts could be used to unlock it. The downside to this is that now there are more accounts to keep track of and that could potentially be compromised.

Some applications have a specific account which is the only one that can truly do everything. If this account gets locked, then you don't have the luxury of logging into another account and unlocking it. How can you unlock it then? You need to get this answer from the vendor, but I've seen two ways of being able to do this.

- One application I supported allowed the admin account to be unlocked by making a change in a database table. There was a specific table that contained information about accounts. If the Administrator's account was locked, then a SQL UPDATE statement could be executed to change the date value in column "USERLOGONOK" in table "USERS" to some future date. Making this change to any account, including the Administrator account, would unlock it.
- Another application also had a database-oriented solution to unlocking the Administrator account. In their database setting, the value of column "LOCK_TYPE_ID" in table "USER" to NULL would unlock any account including the Administrator's account.

In both of these applications actually unlocking a locked Administrator account wasn't particularly difficult, but you had to know how to do it. If you were in an emergency situation and needed that account locked immediately, you certainly didn't want to open a ticket with the vendor and wait for a response. The moral of the story is to know how to do this long before you need it.

29.9.2 Modifying the administrator password

Changing the administrator account password for an application may be significantly more difficult than changing a typical user's password so it's important for you to know how to do this in advance. There may be times when changing this password must be done immediately. For example, what if the other administrator gets fired or quits? He or she knows the password and it would be in everyone's best interest if it gets changed before any mischief gets done. Another potential situation is when it appears likely that someone else has been accessing the admin account.

It's usually relatively easy to change the typical user's account. There might be a "Change password" button or link on the main screen of the application. You might have to go to a preferences page to get to that link. Unfortunately, it isn't always as easy to change the Administrator's password. One application I support requires an update be made to a database table.

On another application, the process was even more complicated. This application stored the password in an encrypted state in a configuration file. The steps to change it were:

1. Stop the application
2. Modify an entry in a configuration file to contain a clear text version of the new password
3. Run a specific utility that would encrypt the password in the configuration file
4. Start the application

If you don't already know how to change the Administrator password, then you should contact vendor support and get the details on how to do this. I would also advise you to practice the process by changing this password on a test, DEV, or QA environment. There is no better way to confirm that the instructions are accurate and that you understand them than to actually make this change a time or two.

If you ever modify the Administrator password, you need to know all of the locations where it might be used. Failing to change it in any locations where it's being used could cause processes to fail. Some examples of where it might be used include the following locations:

- Hard-coded into a script
- Used by a scheduled task
- In a SQL statement coded into a batch file

29.9.3 Shutting down the application in an emergency

There will be times when you need to shut down the application immediately. For example, something might have gone wrong and the longer it stays running, the worse the damage that is being caused. To ensure that you can stop that application as quickly as possible, you should have the process documented if it is at all complicated. If the process is a multistep one, then it would be best if you wrote a script to do it. Having a script in place would be both faster and less error prone than performing the steps manually. Of course, this script needs to be developed and thoroughly tested on a nonproduction environment.

One other thing to keep in mind before shutting down the application is what authorization is needed. Do you need approval before stopping the application in an emergency situation? If so, who needs to give approval? Do you need to call them, e-mail them, or IM them? What is the protocol if you're not able to reach the approver in a timely manner? Are you allowed to restart that application after a good faith effort to make contact?

29.9.4 Rebooting the server immediately

If you can remotely connect to a Windows server, you can reboot it by clicking the Start icon and selecting "Shut down." On the shutdown Windows screens, select option "Restart" in the drop-down list box labeled "What do you want the computer to do."

Another way to restart a Windows server is to user the shutdown command. You should confirm in advance that your account has the required privilege to remotely shut down servers. Thankfully, this permission isn't given to everyone. The format of this is command is

shutdown /m \\computername /r /t:01 /y /f

Where the parameters are:

- /m \\computername—Specifies the remote computer to be shut down. Omitting this parameter will cause the computer on which the command was entered to be shut down
- /r—Causes a restart instead of a shutdown
- /t:xx—The time (in seconds) to delay before shutting down the remote computer
- /y—Answers "yes" to all prompts that are displayed during the shutdown process
- /f—Forces all currently running programs to quit prior to the shutdown occurring

Rebooting a server isn't a difficult thing to do, but some organizations have even tighter restrictions about rebooting a server than stopping and restarting an application. Be sure you're following all protocols before restarting a server.

One thing you need to be sure of is that you request that the server be rebooted as opposed to just shutting it down. If you stop it instead of rebooting it, then someone who has physical access to it might have to start it up again. If you aren't at the same location as the data center, making this mistake could delay the server's reboot until you contact someone at the data center who can walk over to it and physically restart it.

29.9.5 Restoring the database from a backup

If you are backing up your application's database on a regular basis that's great and you should be applauded. But you need to know how to restore the database from a backup to be able to use any backups that have been created. In an emergency, you'll need to know the answers to the following questions:

- What are the steps to restore from a backup?
- Are all of your backup's full backups or are incremental backups created on some days of the week? If some backups are incremental, how does that impact the steps needed to perform a recovery?
- Who has to perform the steps to perform a restore? Specifically, can the Application Administrator do this or does a DBA have to get involved?
- How many distinct backup files exist? By this I mean, are there separate backups done of the database and of files from the application server? If so, are both sets of data being backed up at the same time? When a restoration is being done, do both sets have to be restored at the same time? Do the sets of backup files have to have been created at the same time?
- How many databases does the application have and how does this impact performing a recovery? This answer to this question might not be as obvious as you think. For example, one application I support has three separate databases: a report database, a workflow database, and an application database. Another application had four distinct SQL Server databases.
- How long does it take to restore the database from a backup? Does that include any required time to transfer files from one server to another?
- When was the most recent backup performed?
- How many sets of backup files are retained?
- Is it possible to recover an older set of backup files from tapes or an offsite storage facility? If so, how long does it take to have the CDs, DVDs, or tapes delivered?
- Where are the backup files? For example, are they on the application server, the database server, or a SAN server?
- What is the naming convention of the backup files? Is the date and time they were created embedded in it?
- Are DEV, QA, and Production backup files stored in the same location? Are they named in such a way that you can easily distinguish between them? For example, are they in separate directories or are they named differently?
- Can the backup from one environment be restored to another environment? For example, can the backup files from PROD be loaded onto the QA environment? If this can be done, are the steps to do it the same? For one application that I support the process to restore the application from one of its own backups is simple and quick, about 30 minutes. But to migrate a PROD backup to the QA server takes about 6 hours and requires a great number of manual steps.
- How often is the restore process performed to verify that it works? When was the last restoration test performed? Did it work?

It would be a very good idea to periodically test the process to restore the application's data from backup files. This can be done on the DEV or QA environments so it won't impact availability of the production environment. I would especially advise testing this after any significant changes have been made in the application's environment. For example:

- After a significant upgrade has been done to the application. For example, after a major update (from version 4.0 to version 5.0) but not necessarily after a minor upgrade (from version 5.4 to version 5.5).

- After any significant change in the database engine.
- After any hardware changes like new disk drives, servers, etc.
- After any change in personnel such as new Application Administrators or a completely new DBA team.

29.10 "Read_Me.txt" FILES

Files with the name "Read_Me.txt" can be created and used for documentation purposes. Most administrators will recognize that the name implies the file is significant, should be read, and shouldn't be deleted. Occasionally, you might need to create a Read_Me.txt file to include information that needs to be seen by all Application Administrators. One word of caution is not to overuse files like this. If every subdirectory on the system contains a Read_Me.txt file, that file name ceases to hold any significance. You might want to reserve them for situations like:

- To explain the purpose of an infrequently touched file.
- To explain how the backup process works and what files need to exist for that to succeed.
- To explain the purpose of initialization or properties type files.
- To describe the important of specific files to the monitoring process.

29.11 VERSION PLEASE

Every application has a version. There will be times when you need to know what version you are running. For example, when you open a ticket with the vendor's support desk, they will almost always request that information. You need to know which version of the application has been installed. Each application is slightly different, but the following are some of the ways I've seen to get the application's version information:

- In a configuration file
- Displayed on the Help | About screen
- Displayed on the logon screen
- Entries written in a log file each time the application is started

Knowing the version doesn't only apply to the application itself. The need to know what version is running also applies to support software that is running on the server. Some examples of software that you might need to find the version of include the following:

- IIS—Internet Information Services
- Apache Web Server
- Database client software like Oracle Client
- JRE—Java Runtime Environment
- JDK—Java Development Kit
- WebLogic

29.12 PERFORMANCE

It wouldn't surprise me if the first words from the first computer user to the first programmer were "It's great, but could you make it run faster?" It's human nature to want our tools and toys to run faster and faster. Unfortunately, the current generation of enterprise-level applications are incredibly complex. Making them faster isn't easy, especially for an Application Administrator who doesn't have access to the source code, control over the overall design, control over the network, control over the database engine, control over the user's desktop, etc.

Without a doubt you will get complaints from users that the app is running slow, very slow, or even unusably slow. You have to decide if the system is actually slow or possible the user could just be complaining. Can you prove or document its performance one way or the other? If you have baseline performance statistics, you will have something to compare current performance against. Such statistics can be captured and expressed in at least two ways:

1. Measure server statistics like % of Processor Busy, Disk Activity, level of I/O traffic currently occurring, etc., when the application is performing normally.
2. Time the typical activities that users do in the application. For example, activities like login, common searches, sorts, running an existing report, modify an entry, add an entry, bringing up a screen that's deep in the application when performance is normal.

When the inevitable complaints arrive, you can measure current activity or performance and compare it to the baseline statistics that were recorded. If there is a significant difference, then user complaints are probably justified. Recording statistics on the server can't be captured using one of the performance tools described later in this section. Unfortunately, gathering timing information for typical user activities might not be so easy to automate. It might require your stepping through the application and actually timing the results. It would be more representative if you captured these results on multiple occasions.

To be prepared for the inevitable requests for better performance, there are some ways that you can be prepared in advance. Some of these preparatory steps include the following:

• Gather your baseline performance statistics as described in the previous paragraph.
• Gather stats over several types of time frames: early morning, mid-day, month-end, etc.
• What statistics would be useful and how do you get them?
• Does the app have a set of internal tests that provide information on performance? One application I supported had this ability. You could kick off a screen that would make 500 connections to the database, perform 500 reads, perform 500 writes, etc., and display the average required time. The only downside to this tool was that it put quite a strain on the system when you ran it.
• The tools that are available to provide you with performance information depend greatly on the operating system that's running on your server. For example, Perfmon (Performance Monitor) gathers statistics on a Windows-based server. On UNIX and Linux systems, commands like time, netstat, ps, and top can provide details regarding activity on the application server.
• Tools to gather statistics at the browser level are also available. Firebug is an open source tool that can be used to capture statistics on HTTP traffic for the Firefox browser. Fiddler is another open source tool that captures HTTP traffic on an Internet Explorer browser session. Tools like these can provide insights into what is coming into and out of your browser and potentially why it's taking so long.
• Network level tools like open source packet analyzer Wireshark can be used analyze network traffic. Once you gain experience with such tools, you'll have a much deeper understanding of what's being passed back and forth across the network from the user's workstation to the application server to the database server.

Once you determine that the system is running slower than normal what do you do? The first step is to isolate the problem. Is the performance problem only occurring for a single user? If this is the case, then request that they clear their Internet browser cache, reboot their workstation, and log into the application again. Surprisingly, this has been known to clear up a significant percentage of problems that users encounter.

If multiple users are reporting the same problem, then it's a legitimate issue that must be investigated and dealt with. The first step is to try to isolate the problem to a specific area of the application's landscape. For example, I would investigate the following areas in this specific order.

- Does it appear to be an application server issue? If the application server's CPU is 99% idle, then this likely isn't the problem. Other resources that should be examined on the application server include the amount of memory being used, the amount of disk I/O activity, and the amount of network traffic being generated. If none of those statistics are abnormally high, then you can probably safely rule out the application server as the source of the problem.
- Could it be a database server issue? Unfortunately, most Application Administrators don't have the ability to remotely log onto the database server. Given this reality, your primary alternative is to contact the DBA team and ask them if it appears the database server is overloaded or acting sluggish. If you do happen to have access to the database server, then check the same statistics that you checked on the application server, i.e., CPU activity, memory usage, disk I/O, and network activity.
- If you didn't find any issues on the application server or the database server, then the network is then next component to focus on. Unfortunately, it isn't always easy to investigate potential network performance issues. You'll likely have to rely upon the expertise of your organization's network team. Showing them the current vs. baseline performance statistics should help to convince them that there is indeed an issue.

29.13 APPLICATION ADMINISTRATOR'S MANUAL TEMPLATE

There are certain things that the Application Administrator of every app needs to document. With this in mind, you should consider creating an Application Administrator's manual template for the entire organization. It could be copied and customized for every application that you or your group supports. Most of these items will take only a page, some only a paragraph. Having all of this information in a single place will be invaluable for you late at night, your replacement, your boss, etc. Writing and assembling this document, in advance, may allow you to enjoy your vacation days without being interrupted by a frantic call from your backup.

I hate referring to something as a "living document," but that term is quite appropriate for this documentation. You need to keep it up-to-date. If you write it and never review it then it will quickly become obsolete and useless.

Potential topics that apply to virtually every application include:

- Startup procedures
- If multiple servers exist, you need to include the sequence in which they should be rebooted
- Shutdown procedures
- If multiple servers exist, you need to include the sequence in which they should be stopped
- Emergency shutdown procedure
- Adding, dropping, disabling, enabling a user
- Killing a user's session
- Finding out what users are in the system
- Configuration files
- Topology files
- Files that need to be preserved across an upgrade. Usually, these include customizations that exist only for your installation. The vendor's upgrade will likely either overwrite these files or purge the entire directory where customizations reside
- Administrative passwords and logons

- Services or daemons on the server that are specific to this application
- Recompiling the application
- Bringing up the Administrative console mode
- Where the log files are, what they are, how often they are created and archived
- URLs to get to the application
- Current version of the application and how to find it
- Current version of the operating system and how to find it
- The amount of RAM and disk space the server(s) has
- Name and location of all servers
- Database details
  - DB server name
  - DB logon the application uses
  - DB password the application uses
  - Connection string the application uses
  - Version of the database software
- Load balancing details if it is applicable to this application
- FTP server if this application uses one to import or export files
- Procedure to bounce the application
- Procedure to bounce the server
- DNS names being used
- Backup details
  - How often is it done?
  - Where is the backup sent to?
  - What tool is being used to create the backup?
- Contacts
  - Vendor
    - Phone numbers
    - Website URL
    - Support e-mail address
    - Your license #
    - The product name and version you're running
    - Your ID and password when logging onto the vendor's website
  - DBA team
  - Data center
  - Network personnel
  - User community, specifically the people that have to approve bounces
  - Application business "owner"
- Overview of getting assistance from vendor
  - Do you call an 800 number?
  - Do you submit a request by e-mail?
  - Do you post your request on a website?
  - Is their contact information for you accurate? You don't want to be waiting for a call from them only to find out they've been calling your old telephone number
- Details for a baseline performance load
- Overview of steps to roll out a patch or upgrade
- Maintenance outage window for the application. For example, Sunday night from 10 pm until midnight Central time

- Landscape documentation that lists application servers, database servers, IP addresses, etc.
- Data feeds into and out of the application
  - How often are files imported or exported?
  - File layout
  - What process imports the data?
  - How are error situations handled?
  - Who to contact if a problem occurs?
  - Any other applications it depends on or depend on it?
- Overview of your DR (Disaster Recovery) procedures, hardware, and locations
- Failover procedures, including a recovery from backup tapes
- Steps to rebuild the system from scratch
- Are there any scheduled tasks on the application server?
  - What does each do?
  - How often do they run?
- What reports come out on a regular basis?
  - Who are these reports sent to?
  - How are they scheduled?
  - Report schedule times should be staggered to avoid overloading the system
- Process to modify, add, or delete a report

Things Will Happen That You Don't Want to Think About

In spite of our hopes and wishes, bad things happen in everyone's lives. In the course of an Application Administrator's career, some things will happen that you would prefer didn't happen. There is nothing you can do to prevent them, but being properly prepared can minimize the damage they will inflict. The key to preparation is to spend some time thinking about what could happen and how you can prepare for it.

The sections in this chapter describe some situations that can occur in your world. Some are more likely to happen than others and some are more damaging than others, but you're likely to see at least some of these problems at some point in your career. If you experience or envision situations that aren't listed here, you should document your plans regarding how you will respond.

30.1 THE APPLICATION HANGS UP

Sooner or later the application that you support will become unresponsive or hang up. In most cases, rebooting it will solve the problem, but that's just slapping a band-aid on the problem. You really should put more thought into plans for preventing, detecting, and analyzing the problem. The following sections describe some steps for dealing with applications that simply stop working.

30.1.1 Notifications

How will you find out that the application has become unresponsive? I can guarantee that if you don't immediately notice the problem that your user community will notice it very quickly. Depending on your relationship with that group, one of them might contact you right away. If they don't know you or know of you, then they might open a ticket with the organization's help desk. If no such tool exists, then they'll sit at their desks and curse you and the application as they try to e-mail or call anyone they can think of in their organization and yours for help.

A better solution than having users discover the problem would be to have some level of automated monitoring in place for the application. For example, if the application relies on a specific process or service, then monitor that process or service. If it stops, then the monitoring script or package should send out notifications of the problem.

This leads up to the questions of who, how, and when.

- Who should be notified? Most likely, there will be a list instead of a single person who gets notified. Some likely candidates include: the Application Administrator, the backup Application Administrator, the Business Owner of the application, and possibly someone in the Data Center. Every organization will come up with a different list of who to notify.
- How should they be notified? The obvious choices are to send out e-mails or text messages depending on what electronic devices your staff routinely carries.
- When should they be notified? This question becomes very important about midnight. Some applications need to be running 24 hours a day, 7 days a week. If your application is one of them,

then alerts should be sent out whenever it becomes unresponsive. On the other hand, if no one will be using the application until Monday morning at 9 am, do you really need to get a call at 2 am on Saturday? A realistic assessment of the level of support needs to be done and the monitoring process should be set up accordingly. Perhaps a text message is sent out between 7 am and 10 pm Monday through Friday and an e-mail is sent after hours and on weekends. Monitoring tools usually let you configure what types of alerts are sent and when depending on the severity of the issue (as defined by you).

A caveat is needed here on the limits of monitoring. It's entirely possible that the critical process or service hangs up but doesn't technically stop running. From the user's viewpoint, the application appears to be dead, but on the server the process is still active. In a situation like this, a monitoring process may not send out any notifications. There will be times when your users will act as the ultimate judges of whether the application is working or not.

30.1.2 Balancing a quick restart vs. gathering information

When the inevitable hang-up of the application occurs, your natural inclination may be to start the application back up again as quickly as possible. While that's understandable, it might not be the best decision. If you don't learn what caused the problem, then you'll never be able to do anything to prevent it from occurring again. So instead of simply restarting the application, it would probably be a wise investment to spend a few minutes gathering information about the state of the application before restarting it. Some of the information you should attempt to obtain is described in the following section.

30.1.3 Gathering information about the hang

A list of possible sources of information that are potentially valuable include the following:

- Are the application's services or processes running? If you haven't already written a script to gather this information, this is one more good reason to do so.
- Are some or all of the server's resources being over utilized? For example, is the CPU utilization rate abnormally high? Is all of the available RAM being used? Is the system page swapping like a banshee? What percentage of network bandwidth is being used?
- Capture a set of log files that the vendor support team typically requests. Again, if you haven't written a script or batch file to copy log files to a temp location, this is a good reason to do it.
- How many users are logged into the application and what are they doing? You might not be able to obtain this information if the system is hung up. On some systems, this information might be available via a log file or in the database.
- Is the database accessible? It only takes a few seconds to make a quick connection to the database using Toad or SQL*Plus. You should consider writing a script to test the database connection. If the application has a table that contains the list of active users and their most recent actions, you could write a script to select those rows and write them to a text file. This might be useful knowledge when troubleshooting the cause of the problem. If you can't establish a connection to the database, then that's a valuable piece of information.
- Capture a screenshot of any error messages that have been displayed. These would more likely have been displayed on user screens than on the server console.
- If the vendor support group has requested that they be given a core dump when the application hangs, then now is the time to create it if one hasn't been created.
- One last source of information is to look at operating system-level log files. On a Windows server, these can be accessed by opening the Event Viewer.

30.1.4 **Restarting the application**

Once you've extracted every crumb of information from the system, it's time to restart the application. The next decision you need to make is whether to simply restart the application or completely shut it down first. It might seem quicker to just start it back up, but doing that might leave some processes or services in an unknown state plus there may be a risk to the database. The right answer to this question will be dictated by:

- Instructions in the Administrator's Guide
- Advice given to you by the vendor Support Group
- Your experience with previous situations where the application hung up

How long will it take to restart or shut down and restart the application? It's important to know this so you can recognize situations when the application isn't coming up cleanly. If it normally takes 10 minutes to come up from scratch and you've been waiting 30 minutes, then it's likely that you have a more significant problem on your hands than you previously thought.

Does the application display or log messages documenting that the application successfully completed step "*x*" of "*y*" possible steps during the startup process? If this information is available and the application has a history of not coming up cleanly, then you need to be an expert on recognizing where in the startup process the application is at.

30.1.5 **Alert the user community**

Once the application is completely operational, who do you need to notify? Some potential people on this list are:

- The Business Owner of the application
- The person who originally reported the problem
- The Data Center team
- The team responsible for the monitoring package that reported the problem
- Your boss
- Your partner or backup so he or she doesn't waste time investigating something you've already taken care of
- The users

30.1.6 **Getting to the root of it all**

If you don't figure out what caused the problem, then it's very unlikely that it will ever be fixed. An investigation to figure out what caused a problem is frequently referred to as a root cause analysis. Unfortunately, doing a root cause analysis usually:

- Takes a significant amount of effort
- Takes time
- Requires specialized expertise

I would love to tell you that every time one of my applications crashed, that through hard work and diligence I was able to arrive at the root cause of the problem. I'd love to be able to tell you that, but it would be a lie. In my experience, most of the time you are able to come up with an educated guess of the cause, but you won't be able to definitely prove it. The reality is that applications, databases, support software, and operating systems are all incredibly complex. They contain millions of lines of code. The error could be just about anywhere in that mountain of code.

Realistically, the best that you can hope for is that if the problem is one that recurs the application vendor will eventually determine its cause. By gathering your logs, error messages, etc., you're helping provide them with the information they need to solve it. I used the word "eventually" quite deliberately earlier in this paragraph. If the vendor does identify the root cause and fixes it, you might not see the fix for months.

30.1.7 Create an incident report

Every outage should be documented by an incident report. These reports don't have to be long. They can consist of just the following sections:

- Overview of the impact
- Description of the steps taken, by whom, and when
- Total down time
- Root cause or your best approximation
- If this seems to be a recurring problem, the dates when it's happened before

There are several reasons that you want to create incident reports. Some of them are

- It helps you recognize outages that are caused by the same or similar problems or situations
- It documents that you promptly and consistently handle outages and get the application back up in a timely manner
- It documents the total amount of down time
- Provides documentation of each outage in case someone tries to exaggerate the number of times the application has experienced an outage
- Might be required by the auditors

30.2 SERVER CRASHES

Hardware and software are significantly more reliable today than they were back in the bad old days. Servers don't crash as often, but eventually your server could crash. When it happens, it's much like when an application hangs up but scarier.

One difference between an application hanging up and a server crashing is that the server problem has the potential to affect more users. If the server is hosting multiple applications, then all of the users for each of the applications are being affected.

The steps that you need to take in this situation are very similar to what you do when an application hangs up. I don't want to duplicate the last chapter, but will include the same sections and only list steps to be taken that are different.

30.2.1 Notifications

If your organization has a monitoring package in place, then it will certainly be set up to recognize that a server has crashed. If you need to write scripts to recognize a server crash, the best approach would be to have a script or batch job on another server periodically pings the application server. If there is no response, then it's a pretty good bet that the server is hung up or has crashed.

The list of who should be notified if a server crashes is pretty much the same people who are notified when an application stops. The only differences are that if the server hosts multiple applications, then multiple Application Administrators need to be contacted. Since it's a server problem, then someone in the Data Center will definitely need to be contacted.

30.2.2 **Balancing a quick restart vs. gathering information**

The balance between a quick restart versus taking the time to gather information doesn't change just because a server has gone down. It's still better in the long run to take a few extra minutes to learn as much as you can about the problem before restarting the server and bringing the applications up.

30.2.3 **Gathering information about the crash**

Generally, if the server crashes, then the responsibility for gathering information on the problem belongs to the data center or server team. It wouldn't hurt for you to gather application log files once the server comes up, but the data center team should be running point for this problem.

30.2.4 **Restarting the server**

Typically, it is the responsibility of the data center team to restart the server. In many cases, an Application Administrator can't do this because he or she doesn't have access to the data center. The question of who can authorize the application be restarted is moot if the server is down.

One wrinkle that has to be considered is the server is restarted whether the application is launched automatically? There might be some cases when the System Administrators would like to bring up the server without any applications coming up. For example, they might want the opportunity to see whether the operating system is acting normal before adding an additional load onto it. Is it possible to prevent the application from coming up automatically when the server comes up?

If the application has to be has to be started up manually do you know how to do that?

- Is this process documented?
- Where is the documentation?
- How do you handle the situation if the application doesn't come up as expected?

Once the server is up, you have to confirm that the application is up and running. The following questions need to be answered:

- Who is responsible for verifying that the application is up? Can the Application Administrator do this or is it the responsibility of the application's Business Owner?
- How do you confirm that the application is operational?
- Is this test or process documented?
- What actions are taken if the application doesn't come up correctly?

30.2.5 **Alert the user community**

The same cast of characters needs to be notified that the server has been rebooted and the application is confirmed to be operational. Whoever has the responsibility to do this after the application has been restarted should also be responsible after the server has been rebooted.

30.2.6 **Getting to the root of it all**

Once the dust has settled, someone needs to figure out why the server died in the first place. Most likely, the responsibility for this will be assigned to the data center team rather than the Application Administrator. They might request input from you, such as the application log files, but this should be their task not yours.

30.2.7 **Create an incident report**

You'll still want to create an incident report for a server crash. The layout should be the same as when the application hangs up. The biggest difference would be that under the root cause you would just include any information that the data center team provides instead of researching this for yourself.

30.3 **DATABASE DILEMMAS**

Since the majority of applications store their data in a database, typically a relational database, any problems that occur with the database will have a significant impact on the application.

Perhaps the worst database-related dilemmas are when application data is lost. Some of the causes for data to be lost include:

- Application problem—if the application has coding or logic errors, then it's possible that data can be lost or simply not saved when it should be. If you suspect this to be the cause, then you need to test the circumstances under which data was lost more than once to confirm that a problem exists. If the data is lost repeatedly, then open a ticket with the vendor support group to report the issue. With luck, they will provide a work-around that can be used until a patch that fixes the error becomes available.
- Human error—realistically this is the most likely cause of data being lost. Either the user doesn't understand how to properly use the application or he needs additional practice to get up to speed with the application. Providing more training is definitely an option in this circumstance.
- Database issues—the chances of the database actually being the cause of lost data are very, very slim. The major commercial database engines are complicated, but extremely well tested before being released. Furthermore, they are being used by hundreds of thousands if not millions of installations on a daily basis. If they were losing data, it's almost a certainty that such a problem would have been reported already. I'm not saying this can't happen, but the odds against it are extremely long. It's much more likely that the cause of lost data is a human error, a misunderstanding, or an application error than a database error.

30.4 **MOVING**

Moving an application doesn't happen very often, but is something that could be in the future of your application. None of the types of moves are much fun, but it's doubtful that an Application Administrator will be able to stop these types of events once they start in motion. Some types of moving events are described in the following sections.

30.4.1 **Reasons for moving to a new server**

There are several understandable reasons why the application might be moved to a new server.

1. The end of life of the current server is approaching or has arrived. This type of move is inevitable if the application is used by your organization long enough. Servers have a life expectancy of about 5 years. They can be kept running after that but it becomes difficult to find replacement parts, the vendor is no longer willing to support it, or the price/benefit ratio of a replacement server is too attractive to ignore.
2. The application has outgrown the current server and needs to be moved to a bigger, more powerful server. This is actually a good problem to have. It indicates that the application is being widely used. This almost certainly means that its value to the organization is appreciated.

3. The physical server is virtualized. This too is probably a good problem to have. It means that many of the maintenance issues associated with a physical server will be transferred to the group that supports the virtual servers in your organization. Moving to virtual servers has other benefits, including the following:
   * It's easier to allocate resources like additional processors, memory, and SAN space to a virtual server than a physical server
   * Since multiple virtual servers are hosted by a single physical server, the cost of each virtual server is typically lower that costs for a physical server
   * Snapshots can be taken of virtual servers and used to recreate it if it becomes corrupted or crashes. This ensures that the down time of a virtual server will be minimal.

30.4.1.1 Steps for moving to a new server

What do you need to do to ensure a smooth, uneventful transition to a new server? The first step to making a smooth transition is to have a checklist that lists the steps needed to make this move. By doing this, you can identify potential bottlenecks and schedule people to work in parallel to complete the project in the least overall time. Tasks on this list might include the following, but of course every plan will be different.

1. Verify that the proposed hardware and operating system meet the application's requirements
2. Acquire the server(s) and load the operating system onto it/them
3. Grant access to the server to the Application Administrator team
4. Open the required firewall ports, for example, to the database server, report server, mail server
5. Load support software like IIS, Apache, database client, etc., on the server(s)
6. Load the application software onto the server(s) and apply all the latest patches and updates
7. Acquire and install the application license file if required. Sometimes, licenses are hard-coded to a specific server, so moving to a new server(s) might require a new license
8. Configure the new application environment to access a copy of the production database. This ensures that testing will use realistic data, but won't corrupt production data. If your database contains PII (Personally Identifiable Information), then you may need to modify it or mask it before tests get access to it
9. Perform UAT (User Acceptance Testing) of the application on the new server
10. If the UAT was successful, then schedule the migration outage with users
11. Users are no longer able to access the old server(s) from this point on
12. Point the new application environment to the production database
13. Perform final testing on the new server(s) before it's turned over to the users
14. If testing was successful, then enable access to the new environment for users
15. If the old server is being left online for a while, be sure to disable all reports, extracts, and alerts that it creates. If you forget to do this, the users may receive duplicate reports or export files may be created by both the old and new servers
16. After a suitable interval, several days or weeks, decommission the old server(s)

The steps for moving to a new server include many of the steps that were performed when installing the application on the original server. If you kept accurate notes and screenshots, then this documentation can be of great use when moving the application to a new server. Drag it out and take advantage of your foresightedness.

30.4.2 Physically moving a server

Moving a server can take several forms. Some of them are listed here:

* From a desk or wiring closet to an actual data center
* From one data center to another

The steps might involve physically moving the server from its current location, for example, a desk in a cubicle or a wiring closet, to a formal data center. This might be occurring because the responsibility for the application is shifting from the development group to a formal support group. It might also occur if an organization "matures" and realizes that its hardware needs to be gathered into an appropriate facility that has physical security, adequate environmental controls, and redundant support (power and telecommunications connectivity).

If the effort is just physically moving the server, the list of steps would be something like the following.

- Coordinate the move date and time with the user community
- Back up the database
- Back up the application software and associated files
- Physically move the server to its new location, e.g., the data center
- If the server will be moving from one LAN to a different LAN, this might affect security or firewall ports
- Verify that the server has power and telecommunications connectivity
- If the server's IP address has changed, then update its DNS entry
- Test connectivity to other subsystems like the database, backups, and messaging
- Test the user's ability to access the application
- Perform a UAT to verify that the application is working correctly
- Inform the user community that the application is available again

30.4.3 Moving to a vendor-hosted ASP (application service provider)

Many vendors offer to host their application for clients who would access it over the Internet. Basically, the client's users access the application that is running on the vendor's server(s). This method of application delivery has several names, for example:

- ASP—Application Service Provider
- On-demand software
- Software as a Service (SaaS).

Some of the advantages of an ASP model are that the vendor takes on many of the routine activities that had traditionally been the responsibility of the in-house staff

- The client doesn't need to acquire or maintain application servers, OS licenses, related infrastructure, and data center space
- The client doesn't need to maintain database servers
- The client doesn't need to perform backups. Be sure you know exactly what backups the vendor is doing and how long they are being kept. If a user inadvertently deletes some critical data, you'll want to know whether the vendor can restore it, how long the process will take, and how much it will cost
- The client doesn't need to apply upgrades to keep the server or the application up-to-date

ASP is not without disadvantages. Some of them are:

- The cost of the application may be greater than an on-premise installation, but a careful financial analysis has to be done comparing costs over several years
- Loss of control of the application
- The organization's data resides on databases and drives outside of the data center
- Unless you specifically contract for it, there probably won't be a TEST or QA environment
- You're trusting your data, your reputation, and your ability to access the application to someone else
- Security of your data is total dependent on the vendor's security expertise

- Your organization will have minimal control over upgrade schedules
- Your organization will have minimal or no ability to analyze or deal with performance issues

If you're currently hosting the application on internal servers and the decision is made to move to an ASP environment, then you'll need to participate in this change. You might not be enthusiastic about this change, but you'll have to be a good team player and support it. The basic steps that are necessary to perform this migration are:

- Export your database and provide it to the vendor
- Provide any customizations developed locally to the vendor
- Provide any locally developed reports to the vendor
- The vendor builds a system based on your data, customizations, and reports and makes it available for testing
- UAT (User Acceptance Testing) is performed on the ASP-hosted application by a selected subset of the user community
- If the testing is successful, then coordinate with the users for a cutover date and time
- On the day of cutover, access to the internally hosted application is disabled or users access is reduced to read-only
- The final export of your database is done and is sent to the vendor
- Vendor loads your final database export on their servers
- Disable any reports, data exports, or other processes on the internally hosted version of the application
- UAT is performed on the ASP-hosted application
- If the testing is successful, then users are given access to ASP-hosted version of the application
- All users are given the new URL to access the ASP-hosted version of the application
- After several days or weeks of using the ASP version, the internal application servers are decommissioned

30.5 VENDOR CHANGES

Once your organization has licensed and installed a vendor's application, then you don't want any changes to occur to the vendor. You want them to just keep doing what they're doing without creating any waves. One of the more unsettling things that can happen is that you are notified by the vendor that things on their end are changing. Some examples of such changes are described in the following sections.

30.5.1 Your vendor gets acquired

The world of software application vendors is a constantly changing one. You may think that your vendor is too big or too independent to be acquired. If that's what you think, then you're probably wrong. Even clients of the largest vendors can find out that their vendor is being acquired by an even bigger fish in the corporate application ocean.

What should you do if the vendor you licensed an application from is acquired by another company? You need to listen carefully to what is being said in any announcements you receive or any press releases that come out. You also need to look at other products and services the acquiring vendor currently offers. For example:

- Does the acquiring vendor offer an identical or similar application? If this is true, then you need to be prepared for the likely eventuality that the application you rely upon may be discontinued.
- Does the acquiring vendor claim that they will continue to support the application they just acquired? At the time the acquisition is announced, you have no idea of their true intentions. All you can do is

look at their past behavior and similar products they currently market. If they don't have an application like the one you license, then there is a good chance they are telling the truth. On the other hand, if they have a history of acquiring software vendors and discontinuing their product line, then you need to face the truth that your application's days may be numbered.

- Will they roll it into their own suite of products? This is more likely if they have no competing product or their internal product has a significantly smaller market share than the application that was just acquired.
- Will they let the acquired application die on the vine and force you to migrate to their application? Maybe. Only time will tell.

30.5.2 Your application is being retired by the vendor

Another communication that you never want to receive from your vendor is that they have decided to retire or discontinue the application that you licensed from them. If you receive an announcement along this line, then there are things you should do and questions that you should be asking. Among them are:

- Make sure the business users and departments are aware of the vendor's plans. They will probably have the most influence in determining the strategy in dealing with this situation.
- How long will they continue to support the application? What does "support" actually mean? Is it providing patches and updates? Break/fix support? Troubleshooting problems? Or just taking calls and referring you to the manual?
- Is the vendor adding this application's functionality to another product that your organization could migrate to?
- Will the source code of the application be made available?
- Is there the possibility that third-party support will be available for it after the vendor stops supporting it? What expertise will this entity have?
- Would it be possible to hire ex-employees of the vendor that have experience with the application? Would this expertise and access to the source code provide you with adequate support of the application?
- Can you live without support provided by the vendor or a third party? If the application is very stable and doesn't require periodic data updates, e.g., tax information changes, then it's possible that you can limp along without support.
- Is it conceivable that your organization can network with other organizations that also license the application and support each other once the application is retired? In some fields, the thought of such cooperation is inconceivable. In other areas, it's already occurring.

30.5.3 Migrating to a product from another vendor

If the vendor has been acquired or has chosen to retire the application, there is a possibility that your organization will decide to replace it. If this is the game plan, you will need to start gathering information about potential replacement products as soon as possible. The replacement process will take longer than expected. The end of support by the current vendor will arrive much quicker than you expect and it's best not to be caught unprepared.

There are other reasons why an organization decides it's time to migrate to another product from a different vendor. The reasons for making this decision are numerous. Some examples are:

- The current application doesn't offer features you feel are important
- The current application isn't keeping up with changes in the industry
- Support from the vendor for the current application isn't at the level you expect
- The cost of the current application is deemed to be excessive
- Users aren't happy with the current application

Steps that need to be taken to migrate to a new application include the following:

- Acquire benchmarks of potential replacement products.
- Ask potential new vendors about their experience with migrations, especially from the product you're currently using.
- Ask the potential new vendor if they can migrate data from the current application to the new application. Application databases are typically very complex. If the new vendor has experience migrating data, then you should seriously consider having them perform this step.
- Can you recreate your existing customizations on the new product?

30.5.4 Avoiding vendor changes

One method of avoiding all of the vendor changes that are being described is to rely on applications that are built on Open Source technology. Those applications aren't "owned" by anyone in the traditional sense. They are developed and enhanced by a volunteer community instead of a single corporation. If such an application is available and you choose that route, your organization will need to be more involved in it than in a traditional licensed application. Of course, if there is no open source application similar to what you are using, then this option isn't available to you.

30.6 CONSOLIDATION, MERGERS, AND ACQUISITIONS

Organizations in the United States and other countries seem to constantly undergo a process of consolidations, mergers, and acquisitions. What will the impact on the application you support (and your job) if your organization acquires another company or is itself acquired? While there is no way to be certain of this in advance, it doesn't hurt to at least consider what might happen.

Reducing costs has been something of a Holy Grail for the last decade or so. One way management can reduce costs is to consolidate multiple, similar applications into one application. This is a reasonable thing to do and you can be fairly sure it will continue to happen in the future. The biggest question is will the application you support be the "mergee" or the "merge-ed"?

If your organization is involved in a merger or acquisition, you have to ask if the other organization has an application that provides the same function as the one you support. If the answer is "yes," then there is a good chance that one or the other will be discontinued eventually.

- The $64,000 question is which one will be retained?
- If your application is retained, how will you absorb the other application's users and functionality?
- If your application isn't being retained, how will it be migrated to the other application?
- If your application isn't going to be retained, what are the chances that you will be let go or transferred?

Whether your application stays or is decommissioned, there will be a lot of work to do. Some steps that will need to be taken include the following:

- Identifying customizations that need to be retained
- Data migration, i.e., exporting data from one application and importing it into the other
- Retraining users
- Retraining administrators
- Update network access, firewall ports, backups, etc.
- Decommissioning or re-using servers

30.7 ADDING A NEW OFFICE, DEPARTMENT, OR DIVISION

What will the impact on your application be if your organization expands? Would usage of the application be impacted if a new office were opened? What if a new department or division needed to start using it? While this may not happen in the near future, in the long run it could happen. If you can have at least cursory answers to the following questions, you'll be able to react to such possibilities more quickly.

- Will additional hardware be needed?
  - Will this be the nudge to move to a bigger server? A virtual server? A cluster? A load balanced environment?
- Will the licensing agreement with the vendor need to be altered?
- Will new users need to be trained?
  - If so, who will do it and when?
- Will software need to be installed on the new users' workstations?
  - If so, who will do it and when?

30.8 INPUT AND OUTPUT FILES

Many applications deal with files that are input into the application or created and exported by the application. Occasionally, these processes don't work like they are supposed to. If this happens, then the situation needs to be corrected as quickly as possible. The reason that expediency is needed is that these files frequently drive other processes. For example, if new users are added to the HR application, they might be included on a file sent to the payroll application. If that file isn't correctly created, exported, received, and imported, then the new employees may not get paid during the next run of the payroll application.

Unfortunately, when a process runs successfully for a lengthy period of time, people tend to forget the details about how it exactly works. If these processes aren't well documented, then it can take time to refresh the institutional memory needed to reestablish the expertise needed to correct problems.

The cause of problems with import or export file processes can be something as simple as the situations in the following list:

- Running out of disk space
- A user account being used becomes disabled, possible because he or she quit or retired
- A process that was running on a desktop computer doesn't run because the computer isn't turned on or has been decommissioned
- A slight change to a database table makes a SQL query invalid
- A database view is dropped or not recreated after a table has been modified
- An index is created in a database which doesn't allow duplicate keys
- The existing FTP server is no longer available
- A scheduling entry became corrupt
- A scheduling entry is inadvertently deleted
- The layout of the file was changed by the process that creates it
- The server that creates the file wasn't running when the process should have run
- Daylight savings time changes affect one location but not the other
- A file name that doesn't match the expected format

Documentation of export and import processes needs the details of the files that are being handled. If they aren't in the documentation, then anytime a problem occurs whatever you learned when you resolved it should be added to the documentation. For example, details like the following should be included in the documentation.

- How many files are being imported or exported
- The layout of the file, e.g., all of the fields in it and their respective sizes and data types
- The naming convention of the file, including the file extension
- When the file(s) are created
- The name of the process that creates or processes each file
- The account that each process runs under
- Where each process runs (application server, database server, web server, FTP server, user workstation)
- How is the process scheduled?
- What should happen if the process fails? Who should be contacted?
- What should happen if an expected file doesn't arrive? Who should be contacted?
- What should happen if the input file has an error? Missing field, record too long, etc.
- How to handle duplicate files, i.e., if yesterday's file arrives instead of today's file?
- Will processing a duplicate file cause problems?
- What happens if an unexpected file arrives?

30.9 RUNNING LOW ON DISK SPACE

Most applications require disk space to function correctly. Exceptions to this generalization include embedded applications, but that type of program isn't the topic of this book. If the amount of free space on the server drops below a minimal level, the server can perform badly. It might make an application unstable, produce errors, or perform extremely slowly. In the worst case scenario, the application server itself could crash and refuse to reboot.

You need to do anything you can to make sure your server never reaches this situation. Some steps that can be taken to assure this are described in the following sections.

30.9.1 Start playing with a full deck

Most applications have a checklist of requirements that need to be adhered to before installing the software. Invariably, one of the entries listed is a reference to the amount of disk space that is available *after* the installation of the operating system, support software, and the application itself. Make sure that the amount of available disk space meets or exceeds the requirements of the application.

30.9.2 What's using all the space?

As the administrator, you need to have a handle on what is using disk space on the application server. It doesn't take long to run a search every week or two for the largest files on the server's drives. After doing that a few times, you start to recognize where all the disk space is going. For example, is it being used by the following areas?

- Log files
- Reports
- Core dumps
- Temp files
- Backup files

- Old versions of the application
- Download files that were used during patches or upgrades
- Import or export files
- Large reports

Can the unusually large files on the server be deleted? Or are they still needed by the application? If they can be deleted, then how will you do it? For example:

- Manually after you launch a search for large files
- Via a script that you kick off on a regularly basis
- Better yet, can they be deleted automatically by a script that runs regularly

One warning is imperative here. There will be some very large files on the drives that cannot be deleted. For example, executable files associated with the operating system and the application, library files, the current set of backup files. Be absolutely sure about a file before you delete it.

30.9.3 **Monitor it**

Do you have a process in place that monitors the server? If so, then the amount of available disk space is one of the metrics that absolutely needs to be monitored. If not, then this ability should be added even if it's as simple as a script you've written that's launched once or twice a day.

Will an alert come out when the server is running low on disk space? Exactly what alerts will come out?

- Are there different types of alerts, for example, warnings vs. critical alerts?
- Who will receive these alerts?
- How are alerts sent out? For example, by e-mails, text messages, or pages?
- How many times will an alert be issued? Just once or will the alerts continue to come out until the situation no longer exists?
- Will a "returned to normal" alert be issued when the amount of free disk space returns to the required amount?

Does your monitoring process provide a chart or report showing how much disk space was available last month, last week, or last night? Retaining statistics like that would be extremely useful for predicting disk space needed for future growth. Just drawing a line that extends the usage trend might show you when the available disk space will be exhausted. Of course, this assumes that all of the measurements are recorded after the large files describes in Section 30.9.2 have been deleted.

30.10 **DISASTER RECOVERY (DR) PLANS**

A Disaster Recovery plan needs to be developed for every application. These plans need to lay out what will happen if the production facility or a significant portion of it is no longer available. You hope that you'll never need to use this plan, but you can't let hope be your DR plan. Chapter 12 describes Disaster Recovery plans in detail so rather than repeat the information here, please refer to that chapter of the book.

30.11 **RAMPING UP AND RAMPING DOWN**

It's possible that the organization's use of the application could change significantly in a very brief period of time. Some examples are:

- Your organization undergoes a merger or acquisition and your application is the one chosen to be retained
- The vendor releases new components for the application that other departments in your organization desperately want to start using
- In a cost-cutting measure, one half of your users are laid off
- New government regulations go into place which mandate that additional controls be used by organizations like yours. It just so happens that your application provides those exact controls.

Admittedly, the odds of such a dramatic need to ramp up or down are slim. It is very plausible that usage of the application could significantly change over a longer period of time, say a year or two. Do you know what it would take to ramp up or ramp down your application in terms of the following elements?

- The absolute number of registered users
- The number of sites where it's being used
- The number of data centers where the application servers are located
- The number of processors in the application server(s)

30.12 GETTING A NEW COMPUTER

Whether it's you or your users, getting a new computer is something that happens periodically. What isn't always recognized is how disruptive and time consuming this event can be. Unless you've been through this process recently, the downside of getting a new computer might be a surprise to you. A little planning upfront will significantly reduce the headaches that moving to a new computer can cause.

30.12.1 Overlap

If at all possible, try to have the old computer available for a while after you begin using the new one. I guarantee you that there will be something on the old computer that you forget to migrate to the new one. A week would be a good overlap, but 2 weeks would be even better. If possible, try to retain the old computer until at least the beginning of the next month. It's possible that there are things you do at the beginning of each month that you've overlooked.

30.12.2 What is on the old computer?

The first step to do when moving to a new computer is to create an inventory of the software that is on your old computer. This step is probably going to be harder to do than you realize because it's easy to forget what was loaded onto your old machine over time. Some of the software were already on it when you got it and other programs were added one by one over the months or years that you've been using it.

How can you or a user find out what programs are installed on computer? There are several methods for acquiring such a list. Some methods or tools are listed here:

- On a Windows PC, open the Control Panel | Add/Remove Programs and look at the list of programs that are listed.
- On a Windows computer, select the Windows Icon and then "All Programs." The screen you'll see at that point will show you applications that have been loaded on the computer.
- In a command prompt, entering the following command will create a text file with a list of software loaded on a Windows computer: wmic /output:Software_List.txt product get Name, Version, Vendor, InstallDate, InstallLocation, PackageName

30.12.3 **Loading programs on the new computer**

Once you figure out what's on your computer, then you need to decide what needs to be loaded on the new machine. Just because something was loaded on your old machine doesn't mean it has to be loaded on the new computer. Some reasons why you might choose not to load it include:

- It was loaded on the machine when you received it and you never used it
- It's a package that you no longer need
- You've identified a better tool or utility to replace it
- The version on the old computer is outdated
- You're no longer supporting the application that it was needed for

Before you start loading software onto the new computer, you need to do a little more research on the software running on the old machine. For example:

- Which packages do you have installation disks for?
- Which were installed from one of the organization's network drives?
- Which were downloaded from a website?
- Which programs are free and which ones are licensed?
- Do you have the License Key for the licensed packages?

I recently received a new laptop and went through this process. The following is some of the software that I had to install on it. This is the list that I recall, but it's likely that I forget a package or two along the way.

- SQL Developer
- Oracle Client
- Database drivers (ODBC, JDBC, Oracle)
- WinRar
- FileZilla
- Juniper VPN
- Process NT
- Java Development Kit (JDK)
- Notepad++
- WinSCP—Windows Secure Copy program
- PuTTY

30.12.4 **Personalizations**

If you're like most people when you get a new computer you want it to be set up as similar as possible to your previous one. People are creatures of habit and want to be able to do things the same way that they used to be able to do it. If that description fits you, then here are some things that you might need to set up on the new computer:

- Desktop icons
- Your favorite Internet browser if it doesn't come preinstalled
- Bookmarks or favorites in your Internet browser
- Personal folders file in Outlook or other e-mail package
- Contact list in your e-mail package
- Oracle tnsnames.ora file
- Tasks you set up in the Windows Task Scheduler or other scheduling tool

- Local printers that you've defined
- Network drives that you've mapped
- ODBC (Open Database Connectivity) DSNs (Data Source Names)
- Passwords for applications or connections that your old computer has remembered. Do you know all of these passwords? If not, how can you recover them?
- Will the IP address of the new computer be the same? Does it matter?
- Destinations in the "Send To" option when you right-click a file
- Applications that are started up when your computer boots up
- The defaults for how Windows Explorer presents files, folders, etc. For example, are known file extensions displayed or hidden? Is the full path shown in the title bar? Are icons or thumbnails displayed?

30.12.5 **Training time**

If you get a new computer, it's very likely that you'll also be getting some new software. It might have a newer operating system loaded on it. Business-related software like a word processor or spreadsheet application might be different or a newer version. Regardless of what new software it is, it will take time to become as productive with it as you were with software that you were familiar with. Be sure to factor in the time it will take to come up to speed on any new software if you're estimating what the impact of getting a new computer will be.

The End of Days—
Decommissioning an Application

31

All good things come to an end and the life of an application is one of them. At some point, the decision may be made to shut down the application. This is referred to as decommissioning the application. Other phrases describing this are to "retire the application" or to "sunset the application."

This chapter focuses on tasks related to the application being decommissioned once the decision has been made. It won't cover any of the following tasks. There are many other books available that provide this information.

- Choose or design a replacement application
- Estimate the cost of the replacement
- Estimate the cost of maintaining the current application
- Project savings that can be realized by decommissioning the application
- Test the replacement software
- Write a project plan to manage all of the above

31.1 REASONS TO RETIRE AN APPLICATION

There are many reasons for deciding to retire an application. Each organization will have its own process of reviewing the reasons and weighing them. Some possible reasons are:

- The business need for the application no longer exists
- It's no longer actively being used, but is simply a repository of historical information
- Current applications offer newer technology, for example, they support mobile devices or BYOD
- It's functionality is being consolidated with another application, possibly due to a merger or acquisition
- The vendor no longer provides support for it
- The vendor has been acquired, and you have serious doubts about the new owner's long-term intentions to support the application
- Vendor maintenance fees and ongoing licensing costs are deemed prohibitive for what you're getting
- The custom hardware it runs on is aging and unmaintainable
- The IT skills to maintain the application are no longer available
- Keeping it running is consuming a significant amount of IT resources
- It isn't secure and making it secure isn't feasible or would be prohibitively costly
- The organization is moving to an ASP or SaaS hosted environment possibly from the same vendor
- The organization wants to move to a cloud implementation, and the current package isn't compatible with that architecture

31.2 WHO HAS THE FINAL DECISION-MAKING AUTHORITY?

The person or group that makes the final decision on whether or not an application gets decommissioned isn't likely to be the Application Administrator. That power belongs to the group that is paying the bills, is actually using the application, and is getting value from it. The Business Owner is the most likely person or group making this decision. There were probably ones that originally decided to bring in the application. It belongs to them and they're paying for it so it only makes sense that they have the power to decide when it's time to get rid of it.

The team that supports the application, including the Application Administrator, has a technical role to play but doesn't make the final decision. They can provide advice and recommendations based on experience and industry-wide best practices. For example, they can provide advice on the following areas:

- Provide advice on what to replace the application with
- Provide estimates of what it costs to maintain the existing application
- Provide a list of tasks that need to be done to decommission the application
- Provide a timeline for retiring the application

31.3 WHAT ABOUT THE DATA?

Perhaps the most complicated factor related to decommissioning an application is what will be done with the data? The following sections describe common options for handling data from an application that is being retired.

31.3.1 What data needs to be retained and for how long?

Before making a decision about what to do with the data, you need to know if there are any legal obligations to retain it. If there are no government rules or regulations, then your options are more flexible.

The legal obligations for retaining data are a labyrinth. The rules in the United States alone are extremely complicated. Each government organization, e.g., the IRS, OSHA, EPA, Commerce Department, Customs, all seem to have their own retention schedule. Major pieces of legislation like the Sarbanes-Oxley Act or HIPAA have unique retention schedules. To make sure that you have accurate, up-to-date information you need to consult with an expert in this field.

How long do different types of data need to be retained? Some examples are listed here, but be aware that these are just generalizations. Also, you must realize that regulations can change drastically virtually overnight. Don't make any decisions based on the following durations listed here. By the time this book is printed, they may no longer be accurate.

- Incorporation documents—permanent
- Contracts—7 years to permanent
- Business Records, e.g., canceled checks, payroll checks, bank statements, invoices—6 years
- Payroll records—3 years
- Fair Labor Standards Act-related documents—at least 3 years
- Employee records—3 years
- Audit records—7 years after the audit
- Family and Medical Leave Act—minimum of 3 years
- Customs Duty Records—5 years from the data of when duty was paid on imported goods
- OSHA-related records—5 years after an incident is reported
- Immigration I-9 forms—3 years after hiring date or 1 year after employment ends, whichever is later

If your organization does business in multiple countries, it's possible that the same piece of data will have drastically different retention requirements in each country. You need to consult with legal experts in each country before making the decision to delete any data. Even without the weight of law, there are probably very good business reasons to want to hold onto the data for a period of time.

31.3.2 Extract data from the existing system

From a technical viewpoint, extracting data from the database of the existing application can be difficult. Databases that support applications are typically large, contain lots of data, and are composed of many, possibly hundreds or even thousands of tables. They were designed to be flexible and minimize data duplication, but not to be easily understood.

If you need to extract data from the existing application, it can be done, but it's never easy. Some options for accomplishing this are listed here. These options are listed roughly in order of preference.

- The best option available is if the application has an export functionality that allows logical groupings of data to be exported. If this feature exists, then it should be at the top of your list on how to extract data. When running this utility, try to get the data as widely and deeply as possible. By this, I mean include all columns that are related to the object if possible. By "deeply," I mean to not filter out any rows, i.e., include all dates, all countries, all departments, all statuses, etc. You want to export every row of data that you possibly can.
- If the application has a reporting package, then you can use it to create reports that pull the data you want. The reporting software, especially if it has a drag and drop interface, is likely to present data at the logical level instead of at the physical level. This means that you don't have to understand how the database tables are related to each other because the reporting package has that logic built into it. The preferred output file type would be CSV or tab-delimited files. If possible, exclude page headers, column headers, pages number, creation date of the report, etc., from the reports. Extraneous details like this will just need to be trimmed out before the files can be used as input to the replacement application.
- If the two previous options aren't available, then the next best option is to write SQL queries that select data directly from the database. This is assuming that the database is built on a relational model, that you have a tool like SQL*Plus or Toad, and that you have an account that enables you to connection to the database. Before writing the queries to pull rows from the database, you'll have to spend some time poking around in the tables to get a basic understanding of what's in each of them. It would be worth seeing if any documentation exists that explains the major tables and how they are related. Check on the vendor's website or on the user group website if one exists.
- Screen-scraping refers to a technique where a program reads the output or "screen" of another program. The data read, i.e., "scraped," from the screen can be saved to a file or a database. Screen-scraping programs were used frequently on the old "green screen" terminals that were connected to mainframe computers. It's tricky but possible to write a screen-scraping program to extract data from a PC or graphical workstation. This option is one of the least desirable ways to extract data because of the time and effort it takes to develop the software to properly screen-scrape.

31.3.3 Will the data be migrated to another application?

If data from your existing application needs to be migrated to the new application, then you should consider including this requirement in your RFP (Request For Proposal) that's sent out to potential bidders that are interested in providing you with the new software. If the vendor that is providing the new software has experience migrating data, then they probably have tools available to them for doing this. They might also have experience with the specific application that you're decommissioning. By delegating this activity to the new vendor, you avoid having to recreate the wheel.

If the vendor that is selected doesn't have experience in this area, then you will need to determine how the data will be extracted from the current application and imported into the new application. The options presented in Section 31.3.2 should at least be considered as possibilities.

31.3.4 Keeping data accessible

If the data isn't migrated to a replacement application, how will it be accessible? Some options that are possible include:

- Keep the data in the CSV (Comma Separated Value) files that were created if it was exported from the original application to CSV files. CSV files can be opened with a text editor or a spreadsheet program like Microsoft Excel. Basic searches can be done using a text editor, but more complicated searches would be more difficult to accomplish with that type of tool.
- Convert the CSV files to spreadsheet files, e.g., xls files. Users are frequently accustomed to working with spreadsheets so their level of familiarity with this tool is probably high. One drawback is that some spreadsheet programs have limits on the number of rows they can handle. If your data set exceeds the spreadsheet's limit, you might need to split the files into multiple pieces. If this is required, it's inconvenient for both you and the users if they want to see all of the data in a single view.
- Create a very simple relational database and import the data into it. There are a number of relational database engines that are either free (MySQL) or offer scaled back versions that are available for free (Microsoft SQL Server or Oracle). If the database offers a graphical reporting tool, then your users can filter, sort, and search the data to their hearts content.

31.3.5 Archiving the data

If the data has to be retained but doesn't have to be online, then it can be archived for historical purposes. Some questions that need to be considered when archiving data are:

- Does your organization have a storage management team that handles data that is being archived for the long term? If so, then you should get them involved in this effort from the very beginning.
- Will the data have to be compressed when it is archived? This could make a very significant reduction in the volume of data being stored. If compression is applied, how will you guarantee that the algorithm to uncompress the files will still be available in the future?
- Will the data be encrypted when it is archived? Is this a legal requirement, an organizational policy, or a preference? If so, how can you guarantee that the algorithm to decrypt the files will still be available in the future? Where and how will the key(s) to decrypt the files be stored? Who is in charge of the keys? What are the alternatives if the keys are lost or corrupted?
- What media will be used to archive the data? Some examples are tape, hard drive, DVD, or flash memory card.
- No physical storage media endures forever. How long will the chosen media typically last before it becomes unreliable?
- All storage media technology eventually are replaced. As new technologies become mainstream, the older ones become obsolete. If your data is stored on a media that's becoming obsolete, will it be migrated to a newer media? Will someone remember to do this 5 or 10 years down the road? Or will you wake up one day and find out all of your data is on a technology that can no longer be read?
- Does the archived data need to be in a read-only format? Does the selected media allow or enforce this?
- What documentation about the format of the files needs to be retained with the files?
- Where will the media be stored? In-house? With a firm that specializes in long-term storage of data?
- How will people in the organization learn that the data has been archived?

- If someone needs to be access the archived data, how will they do that? Is there a formalized process for making and fulfilling such a request?

One word of advice is to verify that the media can be read immediately after it has been created. If there was a problem creating the archived copy, then you'll want to know about it sooner rather than later. By verifying that you can access the archived media that provides at least some assurance that it was properly created.

31.4 STEPS TO SHUT DOWN AN APPLICATION

If the application is being replaced with another software package, the schedule for shutting it down will be heavily dependent on when the new application is available, installed, tested, and certified. Be sure to keep your schedule flexible because it's possible or even likely that the replacement application won't be delivered on time.

One thing to remember is that you're not just decommissioning your production application. You're also shutting down and decommissioning any test servers, development servers, DR servers and QA servers in the application environment. Many of the steps you perform to shut down the production server will have to be duplicated on the other servers as well.

31.4.1 Back up everything

Back up everything related to the application that you can think of. If you never need it, then you haven't lost much. This includes:

- The database
- Execute a SQL query to list all the tables in the database along with the column names, data types, etc., in each table. It's also useful to get a row count for each table. If you don't know how to do this, ask your DBA to assist you
- Source code, if you have it
- Set up files, configuration files, ini (initialization) files, etc.
- Documentation from the vendor
- Any documentation that you, your associates, or predecessors wrote
- Scripts or batch files
- Log files
- Incident reports documenting when the application went down
- Print out all the system and environment variables on the server
- What accounts were used to access the application, specifically the Application Administrator account?
- What accounts were used to access the database?
- Run a netstat command to list all the open ports on the server

31.4.2 Document every step along the way

When you're in the process of shutting down an application, it's a good idea to document everything along the way. You will probably never need it, but it's a good idea to have a record of what you have done.

If you write up this documentation when you shut down the first environment, e.g., the development server, then it can be used (and improved) when you shut down the next environment, e.g., the test server. If you shut down the environments in the order of development, test, quality assurance, then by the time you shut down the production environment the documentation should be accurate, complete, and quite valuable.

31.4.3 **Inputs and outputs**

If your application creates any output feeds or received any input feeds, then you need to fully understand how these will be handled after it has been decommissioned. Examples of the questions that need to be asked are:

- If the application is being replaced by new software, will it continue to need the input file(s)? If so, then the new vendor needs to be aware of this requirement. An example of an input file(s) should have been provided in the requirements document.
- If the application isn't being replaced, then the group that provides the input file(s) should be informed that they can stop creating and transmitting these file(s).
- Does the need for the output file(s) created by the application continue to exist? If so, then the new vendor needs to be aware of this requirement. An example of an output file(s) should have been provided in the requirements document.
- If no new software is being acquired to replace the decommissioned application, then someone needs to determine how the output files will be created in the absence of this software.

31.4.4 **Disable jobs**

If the application required that jobs be scheduled on the application server, report server, database server, ftp server, or any other server, then those scheduled jobs need to be disabled or completely deleted. Examples of jobs that might have been scheduled include the following:

- A process to created backups
- Jobs to delete old log files
- A process to create an output file to be fed to another application or system
- A process to receive an input file and import it into the application
- Jobs that monitor the application server
- Reports that are created

Different servers might have different scheduling packages running on them. For example, Linux or UNIX servers will probably use cron to schedule their jobs. A Windows server might use the Task Scheduler. The organization might use an enterprise scheduling package like Control-M. When searching for scheduled jobs, be certain that you look for all of these types of schedulers and jobs that might be running on them.

31.4.5 **Start saving money**

Once the application has been decommissioned then you want to make sure that your organization is no longer paying out money it doesn't have to. Make sure your Accounts Payable department knows not to pay any invoices for this application after a specific date. Any payments for an annual licensing payment, maintenance fees, or consulting charges by the software vendor should be rejected outright or at least investigated before being paid.

31.4.6 **Reselling your license**

Does your contract with the vendor allow you to resell or sublease your license to another organization? If this is allowed (or at least not disallowed) in the contract, then you should determine whether it's worth pursuing. The reality might be that it's legal but economically wouldn't be doing, but it's worth at least looking into the possibility.

31.5 NO APPLICATION IS AN ISLAND

Even if it's your application that is being decommissioned, you're not the only person or group that will be affected when an application is retired. There are a number of other groups in your organization that will have to make some changes or at least be notified when an application is decommissioned. The following are examples of groups or teams that you should consider notifying:

- DBA team—will stop the database and drop it if necessary. This frees up CPU cycles and memory on the database servers as well as disk space.
- Security team—will close the ports that were opened to allow the application to communication with other servers across the network.
- Backup team—backups of the application server(s), and possibly the database server, will no longer be needed. Any reports that are sent out documenting the results of the backups can be discontinued.
- Monitoring team—monitoring the application server(s) will no longer be required so the monitoring team can remove this server(s) from their list.
- Messaging team—will remove the application server(s) from their list of servers to accept and forward messages for.
- AntiVirus Team—will know that they can stop updating the AV definition files on the application server(s).
- System Administrators—will either decommission the server or rebuild it so it can be used for another application. This may free up some rack space if the server has reached its end of life and is being disposed of. At a minimum, they can turn off the server to save electricity and A/C until the server is needed for another task.
- VM team—will drop the virtual server.
- DNS team—will remove any DNS entries that were created specifically for this application.
- SAN team—will free up any space on SAN drives that have been allocated to this application server.
- Update team—the team that controls when updates or patches are pushed out to servers can take your server(s) off the list of machines that need to be updated.
- VPN team—if your users will no longer be using VPN access to the organization's network, then they can be removed from the authorization list. This change might not be applicable because all of the users might need to retain their VPN account so they can access the network and other applications.
- AD team—can any of the application's users be removed from the Active Directory database? Again, this change might not be applicable because all of the users might need to retain their AD credentials to access the network and other applications.
- Training team—can the training team shut down any LMS (Learning Management System) courses for the application that is being decommissioned?
- Service desk, aka Help desk—needs to be told to no longer process requests for the application. If they get calls about an application that has been decommissioned, they should inform the caller that this application is no longer operational.
- DR facility—if your application has a DR server or servers, they can be decommissioned as well. This may free up one or more servers that can be used for other applications. The decommissioned application should also be taken off the list of applications that need to be brought up should the DR facility be activated. There is no sense bringing up an application in the DR facility that has no production version running.
- Auditors—will no longer have to audit your application. Of course, they may need to audit the decommissioning process, but after that they are likely done with this application.

- User workstations—did this application require that any software be installed on the users' workstations? If such software exists and needs to be removed, the next question is whether the user is able to remove it or not. Some organizations "lock down" user workstation so the users aren't able to load or unload software on them. Depending on whether users have access, you would need to send out explicit instructions telling users how to remove it or coordinate with the Desktop Software team to have them remove the software.

31.6 DOCUMENTATION

What will the impact of the application being decommissioned be on documentation? Some examples of documentation that might need to be updated include the following:

- DR documentation that refers to the decommissioned application needs to be updated to remove those references. Alternatively, you might need to update it with details of the replacement system.
- The Playbook that the Help Desk uses to respond to problems regarding the application needs to be updated. If nothing else, the Help Desk should know that the application is no longer operational.
- Access documentation showing who has access rights to applications will need to be updated to reflect this application's demise.
- Phone lists maintained by the organization showing the contact person for each application should be edited to remove the application being retired. Removing these references eliminates the risk of someone being called accidentally in the middle of the night.

Does any of the documentation written for the application need to be put into long-term or permanent storage? If so, does it need to be a hard copy or could an electronic copy be archived? The answer to this might be dictated by a regulation, rule, or law.

31.7 SECURITY

Does this application have any security implications? For example, does it:

- Contain material that your organization considers sensitive or confidential?
- Contain information that the organization would consider proprietary?
- Contain PII (Personally Identifiable Information) of customers, clients, employees, investors, patients?
- Require dedicated service accounts to run scheduled tasks or jobs? If the application goes away, can any service accounts be deleted?
- Require that any users have network credentials specifically to access the application? If the application is decommissioned, could the network credentials of any users be revoked?

If the application did contain secure data, then additional consideration has to be given to the manner in which the files, servers, or drives are disposed of. For example:

- If all disk files and the data they contain are encrypted from the time the files are created, then when a file is deleted or a drive is decommissioned the danger of data being extracted from the drive is significantly lower. Drives are available that encrypt the data as it is being written to the drive and decrypted as files are read from the drive. If security is a major concern of this application, then disk drives that automatically encrypt files should be employed.

- Most technically literate people realize that when a file is deleted from a computer's hard drive, the data doesn't really go away. What actually happens is that an entry in the File Allocation Table (FAT) is changed to indicate that the sectors (areas) of the drive previously allocated to the file are now available to be allocated to another file. The contents of the sectors are never actually removed. Utilities are readily available that can resurrect a file that has been "deleted."

- One method of preventing deleted files from being read later is to repeatedly overwrite its sectors with random patterns of ones and zeros. The principle here is that after this is done, no one will be able to detect "ghost" images of the original values. There are several ways to achieve this. One is to purchase disk drives that have this specific capability built into them. Another is a load and use a utility that does the same thing.

- Relational databases system use physical disk drives and files to contain the logical tables that they manipulate. If the database isn't using encryption to protect the data, then any disk space released when a database is dropped could potentially be studied and possibly expose the confidential data that it held. If encryption isn't performed, then the process of repeatedly writing random ones and zeros should be considered as a security measure when a database is dropped.

- Data extracted from the application being decommissioned also needs to be protected if it's being imported into the new system. The extraction files need to be encrypted until they are imported into the replacement application. At that point, the extract files need to be deleted and properly obscured by the process of repeatedly writing random ones and zeros over the files sectors.

- If there is no replacement system and the data is being archived then it needs to be secure. Archive files should be secured with an encryption algorithm that is considered currently unbreakable. One other thought is that what is considered unbreakable today might be easily broken 5 or 10 years from now. If your data is going to be archived for the long term, you might need to re-encrypt at future date with state-of-the-art algorithms at that point in time.

31.8 RELEASING THE SERVER

Once the application has been decommissioned, what will be done with the server(s)? If they are relatively new, they could be reused within the organization for another application. If they are at or near their end of life, then it might not make sense to retain them. If the application is running on a virtual server, then the physical server will probably stay in place to host other virtual servers.

If any hardware is going to be disposed, you'll want to make sure it's done in an ecologically sound manner. Dumping it in a landfill or shipping it off to a third-world country with more lenient regulations doesn't cut it. Computers contain heavy metals that can be significant pollutants if they aren't disposed of properly. Saving a few dollars in the short run could be a significant embarrassment later on if your lack of attention to environmental regulations is revealed.

Another option would be to donate your surplus hardware to a nonprofit. Two concerns that need to be dealt with before doing this are:

- Have the disk drives been sufficiently cleansed? If this isn't done, the potential for loss of corporate information exists. See the earlier section that describes utilities that repeatedly write random ones and zeros to disk sectors so deleted files can't be recovered.

- Before donating any servers to a nonprofit, you need to make sure that any software left on them can legally be transferred. For example, if your organization licensed copies of a word processing program, you might be violating your license agreement by transferring the servers to another organization.

31.9 THE REPLACEMENT APPLICATION

If the existing application is being replaced by new software there will be additional considerations in your decommissioning process. Some of these points are described in the following sections.

31.9.1 Last minute details

Will you need to extract and retain any additional information from the existing application? For example

- A list of all users who can currently use the application. This might be needed to set up the replacement application.
- Will users log in with the same IDs and passwords in the replacement system? If this is required then you'll have to export this information from the existing system.
- A list of the security groups that have been defined in the existing system.
- The group(s) that each user is assigned to.
- Screenshots of customized screens that have been developed or modified.
- Workflow steps that application imposes, including who is responsible or authorized to advance the task at each step in the process.
- Custom reports that were written by your team or by the users.
- Days and times when all reports are scheduled.
- The distribution list for each report that is to be sent out to users.
- Customized icons or backgrounds.

31.9.2 Maintaining the outgoing system

New applications don't arrive overnight. It takes time for each of the following steps:

- Research what other packages are available
- Develop and send out the RFP (Request For Proposal)
- Examine the proposals that are received
- Select the best proposal
- Negotiate a contract
- Have the COTS (Commercial Off the Shelf) software customized to your organization's needs
- Installation
- Loading data

What is happening with the existing application while all of that is going on? Specifically, are updates or patches being applied to the current software during this process? There are pros and cons to each possible answer.

- If changes are being made to the existing app, then the replacement system is being forced to hit a moving target.
- On the other hand, there will be changes that have to be made. Patches that affect security need to be installed. Patches that make fixes needed to get the work done need to be applied.

31.10 USER ACCEPTANCE TESTING OF THE NEW APPLICATION

As the Application Administrator of the existing application even if you're not involved in selecting, acquiring, or installing the new application, there will be some impact on you. If nothing else, the experienced users of the current application may be involved in the testing of the new software. This might mean that for a certain period, less experienced users will be working with the existing system. This might result in additional questions for you or bug reports that turn out to be caused by user errors. Make sure that you're very patient if this turns out to happen.

It's very likely that you'll be approached with some very detailed questions about how the current application works. This likely means that someone has encountered a situation that wasn't addressed during the RFP or customization phases. They'll want to see how it works on the existing system to confirm that the replacement system is handling it correctly. Obviously you need to deal with such questions with the utmost professionalism.

31.11 PARALLEL TESTING IS EVEN HARDER THAN PARALLEL PARKING!

Testing the new application while the existing application is still running is referred to as parallel testing. It's likely the best method of making sure that the new system produces the same results from the same input as the existing software. Unfortunately, it isn't easy to properly perform parallel testing. It requires the following:

- The databases in both applications must be functionally identical when the parallel testing begins. This by itself isn't trivial to accomplish.
- The same input must be entered into both systems at roughly the same time. This applies to both data feeds and manually entered data. The group doing the data entry will be handling double their normal work load. If a significant amount of data is entered into the system on a daily basis, then this can become overwhelming.
- Manually entered data that is entered into both systems must be identical. If the data entered into both systems doesn't match, this can cause outgoing data files or reports to differ. This can easily cause someone to investigate potential problems in the new system only to find out they can be attributed to inconsistent data entry activity.
- Outputs from the system, i.e., outgoing data feeds and reports, have to be compared to ensure that they are identical. If these comparisons can be automated that is wonderful. If not, then it has to be done manually.

31.12 RECOMMISSIONING THE APPLICATION

Is there even a remote possibility that the application will ever be needed again? Don't laugh and immediately say no. Stranger things have happened. Just to be on the safe side, you shouldn't decommission either the current software or hardware until it's obvious that the new system is going to work as advertised and there will be no last minute need to revert to the decommissioned application.

Things Every Application Administrator Should Know

32

There are things that every Application Administrator should know about regardless of the type of application that is being supported. You'll eventually figure them out because you'll probably find yourself bumping into them over and over. Knowing about them in advance might make the learning process just a little bit easier.

32.1 UNDERSTAND THE APPLICATION!

Not everyone will agree with this, but I think it's very important to have a good working knowledge of the application that you're supporting. You don't have to be an expert, but you should have a sound understanding of what it does. Some examples of what you should know include:

- Can you summarize what the application does for the company in one or two sentences? For example, does it send out invoices to customers, prepare checks for vendors, perform budgeting forecasts, or track legal contracts?
- Does the application have certain times of the year when it is heavily used? Do you know when they occur and why?
- During conversations with members of the user community, do you understand most of the commonly used abbreviations or technical terms they are using?
- Do you know how the users got the work done before the application was installed?
- If the users drew up a "wish list" of ways the application could be improved, would you be able to predict any of their wishes?
- If a user explains the steps needed to get to the screen where an error is occurring, will you have a pretty good understanding of how to reproduce their steps?

If you don't have this level of knowledge then coordinate with one of the more experienced users to sit with down them and learn about it. They'll almost certainly be happy to help because they know that the better you understand the application, the better you're able to support it.

32.2 FILES

Files will constantly be in your work life. You'll be loading them, comparing them, creating them, and deleting them. To be as efficient as possible, you'll want to know as many tricks as you can when it comes to working with files. I can't say that I know every trick, but the following sections should have some advice for just about everyone.

32.2.1 File name and locations

Files aren't abstract. They reside on a drive somewhere and have a name. Some points that you need to know regarding files are:

- A fully qualified file name is a way of referring to a file that includes the complete path where the file is located. When a fully qualified file name is specified, it can only refer to a single file. On a UNIX or Linux computer, this would include the path name starting at the root directory, e.g., /Examples/ Chapter32/this_file.txt. For a Windows file, the drive letter would be included, e.g., C:\Examples\ Chapter32\this_file.txt.
- A symbolic link is an object that points to another file system object. The target of a symbolic link can be either a folder or a file. This feature is available on Linux, UNIX, and Windows computers. One reason why a symbolic link would be used is for the flexibility. The folder or file can be moved to a bigger or faster drive on another server. As long as the link is updated to reflect the new location, any person or program referring to it wouldn't know that a change had been made.
- Universal Naming Convention (UNC) is a naming convention that is used to map network drives across a LAN. The format is \\server\share\file_path. For example, \\FileServer1\D$\Accounting\.

32.2.2 File types

There is an extremely wide variety of types of files, and sooner or later, you'll probably bump into most of them. Some of the ones that are more common are briefly described here. No list can contain all file types because new ones are being created regularly. Also, there is nothing to stop an application developer from picking a random collection of letters and using that as a new "standard" file extension.

- 7z—a compressed file used by the 7-Zip compression utility
- bat—batch files, frequently on Windows computers. It holds commands that will be executed when the batch file is launched
- cab—cabinet files are a form of compressed files typically used by Microsoft for installations
- cmd—a command file, aka batch file, that holds commands which will be executed when the file is initiated or launched
- csv—Command Separated Values files are frequently used to hold data. They can be opened by text editors. Microsoft Excel is also able to open and display them in a spreadsheet format
- evt—an evt file is used to save a list of events from the Microsoft Event Viewer utility
- ear—"Enterprise ARchive" files are used by Java to hold multiple files in a single archive
- html—Hypertext Markup Language is the primary markup language used for creating web pages. Web browsers, e.g., Internet Explorer, Firefox, Safari, and Chrome, interpret these files and render them into the screens that are seen by users
- iso—ISO files are images of an optical disk, i.e., a DVD or CD. ISO files are frequently used for downloading software or patches
- jar—Java ARchive files are used to aggregate and compress multiple Java class files and other related files
- mdb—database files used by Microsoft Access, specifically by versions 2003 and earlier
- mime—Multipurpose Internet Mail Extension—a file type used for e-mail
- msi—MSI files are used by the Microsoft Windows Installer for installing software
- pdf—Portable Document Format files are used to create and documents independent of the computer hardware and operating system it is being used on. This file type was developed by Adobe Systems
- ppt—PowerPoint files used to create presentations
- rar—compressed files created by the WinRAR compression and archival tool
- tar—Tape ARchive files are compressed files created by the UNIX tar command
- xls—Excel spreadsheet file. The most recent versions of Excel create files with an extension of xlsx
- xml—eXtensible Markup Language—many applications use XML files for input or to hold configuration details
- zip—compressed file created by the Zip or WinZip compression tool

32.2.3 **Association between file types and a program**

On a Windows computers, when you double-click on a file, a program that has been associated with that file type will start executing and will open the file that was double-clicked. For example, if you double-click on a file named "my_notes.txt," then typically Notepad starts up, launches, and opens that file. There are many file types associated with specific programs or actions. Some are set up when the operating system is loaded and others are added by applications. If Windows doesn't recognize the file extension, then you will be prompted for the program to be associated with the extension type.

Even if a file type is associated with a program, you can force it to be opened with a different program. Right-click on it in Windows Explorer and select the "Open with" menu option. A list of alternate programs will be displayed in a submenu. Select the program that you want to use to open the file.

32.2.3.1 *Listing file type associations*

The steps to view a list of file extension types and the program that has been associated with each file type seem to differ on each version of Windows. The following steps will be performed:

- Open the Control Panel by clicking the Start button and then click the Control Panel link
- Click the Folder Options tab
- Click the File Types tab.

The list box will contain each extension and the program associated with it. Figure 32.1 is a screenshot of the Folder Options window. To see additional details for an extension, select it.

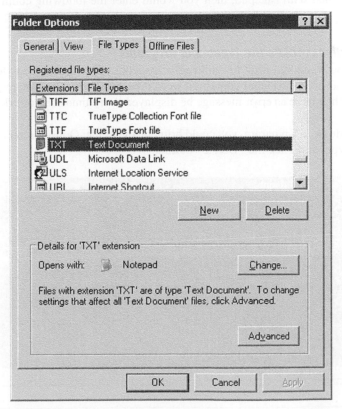

FIGURE 32.1

Folder Options window. (For color version of this figure, the reader is referred to the online version of this chapter.)

There is also a method of seeing file associations via the command line. There are two commands involved in the process.

1. assoc—This command display the file type associated with each file extension.
2. ftype—This command displays the program that will be opened when files of a specific file type are double-clicked.

Figure 32.2 shows a command prompt window with the output of these two commands. The output from both commands is lengthy, so it was piped to the "find" command to filter out unwanted output. The "assoc" command shows that four file extensions are tied with the "txtfile" association. The "ftype" command tells us that all file extension types associated with "txtfile" will cause the Notepad program to be launched and the file that was double-clicked will be opened.

32.2.3.2 Associating file types with a program

If a file type isn't currently associated with a program, there are multiple ways to create the association. The easiest way is to right-click on the file in Windows Explorer and select the Open option. You will be prompted with a screen asking whether the computer should decide what program to use or you can select from a list of programs to open the file. If you opt to make this decision yourself, then you can choose from a list of existing programs or you can browse to find another program.

If you're a hard-core command line user, then this association can also be done from there. Parameters can be passed to the "assoc" command to establish an association. For example, if you wanted all files with extension "mylog" to be opened with Notepad, then you would enter the following command:

```
assoc .mylog=txtfile
```

32.2.3.3 Steps to disassociate file types and programs

There may come a time when you want to remove the association between a file extension type and a program. For example, if a server no longer contains a word processing program, you might prefer to eliminate the association rather than have an error message be displayed every time someone double-clicks a file with that extension.

To disassociate a file from a program, you could bring up the Folder Options screen shown in Figure 32.1, select the extension type, and click the "Delete" button.

FIGURE 32.2

Command prompt options for file associations. (For color version of this figure, the reader is referred to the online version of this chapter.)

The "assoc" command can also make this change. By entering an extension type without specifying an association, any existing association is removed. To remove any association with the extension ".doc," enter the following command:

```
assoc .doc=
```

32.2.4 Accessing files on other computers in windows explorer

There will be many times that you need to deal with files that are on another server. For example, you might want to look at a file on the DEV server while you're on the production server. Or you might want to copy a file from DEV to QA server. One way is to move the file you need to a drive that is common to your PC and the server. For example, this might be set up as your "Z" drive. This method will work, but requires that you move or copy the file twice, i.e., from the DEV server to the Z drive and then from the Z drive to the QA server. It also requires that you remote to the server in question.

A simpler way to accomplish this is via Windows Explorer. Assume that you have a remote session open to application server app001 and you want to access a file from application server app002. A very quick way to access it would be to open Windows Explorer and in the Address field enter \\app002\d$. Figure 32.3 shows what the field should look like. After doing this, all of the files and directories on the D: drive on server app002 will be displayed in Windows Explorer just as if they were in local. This assumes that you have access to the server and that the D: drive is shared.

Another easy method to move a file from one server to another is to use the "Save As" function that is built into many programs like Notepad, Microsoft Word, and Microsoft Excel. This technique can even be used to save a file attached to an e-mail to another server. Figure 32.4 is a screenshot demonstrating how this technique can be done. To save a file to server app002, follow these steps:

1. Select the File | Save As menu option in Notepad or another program. The normal file browser screen will be displayed.
2. In the "File Name" field, enter the destination server and shared drive in the format shown in Figure 32.4.
3. Press the Enter key.
4. The main area of the browser screen will show the directory structure of the destination server. You can drill down to a subdirectory by double-clicking it the same way that you do in Windows Explorer.

32.2.5 Hidden files

Most operating systems provide the ability to hide files from anyone who is looking at the contents of a directory. It seems that the intent isn't so much to make them completely inaccessible as much as it is to keep them out of sight. They are easily accessed if you know how to look for them.

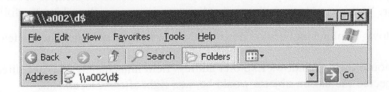

FIGURE 32.3

Accessing files on another computer. (For color version of this figure, the reader is referred to the online version of this chapter.)

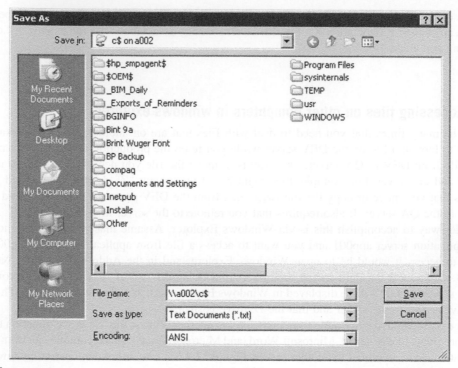

FIGURE 32.4

Save As to another server. (For color version of this figure, the reader is referred to the online version of this chapter.)

On UNIX and Linux computers, directory and files names that begin with a period are hidden by default. Typically, configuration files are hidden. To include hidden files and directories in the output of an "ls" command, the -a flag needs to be included. For example:

```
ls -a
```

On a Windows computer, files, folders, and drives can be defined to be hidden. Hidden files are by default not displayed in Windows Explorer. You can change this setting in the following manner:

1. In Windows Explorer, select menu option Organize | "Folder and search options"
2. Click the tab that is labeled View
3. In section "Hidden files and folders," select option "Show hidden files, folders and drives"

You don't usually expect that a vendor will deliberately hide files or directories but it can happen. A coworker showed me a way to display them. We had just run a process that died with an error. The process should have created several log files in the directory C:\Users\Kelly.Bourne\Documents\Rentview, but we didn't see it in Windows Explorer. We were able to drill into the directory in question by taking the following steps:

1. Opened Windows Explorer and drilled down to the point where we knew the hidden directory should exist.
2. Clicked the mouse in the Windows Explorer address field immediately after the directory name where we expected the hidden objects would be, i.e., right after "\Documents."
3. Manually added the name of the directory that was being hidden, i.e., "\Rentview."
4. Pressed the Enter key.

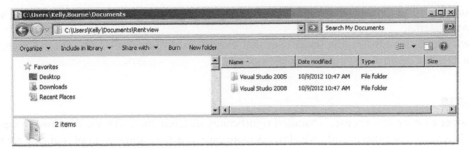

FIGURE 32.5

Revealing a hidden directory. (For color version of this figure, the reader is referred to the online version of this chapter.)

Figure 32.5 shows the Windows Explorer just before I pressed the Enter key. After that, the expected directory appeared in the right-hand pane. We were able to drill down into that directory in the normal manner, i.e., by double-clicking it in the right-hand pane.

32.3 UNIX VS. WINDOWS

There are a number of differences between UNIX and Windows computers that can trip up an Application Administrator that isn't careful. Some of the more significant differences are listed in the following sections.

32.3.1 Root vs. administrator

Every computer system needs an account which is capable of doing everything. Traditionally on UNIX and Linux systems, this account is called "root." On a Windows system, it is called the "administrator" account. Other names that you might hear for these accounts are superuser or admin.

32.3.2 Files

There are significant differences regarding how files are handled by UNIX and Windows. Some of the major differences are briefly described in the following list:

- In UNIX, a file name is a pointer to an inode (index node) which is where metadata about the file is actually stored. Inodes allow UNIX to have a great deal of control over files. For example, it tracks how many processes have the file opened and won't allow the file to be deleted as long as one or more processes have it open. Windows has no concept similar to inodes.
- UNIX systems allow multiple filenames to refer to the same disk file. This concept is referred to as a "hard link." This is allowed because the different file names are simply pointing to the same inode.
- In a Windows system, the "top" of a path is typically a drive letter, for example, C:\Windows\system32 \some.dll. On a UNIX system, it is referred to as a mount point.
- The slashes used in file paths are different. UNIX systems use the forward slash (/), while Windows users the backslash (\).
- UNIX allows a wider selection of characters in file names than Windows. For example, Windows won't allow characters like <, >, :, \, and I.

- Permissions used to control who can access files are significantly different between UNIX and Windows systems.
- Windows maintains information on its files that have no equivalent on UNIX. For example, the attribute bits for "archive," "hidden," and "system."

32.3.3 **Case**

Case, i.e., upper case vs. lower case, is handled significantly different on UNIX vs. Windows systems. In general, UNIX is less case sensitive while Windows is more case sensitive. Some examples of case sensitivity are:

- File names in Windows are case insensitive, while in UNIX they are case sensitive. This means that the file names Example.txt and example.txt would refer to the same Window file, but different files in UNIX.
- Commands in Windows are case insensitive, e.g., both "dir" and "DIR" will work. In UNIX, the command "ls" works, but "LS" isn't recognized.
- User names are case sensitive in UNIX, but not in Windows.
- Searches done on UNIX are case sensitive, but searches on a Windows system are case insensitive.

32.3.4 **End of the line**

Windows and UNIX use different characters to indicate the end of each line in text files. The symbol used by UNIX is the line feed character (\n). Windows uses two symbols, the carriage return and line feed (\r\n).

If you're transferring files from one type of system to the other, then this concept will be important to you. If a program reading a file encounters an unexpected line terminator, it's likely to crash.

If you need to convert line terminators from one style to the other, there are utilities available to do this. The "dos2unix" command on a UNIX system converts a file from the DOS or Windows format to UNIX. A freeware program called Unix2DOS will convert a file with the UNIX style termination to the Windows format.

32.3.5 **Getting help**

The standard method of getting information on a UNIX or Linux system is to enter the "man" command at a shell prompt. The parameter that needs to be passed is the command that you want information on. For example, the command "man mkdir" would return details on the "mkdir" command.

On a Windows system, the equivalent method is to enter the command name followed by the forward slash and question mark at a command prompt. For example, entering "mkdir /?" would return details for the "mkdir" command.

32.3.6 **CLI vs. GUI**

Historically, UNIX and Linux systems use a CLI (Command Line Interface) to interact with users. Windows users have primarily used a GUI (Graphical User Interface) to interact with that operating system. This isn't to say that Windows users don't or can't use the command prompt to achieve their goals. There are also GUI tools for UNIX systems that allow users to drag and drop, etc.

An application Administrator should be comfortable using the command line interface (CLI) for both Windows and UNIX. If you become accustomed to a specific UNIX GUI tool, there is no guarantee that it will exist on every UNIX server that you will work with. Instead of needing a GUI tool loaded, it would be more efficient to develop at least a minimal level of proficiency with UNIX commands at the command line level.

32.4 COMMAND LINE COMPONENTS

The contents of a command line are the command itself, zero or more parameters, and zero or more options. Options are also called flags or switches. There can also be pipe symbols and a file to write the output to.

Parameters are frequently disk files. For example, the command might require a parameter that indicates where the command's output should be written. Commands may have multiple parameters, for example, an input file and an output file may both need to be specified.

Options modify the operation of the command. Depending on the operating system or the shell, any options being used might be preceded by a hyphen or a forward slash. Options might or might not be case sensitive.

If you have any questions about the parameters or options a command is expecting, then use the "man" or "help" commands to display more information on the command. Better to take a couple of extra minutes, get it correct, and then have the command do something unexpected and possibly destructive.

32.5 PIPES AND REDIRECTS

As an Application Administrator, you will be using the command line interface on a regular basis. There will be times that you need to capture the output from a command. Perhaps, the easiest way to do this is to redirect its output to a file. For example, the following command writes the list of files and directories to a file named output_list.txt:

```
dir > output_list.txt
```

The redirect symbol can also allow you to use the contents of a file as the input of a command. Personally, I've used this but not as often as the output redirect. The following command would feed the contents of files input.txt to the sort command. The output of the sort command would be sent to file output.txt:

```
Sort < input.txt > output.txt
```

The pipe symbol (|) allows you to feed output from one command to be the input of a second command. The most common usage I've found for this is when I need to search the output of one command for a specific string. For example, the following command searches the output of the netstat command for port 1521:

```
netstat -a | find "1521"
```

32.6 DOS COMMANDS THAT CAN SAVE TIME AND TROUBLE

If your background is primarily on Windows computers, then you are probably accustomed to using a GUI for everything. You shouldn't discount the possibility that, at times, commands entered at the command line can save time.

One simple example is if you need to create a number of subdirectories in a directory. You could easily right-click in Windows Explorer and select New | Folder and then enter the desired subdirectory's name. It's much quicker to open a command prompt in the desired directory and simply enter "mkdir directory_name." If the new subdirectory names are similar, you could use the up arrow key to display your last command and change it to reflect the new directory name.

The "rm" or "erase" in a command prompt is more efficient than using the Windows Explorer to delete files because the GUI alternative moves the files to the Recycle Bin. If you're trying to delete a large number of files by moving them to the Recycle Bin, this can slow down the process significantly. It might be advisable to use the "erase" command instead of "rm" just because it's harder to enter it by mistake.

One more example of a command that can be run in a Windows command prompt is "Robocopy" or "Robust File Copy." This command replicates directory and the subdirectories under it from one location to another. This command is extremely useful when you need to synchronize files on two computers.

Granted I've mentioned only a couple of CLI commands, but the point is to not assume that a GUI is faster and easier than the command line. If you keep your mind open, you might find alternate and more efficient ways to get your work completed.

32.7 TESTING BASICS

Testing applications will be a regular, if not constant, activity that an Application Administrator will be involved in. You may not test the entire application, but there will be pieces of the application that only the administrator can access so you'll always have some involvement in the testing activities.

Situations when testing will be needed include the following:

- After the initial installation of the application
- After each upgrade
- To document performance before and after significant changes are made to the system.

Software testing comes in a variety of flavors. Each type of testing is applicable during specific times during the application's life. The following sections describe types of testing and when each is typically performed:

- Unit testing—doesn't really apply to users of third-party applications. This type of testing is done when the application is being developed. As each unit, aka module or subroutine, is completed it is tested to verify that it meets the specifications.
- UAT (User Acceptable Testing)—is done when the application is initially installed to verify that the application does everything that the specifications dictate. UAT testing is also done after each upgrade is applied. Sometimes organizations don't do a UAT after each upgrade and regret it when their upgraded production environment experiences problems that were apparently introduced by the upgrade or patch.
- Performance testing—is done to measure how the application is performing. It could be done when the software is installed. Another situation when performance testing is performed is before and after significant changes are made to the system, for example, when moving from a physical server to a virtual server or before and after moving from local drives to SAN drives. Examples of performance testing would include timing how long it takes to do the following actions:
  - Bring up specific screens
  - Run some of the more complicated reports
  - Import a significant quantity of data
  - Create an export file for another department, vendor, or business partner.
- Stress testing—is typically done when the software is installed to validate that it meets the specifications provided to the application vendor. Stress testing might verify that a certain number of users are able to simultaneously log onto the application and response time remains within the specified time period.
- Regression testing—is done to confirm that changes to the software haven't caused problems with existing functionality. Running a UAT after each upgrade is a form of regression testing because you're trying to confirm that the upgrade hasn't broken existing functions of the application.

- Parallel testing—is done by running both an existing application and the new system simultaneously for a period of time. The purpose of parallel testing is to confirm that data displayed, reports created, etc., by both systems are identical. Parallel testing is valuable but difficult to implement because both systems have to be maintained, e.g., users have to enter new data into both systems to keep them synchronized.

32.8 BASIC SQL

SQL, i.e., Structured Query Language, is the *de facto* language used to interact with relational databases. If your application stores its data in a relational database, then SQL is being used whether that database involved is Oracle, Microsoft SQL Server, DB2, or MySQL.

As an Application Administrator, you don't need to be a SQL expert, but you need to understand the basics. You have to know how to write, execute, and debug some basic SQL statements. These statements will be executed in a tool like SQL*Plus, TOAD, or SQL Navigator.

The SQL statement that you will almost certainly use the most is the SELECT statement. This statement is used to select, i.e., read, data from the database. The basic structure of a SELECT statement is shown here.

```
SELECT table.column
FROM table
WHERE conditions
ORDER BY columns;
```

Other SQL statements that you might encounter are:

- UPDATE—modifies the values of existing rows in a table in the database. Unless the vendor specifically tells you to perform an UPDATE statement, you shouldn't do this on your own. The reason is if the WHERE clause of an UPDATE statement isn't correct, you can change the wrong rows. It's possible to inadvertently modify every row in the table.
- INSERT—adds rows to a table. One danger of writing and executing INSERT statements is that tables in the database have relationships, i.e., rows in one table are tied to rows in other tables. If you don't understand these relationships, you can easily corrupt the database.
- DELETE—removes rows from tables. If the WHERE clause of a DELETE statement isn't written correctly, you could delete every row in the table. Obviously, the DELETE statement should be used with extreme caution.
- CREATE—used to create database objects like tables, view, indexes, etc. It's unlikely that you will ever write or execute a CREATE statement when supporting an application.

32.9 ADVANCED USES OF EXCEL

You may think of Excel as only something that users need to be familiar, but it offers many functions that even an Application Administrator can use. The more mundane uses of Excel are to create forms that users can complete to report problems, request access, identify enhancements, etc. These are useful because users are probably already familiar with Excel and how it's used.

A knowledgeable Excel user can quickly and easily use it for more advanced purposes. One example is to quickly and accurately create SQL statements or scripts. For example, say you need to drop 500 tables that have names which include an ascending numeric sequence, e.g., Table_001, Table_002, etc. You could do this manually or use Excel to create a file with 500 separate DROP statements in it. To use Excel to create this file, perform the following steps:

- Enter "Table_001" into cell A1.
- Click on the bottom right corner of that cell and drag it down.

- Subsequent rows will be populated with Table_002, Table_003, etc. Extend this as far as needed.
- In cell B1, enter the value ="DROP TABLE" & A1 & ";".
- Click on the bottom right corner of this cell and drag it down, so it's copied to all the rows that have a value in column A.
- Subsequent rows will be populated with the same formula.
- Select all the cells you want in column B, copy them, and paste them into Notepad.
- Save the file as Drop_Table_script.sql or an appropriately named file.

Figure 32.6 shows how the Excel sheet should look like after the above steps are performed. By executing this SQL file in SQL*Plus, all of the "DROP table" statements will be executed.

This same technique can be used to create:

- INSERT statements to insert test data into a table
- UPDATE statements to modify existing data in a test table
- DELETE statements from a test table

The potential for using Excel to create SQL scripts and batch file content is limited only by your imagination and cleverness.

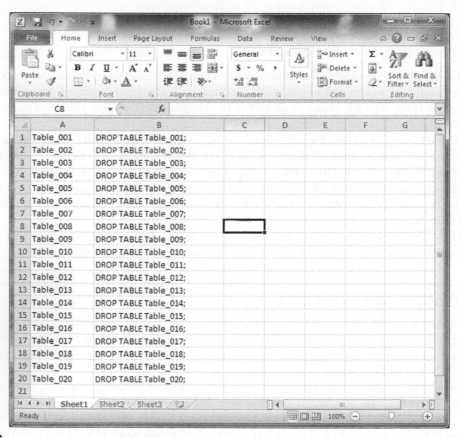

FIGURE 32.6

Using Excel to create SQL statements. (For color version of this figure, the reader is referred to the online version of this chapter.)

32.10 **URLs**

An URL, uniform resource locator, is the address of a web page that is entered into an Internet browser to display the desired web page. You won't be writing the code that interprets or processes URLs, but you'll have to understand what they look like. It will be extremely useful if you are able to quickly spot errors in an URL that a user might have entered accidentally.

An URL has the following parts:

- The schema name also called the protocol. Examples of the schema name are http, https, ftp, gopher, and wais.
- The domain name, also called the IP address, is the destination location of the URL. This can be expressed as a domain name, e.g., google.com, or its IP address. Domain names are case insensitive. The domain name is separated from the schema by a colon and two forward slashes (://).
- An optional port number can be included after the domain name, e.g., google.com:80. If no port number is provided, the default port for the schema will be used. A colon is used to separate the port from the schema.
- The path specifies the requested resource. The path value is case sensitive, but some servers treat it as case insensitive. An example of a path is "example/URL." The path is separated from the domain (or port number if one exists) by a forward slash.
- The query string is an optional field that holds data being passed to the application running on the web server. For example, it might be an account number, order number, or customer ID. If multiple values are being passed, they are separated by ampersands. The query string is separated from the path by a question mark (?).
- The fragment identifier is an optional value at the end of the URL. It points to a subordinate resource of the primary resource being called, for example, a page or document. Fragment identifiers are separated from preceding elements of the URL by a hash mark (#).

32.11 **HTML**

HTML (HyperText Markup Language) is the primary markup language that is used to create web pages. The codes in HTML tell web browsers how to render, i.e., display, the page. If you support a web-based app, you have to at least recognize HTML when you see it. A very short list of the visual elements that HTML tells the browser to display includes:

- Fonts
- Colors
- Normal, bold, or italics
- Underlined or strikethrough
- Line breaks
- Images
- Tables

32.12 **XML**

XML (eXtensible Markup Language) is a markup language used to encode documents that are readable by both humans and machines. It consists of elements and attributes that are preceded and followed by tags. Start tags begin with a less than symbol (<) the code for the tag and then a closing greater than symbol (>). An example is <section>. End tags are similar to start tabs, but include a forward slash, for example, </section>.

It's fairly common for applications to use XML files to store their configuration settings or parameters. Data files created by the application or imported into the application might be in an XML format. Typically, the file extension of an XML file is ".xml," but not always.

XML files can be edited with any text editor or word processor. If you are going to be dealing with them frequently, it's more convenient and productive to use an editor that "understands" XML. For example, it might show XML tags in a different color or it might line up matching tags. If you add a line with a tag, the editor will typically automatically add the closing tag for you. One text editor that works well with XML files is Notepad++.

32.13 WANs, LANs, AND VLANs

If your experience with networks is relatively limited, then there will probably be some concepts, terms, and phrases that you don't understand. A very brief explanation of some networking terms that an Application Administrator is likely to encounter are presented here.

- Bandwidth—the amount of data that can be moved through a network at one time. Bandwidth is measured in bits per second.
- Internet——The Internet is the collection of all networks that are interconnected.
- Intranet—a private network used exclusively by one organization.
- LAN—local area network, computers in close proximity that are connected to each other.
- Network—a system that sends data to and from multiple computers.
- Network card—a device that allows a computer to communicate with the network. Frequently called a Network Interface Card or NIC.
- Ping—a command that sends a message to another computer to determine if it is connected to the network.
- Router—a device that connects multiple LANs together. Routers are what enable communications to flow from a computer on one LAN to a computer on a different LAN.
- Switch—a device that forward packets between computers on the same LAN.
- TCP/IP—Transmission Control Protocol/Internet Protocol, the standard protocol used to connect computers on the Internet.
- VLAN—virtual LAN, a technique of grouping some computers that are on a LAN together. If these computers exchange messages primarily between each other and not with other computers on the LAN, grouping them together on a VLAN can make the network more efficient.
- VPN—Virtual Private Network, a network that uses software to "tunnel" through the Internet to create a private connection between two computers.
- WAN—a network of computers that spans a larger area, for example, a state or country.
- WiFi—Wireless Fidelity, combination of hardware and software that allows network communications to be sent from one computer to another without the use of wires or any other physical connection.

Education

The IT industry is so broad, so complex, and moving so fast that it's almost a full-time job to keep up. It isn't possible to be an expert in every area, so you have to focus on what's most important to you right now. The following sections describe some areas where education can be of the most assistance to you.

33.1 AREAS WHERE APPLICATION ADMINISTRATORS MIGHT NEED IMPROVEMENT

Everyone has strengths and weaknesses. One Application Administrator might have a very technical background. Her biggest weakness might be her limited understanding of the business that the organization is in. Another Application Administrator might have come through the ranks of the user community. Learning additional technical fundamentals might be of the most benefit for him.

The following sections outline some areas where you can focus your educational time and dollars. Since both your time and training dollars are limited, choose carefully to ensure you maximum the return on your efforts.

33.1.1 The application

If you've been supporting this application for a relatively short time period, then you might see the most return on your training investment if you focus your educational efforts on it. Some of the specific areas you can learn about are described in the following sections.

33.1.1.1 Technical aspects of the application

Every enterprise-level third-party application has many, many moving components. There will almost certainly be pieces of it that you're not familiar with. Learning more about the technical side of the application can help you during many activities including:

- Installations
- Upgrades
- Customizations
- Importing and exporting data
- Troubleshooting

33.1.1.2 How the organization uses the application

Learning more about the business background or the organization is definitely worth the effort. If possible, try to understand how your application is being used and what makes it valuable to the organization and the basics of its functionality. This type of knowledge will make understanding the users easier for you.

33.1.1.3 Enhancing the application

Does the application include optional packages that could make it more valuable to your organization? If you understand both how the organization uses the application and what optional features the application offers, then you would be in the position to recommend to management which optional features might provide additional useful functionality.

33.1.2 Technical areas outside the application

If your application-centric knowledge is strong, then focusing on the technical side of the landscape might be your best course of action. The sections that follow describe just a few possible areas that might be of value to you. Review them, but don't be limited by this list of technical topics.

33.1.2.1 Network fundamentals

It's my experience that to many IT personnel, the "network" is a bit of a mystery. Becoming more knowledgeable about networks will benefit most Application Administrators. Even if you won't or can't make changes to the network, you can at least have a knowledgeable conversation with the Network Administrators if something is wrong with the network. Having a working knowledge of areas like DNS, DHCP, routing, IP addressing, etc., can only help you.

33.1.2.2 Security

The areas of IT security are almost endless. Educating yourself about any form of IT security will be of great value to both you and your employer. Some areas that you can dig into include:

- Network security
- Database security
- Identification and Authentication
- Server-level security
- Application-level security
- Security for web server software, e.g., IIS or Apache
- Minimizing the attack surface of your application servers

33.1.2.3 Database fundamentals

It's pretty safe to assume that any enterprise-wide application you're supporting is built upon a relational database. If you don't already have knowledge of relational databases, then this is an area that offers a lot to learn about. Some potential topics that you can learn more about include:

- SQL basics
- Database tuning
- Primary and secondary keys
- Indexes
- Views
- Stored procedures
- The structure of the application's database
- Database backup and restore processes

33.1.2.4 Advanced SQL

Section 33.1.2.3 referred to learning about database fundamentals, including the basics of SQL. Once you've mastered the basics of SQL, there is still a long way to go before you can consider yourself an expert on the topic.

33.1.2.5 Web application fundamentals

If your users use a web browser like Internet Explorer or Firefox to interact with the application, then your application is web based. If you aren't already familiar with the fundamentals of web applications, then this should be one of the first areas you dig into. Knowing the fundamentals of web applications will help you to set up, tune, and troubleshoot the application.

Some potential topics you'll want to learn about include:

- Basic structure of web pages
- HTML
- Cascading Style Sheets (CSS)
- Accessing the data
- Hosting
- Common errors
- How a web site is recognized by search engines
- The Internet vs. the World Wide Web
- URLs
- Supporting a website

33.1.2.6 Scripting languages

A scripting language is a computer language that doesn't have to be compiled. One advantage of scripting languages is that the code can be quickly edited and reexecuted. They are used in a variety of manners including:

- In script files, aka command files or batch files
- On the client side of web applications
- On the server side of web applications

Learning even a single scripting language is worth the effort. Just a few examples of scripting languages include:

- JavaScript
- PHP
- Python
- Perl
- Ajax
- Rexx

33.1.2.7 Performance monitoring and tuning

Performance tuning a computer system is a very difficult undertaking. The number of moving pieces seems to grow almost exponentially with each generation of software. If you learn enough about this topic to improve the performance of the applications you support, you'll be doing a significant service to the organization and the users.

33.1.3 Soft skills

The days are long gone when technical personnel would be sequestered in a room and never interact with upper management, users, clients, or vendors. These days virtually everyone has to be ready to make presentations, field questions, or interact with the rest of the organization. For the hard-core techies among us, this can be a daunting requirement. One way to make this experience easier is to improve the so-called soft skills at your disposal. Some soft skills are described in the following sections.

33.1.3.1 Writing

Everyone in the organization needs to be able to write in a concise and coherent manner. Even the most hard-code technical types will need to write documents like:

- Incident reports
- Test plans
- Application overviews
- How-to guides for the users
- Playbooks
- Proposals
- Recap of conference calls or meetings

33.1.3.2 Verbal communication skills

It would be hard to overestimate the value of being able to communicate verbally effectively. Whether it's making a presentation to a group or explaining to the boss or users why their request is far more complicated than it seems. Throughout your entire career, you'll be communicating with your supervisor, users, management, vendors, other Application Administrators, and other technical personnel. If you can't put together a coherent sentence, then improving your communication skills might well be the best place to being improved your soft skills.

33.1.3.3 Project management

The range of projects that need to be managed ranges from hundreds of man-years down to a few man-months. If you don't have any experience or training in the art of project management, then a "project" that includes just a few tasks might overwhelm you. Learning the basics of project management is definitely a worthwhile investment. Even if you never have to create a formal project plan for a relatively small effort, it might be valuable to develop one strictly for your own use.

If you find yourself doing more and more project management-related work and enjoy doing it, you might want to become certified in this area. The Project Management Professional (PMP), offered by the Project Management Institute, is one of more recognized certifications for project managers. It takes time and effort to become certified, but you'll learn a great deal about the field and be a recognized professional in it.

33.1.3.4 Leading meetings

Eventually, almost everyone will be required to lead a meeting. This may involve a team assembled in a local conference room or it may be a conference call with team members dialed in from around the world. No matter where or how many are attending, the meeting will be more productive if the leader is effective. Some methods of improving how meetings are managed include the following:

- Every meeting should have a defined and recognized purpose
- Distribute an agenda for the meeting in advance
- Use effective visual aids when appropriate
- Encourage discussion and participation by everyone, but keep the discussion on topic

- At the end of the meeting, summarize what was discussed and agreed to
- A recap or minutes from the meeting should be written and distributed to attendees as soon as reasonably possible

33.1.3.5 Budgeting basics

Many technical types have little or no understanding of how the budgeting process works in their organization. Learning more about budgeting basics can help you in several ways:

- You'll know the process for submitting requests for additional hardware, software, and training
- If your request for funding is turned down, you'll be in a better position of understanding why and increase the chances of it being approved the next time
- It can enhance your chances of being promoted to a management position

33.1.3.6 Staff supervision and management

Learning more about how supervisors and management do their jobs is good for everyone to do. It will give you a better understanding of what they do and why they do certain things. By knowing more about those positions, it will give you a better insight into whether or not you would be interested in a supervisory position.

33.1.3.7 Your industry

It's always possible to learn more about the industry that your organization is in. You can learn more about its background, current happenings, government influence, future trends, etc. Having more information on the background can help you understand the application your support and the ways in which it is being used.

33.1.4 Future trends

The IT field is changing constantly and it seems that the rate of change is accelerating. There are numerous future trends that seem to be far off right now but will arrive much sooner than anticipated. It isn't possible to be an expert on every future trend, but if you can keep up with several that are most likely to impact your industry or organization, then you'll be ahead of the game. Just a couple of trends that are either coming in the future or have already arrived are listed in the following sections.

33.1.4.1 Virtualization

Replacing physical servers with virtualized servers is already a reality for most data centers. If your organization hasn't yet made this move, then it's probably just a matter of time until it does. You need to determine if your applications are certified by the vendor to run on virtual servers. If so, which types of virtualization software is it certified for?

Servers aren't the only devices being virtualized. User desktops are also able to be converted to a virtual device. The concept is that the operating system runs on the local, i.e., desktop, hardware but the software was accessed from a remote server. One of the downsides to virtualized desktops is that it requires constant network connectivity to the server where the image is being accessed.

The advantages of virtualizing a desktop include the following:

- If the desktop is lost, stolen, or damaged, a new virtual device can rapidly be created.
- Virtual desktops don't contain any data so if they are lost or stolen, no confidential information is lost.
- Virtualized desktop can be cloned from a standard base. Having identical servers makes it easier to ensure they have all of the needed support software on them.
- Your DR plan can include creating virtualized desktops to replace any lost at the primary facility.

- Applying upgrades to virtual desktops is easier than installing them on physical devices.
- If a virtual desktop gets infected with a virus, Trojan horse, or other malware, it can be dropped and quickly rebuilt.

33.1.4.2 Cloud computing/SaaS

Cloud computer is a widely used phrase used to refer to an arrangement where an organization rents computing power without necessarily knowing or caring where those servers are located. This shifts the burden of supporting servers from the user's organization to a support organization, for example, Amazon and its Elastic Cloud Computing offering.

The advantages of cloud computing for most organizations include:

- It is more agile, e.g., computing power can be added or subtracted almost at will
- The vendor will claim that the cost is reduced
- Better performance is promised by the vendor
- Reliability
- The maintenance burden is handled by the vendor

If your organization is thinking about moving its data center or at least some of its servers to the cloud, then you need to understand how it might affect your application. For example:

- Is the application certified to work in a cloud environment?
- Does the cloud vendor have experience with your particular application?
- Have other clients using this application successfully migrated it to the cloud?
- Is cloud computing secure enough for the application's security needs?
- Is there likely to be a performance impact if the application is moved to the cloud?

Vendors often host SaaS (Software as a Server) applications in a cloud. One major advantage of doing this is that the cloud is flexible. If demand for the application increases, then additional (cloud) computing resources can be allocated to application so user performance is maintained.

33.1.4.3 Open source software

Open Source Software (OSS) refers to software that is freely distributed, including the source code. The copyright holder of the software allows anyone to examine, modify, and redistribute the software. It's possible that an Open Source Software application might exist that fulfills the needs of your organization. If this is a possibility, then your organization might consider utilizing it instead of a licensing a product from a third-party vendor.

Before diving into the open source waters, you need to be aware that there are disadvantages to this approach to acquiring software. Some of these disadvantages are:

- Migrating from your current application to the OSS will have to be done without a vendor supporting you
- The OSS application might not be exactly what you need, so your organization needs to be prepared to modify it or accept its limitations
- Supporting an Open Source application requires a more technically savvy staff
- If problems occur with the application, you can't just pick up the phone and expect a vendor to fix it. There might be individuals or a group that supports it, but you or your staff needs to be capable of digging into the source code to resolve problems on your own
- The quality of the documentation that comes with the application might not be at the level you're accustomed to
- Utilities to support the application might not be available like they are for a third-party product

33.1.4.4 Outsourcing

It seems that sooner or later almost every organization considers outsourcing as a way to cut costs. Outsourcing can impact you if the vendor decides to outsource its development team or support group. If this happens, the best advice I can suggest is to be patient and keep an open mind. If you've developed a network of other Application Administrators, you might turn to them as your first level of support if something goes wrong. If they aren't able to help you, then open a ticket through the vendor's support group.

33.1.4.5 Data visualization

As organizations accumulate more and more data, it becomes increasingly difficult to make sense of it all. One technique being used to make sense of it all is data visualization. Displaying data in a graphical format is commonly associated with data visualization.

Does the application you support include any data visualization tools? If there are no tools currently provided with the application, is the vendor promising that such tools will be available in the future? An alternative would be to export data so a visualization tool like Tableau can access it and create graphically oriented presentations of the data.

33.1.4.6 Mobile applications

Being accessible by mobile devices, e.g., smart phones and tablets, seems to be the latest topic *du jour* for enterprise-wide applications. Is this something that people in your organization are starting to talk about? If so, then you might start thinking about questions like these:

- What types of hardware will your mobile users have? iPhones, iPads, Android phones, etc.
- Does it make any sense for your application to be accessed by mobile users?
- Can the application you support be accessed by a smart phone or tablet?
- How many users of the application would want to access it from a mobile device?
- Is that number growing?
- What are the security requirements of the application? Would accessing it from a mobile device likely violate the security requirements?
- Could the application be modified or reconfigured to make it more secure?

33.1.4.7 BYOD—bring your own device

BYOD seems the next step after mobile applications. It simply goes one step farther down the path toward supporting basically any device that a user wants to access the application with. All of the questions that were listed in Section 33.1.4.6 are equally applicable to the BYOD trend.

33.1.4.8 Virtual patching

Virtual patching is a method of applying a quick repair to address a specific vulnerability of an application. It isn't meant to be a comprehensive or long-term solution. A significant shortcoming of virtual patching is that it doesn't correct the inherent defect in the application; it figuratively covers the problem with a band-aid until a permanent fix becomes available. If your application vendor provides virtual patches, then you need to at least consider accepting them and loading them.

33.2 OPPORTUNITIES FOR EDUCATION

The opportunities for educating oneself in our profession are almost limitless. With a little imagination and a reasonable amount of hard work, anyone can improve their knowledge of virtually any topic in the profession. Some of the more obvious resources that you can take advantage of to educate yourself are listed here.

33.2.1 Vendor training

Application-specific training provided by the vendor is usually the best source of training you can find. If your employer has ponied up to send you to vendor-supplied training, then you want to maximize what you learn while in vendor training classes. Some tips for getting the most out of those classes are:

- Don't go in cold. Read any available manuals, help screens, Dummies books, etc., before the class starts. Having a good foundation about the application will help you absorb the material that's going to be presented to you.
- Work with the application as much as possible before the class. Any hands-on experience will be a significant benefit.
- Come with plenty of questions. Write them down before you attend the class and write the answers down when you get them. Talk to coworkers, users, your predecessor, etc., and ask if they have any questions about the application that they would like to have answered. When it comes to your list of questions, the more the merrier.
- Review the material every day after class. It would certainly be more fun to head off for margaritas after class is over for the day, but reviewing the information while it's fresh in your mind will help cement it in your memory. This is the time to update your notes—or write them if you didn't during class.
- If the class involves hands-on labs or assignments done as a group project, don't rely on someone else to figure things out. This might look like the easy thing to do at the time, but you'll be wasting an opportunity to learn from the experts.

If you're fortunate, your vendor will provide other training avenues. For example, webinars (live or on-demand), white papers, or newsletters. You should take advantage of any educational opportunities that are available to you.

33.2.2 Learning from the application itself

If there are no classes for the application or your employer won't send you to them, don't despair. There is a lot you can learn by yourself if you're willing to work at it. Some sources are listed in the following sections.

33.2.2.1 Vendor documentation

Vendor-supplied documentation on the application may not be light reading, but it usually provides an incredible amount of information. Be warned in advance that it might be a little dull, it might not be extremely well written, and it's certainly not going to be made into next summer's blockbuster movie, but it's readily available and usually it's free. Who could ask for anything more?

33.2.2.2 Experiment with the application

Some people learn best when they're doing something rather than reading a document. For these types, the best learning opportunity might be to experiment with the application. Work your way through the manual and then test what is being discussed. Of course, it goes without saying that this testing should be done on a development or test environment. Playing around with the production version of the application could get you fired.

33.2.2.3 Help on the server

There will be many technical aspects that you need to learn about that aren't in the vendor's documentation. Tools, commands, and techniques that are related to the server's operating system won't be documented in application's documentation. Instead, you should turn to documentation provided by the operating system. Two examples are the UNIX/Linux man pages or the Windows Help system.

33.2.3 Internal LMS (learning management system)

Many organizations provide an internal Learning Management System. These LMSs may not have courses geared toward the technical level you require, but it never hurts to check.

33.2.4 Classes

If the application you're supporting is widely used, then it's possible that courses on it will be provided by entities other than the vendor. Some possible providers are listed in the following sections.

33.2.4.1 Local university

Most universities don't provide classes geared toward specific applications, but it takes only a few minutes to check their online course catalog. You many not find a course that's specific to your application but may find one on another topic that interests you.

33.2.4.2 Community college

Your local community college is probably more likely to have a course specific to your application than a university. Again, if you don't find a course specific to your application, but there are probably many on topics that you are interested in or recognize would be valuable to know more about.

33.2.4.3 Training organizations

Most medium-to-large cities have at least one or two companies that provide training to the IT industry. Many of their courses are likely to be geared toward preparing for the tests associated with a certification. Other courses might be on programming languages. If your application is widely used, then it's possible they might offer a course or two on it.

33.2.5 Books

If the application you support has a significant market penetration, then there is a very good chance that at least one book has been written about it. For a $25-30 investment and a week or two of applied effort, you may be able to raise your expertise level from beginner to advanced.

33.2.6 White papers or presentations

If you search diligently on the Internet, you can probably find about anything. One of the things you might find is white papers or presentations on your industry or the application that you are supporting. Of course, everything you read on the Internet has to be taken with a grain of salt. A presentation put together by a marketing guy from the vendor isn't likely to present a balanced view of the application. With that in mind, it never hurts to read anything and everything related to the application.

33.2.7 Blogs

There are many valuable blogs that are absolutely worth reading on a regular basis. While you might not find one devoted to your application, some of them cover topics like software development, testing, security, change control, etc. Any blog with industry background information you find is worth at least looking at.

33.2.8 Trade journals

The number of trade journals that are published regularly is astounding. If you poke around on the Internet, you'll very likely find at least one or two that covers your industry. Some are hard copy versions that are delivered by the Post Office and others are e-copies that arrive by e-mail. One feature that is hard to beat is that most of them are free.

33.2.8.1 Technical

The IT industry is blessed with a wide variety of trade journals. The subjects they focus on range from hard-core programming to networking to security to high-level topics suited for a CIO or CTO. Many of them are either delivered to your desk for free or can be read online for free.

There are also a number of technical e-newsletters that will be sent directly to your e-mailbox. Once you start getting one of these missives, it seems that your name gets passed along and very soon you'll be getting more than you can possibly read.

33.2.8.2 Industry specific

It's a very good idea to keep up with the industry that your organization is part of. I'd be willing to bet that no matter what industry you're involved with, there are specific trade journals for it. I did a quick search and found that www.wikipedia.org has 254 pages listing "Professional and trade magazines." If you can't find your industry in that list, then you're in a pretty obscure field.

33.2.8.3 General business

Business trends and climates affect all industries, so it's a good idea to be informed about the general business climate. There are many publications that provide coverage of basic business information.

33.2.9 Webinars

If you don't enjoy reading technical publications, then you might be more amenable to acquiring your educational material from webinars. I seem to get two or three invitations to webinars on technical topics every day. Some are live and others are prerecorded. The live ones allow you and the other members of the audience to participate by asking questions. The biggest advantage of prerecorded webinars is that you can watch them when it is most convenient for you.

33.2.10 The Internet

The Internet probably provides more information on more topics than any other resource available to the average person. It's convenient, it's free, and you can access it from almost anywhere. By running a search on a topic, you're likely to turn up a white paper, a blog, a webinar, or a college class that provides timely and pertinent information. Of course, whenever you're relying on information from sources that you're unfamiliar with, you need to be a little cautious. Don't believe everything that you read, especially if one particular source seems to be significantly different than what other sources have to say.

33.2.11 User groups

Does a User Group exist for the software application that you support? If it does, then it's probably worth your while to check it out. If one doesn't exist, then perhaps you have the opportunity to form one in your area. Some user groups provide the following resources to their members:

- An annual meeting with vendor presentations, user presentations, and classes
- A local user chapter with monthly or quarterly meetings
- A website with a knowledge base or extensive FAQ list
- Opportunities to network with fellow professionals

33.2.12 Conferences

If your application vendor or user group has an annual conference, you should attend it if you can. If there is no user conference or you can't attend, then see if there are IT or industry conferences being held closer to home. Looks for ones where your vendor might be exhibiting or presenting. While these may not offer details on your application, they can provide you with valuable information on the IT field and opportunities to network with IT professionals in your area.

33.3 POTENTIAL PERSONAL GOALS RELATED TO EDUCATION

Having professional goals is a way to help ensure you do more with your life than show up and collect your paycheck every week. The following sections are just a few possible goals that you might consider.

33.3.1 Present sessions at user conferences

If you've discovered a better way to do something or are involved in a unique way of using the application, you should consider presenting a session at the next user conference. The first step is to submit a proposal when the conference puts out their call for papers. This usually occurs about 6 months before the conference is held. While public speaking can be a little scary, it's an exciting experience to present information to your peers.

You may not be paid for doing your presentation, but many conferences waive the admission fee for their speakers. Since conferences can easily cost a thousand dollars, this is a fairly generous compensation for your time and effort. If your organization doesn't usually pay for conferences, being able to attend for free might help sway their decision.

33.3.2 Write articles in trade journals

All of the trade journals that are being printed every month need articles to fill them up. In my experience, the editors of those journals are happy to consider proposals from IT professionals that want to write about their jobs, applications, or techniques. If you submit a well-thought-out proposal about your application, a new technique, or a current trend, don't be surprised if it is accepted and you find yourself a published author.

33.3.3 Blog

Anyone can blog about their application or the profession in general. It's my feeling that if you take the time to organize your thoughts and put them down on paper, it's a learning experience. If you take the time and effort to blog about your professional life, you might end up seeing things in new and better light.

33.3.4 Degrees

Getting a degree is a significant undertaking, but can be both personally and professionally rewarding. Taking classes either at a local university or through an online program can help advance your career at your current employer or in a future position. Make sure you give this decision some thought to ensure you enroll in the most appropriate program for your professional goals.

33.3.5 Certification

Is it worth getting certified? If the certification you're considering is directly applicable to your job description, then this may be a very obvious decision. If the certification isn't so closely aligned to your everyday work, then getting certified should be either something you really want or an area that you are planning to transition to in the future.

Some things to consider before heading down the certification path are:

- Is the certification recognized and highly regarded in the field?
- How many tests does it take to become certified?
- How frequently does the certification need to be renewed?
- Does the underlying topic change so frequently that the current certification will be obsolete in the near future?
- Will your employer pay for some or all of the costs of books, classes, or tests?

33.3.6 Write a book

One area of personal development that you should at least consider is writing a book. If the application you support has a significant market share, then a good book on the subject might sell well. If there are no competing titles, then it's even more likely that it will sell well.

33.4 EDUCATING THE USERS

Educating the application's users might not be your responsibility, but it's reasonable to assume that better educated users require less support. If you can help educate them without jeopardizing your level of support for the application, it's probably a good thing to do. And, it will give you opportunities to hone your presentation skills.

There are many ways that training material can be present to the users. Some examples are:

- If your organization has an in-house training department, then involve them in this effort
- Instructor-led classes
- Prerecorded classes that users can view at the own time and pace
- A list of FAQ (Frequently Asked Questions) that have been asked by present or past users
- A wiki with information about the application

Some topics that should be considered are described in the following sections.

33.4.1 Computer basics

If your users are relatively new to computers, then providing classes or materials on basic computer skills would be very valuable. If possible, emphasize computer skills that are needed while using the application. For example, copying and pasting operations, creating and updating spreadsheets, or search concepts.

33.4.2 Application basics for new users

If the application has a relatively high number of new users, then classes or material geared toward new users would be especially valuable. Anything that helps get them up to speed quickly will be useful. An additional advantage of providing solid training for new users is that they'll be less likely to have to interrupt their coworkers with questions.

33.4.3 Advanced application topics for current users

Once educational material has been developed for the new users, then consider developing more advanced materials for your existing users. Even users that have been working with the application for a while probably have gaps in their knowledge of the application.

Parting Advice

It seems like everyone wants to give you advice: your mother, your siblings, your spouse, your boss, and the weirdo who lives next door. I'm no exception. The only difference is that the advice I'm offering applies only to your position as an Application Administrator. I wouldn't think of giving advice on what to wear or how to deal with your obnoxious brother-in-law. This chapter contains advice that didn't fit into the previous chapters. I hope this will help you in your role as an Application Administrator. Maybe it will help you in other aspects of your life.

34.1 DO NO HARM

Part of the physician's credo embodied in the Hippocratic Oath is "first, do no harm." An Application Administrator should follow the same guideline. If there is a reasonable chance that something you're about to do can cause harm to the application, then don't do it. If you absolutely have to do it, then consider doing it only under the following circumstances:

- Test it on your development or test system first. If it doesn't damage those systems, then elevate the change to the production system.
- Back up everything before making any changes. Depending on exactly what is being changed, this might mean making a copy of the configuration file you're about to change, backing up an entire subdirectory, or making a backup of the database.
- Document the current setup. For example, you might need to capture screenshots of how the system looks like before and after making the change as well as the steps taken to make the change.
- Make this change at a time when users won't be impacted. For example, don't make it just before the busiest time of the year.
- If the environment is virtualized, i.e., the application is running on a virtual server, see if the virtualization team can create a new server for you to test this change on. Change it first on the "sandbox" environment. If the change has the expected result, then change the production system.

34.2 ALWAYS TRY TO BE IN THE DRIVER'S SEAT

People learn in different ways, but one common way that people learn best is if they are performing the actions themselves instead of watching someone else do them. If you learn best by doing, then always try to be the one "driving" when something needs to be done on the application. By "driving" I mean you should be the one who's actually sitting at the keyboard making changes to the system. This applies in the following situations and many others that you might encounter:

- When a vendor technician is working with you to install software
- When someone is handing off support responsibility of an application and wants to demonstrate it to you
- When you're working with a user to understand the problem or error they're experiencing
- When you're working with a vendor technician to investigate and resolve a problem

In addition to being a better way to learn how to do things, being in the driver's seat also has the following advantages:

- Being the "driver" allows you to control the pace of the activity. If you're watching the vendor technician do an installation, he or she might be moving so quickly that you can't see and understand everything that is being done. By doing it at your pace you have the opportunity to see what is being done.
- You can pause the action and take notes of what is being done. If you try to take notes while someone else is driving, then you're likely to miss steps while your eyes are off the screen.
- You can capture screenshots and paste them into a document. If someone else is driving, then they may change the screen before you are able to capture it. You would also be likely to miss some of the activities while you're pasting screenshots into your document.

34.2.1 When you're the copilot

There might be times when you can't "drive" the session. When someone else is driving, it's still possible to pick up tips from them. Everyone does things differently and their way of doing something might be better than the way you normally do it. If you watch a coworker, vendor technician, or one of your data center guys closely, you just might learn something valuable. Whenever you're in a situation where someone is showing you something on the screen, always be looking for the opportunity to learn better techniques for doing things. And don't hesitate to ask questions if you see someone do something you don't understand.

34.3 DON'T USE THE ADMIN LOGON UNLESS IT'S ABSOLUTELY NECESSARY

As an administrator you will have access to the admin account for the application. You might also be able to log onto the server using the root or super user account. While it might be easier to always log into either the application or the server as the admin account, you should avoid that temptation. Some reasons for using an account with a lower access level are:

- Since admin has virtually unlimited access, you can unintentionally make widespread and unintended changes, deletions, etc., within the application or on the server.
- While logged in as admin, you can inadvertently install a virus, Trojan horse, worm, or other form of malware and give it administrative rights.
- If multiple people know the admin account password, then there is very little accountability of who made what change. By logging in as yourself whenever possible, it will be easier to track who made which changes.

Instead of automatically logging in as the admin account, you should log in using your personal account and only use the admin account when you absolutely need to. You might also consider using the following commands in these cases:

- su—this command allows an authorized user to switch to another account, for example, the root account. You could log onto the server as yourself and switch to an account that is authorized to make changes to the application's files or directories.

- sudo—available on UNIX and Linux systems, the sudo command allows authorized users to execute commands as either the root account or another specified account. It essentially gives you the power of the root account with the risk of always being logged in as root.
- runas—on Windows systems, the "runas" command is roughly the equivalent of the UNIX sudo command. It lets you start a command shell as the administrator.

34.4 UNDERSTAND WHAT YOU'RE DOING

Don't get into the habit of blindly follow a checklist to complete a task or a process. Understand why you're doing each of the steps in the process. If you don't understand what each step does, then ask someone about it. Potential sources for learning more about the process are the Administrator's Guide, the vendor support group, other Application Administrators that you've networked with, or the coworker that supported the application prior to you.

A major danger of blindly following a checklist is that if something unusual happens you won't know how to respond. And according to Murphy's Law, this will probably happen at a time when no one will be available to help you.

34.5 DO THINGS THE EASY WAY

When performing tasks like an install or an upgrade, you might find yourself repeatedly entering the same values over and over. Some examples of these values are file names, logins, passwords, server names, application names, etc. Keeping an instance of Notepad open with the values in it from which you can copy and paste them will help avoid typos and speed up the process.

34.6 THE EYES HAVE IT

The value of having a second set of eyes looking at a problem can't be overstated. I can't count the number of times I've had a problem with a piece of code or an application's configuration settings. It seemed like continuing to stare at it only made the problem harder to solve. When I finally broke down and asked a coworker to take a look at it, they always seemed to spot the error within seconds.

There comes a point when it just doesn't make sense to stare at it any longer by yourself. Once you reach that limit don't be afraid to ask for help. It's a rookie mistake to think that asking for help is a sign of weakness. Your coworkers will be more than willing to help you just as you are happy to help them when they ask you for assistance.

If you're the kind of person that absolutely loathes asking for help, here are some tricks to help you see the solution to a problem that you're stuck on:

- Take a break—Get up and walk away from your desk for a while. Go get a soft drink or a cup of coffee. Getting your mind off the problem for a few minute will frequently unblock your mind and then the solution will suddenly appear to you.
- Work on something else for a while—This approach has the additional benefit of being productive while you're letting your subconscious work on the original problem.
- Sleep on it—If obtaining a solution isn't time critical, then sleep on the problem overnight. In my experience, if I completely put a problem out of my mind, then the solution will come seemingly out of the blue.

- Try examining it from a different angle. For example, read the code from the bottom to the top. Physically looking at the code or file differently might allow you to think of it differently and might enable you to see the solution.

34.7 DOCUMENT, DOCUMENT, DOCUMENT

If there's one trait, I think all Application Administrators should have is the ability to document what they do. Any problem or situation that happens today is likely to happen again in the future. By documenting it the first time it's encountered you will make it much easier to repeat the process in the future. This is especially true if the situation doesn't recur for months or years. Good documentation will also help your backup or successor handle the problem.

Try to create your documentation as soon as possible after you fix something or make a change. The longer you wait to create the document, the more likely it is that your memory will start getting fuzzy and mistakes will creep into your documentation. Ideally, you would be capturing screenshots as you're performing the activity and pasting them into the document with some very brief notes. As soon as the activity is complete, then update the documentation with full details. Once you're done with your initial pass of the document, then review it and update it as necessary.

If having screenshots in a document will make it more helpful, then by all means include as many as are appropriate. Make sure each screenshot is accurately labeled. It also helps if screenshots in the documentation appear in a logical, chronological order. Develop a document template that you can reuse so that all your documentation has a familiar format and layout along with key information (title, description, data created, revision history, etc.).

Examples of situations that should be documented include the following:

- Software installations
- Applying updates
- Errors encountered by users
- Running the backup process
- Migrating data from one environment to another, e.g., from PROD to QA
- Putting the application into single user mode
- Changing the Administrator password
- Unlocking a user account
- Shutting down the application
- Bringing up the application
- Making changes to configuration files
- Capturing log files to send to the vendor support group

34.7.1 Make it easy to find your document

Any documentation you keep will be even more valuable if you can find it quickly. Some tips for making it easier to perform searches for your documentation are:

- Keep all of your notes documents in a known location. Since I support multiple applications, I've created a separate documentation subdirectory for each of application.
- All document files should be named appropriately.
- Each document should have a meaningful title inside the document, preferable at the top.
- Include the date that the document was created and the most recent date it was updated.

- A year from now you may not be able to recall the exact phrases used in the document to describe a problem or situation. This problem can be minimized by having a "Keywords" section in the document. In that section, you can include a variety of phrases that can be used to describe what the document is about. This can make future searches more effective.

34.8 BE CONSISTENT

When it comes to the tasks an Application Administrator performs daily, being consistent is definitely a virtue. Doing things consistently will result in fewer mistakes and less time spent searching for things. It will also make life easier for your successor or backup.

Some examples of how you can be consistent include:

- Whenever possible, do things the same way on each of your environments: DEV, QA, DR and Production. For example, if the application is installed in D:\Program Files\MyApp on the production server, then it should be set up that way on all of your servers.
- Configuration settings should be as similar as possible. One obvious exception would be that the values for server names will be different for each environment. For example, they might be app_dev, app_qa, and app_prod or something similar to that.
- IIS website names should be as consistent as possible. Again the names might need to include an indication of whether the site is the development, QA, or production website.
- Permission setups for directories and files should be consistent across your development, QA, and production servers.
- File naming conventions should be consistent. For example, all log files should have the ".log" extension. All script files should have extensions of either ".bat," ".cmd," or ".scr."
- For a third-party application, you probably won't have control over the names of database tables and columns. If you do have the ability to influence database object names, then try to be consistent. For example, if there is a column holding the User_ID, then name it consistently in all database tables. Don't call it "User_ID" in some tables, "UID" in others, and "ID" in still other tables. Anyone who has to figure out the relationships between tables will appreciate the consistency.
- User names should be as consistent as consistent as possible. For example, your convention might be fname.lname@email-address. Once a convention has been selected, then don't make exceptions unless it's absolutely necessary.
- Position all scripts or batch files that you've written in the same location on all of your application servers. For example, in the D:\Scripts directory.
- Report names should be meaningful and indicate what the contents of the report are.

34.9 CLEAN UP AFTER YOURSELF RIGHT AWAY

Clean up after completing installs, upgrades, exports, capturing additional logging details, etc. By this, I mean you should delete files, logs, and subdirectories that are no longer needed once you are done with a task. If you don't delete these files right after you're done with them, it's very likely that you'll forget to do it or will get busy and never get back to this task. The result will be an accumulation of old files that are no longer needed. They'll do nothing other than confuse you and consume disk space. At some point in time, when you're forced to go back and clean up the files, it will take a LOT longer to sort through everything and figure out what can be deleted and what needs to be retained.

34.10 ALWAYS CHECK YOUR JUNK E-MAIL FOLDER

Always check your junk mail folder if you're missing an e-mail from any of the following sources:

- The application server
- The report server
- The vendor
- A support technician working for the vendor

I've spent too much time trying to figure out why an e-mail wasn't received when in fact it did get sent but had been automatically moved to my e-mail junk folder. Two recent examples where this bit me are:

- I couldn't figure out why I wasn't getting the e-mail sent out when the nightly backup process completed on a QA server. I checked the task that performed the backups and found that it had succeeded. The backup files created by the process existed. There were no errors in any log files. Finally, it dawned on me to look in the junk folder and there it was. I have no idea why identical e-mails from the development and production servers were accepted but the one from the QA server was diverted into the junk folder. Just one of the many mysteries of life.
- I was expecting a response from the vendor technician working with me on a problem. It never showed up, at least that's what I thought. I had received all of the e-mails generated by the vendor's support website, but in this particular instance the technician had sent the e-mail to me from his corporate e-mail account. For some reasons, my e-mail package thought it was spam and moved it to the junk folder.

34.11 TRUST BUT VERIFY

I don't mean to be a paranoid kind of person, but there are a number of situations when it just makes good sense to verify what someone has told you.

- If a user reports that the application didn't come up for them or that something which worked yesterday no longer works, you should verify it for yourself before investing time into figuring out what happened.
- If a vendor provides you with logon details to the website where you'll download files, you should verify that those details will enable you to log in immediately after receiving them. If they don't let you log in them, it's best to report that back to the vendor ASAP.
- If a vendor tells you that a certain change won't affect the users or won't take the system down, you need to verify this on a DEV or TEST system before making the change on Production. No one is perfect and that includes vendor technicians.

34.12 DON'T RUN SCHEDULED JOBS UNDER YOUR ACCOUNT

If you have jobs scheduled on application servers don't have them run under your personal account. If an account for this type of activity doesn't already exist then create a service account for this task. Reasons for not using your personal account include:

- Your account password probably needs to be changed every 30, 60, or 90 days. When you update your password, you'll also have to remember to update it on every application server where a scheduled job exists. If you forget to update the password on a server, then any task scheduled on it will fail then next time it runs.

- If you quit or get fired, your account will be disabled. The next time that a task using your account runs it will fail.
- No one else besides you will be able to modify the details of the task without knowing your password. Industry best practices are to not share passwords of personal accounts.
- If your application is audited this might be uncovered, then you'll be asked to explain why you chose to do it this way. There really is no justification for using your account, so this question could become very uncomfortable.
- Your backup might need to know your password to change the task while you're sick or on vacation.
- Looking at this from the opposite viewpoint means that someone else in your organization used their account when scheduling a task. If it fails to run, then you won't be able to modify it without knowing their password.

34.13 DON'T TRY TO HIDE YOUR MISTAKES

Everyone makes mistakes occasionally. Eventually you'll make a mistake in your position as an Application Administrator. In my experience, the best course of action is to admit your mistake, correct it, and move on. It might be embarrassing to admit you messed up, but everyone, including your boss, has made mistakes before. Your recent mistake wasn't your first and I can guarantee that it won't be your last.

Even worse than making a mistake is trying to hide it with lies. Never forget that many times people end up getting a greater punishment for the cover-up than the original crime. Think of Richard Nixon as well as other politicians, business executives, and a well-known home decorating maven.

34.14 GET THE MOST OUT OF VENDOR TECHNICIANS

During your tenure as an Application Administrator, you'll spent a considerable amount of time on the phone with technicians from the vendor's support group. You'll want to do whatever you can to get the most out of the time spent with them. Some advice for maximizing the learning potential of your sessions with vendor techs include:

- If you're doing a shared terminal session, always drive. This ensures the session is run at your pace instead of his or hers. He or she is probably so familiar with the steps they're performing that they forget not everyone knows the application as well as they do.
- If you're doing a shared terminal session, take screenshots and save them to a document while you're performing the steps. Tell the tech what you're doing so they understand the time lags while you paste screenshots into your document and save it.
- Always ask questions about what is going on if you don't understand a step or a command. Don't pretend to understand something just because you don't want to appear ignorant. It's obvious that the tech will know more about the application than you do. Don't be ashamed of this reality.
- Always ask the vendor technician if he or she has a cheat sheet, crib notes, or internal documentation on what you're doing. You may or may not get anything by asking, but it's worth a try. If they have documentation like this, then it's likely to be more valuable than the "official" version.

34.15 **THINGS ALWAYS TAKE LONGER THAN EXPECTED**

It's my experience that most things in life take longer than you expect them to take. This includes cooking, cleaning, and auto repairs. An area that this also applies to is fixing applications. Installs take longer, exports take longer, resolving problems takes longer, and scheduling time with a vendor technician takes longer than expected. If a task has a hard deadline and you wait until the last minute to start on it, then you'll almost certainly miss your deadline. So some very wise advice is to make realistic scheduling estimates and start early.

34.16 **FINAL WORDS**

Being an Application Administrator for the past 6 years has been a great experience for me. I've grown professionally, learned how the corporation works, worked with some very competent professionals, and, hopefully, helped many users. I hope that your position as an Application Administrator is as fulfilling to you as mine has been to me.

There are a number of characteristics that I've seen in effective Application Administrators. I think that the following traits have contributed to their, and hopefully my, success. They might help you in your professional life as well:

- Be willingness to go the extra mile for users
- Have a positive attitude
- Assume responsibility for your actions
- Retain a sense of curiosity
- Be willing to learn new ways of doing things
- Always happy to help a coworker

Index

Note: Page numbers followed by *f* indicate figures and *t* indicate tables.

Printed and bound by CPI Group (UK) Ltd, Croydon, CR0 4YY

03/10/2024

01040324-0016